AMERICA'S MINORITIES AND THE MULTICULTURAL DEBATE

AMERICA'S MINORITIES AND THE MULTICULTURAL DEBATE

An Editorials On File Book

Editor: Oliver Trager

Facts On File
New York • Oxford

AMERICA'S MINORITIES AND THE MULTICULTURAL DEBATE

Published by Facts On File, Inc.
© Copyright 1992 by Facts On File, Inc.

Library of Congress Cataloging-in-Publication Data

America's minorities and the multicultural debate/ editor, Oliver Trager
    p. cm. — (An editorials on file book)
Includes bibliographical references and index.
ISBN 0-8160-2815-X
  1. Minorities—United States. 2. United States—Ethnic Relations.
3. United States—Race Relations. 4. United States—Civilization.
5. Pluaralism (Social sciences)—United States.
6. Intercultural education—United States.
  I. Trager, Oliver. II. Series:
Editorials on File book.
E184.A1A639 1992

305.8'00973.dc20   92-3973
                                                       CIP
                                                        AC

Printed in the United States of America

9 8 7 6 5 4 3 2 1

This book is printed on acid-free paper

Contents

Selected Bibliography

Low, W. Augustus & Clift, Virgil A. (eds.), *Enclyclopedia of Black America*, McGraw-Hill, Inc. 1981. Da Capo Press, 1984.

Berman, Paul (ed.), *Debating P.C.*, Bantam Doubleday Dell Publishing Group, Inc. 1992.

Jibou, Robert M., *Ethnicity & Assimilation*, State University of New Yor Press, 1988

Preface

Since the civil rights struggles of the 1950s and 1960s, the United States has striven to overcome the inequities and confusions implicit in issues involving race, ethnicity, gender and class.

A century after the great wave of immigration to the United States, the classic image of America as a "melting pot" is subject to debate. New immigrant groups clash with entrenched ones, and diverse elements of society – ethnic groups, women and sexual minorities – are asserting their identities and contending for their share of power.

Questions of race and ethnicity have sparked renewed national debate. What is "political correctness?" Should multiculturalism be reflected in a national education policy? Are job quotas necessary to ensure employment opportunities for minority workers? How have judicial rulings affected minorities? What are the consequences of racial and ethnic stereotyping? Has the entertainment industry been sensitive to racial

and ethnic stereotyping? How will the future of women in the workplace be affected by the attention focused on the issue of sexual harassment during the confirmation hearings of Supreme Court Justice Clarence Thomas? What challenges does the women's movement face in the 1990s?

In *America's Minorities and the Multicultural Debate* the country's leading newspaper editorial writers and cartoonists examine some of the key issues facing the country, from its schoolrooms to its courthouses. The editorials included in this volume represent a wide range of views expressed over the course of the last five years. They were chosen from more than a hundred major newspapers in nearly all fifty states without regard to balancing or favoring points of view. They were written to stimulate public awareness of issues that go to the heart of our identity as a nation

May 1992

Oliver Trager

Part I: Racism in America

"Race" has only one scientific meaning and that is a biological one. It refers to a subdivision of a given species members whose inherit physical characteristics that tend to distinguish that subdivision from other populations of the same species. Although this definition is as precise as possible, scientists realize that there are no clear-cut subdivisions in the single species called man, Homo sapiens. More people belong to categories between subdivisions than belong to the subdivisions themselves, and many individuals have characteristics that place them in several categories simultaneously.

Culture may be said to consist of the sum total and organization of a group's behavior patterns, and it is an anthropological axiom that any cultural phenomenon must be understood and evaluated in the total cultural setting. Anthropologists assume, for example, that if an American white baby and a Chinese, or a Norweigian and a Congo black, were switched at birth and each were then fully accepted as "belonging" in its new home, each individual would grow up to accept the cultural patterns, attitudes, and beliefs of its adoptive, rather than its biological family. According to this view if the positions of black and white people in the United States had been reversed, black people would feel the way white people now feel and vice versa. The same thing would be true of northerners and southerners.

Since slavery, the difference in the experience of blacks and whites has been large, and has led to a gap in the way many whites and blacks perceive themselves and their relation to one another. That chasm has widened to the point of constituting a social crisis - a crisis based on the attitudes of many American whites, who do not yet accept blacks as their equals, and of Afro-Americans, who are no longer satisfied with anything less.

The complexity of the race problem in sociological terms can be seen in the white-black disparity in socioeconomic levels, in occupational distribution, in education, which is the result of generations of blacks having to face poor schools, job discrimination, and exclusion from cultural opportunities available to white people. Also at work are psychological barriers such as the long-established ways of looking at a situation from different points of view, an inability to see things from others' points of view, of thinking in terms of "we" and "they," or of "my people" and "your people." The combined forces of history, tradition, and habit serves to maintain the status quo.

Finally, myths support the situation: myths of biological differences between the races that influence behavior as much as if they were actually true. Some of these myths come down as part of history and tradition; others arise in the stress and strain of daily contact and are related to the fears that develop when established and familiar social patterns are threatened.

When these factors are viewed as a whole they make an easy definition of racism nearly impossible. Racism has many interpretations and connotations, some of them emotional, depending upon the source of the definition. However, reliable definitions are found in *Webster's Third New International Dictionary* (1965) and in a clearinghouse publication of the U.S. Commission on Civil Rights (*Racism in America and How to Combat It*, 1970). Webster's definition states that racism is "the assumption that psychocultural traits and capacities are determined by biological race and that races differ decisively from one another which is usually coupled with a belief in the inherent superiority of a particular race and its right to domination over others." The civil rights commission defines racism in this way: "racism may be viewed as *any attitude, action, or institutional structure which subordinates a person or group because of his or her color.*"

Two major descriptive categories of "racism" came into widespread usage during the 1960s and 1970s were institutional racism and scientific racism. Institutional racism may not necessarily involve intent, because it may be submerged in the history, structure and function of the institution. The fact that there are, for example, white suburbs and black ghettoes does not necessarily mean that dwellers in either are racists. Most would have no intent or knowledge whatever of their being so, and they would resent being called racists. Yet, the structure of residential housing in the United States effectively subordinates a group because of its color.

Any scientific or pseudoscientific view of race that equates racial differences with racial superiority or inferiority may be defined as scientific racism. The authority of science as a discipline of study has long been called into such debatable areas as the relative importance of heredity or environment.

The principal reason for the persistence of racism, antiblack or otherwise, is that Americans absorb the racial values of their society just as they do its economic, political and social values.

The Ku Klux Klan is perhaps the best-known catalyst for racist sentiments in the U.S. The KKK is a white supremacist organization that grew out of the Civil War and Reconstruction and sought to maintain white supremacy in the South by various means, including terrorism. Founded in Pulaski, Tenn. in 1866 and organized a more formal basis in Nashville, Tenn. a year later, activity peaked shortly after the Civil War and in the 1920s. Today, the KKK is no longer an "invisible empire" and is enjoying something of a renaissance with membership throughout the country. This was recently dramatized by the rise of former KKK Grand Wizard David Duke in his unsuccessful bids for the governorship of Louisiana and the U.S. presidency.

Since the civil rights movement of the 1950s and 1960s the liberalization of racial ideas over the last generation has been slow but sure. However, despite the disappearance of racial inferiority or superiority and a widespread sense that such ideas are no longer tenable, America contains to find itself troubled by the issues of race.

Anti-Semitism Charges
Spread Worldwide

Germany and Austria were experiencing a proliferation of Nazi-oriented computer games, according to reports April 20-May 9, 1991. A spokesman for the Simon Wiesenthal Holocaust Study Center in Los Angeles April 30 said that there were about 140 games with titles such as "KZ Manager" (KZ was a German abbreviation for concentration camp) and "Aryan Test."

"KZ Manager," which used Turks (many of whom worked in Germany) as victims, challenged the player to operate a death camp efficiently. Jews were also commonly victims in the games, the reports said.

The computer programs, most of them written for German-language users, had come to public attention after the Austrian newspaper AZ April 20 reported that the games had spread "explosively" among high school students. Austrian polls said about four in 10 high school students had heard of the games. The Wiesenthal center said it did not know who was producing the games.

Prodigy Services Co., operator of the Prodigy computer network, had drawn criticism from the Anti-Defamation League of B'nai B'rith for carrying anti-Semitic messages, the *Wall Street Journal* reported Oct. 22, 1991.

Prodigy, which was a joint venture of International Business Machines Corp. and Sears Roebuck & Co., operated one of the most popular personal computer networks in the U.S., with 1.1 million members. Its members communicated with each other through their computers and a telephone link-up. Members had access to dozens of different Prodigy "bulletin boards," each of which transmitted messages on an individual topic.

Prodigy, which described itself as a family service, had a reputation for engaging in more extensive screening and censoring of the messages on its bulletin boards than its chief competitors. Company policy prohibited the transmission of bulletin-board messages that contained "obscene, profane or otherwise offensive references."

According to the *Journal*, the ADL had complained to Prodigy after the group discovered that Prodigy had allowed a bulletin-board discussion on the subject of whether the Nazi Holocaust – in which an estimated six million Jews died – was a hoax. Prodigy was also said to have allowed the transmission of messages such as one that contained the statement "Hitler had some valid points."

Prodigy officials responded Oct. 23 by "amplifying" their ban on offensive material. Company officials said the ban would now include material that was "grossly repugnant to community standards." However, they said the ban would not cover such messages as the Holocaust-hoax discussion that had been transmitted on its bulletin boards.

At the same time, they noted that the statement about Hitler quoted by the *Journal* had not run on a bulletin board but had been sent as a private piece of electronic mail from one subscriber to another and thus was not available to all users. Since it was private electronic mail, it was not subject to review or censorship.

Mel Salberg, national chairman of the ADL, Oct. 23 said, "We were pleased to hear that they have modified and amplified their guidelines to define as offensive notes that are grossly repugnant." But, he said, the ADL found "unacceptable" the decision to allow continued debate on the Holocaust-hoax theory and other comments Salberg labeled as "Israel-bashing."

In another development, the Justice Department Nov. 17, 1991 filed suit against the newly created village of Airmont, N.Y., charging that its zoning proposals discriminated against Orthodox Jews. The suit was said to be one of the first filed by the department on behalf of a religious group.

The town of Ramapo, N.Y., which had seen a large influx of Orthodox Jews in recent decades, had authorized the creation of Airmont in April. Supporters of the Airmont proposal had campaigned on a platform of zoning restrictions that included a ban on the construction of synagogues in private homes.

The New York Times
New York City, New York, January 15, 1992

Bradley Smith is a Californian who acknowledges that the Nazis were cruel to Jews but who denies that the Holocaust ever happened. He has tried to expound his views in a 4,000-word essay submitted as an advertisement to several college newspapers — giving headaches and heartaches to student editors. In the process he gives the public some valuable, if unintended, lessons in the workings of a free press.

Many readers would blanch if they came upon Mr. Smith's pseudo-scholarly tract. Yes, he concedes, Jews were mistreated by the Nazis, and "many tragically perished in the maelstrom." But the idea that Nazi Germany exterminated six million Jews, Mr. Smith contends, is an irresponsible exaggeration. Gas chambers? A myth. Those actually were "life-saving" fumigation shelters to delouse clothing and prevent disease.

Should college editors risk appearing mercenary by taking money for publishing such trash? Should they risk playing censors to protect other young minds by refusing the ad? Is there some middle course, like printing the ad but with appraisals of its bizarre musings?

The dilemma is acute, just as it can be for commercial newspapers when confronted with ads that offend decency, patriotism or commonly accepted history. But the first lesson here is that it is their dilemma and not a First Amendment question. That great ordinance directs that Congress make no law abridging free expression. Government may not censor Mr. Smith and his fellow "Holocaust revisionists," no matter how intellectually barren their claims. Whether to publish their ads is something for the newspapers to decide.

The second lesson is that there's probably no right answer to the question of how they should decide. College editors have come out in different ways. Newspapers at Harvard, Yale, Brown and the University of California turned the ad down. Those at Cornell, Duke, Northwestern and Michigan printed it, sometimes citing free speech.

Perhaps the most creative response was that of the student editors at Rutgers University. The Daily Targum newspaper rejected the Holocaust tract as advertising but ran the text in its news columns, along with an editorial denunciation and comment by invited authors. The editors thus transformed revulsion into education.

The public does not usually require protection from bad ideas. Even so, initial instincts in favor of publication may sometimes yield to exceptions, against quackery, for instance, or on behalf of taste or fairness. The Times, for instance, has from time to time refused advertisements — like one insisting that a politician killed in a plane crash had himself sabotaged the flight; that claim seemed unjustly unanswerable.

Denying the Holocaust may be monumentally more unjust. Yet to require that it be discussed only within approved limits may do an even greater injustice to the memory of its victims. To print or not to print? The diversity of responses from diverse editors demonstrates something more important than the answer. When there is free expression, even the ugliest ideas enrich democracy.

DAILY NEWS

New York City, New York, August 21, 1987

POPE JOHN PAUL'S LETTER on Jewish suffering during the Holocaust said all the right things. It was released Wednesday, and two days later the sighs of relief could still be heard.

Said the Pope: "We Christians approach with fearsome respect the terrifying experience of the extermination, the *Shoah*, suffered by the Jews during the Second World War, and we seek to grasp its most authentic, specific and universal meaning . . . it is not permissible for anyone to pass by with indifference."

The timing of the letter is crucial. The Pope had scheduled a ceremonial meeting with American Jewish leaders during his upcoming visit to the U.S. Many leaders, in the wake of the Pope's audience with Kurt Waldheim, threatened to stay home in protest.

Reaction to the letter has been highly encouraging. Elie Wiesel, for instance, called it "gratifying."

The Pope will be taking up the Waldheim problem, along with other related issues, in a meeting with Jewish leaders at his summer home Sept. 1. If this wise and well-timed letter is any indication, Jewish-Catholic relations are looking up again.

The Boston Herald

Boston, Massachusetts, August 16, 1991

The desecration this week of Plymouth Rock is upsetting not just because an American symbol of freedom was spray-painted with the Nazi symbol of repression, but because this defilement was not an isolated incident.

In fact, less than 48 hours later a newly built Newton library — in fact, one not yet even open to the public — was similarly defaced with swastikas.

Police say they don't know yet whether the Plymouth crime was motivated by hate or ignorance, or whether the people responsible knew what the swastika they spray painted backwards represented.

But whoever did it knew at the very least that the swastika is a hateful reminder of concentration camps and the extermination of European Jewry. There are few alive who are totally ignorant of this period of history.

What happened in Plymouth and in Newton is happening nationally. Hate crimes against Jews are on the increase for the fifth straight year. Predictions are that hate crimes motivated by race, religion, and sexual preference will hit a record high in 1991.

If there is a ray of hope in all this, it may be that the public outcry against such acts of hatred and vandalism is usually so immediate and so passionate.

When a cemetery is destroyed, when property is defaced, when a rock is painted with a swastika, people become outraged. "Words can't express the vulgarity of it," said Duxbury resident Bill Hann, about the defacement of Plymouth Rock. "I think it's disgraceful," said Patricia Smith, a tourist from California.

Yet when people are attacked and defiled, the outcry is not as great. Just look at the barrage of epithet-filled abuse that wrecked an East Boston-South Boston basketball game Tuesday night. Where is the outcry for those young men?

Perhaps the logic is that a person can provoke hate. Who can ever be certain who started a fight? Who said what to whom? Thus, the Southie incident is officially "under investigation."

An inanimate object, of course, can't be held responsible for what happens to it at all. But while rocks and libraries don't feel the sting of an epithet hurled in hatred, individuals do.

Plymouth Selectman Alba Thompson's comment that what happened in Plymouth is "not a community problem," but a "country problem with skinheads who think they are making a statement with this type of vandalism," is absolutely correct.

The statement being made is that hate lives. The swastikas may have been scrubbed off Plymouth Rock and removed from the Newton library, but the sad fact is that the hate that put them there lives on.

The Chattanooga Times

Chattanooga, Tennessee, October 2, 1990

The United States has often been described as a melting pot, but Stuart Lewengrub, southeast regional director of the Anti-Defamation League of B'nai B'rith, thinks that image is counterproductive. "We're not a melting pot," he said here recently. "We're a mosaic." His choice in images reflects ADL's emphasis on educating Americans to appreciate the diversity of the population that makes up this great nation.

The melting pot brings to Mr. Lewengrub's mind a "tasteless soup" in the making of which differences have been boiled away. A mosaic, by contrast, creates of many different pieces a beautiful whole, losing none of the unique qualities of its individual parts in the process. Progress toward a society free of racial and ethnic prejudice will accelerate, Mr. Lewengrub believes, when Americans can look at their nation and see the differences in its people as good and healthy rather than somehow threatening.

Unfortunately, however, there are still many times when some Americans lash out at those who are different. Since the Iraqi invasion of Kuwait precipitated the current crisis in the Middle East, for instance, the number of Arab Americans subjected to insults and intimidation has jumped sharply. Misguided people, angry at Saddam Hussein, have vented that anger on neighbors who have nothing to do with the problem. It is thoughtless, groundless and ugly victimization of the innocent.

The Anti-Defamation League fights against that kind of activity, whether it is directed against Jews, or blacks, or Arabs. Mr. Lewengrub noted that the ADL recently issued a strongly worded statement condemning the surge of anti-Arab activity in this country, adding that he hopes Arab Americans will also condemn such activity aimed at Jews. And it is true that all people of good will must commit themselves to resisting mindless prejudice, whoever its target may be. For to the extent that prejudice exists, it degrades our society. Left unchallenged, it can fuel political extremism which can be dangerously destabilizing.

Mr. Lewengrub reported during his recent visit to Chattanooga that membership in political organizations which base their philosophies on racial or ethnic hatred is diminishing in numbers. But the hard core remains and is increasingly violent.

It is also increasingly sophisticated, seeking to hide its vulgar racist message behind a more palatable image. In Tennessee and other states, he said, political candidates with thinly veiled racist platforms are experiencing a disturbing degree of success. Americans must be attuned to the themes which betray the underlying values of these politicians and groups, and reject them as the antithesis of American principles, as would-be destroyers of the beautiful American mosaic.

DAILY NEWS

New York City, New York, August 7, 1987

The static over Pope John Paul's meeting with Kurt Waldheim may have subsided. But the anger and dismay generated by that meeting is as fresh as ever. That, it seems obvious, is why the Pope now plans to meet at the Vatican with Jewish leaders prior to his September trip to the U.S.

Early reports suggest that expectations on both sides are sensible and modest. No dramatic confrontations. Just a thoughtful conversation between reasonable people about a potentially explosive situation.

In the face of the agonies of moral and doctrinal feelings on all sides of the controversy, that is very, very welcome. And—it is to be hoped—useful.

The Evening Gazette

Worcester, Massachusetts, July 9, 1987

Efforts by two American Protestant denominations to undo centuries of prejudice against Judaism and Jewish people show how deep-seated such attitudes have been. The moves are particularly welcome in a time of sporadic outbursts of anti-Semitism.

The United Church of Christ at its recent national convention approved a major position paper that included such statements as "Judaism has not been superseded by Christianity" and "God has not rejected the Jewish people."

The Presbyterian Church (U.S.A.) debated a similar affirmation of Jewish faith at its convention last month, but discussion broke down over the statement's strong support of the state of Israel. The UCC statement did not mention Israel or Zionism. Both denominations have done extensive missionary work among Arabs in the Middle East.

Many of the pogroms and much of the persecution of Jews throughout European history were based on theological arguments that Jews had been responsible for the crucifixion of Jesus or that Christianity had supplanted Judaism in God's favor. The Nazi Holocaust is seen by some as growing out of those positions.

The Roman Catholic Church, during the Second Vatican Council, rejected the notion that Christianity had taken Judaism's place or that Judaism's ancient covenant with God had been supplanted. This position was reinforced as recently as last year when Pope John Paul II preached at a synagogue in Rome. But the modern state of Israel remains a troublesome issue for the Vatican, which counts many Catholics among the Arab nations, particularly in Lebanon. The Vatican has never established diplomatic relations with Israel.

People of good will find religious persecution of whatever form abhorrent. But sentiments of long-standing often defy logic and are difficult to dislodge. The United Church of Christ statement and the continuing Presbyterian debate are valuable expressions of tolerance and respect for one of the world's most ancient religions. They should go a long way toward advancing relations between Christians and Jews.

THE DAILY OKLAHOMAN

Oklahoma City, Oklahoma, June 22, 1987

CHURCHES have been getting involved in social and political issues for years, and the public ought to be as interested in these activities as the more sensational behavior of some television evangelists.

A case in point is the 3.1 million-member Presbyterian Church (USA). At their recent general assembly, delegates elected a woman as their leader, adopted a controversial document on Christian-Jewish relations, and took positions favoring homosexuals.

The church's new moderator is Isabel Wood Rogers, a Richmond, Va., teacher who spent a six-month sabbatical working in a program for battered women and rape victims. She succeeds the Rev. Benjamin Weir, a former hostage in Lebanon.

As chief spokeswoman for the church, she may be commenting frequently on a paper which affirms "God's promise of land" to the Jews, but explicitly does not endorse the Jews' claim to what is now Israel. Further, the document urges Presbyterians to fight bigotry and prejudice against Moslems and Arabs in the United States.

Another action that might prompt some interest was a decision to ask federal and state governments to rescind laws governing private sexual behavior between consenting adults, and to pass laws forbidding discrimination based on sexual orientation. A new church study to be undertaken on sexuality may recommend lifting of the current ban on ordination of "unrepentant" homosexuals.

A move to put the church on record as advocating tax resistance and civil disobedience to nuclear defense policies apparently has not been successful. But activists in the denomination persist in pursuing other avenues of dissent.

Prominent among these is the sanctuary movement, which combines the harboring of illegal aliens with the political stance of opposition to U.S. government policy in Central America. In 1985, the denomination contributed $100,000 and considerable staff time to the legal defense of church workers indicted for conspiring to violate immigration laws.

The church's endorsement of sanctuary is being challenged by a Nashville-based caucus — Presbyterians for Democracy and Religious Freedom — which contends that local church members don't favor the idea. The group points to a survey of the 11,621 Presbyterian congregations which showed that only 1.2 percent of those responding had agreed to become sanctuary churches. Nearly 80 percent reported they had either studied and rejected sanctuary status or had no plans to take up the issue.

With so many issues on the minds of Presbyterians, they may be hard pressed to find time to worship.

Newsday

New York City, New York, August 23, 1987

At a rather chilly time in Catholic-Jewish relations, Pope John Paul II has made an extraordinary gesture of conciliation that should go far to warm the atmosphere at his scheduled meetings next month with American Jewish leaders.

Jews were not alone in being perplexed by some of the Pope's actions and statements in recent months. His audience in June with Austria's President Kurt Waldheim, so recently unmasked as an accomplice in Nazi war crimes, was only the latest source of bewilderment. When John Paul went to West Germany in April to begin the beatification of Edith Stein, a convert from Judaism who died at Auschwitz, he had copious and much-deserved praise for Catholics who had defied the Third Reich but nothing to say about those elements in the German Catholic hierarchy that had not. And in May, when he visited the Maidenek extermination camp in Poland, he listed 14 nationalities of victims but failed to mention that the vast majority were Jews.

These were unsettling omissions. History records that, sometimes by deed and sometimes by silence, the German church played a role in Adolf Hitler's rise to power. Maidenek, like Auschwitz and many other concentration camps, was set up and run as a murder machine for Jews. Although millions of Christians died in them, Jews were uniquely singled out for total destruction.

If the Pope was perceived as less than fully responsive to these facts, he has now addressed them in a profoundly meaningful manner. In a letter to the president of the National Conference of Catholic Bishops, he acknowledged a the need for Christians to "approach with immense respect the terrifying experience of the extermination, the *Shoah*, suffered by the Jews during the Second World War." That experience, he wrote, should remain "before the eyes of the church, of all peoples and of all nations, as a warning, a witness and a silent cry," and "it is not permissible for anyone to pass by with indifference." John Paul offered the church's sincere sorrow for suffering endured in the past, and fraternal solidarity for the future.

This declaration deserves to be studied around the world, in Catholic churches and elsewhere, as a powerful moral directive about the necessity to take a stand against bigotry and human suffering. It holds special lessons for the young in Germany and Austria who want to come to terms with the past. It's a text that deserves the wider currency and enduring status that encyclicals receive; perhaps its sentiments will some day be expressed in that more weighty form.

THE KANSAS CITY STAR
Kansas City, Kansas, July 5, 1987

The recent meeting between Pope John Paul II and Austrian President Kurt Waldheim further frayed relations between Roman Catholics and Jews. The pope never publicly mentioned charges that Waldheim committed Nazi war crimes, and Jews were justifiably angry.

Now Cardinal John J. O'Connor of New York has proposed a quiet-time idea that may help. He says Catholics and Jews should hold a joint prayer service as a start toward healing divisions. The purpose of the service would be "not to dialogue, not to give speeches or argue or debate, but simply to pray together for increased mutual understanding and a peaceful resolution of a regrettable difference," says the cardinal. It may seem like a naive way to undo such damage but it makes much sense.

Not only would it allow Catholics and Jews to gather in peace under one roof but it would allow both groups to take a deep breath and to seek help from a source outside themselves, a creator both groups worship.

Cardinal O'Connor, who visited Israel earlier this year and who has tried to improve Jewish-Catholic relations, knows a prayer service is only a beginning and other efforts would need to follow it. But if the idea works, it would result in Catholics and Jews talking quietly with their God. And surely that's better than yelling at each other.

THE PLAIN DEALER
Cleveland, Ohio, August 23, 1987

Relations between the Vatican and Jewish leaders, seriously strained in recent months, may begin to mend as a result of a remarkable letter from Pope John Paul II to Archbishop John L. May of St. Louis, president of the National Conference of Catholic Bishops. In the letter, the pope describes Jews as "our elder brothers in the faith of Abraham." That description of bonding surprised and pleased Jewish spokesmen more accustomed to thinking of the papacy as favoring proselytizing of Jews.

The letter is considered a sincere and sensitive effort to assure Jews that John Paul fully recognizes their unique role in the Holocaust, a perception that was put in doubt by earlier papal actions, particularly the reception of Austrian President Kurt Waldheim at the Vatican. Waldheim, an officer in Hitler's army, has been linked to war crimes in Greece and Yugoslavia and, as a result, has been barred from entering the United States.

Jewish dismay over the Waldheim episode threatened to disrupt a scheduled meeting between the pope and Jewish leaders in Miami next month. To head off such an unpleasant possibility, the Vatican agreed to receive a group of Jewish officials Sept. 1 to discuss their concerns over Roman Catholic attitudes towards the Jews.

The pope's letter represents a major step forward in establishing a framework of communication between Roman Catholics—and, by example other Christians—and Jews. Far from seeming to minimize the sufferings of Jews under the Nazis, the pope considers the Holocaust to be for all countries "a warning, a witness and a silent cry."

Obviously, John Paul is concerned that nothing should mar his forthcoming visit to the United States. But it would be wrong to regard his letter to Archbishop May as an exercise in fence-mending for a narrow purpose. The language of his letter appears to be heartfelt, the tone conciliatory. In that light, John Paul's reception of Waldheim appears all the more inexplicable. Some Jewish spokesmen have suggested it simply was an error of judgment on the pope's part. By the same token, his letter could be seen as a welcome acknowledgement of a wrong to be righted.

Georgia County Draws Marchers

One of the largest civil rights actions since the 1960s took place Jan. 24, 1987 in all-white Forsyth County, Ga. Some 15,000 to 20,000 demonstrators from many states marched through the town of Cumming, the seat of Forsyth County, to protest.

The march followed a much smaller one Jan. 17 that had been disrupted by Ku Klux Klan members and supporters. The break-up of that march had brought Forsyth County into the national spotlight.

Predominantly rural Forsyth County was located in northern Georgia not far from metropolitan Atlanta. Its population was about 38,000. The county had been all-white since 1912, when some 1,000 black residents had been driven out following the rape of an 18-year-old white woman, who died of her injuries. Before she died, the woman had accused three black men of the attack. One was subsequently lynched, and the other two were hanged after a quick trial.

The earlier march had originally been planned as a "walk for brotherhood" by Charles A. Blackburn, a Californian who moved to Forsyth County in the early 1980s. He said he wanted to show that "it would be O.K. for black people to come visit Forsyth County." But, amid threats and lack of support, he called off his plans.

THE ATLANTA CONSTITUTION
Atlanta, Georgia, January 26, 1987

If numbers count, then brotherhood and racial harmony won out over hate and racism in Forsyth County on Saturday — and handily, by something better than 10 to one. But was this a victory for the long run or just for the day?

It was unquestionably an accomplishment of historic proportions. Some 20,000 persons — far more than the organizers had dared to hope for — volunteered for the brotherhood march. They convincingly demonstrated the utter unacceptability of the events of a week earlier, when another march in Forsyth County, with the benign theme of brotherhood, had been attacked and aborted by an unexpectedly large turnout of violent Ku Klux Klan members and their allies.

Certainly the message of that sad day could not be allowed to stand, not for the good of Georgia or of Forsyth County. And it as especially stirring that the huge reprove was delivered by a crowd that was about one-third white.

Far from suggesting that the South has not changed, as a few would willfully have it, the events of the last two weekends dramatized just how much it *has* changed.

The change was apparent in the dedicated and skillful protection given the civil rights march this weekend by officers from an array of state and local law-enforcement agencies. It was clear as well in the official embrace that the march received in Cumming. The usual old race-baiters and hate-mongers worked the fringe, but at the center stood both of Georgia's U.S. senators, the major elected officials of Forsyth County and Cumming and the local chamber of commerce. Their message to the marchers was simple and direct: Welcome.

It would be naive in the extreme, however, to suppose that the issues revealed by the violence that caught everyone off guard a week earlier were settled by the second, successful march.

Forsyth specifically, but other counties as well that have harbored a similar racial inhospitableness, are challenged to move beyond mute dislike of the intolerance and ignorance that marked the opposition to the brotherhood marches. In particular, considering the youth of so many of the persons spewing racial hate, the schools would seem compelled to create programs to broaden the understanding of their students. State leadership in that is called for.

For the short term, it seems likely the Klan and other hate groups will try to use these recent events to increase their numbers and spread their sour influence. Wherever that has been so in the past, the experience has been clear: The most effective rebuff is by open, firm, unequivocal opposition from local political, business, religious and civic leadership.

For the long run, the challenge remains the creation of a Georgia, indeed of a nation, in which the habits of racial justice and amiability are so general and so secure that it would not occur to anyone to disrupt or deny them. With thoughtful follow-up, the march this Saturday will have walked us all a long mile closer to that goal.

The Oregonian
Portland, Oregon, January 14, 1987

Are Howard Beach and Forsythe County symbols of the promise or poison of American life? Do they symbolize a growing incidence of racial and religious violence across the country? Or, does their headline value tell more about the general climate of racial and religious harmony in the United States?

The absence of hard statistics leads to answers by anecdote and to misguided calls to require the U.S. attorney general to report annually on crimes that are racially, religiously or ethnically motivated.

It's not that some kind of periodic reporting on racial and religious harassment is unnecessary. Far from it. But the routine gathering of statistics in an office in Washington, D.C., will yield little but a national report that is prey to distortion and politicization and — more important — that does little to erase the ugliness, large or small, that mocks our ideals.

And to what end? The Justice Department investigates and prosecutes federal crimes as well as offers conflict-resolution services to deal with disputes between, for example, community groups and law enforcement agencies.

If the U.S. Civil Rights Commission is not periodically assessing progress toward freeing U.S. society of racial and religious hatred, it should be.

But religious and racial crimes — and their pathologies — are predominantly local and regional matters, best monitored and combated at those levels by private and public bodies sensitive to the area.

One fine example is the Northwest Coalition Against Malicious Harassment, a consortium of public and private organizations in the five-state region brought to life by the squalid activities of the white-supremacist Aryan Nation.

And there is certainly room for other entities — the state of Oregon, for instance — to take a deeper look at race relations in a particular area.

But sending more crime data, notoriously unreliable stuff at best, to Washington will do little to advance racial and religious harmony.

The Birmingham News
Birmingham, Alabama, January 27, 1987

The Forsyth County experience, in which angry whites confronted thousands of civil rights demonstrators in a small town north of Atlanta, is a disturbing reminder that beneath the normally calm surface of our integrated society there remains an undercurrent of hatred and rage. There are still some of our neighbors who hate other of our neighbors because of the color of their skin.

That is a perplexing problem. We can legislate away the legal barriers to equality of opportunity. We can demand that all Americans be treated equally under the law. We can dismantle the barriers that kept some of our citizens out of some neighborhoods, businesses and schools.

But what can we do to change men's hearts?

Gov. Guy Hunt, in his inaugural address as governor of Alabama, said the moment has finally arrived when we can put to rest the forces that have divided us since the days of the Civil War. We agree with him. It is time for us to "move forward together in unity," as Hunt said.

Unfortunately, though, there are some who have not yet gotten the message. There are some who want to cling to the soul-devouring hate that has held our region back for far too long.

Tragically, as we saw in Georgia, some of those who would hold us back are young people — the new generation which should be leading our beloved South to new heights, unfettered by the chains of prejudice.

We do not know what to say to these people that has not already been said. We can only turn with hope to the holy commandment and pray that all will hear: "Thou shalt love thy neighbour as thyself."

The Sun  Reporter
San Francisco, California, April 15, 1987

A number of individuals and important organizations have expressed alarm and some distress on rediscovering that racism is alive and well in the USA. It extends from Howard Beach, N.Y. to Forsyth County, Ga. Moreover, it is fueled and sustained by the overt and covert acts of the chief legal officer of the Reagan Administration, Attorney General Edwin Meese III.

Racism is also rampant in the international affairs of our nation, as examplified in the efforts of the Reagan administration to overtly and covertly assist South Africa in the maintenance and strengthening of apartheid, and by their supporting Savimbi in Angola despite the protest of Blacks, especially through TransAfrica.

We are eternally amazed at the readiness with which the Black leaders and white civil rights advocates and liberals lull themselves into a false sleep, and usually condemn and oppose any person or organization who pricks the conscience of the nation by making them aware that racism is a cancerous disease that will destroy not only an individual, but also the nation, nor will it go away without radical surgery.

The publisher is about to become the present-day Jeremiah, the weeping prophet, who attends church services in San Francisco and notes the fervent manner in which great choirs and the congregations sing the old spirituals and religious anthems, causing Dr. Goodlett to weep because it is obvious that Blacks feel singing and praying will free them from the ravages of racism. However, the fact that freedom and the cause of liberty will require energetic struggle and even the loss of life and limb in an effort to stamp out racism seems never to be understood by the collective Black mind. In fact, racism, institutional and individual, is so entwined in our everyday living that most Blacks do not understand or recognize racism when it is quietly imposed upon us by the establishment.

The recent preliminary results in the election for a successor to Sala Burton contains a reminder of how persons labeled liberals or Black leaders fail to recognize in their normal behavior that they reflect submerged streaks of racism. It becomes difficult to combat the scourge of racism if such seasoned community leaders as John Burton, Agar Jaicks or Willie Brown fail to recognize the hidden manifestations of racism. Despite the opportunity to vote for a Black person or a homosexual, two despised minorities, they utilized their organizations' ties and support to nominate and assist the front runner, Nancy Pelosi.

The process of electing a U.S. President in 1988 will also reflect the refusal of political leaders to deal with the problem of racism in the electoral process. How other than by racism can the Democratic leaders explain their refusal to give racial minorities, youth and senior citizens the same status as the requirement that 51 percent of the delegates be women? The same leaders will vigorously oppose the use of quotas in selecting the minority, senior citizen and youth delegates to the National Convention. How else can they explain the fact that Jesse Jackson, the most knowledgeable candidate for the high office of President, will not even be given the nomination for Vice President?

Now that the American people are newly awakened by the efforts to discuss the celebration of the 40th anniversary of Black entry into the national pastime, baseball, especially as we recall the hard struggle and demands placed upon Jackie Robinson in breaking into this sport, we believe the nation must not be allowed to sleep or ignore the existence of racism. The raison d'etre of this newspaper is to ever keep racism before the public eye.

THE ANN ARBOR NEWS
Ann Arbor, Michigan, January 27, 1987

It is hard not to be profoundly disturbed by events in Forsyth County, Georgia. Perhaps, as The Huntsville (Ala.) Times editorialized, it was too much to expect racism to be wiped out in a generation.

Just when many Americans were thinking that a better-educated country and integrated schools and a more honest portrayal of black people in the national media were contributing to a more tolerant and just society, along comes a setting which could have been lifted from the '60s.

There were the faces contorted with hate again. There were the racial epithets and taunts. In Georgia, America was on display again, and it wasn't something of which we could be proud.

Except for one aspect. Nearly 25,000 demonstrators in one of the largest civil rights demonstrations in the U.S. in a quarter century turned out to protest hate and bigotry. These people, and the bulk of their countrymen, still care about the dream articulated by Martin Luther King Jr.

Saturday's march was a response to a similar march the previous weekend by blacks and whites that was disrupted by Ku Klux Klan members and supporters who pelted the marchers with rocks, bottles and mud.

Incredibly in this day and age, the KKK lives. Not in strength, of course, or in the affections of any but a handful of racists, but just enough to remind all of us that as long as the Klan is on the march, there is no room for complacency.

Men who dress up in white bedsheets and pointy hats and spew racial venom are among the most contemptible elements in our society. Perhaps we err in making too much of one Klan-inspired act of violence in a semi-rural county in Georgia.

Still, racism lives, whether in Forsyth County or in other American communities. The civil rights march in Georgia follows hard on a widely publicized racial beating in the Howard Beach section of New York and speculation about the existence of a white backlash going on all over the country.

Since 1980, according to the Justice Department's Community Relations Service, the number of clashes between racial and ethnic groups has nearly tripled, from 99 to 276.

Note that date. It corresponds with the passing of one national administration and the emergence of another — one which has stood for standstills on affirmative action programs, a de-emphasis on civil rights and voting rights legislation and originally was opposed to the creation of a Martin Luther King federal holiday on grounds of lost worker productivity.

Cause and effect? Perhaps not. But insofar as a national administration establishes a mood and atmosphere for the country in the way it puts its beliefs into practice, it's interesting to speculate on why racial tension appears to be up.

Howard Beach and Forsyth County have shocked the country: Is racial prejudice coming out of the closet again, after a period when we thought it had been put behind us? Is the fact that this is 1987 and the KKK is still burning crosses and stoking the fires of race hatred an indication that education has failed?

Sad to say, demonstrations and protest marches and a leader's martyrdom did indeed rewrite our law books, but they did not end racism. For that, we must continue to follow King's lead — blunting the spear hurled in anger with the powerful weapon of peaceful resistance and giving the lie to segregation by preaching brotherhood.

Incidents which have made national headlines and other examples of racism in local communities should not throw right-thinking Americans into resignation or despair. King's birthday this month is a reminder that there are promises to keep and miles to go before America rests from this great labor.

Ku Klux Klan Gains Nationwide Attention

The Justice Department April 24, 1987 said that 15 white supremacists had been named in three separate federal indictments.

The indictments were as follows:

Firstly, 10 men associated with the neo-Nazi group Aryan Nations had been charged by a federal grand jury in Fort Smith, Ark. with conspiring to overthrow the U.S. government.

Secondly, one of the 10, plus four other men, had been charged by that jury with conspiring to murder a federal judge and a Federal Bureau of Investigation agent.

Thirdly, three of the Fort Smith defendants and a woman had been separately indicted by a grand jury in Denver for depriving radio talk show host Alan Berg of his civil rights – by machine-gunning him to death in 1984.

Seven of the 15 – including the four charged in connection with Berg's murder – were already serving prison terms for other convictions. Louis Beam Jr., a onetime Texas Ku Klux Klan organizer, was still at large. The other seven had been arrested before the indictments were announced. They included two of the most influential racist leaders in the U.S.: Aryan Nations chief Richard Girnt Butler, 69, and former Michigan Klan chief Robert E. Miles, 62.

The 10 defendants charged with sedition were accused of plotting to destroy utilities, pollute water supplies, set up guerilla training camps and kill federal officials and Jews. The alleged conspiracy took place between mid-1983 and early 1985.

The defendants planned to finance their activities by armed robberies and counterfeiting, according to the indictment.

In 1985, more than 20 members of the Aryan Nations's violent splinter group, known as the Order, had been convicted of or had pleaded guilty to crimes that included counterfeiting, arson, and armed robberies that netted more than $4 million. Much of that money had never been recovered.

"It's just another [North Carolina] town," said Virgil L. Griffin, 42, who led the marchers June 7. Griffin, who had been present at the 1979 confrontation, added, "We're going to all of them."

A federal jury in Fort Smith, Ark. April 7, 1988 acquitted 13 white supremacists of charges that they had conspired to overthrow the U.S. government and kill a federal judge and a Federal Bureau of Investigation agent.

Nine defendants were acquitted of seditious conspiracy for allegedly plotting to overthrow the government. Lawyers for the defendants had argued that the conspiracy theory had been invented by the government's key witness, James Ellison, a former member of a paramilitary racist organization who was currently serving a 20-year prison sentence for racketeering and illegal weapons manufacturing.

Two leaders of a white supremacist group were found liable by Multnomah County Circuit Court jury in Oregon Oct. 22, 1990 for inciting the 1988 beating death of a black Ethiopian immigrant in Portland.

The two men were Thomas Metzger, 52, and his son John, 22. The Metzgers were the leaders of the White Aryan Resistance, which was described as a loosely knit organization of white supremacists and "skinhead" youths from across the U.S. who advocated racism, anti-Semitism and neo-Nazism.

The Metzgers and other members of the group were ordered to pay a total of $12.5 million in punitive and compensatory damages.

Neither Thomas nor John Metzger had been charged with actually killing the immigrant, Mulugeta Seraw. Instead, they were charged with intentionally sending an agent to Portland to incite violence against minorities.

THE SPOKESMAN-REVIEW
Spokane, Washington,
August 2, 1988

Crime-fighting, like boxing, is a tactical game. There is a distinct danger in shadowboxing against a perceived threat and missing the knockout punch from the real threat lurking just behind you.

Spokane police, like their counterparts in other Northwest cities, have been bracing themselves to try to repel drug-selling gang members migrating north from Los Angeles. If, instead of a welcome mat, the gangs find police officers who block their initial attempts to set up shop here, it is hoped the undesirables will move on.

Police are well-aware that the possible influx of Los Angeles street gangs, with their semiautomatic weapons and their penchant for using them indiscriminately, must not be taken lightly. But a violent act that occurred in a Spokane grocery-store parking lot early Saturday indicates that another deadly and unpredictable menace *already* is afoot in this city.

Two "Skinheads" demanded to know, ironically, if a young black man was a member of the Bloods, a Los Angeles gang, before they attacked him with knives, inflicting serious injuries. No, the Skinheads are not concerned about keeping the gangs in check; their violence — and the remarks that accompanied their assault — constitutes an act of racial hatred.

The assailants, wearing neo-Nazi insignias, decided to pick on a black man in a relatively deserted setting in the early morning hours. And this is not the first violent incident in the city involving Skinheads; police say three of them threw rocks at a black teen-ager and his mother in downtown Spokane last week. There also have been scattered reports of fights started by Skinheads baiting blacks.

The Skinheads look like kids, with their shaved heads, Army boots and neo-Nazi paraphernalia, but there is nothing childish about the game they are playing. They are emulating racist neo-Nazis who have made their mark on this region's reputation and lifestyle with violence and intimidation.

Just when it had seemed that the climate of fear the racists created is fading, members of minorities once again feel they must be actively on guard against the threat of violence. It will take a concerted effort by police as well as the entire community to guard against any escalation of racist harassment and attacks by Skinheads and others who share their views.

The police must keep all bases covered in order to eliminate threats — both present and potential — to the community. That means playing hardball with both the drug-dealing gangs and the Skinheads.

MILWAUKEE SENTINEL

Milwaukee, Wisconsin, July 18, 1988

What Milwaukee police can do to limit the activities of a group of misfits known as "skinheads" should be done.

The small group of neo-Nazis with shaved heads has started showing up on Milwaukee's East Side and generally has been a nuisance on the Downer Ave. shopping strip.

Some buildings have been defaced with swastikas and other symbols; there have been threats and racial and ethnic slurs; there has been some violence; there have been some arrests.

There is a clear potential for even more serious trouble as area merchants, customers and strollers react with disgust to the bold and brash band of white supremacists.

Police must monitor the group closely. Their behavior demands it; their purposes are not peaceful.

The Miami Herald

Miami, Florida, October 31, 1988

WHITE supremacists, neo-Nazis, anti-Semites, and any others dedicated to demonstrating their bigotry should be on notice: Violate the rights of those whom you love to hate, and you'll be hit where it hurts — in the wallet. That's the message that a Federal-court jury wisely sent this week when it ruled that two white-supremacist groups must pay nearly $1 million in damages to racism protesters.

Held liable were the Invisible Empire Knights of the Ku Klux Klan and the Southern White Knights. At issue were the events of Jan. 17, 1987, when 55 marchers, most of them black, were jeered and pelted with stones and bottles in Forsyth County, Ga. The protesters went to Forsyth after white residents there vowed to exclude blacks. The jury ordered the two racist groups to pay $400,000 each into a pool that will be divided among the plaintiffs. Individuals were ordered to pay damages of $1,000 to $50,000 each.

"When they start paying these bills, they might think the next time they want to go out on a Saturday afternoon and violate someone's rights," said Morris Dees of the Southern Poverty Law Center. The center has led the legal campaign to make the Klan and its members liable for illegal activity.

Last year the center won a $7-million judgment for the mother of a black youth murdered by Klan members.

Attorneys argued this case based on one of several Reconstruction-era Federal statutes that protected the rights of recently emancipated blacks. That entire body of post-Civil War law, widely ignored for at least 100 years, is often the only legal avenue for pursuing certain discrimination cases. It has come to the rescue when state and other local legal systems fail.

The Anti-Defamation League of B'nai B'rith, the American Civil Liberties Union, and other civil-rights organizations report increases in hate groups and racist violence. These laws, crafted to combat 1860s racism, unfortunately still are needed in 1988.

In that light, it's ironic that the Supreme Court has voted to reconsider its 1976 *Runyon vs. McCrary* ruling, which permits individuals to seek punitive damages for private acts of discrimination. This is no time to diminish what is often the last bastion of legal hope for victims of irrational hatred.

ST. LOUIS POST-DISPATCH

St. Louis, Missouri, June 24, 1988

In Kansas City, where the Ku Klux Klan wanted to spread its racist message over a public access cable television channel, the City Council bowed to black political pressure and threw the baby out with the bath water. The council, by a lopsided vote of 9-2, has decided to cancel the public access channel because American Cablevision, with 140,000 subscribers, was about to allow the KKK open access to the channel.

This is thought to be one of the first such actions by a city regulating cable TV in the country — and it is a distressing precedent that ought to alarm people everywhere who are concerned with civil liberties. The immediate issue isn't what the Klan is saying; its message is repugnant and morally bankrupt. Instead, the issue is that a legislative body would cave in to the pressures of an organized interest group and so quickly dispose of the First Amendment right to free speech.

The American Civil Liberties Union has agreed to take the Klan's case to U.S. District Court. That would be in the public interest and should be pursued as far as possible until the Klan's right — which is also your right — is preserved for all users of public access channels. American Cablevision can replace its public access channel with a community programming channel that would allow the Klan — and its opponents — to speak. But programming control would be in the hands of the station instead of those presenting their ideas.

The mistake made in Kansas City is a common one. In seeking to deny the Klan a public forum, a threat is posed to the free exchange of ideas in a free society. While one may sympathize with the blacks, the solution is not to silence offensive views but to allow them to be heard and refuted. If the KKK can be censored, who knows what other opinions could be?

Arkansas Gazette

Little Rock, Arkansas, July 12, 1991

It wasn't so long ago that Ku Klux Klansmen and other white bigots habitually attacked civil rights marchers, shattering peaceful protests. They did it with impunity, and often with official encouragement.

Remembering those days, one might be tempted to condone as just retribution similar attacks in the other direction, such as occurred Sunday in Atlanta. But there's no excusing the incident. A mob of almost 1,000 disrupted three attempted marches by Klansmen and neo-Nazi "skinheads" in support of the South African government. The mob didn't fit any South African necklaces on the marchers — a modest show of restraint — but the mobsters did push and pummel, break the windows of a truck they believed to belong to a Klansman, and burn pro-Nazi literature and flags in the streets. The police, who always seemed unable to protect the civil rights marchers in the old days, were unable to protect the anti-civil rights marchers this time around.

Most importantly, the mob kept the Klansmen and the neo-Nazi skinheads from peacefully demonstrating for their beliefs, thus effectively denying them rights that are promised all Americans in the United States Constitution. The mob might as well have burned that document along with the Nazi pamphlets.

What a simple lesson it is, and how hard for some people to learn: The Constitution is for everybody, not just our crowd and the people who agree with us. Some people not only don't accept that basic principle of American democracy, they won't tolerate those who do. That's why the American Civil Liberties Union is perhaps the most "American" of all organizations. It practices what the Constitution preaches, the principles this republic was founded upon.

No other group that depends on private financial support has ever shown more courage than the ACLU did when it defended the rights of American Nazis to march at Skokie, Ill., home of many Jewish survivors of German concentration camps. The ACLU has always relied heavily on Jewish contributors, many of whom were angered by the organization's action.

Atlanta is a major Southern city with a black mayor. It is hosting a political convention at which one of the stars is a black who has come closer to a major presidential nomination than any other member of his race. Both men are living proof that the nation has made great progress in the last 30 years or so. What happened in the streets of Atlanta Sunday is proof that there can be no resting on the oars. When Klansmen and Nazis are denied their rights, so are we all.

St. Paul Pioneer Press & Dispatch
St. Paul, Minnesota, November 4, 1988

A U.S. Federal court jury wisely sent a strong message last week to Klan members, skinheads, neo-Nazis, anti-Semites and others of that ilk: Violate the rights of those whom you hate, and you'll feel it where it hurts — in the wallet.

The Invisible Empire Knights of the Ku Klux Klan and the Southern White Knights were held liable to the tune of nearly $1 million. The groups were sued because of their actions on Jan. 17, 1987, when they hurled rocks and bottles at racism protesters in Forsyth County, Ga. Marchers gathered in Forsyth to honor Martin Luther King's birthday after white residents there vowed on national television to exclude blacks from their community. Following a lynching incident in the 1920s, black farmer/landowners were literally run out of the county and none have lived in the area since.

Jury members ordered the two groups to pay $400,000 each into a pool that will be divided among the plaintiffs. Individuals were ordered to pay damages of $1,000 to $50,000 each. Most of the award is punitive; each of the 55 plaintiffs will receive only $50 in compensatory damages for injuries and inconvenience.

Richard Cohen, legal director of the Southern Poverty Legal Center and an attorney for the marchers, said he was pleasantly surprised by the level of punishment handed down by the court.

"When they start paying these bills, they might think the next time they want to go out on a Saturday afternoon and violate someone's rights," added Morris Dees, also of the Center. His organization has led the legal campaign to make the Klan and its members liable for illegal activity. Last year, the center won a $7 million judgment for the mother of a black youth murdered by Klan members.

Attorneys argued this case based on one of several Reconstruction-era federal statutes that protected the rights of recently emancipated slaves. That entire body of post-Civil War law, widely ignored for at least 100 years, is often the only legal avenue for pursuing certain discrimination cases. It has come to the rescue when state and other local legal systems have failed.

Given the recent increase in racially and ethnically motivated violence, as reported by groups such as the Anti-Defamation League, B'nai B'rith, and the American Civil Liberties Union, it is clear the laws aimed at 1860s racism are still needed in 1988. That is shameful.

In that light, it is ironic that the Supreme Court has voted to reconsider its 1976 Runyon vs. McCrary ruling, which permits individuals to seek punitive damages for private acts of discrimination. This is no time to diminish what is often the last bastion of legal hope for victims of insane and irrational bigotry.

TULSA WORLD
Tulsa, Oklahoma, October 27, 1988

THE $1-million judgment by an Atlanta jury against two racist groups invites a feeling that justice has been done. Sadly, however, it won't solve a thing.

Of course, the thugs in nearly all-white Forsyth County, Ga., who pelted civil rights marchers with rocks in January 1987 deserve to be punished. And, barring criminal action, monetary punishment is the only recourse. But taking money and property from the defendants will more than likely only fuel their hatred.

The judgment against the Ku Klux Klan and two white supremacist groups responsible for disrupting the march will be paid to 49 demonstrators who filed suit.

There was disagreement among those who filed the suit. Most were happy with the judgment and vowed to get every dime from the KKK. Others, such as Atlanta City Councilman Hosea Williams, dropped out of the suit. Williams said it would solve nothing to impoverish the families of the KKK members. He went so far as to publicly shake hands with and forgive those who had hurled rocks at him.

The Atlanta award is the second major one involving a Klan organization in two years. The other was brought by a mother whose son was beaten and lynched by KKK members.

Both judgments were needed. But neither will end racism or cause the KKK to fold. It doesn't take a lot of money to hate.

The only hope is to stop racism before it starts. Until then, monetary judgments won't make much difference.

THE ATLANTA CONSTITUTION
Atlanta, Georgia, November 7, 1988

If the American Civil Liberties Union (ACLU) is wondering why even its friends are sometimes down on it these days, it might reflect on its claim that Santa Claus must take up with the Christian Knights of the Ku Klux Klan.

The ACLU has filed a suit against the small town of Pelion, S.C., arguing that the Klan should be allowed into the town's Chirstmas parade. "The government simply has no right to judge whether the Christian Knights or anyone else is Christian enough, or politically correct enough, to participate in a public Christmas parade," the ACLU state director says.

Oh, yes it does. It is one thing to defend the free speech and free assembly rights of a group denied a parade permit because its views are noxious. It is quite another thing to argue that community parades must accept every scum-of-the-Earth outfit that shows up — Klans, Hell's Angels, Nazis.

A Christmas parade with the Klan in it would make no sense whatsoever. The ACLU flies in the face of common sense and stretches the U.S. Constitution dangerously by insisting otherwise.

The Constitution may say the Grinch has a right to be a grouch. It doesn't say he has a right to steal Christmas.

DAILY NEWS
New York City, New York, November 7, 1988

In January 1987, the nation was outraged by a violent attack on a group of civil rights marchers by 200 white supremacists in Forsyth County, Ga. The other day, justice was done when a federal court jury awarded nearly $1 million in damages to the marchers—money the attackers are supposed to pay. But will they?

Jeffrey Sliz, a lawyer representing David W. Holland, Grand Dragon of the Southern White Knights, doesn't think so: "These people aren't foolish, and they don't put assets in the name of an organization whose purpose is not very popular. Frankly, I wouldn't trade you a hot dog and a coke for the $800,000 in damages from the two groups."

The jury also ordered the Invisible Empire Knights of the Ku Klux Klan to pay $400,000 and assessed individual damages ranging from $1,000 to $50,000 against Holland. Last year, an Alabama jury awarded $7 million to the mother of a black man slain by members of the klan.

Despite the feeling by many that such damage suits are a good way to address racially motivated violence, one of the best known of the 55 marchers—the Rev. Hosea Williams—withdrew as a plaintiff. Williams said seeking money damages is not true to the civil rights movement's goal of "redemption and forgiveness."

Williams, a well-known movement maverick, is entitled to his opinion. But on this one, he appears off base. Bigotry—especially the kind that erupts into violence—must be dealt with in the most effective manner. If fines help put hate groups out of business, go for it. Even better, make sure they pay. Then justice will most certainly be served.

New York City, New York, March 24, 1988

A loony tunes white supremacist organization is trying to force the American Telephone & Telegraph Co. to abandon its commitment to minority hiring. AT&T, long a leader in employing minorities, isn't happy. For very good reason.

The racist group calls itself the National Alliance. Based in Washington, it promotes the study of the writings of Adolf Hitler. Its leader, a kook named William Pierce, heads a white supremacist church in West Virginia and has written a fictional account of a race war ending with a Hitler-like group running the world. Get the picture?

By owning 100 shares of stock, the group has forced its hiring resolution onto the agenda of AT&T's annual meeting April 20 and the proxies for it. But to its everlasting credit, the company has recommended that shareholders vote it down. Amen.

LAS VEGAS REVIEW-JOURNAL
Las Vegas, Nevada, November 14, 1988

Last week local Nazi-oriented skinheads mixed it up with Jewish protesters in front of the Imperial Palace. The protesters were on the scene to express their objections to casino owner Ralph Engelstad's collection of Nazi memorabilia and Engelstad's past practice of staging "birthday parties" for Adolf Hitler. The skinheads showed up to protest the protest.

Both groups had a perfect right to be there so long as things stayed peaceful. Protests and peaceful assembly (with the emphasis on peaceful) are a time-honored tradition — and an ironclad constitutional right — in this country. When fisticuffs broke out, the police moved in, and rightly so.

Before the brawling began, both groups were legally exercising their constitutional rights.

We also are going to exercise our constitutional right of free speech and say that the skinheads espouse a rancid line of racist swill that anyone of even marginally sound mind will find offensive in the extreme.

These callow youths who shave their heads, sport Nazi regalia and steel-toed boots seem to take pride in their ignorance. These dim-witted cretins pass out literature, for example, claiming the Nazi Holocaust never happened. Here is a quote from a leaflet handed out at last week's demonstration: "In reality, the 6 million Jews who disappeared from the Europe of 1933-45 were smuggled illegally into the USA by (President) Roosevelt and his JEW DEAL."

The know-nothing Neo-Nazis arrive at this conclusion using bogus material produced by charlatans. The Holocaust is historical fact. It's occurrence is not open to question. Thousands of newspaper accounts and miles of film footage taken by allied troops who liberated the death camp survivors across Europe — these alone prove the case for the Holocaust. But we also have thousands of eyewitness accounts, mountains of history books, reams of Nazi documents, hundreds of volumes based on the stories of concentration camp survivors, not to mention evidence directly out of the mouths of the Nazi killers, plus the concentration camps themselves, many of which still stand, complete with ovens and gas chambers. Thousands today bear on their bodies the crude tattoos scratched on their skins by SS guards.

The Holocaust is one of the most carefully and thoroughly documented events in history. To say that the Nazis did not murder millions of Jews and others is the same as saying Hitler never existed and there was no such thing as World War II.

Only those who are willfully and aggressively ignorant can deny the Holocaust occurred. If the boneheaded skinheads had their way, it would happen again, and that's what makes their message so hateful — even if it is legal.

The Hutchinson News
Hutchinson, Kansas, March 9, 1988

A funny thing happened along Jayhawk Boulevard at the University of Kansas Monday evening.

The Ku Klux Klan came to town and discovered that free speech works well, after all.

The discovery was long in coming to KU.

Two weeks ago, when the visit was first revealed, a few black ministers complained, and KU's administrators and faculty fled in terror from free speech. Rather than offend a special interest group, KU canceled the meeting.

After a few days of student outrage, federal mediation and the intervention of student groups, however, the KU administration and faculty discovered a sliver of courage. They decided to allow some free speech, after all. They permitted the Klan creatures to be invited.

The two Kluxers arrived at Hoch Auditorium Monday. They were confronted by 3,000 people outside, 2,000 inside the auditorium. Most of the 5,000 were protesting the Klan, who discovered that free speech works both ways.

Freedom of speech in America allows kooks, nincompoops and even Klan creatures to have their say. But the same freedom doesn't require anybody to listen. Those who do listen have an equal opportunity to express their disgust and outrage. From a melting pot of ideas, truth emerges.

The Klan is probably incapable of learning any truths. But the 5,000 or so protesters rediscovered the virtues of free speech in a robust democracy.

And if Kansas is lucky, the previously terrified KU administrators and faculty even learned that the search for truth on a university campus is a noble undertaking. It is not to be surrendered to any special-interest pressure group.

THE ATLANTA CONSTITUTION
Atlanta, Georgia, July 31, 1988

Do not imagine that the naming of a ballpark for James R. Venable would be unrelated to his Ku Klux Klan background. The former imperial wizard of the hooded hatemongers put the lie to that Wednesday with a vow to erect his own sign proclaiming the Klan connection.

He said he will put up a 12-foot illuminated sign on an adjoining lot he owns, saying something like "This land was donated 30 years ago by James R. Venable, an old Klansman," whether the Stone Mountain City Council honors him or not.

That ought to make the council's next move very simple. It should not even think of concurring in a tribute to the racist, anti-Semitic cross-burners of a bygone era.

Not that it has to. A 1987 city ordinance prohibits the erection of anything like the monument Mr. Venable proposes, and tempers on the council are wearing thin.

Enough is enough. Naming a park for its benefactor under usual circumstances would be one thing. Falling in with an unreconstructed racist, who accuses those officials with second thoughts of trying to curry favor with black voters, is something else.

The council need not argue any further about the honor. The honor is in refusing Mr. Venable's request.

Detroit Free Press
Detroit, Michigan, June 6, 1988

BIGOTS DON'T all wear white sheets. In fact, membership in groups such as the Ku Klux Klan and the American Nazi Party has decreased. However, a new wave of more violent hate groups, such as the National Association for the Advancement of White People, the Aryan Nations, the White Aryan Resistance, and the Order, has been quietly recruiting members.

The crimes members of these groups commit often go unrecognized and unpunished because there is no central agency for monitoring such crimes. A bill called the Hate Crimes Statistics Act would correct that by requiring the U.S. Justice Department to record and publish statistics on crimes motivated by prejudice. The House passed the measure by a vote of 383 to 29. The Senate should act as decisively.

There were 2,900 crimes motivated by prejudice based on race, religion, ethnicity and sexual orientation from 1980 to 1986, according to the National Council of Churches. Those included 121 murders, 302 assaults, 301 cross-burnings, 145 shootings, and 138 bombings.

Minorities have tolerated such violence long enough without the criminal justice system taking action. It's time for the federal government to send the message to hate groups that their criminal activities are traceable and will no longer be tolerated.

Hate Crime Concerns Rise Throughout U.S.

The Southern Poverty Law Center in Atlanta, Ga. reported Feb. 6, 1989, in its annual survey of racist activity, that the white supremacist movement had been revitalized by the emergence of violent, neo-Nazi skinhead youth groups. (Many neo-Nazis were known as skinheads because they favored shaved or close-cropped heads.)

"Not since the height of Klan activity during the civil rights era has there been a white supremacist group so obsessed with violence or so reckless in its disregard for the law," the organization said.

It also claimed that the skinheads had forged ties to traditional racist groups such as the Ku Klux Klan. It said that skinhead individuals had been linked to four racially motivated murders in Western states, as well as attacks on blacks, Asians, Hispanics, Jews and homosexuals.

President George Bush April 23, 1990 signed into law a bill that would require the federal government to keep records on crimes motivated by racial, ethnic or sexual prejudice. The bill, the Hate Crimes Statistics Act, had been passed by the House on April 4 by a vote of 408-18, and by the Senate on Feb. 8 by a vote of 92-4.

Bush hailed the measure as a "significant step to help guarantee civil rights for every American," and he added, "The faster we can find out about these hideous crimes, the faster we can track down the bigots who commit them."

Bush signed the bill at a White House ceremony to which congressional leaders and civil rights groups had been invited. Among those in attendance were the first avowed homosexual and lesbian activists ever invited to a White House ceremony.

The law would require the Justice Department to compile and publish data for the next five years on crimes motivated by prejudice based on race, religion, ethnic background or sexual orientation. The crimes covered would include murder, rape, assault, arson, vandalism and intimidation. Although several states required such monitoring, the new bill marked the first time that the federal government would collect nationwide data on the motivation behind crimes.

The statistics would be used to monitor the extent of hate crimes, to determine law enforcement priorities and to suggest possible changes in the law.

The major opposition to the bill had come from conservative lawmakers who were opposed to the inclusion of "sexual orientation" as a category together with race and religion. According to gay rights activists, the new legislation would be the first federal law relating to civil rights that included the classification of sexual orientation.

Conversely, racist and anti-Semitic attitudes were on the decline in America, according to an analysis of several existing surveys released Jan. 7, 1992. The analysis, which had been conducted on behalf of the American Jewish Committee, showed that, in general, Americans were growing more tolerant of all minority groups.

The analysis had examined the results of several major national surveys dating back to 1958, including the annual General Social Survey, conducted by the National Opinion Research Center in Chicago. The report was written by Tom Smith, director of the General Social Survey.

The report showed that survey respondents had reported more positive opinions about all minority groups in 1990 than they had in the past, when asked to rank the social standing of 37 different groups. The groups that posted the highest increases in positive responses were Japanese, blacks and Chinese, although all three groups, remained in the bottom half of the social-standing rankings. (The groups at the top of the ranking were native white Americans, "people of my own ethnic background," British, Protestants, Roman Catholics, French, Irish, Swiss, Swedes and Austrians.)

Minneapolis Star and Tribune
Minneapolis, Minnesota, February 2, 1992

Hate crimes are making headlines in the Twin Cities and maybe that's good — the headlines, not the crimes. It's an opportunity to take a hard look in the mirror.

If anything positive can come from the latest outbreak — racist and anti-Semitic mail sent to Minneapolis police officers and civic leaders — it's the realization that some people haven't outgrown the rawest forms of bias. But another message must prevail: This community will not tolerate outbursts of racial hatred.

It's a sad commentary when the murder of a black man who worked 30 years for racial justice unleashes racial hate. Minneapolis Police Chief John Laux was right in promptly asking the FBI to investigate racist, threatening letters to black officers. If police are targets, who will be next?

Indians, African Americans, gays and lesbians and others have warned that this is a time of danger. The Anti-Defamation League recorded 307 hate crimes in 1990, up from 253 the year before. The 1990 cross-burning in St. Paul is before the Supreme Court in a test of the city's hate-crime ordinance, but apart from constitutional questions, the incident is a reminder of the vicious forms in which racial hatred can appear.

Modern white supremacy embraces a broader spectrum of hate, including Jews, Asians and Hispanics, and is prone to more sophisticated techniques than the old-line Klan. The movement's members tap into computerized message boards and fund-raising lists. Their message is on cable TV, protected by the First Amendment. But whether manifested in high-tech harassment or old-fashioned violence, acts of racial hatred cannot be ignored. They must be actively countered, in the Twin Cities as elsewhere, by people of good will.

The banner of local civic pride carries the pleasant if dull slogan "Minnesota nice." A proud community will recognize its faults, too, and try to cure them. The unpleasant, abrasive slogan is "Minnesota ugly." It stands for racial hatred. Blot out the slogan. Blot out the hate.

Chicago Defender

Chicago, Illinois, February 9, 1991

For the fourth straight year anti-Semitic incidents increased in America. Last year, 1,685 of the bigoted occurrences tainted our nation. Those distressing statistics were recently released by the Anti-Defamation League and they certainly don't speak well of how well some Americans are respecting the life, liberty and pursuit of happiness of our Jewish brothers and sisters.

Reports have shown that since the war with Iraq, there has been an increase of verbal taunts and brutal assaults against Arab Americans. The stupid and ruthless treatment of their own didn't stop with the violence against Arabs and Jews. Hate crimes against African Americans also surged in various areas of the country in 1990.

It's important for leaders *and* grassroots individuals to be concerned about the rise in hate crimes. After all, such crimes have caused the destruction of lives, the vandalism of valuable property and the disruption of innumerable families.

After the U. S. Civil War ended, the violence of hate crimes escalated and had a grievious impact on communities in rural areas and cities across the United States. From that period on, media and law enforcement organizations have listed incidents where individuals of a particular racial or religious group were beaten, unfairly imprisoned, lynched, or brutalized.

The U.S. government, in passing the Bill of Rights and instituting laws like Brown vs. the Board of Education, did much to protect the rights of every American. Our country deserves credit for such positive efforts in attempting to make the principles espoused in the Declaration of Independence and the U.S. Constitution work for *all* the nation's people.

It is tragically sad the federal government was directly responsible for over two centuries of the American slave trade and the racist Dred Scott decision. Also, the ill-advised withdrawal of federal troops from Southern states, which resulted in the premature end of the Reconstruction Period that left ex-slaves defenseless against an onslaught of bigoted, reactionary actions by the area's whites. There was also the incarceration of Japanese Americans during World War II.

These bigoted, repressive acts have, over the years, helped racists and anti-Semites feel comfortable in their hate crime activities. The relatively small number of prosecution and imprisonment for hate crimes has also given bigots more courage to commit their stupid acts.

How can the average American change things? Two good ways any individual can help to limit the spread and impact of hate crimes is to (a) develop a geniune respect for the rights and property of others and (b) refuse to be a part of the bigoted action. Our nation *must* reverse the appalling number of hate crimes that still plague its citizens, otherwise, we will not be able to live out the great creeds upon which our wondrous nation was founded — and that would truly be *an American tragedy*.

The Gazette

Cedar Rapids, Iowa, February 23, 1991

A WAVE of intolerance continues in the United States, with much of the trouble occurring on college campuses. Each incident is worrisome, whether based on race, ethnicity, religion, gender or sexual orientation.

Most noticeable, perhaps because of the gulf war and the focus on non-combatant Israel, is the surge of anti-Semitic incidents. The 1990 total was a record 1,685. It was, according to the Anti-Defamation League of B'nai B'rith, the fourth straight year of increases. Of the 1,685 anti-Jewish acts, 927 were vandalism and 758 were harassment, assaults or threats against Jews or Jewish institutions.

Twelve years ago, when the ADL began its audit of anti-Semitic incidents, we thought such intolerance was on the wane. After all, ignorance is the real villain. And chipping away at anti-Semitism seemed no more complicated than improving the schooling of the populace.

Which shows how much we knew. Enlightenment is *not* a byproduct of general education. Today college campuses themselves have just seen a four-year surge in anti-Semitism. Ninety-five incidents occurred at 57 institutions last year, compared with 69 at 54 campuses in 1989.

How to explain it? Arthur J. Kropp, president of People for the American Way, says (concerning anti-Semitism and other forms of intolerance on campuses), "Bigotry doesn't start at the college gate. Campus life is a microcosm of a society bitterly divided along racial, religious and other lines. As one administrator told us, 'The intolerance that is so rampant is largely due to the fact that most of our students come from highly segregated environments and their first experience with difference is on the campus.'

"But colleges have always been the crucible of conflict and change in our society, and this issue is no different. As they prepare our young people to join the workforce, colleges should be teaching them the fundamentals of getting along in the workforce. . . . If our nation is to thrive in the next century, mastering 'multicultural literacy' — the skill of understanding and respecting cultural differences — must become an indispensable part of the college experience as Lit or Math."

But danger lurks there, too, according to Kropp. "Education officials should not rush headlong into hasty or ill-planned schemes to minimize these incidents, which they view as embarrassing. . . . Too many schools are clamping down on free speech in the name of combatting words that hate. That's the last lesson we should be teaching — fighting intolerance with more intolerance."

Still, "multi-cultural literacy" seems the most promising approach to fighting anti-Semitism and other forms of bigotry. Two new ADL programs, "A Campus of Difference" and "A Workplace of Difference," increase students' and workers' awareness of cultural and ethnic diversity.

We would like to be optimistic. But anti-Semitic acts and other hate crimes seem to occur in cycles. They subside during times of relative prosperity, only to return during recession. Financial problems invariably are blamed on shadowy "Jewish bankers in the East."

Hatred toward Jews, blacks, Catholics and other minorities is persistent and insidious. "Multi-cultural literacy" had better remain a required course well into the 21st century.

The Hutchinson News

Hutchinson, Kansas, February 20, 1987

A jury in Alabama may have found a way to communicate with the Ku Klux Klan.

The jury hit the Klan with a $7 million damage judgment.

An all-white jury of Alabamians took a few hours last week to decide its message to the state's Klan. But when it decided, wow. The jury assessed the damage award against the Klan because two Klansmen murdered a black teen-ager.

The $7 million was levied against the two murderers, six past or present members and the entire United Klans of America Inc.

The scum probably can't pay even a part of the award, but in the process of not paying, the Klan may be driven into bankruptcy. That isn't the appropriate place for the Klan to be driven, but there is something poetic about the idea that the Klan, which is bankrupt intellectually, would be done in by being driven to financial bankruptcy.

This is also something like the way the nation got rid of Al Capone some years back, and a technique that works with other criminals today.

With or without the financial bankruptcy of the Klan this time, however, more communicating will probably be needed in the future.

The disease that leads to outfits like the Klan lingers, but it will surely be held in check better if those afflicted with the disease are held accountable for their actions, both criminally and financially.

ST. LOUIS POST-DISPATCH

St. Louis, Missouri, May 24, 1987

A recent jury verdict against the nation's largest Ku Klux Klan group ought to serve as a warning that juries — even all-white juries in the South — are growing less tolerant of the terrorism waged by this outfit. The Klan and six of its former and current members were hit with a $7 million judgment in connection with the slaying of a 19-year-old black man, Michael Donald, in 1981 in Mobile, Ala. The judgment was won by the victim's mother. Because the Klan unit had few assets, the group was ordered to turn over its $250,000 headquarters to satisfy the judgment.

Civil rights lawyers may be overly optimistic in assuming the court ruling will mean the end of the Klan, but the action certainly speaks highly of the jury in deciding to make the organization pay a heavy price for its hate. The Klan's behavior shows it always has felt itself above the law. The heinous crimes in which its members have been implicated include the widely publicized murder in 1965 of Viola Gregg Liuzzo, a white civil rights worker from Detroit. She was slain while in Alabama to take part in the historic civil rights march from Selma to Montgomery.

Murder for any reason is unconscionable, even more so when committed by a group that kills at random simply to show its strength. The judgment may be of little consolation to the mother of the youth who was beaten to death, his body left hanging from a tree. But the jury has taken a major first step toward eradicating this kind of repulsive activity by making a hate group liable for its members criminal behavior.

FORT WORTH STAR-TELEGRAM

Fort Worth, Texas, February 17, 1987

The ruling handed down by a federal jury in a damage suit against the United Klans of America provides a valuable weapon for use in the fight against organized racial terrorism.

The awarding of $7 million in damages against the Klan for the 1981 murder of a black teen-ager in Mobile, Ala., serves notice to the Klan and similar hate groups that lynching can be very costly to them.

The mother of the youth, who had been beaten and strangled and left hanging in a tree, says the money means nothing to her because it won't bring her child back, but "she's glad justice was done."

In this case, justice was done in a way that will hit the Klan in its collective solar plexus. While the money, which is likely to translate into transferring the title to the Klan's national headquarters to the family of the victim, means nothing to the mother, it means a lot to the Klan.

Merely convicting a couple of Klan stooges who did the actual deed and sentencing one to life imprisonment and another to death was not appropriate justice. The actual murderers were themselves victims of the insidious poison dispensed by the Klan leaders. Those two are expendable to the organization.

The damage award inflicts punishment upon the Klan where it will really hurt. The loss of such a sum will put a severe drain on the Klan's resources and diminish its ability to organize and recruit. It won't put the Klan out of business altogether, unfortunately, but it could put it out of the lynching business.

Klan leaders should be able to see that the precedent set in this lawsuit has placed too high a price on their brand of terrorism for the organization to continue to perpetrate such atrocities.

The Boston Globe

Boston, Massachusetts, December 19, 1987

Poor Dwight McCarthy. Perhaps he should call the Utah Civil Liberties Union. His radio talk show, the Aryan Nations Hour, was canceled because of protests by people he feels are racially and morally inferior – a "liberal-Marxist-homosexual-Zionist coalition."

McCarthy, 37, began a weekly program on Dec. 5 to express Aryan Nations' disgust with the way America is going – recognizing rights and liberties for all manner of undesirables. McCarthy said he was within his free-speech rights to express his views on how to make the country safe for decent white folk.

And what thanks does he get? Some of his fellow citizens formed a group called Utahans against Aryan Nations, and, together with several hundred subscribers to the already-cited philosophies, staged a rally six blocks from the radio station.

Businesses with advertisements on the station – KZZI – put profits before purity and caved in to the pressure from the communist-leaning melting-pot contingent – the NAACP, the Anti-Defamation League, the National Or-ganization for Women and other equally radical groups. That probably explains the desire of Aryan Nations to take several states and set up their own country.

Station owner John Hinton said that he lost virtually all his advertisers and that the show was canceled. Hinton said that although he does not agree with Aryan Nations' views, he felt McCarthy had a constitutional right to buy time from the station. Hinton has a right to his opinion. Surely McCarthy – and Hinton – can find a champion somewhere in that vast crowd of constitutional wits who take the defense of liberties to the point of absurdity – like opposing Christmas creches.

McCarthy had belonged to Aryan Nations for five years before deciding to "come out of the closet," only to find that people "hate us because we are white." That is not the reason, but it is useless to try to explain anything to someone who goose-steps through life as a member of hate organizations. McCarthy may no longer have a radio show, but there is always the closet.

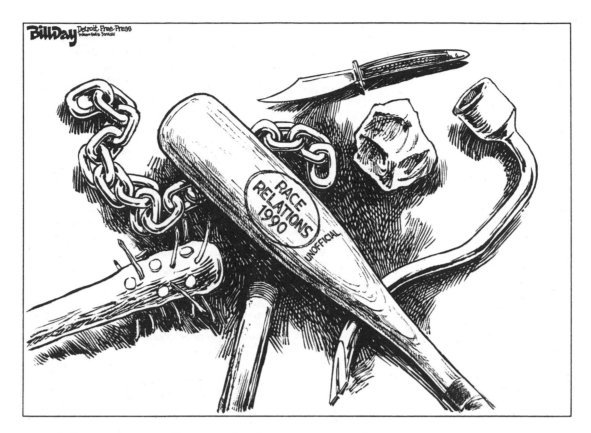

Birmingham Post-Herald
Birmingham, Alabama, February 17, 1987

For being black and in the wrong place at the wrong time, Michael Donald was lynched.

For contributing to Donald's death by fostering a climate and a tradition of violent hatred against blacks and other minorities, the United Klans of America has been ordered to pay $7 million to Michael's mother, Beulah Mae Donald.

One can lament the fact that the judgment by an all-white jury in U.S. District Court in Mobile comes a century — and too many victims — too late. But one can also rejoice, because this jury's verdict may well put one Ku Klux Klan group out of business as an agency of violence and brutality.

The fatal attack on Donald was particularly vile. It was sparked by the failure of a predominantly black Mobile Circuit Court jury to reach a verdict in the murder trial of Josephus R. Anderson, a black man accused of shooting Sgt. Albert Eugene Ballard, a white Birmingham police officer. That March 1981 trial wasn't even a local issue; it was moved from Birmingham to Mobile on a change-of-venue motion. (Anderson was convicted, three trials later, in 1985.)

On the evening of the hung jury in 1981, Michael Donald was snatched from a Mobile street, then beaten and strangled. His corpse was hung from a tree. Two members of the United Klans were convicted of the crime in 1984. It was said during their trial that Donald was killed to demonstrate Klan strength and to intimidate black jurors. The Anderson trial's hung jury was cited as the event that provoked the killers.

Now the slow, and in this instance sure, wheels of justice have turned. Last week's verdict punishes the United Klans — even though its assets will likely prove far less than $7 million — and sends a message that we hope chills the spine of anyone who has a hooded white robe in his closet: Our society will not tolerate the rule of the whip, the rope and the gun.

If, as members claim, the Klan is merely a political organization, a kind of white NAACP, then let it confine its activities to the constitutionally guaranteed exercise of free speech and association.

The Klan has had a comeuppance coming for a long time, and of late has been getting it. In recent years, we have seen more of its members in court than in the streets or meeting halls.

We would like to think the Mobile jury's verdict is the final blow that ends Klan violence and brutal intimidation once and for all, although experience tells us otherwise.

But if the decision stands, it will be a clear warning, and a legal precedent to guide future cases. If the decision is overturned on appeal, it will still have a chilling effect on hate groups. While the jury's race and Deep South location should be of no significance, it does emphasize the message: Klan violence will not be tolerated by any decent person, white or black.

THE ATLANTA CONSTITUTION
Atlanta, Georgia, February 17, 1987

Last week's $7 million judgment in federal court against the United Klans of America Inc. and six of its members in a civil-rights lawsuit in Mobile is a momentous decision. It grants redress to the family of a black teenager murdered by two Ku Klux Klansmen in 1981 and serves the broader interests of public justice as well.

The ruling holds the United Klans legally responsible for the racist violence and terrorism of its members and sends a strong message to other hate groups that foment violence: There is a price for such culpability beyond the legal penalties for any specific laws that are broken. The ruling, that the corporate Klan and its members had conspired to violate the black teenager's civil rights, gives the nation added ammunition with which to fight a seeming growth in racial violence and hooliganism.

In the Mobile case, Michael Donald, 19, was abducted at random from a street near his home. He was beaten savagely, slashed with a knife and hanged from a tree. One of the Klansmen convicted for the murder said the killers were acting on orders from Klan leaders and that the murder was committed to bring publicity to the Klan and intimidate blacks from serving on Alabama juries.

The lawyer for the victim's mother said the financial award could put the United Klans out of business. Let's hope so. Maybe financial bankruptcy will prove more lethal to the Klan than its moral bankruptcy.

Omaha World-Herald

Omaha, Nebraska, June 15, 1987

It was almost an article of faith in some liberal circles that the election of Ronald Reagan in 1980 marked the beginning of a golden age for right-wing extremists. A new report by the Anti-Defamation League of B'nai B'rith demonstrates how unfair that assumption was. The opposite has happened, according to the report, entitled "The Hate Movement Today: A Chronicle of Violence and Disarray."

Membership in such extremist groups as the Ku Klux Klan, Posse Comitatus, the Aryan Nations and American Nazi organizations has declined since 1981. Authors of the report gave the Justice Department under Reagan credit for "a superb job" of reducing the influence of extremist groups.

The report lists a number of cases brought by the Justice Department against right-wing fanatics and extremists. Not since Franklin Roosevelt's wartime prosecution of Nazi sympathizers and seditionists were so many right-wing extremists put on trial, the report said.

It has been said that the Reagan administration has made conservatism respectable. Right-of-center think tanks such as the Hoover Institution and the Georgetown Center for Strategic Studies have achieved mainstream political influence. Some magazines of commentary have become more conservative. As for some people who might otherwise be drawn to the far right, the B'nai B'rith report suggests, the Reagan administration has provided a mainstream alternative.

With Reagan's election, conservatives lost some of their sense of isolation and powerlessness. Conservatives had not held so much political power in the United States since Herbert Hoover's presidency. The Reagan administration made no secret of its convictions on a broad spectrum of issues.

The B'nai B'rith report helps to set the record straight. The past few years have been anything but a golden age for right-wing extremism. Vigorous prosecution of hate groups and a trend toward popular support for sensible conservative causes have dried up some of the support for the hate-filled fringe.

TULSA WORLD

Tulsa, Oklahoma, February 16, 1987

THE family of a black teen-ager who was brutally murdered by Klansmen six years ago has been awarded $7 million in damages against the United Klans of America and six present and past Ku Klux Klan members.

An all-white federal court jury awarded the sum to the family of Michael Donald, 19, who was beaten, strangled and left hanging in a tree in Mobile, Ala., in April 1981.

The verdict is expected to give the Donald family title to the Klan's national headquarters building in Tuscaloosa, Ala., and may bankrupt the organization.

Good.

One of the more disgusting media trends in recent years has been the laundering of the Klan to the point that the organization has become an accepted voice for a legitimate American viewpoint. It's not unusual to find a robed, hooded Klansman on the air debating, say, an NAACP spokesman and a TV personality. One highly regarded cable TV interview show had just such an encounter in the past week.

To legitimize the Klan in this fashion — to provide it with a forum — is repugnant.

The Michael Donald lynching — right here in the 1980s — is a horrifying reminder that the Klan is what it always has been, an outlaw terrorist band of thugs hiding behind robes and masks. If the huge award given his family helps blot out the Klan as a formal organization, the entire country will be better off.

Los Angeles Times

Los Angeles, California, February 17, 1987

In 1981 a young black man named Michael Donald was kidnaped as he walked to a store in Mobile, Ala. Soon after, his badly beaten and strangled body was found hanging from a tree in a racially mixed neighborhood. In 1984 two men who were members of the United Klans of America, the largest of the Ku Klux Klan organizations, were convicted of his murder. One was sentenced to death, the other to life imprisonment. Now, in what is seen as a landmark civil case, a federal jury has held the United Klans of America and six of its current and former members liable for Donald's death. The jury also has awarded Donald's family $7 million in damages.

The assets of the United Klans of America and other defendants in the case probably amount to only a tiny fraction of these damages. The likelihood is that the judgment will effectively put the 2,500-member organization out of business. That was precisely the purpose of the suit. Morris Dees,

an attorney for the plaintiffs, said his aim was to establish that all Klan chapters can be held civilly liable along with their members for criminal actions. "They may get away with killing and maiming here, there and yonder," Dees said after the verdict was returned, "but they're going to have to know that their houses are at stake, that their jobs are at stake and their property is at stake when they hurt somebody."

Why was Michael Donald killed? In a repentant statement to the court, one of the men convicted of the crime said that Donald was a random victim, abducted and slain only to demonstrate the strength of the Klan in Alabama and to intimidate blacks from serving on juries. The jury that held the United Klans of America liable in the death of Donald was, as it happens, composed only of whites. It heard testimony of a chilling atrocity. Its precedent-setting award should go a long way toward preventing other atrocities.

FORT WORTH STAR-TELEGRAM

Fort Worth, Texas, February 17, 1987

The United Klans of America was found as guilty of promoting murder as a civil jury is able to find last week.

It was a landmark finding, one that follows criminal prosecutions of Klan thugs — such as the murder convictions of two Klansmen who killed Michael Donald in 1981 — with unprecedented civil penalties against the organization that spawns such violent hatred.

The verdict by an all-white jury in Mobile, Ala., was a dramatic step in placing not only the Klan but perhaps other organizations based on violent racism beyond the limits of society's toleration.

Whatever vestiges of a falsely romantic past still cling to the Ku Klux Klan, it has always been, in modern terminology, a terrorist organization. Behind its white-sheeted demonstrations, its cross-burnings, its trumpeting of a doctrine of racial superiority — at times directed at Jews and Catholics as well as blacks — there has al-

ways been the threat of violence and death. It has been a threat frequently carried out.

If it quacks like a terrorist and walks like a terrorist, then what is it but a terrorist?

It is part of U.S. policy vs. international terrorism to try to find and attack the support organization behind the individuals who commit terrorist acts. The civil jury in Mobile applied that same reasoning to domestic terrorism.

Technically, the jury awarded $7 million in damages to Donald's family. The young victim's mother may wind up owning the United Klans' headquarters building in Tuscaloosa.

There is delicious irony in that, but it is the fact that responsibility for fomenting deadly violence was pinned on a corporate organization that matters.

That finding, as well as the financial penalty, takes away the Klan's pretensions to respectability and spells out America's — including the South's — utter disapproval of racial terrorism.

THE TENNESSEAN
Nashville, Tennessee, July 1, 1987

A history lesson on an old, established organization with strong Southern roots is obviously in order.

The Grand Titan of the Ku Klux Klan in Tennessee made a statement last week that was absurd to the point of being ridiculous. The Titan, Mr. Henry Ford, described his organization as being "based on love."

Most people, especially people who grew up in this region, know better. Most people know that the Klan was founded on hatred, and nurtured by lies. Most people realize that the organization wouldn't exist at all were it not for the ignorance it feeds on. Most people know it stands for the rankest sort of racial discrimination and anti-Semitism.

It is tempting to simply ignore Mr. Ford and his statement. It's tempting to ignore the rally and cross burning that the Klan has planned this weekend in Murfreesboro.

But just as history holds the truth about the founding of the Klan, history also holds some sad chapters on other movements based on hate. Because they were ignored, some of those movements were able to move from talk to action. Because they were not exposed, some of those groups, including the Klan, were able to become catalysts for blatant discrimination and torture.

Groups like the Klan are constantly reaching out to people who don't understand them, especially to young people, and glossing over their message just enough to try to lure in new converts. Their existence is an embarrassing fact. But their growth and spread would be a tragedy.

When the Murfreesboro city council learned of the Klan's plans for a march, it voted to designate this as Racial Harmony Week in Murfreesboro. That was a wise decision. The Klan proclaims that it has many enemies — it hates virtually all people who are not white, not Christians, and not heterosexuals. But its greatest enemy is not a color of skin or a religious belief. Its greatest enemies are tolerance and understanding. ■

CHICAGO Sun-Times
Chicago, Illinois, October 14, 1990

The Ku Klux Klan's misuse of the Mister Rogers persona in racist telephone recordings amounts to more than simple abuse of any license for hyperbole in political messages. It was a disgusting and obscene outrage for the Missouri Klan to link the popular host of a children's television show to the venom and bigotry espoused in the tapes.

The recordings used imitations of Rogers' gentle voice and melodious speech pattern, and a federal judge in Kansas City acted promptly in ordering the Klan to halt its infringement on trademarks and copyrights associated with "Mister Rogers' Neighborhood." The Klan was ordered to turn over the recordings, which represent the antithesis of the values emphasized by Rogers—brotherly love and cooperation in a multicultural society.

Unfortunately, the telephone number of the Klan recording was widely circulated among Missouri schoolchildren before community and religious leaders were able to alert the TV show to what was happening.

A careful monitoring of Klan messages should nip further such outrages a lot earlier.

THE ROANOKE TIMES
Roanoke, Virginia, February 17, 1987

IT'S ABOUT time somebody hit the Ku Klux Klan in the pocketbook, where it hurts.

A federal jury in Mobile, Ala., has awarded $7 million in damages to the family of Michael Donald, 19, whose body was left hanging in a tree. The family and the Alabama arm of the National Association for the Advancement of Colored People had sued the United Klans of America, holding it responsible for the death of the young black man.

This bit of retribution comes on top of the conviction of two Klan members in the slaying. One of them, Henry Francis Hays, 32, was sentenced to death. The other, James Knowles, 24, received a life sentence. Both were co-defendants in the civil suit.

Knowles testified that Donald was abducted at random from a Mobile street and killed "to show Klan strength in Alabama." According to testimony, the local Klan was angered by an unrelated trial in which a black was accused of murdering a white police officer in Birmingham.

The plaintiffs charged that other Klansmen conspired to violate Donald's civil rights because they either knew of plans for the murder or knew it had been committed and kept silent.

"I was acting as a Klansman," said Knowles, who pleaded for a verdict against him and the Klan. In a closing statement, he apologized to Donald's mother and declared, "God knows, if I could trade places with him, I would."

The conviction of Hays and Knowles and the death sentence for Hays represent major achievements for justice in a region where justice for too long depended upon skin color. But convicting the direct perpetrators without punishing the organization behind them is like convicting Mafia hit men without touching the crime czars who give them their contracts.

The Ku Klux Klan's attitude toward blacks is so manifest it needs no documentation here. The organization's literature, public statements and violent actions are an unsavory part of American history. When it exhorts to hatred and violence, it should not escape organizational responsibility if its members act upon its exhortations.

Until the Klan is held responsible as an organization, it can always find mindless brutes willing to translate its doctrines into violent action. Those who enroll in the Klan and bankroll its programs should be made to understand that they can't hide their dollars behind hoods and sheets; that the Klan will be held financially responsible for the excesses its policies generate.

The Donalds are expected to acquire title to the national headquarters of the United Klans — a 7,000-square-foot building in Tuscaloosa.

State Sen. Michael Figures, attorney for the Donalds, expressed the hope that the ruling "would make sure Donald's death was the last Klan lynching."

The Klan seems unsure whether to appeal its case. It was, after all, found guilty by an all-white Southern jury. The Klan is unlikely to find a more sympathetic audience among federal judges. Their robes are black, not white, and they don't wear hoods.

New York City Racial Killing Stirs Conflict

The Aug. 23, 1989 fatal shooting of a black teen-ager in a predominantly white neighborhood in Brooklyn, N.Y. inflamed racial tensions throughout New York City.

The black youth, 16-year-old Yusuf K. Hawkins, was killed in the Bensonhurst section of Brooklyn, where he had traveled with three friends to answer a classified newspaper advertisement for a used car.

Hawkins was shot twice in the chest at close range after he and his friends were chased by a gang of as many as 30 white youths. The youths reportedly had been waiting to ambush a group of blacks and Hispanics who had been invited to a birthday party given by a local white girl. None of the other three blacks was injured.

Police filed charges Aug. 25, against five of the Bensonhurst youths. The five – Keith Mondello, 18, Pasquale Raucci, 19, Charles Stressler, 21, Steven Curreri, 18, and James Patino, 24 – were charged with assault, riot, aggravated harassment, menacing and violating Hawkins's civil rights. All except Patino were also charged with criminal weapons possession.

The alleged gunman, Joseph Fama, 18, fled the neighborhood after the shooting, but surrendered to police in upstate Oneonta, N.Y. Aug. 31. He was charged with two counts of second-degree murder, as well as assault and other charges. He pleaded not guilty at an arraignment in Brooklyn Sept. 1.

The attack was widely viewed as the most serious racial incident in the city since a black man was chased to his death by a group of whites in the Howard Beach section of Queens, N.Y. in December 1986.

Several protest marches were held in Brooklyn in the wake of Hawkins's death. In the largest demonstration, about 8,000 people attempted to march across the Brooklyn Bridge into Manhattan Aug. 31 as part of a "Day of Outrage and Mourning" to protest Hawkins's killing as well as the recent murder of Black Panther leader Huey P. Newton. The crowd confronted dozens of police officers who attempted to stop them from crossing the bridge. In the ensuing melee, 44 policemen and two civilians were injured.

THE ARIZONA REPUBLIC
Phoenix, Arizona, September 1, 1989

IN both Utah and New York, racial hatreds are flaring, and the inevitable opportunists are sniffing out whatever advantages the situations seem to offer.

Demagogues are especially conspicious in New York, possibly because their identities became so well established during the Tawana Brawley affair. Ms. Brawley, it will be recalled, was the young black woman who kept New Yorkers on edge for months with her story, subsequently disproven, of an abduction and attack by white men. The Rev. Al Sharpton, whose strenuous proddings kept the Brawley case alive, now has adopted the cause of Yusuf K. Hawkins, a young black man of promise ambushed last week by a group of white punks.

At the funeral of Mr. Hawkins Wednesday, Mr. Sharpton stopped within inches of urging a racial *jihad*. "I don't know who shot Yusuf, but the system loaded the gun," he cried. "I want you to know, Yusuf, we're not going to let you down! They're going to pay this time!"

Mayor Edward Koch and Gov. Mario Cuomo were allowed into the church only after being detained for an hour by the "security forces" of Louis Farrakhan, leader of the black-extremist Nation of Islam and a notorious anti-Semite. Once inside, they were booed and taunted by people who had been worked into a lather by Mr. Sharpton.

Meanwhile in far-off Utah, racism is being blamed for the death sentence of William Andrews, convicted in a multiple murder in Ogden. Mr. Andrews and an accomplice, subsequently executed by lethal injection, poured Drano down the throats of four victims and taped their mouths shut. The men thought this would be fatal, but when they saw that it only caused excruciating pain, Mr. Williams's accomplice shot and killed three of the four.

Those seeking clemency for Mr. Williams, who is black, argue that lethal injection was a fit punishment for the trigger man only. The death sentence for Mr. Williams they impute to racial prejudice — widespread, they say, in largely Mormon Utah.

Racism does in fact exist in Utah — and in New York and every other state — and we should do our utmost to combat it. But racism is scarcely alleviated by awarding torture-murderers victim status. Nor is it alleviated when New York officials, who have made three arrests so far and are proceeding diligently toward prosecution, are blamed for the senseless death of a young black man at the hands of a mob.

While all men are brothers, not all men know it, and this is true of blacks as well as whites. We are brought no closer to understanding by Al Sharpton, to whom racism is the last refuge, than by those white cretins who turned out this week to heckle Mr. Hawkins's mourners in New York.

The Honolulu Advertiser
Honolulu, Hawaii, September 9, 1989

Just because different races live close to each other, as they do in Hawaii, is no guarantee of race harmony or even tolerance.

In New York, a young black man named Yusef Hawkins ventured into Bensonhurst, an Italian-American neighborhood, with three friends to look at an advertised used car. Hawkins was chased by 30 white youths with baseball bats. One of the whites pulled a gun and shot Hawkins to death.

This is a sad echo of other incidents. A few years ago, several blacks passing through mostly white Howard Beach were chased by a crowd until one black died crossing a freeway to escape. A white woman jogger was beaten, raped and left for dead in Central Park; a gang of young blacks (and one Hispanic) is charged in the case.

Blacks are watching the Bensonhurst case to see whether the white bat-wielders and gunman are labeled "savages" as were those arrested for the Central Park attack. They should be.

At first, some in Bensonhurst showed little remorse, saying there are black neighborhoods where whites are not safe. While true, that doesn't excuse violence anywhere.

Sadly, these cases are becoming too common in New York to be dismissed as "isolated." They show again that laws may outlaw discrimination, but have not ended hatred and intolerance.

In Hawaii, we sometimes fall short of our ideal of a benevolent racial and cultural mix, though our lapses seem small compared to problems elsewhere.

We can take comfort that, whatever frictions exist between races here in Hawaii, they rarely end in brutal violence. But we would be foolish to forget that racial harmony requires constant fine-tuning.

THE KANSAS CITY STAR
Kansas City, Missouri, September 9, 1989

There have been several explanations for the death of Yusef Hawkins, a black 16-year-old who was in a predominantly Italian-American section of Brooklyn when he was gunned down, allegedly by Joseph Fama, 18.

Some people say Hawkins, who was accompanied by friends, also black, was attacked because he was in the *wrong* neighborhood.

Others say Hawkins, who reportedly was in search of a used car to buy, was surrounded by white teen-agers because of a possible link to an interracial romance that soured.

Of all of the excuses for what happened Aug. 23. none—not even the fact that such tragedies are considered normal in racially polarized New York—is good enough to justify the shortening of Hawkins' life by a savage mob of about 30 young white men.

Far worse than this senseless murder, as if worse were possible, is the way some Bensonhurst residents have received peaceful demonstrators who marched through the Brooklyn community to protest the killing.

The demonstrators, including several religious persons and people of mixed races, were jeered and slurred. Signs read: "Long live South Africa," "You savages," and other insults directed at black Americans.

Some white residents had the audacity to wave American flags, as if Old Glory stood for gang killings of innocent Americans of any race. This use of the flag is more disgraceful than burning it. Since when does patriotism mean that Hawkins or anyone must die this way?

Surely the counter-demonstrators of Bensonhurst are not so ignorant, so deeply involved in their turf battle or so committed to their sick convictions that they fail to recognize their foolishness? Patriotism is a specious argument. So is unconditional support for the white mob that surrounded Hawkins and friends.

The kind of reception given peaceful demonstrators in Bensonhurst was bound to conjure up the Rev. Al Sharpton, Louis Farrakhan and their ilk. Naturally, combative individuals, not the rational and cool-headed among New York's black political and religious leadership, are given more media power than they actually possess in these tense times.

And, people who have traditionally been denied equal rights and protection under the law because of their race are more likely to accept leadership from others, charlatans among them, who are better at drawing crowds than bringing a solid criminal case to the courts.

Does Bensonhurst remind us of Howard Beach? Yes. Is Hawkins' murder retribution for the "wilding" in Central Park? No. Each was a condemnable, criminal act. Each victim deserves justice.

The Providence Journal
Providence, Rhode Island, September 1, 1989

Yusuf Hawkins was buried on Wednesday. The black teenager from the East New York section of Brooklyn was yet another innocent victim of the racial tensions that haunt American society. His murder ought to inspire sober reflection and renewed determination to overcome our nation's legacy of racism; it would be doubly tragic if this vile deed should become the occasion for further exacerbating racial divisons.

On the night of August 23, Mr. Hawkins and three black teenage friends went to the predominantly white Bensonhurst section of Brooklyn in answer to an advertisement for a used car. As they walked along 20th Street near Bay Ridge Avenue, they were accosted by a dozen or so white youths, armed with baseball bats, golf clubs and, most ominously of all, at least one revolver. Within minutes, Mr. Hawkins was dead from bullet wounds.

Why such a senseless end to a promising young man's life? The immediate cause seems to have been the white youths' mistaken belief that the Hawkins party consisted of acquaintances of a young white woman from the neighborhood, a former girlfriend of one of the assailants, who was now dating black and Hispanic men. In short, Mr. Hawkins had the misfortune of walking into an atmosphere poisoned by sexual jealousy and racial animosity.

Regrettably, there are few more socially volatile combinations than race and sex. This was made plain by the public revulsion earlier this year when a young white woman, innocently jogging in New York's Central Park, was accosted by a mob of nonwhite youths, who proceeded to rape her repeatedly and beat her nearly to death.

Such events should not be allowed to become counters in a sordid game of racial one-upmanship. They should be handled through recourse to the criminal justice system. That is how the Central Park horror is being treated, and the same is true thus far with the killing of Mr. Hawkins. On the very day of his funeral, two suspects in the attack were indicted on multiple charges, including second-degree murder, which would bring prison terms of from 25 years to life upon conviction.

It would be sadly ironic if the death of Yusuf Hawkins, a victim of white racism, were now to be manipulated by black racists. It was disquieting to note that such people as the Black Muslim leader Louis Farrakhan and the Rev. Al Sharpton, impresario of last year's Tawana Brawley affair, were prominently on display at Mr. Hawkins' funeral services. Their contribution is neither necessary nor desirable, for as Brooklyn District Attorney Elizabeth Holtzman has properly said, the case against Mr. Hawkins' assailants "does not involve politics; it involves murder."

The Star-Ledger
Newark, New Jersey, September 5, 1989

What is happening in New York is deeply disturbing and points up a negative trend that is more than regional and threatens the democratic concept of an American melting pot.

Of course, the subject is racism, and the raw, unsettling symptoms of this social malaise have seethed to the surface in New York. They are starkly evident in such deplorable, senseless incidents as the Bensonhurst killing of an innocent black teenager, the Howard Beach racial rampage and the "wilding" episode that resulted in the assault and rape of a Central Park jogger.

In composite, these anti-social eruptions chillingly reveal that racial violence is on the upswing, and its backwash leaves an ugly taste. Much to the distress of most decent Americans, violence emanating largely from racial bias has escalated.

Most Americans would concur that there is an urgent need to get to the bottom of a problem with ominous overtones. As difficult as it may be to fathom, racial violence seems to be taking on a dismaying, disruptive continuity in American society.

The senseless murder of Yusef Hawkins dredges up a different kind of fear, primarily because it is occurring in what should be an enlightened age of heightened racial tolerance and understanding, in an America that should have learned from the painful lessons of its past.

The frightening aspect is that a young man who, according to one of the assailants, was not even the intended victim, was set upon by a gang determined to show "those folks" that they were not welcome. It points up the resurgence of a mindset that should have been eradicated years ago.

Dr. Martin Luther King Jr., himself a victim of racial violence more than 20 years ago and whose birthday is now a national holiday, dreamed of a nation where a man is judged not by the color of his skin, but the content of his character. Twenty years later, a life can still be wiped out by being in the "wrong" neighborhood.

If Americans are to be true to the beliefs and concepts that we all hold dear, racial violence must be attacked with the full velocity of our moral arsenal. That attack must come from every corner with a passionate, vigorous commitment.

Wisconsin ▲ State Journal
Madison, Wisconsin, September 7, 1989

The racial anger that burns and itches just underneath America's skin has surfaced repeatedly in recent weeks, yet no one in a position of leadership has asked the basic question: What has changed? Why now?

In the predominantly white Bensonhurst section of New York last month, four blacks were attacked by 30 young toughs for no apparent reason other than the jealous fantasies of one of the mob's white instigators. One black youth, Yusef Hawkins, was shot to death.

Were the people of Bensonhurst shocked, even shamed, by this unprovoked murder? Not exactly. When about 250 demonstrators showed up Saturday to protest the release of six whites implicated in the attack (the suspected gunman is still at large) the closest they came to sympathy were shouts of "Niggers, go home," "Monkeys," and "Long live South Africa."

In Virginia Beach, Va., an annual fraternity festival of students from mostly black colleges erupted into Labor Day weekend clashes between students and police. More than 40 people were injured, 260 people were arrested and about 100 stores were inexplicably looted.

In a curious example of life imitating art, there were reports that some of the students chanted, "Fight the power," a phrase from the hit film "Do the Right Thing," which is about racial violence in New York City.

Undoubtedly, the debate will now center on questions about police actions *after* the bottle-throwing and looting began. But will anyone ask what causes blacks to trash merchants in Virginia Beach? Or what causes whites in New York to shout the worst racial slurs possible?

The answers are important because the incidents are not isolated. Black separatism is making a comeback. White skinheads, neo-Nazis and Klansman rallied last weekend near Atlanta.

Closer to home, Wisconsin has seen its own ugliness. It was only a few months ago that racial taunts (and a few rocks) were hurled at Chippewa Indians seeking to exercise their treaty rights to spear fish.

Currents of racism have always run deep in this country. Only the most naive among us believe it will ever be eliminated. But only a true pessimist would have believed that overt incidents of racism would be commonplace today, 35 years after the start of the modern civil-rights movement.

President Bush has promised a "kinder, gentler" America, but increasingly we're seeing a nation that can be mean-spirited and ugly. Remember your own campaign theme, Mr. President, and back up your warm words with cold, hard proposals. It's time, Mr. President, to "do the right thing."

BUFFALO EVENING NEWS
Buffalo, New York, September 15, 1989

THE FOURTH SUSPECT indicted on murder and manslaughter charges in the Bensonhurst, New York City, killing of a black teen-ager was 19 years old, the same age as one of the others indicted before him and only a year older than the other two.

Not only were those involved in the murder relatively young, but so were most of those who gathered to hurl vicious racial taunts at demonstrators who converged on the site of the shooting to display their outrage.

It is perhaps that aspect of the Yusef Hawkins slaying, the Howard Beach killing and several other racial confrontations that is most ominous. It puts the focus most squarely on schools as perhaps the best hope of combating what some see as a rising tide of racism.

It does not seem so long ago that the "younger generation" was supposed to hold the key to change. Veterans of the civil rights struggle optimistically thought a new world they ushered in would result in children being raised relatively free of bigotry.

But it turns out that those same children are now young adults who grew up with little knowledge of that struggle and in an era when the Reagan administration attacked the programs that sprang from it. Many of them are the very ones instigating much of the racially inspired violence in New York and elsewhere.

When New York City police estimate that 70 percent of all bias crimes are committed by persons under 19, and when U.S. Justice Department figures show that the number of racial incidents in schools climbed by 50 percent between 1986 and 1987 even as the overall number dropped slightly, it is obvious that the generations that missed the civil rights experience also are missing something else.

It is just as obvious that many are not getting that something growing up in ethnic enclaves, exposed only to others of their own race. With groups like the Ku Klux Klan and the Skinheads actively recruiting these young people, the schools that hold them as a captive audience offer the best hope of a countervailing influence to break down the walls of ignorance and the bigotry that it spawns.

It is too late to save Yusef Hawkins, who was attacked by strangers after going into an unfamiliar neighborhood to look at a car for sale there. But school officials in Bensonhurst have belatedly recognized the need. After meeting with local civic leaders, they agreed to expand the human relations curriculum and develop specific plans for classroom instruction, assemblies and counseling in racial tolerance.

It took a savage murder to prompt Bensonhurst — where prior incidents should have served as a warning — to re-evaluate the role of its schools in heading off this resurging menace.

It should not take so tragic an incident to spark other areas — including Erie County, where minority college students felt compelled to take legal action against nightclubs they feel discriminate — to undertake a similar assessment of what its young people are learning or not learning about bias.

Newsday
New York City, New York, August 29, 1989

"We are not going to allow New York City to become South Africa. We will walk in Bensonhurst, Howard Beach or anywhere else we please." — the Rev. Timothy Mitchell, pastor of Ebenezer Missionary Baptist Church, Queens.

Mitchell, of course, is absolutely right. And Sunday's peaceful march through Bensonhurst, led by Mitchell, tried against considerable odds to make a simple but seminal point — one that is well worth reiterating:

Black or white, rich or poor, native or immigrant, Christian, Jew or Moslem — New Yorkers must be able to *exercise* their inalienable right to live, work, shop and, yes, walk anywhere in this city. No ands, ifs or racist buts. No one should have to fear winding up like young Yusef Hawkins — dead of two gunshot wounds at the age of 16 because a white gunman, backed up by a gang of bat-wielding punks, didn't want blacks (or Latinos) setting foot in predominantly white Bensonhurst.

Yet even in the wake of this racially motivated tragedy in Brooklyn, Mitchell's message isn't getting through to everyone. As Mitchell, the Rev. Calvin Butts of Harlem's Abyssinian Baptist Church and others gathered at the spot where Hawkins was killed last week and marched through the neighborhood, hundreds of angry Bensonhurst residents lined the sidewalks Sunday, many yelling vile racist slurs.

Was this patently bigoted behavior representative of the mind-set of most who live in this largely white enclave? We hope not. We will continue to believe, until otherwise persuaded, that the majority in Bensonhurst are more like the Rev. Charles Fermeglia of St. Dominic's Roman Catholic Church. This priest knows racism when he sees it. At mass on Sunday, he noted flatly, "Sometimes our religion does not reflect the way we live."

Sunday's jeering "counterdemonstrators" weren't the only provocateurs out in force this weekend. Sadly, Saturday's protest march was led by the Rev. Al Sharpton, who is in part responsible for shamelessly distorting whatever actually happened to Tawana Brawley. No one, black or white, from Bensonhurst or elsewhere, can be faulted for boycotting a Sharpton-led march.

But Sunday's march — organized and run by credible civil rights leaders, including Mitchell and Butts — was a different matter. Still, there were too few white faces, prominent or otherwise, among the marchers. If there are more protests, and there may be, they ought to be interracial ones — if only to drive home everyone's responsibility to respect human rights and ease racial tensions.

Los Angeles Times

Los Angeles, California, August 30, 1989

The recent murder of a black teen-ager in Brooklyn was more than a crime of passion. It was more than a case of mistaken identity. It was a racial murder. The painful lesson of history is that such tragedies are compounded if the authorities— or, for that matter, any of us—look away from that repellent fact. This country has come a long way since those terrible days when Southern trees bore strange fruit, but not far enough to forget.

The victim, Yusef Hawkins, 16, went last week to the Bensonhurst section of Brooklyn to check out an ad for a used car. It is the kind of thing teen-agers do all the time. In this case, Hawkins and three friends were in hostile territory. They were confronted by as many as 30 white youths wielding baseball bats, according to police accounts.

The subtext to this tragic confrontation reads like a primer of racial stereotypes and white anxiety: The white youngsters mistakenly thought Hawkins or someone in his group was the new black boyfriend of a white girl who had rejected a young white man from the neighborhood.

The black teen-agers were singled out because they were black and only because of their race. Hawkins was killed because he was black. The racial hostility became clear when an elderly white woman who lives in Bensonhurst told Times reporter David Treadwell that black people were not wanted in that neighborhood. "Chase them, beat them up a bit, give them a black eye but don't kill them. They're human beings". It became even clearer when black marchers mourning the young man's death were met by white youths hurling racial epithets and insults during a weekend protest in Bensonhurst.

As racial tensions worsen, there can be no shrinking from the truth. New York's political, civic and religious leaders must make it perfectly clear that racial attacks will not be tolerated. New York Mayor Ed Koch can make that point most emphatically by rallying the entire city to the necessity of racial harmony.

Mayor Koch has condemned the racial assault but not without adding somewhat defensively that he cannot mold the attitude of every teen-ager and that his city has no monopoly on racism or murder. That may be true, but across America confrontational politicians, like Koch, have been all too ready to further their own careers by playing to the passionate animosities engendered by racial and ethnic differences.

The Bensonhurst murder is the most recent indication of New York's racial tensions. It is being compared to Howard Beach, where a white mob chased a black man to his death in 1986. It is also being compared to Central Park, where a white woman was brutally assaulted while jogging earlier this year; six black and Hispanic teen-agers have been charged.

The mugging in Central Park evoked a national outpouring of public anguish. In contrast, the Bensonhurst murder has prompted mere murmurs of condemnation. Coming to terms with the meaning of that disparity will not bring Yusef Hawkins back to life, but it will erase the fiction that his death was just another of those inexplicable, unavoidable urban tragedies.

St. Petersburg Times

St. Petersburg, Florida, August 31, 1989

Last week 16-year-old Yusef Hawkins took a trip across Brooklyn with three teen-age friends. He found himself in a neighborhood much like his own — blue-collar, with an emphasis on upward mobility and community pride.

Hawkins and his friends were black, though, and the Bensonhurst address that had been their destination was in a mostly white area. The young men must have known about Bensonhurst; recognizing the invisible boundaries that carve cities along the lines of race, ethnicity and class is a basic element of any urban child's education. Yet they also must have assumed — as any American should be able to do — that no harm would come of taking a first-hand look at a used car they had seen advertised.

In this case, a basic assumption of freedom proved to be a fatal miscalculation of danger. The would-be car hunters were met by a gang of white youths, who attacked them with bats and then shot Hawkins, who died.

The reason for the attack was a shameful combination of racism and mistaken identity. It had been rumored that a black teen was invited to a local girl's birthday party that night, police said, and neighborhood youths were planning to hurt him when and if he dared to arrive. Yusef Hawkins and his friends were unlucky enough to cross their paths first.

The ensuing week has brought nothing but ugly interchanges, made worse by their sad predictability. When a group of ministers led a protest march through Bensonhurst, angry bigots tried to shout them down. The young girl who had the birthday party is now under police protection, intimidated by her own neighbors. New York mayoral candidates have seized the incident shamelessly, shaking it for all its political worth.

Every day, the tragedy is re-examined and the principals retried by the ordinary people who must continue to survive together after the marches are over and the politicians have moved on to fresher bait. The more Bensonhurst's wounds are probed, the more racial tensions seem to rise. Here are just a few of the comments reported by the *New York Times*:

"After this incident we feel cut off," said Warren Alexander, who lives across town, near Yusef Hawkins' family. "The lines are set. They are drawn. The message is, 'Don't cross.'"

"A 16-year-old boy should be allowed to go where he wants to go," said a Bensonhurst resident who would not be identified by name. "There's no such thing as off limits, this is not Russia."

Richard Gonderson, a young sanitation worker, gave voice to the hopeless thinking that sums up white America's continued failure to master bigotry: "I'm racist against black people who are racist against me."

The investigation of Yusef Hawkins' death and the trial of those who murdered him should not be conducted in the streets and on the soapboxes, as has happened all too frequently in recent years. In the absence of strong federal leadership from the White House and the Justice Department, cities and neighborhoods have been left to deal with racially motivated violence as best they may. Often, that isn't very well.

A shocked nation waited in vain for decisive Justice Department action on the mounting roster of racial attacks during the 1980s, culminating in the Howard Beach incident. President Bush should take this opportunity to set a meaningful standard of leadership for the coming decade by focusing federal attention on the aggressive prosecution of civil rights violations in the Bensonhurst case. Left alone to lick the wounds caused by racially motivated violence, neighborhoods cannot heal.

THE CHRISTIAN SCIENCE MONITOR

Boston, Massachusetts, September 6, 1989

THE racial killing in the Brooklyn neighborhood of Bensonhurst has at least one root cause in the kind of latent racism reported recently in our hometown.

The Federal Reserve Bank of Boston finds a clear racial pattern in mortgages approved for homeowners in the city. Even when economic factors are discounted, predominantly black communities are 24 percent less likely to get such mortgages. The disparity is even greater between all-white and all-black neighborhoods in Boston. Other cities have the same problem, which doesn't come as any revelation to those who have been working against "redlining" for years.

Lenders are not charged with denying home loans simply on the basis of race, and there are other factors involved – unwillingness of some real estate agents and developers to generate business in minority communities, unwillingness of would-be homeowners to move to certain neighborhoods. Still, the issue really is one of race and the kind of institutional barriers to social desegregation that remain long after the most overt forms of racism have been declared illegal.

The Community Reinvestment Act of 1977 requires lenders to meet local credit needs, but doesn't have any real enforcement teeth. Maybe it should, as Rep. Joseph P. Kennedy 2nd (D) of Massachusetts suggests, especially since the savings and loan industry is about to be bailed out by taxpayers at a cost of hundreds of billions of dollars.

More helpful will be the lending industry's acknowledging that the problem exists and that it has an obligation to do something about it. As Bank of Boston president Robert Mahoney said, "It's not only the law, it's the right thing to do. And it's not charity, it's good business."

Bensonhurst was a tragedy. It would be good if one of its roots could be identified – and dealt with – in Boston.

Boston Murder Hoax Revealed

A man who gained nationwide sympathy following an alleged robbery attempt in October 1989 in which he was wounded and his pregnant wife was killed, committed suicide by jumping from a bridge into Boston Harbor Jan. 4, 1990 after learning that police had identified him as the main suspect in the case.

The 1989 shooting of 29-year-old Charles Stuart and his 30-year-old wife, Carol, had attracted national media attention as an example of apparently random urban violence. It had also stirred racial tensions in Boston, since Stuart, who was white, had claimed that the assailant was black.

According to the story Charles Stuart told police at the time, he and his wife, who was seven months pregnant, had been attacked by a man who had jumped into their car as they were leaving a childbirth class in Boston on Oct. 23, 1989.

Stuart said the assailant had forced them to drive to an inner-city neighborhood, where he had robbed them, shot Carol in the head and shot him in the stomach before fleeing. Stuart had reached police by calling them on his cellular car telephone. Tapes of his dramatic plea for help had been broadcast on radio and television stations across the country.

Carol Stuart died Oct. 24 after arriving at the hospital. Her baby, named Christopher, was delivered prematurely by Cesarean section, but he died 17 days later.

In a twist to the case, however, Boston police revealed Jan. 4, 1990 that Stuart's brother, Matthew, had approached investigators on Jan. 3 and implicated Charles in the shooting. According to police officials, Matthew told them that as a result of an arrangement he had made with Charles, he had driven to the neighborhood in which the shooting apparently took place and picked up Carol's handbag from Charles, together with a revolver Charles was believed to have used to shoot his wife and himself.

Matthew said he had taken the bag and the gun to the Boston suburb of Revere, where he threw them into the Pines River. Police divers recovered the handbag from the river on Jan. 4 and a .38 caliber revolver that was believed to be the murder weapon on Jan. 9.

Matthew's lawyer said his client had decided to come forward after Charles Stuart had identified a black man, William Bennett, in a Dec. 28, 1989 police line-up in which he claimed that Bennett resembled the man who had shot him and Carol.

Although police refused to speculate on Stuart's reasons for murdering his wife, news accounts reported that he had taken out several large insurance policies on her. Other reports suggested that Stuart had been romantically involved with a young woman who had once worked at a fur store he had managed.

Black leaders in Boston Jan. 4 criticized city police, the local media and Mayor Raymond Flynn (D) for their response to the case. They accused all three of inflaming racial tensions in the wake of Carol Stuart's death.

Following the purported attack, Flynn had ordered 100 extra policemen into the predominantly black Mission Hill neighborhood where the Stuarts' car had been found. Residents of the area claimed that police had broken into their apartments and had routinely stopped and frisked young black men. Some blacks charged that white residents of Boston had treated all black men as if they were suspects in the weeks following the killing.

In his State of the City message Jan. 10, Flynn defended the "aggressive police response" to the Stuart case, but said he would be willing to support an investigation of possible civil rights violations. He noted that the Stuart case had damaged race relations in Boston, and he accused Charles Stuart of "hurt[ing] everyone, especially the residents of Mission Hill ... It appears that [he] has perpetrated a giant fraud on this city."

THE DENVER POST

Denver, Colorado, January 9, 1990

THE BIZARRE case of Charles Stuart, the Boston man who now appears to have been the perpetrator rather than the victim of a brutal inner-city street attack, should cause all Americans to re-examine their thinking about the links between crime and race.

Like the celebrated fiasco involving Tawana Brawley, the black New York teenager who falsely claimed to have been kidnapped and raped by a gang of white men in 1987, the Stuart case was widely regarded initially as evidence that racial tensions had reached new heights of unspeakable violence.

In view of the notorious Howard Beach incident in New York, as well as the vicious beating earlier last year of a white female jogger in Central Park, it was easy to believe the story that Stuart told in October — of his pregnant wife being shot to death, and himself wounded, by a black assailant who mistook the white couple's car phone for a police radio.

Even now, the notion that the 29-year-old former football star staged the whole episode strains credulity, like the plot of a second-rate TV movie. And the fact that an innocent black man whom Stuart had picked out of a lineup could easily have been convicted of these heinous crimes — Massachusetts was surely ready for revenge, after letting Willie Horton get away — makes the ruse even more incredible.

Stuart has now committed suicide, after learning his brother had tipped off authorities and transformed him into the chief suspect.

The mysteries he has left behind should prompt all who have heard about this case to ponder not only the malevolence at the bottom of the human soul, but also the superficiality at its surface.

The Evening Gazette

Worcester, Massachusetts, January 9, 1990

Perhaps we will never learn all of the details of the slaying of Carol Stuart and the subsequent suicide of her husband. But one thing seems perfectly clear: Society must not be so quick to leap to conclusions before all the facts have been assembled.

Because Charles Stuart identified a "tall black man" as his pregnant wife's murderer, police came down hard on residents of Boston's Mission Hill section. Willie Bennett, a black man with a police record, was named as a suspect, and some have charged that investigating practices bordered on harassment.

Worse yet, fear swept sections of the city. People were afraid to go to Brigham and Women's Hospital, where Carol Stuart had her last birthing class just before she was shot, or other institutions in the inner city. Suburban residents bemoaned the dangers of Boston, where such a heinous crime could be committed.

The issue of race and class has become the focal point of the case. Boston was labeled as a city of "racial unrest." The Willie Horton case was remembered. There were renewed cries for the death penalty.

Charles Stuart jumped to his death from the Tobin Bridge after his brother denounced him as Carol's killer, and some circumstances of the crime may remain a mystery.

But the question is inescapable: Would the case have attracted the same amount of attention and outrage if a white man had been fingered as the suspected attacker of a black middle-class couple from the suburbs?

We don't pretend to know, but do suggest that white Bostonians, indeed white Americans everywhere, search their conscience for the answer.

It would be unfortunate if this tragedy, almost solely the doing of Charles Stuart, served to widen the gap between blacks and whites.

Charles Stuart ignited a bonfire of prejudice, fear and overreaction. It can be removed only through compassion, understanding and reconciliation.

THE SPOKESMAN-REVIEW

Spokane, Washington, January 10, 1990

Charges and countercharges are flying in Boston over an incredible case of deception. What was a dramatic tale of a robber slaying a pregnant woman now is believed to be a sordid tale of the woman dying at her own husband's hand.

National media gave tremendous ink and air time to the tragic events, including a 13-minute recorded conversation between a dispatcher and the seriously wounded and supposedly distraught husband, talking on a telephone in his car in an attempt to help rescuers pinpoint the couple's location.

Now, more than two months later, Boston is in shock. Carol Stuart's husband, Charles, who committed suicide this week, had become the suspect in her death.

Boston's black community is up in arms over the fact that Charles Stuart chose to point his finger at an innocent black man as the perpetrator of the crime, as well as the fact that Boston found that scenario so easy to believe. The black community also says that if the shooting victims had been black, the tragedy would not have received anywhere near the amount of attention that it did.

Dealing with similar situations differently based on race is not a new charge leveled at the media and law-enforcement agencies, but this is a poor test case. The sheer drama and unusual aspects of this tragedy — an anguished, rambling call to a state police dispatcher who coolly tried to reassure the caller while also trying to identify the car's location through the sound of nearby sirens — guaranteed intense media attention, regardless of the victims' race.

For now, what this case does show in disturbing detail is how the location of the crime — in Mission Hill, a low-income area with a large minority population in Roxbury, Mass. — affected the response. Almost certainly, city officials would not have allowed or condoned law-enforcement officers tossing civil liberties aside and making indiscriminate stops of citizens in a middle-class neighborhood in search of the culprit.

A thorough, independent investigation of the Carol Stuart murder case and the way it has been handled by police, prosecutors and the media — something that is being called for by black community activists in Boston — is mandatory. The results would be instructive not just for Boston but also for the many other cities in this nation where the same kind of response easily could occur.

The soul-searching arising from this tragedy will not make Boston or any other city immune to such a deceptive sequence of events in the future. And the right combination of circumstances will always make people angry and empathetic and quick to rush to judgment.

Common people, however, are not in charge of dealing with such situations; that is left to supposedly cooler-headed officials who must employ analytical skills and the kind of methodical, thorough investigation that ultimately gets at the truth.

Minneapolis Star and Tribune

Minneapolis, Minnesota, January 9, 1990

When Charles Stuart committed suicide after becoming the prime suspect in his pregnant wife's murder he brought a bizarre end to a bizarre case. Stuart also gave other Americans reason to think hard about why they had so unquestioningly believed the lie he told last fall — that a black mugger killed his wife and wounded Stuart after invading their car near Boston's mostly black Mission Hill neighborhood. Residents of Mission Hill are angry about the cloud cast on them. They have reason to be.

The story was full of dramatic elements. But its impact depended heavily on the way it was cast by police, news media and a credulous public as a fatal encounter between middle-class, white suburban professionals and violent inner-city blacks. The episode thus became a classic example of racial stereotyping. And it was a lie.

Another lie was the story told last week by a white prosecutor in Camden, N.J., who claimed to have engaged in a running gunfight with two black drug dealers. The prosecutor has now admitted it was all a hoax and has resigned. But his story, like Stuart's, attempted to play on white stereotypes of inner-city blacks.

It can work the other way too. Black teenager Tawana Brawley made the news two years ago with a claim that she was abducted and raped by a gang of white men and left in a plastic garbage bag, smeared with feces and with racial epithets scrawled on her body. It's now clear, however, that she faked the whole thing.

In retrospect, all three stories might have been recognized as implausible. But as their tellers knew, one way to lend their lies credibility was to play on racial prejudices and fears. In Stuart's case, somebody might have recalled that most murder victims are killed by members of their own families. Yet Stuart was able to divert attention from the possibility of his own guilt by making his wife's murder appear to have been a racial incident.

A Boston black leader wonders "what hope we have for justice in a country that took this man's lie and made him and his family a symbol of national mourning." Perhaps the best hope is that the impact of the truth will force people to recognize the extent of prejudice. Similar situations will be prevented only when Americans — white and black — abandon their all-too-easy readiness to believe the worst of the other race.

The Philadelphia Inquirer
Philadelphia, Pennsylvania, January 7, 1990

It was the Tawana Brawley case in reverse: A white suburban couple attending a child-birthing class at a Boston hospital are seized by a drug-crazed black gunman; he forces them to drive to a secluded spot, then kills the pregnant wife and wounds the husband, who plaintively calls for help on his car phone. The resulting uproar further divides a racially divided city — all for nothing. Last week, evidence came to light that the young husband, Charles Stuart, had staged this unspeakable crime. Before the authorities could arrest him, he took his own life.

In the Brawley case, a black teen-ager concocted a story about abduction by white racists that became a national cause celebre. A special prosecutor had to be appointed to quell black concerns about unequal justice, but a grand jury still concluded that Ms. Brawley had lied.

The two stories are linked not just by their phoniness, but by the way they played to racial fears and stereotypes. Black men from the inner city *do* commit a disproportionate number of violent crimes, particularly in the age of crack. (Their victims, it should be noted, are also disproportionately black.) Virulent white racism *does* still exist, and the justice system in this majority-white nation often isn't color-blind.

What gets lost in all the emotion, however, is any sense of proportion. Most blacks are not criminals, and most whites are not ugly racists. In general, whites and blacks have little to fear from each other. But the overall climate of fear and suspicion — and these cases show how close to the surface it lies — undermines our society at least as much as the individual acts of hatred and violence at the extremes.

Last week, Inquirer staff writer Ginny Wiegand told the story of Rosa Toussaint, a young woman of African and Hispanic heritage who moved to Philadelphia early last year with her two children, took a job as a social worker and bought a house in Kensington. Eight days later she fled, after neighbors threw rocks through her living room window, dumped trash at her front door and called her "nigger." Friends and even sympathetic strangers subsequently tried to help her, but she eventually decided to move back to Huntsville, Ala.

Now it's easy to decry the racists in Kensington who drove her away, but Ms. Toussaint's indictment of Philadelphia was broader than that. She said she finally got tired of living in a city where "every week, everybody black and white is fighting each other." In her apartment complex back in Alabama — that's right, *Alabama* — blacks and whites live in peace. "I walk in the street and the white person says, 'Hi,' and always says something nice about the children," Ms. Toussaint said. "That means a lot to me."

This city may not be able to eradicate crime and overt acts of racism anytime soon. However, the great majority of blacks and whites who are neither criminals nor racists could do a lot to improve the atmosphere by putting their preconceptions aside and, in the simplest of ways, just being nicer to each other.

The Boston Globe
Boston, Massachusetts, January 5, 1990

An innocent suburban couple awaiting the birth of their child and returning home from a Lamaze class is attacked by a crazed urban monster. A wounded husband calls the police by cellular phone, and his pleas are replayed by a camera crew on the scene. The saga was so startling that Dan Rather had to remind his CBS audience that this was not simulated, but real.

On October 23, when the Stuart shooting occurred, Mayor Flynn held a press conference and called out "every available detective." Others cried out for the death penalty. Early reports described the assailant as a tall black man, and any one fitting that description braced himself for harassment. The issues of race and class were hashed and rehashed.

Now, if the bizarre denouement of this tragic story points to Charles Stuart himself, these questions are worth asking: Is Reading safe to drive through at night? What is it in Reading's pathology that leads to such violence? These questions are not fair to the Stuarts' hometown, of course, but they were asked about Mission Hill, the site of Carol Stuart's death, and of Roxbury, site of so many other murder victims whose deaths were less elaborately reported.

The media's role in this case has been criticized by public officials, particularly in covering a suspect in Carol Stuart's murder, Willie Bennett, exonerated yesterday. No newspaper or television station ordered him into a lineup for Stuart to identify. That development was news, and the Globe reported it responsibly.

Bad news is news, alas, and the fiction-like saga of Charles Stuart had all the elements of classic tragedy. We still mourn for Carol Stuart and her family, and we hope that Boston's Mission Hill, now that its name has been restored and its residents vindicated, can shake off the stigma of this spectacular case and participate in a more prosperous future.

Boston, Massachusetts, January 10, 1990

The element of the Stuart murder case that sets it apart from others equally stunning and equally tragic is the way in which Charles Stuart was able to divert suspicions from himself – suspicions that are usually the first thing investigators focus on when a man's wife is murdered.

Charles Stuart, it now appears, cleverly played upon suburbanites' fears about urban crime and upon the racism which tears at Boston's social fabric. In the same way that the case has pulled back a curtain and revealed one young couple's life to be less idyllic than it had seemed, it has yanked aside the shades which conceal that racism from the eyes of all except those whose lives are daily diminished by it.

Some in Boston's black community have now made serious charges about the conduct of the police officers investigating the Stuart case – and about the acquiescence of the white community in that conduct. They have called for an investigation of these charges.

During his six years in office, Mayor Flynn has attempted to be a force for unity between the city's diverse and often antagonistic neighborhoods. Tonight, when he delivers his State of the City address, he has an opportunity to assume that role again – and there can be no time when that healing quality is more needed.

If Flynn decides an investigating committee is appropriate, he should ask it to look beyond the Stuart case to some underlying issues.

The police have a difficult and dangerous job. But the Police Department's "search on sight" activities may have created tensions in the black community that were exacerbated by the murder of Carol Stuart. A study might also consider whether a civilian review board would be helpful –not only in defusing tensions but also in providing the police with a broader view of the neighborhood in which the crime occurred.

Such an investigation will be most useful if it provides a blueprint for police conduct in the investigation of future crimes, no matter who the victims or where they occur.

Roanoke Times & World-News

Roanoke, Virginia, January 11, 1990

THE BIZARRE murder case that came unraveled last week in Boston is not simply a tale of a man caught in a lie about who killed his family. It is also a tale of how a city got caught up in the man's story, made more believable because of its racial element. It's a tragic story, all the way around.

Charles Stuart jumped to his death in Boston Harbor last Thursday after 'earning that he had become the prime suspect in the death of his wife. His story had been that a black man had jumped into his car outside Boston Hospital after a childbirth class, and had shot him and his pregnant wife. Carol Stuart was mortally wounded, and Charles Stuart was shot in the stomach. Their baby son was delivered by Caesarean section, but survived only 17 days.

The story related by Charles Stuart was of horrifying urban crime: A young, white, suburban couple is accosted by a black man who tries to rob them and then shoots them. The couple had done nothing to provoke this treatment, except venture into a racially mixed neighborhood in the city. The message: City streets aren't safe for law-abiding whites.

But it apparently was all a lie.

The true story also horrifies: A city bought Stuart's story and turned on its black citizens in an effort to solve the case. Residents of the neighborhood where the murder occurred said police harassed black men there following the October shootings.

The family of the prime suspect, William Bennett, protested that he was being framed, but few people listened. Bennett had a criminal record. Stuart reportedly had picked him out of a police lineup. Bennett was never charged, but he might as well have been. The news media linked his name and face to the crime.

This case parallels another recent hoax — that by Tawana Brawley, a black girl in New York who claimed she'd been sexually abused by white men. Both Brawley and Stuart relied on racism to give their lies credibility. And in both cases, the ruse worked for a while.

The message in both the Brawley and Stuart cases is that Americans are very willing to believe that one race will mistreat the other. They're so willing to believe that they'll trust accusations on flimsy evidence. As long as Americans believe in racial hatred, it will persist.

St. Petersburg Times

St. Petersburg, Florida, January 8, 1990

For weeks, Charles Stuart was viewed as the heroic victim of a horrible crime. Shot in the abdomen, his pregnant wife slowly dying from a bullet to the head, he used his automobile telephone to direct police to the predominantly black Boston neighborhood where the couple was finally found. Stuart, an affluent young furrier, was still hospitalized when his wife was buried. Later, the community mourned the death of the couple's 17-day-old son, delivered by Caesarean section just before Mrs. Stuart died.

Stuart told police that he and his wife had been robbed and shot by a black assailant who commandeered their car as they returned home from a birthing class at a local hospital. Accounts of the crime, including the release of the recording of Stuart's desperate phone call to police, aroused the sympathy — and the fears — of millions who read and heard about the terrible fate of the young, successful white couple with whom so many could identify.

Now the Stuarts' story has taken a bizarre turn. If police investigators are correct, Stuart was the perpetrator of this crime, not one of its victims.

Beyond that, police believe Stuart concocted his entire story in a way especially designed to win sympathy and divert attention. They say he drove to a poor, predominantly black neighborhood to commit the crime and then invented a vicious black gunman to blame it on. In the weeks following the shootings, dozens of black men in Boston's Roxbury and Dorchester neighborhoods were subjected to random searches and interrogations.

Just before Christmas, Stuart even went so far as to give a positive identification of a black suspect in a police lineup. If Stuart's brother had not finally come forward with evidence that changed the focus of the investigation, that suspect, William Bennett, might have been tried and convicted of murder on the basis of Stuart's false testimony.

Now Bennett has been exonerated, and Stuart — the supposed "victim" of a ghastly crime — is dead, having committed suicide after learning that he had become the prime suspect in the case.

As the true story of the Stuarts' deaths becomes clear, a new set of victims emerges: Bennett, who was accused of a murder he didn't commit; dozens of black men who were brought under suspicion solely because of their race and gender; an entire community unfairly identified with a crime that never happened, at least as it was originally described; and an entire city stricken by fear of a threat that never existed.

The hysteria surrounding the Stuart case seems to have caused some people — including police, politicians and journalists — to forget much of what they know about crime. Criminals, as well as their victims, come in all ages, races, genders and socioeconomic groups. The great majority of violent crimes involve people who know each other: husbands and wives, best friends, next-door neighbors and other acquaintances. The threat of random violence is real and growing, but people tend to exaggerate it — even as they underestimate the dimensions of the modern epidemic of domestic violence, as well as other forms of crime that do not neatly fit our stereotypes.

No one can be blamed for having originally accepted Charles Stuart's story at face value, or for having reacted to it with special empathy. That's human nature. However, those who do not believe that their response was tinged at least to some degree by their unconscious racial and social assumptions should ask themselves this question: Would they have reacted to the Stuarts' story as emotionally or as credulously if it had involved a poor black couple, an affluent neighborhood and an imaginary white assailant?

The Des Moines Register

Des Moines, Iowa, January 15, 1990

The racial tension that flared in Boston following the bizarre Carol Stuart murder case was a disheartening prelude to today's observance of Martin Luther King Jr.'s birthday. It was an ugly reminder that too little racial understanding has been achieved since the assassination on April 4, 1968, of the remarkable man who had a dream of equality for all people.

Charles Stuart committed suicide this month, shortly after his brother told police Stuart had planned and executed the October robbery and shooting of his pregnant wife and then shot himself to cover up the crime.

A black man with a raspy voice had forced his way into the white couple's car as they were leaving a birth class and shot them in a robbery attempt, Stuart had told the Boston police, feeding the worst kind of stereotype.

While Stuart's death cleared a black man, paroled convict William Bennett who became the prime suspect in the case, black leaders were outraged.

They contended that Bennett had been railroaded and that law officers were all too ready to narrow their search for the killer to the black community.

Surely this souring of race relations would have saddened King as it should dismay everyone. Despite the advances over the last two decades in the way whites, blacks and other minorities all think about each other, suspicion, disdain and misperception all too often come into play.

In 1967 King gave a speech at Grinnell College the day before he was to begin serving a jail sentence in Birmingham, Ala., as a result of his courageous civil-rights work.

King spoke powerfully about how everyone must learn to live together as brothers or perish together as fools.

He said everyone must struggle unrelentingly to eliminate every aspect of racial injustice.

"To be sure, we have made some strides in the struggle to make racial justice a reality, and I would not want to overlook the progress that has been made, but it is necessary for all to see that the plant of freedom has grown only a bud and not yet a flower, and we must realize that racism is still alive all over our nation, North and South, but anybody who lives by the racist creed is sleeping through a revolution," he warned.

Still it can be said America has made progress. Still it can be said racism is alive all over our nation. Iowans, like everyone, must not feel defeated by its presence, but must recognize it, and then struggle against it.

Videotape Shows
L.A. Police Beating

An onlooker took a videotape of Los Angeles police officers apparently beating a suspect who had been stopped for a speeding violation early March 3, 1991. The videotape was aired on national television news programs March 4-5.

The videotape was taken by George Holliday, 31, who said he witnessed the incident from his balcony window. Holliday said he saw about 10 police cars stop a car that they had apparently been chasing. The police officers apparently ordered the driver, who was later identified by police as Rodney Glenn King, 25, to get out of the car and lie face down on the pavement.

The two-minute videotape showed King lying on the ground and being kicked and beaten with nightsticks by several police officers. After being treated at a hospital for nearly two days, King was booked on investigation of evading police officers.

Probes into the hearing were launched by the Federal Bureau of Investigation, the Los Angeles Police Department's internal affairs division and the local district attorney's office. After viewing the videotape March 5, Los Angeles Mayor Tom Bradley declared, "This is something we cannot and will not tolerate."

The American Civil Liberties Union of Southern California reported March 5 that it received "frequent" complaints about police brutality in Los Angeles. According to Ramona Ripston, the group's executive director, more than 35% of the calls received by the local ACLU concerned police abuse.

The Pittsburgh
PRESS
Pittsburgh, Pennsylvania, March 10, 1991

At the outset of the Persian Gulf War, the nation looked with horror at television pictures of the bruised and swollen face of Lt. Jeffrey Zaun, a Navy airman who had been captured by the Iraqis. Thinking he had been mistreated by his captors, Americans were outraged and rallied solidly behind the war effort.

The treatment of Lt. Zaun, now free, "wasn't that bad," his father said, and it is now thought the flier wasn't beaten, that he was injured when he ejected from his aircraft.

But the nation now has watched a beating of almost unbelievable ferocity, administered not by a crazed war enemy but by a band of 15 Los Angeles police officers. It's time again for outrage and a rallying behind an effort, this time to bring police, not a foreign dictator, under control.

The beating administered to Rodney King, a black man who was driving a car that allegedly had been traveling at more than 100 mph, was recorded on videotape by a man who lives near where police finally caught up with him.

It showed police, all white, repeatedly clubbing him, some using both hands to swing their nightsticks with brutal force. He also was hit with a jolt by a stun gun and kicked while he lay writhing on the ground.

In all, he was clubbed more than 50 times and kicked at least seven times by several officers while others, including California Highway Patrol police, watched impassively. He suffered a broken leg and a bruised arm and "the side of his face was deformed," said his wife.

At the outset, before a national outcry made him seek felony charges against three of the police who administered the beating and administrative charges against all 15 who were at the scene, Los Angeles Police Chief Daryl Gates wasn't all that upset. "Even if we determine that the officers were out of line, it is an aberration," he said.

Out of line? A man was beaten, kicked and jolted, hospitalized for two days and the chief thinks it may have been "out of line."

It was so far out of line it was repulsive. The entire force is so far out of line that the Los Angeles chapter of the American Civil Liberties Union gets about 55 calls alleging police brutality every week. Indeed, in the last five months, the 8,300-officer police department has had to pay awards ordered by juries in two abuse cases and to settle another, at a total cost of $1,390,000.

If the latest case isn't pursued vigorously, it will end as did a similar one in Pittsburgh in 1989. Because a videotape of a Pittsburgh policeman punching a rock fan at the Civic Arena was inconclusive and there was no corroborating evidence, the officer was cleared.

That must not happen in Los Angeles. All evidence — and there is plenty of it, including eyewitnesses besides the videotape — must be meticulously gathered. And it must be presented in separate investigations begun by the FBI, the Los Angeles County district attorney's office and the police department's Internal Affairs Division.

We fear that brute force, more than is necessary to subdue a suspect, is not, as Chief Gates said, an "aberration" but too often a characteristic in police work. That's not the type of government that Lt. Zaun and his fellow members of the armed forces were fighting for.

As for Chief Gates, a 41-year civil servant with the police department, he maintains that he has "absolutely no thoughts of retiring" over the incident. Even though he can't be fired, it wouldn't be any great risk to bet he changes his mind in the very near future.

The
Evening Gazette
Worcester, Massachusetts, March 12, 1991

The videotape of the beating of a handcuffed suspect by Los Angeles police is a sickening document of sheer, mindless brutality.

In what can only be described as a police "wilding," officers took turns kicking and clubbing the man. More than 50 blows were struck.

Except for the presence of an amateur photographer, complaints the victim might have made after the fact may well have been dismissed. The visual record leaves no doubt that the beating occurred and was unjustifiable.

Beyond its sheer brutality, there are several troubling aspects to the incident. One is the dubious credibility of the official arrest report, which said the suspect's subcompact car was traveling 115 mph.

Even more troubling was that other officers present, including a supervising sergeant, made no attempt to halt the beating.

Even after seeing the videotape, the police chief failed to act decisively. Only after intense political and media pressure was it decided that three officers would face criminal charges; a dozen others at the scene will face only an internal departmental review.

The reluctance of police administrators to take steps to curb such rogue behavior is a betrayal of police officers as well as the public. In addition to the injuries inflicted on their victim, those renegade cops have given a black eye to all 8,000 members of the L.A. Police Department.

They also have besmirched the integrity of police officers across the country who strive to do a difficult job with fairness and compassion.

The public's shock at the orgy of violence is justified. Americans expect to see such police excesses in places like Johannesburg, Bucharest and Baghdad, not in the United States.

Indeed, such brutality has no place in legitimate police work. Nor does it have any place in a nation that prides itself — correctly, for the most part — in being a compassionate, enlightened democracy.

SYRACUSE
HERALD-JOURNAL
Syracuse, New York, March 8, 1991

Maybe it's time for all good citizens to arm themselves — with a video camera.

It's certainly long past time for swift and sure justice to be served upon some sick, sadistic cops.

We're talking about the Los Angeles police officers who apparently mercilessly and brutally beat a black motorist they had stopped early Sunday. The police officers delivered at least 30 blows with nightsticks and a flurry of kicks to the man's prone body.

We know this because it was captured on videotape by an amateur photographer. Other eyewitnesses said the cops "were all laughing and chuckling, like they had just had a party" after they had meted out their version of roadside instant justice. The same witness said the victim pleaded with the cops to "please stop, please stop" as they unloaded their blows like they were swinging a baseball bat at an intramural charity ball game.

For the nation, the seeing is a good part of the telling. That grainy, gruesome, almost surrealistic videotape was shown over and over on television news programs.

Whether this is an ugly racially motivated incident or just another case of police brutality isn't clear yet. The Los Angeles Police Department isn't saying if any of the cops involved in the gang-style beating are black.

What is known is that during the course of the internal police department investigation, and separate probes by the Federal Bureau of Investigation and the Los Angeles County District Attorney's office, the cops who participated are riding desks instead of patrol cars.

That's outrageous. They should have been instantly fired, with criminal charges as hotly pursued as they would be if it were a police officer on the other end of the nightsticks and kicks. But it took several days of nationwide outrage to inspire the Los Angeles police chief to call for criminal charges against three of the cops involved.

We agree there are two sides to every story, and we've yet to hear the circumstances which propelled the officers into their unrelenting fury. Police reports say the victim of the beating tried to charge at the officers after he was stopped for speeding, while eyewitnesses say the man offered no resistance to the cops — only pleas to stop the blows. We don't know why fellow officers stood nearby and didn't arrest their "brothers" on the spot, but we can only guess it was fraternal instincts.

What is crystal clear from the tape is that they went way beyond any force needed to subdue a suspect, and served up a savage, relentless beating.

We believe this is more than an aberration, one case of Officer Friendly flying off the handle once and getting ugly. We just got "lucky" this time and caught on videotape some cops who were issued attitudes with their badges and nightsticks — and will pay the price.

For any others considering stepping over the line, be warned. While the ease of use and proliferation of video cameras may mean you can capture drunks on the camera in your patrol car, there may also be a citizen nearby with one aimed at you.

It's a sad commentary that we should even contemplate a call for Americans to consider arming themselves with camcorders. It's sad we'd even be driven to imagine this desperate twist on Big Brother watching, to imagine TV programs called "America's Brutalist Home Videos."

But these were sad, telling pictures of the law in action in 1991.

THE PLAIN DEALER
Cleveland, Ohio, March 11, 1991

Police who brutalize the public should have no badge to hide behind. Such subversion of police power, as apparently happened in Los Angeles last week, is inexcusable.

What perhaps is most immediately troubling, however, is that officials have shown little outrage and even less inclination to vigorously pursue long-standing allegations that Los Angeles police routinely brutalize minorities.

But that was before an amateur cameraman captured one of the beatings on videotape. Now everyone, it seems, is anxious to probe L.A.'s "finest."

The furor involves the case of Rodney Glenn King, who is 25 and black. Los Angeles Police Department reports said he was stopped after a car chase. At that point, the eyewitness accounts — and the videotape — veer from the "official" version of events.

Police said King went after one of the officers who stopped him, provoking the beating. Witnesses saw no such resistance, only a man pleading with the 15 police around him to stop.

The three-minute videotape, portions of which were played on national television, adds frightening credence to the witnesses' version. It shows three of the 15 police officers taking turns kicking and clubbing King as he lies on the ground. The prostrate man took as many as 56 blows from police cudgels. It's a three-minute obscenity.

L.A. Police Chief Daryl F. Gates said he would seek felony criminal charges against the three officers who administered the beatings, and that all 15 who were present would face departmental charges.

> *The three-minute videotape shows three of the 15 police officers taking turns kicking and clubbing King as he lies on the ground. The prostrate man took as many as 56 blows from police cudgels.*

But those who stood by and did nothing, particularly the sergeant in charge at the scene, might as well have had their hands on the clubs. They, too, should face punishment.

And what about earlier complaints against the department? Despite an increase in complaints to the Police Misconduct Lawyer's Referral Service in Los Angeles about excessive force toward minorities, few police officers have been prosecuted.

Gates has a history of making racially insensitive remarks. Those comments surely set a department tone that tacitly approves harsh treatment of minorities. It is debatable whether Gates would have seriously disciplined *any* of his officers had the King beating not been taped.

The public should not have to be armed with video cameras to protect themselves from police wrongdoing. Neither should it take a piece of film to spur action to ensure that those who uphold the law hold themselves to the same standard of justice.

The
Des Moines
Register
Des Moines, Iowa, March 9, 1991

Judges often measure right or wrong by whether an action "shocks the conscience." An amateur videotape showing Los Angeles police officers savagely beating an unarmed man clearly shocks the conscience.

Television viewers across the country were exposed to the horrifying scene Tuesday night. It was captured on video by an unobserved bystander who was testing out a new camcorder. The tape was turned over to CNN, which broadcast it. While as many as 10 officers stood by, three officers repeatedly beat Rodney Glen King, 25, of suburban Los Angeles with billy clubs and kicked him in the head.

While there has been a surfeit of investigations proposed by state and federal authorities, the Los Angeles Police Department's response has been disappointing. Officers involved in the incident sought to defend the brutality by saying King — who was clocked speeding up to 115 miles an hour prior to his arrest — resisted arrest, though that was clearly contradicted by the 2-minute videotape and eyewitnesses.

The department for days slammed the lid on any further information about the incident, refusing to identify the officers involved. Thursday, Police Chief Daryl Gates said criminal charges would be filed against three unnamed officers, but none of the others.

Gates' immediate reaction — that the public should not judge the whole department by the tape — was especially weak in light of the troubling rash of brutality complaints against L.A. police lately. Gates himself has drawn fire for shoot-from-the-lip comments, such as his remark to a U.S. Senate committee that casual drug users should be shot.

If the beating weren't enough, Los Angeles authorities held King in the county jail for more than three days after his arrest. He was finally released — confined to a wheelchair with his leg in a cast and his face distorted by swelling and bruises — only after the district attorney concluded there was insufficient evidence to file criminal charges.

The LAPD owes King an enormous apology, and the public a full accounting of what happened.

The Chattanooga Times

Chattanooga, Tennessee, March 11, 1991

Lashing fast and hard with their nightsticks, with full, two-fisted, baseball-bat swings, Los Angeles police officers furiously clubbed a downed man. Several kicked and stomped him. The club-swinging men waded in again, senselessly raining blows on the prone man, evoking an image of savage sharks in a feeding frenzy.

The man, who had been kneeling or trying to rise to his hands and knees, finally collapsed to the ground, rolling over on his back. Still, officers pummeled him with nightsticks on his chest and belly. One attacked his legs, whacking viciously at one of the man's limbs.

A witness, a 52-year-old nurse, told reporters she could hear the victim, Rodney Glenn King, pleading, "please stop, please stop." After the beating, she said, the policemen "were all laughing and chuckling, like they had just had a party."

Mr. King, struck more than 50 times, was hospitalized with a broken leg and multiple bruises. His wife said "his whole face looks deformed." He says he is lucky to be alive. He's right.

Anyone who saw the full videotape of the beating, taken by an amateur photographer from a nearby balcony, could not fail to be astonished and repulsed. Mr. King was cruelly, wantonly beaten — in the presence of more than a dozen police officers. If the unarmed Mr. King ever could have presented a threat when he was stopped for speeding, the beating continued for so long while he was helpless on the ground that one cannot possibly imagine a connection between the reason he was stopped and the motive for the beating.

Seen on national news programs, the beating outraged the nation, and rightfully so. It is a vivid demonstration of police brutality and a painful reminder that the justice this nation claims to protect for ourselves and others can be subverted and corrupted in a flash in our own backyard.

Amid the publicity, Police Chief Daryl Gates said he will bring felony charges against three policemen who attacked Mr. King and discipline the sergeant on the scene and 11 other officers who should have interceded but did not. It is the very least that should be done. The assault on Mr. King, who is black, reinforces frequent charges against Los Angeles police of brutality toward blacks and Hispanics. And it makes more urgent the speedy investigation promised by local, state and federal authorities into the assault.

Those investigations should look not just at officers' conduct but also at the police department's leadership. Chief Gates is a magnet for complaints of insensitivity to brutality charges. In one instance, he said blacks die as a result of choke holds because their bodies are somehow abnormal. In another, he asserted that an El Salvadoran resident killed by a policeman had no place in the United States. He told a U.S. Senate committee that casual drug users should be shot.

Police brutality is not unique to any one jurisdiction, however, nor is the issue of departmental leadership. The occasional incidents of brutality — here and elsewhere — make the assault on Mr. King relevant everywhere. Policemen and public authorities with high standards of human decency must accept the challenge of always reinforcing those standards. They, and the rest of us, must also publicize our revulsion of brutality and reject any rationalization for its perpetrators.

The Oregonian

Portland, Oregon, March 9, 1991

The Los Angeles Police Department's 8,300 men and women are all under a cloud because of the brutal beating administered to a black motorist by rogue LAPD officers.

Many Americans have seen the television tape of cops mercilessly whacking Rodney Glenn King, 25, as he lay huddled on the ground in suburban Los Angeles last Sunday.

It followed what the California Highway Patrol alleged was a high-speed chase during which King's 1988 Hyundai hit 115 mph.

King says it was low-speed, more like 45 mph, and he didn't pull over as quickly as he should have because he was on parole and afraid that even a traffic stop might send him back to prison.

Twelve other LAPD officers, several highway patrolmen and even two school police were gathered around King when three Los Angeles cops went berserk.

They stunned King with Taser guns that administer electric shock, kicked him seven times, stomped him and rained at least 53 blows on him with police batons. One blow broke his ankle. King wasn't resisting, but appallingly, no one moved to stop the cruelty.

Unknown to the police, a plumbing company manager with a brand new video camera, George Holliday, 31, was taping it all from his second-floor apartment balcony.

It would be comforting to be able to say this incident was a temporary aberration, an isolated moment of madness. But it wasn't.

The Los Angeles police involved ignored most of a dozen witnesses, including two in King's car and others around the apartments, and wrote reports to justify their own version of events. They didn't test King for blood-alcohol content because he was so badly mauled he needed immediate medical attention.

The three patrolmen and their on-scene supervisor, a sergeant, were later suspended. Police Chief Daryl F. Gates recommended felony assault charges against the three, and all 12 LAPD officers who watched will be subjected to disciplinary hearings. The two school policemen were reassigned for not reporting the incident.

The FBI, highway patrol, Los Angeles County district attorney's office and police Major Crimes Unit and Internal Affairs Division are all investigating, with U.S. Department of Justice civil rights enforcers looking over their shoulders. Mayor Tom Bradley has asked his civilian Police Commission to examine departmental training, procedures, command structure and any patterns of abuse.

Thousands of angry calls protesting the beating have poured in to the mayor's and chief's offices and the American Civil Liberties Union, some of them from other police.

Well they should. This incident is reminiscent of the worst police abuses during the civil rights marches of the 1960s or the Chicago police riot of 1968. Have we come no further than this?

Omaha World-Herald

Omaha, Nebraska, March 10, 1991

Los Angeles police officers outraged people of good will everywhere when they beat an unarmed man. If anything positive is to come of the incident, police officers across the country will recommit themselves to the idea that a badge is not a license to brutalize another human being.

Fortunately, an onlooker had a video camera and recorded the beating, during which Rodney King was knocked to the ground, surrounded by officers, immobilized with a stun gun and clubbed more than 50 times. The camera captured images of officers kicking King as he lay on the ground.

The officers attempted to justify their actions by saying that King made a threatening move and needed to be subdued. They pointed out that he had been stopped after a high-speed chase during which speeds had reached 115 mph.

King was wrong to flee when the officers tried to pull his car over. He endangered the lives of others when he operated his car at speeds that were grossly irresponsible. And if he made a threatening move as the officers approached, he was wrong to do that, too.

But what the officers did to him exceeded any reasonable, humane limits. He was already subdued. What kind of men would behave so brutally?

Fortunately, the officers who abuse their authority are few. And appropriately, their chief has urged prosecutors to file criminal charges against three of the officers. Bill Frio, a spokesman for the Los Angeles Police Department, said, "The average citizen out there must realize those officers don't represent a department of 8,400 officers."

Frio is right. Renegade cops don't represent all officers. Unfortunately, their actions reflect on their fellow officers.

The country needs more police commanders with William Rathburn's approach. Rathburn, who took over as chief of police in Dallas this week after moving from Los Angeles, referred to the beating as an example of gross criminal misconduct.

"That kind of behavior will not be tolerated in Dallas — period," Chief Rathburn said. "I'm trying to clearly communicate not just my expectation, but my demand, that everyone be treated with dignity."

What happened in Los Angeles might have been a rare occurrence. But even once is too much. The use of excessive and unnecessary force by the police, even when the victim may be suspected of a crime, is intolerable. It should be punished whenever it occurs.

"THESE BLACK PEOPLE ARE SO SELF-DESTRUCTIVE. TIME AFTER TIME AFTER TIME THEY RUN INTO OUR NIGHT STICKS."

Minneapolis Star and Tribune

Minneapolis, Minnesota, March 15, 1991

No one could responsibly argue that the video-taped beating of a black motorist by Los Angeles police officers represents normal police behavior. But neither is every case of police misconduct so vividly documented. That terrible incident is a reminder of why it's so important that law-enforcement personnel be held to the highest standards of discipline and accountability.

Not everyone, however, seems to agree. Rep. Phil Carruthers, DFL-Brooklyn Center, has introduced a bill in the Minnesota Legislature that would severely undercut the ability of police agencies to discipline officers and hold them accountable for their actions. Gratuitously referred to as the "Peace Officers' Bill of Rights," the measure would instead trample the right of ordinary citizens to have their complaints about police misbehavior heard and effectively resolved.

The bill would do this by surrounding accused officers with a protective wall of procedural rules and red tape. The result, at best, would be to make it more difficult, time-consuming and costly for police administrators to carry out disciplinary actions.

And it's not as though police officers aren't already adequately protected in such situations. Like other public workers, police, troopers and sheriff's deputies are covered by collective-bargaining agreements, civil service rules, departmental personnel policies, veterans preference laws and a host of other requirements to assure fair and reasonable disciplinary treatment. By going beyond these requirements, the bill would make police officers a privileged class with employment rights that other public workers, and other citizens, don't share.

Especially worrisome is the chilling effect that the measure would have on the investigation and even the filing of complaints. Agencies that technically violate any of the proposed rules could be sued for civil damages — whether or not the officer involved suffered harm. And a proposed requirement that no officer could be interrogated except on a written and signed citizen complaint, a copy of which has been furnished to the officer, could intimidate many potential complainants and even prevent departments from conducting investigations based on their own evidence.

Many sheriffs and police chiefs are appalled by the bill. Legislators and citizens should be too. This would be more than just a bad law; it would be an open invitation to bad law enforcement.

THE DENVER POST

Denver, Colorado, March 7, 1991

AMERICANS were horrified by the images on their TV screens Tuesday night: a group of white cops surrounding a black man on the streets of Los Angeles, kicking and beating him senseless.

As horrifying as the beating was, the sight of other cops standing idly by — simply watching the brutality — was equally as shocking. Never has there been, or is there likely to be, more dramatic evidence of the protective "brotherhood" cops have to protect themselves from charges of brutality.

The scene mocked the very value of justice in America. We can only hope that most police officers in the country were as appalled as the rest of us by what they saw.

The blood-chilling video, taken by the resident of an apartment building across the street from the scene of the assault, ought to become standard viewing in every police training academy in America.

That one scene, played out by a dozen bad cops among the tens of thousands of honest ones in this land, has done more to damage police-citizen relationships than a generation of community-relations officers could repair. It will be a long, long time before the images are erased from the American mind.

There is a simple, common-sense lesson for cops in this incident: Always assume that your behavior is being videotaped. In this day and age, it very well could be.

And then ask yourself, "Would I mind seeing this on national TV?"

Los Angeles Times
Los Angeles, California, March 22, 1991

The Los Angeles City Council's first public discussion of the Rodney King beating was a model of the recreant politics of avoidance. The council, ostensibly, summoned Police Chief Daryl Gates to explain more about a 1985 police brutality case before it would agree to pay a $265,000 settlement.

Countless times before, the council has routinely signed off on such legal settlements. But with the King case highlighted daily in the news over the last two weeks, the council decided to use the opportunity to ask Gates more about the beating. Fair enough, except that this same council voted down the direct opportunity to question Gates about the King beating last week.

When Councilman Michael Woo put forth a motion to do just that, he couldn't get enough support from colleagues. The council, it seems, was only comfortable daring to ask questions if it could do so indirectly through the 1985 case—which, before the King attack, would have received barely a raised eyebrow from most council members.

The savage beating of King, an unarmed black man, at the hands of Los Angeles Police officers has been so riveting a case of brutality that it has caught the attention even of President Bush, who on Thursday called the beating "outrageous."

With that sort of national interest, you'd think the city's legislative body would be eager to ask lots of tough questions of the police chief. That's what's expected when you are the boss. You get the glory when your troops do well, and you have to answer when they don't.

Yet it was the council that seemed to be on the defensive Wednesday, mostly prefacing any remarks with 1) how shocked it was by the beating and 2) how much it supports LAPD officers, most of whom are fine cops. Certainly.

But by avoiding the difficult issue of whether Chief Gates should step down for the good of the city—as many now believe he should—most of the council members seemed to be tripping over each other, trying to dodge the very leadership they claim to want.

Los Angeles, California, March 16, 1991

The first and, we trust, not the last indictments were announced Friday in the now nationally infamous police beating of motorist Rodney King. More indictments are expected, as the Los Angeles County Grand jury looks further into the disgraceful incident.

Citizens of Los Angeles and beyond continue to be deeply disturbed by the beating almost two weeks after it happened; that's a measure of the tremendous revulsion generated by the videotaped pounding.

The five indictments rightly go beyond what Chief Daryl F. Gates had recommended. Even so, descriptions of the charges do not do justice to that unforgettable image of gang-like assault now burned into the national consciousness; they tell only part of the story. Still, it is some story they tell.

Charge 1: Alleges that Officers Laurence Powell, Timothy Wind, Theodore Briseno and Sgt. Stacey Koon assaulted King by force likely to produce great bodily injury and with a deadly weapon. Charge 2: Alleges that officers Powell, Wind, Briseno and Koon "did willfully, unlawfully, under color of authority and without lawful necessity assault and beat" King. Charge 3: Alleges that Powell "knowingly and intentionally made statements in the [police] report which he knew to be false." Charge 4: Alleges that Koon intentionally made statements he knew to be false. Charge 5: Alleges that Koon knew a felony had been committed and "did harbor, conceal and aid" Powell "with the intent that he might avoid and escape from arrest, trial, conviction and punishment."

The investigation is ongoing and the evidence-gathering is proceeding. The other 11 officers present at the beating of King also should come under scrutiny for possible prosecution. At the federal level, Justice Department civil rights lawyers are considering ways to bring federal charges against some of the officers who stood by and watched; on some level, such inaction could be deemed to be as reprehensible as doing the evil deed.

The FBI and Justice Department already are aggressively investigating the beating to determine if any of the officers should be prosecuted on a charge of violating King's civil rights. Federal policy typically postpones action until state proceedings have been completed, but because of the outcry, parallel investigations are proceeding, as well they should.

Prosecutions are typically and often necessarily lengthy procedures. The defendants deserve their day in court. But justice must be done. Court action is one way.

Los Angeles, California, March 29, 1991

The Rodney King beating has brought to the surface ugly problems in Los Angeles: not only the allegations of police brutality, but the now exposed factionalism among races and ethnic groups and the tensions between longtime city powers who fear too much change and new-line city powers who fear too little.

With the political winds full of volatile elements, the easiest, safest—and the most timid—response for an elected official is to do nothing. That's why Los Angeles City Councilman Michael Woo deserves credit for taking an unequivocal stand in calling for the resignation of Los Angeles Police Chief Daryl F. Gates. Woo believes, as do many other responsible people, that the chief, "by pitting his personal supporters against his critics . . . has placed himself at the center of a fight which threatens to tear this city apart."

Given the crisis of public confidence in the Police Department, the national shame the beating brought upon the entire city and the controversy the chief has brought upon himself during his tenure, Woo's stand shouldn't be courageous. But it is, compared to some council members, who can't seem to decide, after three weeks of exhaustive public discussion, whether they support Gates' indefinite continuation as police chief. "Let's wait and see." "It's not really the council's job," some members have said. "We don't want to just add rhetoric." Really? Funny, that's never stopped council members from jumping into U.S. foreign policy, rhetorical guns blazing.

Some city officials simply are afraid to take a stand on the city's biggest controversy in recent history. Council members Joel Wachs, Ruth Galanter, Robert Farrell and Nate Holden say they have no position whatsoever on Chief Gates' tenure. Mayor Tom Bradley, although he's more than hinted that he wants Gates out, has been no model of clarity on this issue, either. And clarity is what's needed, whether the position is in favor of or against Gates as police chief.

Absent political leadership to give voice and positively channel public frustration—which is particularly strong among African-Americans—others step in to fill the gap. Enter Al Sharpton, the New York preacher-activist who has a proven knack for showing up in racially tense situations and making them more so. He describes himself as a "loose cannon," a point on which we agree.

Sharpton is just what Los Angeles doesn't need. But when you've got a town full of duck-and-run politicians, it invites others to take up the leadership mantle. And when that happens some people will follow—no matter, unfortunately, where they are being led.

Chicago Defender

Chicago, Illinois, March 20, 1991

The recently released transcript of the beating of an unarmed African American motorist by a number of Los Angeles police officers contains ominous statements. The conversations relayed to the Police Department by various officers from portable transmitters in their squad cars were chilling in their effect, and cause for deep concern. For example:

• One officer transmitted the message, "Oops!" The receiving unit replied, "Oops what? The original transmitter responded he hadn't "beaten anyone this bad in a long time." The other unit replied, "Oh, not again. Why for you do that? I thought you agreed to chill out for a while. What did he do?"

• After the victim, Rodney G. King, was beaten, Sgt. Stacey Koon is recorded on the transcript as typing the following message to a police dispatcher: "You just had a big-time use of force. Tased (meaning a stun device that uses darts) and beat the suspect...pursuit, big time."

• The reply from the Police Department: "Oh well. I'm sure the lizard didn't deserve it. Ha, ha. I'll let them know, OK?"

• After the incident, a squad car carrying two of the officers charged in King's beating responded to another unit's report of its narcotic's surveillance by transmitting this message: "Sounds almost (as) exciting as our last call...it was right out of 'Gorillas in the Mist'" — the title of a film about a scientist who studies gorillas in Africa. The other squad car responded, "Ha. Ha. Ha. Ha...Let me guess. Who be the parties?"

• The individual heading the police investigation of the matter said of the previous statement: "Based on the look of it, there is every appearance of a racial comment."

• Koon also made the following statement: "I'm gonna drop by the station for a fresh Taser and darts. Please have the desk have one ready."

These words show a callous disregard for human safety, a lack of concern for the mission and goals of honest police work, a Nazi-like attitude towards the common person, and disrespect of the fact that taxpayers' dollars pay police salaries.

The most frightening aspect of the transcript is it shows the policemen's warped attempts at humor. Such bizarre, comedic references are not funny. It is strange and possibly pathological because it represents actions that can seriously injure or even kill innocent individuals.

The ongoing investigation into the matter deserves the most serious effort. There must be no cover-up or attempt to soft-pedal the issue or sugar-coat the officers' reprehensible conduct. In the final analysis, every step must be taken to ensure that all the guilty parties are punished appropriately for the harm they have caused and the terrible example they have set.

The Providence Journal

Providence, Rhode Island, March 19, 1991

That recent incident in Los Angeles involving what appears to be a clear case of police brutality — fortuitously captured on videotape by a private citizen — may produce at least one beneficial result: Attorney General Richard Thornburgh has announced that the Justice Department will undertake a nationwide examination of the issue.

The department's research arm, the National Institute of Justice, will review all complaints of police brutality submitted to the federal government over the past six years. The study will try to determine whether there are any geographical patterns to the allegations. This will help pinpoint communities that may be particular troublespots, and allow officials to consider whether such municipalities need to improve their police departments' training methods or internal disciplinary procedures.

This study should be well worth the effort. Police brutality simply cannot be tolerated. As Mr. Thornburgh stated when announcing the planned study: "Responsible law enforcement officers condemn acts of police brutality by anyone in law enforcement. Those engaged in law enforcement must be among the first to assure the observance of the civil rights and civil liberties of all citizens." No sensible person can disagree with those sentiments.

The issue of police brutality is far too important to be hushed up or treated lightly. Yet having said as much, it is equally important not to go to the opposite extreme by allowing the legitimate furor over a particularly brutal incident (such as the one in Los Angeles) to undermine the reputations of all police officers and their departments. After all, allegations of police brutality are just that: Allegations. While some are undoubtedly true, others are just as likely to be false. People taken into custody are naturally inclined to try almost anything to get out of their predicament — including making false accusations against arresting officers.

It is well to bear in mind that the difficult conditions under which police go about their work often involve instances of heated verbal confrontations and intense physical clashes. As a result, the line between appropriate and excessive force, difficult enough to draw in theory, becomes even more so in practice — especially since officers may find themselves having to make that decision instantaneously, and in the midst of dangerous or chaotic circumstances.

Of course, understanding the factors that may lead to police brutality is not the same as justifying such conduct. The police have an important task: They serve as guardians of life, liberty and property. But the ancients posed a question that remains pertinent to this day: *Quis custodiet ipsos custodes?* — who will guard the guards themselves? Society necessarily gives police officers enormous power. It must take care that this power is not abused.

FORT WORTH STAR-TELEGRAM

Fort Worth, Texas, March 20, 1991

Los Angeles Police Chief Daryl Gates misses the point. The issue in his city — and across the land — is not whether a paroled convict will "straighten out" his life after being brutally beaten by police officers, but whether a rogue police force ever can be straightened out while commanded by Gates.

Gates should not be made a scapegoat for an "excessive-force" problem that plagues responsible officers across the nation and diminishes respect for the law. But Gates should resign because if he really does not understand the hue and cry caused by the videotaped beating of Rodney King — and he seems not to understand it — then he is too limited to run a police department in a sprawling, multiethnic city like Los Angeles.

The King beating has focused the nation's attention on police brutality in a new way and also has focused a spotlight on Gates' peculiar brand of police administration.

In the past, the chief has been guilty of too many instances of racist statements and his department has committed too many acts that were beyond the scope of legitimate police tactics for him now to make a believable claim that he is in no way responsible for its excesses.

True, the fault is not all his. Taxpayers and city leaders share it. Los Angeles has one of the nation's worst police-to-population ratios, providing an invitation for outnumbered and frustrated cops to use excessive force.

But there is not likely to be improvement in the Los Angeles police, or a healing in the community, without fresh leadership and a new attitude — something that Gates, in his state of denial, appears unable to provide.

Riots Erupt in Los Angeles after Acquittal of White Policemen

A California Superior Court jury in suburban Simi Valley April 29, 1992 acquitted four white Los Angeles police officers on all but one charge stemming from a March 1991 beating of black motorist Rodney G. King. The beating, videotaped by a resident of a nearby apartment complex, was broadcast around the world and provoked outrage at police brutality nationwide. In the hours after the verdict was announced, looting and violence broke out across the predominantly black and Hispanic South-Central section of Los Angeles despite appeals for calm from city officials and black leaders. As the sun set, the attacks grew increasingly more violent, and more than 100 arson fires engulfed much of the area. About a dozen people were reported killed by day's end.

Los Angeles Mayor Tom Bradley (D) April 29 declared a local state of emergency, and California Gov. Pete Wilson (R) ordered the National Guard to report for duty, to assist local police trying to control the growing anarchy. The riots were said to be the worst since the August 1965 Watts riots in Los Angeles in which 34 people were killed over six days.

The 81-second videotape of the beating, the prosecution's key piece of evidence, showed police officers repeatedly kicking King and hitting him more than 50 times with their batons as he lay on the ground. Nonetheless, the jury acquitted Sgt. Stacey Koon and officers Timothy E. Wind and Theodore J. Briseno of all charges against them, including assault with a deadly weapon, excessive use of force by a police officer, filing a false report and acting as an accessory after the fact. The fourth defendant, Officer Laurence M. Powell, who was seen delivering most of the blows, was acquitted on charges of assault with a deadly weapon and filing a false police report.

The jury, after deliberating for 32 hours over seven days, deadlocked on a single count accusing Powell of assault under covor of police authority. Judge Stanley M. Weisberg said he would hold a hearing May 15 to determine if Powell would be retried on the charge.

Koon, Powell and Briseno had been suspended without pay since the incident. Wind, a rookie at the time of the beating, had been fired.

Remaining anonymous, as they had during the trial, several jurors spoke with national news organizations April 29 explaining how the jury had reached its verdicts. One woman told KNBC-TV in Los Angeles that she had voted for acquittal because King had resisted arrest and was "in full control" of the situation both before and during the beating.

The six-man, six-woman jury that acquitted the police officers had no black members. It was made up of 10 whites, one Asian and one Hispanic. Simi Valley, where the trial was held, was located 45 miles (70 km) northwest of Los Angeles in Ventura County. It was a predominantly white bedroom community where many police officers and firefighters lived.

(In July 1991, the California Second District Court of Appeal had granted a change of venue to avoid having the judicial process tainted by pretrial publicity. Judge Weisberg chose the new venue in November 1991, after the first judge in the case, Judge Bernard Kamins, was removed by the appeals court in August.)

Late April 29, the U.S. Justice Department, which had not yet acted on its own investigation of the beating, said it would review its findings to determine whether to charge the officers with violating King's civil rights.

In a televised address, Mayor Bradley, who was black, appealed for calm and expressed outrage at the verdict, saying, "Today the system failed us." He added, "The jury's verdict will never blind us to what we saw on that videotape. The men who beat Rodney King do not deserve to wear the uniform of the L.A.P.D."

Minneapolis Star and Tribune

Minneapolis, Minnesota, May 1, 1992

Justice may yet prevail, in the case of Rodney King, the bludgeoned black motorist known worldwide through a videotape of his mauling. It had better. Otherwise, this week's incomprehensible travesty will split further the fraying seams of race relations in America.

But justice will not prevail if law enforcement officials anywhere interpret the acquittal of four white Los Angeles policemen to mean that their beating of King was acceptable behavior. It will not prevail if the four escape discipline by their department or if the U.S. Justice Department fails to bring federal charges against them. Hope still glimmers because the four do face disciplinary proceedings. It glimmers because federal prosecution is possible.

Outraged, Los Angeles Mayor Tom Bradley spoke for many of us: "The jury's verdict will never outlive the images of the savage beating." For the images were clear. On that awful March night in 1991 the four police officers repeatedly kicked King where he had fallen, shocked him with a stun gun and clubbed him 56 times. To suggest that this was minimum force, even against a powerful suspect resisting arrest after an auto chase, defies common sense.

After hearing seven weeks of testimony, jurors nevertheless found the officers innocent of assault and of using excessive force. Members of the nonblack jury, which included one Hispanic and one Asian, insisted that racism was not a factor. They said that King could have stopped the attack by submitting.

We have no reason to doubt the jurors' integrity, no reason to doubt their belief that the four are innocent under California law. But even at this distance the violation of federal civil rights laws looks clear. Prosecutors should act accordingly. The Los Angeles Police Department should move fast, too, heeding the advice of former policeman Bradley: "The men who beat Rodney King do not deserve to wear the uniform of the LAPD."

■

Outrage at the verdict is understandable, but fire-bombing, looting and killing are intolerable. They can spell the collapse of an entire community. The 1960s urban riots taught that it is sometimes impossible to rebuild with money a broken belief that living and working together is a worthy commitment. Without bonds of community and faith in opportunity, the future of America's cities will become as desolate as south-central Los Angeles.

THE WALL STREET JOURNAL
New York City, New York, May 6, 1992

"The big racial conflict in Los Angeles shocked the whole world and it enabled the people to see that the phenomenon of human-rights violations in the U.S. is much more serious than people imagined." Thus, an almost gleeful commentary in Monday's People's Daily in Communist China. And, "American blacks and minorities are subjected to discrimination of every kind in American society. Their human rights are not respected and guaranteed as they should be, and that is the real reason for this tragedy."

What happened in Los Angeles and some other U.S. cities does indeed reflect complex and unattractive social pathologies. Crime is a serious problem in American cities, but that is partly because civil-liberties protections set high standards of proof, not because those protections don't exist.

The headline of Monday's People's Daily diatribe was "Evil Consequences of Racial Discrimination." Yes, de facto racial discrimination still exists in the U.S. But American public policy today is in no way aimed at explicitly crippling minority cultures, as China continues to do in Tibet, Xinjiang and Inner Mongolia.

The U.S. system of justice is based on the presumption of innocence. Unpopular verdicts have happened before and will again because of the heavy burden this places on the prosecution. China, of course, does not have that problem; there is no presumption of innocence and indeed, sentences are often decided before the trial. The conviction rate in Chinese courts, according to the U.S. State Department, hovers near 99%.

In the aftermath of Los Angeles, Americans will be able to discuss among themselves the causes of the riots and to consider how to respond to one of the most troubling events of recent times. China's citizens, by contrast, have not had the opportunity to discuss the Tiananmen events of June 1989 in any honest way. Instead, in Beijing, workers had to write a *renshi*, or "understanding," of the turmoil that showed their approval of the crackdown. There has been no opportunity for the public soul searching that America has already begun, no chance to question the government's version of events.

Free societies may indeed stumble and sometimes fail. Controlled societies acknowledge no such failure. We know which we prefer.

Wisconsin ⌂ State Journal
Madison, Wisconsin, May 3, 1992

As the rioting spread last week in Los Angeles, it quickly became apparent that what began as a show of anger and frustration over the acquittal of four white police officers in the beating of Rodney King had turned into an episode of "L.A. Lawlessness." Thugs of all colors took to the streets, not to register a political protest, but to rob, plunder, burn and hurt.

Within a day, the sickness in the streets of Los Angeles had spread to other cities and states, including Wisconsin. People who may never have heard of, nor cared about, Rodney King were committing horrible acts in his name. As former Madison affirmative action officer Eugene Parks remarked with a mix of anger and sadness, "What the jury decided was wrong, but what I see happening now is 10 times wrong."

The chaos in Los Angeles and the copycat violence in other cities could serve only to worsen the already fragile condition of race relations in the United States. Some people watching the mayhem will conclude that core cities have become so dangerous that police are justified in using any means necessary. Others will see black and white looters tearing apart Hispanic- and Korean-owned stores and conclude that envy, not racism, is to blame.

The Los Angeles riot will carry a huge economic price, and it will be paid by those who can least afford it. The Watts section of Los Angeles never fully recovered from riots there in 1965; how many decades will it take for reinvestment to occur in south-central L.A.? How many more jobs and services will join the exodus from central cities? Talk about fouling one's own nest.

Hardest to accept is the notion that because of one verdict in Simi Valley, the criminal-justice system is beyond repair. There is no substitute for the jury system. It is not perfect, but it is preferable to any other system of justice in the world. Black and white leaders who were shocked by the acquittal of the officers who beat King should be careful not to condemn an entire system — a system that has worked many times in the past to the benefit of minorities, and which may be all that stands between order and tyranny.

Even though the videotape of King's ordeal seemed conclusive, those officers were presumed innocent until proven guilty. That's the way our judicial process works. Ironically, some of the know-nothing looters who have been filmed with VCRs and stolen clothing in their arms will deserve the same "presumption of innocence" should they be arrested and brought to trial.

No one is blameless in Los Angeles — not the cops, the courts, the rioters, the news media or the political leaders who have failed to lead. But as Rodney King himself said, the time for finger-pointing is past. It is time to get on with the tasks at hand: Calming the anger and fears that divide blacks and whites, and working to achieve true justice for all, so someday crimes like the beating of King and the looting of L.A. will be just ugly memories of days gone by.

The Houston Post
Houston, Texas, May 1, 1992

THE RIOTING and looting in Los Angeles is the work of a multiracial mob acting in the guise of exacting justice. It is not justice to commit arson, terrorize business owners and beat up motorists.

What has been happening is tragic. And hard-working, law-abiding blacks are among the victims. Black shops are being looted and black neighborhoods are going up in flames in the wake of a case in which four white Los Angeles police officers were found innocent of the videotaped beating of a black man.

Even more sad is the videotape of rioters pulling people from their cars and beating them senseless — Precisely the kinds of acts they supposedly were protesting.

There is no doubt that most of America is sickened by the events surrounding this case: Motorist Rodney King trying to outrun police officers and being combative when officers finally cornered him; the officers beating King while he seemed helpless on the ground; the verdicts of innocent that said the officers did not use excessive force; and the subsequent killing of at least 12 people and the looting and burning in L.A. All low points.

Mostly peaceful demonstrations were held in other cities. However, protesters smashed shop windows in downtown San Jose, Calif., and Atlanta, and in Madison, Wis., someone shattered the windshields of 34 police squad cars parked at a garage. A note at the scene said "Justice for King."

Few court decisions have prompted such nationwide response. Those denouncing the verdict included black leaders, police officers, civil libertarians and ordinary citizens, all of whom said what they saw on video did not square with the jury's decision.

New York's first black mayor, David Dinkins, expressed fear that "if cooler heads don't prevail . . . a whole lot of brothers and sisters and innocent people are going to get hurt."

President Bush said the verdict in the case "has left us all with a deep sense of personal frustration and anguish." In a speech in the White House briefing room, the president pleaded for calm, denounced "murder and destruction in the streets of Los Angeles," and called for "all citizens to . . . abide by the law." He pledged federal help to maintain law and order.

Numerous black leaders demanded that federal civil rights charges be brought against the officers.

U.S. Attorney General William Barr, who discussed the matter with Bush, said the Justice Department could use federal civil rights laws to prosecute the officers. He is sending a top aide to Los Angeles and accelerating a federal probe of the case.

So this thing is not over yet. Black leaders ought to stop simply condemning the jury decision and start calling for calm while the justice process is given time to run its course.

THE SAGINAW NEWS
Saginaw, Michigan, May 3, 1992

More than the mobs and the fires, the gauge of last week's outrage in Los Angeles was the reaction of the police.

The rioters may have lashed out in genuine fury at the acquittals of the white policemen who clubbed Rodney King, a black motorist, not knowing they were caught on a home candid camera.

Some, of course, also may have used the miscarriage of justice as an excuse to burn and loot.

You would expect police officers, however, to look on the verdicts with a different eye.

They also feel the pressures of the streets. They also would look for reasons why the King beating could happen. They would praise the jury. Wouldn't they?

Mostly, they didn't.

At the trial, an L.A.P.D. official testified that the beating broke department rules, if not the law.

Darryl Gates, the chief who is on his way out, pre-taped a call for calm — from his officers. He did not expect an acquittal.

Then the jury came in and defied expectation, logic and sense.

One defendant told the court he tried to stop the beating. That was almost a mistake. This jury might have accused him of undue interference with his fellow officers.

Saginaw Chief Alex G. Perez said one bad decision "taints the rest of the profession."

Saginaw Township Chief Kenneth P. Ott could not conceive of anything that would justify the evidence of the tape.

One juror said the tape wasn't all the evidence. True enough, King was no angel. The police were right to subdue him. The jury concluded they were also right to smash him mercilessly as he curled and twitched.

The verdict said that anything the police do is "reasonable." In the one mistrial, incredibly, only four jurors thought the beating should have stopped sooner.

In the face of the truth, this jury found a way to lie to itself. That is frightening.

But it is a source of some relief that so many other police officers, seeing the tape and probably guessing the rest, reached personal guilty verdicts.

Sanctioning the actions on that tape, as the jury did, bestows an unlimited power that the police must not have, and the vast majority of officers do not want. Blindly, the jury committed an injustice against the police themselves.

The Wichita
Eagle-Beacon
Wichita, Kansas, May 7, 1992

"Can we all get along? . . . Let's try to work it out." pleaded Rodney King last week as riots engulfed Los Angeles after the acquittal verdict of the four police officers who beat him.

Of all the words written and spoken in the past week, Mr. King's appeal is the most poignant and goes to the heart of the crisis facing America. The riots were a tragic reminder that this nation has an incredible amount of work to do in creating a society where the most diverse collection of people ever gathered under one government can live in a semblance of harmony.

A step toward that kind of society could begin today in Wichita when 15 organizations, including the Wichita Ministerial League, Project Freedom and Church Women United, sponsor a march and rally. The event begins at 3:30 p.m. in A. Price Woodard Park, next to Century II.

Rally organizers say their message will be solidarity and justice. Those are noble sentiments, but the anger that the King verdict generated will not go away with eloquent rhetoric or multiracial marches.

Many Americans saw the Los Angeles riots and felt deja vu. Watts. Detroit. Newark. Places that not so many years ago experienced similar violence, caused in part by the same sense of frustration and alienation that aggravated the destruction in Los Angeles the past week.

Likewise, the same blame-laying that greeted the urban riots in the 1960s has reappeared in 1992. Some people want to absolve the rioters of all responsibility, saying they were motivated by justifiable outrage. Other people say the rioters were simply thugs out for a good time.

But most reflective Americans realize that something is fundamentally wrong with a society that periodically erupts in racial hatred. Those same Americans understand that unless the country accepts the plea of Mr. King to find some way to live together, the American experiment in democracy will be a failure.

Today's rally is a positive reaction to the events in California. Yet most Americans have heard it all before. The challenge is to find ways to forge a more perfect society after the TV cameras are gone and the ashes have been doused.

The State
Columbia, South Carolina, May 2, 1992

A JUROR in the Los Angeles police-beating case said that race was not involved in the jury's decision and that, given the totality of the evidence and the instructions given by the court, she was comfortable that the verdict was a correct one.

That said, let us hasten to add that the videotape of the assault on the black motorist by four L.A. policemen led us and, we think, most people around the country to believe that standard police training and procedure were ignored and that grossly excessive force was used in making the arrest. By all appearances, the acquittal by a jury that included no blacks was the kind of verdict that can be incendiary, particularly given the public's months of exposure to the tape on TV.

An outpouring of anger, therefore, was predictable and understandable. But a single beating, even one under these circumstances, does not justify mindless mayhem, an outbreak of criminality on a massive scale.

"There is no reason for this, no reason for the violence, no reason for the killing, no reason for the arson," said Philadelphia Police Commissioner Willie Williams, a black officer who has been chosen to replace L.A. Chief Daryl Gates. Mr. Gates is being forced out as a result of the beating by his officers.

"All of those involved should be prosecuted to the full extent of the law," Commissioner Williams added. That would take a bit of doing. More than 3,000 have been arrested in Los Angeles alone at this writing, and the riot there leaped like a brushfire to other cities.

The number of arrests will surely rise. So, sad to say, will the number of deaths (31 after two nights of rioting and looting), the number of injuries (1,200) and the number of fires (1,500). Already the riot is of the dimension of the one in the Watts section of Los Angeles in 1965.

What we saw on the faces of looters was not understandable rage but unforgivable glee. It was opportunism run rampant. Why are you doing it, a woman with a armful of clothes was asked. "Because it's free!" she replied with a grin.

No, not free. Not free at all. Public concern over the verdict has been converted to public outrage over the violence. Millions of dollars, private and public, have been wasted, some of which could have been directed at social problems. Jobs are lost in the affected neighborhoods, perhaps never to reappear. Years of effort to build racial and ethnic trust go for naught.

But we must start again. Begin a dialogue immediately, counseled Philadelphia's Williams to those manning his future post. And the federal government is right to consider whether the acquitted policemen violated the victim's civil rights. Legitimate urban problems must get more attention.

But most of all, African-Americans, indeed all people, must remember that, as Dr. Martin Luther King fought tirelessly and successfully for the civil rights of the black race, his method, his trademark, was non-violence. That legacy should be the guide to the future.

The Union Leader

Manchester, New Hampshire, May 1, 1992

There is no question about it.

The widespread public perception is justified that the California jury decision acquitting four white Los Angeles police officers in the videotaped beating of black motorist Rodney King was a grotesque miscarriage of justice.

So revealing and revolting was this showing of the repeated clubbing of King by police officers who rained 56 blows on him for a seemingly endless one minute and 21 seconds, breaking bones in his leg and face, that it seems certain that the accused, however well trained they were supposed to be, were out of control.

Since it is an awesome power that society bestows on law enforcement officers charged with acting on the people's behalf, it is all the more ugly a spectacle when that power is abused.

And yet, a carefully selected jury of the police officers' peers acquitted them of all but one assault charge and declared a mistrial on the latter, one officer's alleged use of excessive force.

What does that mean?

Most obviously, it means that juries are not omniscient.

It means also that the very best instrument of justice available under our system of law, a properly instructed jury, weighed all the evidence, including the videotape played at various speeds, and concluded that — contrary to almost universal public perception — it failed to undermine the officers' presumption of innocence.

Cause for outrage? Sure. Indeed, our outrage is constrained only by the knowledge that juries generally are conscientious to a fault and have a far better grasp of the totality of the evidence than does the public and the news media. The jury, literally, is us —presumably the best of us.

Nevertheless, it stretches the bounds of credulity to accept defense lawyers' premise that that is the case here. Perhaps, just perhaps, if the news media are now as diligent in seeking out this jury's rationale as they were in prejudging the case, the public's perspective will change.

We doubt it. But closed-minded refusal at least to acknowledge the possibility is unacceptable.

Granted, the other possibility seems more likely: that the passage of time will affirm the appearance that justice was mocked outrageously in the Rodney King case. Only one phase of this case has been concluded.

As to the deaths, beatings, property damage, arson and looting in Los Angeles that occurred a few hours after the acquittal, some of it may be attributable to blind rage, and to that degree, while not excusable, is at least understandable. But it clearly was fueled also by violence-prone, thuggish opportunists calculatingly looking for an opportunity to exploit the mood of the moment —people who don't give a tinker's damn about either justice or Rodney King.

The Washington Post

Washington, D.C., May 11, 1992

THE CENTRAL finding of the Christopher Commission, a panel formed to analyze the Los Angeles Police Department after the beating of Rodney King, was prophetic. The LAPD, the commission said, was an insular force that hadn't had new leadership from outside its ranks since 1949. It was remote and even contemptuous of the communities it served. And in the crucial first hours of the riot on April 29, in what would soon become the nation's deadliest urban disturbance since the Civil War, the police force was headless, perplexed and unwilling to risk itself early on.

At Normandie and Florence avenues, where the riot began and where the images of beating victims such as truck driver Reginald Denny were later captured on videotape, 25 officers had begun to make arrests. According to radio news accounts, some of those officers believed they could have maintained control until reinforcements arrived. They were ordered to pull out. The tactic might have made sense had police quickly regrouped and moved back into the fray. Instead, LAPD officers remained in staging areas for as long as two hours as orders from superiors were constantly changed.

For 90 minutes, according to the Los Angeles Times, as the arson and vandalism spiraled, Police Chief Daryl F. Gates was not at his post. Chief Gates was at a fund-raiser held by the opponents of a June voter initiative that could dramatically scale back the power of his office.

Some good has emerged from the Rodney King affair, and it has come in terms of a much-needed leadership change in the LAPD. Chief Gates, who ought to step down now, departs in June. His successor is a person who could break down some of the insularity noted by the Christopher report. Willie L. Williams established a solid reputation as chief of the Philadelphia police as one who is capable of reforming a tarnished department and building ties—not walls—between police and citizens.

There are more law enforcement choices for Angelinos than the ugly aggressiveness of the King arrest and its opposite—a tentative and curiously confused response to violent urban unrest. Recognizing that would be the quickest route to a police force that is no longer so alienated from the populations it serves.

The Record

Hackensack, New Jersey, May 8, 1992

SOMETIMES, there simply are no easy solutions to serious problems.

Take the case of the change of venue that resulted in the Rodney King brutality trial being transferred to predominantly white Simi Valley. There, in a decision that is hard to understand, a jury with no blacks acquitted the four Los Angeles police officers who were charged.

In reaction, New Jersey state Sen. Richard Codey, D-Essex, is introducing a measure requiring that criminal cases be moved to areas with similar population characteristics. Mr. Codey's bill would stipulate that judges move trials to areas with similar racial, ethnic, and income profiles. New York City Comptroller Liz Holtzman, a Democratic candidate for the U.S. Senate, and Rep. Major Owens, a Brooklyn Democrat, have called for similar legislation on the national level.

At first glance, the idea looks good. It really was outrageous that the King case was moved to an area where blacks were unlikely to be picked for the jury. Nevertheless, Mr. Cody's bill raises questions.

Would it require, for example, that in the case of a change of venue, the trial of a black charged with a crime in predominantly white Sussex County be moved to another predominantly white county? Would such a measure prevent judges from moving trials to neighboring counties simply because they have different per capita incomes? Even if income had nothing to do with the case? If that were true, defendants and lawyers might find themselves traipsing from one end of the state to the other.

Consider that in New Jersey, there are very few changes of venue. Consider that the best outcome might take place if New Jersey's chief justice, Robert Wilentz, simply urged that his judges employ some sensitivity on the rare occasions that they transfer cases to another county.

Consider also that the New Jersey Legislature — as well as Congress — might be best advised in this case to take an unusual step — and do nothing.

ARGUS-LEADER

Sioux Falls, South Dakota, May 1, 1992

The U.S. legal system usually works well. On Wednesday, it failed miserably.

Incredibly, a jury in Simi Valley, Calif., acquitted four white police officers involved in the infamous beating of black motorist Rodney King.

An amateur videotape of the incident that has been widely broadcast appears to provide clear evidence of excessive force. But Stacey Koon, Theodore Briseno, Laurence Powell and Timothy Wind were acquitted on all but one assault count, and the unresolved charge was set **Editorial** aside because jurors deadlocked.

Within hours of the verdict, parts of Los Angeles turned into a war zone. The rioting continued Thursday. At least 11 people have been killed, approximately 200 injured and 300 arrested.

The details are sickening. Motorists have been dragged from their cars and beaten. Hundreds of homes and businesses have been looted or burned in South Central Los Angeles, a mostly black section.

Although inexcusable, the violent reaction is understandable.

California and federal officials must take decisive action, not only to discourage further violence but to restore public confidence in the judicial system.

Further charges, particularly at the federal level, may be in order.

President Bush said Thursday that the U.S. Justice Department was intensifying its investigation of police conduct in the King beating. Bush, however, didn't help settle the explosive atmosphere any with his initial reaction to the verdict on Wednesday.

"The court system has worked," he said. "What's needed now is calm, respect for the law. Let the appeals process take place."

We also were disappointed with the reaction of Sioux Falls Police Chief Terry Satterlee. He said Thursday that the King beating was an issue of excessive force, not race.

Like it or not, the case clearly has racial overtones.

The jury that heard the case included 10 whites, one Asian, one Hispanic and no blacks.

One juror told ABC newsman Ted Koppel that the fact that King didn't testify may have affected the verdict. That shouldn't have mattered. King wasn't even on trial. Four police officers were on trial.

Portions of the 81-second videotape that have been broadcast nationally are so incriminating that it's hard to imagine what could compel any jury to acquit the defendants. Jurors viewed the tape more than 30 times during the trail, sometimes frame by frame. The juror Koppel spoke to said the tape showed many blows missed King.

But many — too many — connected.

The fact that the officers involved in the beating may escape punishment does not justify violence in Los Angeles, but it certainly undermines the credibility of the justice system.

This is one verdict that must not be shrugged off.

StarPhoenix

Saskatoon, Saskatchewan, May 1, 1992

U.S. President George Bush is wrong. The legal system did not work in the Rodney King case.

It was co-opted by a clever manipulation of racism and class snobery, something Bush himself used to his advantage in the last presidential election campaign.

King is the black man who was beaten senseless by four white Los Angeles police officers while 11 other officers looked on. He was clubbed 56 times and shocked with a stun gun; his face was smashed and his leg was broken. The officers, who were charged with assault and using excessive force, said the force was warranted because King had tried to elude police in a car chase and was unco-operative when he was finally stopped.

Despite the fact that this attempted lynching was captured on video tape, a predominantly white jury agreed with the officers' arguments. They were undecided on whether one officer used excessive force — a mistrial was declared on that charge (however, he was acquitted of assault).

The trial took place in a white Los Angeles suburb where many residents are police officers. None of the jury members were black. They accepted the defence's warning that to find the officers guilty would destroy the "thin blue line" which divides the law-abiding from the lawless.

In reaching its verdict, the jury destroyed another line, the one between justice and injustice. Many Los Angeles residents responded by rioting. Restoring civil order now means restoring moral order to that city. As Rev. Jesse Jackson said, "the predicate for peace is justice."

TULSA WORLD

Tulsa, Oklahoma, May 1, 1992

THE acquittal of four Los Angeles policemen in the videotaped beating of a black traffic offender has, as it should, outraged Los Angeles blacks, and, for that matter, the entire country.

Some blacks reacted in predictably violent ways. By mid-morning Thursday, nine citizens had been killed in a variety of incidents. Cars and buildings were being torched in black sections of Los Angeles.

The acquittals came at the hands of a jury of 10 whites, an Asiatic and a Hispanic in the bedroom community of Simi Valley where the trial was moved because defense attorneys claimed the police couldn't get a fair trial in L.A. proper.

The jurors apparently bought the idea that police should be given great latitude in apprehending suspects. Some of the defendants testified they feared Rodney King, caught by police after a high-speed chase, was on PCP, a drug which inures its user to pain and has been known to imbue incredible strength temporarily.

But the tape made by a citizen of the "arrest" was deadly. The four officers had King on the ground and beat him repeatedly with night sticks. Maybe they were afraid of King, but it looked more like they were enraged. Testimony showed they later taunted King in the emergency room.

The case provides the usual ingredients of major racial confrontations. A crime, outrageous police behavior, and the violent reaction of a relative handful of blacks in general. Deplorable as the decision is, the majority of blacks and whites know that more violence isn't the answer.

No one has any certain solutions to the broad social situation that triggers the Rodney King affairs.

For the long haul, however, there is still hope. It is unhappily true that the progress the country has made in racial relations is not nearly enough. In some ways racial hatreds among small segments of black and white citizens are as bad as ever.

Still, most citizens — black and white — hunger for an end to racial turmoil and continue to strive to achieve that. They must keep their sights on the larger goal and not not allow themselves to be diverted by miscarriages of justice like the King case.

Times~Colonist

Victoria, British Columbia, May 1, 1992

The acquittal of four Los Angeles police officers in the vicious beating of Rodney King defies belief and violates every sense of decency and justice.

It also confirms to the world at large that the United States is still a deeply racist country, in which blacks' civil rights can be violated with impunity by thugs in uniform — who, after all, are simply enforcing order in an increasingly lawless and brutal jungle.

Millions of people worldwide had seen the prosecution's central evidence long before it was presented and endlessly replayed and analysed in court: the infamous videotape shot by an onlooker. It shows King, lying on the ground, surrounded by officers who systematically deliver kicks, shocks with a stun gun and no fewer than 56 club blows.

That assault left him with a broken leg and shattered facial bones. In any other democracy, such damning visual evidence would have been enough — virtually guaranteed — to convict the accused assailants. But the American justice system allows remarkable scope for legalistic manoeuvres and manipulations to skew the result.

In this case, apparently, the defence lawyers were able to convince the jurors that they couldn't even believe what they had seen with their own eyes. Or if they did, that it wasn't the whole picture. Despite their numerical strength, it was claimed, the officers were terrified of King's potential for violence. Lawyers spoke of the officers' "reasonable perceptions" and urged jurors to stand in their shoes that night.

Surpassing their courtroom tactics, however, was the defence lawyers' coup in influencing both the choice of location for the trial and the jury's make-up. Not only was the trial held in a predominantly white suburb (known as a bedroom community for police), but there was not a single black on the jury. According to the Associated Press, only six blacks were among 400 prospects summoned for jury duty. The two blacks who did get as far as the jury box were removed by defence challenges.

Clever types, those lawyers, but there's nothing to celebrate in this travesty of justice. The Rodney King verdict and the inevitable bloody aftermath will stand as one of the most shameful episodes in American history. Canadians should be embarrassed for their neighbors.

The Seattle Times

Seattle, Washington, May 1, 1992

THE senseless killings, looting, and arsons engulfing central Los Angeles are, in President Bush's words, "tragic for our country." Rioters and vandals are using anger over the not-guilty verdicts in the Rodney King case as an excuse to inflict murderous mayhem on their own community.

National Guard troops have been sent in to curb the violence and a dusk-to-dawn curfew has been imposed. But military control alone will not restore peace or civic cooperation to riot-torn areas. Leadership from the White House is needed. Bush can reduce tensions in the city by pressing for federal prosecution of the four officers who beat King.

Attorney General William Barr announced yesterday that Justice Department staff will go to L.A. to investigate the case. Bush should not wait for Barr's formal report — which may take days to complete — to state his personal commitment to ensuring that justice is done.

Although the law against double jeopardy prevents the state of California from retrying the four officers, they can be prosecuted for assault in the federal system. Several Civil War-era statutes that make the violation of an individual's constitutional rights criminal would apply.

Bush has an important role to play. He can calm public rage by assuring Los Angeles residents that the judgment of one jury in Simi Valley isn't the last word.

ALBUQUERQUE JOURNAL

Albuquerque, New Mexico, May 1, 1992

If that California jury accurately reflected modern American attitudes about brutal police in a violent society, then the American ideal of the rights of the individual has lost out against the passions of the majority.

If the American middle class declines to condemn storm trooper tactics against those they identify with violence and lawlessness, then we have a two-tier standard of police conduct in this country — anything goes by the police in protecting "us" against "them."

"Today, this jury told the world what we all saw with our own eyes wasn't a crime," said Los Angeles Mayor Tom Bradley. "Today, that jury asked us to accept the senseless and brutal beating of a helpless man."

Many in the minority community say such brutality by the police is not that rare — that the rarity in this case was the chance circumstance of a citizen with a video camera. Captured in the 81 seconds of videotape was the spectacle of the four officers kicking and clubbing King while he writhed on the ground. King suffered multiple broken bones from the boots and the 56 strokes of the officers' metal batons. The sergeant in charge at the scene testified he felt threatened by the prostrate King.

Lame duck Los Angeles Police Chief Daryl Gates was right when he said "I do not think there are any winners at all in this situation."

Perhaps the biggest losers are police officers across the nation. They will face the anger that will result from the message that such violence is acceptable police work. If the videotape sets the standard of "reasonable" police procedure, some civilians might be constrained to stop more quickly, or exit their cars with their hands in the air — as the jury apparently felt King should have done. Others might be more inclined to respond in kind to the Los Angeles standard of police violence.

It is unfortunate that the brutality of the Los Angeles police will widen the police-community rift across the country. It is also unfortunate that the us-versus-them mind-set of police solidarity with the baton-wielding Los Angeles four just as easily spans the country. Consider the comment of Albuquerque Police Officers Association head Bill Pounders, who, presumably, has seen the King beating videotape. Pounders said he had believed all along that when the evidence was heard, the officers would be cleared. "They were tried by a jury and I'm sure the jury had a lot more evidence than the news media or the public had," Pounders said.

In the usual criminal trial, that is an accurate generalization. But in this case, the videotaped record of the alleged crime has been shared with the world. In this case, *anybody* with a television set can justifiably second-guess the verdict.

The scars of looted and burned-out businesses will mar the landscape of Los Angeles for years to come. The violence and looting is as senseless as the police violence that precipitated it.

The hate the King beating verdict fans between police and minorities in Los Angeles will poison community relations for years to come.

The Rodney King verdict tells the world that in 1992, all U.S. citizens are *still* not equal. The inequality is getting a harder edge — and the ominous fear is that a majority condones it.

LEXINGTON HERALD-LEADER
Lexington, Kentucky, May 3, 1992

Out in Los Angeles, the violence is ebbing and the mourning and rebuilding are starting. But weeping for the dead and re-stocking new stores is simple compared to the real task now, in Los Angeles and elsewhere.

That task is, sadly, the same as it was 25 years ago after riots swept major cities across the nation. It is to assure that justice and opportunity are not different for blacks and whites in this country.

There is no simple way to do that. The acquittal of four Los Angeles police officers has reinforced the fears of many black citizens that they can't get a fair deal from courts and police. Televised images of violence and looting — much of it simple street crime masquerading as a political act — has reinforced some whites' prejudices and fears.

But the difficulty only makes it more imperative that the nation get to work. And as in most instances of national crisis, much of the burden will fall on the office of the president.

Unfortunately, there is little evidence that George Bush cares for the job. His pronouncements on the matter have focused more on the need to restore law and order (to which he can contribute little) than on the injustice of the officers' acquittal and the poison of racism (both of which he can help to remedy) .

The violence of the last few days makes it urgent that Bush's Justice Department pursue possible federal civil rights charges in the beating of Rodney King. And it also poses a compelling backdrop for this year's presidential election.

No president can assure that every jury always produces a just decision. But presidents can work to produce a society that values equal justice and opportunity for all. What are your plans in that area, George Bush? And yours, Bill Clinton and Ross Perot? It is not an idle question.

THE LINCOLN STAR
Lincoln, Nebraska, May 1, 1992

This country will be a long time recovering from the damage inflicted by not guilty verdicts in the Rodney King case.

Millions saw on video tape a group of Los Angeles police beat and kick King as he lay writhing on the street.

Anyone who believes in the American standard — equal justice under the law — has reasonable cause to be absolutely outraged. This verdict appears to trash that standard.

The jury apparently believed the defense explanation: that police are guardians of an endangered society and that in beating King they were simply upholding the "thin blue line that separates law abiding and the not law abiding."

It is an explanation based on reality. Police officers have a difficult and sometimes dangerous job. But they also have a responsibility not to abuse that authority.

KING WAS NOT an innocent bystander. He instigated the confrontation by his own behavior. But it's impossible to justify the subsequent beating as a "managed and controlled use of force." It's equally hard to ignore the racial comments made on the police radio after the arrest.

The suburban jury, with no African-American members, gave us a racist response. There is no other way to explain the decision.

This predominantly white, middle-class, comfortable jury would have undoubtedly responded with greater sympathy had Rodney King been white — even a white two-bit hoodlum, drunk and disorderly. And it's not too difficult to guess the verdict had a white unruly King been beaten repeatedly about the head by a group of black officers.

It was inevitable that the scot-free verdicts, would result in violence and rioting in Los Angeles neighborhoods.

But many white Americans will ask why? It doesn't make sense. Why would people destroy their own neighborhoods and attack innocent victims?

Listen to the outrage in the voices of the mature and articulate black leaders.

"The not guilty verdicts . . . are outrageous, a mockery of justice," said Benjamin Hooks of the NAACP.

FOLLOW THAT outrage, that sense of helpless frustration in the face of unfairness, into a younger, less restrained crowd.

The wanton violence is a physical release of that frustration and rage. It is an irrational but understandable response to an irrational verdict.

However, understanding does not excuse the violence. There is no justification for anarchy, for murder and destroying property. It relieves no poverty. It solves no problems. It cures nothing.

Perhaps there is some redeeming value in this verdict, this shameful miscarriage of justice.

The King verdict paints a clear picture of our glaring flaws, a country unwilling to become comfortable with its own diversity and a racist mentality that, if unchecked, will destroy us.

The King verdict allows us to see what we are, dangerously divided by race and by class.

Thirty years ago Americans who cared about justice joined hands and sang, "We shall overcome."

The King verdict shows what a distance we still have to go.

MILWAUKEE SENTINEL
Milwaukee, Wisconsin, May 2, 1992

The level of violence and destruction in Los Angeles required that the federal government react.

Friday, it did.

Would that the jurors in the Rodney G. King case had acted as responsibly as President Bush did in sending federal law officers to Los Angeles while keeping several thousand Army troops nearby and in reserve — or as King himself did, when he called for calm Friday.

Reaction to the unconscionable acquittal of four white police officers in the King case clearly had degenerated into wanton violence, often committed randomly and with no objective in mind other than to loot, burn and maim with impunity.

Copycat incidents in other cities attested further to the intensity of the reaction to the King verdict.

Rightful outrage at the jury's decision was replaced by the sickening spectacle of thugs and thieves rampaging through the streets of the community, not out of rage over an unjust verdict, but with carnival-like abandon.

Friends and neighbors were dead. Homes and businesses were burned. And yet too many were prepared to write it off to anger and rage.

People were angry. They were outraged. But their cause now lies in the streets, bloodied and burned by swarms of the lawless. The racism evident in some of the violence was as ugly as that of which the King jury stands justly accused.

Once again, America finds itself at risk of plunging into another period of racial and ethnic disunity and division. The King verdict could have been a unifying force as millions of people across the nation — black and white — recoiled against the insensitivity and arrogance of the jury's verdict.

The verdict in favor of four unbelievably brutal officers could have resulted in a thunderous voice raised against racism that neither the Los Angeles Police Department, nor America, could dare ignore.

That opportunity may now have been lost in the fire and haze that filled the sky over Los Angeles.

The News Journal

Wilmington, Delaware, April 30, 1992

By most standards of decent conduct, what we have witnessed in the acquittal of four white Los Angeles police officers by a jury from which blacks were absent was an act of cowardice.

The officers were accused of using excessive force in the beating of Rodney King, a black motorist who had led the California Highway Patrol on a wild, high-speed chase only days after being released from prison. Their defense was that they had conducted themselves properly through "managed and controlled use of force."

Fortunately for posterity, the beating was videotaped by a witness, and the actions spoke louder than either the rationalizations or the verdict. Rodney King was brutalized. The brutality was not "managed and controlled," the justice system was.

More than any event in recent memory, this acquittal rolls back the clock to the mid-1960s when all-white juries (the King jury had an Asian and a Hispanic on it), routinely absolved white police of wrongdoings against black people. It also takes us back to a time when the relationship between African Americans and white Los Angeles policemen was so bad that violence erupted in Watts.

This time, if we are lucky, the violence will not roll from Los Angeles to New York, city by city; but this verdict, the product of a twisted application of justice, will mar us for a long time.

DIARIO LAS AMERICAS

Miami, Florida, May 5, 1992

When some or many persons condemned the forty nine killings so far occurred in Los Angeles, the more than two thousand fires, the assaults and the several thousand people injured as a consequence of the verdict dictated by the jury that acquitted the four police officers who brutally beat the citizen of the black race Rodney King, it seems that they believe —and many times they give the impression— that such criticism by itself implies they agree with the conduct of the jurors who passed judgment favorable to the four antisocial men, four police officers who so brutally and lengthily beat the person captured. To believe this is to fall into an error of interpretation, unless whoever criticizes the outrages occured last week in Los Angeles gives the impression clearly or indirectly, that he or she thinks that the brutal beating against Rodney King was justified and, therefore, the jury who acquitted the four police officers was right.

The beating against Rodney King, proof of which is in a videotape, is totally incompatible with the elementary principles of morality, civilization, justice, safety, as well as contrary to the spirit and rules that should regulate the performance of the law and order bodies.

No matter what the reaction of the captured person was, physical resistance or verbal abuse, four police officers —armed and well trained— are enough to subdue rapidly the person in question without any need for countless blows, although it is said that one of the officers gave forty five blows. If the policemen did not know they were committing a very serious crime, not because they had captured a person but because of the way they did it, this means they do not know the duty of a police officer who, in many aspects, in fact, in fundamental aspects, should be an exemplary citizen. It is fitting to say that the great majority of police officers of all the cities of the United States of America are decent persons and, as agents of law and order, they skillfully practice their rights and obligations.

To all that it must be said again, with deep indignation, insistently, that there is no justification for the multiple and savage crimes unleashed last week against the lives of forty nine innocent people, against private property and against the physical integrity of more than two thousand persons injured in the riots, committed by people who demonstrated to lack the moral fiber to act in the name of justice, not only outside the Law but against the Law. And, in fact, spreading terror, pain an death in the name of justice. One thing can not be confused with the other. The jury's verdit was unfair and what has happened in Los Angeles is terribly unfair.

The Sun

Vancouver, British Columbia, May 1, 1992

OH, Los Angeles. The City of Angels burns as *The Cosby Show* ends. Rioting, looting and killing in the streets while a feel-good TV sitcom that for eight years glossed over the reality of black America puts on its last happy face. In the United States the tragic is never far removed from the banal.

But never was black anguish more profound. Race relations in the U.S. may have been set back a generation by the preposterous verdict exonerating four white Los Angeles police officers who delivered a savage beating to a black man. Is there a single African-American who can believe that justice was done when a jury with no black member decided that the camera lied? That what the whole world saw with its own eyes on videotape was not a crime?

The brutal outburst of violence that erupted after the verdict was entirely predictable, notwithstanding pleas from leaders of the community for peaceful demonstrations of black anger. Yet, even here the police were found wanting, failing to anticipate the depth of the rage the jury's decision would trigger.

Lamentably, these shocking developments could erase much of the progress made since the beating toward the cleaning up the police department, which a commission of inquiry has found to be rife with problems of racism and excessive use of force. The chief has been forced to resign. His (black) successor, not yet on the job, faces a daunting challenge.

But it is not just a police problem, or a Los Angeles problem. And if we think it is only an American problem, we are fooling ourselves.

Edwards Defeats Duke in Louisiana Governor's Race

Former Gov. Edwin Edwards (D) Nov. 16, 1991 defeated State Rep.. David Duke (R) in a runoff gubernatorial election in Louisiana.

According to complete, unofficial returns, Edwards received 1,086,820 votes, or 61% of the total, to 701,024 votes, or 39%, for Duke. Turnout was a record high for a gubernatorial election in Louisiana, with almost 80% of the state's 2.24 million registered voters going to the polls. Edwards would be Louisiana's first four-term governor.

The race, which the *Washington Post* called "the most publicized governor's race of modern times," attracted intense interest in Louisiana and nationwide, largely due to the candidacy of Duke, a former Grand Wizard of the Ku Klux Klan whose ties to radical white supremacist groups had extended into the late 1980s.

Coverage of the campaign solidified Duke's national recognition; 40% of those who contributed to his campaign were from out of state. At the same time, his strong following sent a wave of alarm through much of the nation as many realized that a former white supremacist—whose professed conversion from such views was regarded with suspicion—might win a governorship.

During much of the campaign, the candidates had focused on attacking each other's pasts. Duke blasted Edwards for corruption in his previous three terms as governor. (Edwards had been indicted twice for corruption.) Duke carried over from the primaries his focus on welfare, affirmative action and crime (seen by many as a coded racist appeal). Edwards reminded voters of Duke's extremist past and promised to help the state economically.

Fear of Duke had earned Edwards a remarkable array of support that included Louisiana business interests, incumbent Gov. Buddy Roemer (R) and President Bush, in addition to Democratic and liberal groups and blacks.

According to an exit poll reported in the New York Times Nov. 18, Edwards won support from 45% of whites, 96% of blacks, 44% of Republicans, 73% of Democrats, 59% of men and 63% of women. The poll showed Edwards's support to be stronger among those in the highest and lowest annual family-income brackets, and among those with higher levels of education.

Edwards's margin of victory surprised many observers. Although polls had indicated that Edwards would win, they had been regarded skeptically since such surveys had been found in the past to understate Duke's level of support. Experts had surmised that some Duke voters were reluctant to admit their support for him to poll-takers.

In the primary, Edwards and Duke had received 34% and 32% of the vote, respectively, making the election in key respects a battle over which candidate could attract the 27% of the electorate that had voted for Roemer. Edwards soundly defeated Duke on this score. Exit polls indicated that about 75% of those who had voted for Roemer in the primary turned to Edwards in the runoff.

Some analysts attributed Edwards's success with Roemer supporters—who tended to be professional, business-oriented Republicans—to fears that a Duke victory would harm the economy.

Supporters of Edwards had suggested that a win by Duke would damage the New Orleans convention and tourism industries by prompting groups to cancel meetings to protest his election, and that it would generally decrease the state's attractiveness to businesses and investors. Such fears became a major campaign issue and brought powerful business interests into the election on the side of Edwards (whom they had tended to oppose in the past). Many analysts viewed the issue as decisive in the campaign.

Duke accused his opponents of promoting alarmist scare tactics, and in his concession speech Nov. 5, Duke attributed his loss to "economic blackmail" on the part of out-of-state opponents, as well as to the "liberal media."

The Times-Picayune

New Orleans, Louisiana, November 17, 1991

As the whole world watched, the voters of Louisiana did the right thing. At the end of one of the most polarized and emotionally intense contests in memory, they rejected the race-based candidacy of state Rep. David Duke. Not by a sliver, not merely by a comfortable margin. But overwhelmingly.

Edwin Edwards will be our next governor.

And Louisiana is the winner. Those who watched know what we are made of.

But there is still much to be done.

We must rebuild the economy of Louisiana, still recovering from the ravages of the oil bust.

We must restore the faith of those many voters who made plain their disgust with government. That is a tall order for Mr. Edwards and other public officials, but they would be deaf not to have heard this blast of contempt.

And we must address the sorry state of race relations in our city, state and country. Today, 128 years after the Emancipation Proclamation freed slaves, 37 years after the Brown vs. Board of Education decision banned racial segregation in public schools, and 23 years after the death of Martin Luther King Jr., black people and white people are still divided by fear, prejudice and an economic chasm.

It is a fact of American life, yet at all levels of our society we have failed to confront it. If there is long-term good to come from this day, if the momentum of racism is to be stopped, we must start learning to live with each other. It's time to plant, even if we don't live to see the harvest.

For us in Louisiana, this is also a time to praise and preserve the unprecedented coalition that put aside all differences and worked tirelessly to assure this outcome. From Dave Treen to Sybil Morial, they emerged to challenge Mr. Duke's divisiveness.

Mr. Edwards, whose past brushes with scandal flawed him as a candidate, must work to keep the trust of these diverse Louisianians. Many of them could have remained silent, but chose to stake their reputations on the former governor. That is a risk they should not have to regret taking.

As a newspaper, we reiterate the pledge we made earlier: That we will employ all resources to ensure that Mr. Edwards remains true to his word.

He has said several times he regards this opportunity as a pure gift of history — an unexpected chance to redeem his name as a governor the future might yet admire.

He has his moment. He should seize it. Louisiana deserves it.

The Des Moines Register

Des Moines, Iowa, November 21, 1991

Fresh from his defeat for governor of Louisiana, and now contemplating a run for president, former Klansman David Duke acknowledges that a solid black vote is what kept him from winning the statehouse. But he's not about to toss any olive branches to black voters. Instead, Duke has taken to referring to white voters as his "constituency," while consoling himself that he'd do better in states with smaller black populations.

He probably would. Although Duke ultimately lost to former Gov. Edwin Edwards, it's not reassuring that he carried away more than half the state's white vote. Had it not been for 96.4 percent of black voters casting their ballots for Edwards, in an unprecedented 80 percent black voter turnout, the former Klansman would be expounding his message of hate in the Louisiana state Capitol.

An analysis of Saturday's vote reveals that Duke's race-baiting candidacy appealed most to disaffected white people who disdain government and fear for their economic future. The typical Duke voter tended to be a white Republican or independent with a high-school education or less, Protestant or fundamentalist Christian, with a family income of $50,000 or under.

But the paranoid fears about minorities that have percolated down to that group of voters did not begin with David Duke or other far-right fringe candidates. The Bush administration, too, has played the race card to divide Americans — whether through the disingenuous use of terms like "quotas" to oppose civil rights, images like Willie Horton to breed fear, or simply the failure to address the American public on the priority of fighting racism.

David Bositis, of the Washington, D.C.-based Joint Center for Political Studies (a non-profit, public policy-research institute focusing on race issues), says the Republicans' risky game of race politics is "coming back to haunt them."

As long as the economy was all right, notes Bositis, the party of big business felt free to attack affirmative action and civil rights. Now that the economy is failing, those racially charged messages, already legitimized, provide ammunition in the appeals of a David Duke to lower- and middle-income white voters feeling the squeeze.

The message for both parties, but especially for Republicans, is that it is no longer enough to merely disassociate themselves from David Duke. They must directly attack the myths and innuendos that gave birth to the Duke phenomenon — or be prepared to face at the polls the wrath of the voters who've been made scapegoats.

The Louisiana gubernatorial race demonstrates the immense power of an organized black vote, when those voters are sizable and motivated to vote. According to Bositis, in most states, the proportion of voting blacks is now roughly equivalent to that of whites.

If Duke runs against Bush, the administration may feel that repudiating him is all it owes black voters. That would be a mistake. With or without a Duke in the race, the Grand Old Party is going to have to stop giving respectability to racial politics. The tactic is starting to backfire.

THE DAILY OKLAHOMAN

Oklahoma City, Oklahoma, November 21, 1991

DAVID Duke's seismic journey into American politics may have been stalled by his decisive defeat in the Louisiana governor's race, but it is far from over. He vows to keep moving, his ultimate destination the White House.

The scary thing about Duke is that he combines evil "virtues" with the skills of a clever politician. Employing conservative rhetoric, he was able to convince more than 700,000 Louisiana voters to ignore his Nazi-KKK past and support him.

Duke's message, as Vice President Dan Quayle observed, was "anti-big government, get out of my pocketbook, cut my taxes, put welfare people back to work" and it remains a very popular one. It would play well outside his home state.

If Duke plans to take that message into the primaries against President Bush, as all signs indicate, he may not be alone. Some conservatives would like to see Housing Secretary Jack Kemp challenge Bush, but he seems content to be a critic inside the administration. Former White House aide Pat Buchanan is chomping at the bit, however.

What is shaping up is a heated Republican primary fight in which a sound conservative message is certain to be mislabeled as racist because of Duke. Buchanan's challenge is to stake out a claim to the true conservative agenda and not allow Duke to appropriate legitimate ideas for his own fraudulent purposes.

THE ⬛ SUN

Baltimore, Maryland, November 20, 1991

Edwin Edwards defeated David Duke by the lopsided margin of 61-39 percent. This should have made all liberals, moderates and true conservatives very happy. Yet many voices from among those groups are expressing concern about the Louisiana gubernatorial voting. They say the Duke vote indicates racism is strong and rising in Louisiana, in the South and probably even in the nation.

That is not true. Worry warts should savor the reality of a smashing victory. Sixty-one percent of the vote in any two-candidate race has always been and is still considered a huge landslide. It is a complete repudiation of the loser, when, as in this case, the voting turns in large part on a specific group of related issues. David Duke was clobbered.

For the victor to have been a man with Edwin Edwards' reputation makes the defeat even more striking. He makes Marvin Mandel look like a Googoo (good government type). Forty-two percent of those who voted for Mr. Edwards told exit pollsters that that they believed he was guilty of corruption when he was governor before. An untainted candidate opposing David Duke probably would have gotten even more than 61 percent of the vote.

Those who read the worst in the Louisiana voting of Nov. 16 should consider two other votes on different dates. On Oct. 30 the U.S. Senate voted on S. 1745, the 1991 Civil Rights Act. It passed it 93-5. Southern Democratic senators voted for it 16-0. On Nov. 7 — with national attention focused on the legislation and the civil rights issues that David Duke was running against (including specifically the bill) — the House of Representatives voted for S. 1745 by 381-38. Southern Democratic representatives voted 74-1 in favor.

Some might say that since blacks in the South are almost all Democrats, these margins don't mean that much, that Democrats have to be pro-civil rights to get nominated. But Democratic senators and representative have to run in general elections, too. If there were a strong David Duke-style public opinion down South, you would not be seeing such voting line-ups in Congress. Furthermore, *Southern Republicans voted for the bill, too.* In the House their vote was 24-14 for — this from the most extremely conservative group of representatives in Washington. The leader of the conservative bloc in the House, Rep. Newt Gingrich of Georgia, voted for S. 1745. In the Senate, Southern Republicans, led by Sen. Strom Thurmond of South Carolina, voted 5-1 for the bill.

The vote against David Duke was a great victory for decent Americans. It reflected an American and a Southern commitment to equality and fairness that was also made unmistakably clear by the voting on the civil rights bill.

Rockford Register Star

Rockford, Illinois, November 19, 1991

The small comfort we take in David Duke's loss in the Louisiana gubernatorial election of last Saturday is offset by several disturbing factors, not the least of which is that this robeless Klansman is likely to remain on the national political stage for some time to come. He's still a hero to that disaffected segment of the electorate for whom his thinly-veiled racism bespeaks their own ugly frustrations.

Yes, Duke's defeat in Saturday's balloting was by a wide margin, 61-39 in percentage points. And yes, this erstwhile Nazi probably would have lost by even more had his opponent been more respectable than the dubious Edwin Edwards, who twice has stood trial on racketeering charges. But the fact remains that most white voters in this election, and most who think of themselves as Republicans, voted for Duke.

Moreover, there are millions of Americans in other states, including states outside the Old South, who subscribe to Duke's bogus theory that what is really wrong with this country is that black folks get all the breaks to the detriment of white folks on the bottom of the economic ladder. Tellingly, the 55 percent of whites who voted for Duke generally were less educated and less well off than the 45 percent of whites who voted for Edwards.

There is one school of thought that holds that Duke's popularity, limited though it may be, is *in spite of* his background as a Klansman. The theory is that his message, which is basically indistinguishable from that of certain mainstream Republicans, is the alpha and omega of his appeal. We subscribe, however, to another theory: Duke's background, which he now unconvincingly disowns, is his real calling card; the fact that his message echoes that of more respectable Republicans merely provides cover for those who embrace the basic Klan program but not the hoods and robes.

Either way, there is enough pro-Duke sentiment hither and yon to sustain this peculiar specimen as a national political figure for at least a while. Should he end up mounting an independent candidacy for president next year and siphon votes from the Republican ticket, it would be just desserts for George Bush, whose 1988 campaign sought to make racist appeals to the electorate somehow respectable.

David Duke, let's not forget, is a political stepson of those wonderful folks who gave us Willie Horton.

The Register-Guard

Eugene, Oregon, November 19, 1991

In picking a new governor, Louisianans faced an awful choice between a scandal-tainted ex-governor and a former Ku Klux Klan leader and Nazi sympathizer. Louisiana — as well as the country — breathes easier because the rogue was preferred over the racist.

But Sunday's headlines told the real story of the race. They trumpeted David Duke's loss rather than Edwin Edwards' victory.

From the outset, the contest centered on whether someone with Duke's past — and ill-disguised present — could win the governorship in an American state. That he didn't is a relief, certainly in Louisiana but also elsewhere. But the relief is tempered by what Duke tapped in his campaign — the darker side of the American electorate. It is an electorate that is angry and fearful. It is an electorate eager to blame others, to find scapegoats for frustrations.

In Louisiana, the demagogic messenger was defeated — not necessarily his message. Despite his disreputable background, Duke received 55 percent of the white vote. That's scary.

Emboldened by the avalanche of national attention his candidacy received — even though it was overwhelmingly negative — Duke is now talking about running for Congress, or even president. That's not the danger. The danger is that others, without Duke's Nazi and white-supremacy baggage, will seek to wrap the same dark angers that Duke exhibited into more reputable clothing. Some already have. Remember Willie Horton? Remember "quotas"? Remember "welfare queens"?

Most importantly, remember that what was defeated in Louisiana needs to be continuously defeated — time after time after time — everywhere.

Edmonton Journal

Edmonton, Alberta, November 19, 1991

Picking between the evils in their vote for governor, the citizens of Louisiana made the right choice by electing the corruption-tainted Edwin Edwards over David Duke, apostle of the politics of racism and bigotry. But will the American political establishment learn from this election that it must now begin to deal with the legions of disaffected voters to whom Duke cynically appealed?

Louisiana is some distance from Canada, but it is not a world away. Canadians shouldn't draw too many parallels, but they also shouldn't ignore the economic uncertainty and political alienation that shows up in our own society — witness the widespread distrust of the federal government and the traditional political parties, and the resulting growth (outside Quebec) of the right-wing populist Reform Party. In Canada, as in the United States, traditional politics is shutting out too many people.

Louisiana was an extreme example, if only because Republican candidate David Duke is an extreme case. He baked a poisonous cake of economic fears and racism, turning welfare recipients and blacks into scapegoats for the state's economic problems. In the end he got only 39 per cent of the vote, but that in itself is cause for worry. He also attracted a national audience and made his issues of anti-welfare (code words for anti-black in Louisiana) and "white dignity" a part of the political coin, although still an unsavory part.

Louisiana voters created some unlikely alliances, and turned out in admirable numbers, to defeat Duke. Their only alternative, Edwards, was far from ideal. He was voted out of office before because of racketeering trials and a sleazy private life, but Republicans and Democrats, joined by a vast majority of black voters, banded together to elect him over the menacing Duke. Having no one acceptable to vote for, most Louisiana voters went to the polls simply to defeat Duke and his bigoted message.

It would be a relief if it ended there, but there is no such relief. Duke will be a fixture on the American political scene in spite of his loss in Louisiana. And the economic and social conditions that allowed Duke to temporarily prosper, including a growing tendency to racial scapegoating, remain in place for others of a similar bent to exploit.

American analysts have pointed out that Duke's use of the "race card" is not wholly different from U.S. President George Bush's own positions, insofar as the president appeals to the same voters by attacking affirmative rights programs. The Republican party, in the circumstances, should reconsider its whole use of the race issue in light of the disheartening acceptance of Duke by close to 40 per cent of the Louisiana voters.

Democrats, too, should take a lesson from the Louisiana vote. First, they put forward a candidate who fairly reeks of the machine politics and political cynicism that has alienated voters throughout the United States. Second, they were far too vulnerable to Duke's allegation that they represented only "special interests" — code words for liberals of all aspects.

Likewise, Canadian liberals of whatever stripe should reconsider their own politics. The mood of resentment is occasionally evident in Canada too, reflecting at times the sense of exclusion of too many Canadian voters. If Canada's political parties and governments cannot fulfil their traditional role of mediating between the interests in our national community, they too will be inviting a more extreme politics.

The Hartford Courant
Hartford, Connecticut, November 19, 1991

Read one way, the election returns from Louisiana Saturday were comforting. David Duke, the former Ku Klux Klansman and Nazi sympathizer, lost big. Democratic Gov.-elect Edwin W. Edwards's winning margin of 61 percent to 39 percent was a blowout, a landslide.

The turnout was a reason to celebrate, too — almost 80 percent of registered voters went to the polls. Faced with the prospect of electing a political freak to the highest office in the state, Louisianans arose in massive numbers to say no. Many people, especially African-Americans, registered or voted for the first time.

Louisianans "turned back the merchant of hate and the master of deceit," as the redeemed scoundrel, Mr. Edwards, said.

Still, there was troubling news in the numbers.

Exit polls showed that Mr. Duke, who has filtered gut-level racism through a soothing voice and a handsome face, collected a commanding majority of the votes cast by whites. He was especially strong among born-again Christians, but even won a majority from Catholics. Mr. Edwards is a Cajun, but Mr. Duke took that ethnic group by 56-44 percent. Mr. Duke, a Republican, was supported strongly by less-educated whites and lower- and middle-income white voters.

The white middle class responded warmly to Mr. Duke's politics of resentment, his attacks on welfare expenditures, affirmative action and big government in general.

Not everyone who has questions about affirmative action or the welfare system or the scope of government is a racist, but Mr. Duke cast these issues in tones of black and white. He put a black face on people's problems. In hard times, the demagogues find resonance in scapegoating.

There is little doubt about what he meant when Mr. Duke said in defeat Saturday night that "the majority in this country" would some day assert its "rights."

Sad to say, Mr. Duke's racism was not the decisive factor, at least among whites, in his losing. Mr. Edwards won 96 percent of a record black vote, as expected. But many of the winner's white supporters — which included 75 percent of those who had voted for outgoing Gov. Buddy Roemer in the primary — seemed more concerned about the baleful economic impact of a Duke governorship than they were turned off by the Republican's message of racial hatred.

It was Mr. Duke the embarrassment, the cartoonish Klansman and Nazi of yesteryear who would drive business away, that was defeated, not Mr. Duke the sophisticated racist of today.

That, at any rate, is what exit polls show, and that analysis is shared by the likes of Vice President Dan Quayle, who said that Louisiana voters killed the messenger but not the message. For a spokesman of an administration that has helped to unleash the passions of racial strife, that view is not surprising.

But it is disturbing. The Klan has been called the invisible empire — a conspiracy of the heart aimed historically against non-white, non-Protestant, non-gentile Americans. You don't have to wear a hood or a swastika to pluck those heartstrings. There are plenty of people who aren't burdened by Mr. Duke's baggage who sound just like him. That's why it's important not only to defeat the messenger, but to discredit the message.

LEXINGTON HERALD-LEADER
Lexington, Kentucky, November 19, 1991

The voting is over and the punditry has begun. As you can see from the excerpts printed below, the reaction to the Louisiana election is a combination of relief and handwringing.

There's cause for both. Louisiana and the nation both are better off without a former Nazi in a governorship. But Duke's ability to attract almost 40 percent of the voters — and 55 percent of white voters — is distressing.

Beyond these reactions, the Louisiana vote seems to hold three lessons.

The first is the political impact of the weak national economy. Louisiana is fertile ground for the likes of Duke because it has suffered longer and more deeply than almost any other state in the current recession. Surely, America's political history makes it plain that prosperity is the greatest antidote to demagoguery.

The second lesson is that the Republican Party's emphasis on race in national politics is coming back to haunt it. Republican strategists should survey the wreckage in Louisiana and ask themselves which party will stand to lose more if Duke emerges as an independent candidate for president in 1992.

The third lesson has to do with two sets of numbers. Duke actually got 5 percent fewer votes this time than he did when he ran for the Senate last year. And more than 72 percent of voters turned out for this election in Louisiana.

Compare that to the 44 percent who made it to the polls in Kentucky earlier this month, and you can reach a simple conclusion. Citizens vote when the issues in the campaign are clearly articulated and critical to their future. Both circumstances held in Louisiana this week, and voters responded appropriately.

There's an element of satisfaction in that for even the most dedicated hand-wringer.

Racial Discrimination Focus at PGA Tourney

Australian Wayne Grady Aug. 11, 1990 won the Professional Golfers Association Championship at Shoal Creek Country Club in Birmingham, Ala. The tournament had been surrounded by controversy because of Shoal Creek's policy of excluding blacks from membership.

The controversy over the exclusionary practices at PGA tour sites erupted after the Shoal Creek Country Club's founder said in a June 21 interview with the *Birmingham Post* that the club would not be forced into admitting black members because "that's just not done in Birmingham." The founder, Hall Thompson, said that the club's members included Jews, women, Lebanese and Italians. He added, "We've said that we don't discriminate in every other area except the blacks."

The controversy, which came at a time when golf was enjoying a boom in popularity, prompted some major advertisers to withdraw from television sponsorship of the event.

Shoal Creek announced Aug. 1 that Louis Willie, a black businessman, had been voted honorary membership. He was admitted to the club under an agreement reached with the president of the Southern Christian Leadership Conference, Rev. Joseph Lowery, to call off a planned protest at the PGA Championship. That pact was criticized by Lee Elder, the first black to play in the Masters, as a "sell-out." Jim Thorpe was the only black golfer currently on the PGA regular tour.

The PGA Aug. 3 announced that it would not hold regular, senior or Ben Hogan (minor league) tour events at clubs that had exclusionary policies. The PGA said the clubs with all-white memberships would not be presumed to exclude black members, but that host courses must show "appropriate action to encourage minority membership."

According to a survey by the Association Aug. 7, there were no black members at 16 of the 22 clubs scheduled to host various men's and women's major championships in the coming years.

Augusta National, the host course of the Masters, and the prestigious Baltusrol Country Club in Springfield, N.J. Aug 1 had said that they would seek to enroll their first black members.

Defending PGA champion Payne Stewart Aug. 7 caused some controversy when he accused the press of blowing the story out of proportion and said, "The players have probably made more jokes about [the issue] than anything else."

The Miami Herald
Miami, Florida, August 4, 1990

BUT FOR a simple question and an unguarded response, the issue of racial exclusion at private clubs that seek the limelight would have remained for another day. No, said club founder Hall W. Thompson to a reporter, Shoal Creek Country Club wouldn't be "pressured" into accepting any black members. That's not how things are done in Birmingham, he said.

People have a Constitutional right to pick their friends from as narrow a circle as they wish. What made Shoal Creek different is that it sought the benefits and public prestige of hosting the PGA Golf Championship.

So it invited black golf professionals from the PGA Tour to a club in Alabama that they couldn't join, and it entangled a television network and its sponsors into the appearance of endorsing Mr. Thompson's view.

Quite rightly, although belatedly, many sponsors pulled out. Civil-rights groups threatened to picket, further endangering the championship's projected $30-million boon to Birmingham. Now Shoal Creek is accepting one black honorary member and

processing the application of another. The protest is off, golf will be played.

But the controversy shouldn't be over. Private clubs that discriminate abound even though others now say that they are re-examining their policies. Many discriminatory clubs thrive, courtesy of help from corporations and governments. That help may include cheap use of public land, tax write-offs, and underwriting of events.

While these issues have ground through the courts and legislative bodies, many clubs have changed their bylaws to proclaim open membership, at least for men. But few have made it known that all persons who are sportsmen, have nice manners, and can afford the tab will be accepted equally.

Sports groups that depend on public support in multiracial, multi-ethnic America ought to hold their events only in facilities that welcome all people of like interests, whatever their color or religion or ethnicity. And advertisers who sponsor events at exclusionary clubs shouldn't be surprised if people victimized by discrimination choose to buy competing products.

The Register-Guard
Eugene, Oregon, August 4, 1990

The real world has descended upon the unhurried world of professional golf like a downpour at the 18th hole.

The issue is stark and plain: racism at some of the poshest country clubs in America. The clubs prefer the more genteel description, "exclusivity." The distinction is artificial.

The issue came to a head this week when several major corporate advertisers — IBM, Anheuser-Busch, Toyota, etc. — canceled their television advertising for next week's PGA Championship. Some civil rights leaders had protested the tournament being held at the all-white Shoal Creek Club in Birmingham, Ala. When the Shoal Creek president publicly defended the club's exclusion of black members, the advertisers headed for the exits.

The fallout was immediate and the terminology mind-boggling.

The club agreed to accept a prominent black Birmingham businessman as an "honorary member" to defuse the situation. The businessman, in a monumental display of self-humiliation, accepted the club's "invitation." Civil rights groups, calling the tokenism "an excellent beginning," called off picketing the PGA Championship. The U.S. Golf Association proudly announced that it was taking "a second look" at the membership policies of potential host clubs. The PGA acknowledged that "we could be hurt if we were blind to the situation."

What has yet to be said by most of these groups is that exclusionary membership policies — at country clubs or elsewhere — are wrong. Cruelly wrong. That it took the threat of losing cold cash to force this issue into the open is a sad comment on professional golf. This is, after all, the 1990s.

Yes, private clubs can legally exclude blacks, redheads or people with eye patches. And, yes, there are a few black golf pros. And some, perhaps most, clubs around the country have open memberships. But the PGA should have addressed the issue of exclusivity on its own — and long before now. It should not have been forced into "a second look" by TV advertisers. It should have taken a *first look* years ago, found out which clubs had exclusive memberships and bypassed those clubs in scheduling its tournaments.

THE ATLANTA CONSTITUTION
Atlanta, Georgia, August 5, 1990

At that instant when Hall Thompson, founder of the Shoal Creek Country Club in Birmingham, Ala., told a reporter that his club was segregated and that nobody was going to make it change, a change occurred. A dirty little secret that everyone shared — that many country clubs in 1990 America are segregated — had been dragged out of the national subconscious for all to see.

What happened next was inevitable. Reporters, sponsors and golfing officials who had been attending Professional Golfers' Association functions for years without seeing a single black face responded with outrage to Mr. Thompson's "revelation." It became a matter of national honor that Mr. Thompson and his club get slapped down, lest the rest of us be accused of complicity in his vile attitude.

And so it happened. Last week, Shoal Creek admitted Louis Wille, a well-respected black businessman, as an honorary member, with the promise to admit more black members in the near future. Everyone breathed a sigh of relief at the news: The national honor had been redeemed.

We were — or could again pretend to be — a non-racist society again.

That is not to imply, however, that something important hasn't happened with the desegregation of Shoal Creek, and the impending desegregation of similar clubs elsewhere, including Augusta National here in Georgia.

This controversy was never about anything so mundane as letting black people hit a white ball down a green fairway. Mr. Wille, for example, has admitted that he hasn't played golf in 10 years or so, and was never very avid about it to begin with.

This is about equal access to power. It's about exposure. If rich white men tend to promote other white men, because that's who they are most comfortable with, then maybe it's important they become comfortable with other types of people as well.

With women, for example. Many of the nation's finest country clubs expressly forbid women from membership, an issue that hasn't even been broached yet.

Maybe that's the next dirty little secret we'll have to confront.

Richmond Times-Dispatch
Richmond, Virginia, August 4, 1990

Since a good number of people seem always bent on making a sport out of politics, we suppose it only follows that they would also make politics out of sports. For years now athletes who hail from South Africa have been unjustly slighted or even forced out of athletic events by people who want to protest South African apartheid. And now there is a controversy in Birmingham, Ala., where the Professional Golfer's Association Championship, one of four major golf tournaments held every year, is scheduled to take place Aug. 9-12.

The host course for the 1990 PGA Championship is Shoal Creek, a private club. Shoal Creek, like many private clubs on and off the PGA Tour, has no black members; the controversy was touched off when Shoal Creek founder Hall Thompson said in June that his club could not be pressured into accepting any. (He has since apologized and said his remarks were reported out of context.) Since then protests have been planned, advertisers have canceled tournament spots purchased from the ABC television network and at least one NBC network affiliate has announced it will not carry filmed reports of the championship (it has since reversed itself). In fact, the Pittsburgh Press was so eager to show its moral indignation toward Shoal Creek that it announced it would not send a sportswriter to cover the PGA Championship. And then it was reminded that Oakmont, a private club in Pittsburgh which has hosted several U.S. Opens, also has no black members.

Now it turns out that Mr. Thompson's statement nothwithstanding, Shoal Creek is softening. The club's board has voted to accept Louis Willie, a black insurance company executive active in Birmingham civic affairs, as an honorary member. Further, Birmingham Mayor Richard Arrington, also black, has announced that another black could become a member if he meets

normal membership requirements. Augusta National Golf Club, exclusive home of the prestigious Masters Tournament in Augusta, Ga., has also announced that it is seeking black members.

No doubt the process of black entry into private clubs has been accelerated by the Shoal Creek events, but it surely was under way long before now. Private clubs are social, not political, institutions, and they are free to exclude anyone they like from membership, much as any citizen is free to exclude anyone he likes from his home. It is easy to level angry charges of racism, but social and economic inertia are the primary forces that have operated to leave many clubs exclusively white. As a practical matter there are few people with the means to join these clubs (the entrance fee alone at Shoal Creek is $35,000) and it seems likely that the limited number of blacks among that group would rather spend their time and money elsewhere. As more blacks enter the lofty socioeconomic strata from which private club members are drawn, that inertia will be overcome and more will find entry into the Shoal Creeks of the world.

As for the golfers, most are wisely steering clear of the trouble, pointing out that their job is to play golf, not dispense sociology. Jack Nicklaus did venture out, though, if only to say that private clubs ought to be able to make their own membership decisions and that his own club, Muirfield Village near Columbus, Ohio, is open to all races. Gary Player also had an opinion; he said if he were a black man he would be inclined to protest Shoal Creek himself. Aside from being one of the greatest golfers ever to swing a club, Gary Player is a proud and patriotic South African. Racial bigotry is a defect of the individual human heart, not to be inferred from nationality, nor from membership in a private club.

The State
Columbia, South Carolina, August 2, 1990

THE PGA has hacked its way out of the roughs of the Shoal Creek Country Club of Birmingham, Ala. With luck, its scorecard will reflect permanent gains in Birmingham and elsewhere for more than just the professional golfers the PGA represents.

Shoal Creek is where the prestigious PGA Championship tournament is to be played Aug. 9-12. The club has no black members, which is not uncommon in a land where "all-white country club" is a virtual redundancy — whether north or south of Mr. Mason's and Mr. Dixon's survey line. The touring pros routinely play at clubs which have similar exclusionary practices. Shoal Creek was singled out for picketing and a boycott because its founder said the club wouldn't be pressured into accepting blacks.

The world of professional golf was set on its hindquarters when first IBM, then others, withdrew as television sponsors. The ABC network faced a loss of $2 million in revenue for the Birmingham tournament.

For now, confrontation has been averted in Birmingham, where leaders have reached a compromise. Shoal Creek brought in one black as an "honorary member" and promised that another could become a regular member. Social acceptability at Shoal Creek won't be cheap. The membership fee is $35,000. Old members should have no fears that a more accepting policy will bring in riffraff — not at those prices.

A nightmare of the PGA is that the scenario will repeat as the tour moves from one whites-only club to another. No doubt there is a lot of hand-wringing as clubs weigh the advantages of entertaining celebrity golfers for a week against threats to the established order. PGA leaders say they will examine membership policies in choosing sites for tournaments. There are no threats here, and we hope it leads to further positive results — results that go beyond tokenism to a more general acceptance of people who have earned rights of passage by virtue of business and civic accomplishment.

Part II: Blacks & Civil Rights in America

Protest is deeply rooted in the experience of black American. Even as they were involuntarily and forcibly taken from their African homelands and shipped to the New World, ancestors of today's American blacks expressed protest against enslavement through individual acts that ranged from passive reluctance to starvation, self-mutilation and suicide by drowning. Mutinies at sea were strongly guarded against, but some have been recorded neverhteless – the most publicized uprising having taken place aboard the ship *Amistad*.

Once settled in the New World, slaves continued to battle their condition through deception, malingering, pilferage, flight and rebellion. Likewise, northern free blacks, taking advantage of the freedom of assembly and of speech, met in national pre-Civil War conventions to protest slavery. With the collapse of Reconstruction after the Civil War, and its subsequent replacement with massive discrimination and Jim Crow laws, black Americans made special, organized efforts on behalf of civil rights.

The most meaningful civil rights movement followed World War II. Beginning with the Montgomery bus boycott in 1955 and petering out in the late 1960s, this movement was essentially activist in nature. It drew massive support from blacks and a sympathetic national response. The second movement was variously referred to by such names as the "Negro Revolt," the "Black Revolution," the "Civil Rights Revolution," and the "Second Reconstruction." It had two distinct but interrelated phases: one of direct non-violent action and the other of direct militant action. The

movement climaxed in the late 1960s, most probably in 1968, in the reaction of both black and white Americans to the assassination of Rev. Martin Luther King, Jr.

One of the first notable attempts at direct nonviolent action was made by A. Philip Randolph, president of the Brotherhood of Sleeping Car Porters, who threatened to organize a mass march on Washington, D.C. at the beginning of World War II. The idea of the mass march was revived in the early 1960s and culminated in 1963, when an estimated 250,000 Americans from all over the nation converged on Washington, D.C. to protest discrimination against blacks. Many placards displayed the words "FREEDOM NOW" and the need for fair treatment in such matters as housing and employment were strongly voiced.

The movement of nonviolent direct action found its greatest success in the organized efforts of the Southern Christian Leadership Conference (SCLC), whose roots extended to civil rights actions in Montgomery, Ala. Under the the leadership of Rev. King, the SCLC formed in 1957 after the successful boycott of the segregated public buses of Montogomery in 1955. King's leadership in the boycott emphasized the Christian doctrine that it is better to receive violence than to inflict it upon others. The nonviolent principles and approach that King persued from 1955 until his assassination in 1968 were reminiscent of Mohandas K. Gandhi, the internationally known Indian reformer and nationalist.

In the mid- and late-1960s the work of Malcom X began to impact on the thinking and actions of black America. His speeches on behalf of the rapidly expanding Black Muslim movement helped spread ideas of racial separation, of black self-defense, of nonparticipation in white society or religion and of western decadence and immorality.

The militant phase of direct action of the civil rights movement grew out of Malcom X's philosophy, the failure of civil rights enforcement and the violent treatment suffered by blacks at the hands of white racists, particularly in the South. The Student Nonviolent Coordinating Committee (SNCC) eventually became associated with this phase of the movement. This organization, formed mainly by students from black colleges in the South, was founded in 1960 in order to take more dynamic and more militant action against segregation than that espoused by SCLC. Two of SNCC's primary aims were to desegregate public facilities and to register masses of blacks to vote in the South. Stunned by reprisals in the South, SNCC eventually denounced nonviolence as a technique, particularly after Stokley Carmichael succeeded John Lewis as the national chairman in 1966. About the same time, members of the Congress of Racial Equality (CORE), who had also suffered bitter experiences and reprisals in the Deep South, adopted Carmichael's "Black Power" slogan in 1965. The most violent of the militant direct action organizations was the Black Panther Party.

The civil rights movement was universal and diverse, representing the aspirations of not only black Americans, but of all minority groups of all classes of both genders and in all regions. The movement's impact, however, was particularly manifest in the South, where eight of every ten blacks lived, where segregation and discrimination were most apparent and where the problems of racism and poverty seemed most acute. The nature, extent and diversity of the civil rights movement can, therefore, be best illustrated by tracing its history in selected Southern states. The national dimensions of the movement, however, can be traced through civil rights acts, civil rights cases and civil rights enforcement.

In the 1950s, American liberals continued to believe that securing the right to vote for blacks would be the solution to the problems resulting from racism and the deprivation of civil rights. The Civil Rights Act of 1957 was passed in an effort to remedy these difficulties. The act created a Commission on Civil Rights with the purpose of making a broad study of racial and civil rights questions in the U.S. It gave additional aid to the civil rights division in the U.S. Department of Justice and empowered the Attorney General to institute suits on behalf of blacks who were denied the franchise in federal elections. However, the act, with its many loopholes, proved to be largely ineffective in guaranteeing the right to vote.

During the early 1970s, there was a growing frustration among blacks generally to shrug off black activism and the question of whether it brought about any positive, measurable improvement in the condition of blacks in the United States. Among other things, black Americans pointed to the disproportionately high percentage of blacks on public welfare, the apparent impregnability of de facto segregation in the cities and widespread white opposition against the use of busing to achieve school desegregation.

In the 1980s critics charged that racial poilicies carried out by the Reagan and Bush administrations led to exacerbated polarization. Others pointed to gradual improvements in the position of blacks as evidenced by the growth of a black middle class. In any case, the recent violence in Los Angeles following the acquittal of the four police officers in the Rodney King case leaves no doubt that the problems of race and class have yet to be resolved.

Bush Civil Rights Nominee Rejected

The Senate Judiciary Committee voted Aug. 1, 1989 to reject the nomination of William C. Lucas to serve as the Justice Department's assistant attorney general for civil rights. The committee split, 7-7, on two votes – one to approve Lucas's nomination and the other to send the nomination to the full Senate. (A majority vote would have been needed to advance the nomination.)

The vote was along party lines, except for Sen. Dennis DeConcini (D, Ariz.), who voted with the Republicans to confirm. The remaining committee Democrats had opposed Lucas's nomination on the grounds that he lacked experience in litigation and in civil rights.

Sen. Howell T. Heflin (D, Ala.) had been the only committee member who was uncommitted before the final session began. In the end, he cast the deciding vote against Lucas, explaining that Lucas was "lacking in experience and qualifications."

Committee Republicans accused the Democrats of torpedoing Lucas because he was black – in particular, a black Republican. (Lucas had made a heralded switch to the GOP in 1985, only to be trounced in a bid for the Michigan governorship the next year.)

"It seems to me that we ought to give this black man a chance," Sen. Strom Thurmond (R, S.C.), a former foe of the civil rights movement, told the committee. "Turn him down just because he's black? That's the word that will go out to other countries ... to this country."

Committee Chairman Joseph R. Biden (D, Del.) dismissed Thurmond's implication of racism as a "cynical setup" and said those opposed to Lucas's nomination were concerned about his lack of qualifications.

The rejection was seen as a blow to both President George Bush and Attorney General Richard L. Thornburgh, who had selected Lucas for the post. Administration and Senate Republican strategists said they were searching for some way to salvage the nomination.

The Kansas City Times

Kansas City, Missouri, August 2, 1989

Apparently, William Lucas was less impressive in a meeting Monday with Sen. Howell Heflin than in earlier appearances before the Senate Judiciary Committee.

President Bush's nominee for assistant attorney general of civil rights and the Democratic senator from Alabama met at Heflin's request. Heflin was considered the senator who was the deciding vote on the Democratic-controlled committee.

Neither Lucas nor Heflin would provide details of their talk, but it was obvious by Tuesday's judiciary committee meeting, where Lucas was denied confirmation, that the nominee failed to convince.

The committee was to have voted last week, but postponed action until Tuesday because Heflin wanted to meet with Lucas. One would think that in an informal setting, absent cameras and microphones, Lucas could have shone. Perhaps in this relaxed setting, however, his flaws became more pronounced.

"He's lacking in experience and qualifications, his managerial accomplishments are debatable," Heflin announced Tuesday.

By a 7-7 vote, mostly along party lines, the committee refused the nominee and also rejected a proposal to send the nomination to the full Senate without recommendation. Sen. Dennis DeConcini of Arizona was the only Democrat on the committee to favor the nominee. He was joined by all six committee Republicans.

Were Lucas confirmed, he would have to be propped up at Justice by more experienced lawyers who would be his subordinates. Amazingly and regrettably, Lucas makes even former Assistant Attorney General William Bradford Reynolds, who did considerable harm to affirmative action, look good. Reynolds is an experienced, if misguided, lawyer.

"For assistant attorney general for civil rights, I just think we need a strong voice who will speak out for civil rights and I don't hear that coming from Bill Lucas," said Sen. Paul Simon, the committee member from Illinois. He's right.

So is Project Equality, the national ecumenical and civil rights organization based in Kansas City. It opined, "In the context of his lack of legal experience, we believe that confirmation of this nomination would signal to the country that civil rights are not a major concern of this country."

Lacking a vote of confidence from the Senate committee, the administration can reroute the nominee to the full Senate. It ought not to prolong the inevitable or provide opportunities for greater embarrassment. What is needed is a better nominee.

The Philadelphia Inquirer
Philadelphia, Pennsylvania, July 27, 1989

As a prominent black Republican with experience in law enforcement, William Lucas was a natural for a post in the Bush administration, such as director of the U.S. Marshals Service. Or, had he wanted a switch from the familiar, his losing 1986 race for governor of Michigan earned his appointment as ambassador to a balmy post.

Unfortunately, Mr. Lucas has been mismatched with a job of the utmost importance: assistant attorney general for civil rights. If confirmed by the Senate, he would be the administration's point man in fighting discrimination based on race, sex, national origin, religion and disability. Mr. Lucas, a former sheriff and county executive from Detroit, simply isn't qualified for this job.

There's no way that a private plaintiff would hire Mr. Lucas, who has practiced law only since 1987, to handle a civil-rights case. He has never argued a case in court; he's never even written a legal brief. Nor is his lack of hands-on experience balanced by academic expertise in any area of the law — let alone in the specialized area of civil rights. Yet Attorney General Dick Thornburgh wants to hire him to supervise the roughly 150 lawyers in his department's civil-rights division.

Unlike the specialists chosen to head other sections, Mr. Lucas' principal credential seems to be that, as a black, he knows about discrimination personally and thus cares about it profoundly. That's not enough — especially at a time when the Supreme Court is cutting back on affirmative action and it's not yet clear how different this administration is from the last when it comes to civil rights.

That said, Mr. Lucas deserves a little sympathy for U-turns done by two prominent blacks who had supported him early on. Last month Jesse Jackson abandoned Mr. Lucas as opposition grew, and minor improprieties such as his resume-padding kept coming to light. Last week Rep. John Conyers Jr. (D., Mich.) introduced Mr. Lucas to the Senate Judiciary Committee with more than proforma praise. But a day later, he expressed dismay with the nominee's testimony and withdrew his support.

These switches make it seem as if the case for Mr. Lucas' appointment has slowly deteriorated. Actually, he was wrong from the start.

🏛 The Cincinnati Post
Cincinnati, Ohio, August 3, 1989

Attorney General Richard Thornburgh aptly characterized the Senate Judiciary Committee's rejection of Bush nominee William Lucas: "raw politics."

Not only did the panel refuse to endorse Lucas for the post of assistant attorney general for civil rights, it refused to send the nomination to the full Senate for a vote. The conclusion from the latter action is that committee Democrats thought enough party members might defect to give Lucas a victory on the floor.

Lucas' failing, according to Chairman Joe Biden and his Democratic committee colleagues, was his lack of legal experience. Nonsense. If that were the criterion, Bobby Kennedy never would have been confirmed as attorney general to head the entire national legal apparatus.

Lucas' real sin, aside from being a black Republican, was that he didn't fit the ideological model that Democratic liberals and prominent civil rights activists have established for the job.

Lucas had the temerity to say he supported Bush policies. He also refused to view recent Supreme Court rulings in the civil rights field as cataclysmic, contrary to the line of the civil rights establishment.

What happens now is up to President Bush. He can accept the defeat and select another nominee. Or he can stand up to the committee and give Lucas a "recess" appointment to the post, which would allow him to serve until the end of 1990, at which time the president would have to resubmit the nomination to Senate.

Our view is that Bush should make a recess appointment. Lucas is a successful American who worked his way out of the ghetto and has had many years of law enforcement experience. He has pledged to protect the civil rights of all citizens. His qualifications to do that, not partisan politics, should determine whether he gets the job.

THE SAGINAW NEWS
Saginaw, Michigan, July 27, 1989

Opponents of William Lucas of Michigan, nominated for the top civil rights post in the Justice Department, had better be careful. As with Robert Bork, they just might get what they wish for now, and rue the day later.

The parallel between Lucas and Bork, the defeated nominee for the U.S. Supreme Court, is that both fail the liberal litmus test.

It didn't matter that Bork was a brilliant jurist who thought the Constitution means what it says. It doesn't matter, to some, that Lucas comes before the Senate Judiciary Committee with a lifetime record of personal achievement. They flunk because they do not conform to the establishment of the left.

What set the wolfpack howling around Lucas was his calm acceptance of recent Supreme Court civil rights decisions. A look at the rulings explains why a believer in true equal opportunity would not join the outcry. The court, sensibly, struck down arbitrary quotas; and it said plaintiffs have to prove their cases against employers accused of bigotry.

More to the political point, the position of Lucas mirrors those of the president and of Richard Thornburgh, the attorney general. It is logically absurd to expect a nominee who would have 156 attorneys at his bidding to contradict the policies of those who nominated him.

Logic, however, may be the least of the considerations affecting Lucas.

One case in point was the apparently curious reversal of Rep. John Conyers Jr., who predicted "greatness" for Lucas one day, and withdrew his support the next. The explanation is local politics. As we note below, Conyers at that moment was deciding to run for mayor of Detroit, and backing a recently converted black Republican such as Lucas was baggage Conyers didn't need.

Others simply have a problem accepting the concept of a Republican, never mind conservative, black. They speak in the name of civil rights. But such obstinacy does nothing to advance the cause.

To vilify and destroy William Lucas risks following the eight years of Reagan regression with potentially another eight years of Bush stagnation. The so-called People for the American Way lobby that led the crusade to block a Justice Bork forgets that it brought about a Justice Kennedy — who now is the firm fifth conservative vote on the Supreme Court.

For his part, Lucas reflected on his life and told the committee that "I've earned the right to do the things that are right and I've attempted to do that all of my life. . ."

In the matter of this nomination, the committee and Congress, too, should do the right thing.

THE INDIANAPOLIS STAR
Indianapolis, Indiana, August 7, 1989

Short of giving William Lucas an interim appointment to the post he was denied by the U.S. Senate, the White House should find him another position within the administration.

The Senate Judiciary Committee's rejection of President Bush's nominee as the U.S. Justice Department's civil rights chief was beyond a "cheap shot" — as it was called by White House aides. It was the political lynching of a distinguished American, who happens to be black and conservative.

Lucas' public record is remarkable. Less than 1 percent of the Wayne County (Detroit) detective staff was black when he became its sheriff. After 12 years under his leadership, the percentage was 20. He is a former New York City policeman, a former FBI agent and a former Justice Department aide.

All this placed him squarely on the side of law enforcement. It made him a good candidate for the post the panel denied him. So why was he rejected?

One way to explain it, is that to liberal Democrats, Lucas had done the inexcusable. He switched from Democrat to Republican. Further, he did not pass some civil rights organization leaders' litmus test — a slavish willingness to take orders from them rather than follow the law.

Those leaders wanted him to criticize recent Supreme Court decisions they claim are wrong but which, when studied carefully, merely curb special favors given to one race over another.

Testifying before the committee last month, Lucas said he saw no need to pass legislation to overthrow those rulings. In effect it signified his sincere belief in what some of his critics only pretend to believe — that each person be judged on the content of his or her character, not on the basis of race, ethnicity, gender, age or national origin.

The panel's 7-7 vote on Aug. 2, which blocked his nomination, split on party lines. All Democrats voted nay, all Republicans yea.

The "cover story" for the rejection was that he lacked litigation experience in the civil rights field. Parroting that line was Sen. Edward M. Kennedy, D-Mass., who never faulted the naming of his brother, the late Robert F. Kennedy, by another brother, the late President John F. Kennedy, to be the U.S. attorney general, even though Robert Kennedy had never tried a criminal case.

Peculiar isn't it that one can be denied a Justice Department post for agreeing on legal matters with the president, the head of the Justic_ Department and the Supreme Court?

The Seattle Times
Seattle, Washington, August 2, 1989

WHEN the Senate Judiciary Committee rejected the nomination of William Lucas to be the federal government's top civil-rights officer, it dealt the toughest political rebuke to President Bush since the sinking of John Tower, Bush's would-be defense secretary.

It's arguable whether the committee's 7-7 tie vote on Lucas – amounting to rejection – was justified. But the action now affords the administration a chance to come up with another nominee offering better credentials and promise than Lucas displayed.

Lucas, 61, a black with experience as sheriff and chief executive of Wayne County, Mich., had support from some civil-rights groups . . . and strong opposition from others, notably the National Association for the Advancement of Colored People and the Leadership Conference on Civil Rights. During confirmation hearings, Lucas showed a poor technical grasp of recent Supreme Court civil-rights decisions and their implications.

More important, though, was the appearance that Lucas had at best only a faint commitment to enforcement of civil-rights laws and programs. That's a troubling quality in one who would lead the Justice Department's Civil Rights Division.

During the Reagan years, William Bradford Reynolds used that post to thwart civil-rights progress. As compensation for those lost years, Bush should have found a nominee with a thorough grasp of civil-rights laws and a strong, fresh determination to enforce them.

Perhaps the White House now can bounce back with a new appointee who's better qualified and better received — as was the case when Dick Cheney was chosen for defense secretary after Tower's demise. Surely, across America there are plenty of men and women to be found — respected Republicans — with the qualifications for civil-rights leadership that now is needed . . . and that Lucas seemed to lack.

William Lucas

St. Paul Pioneer Press & Dispatch
St. Paul, Minnesota, August 2, 1989

Despite mounting evidence that William Lucas is the wrong person for the job, the Bush administration foolishly and stubbornly clings to another controversial nomination. The White House is standing by its choice of Mr. Lucas to head the civil rights division of the Justice Department, even though some of his staunchest supporters have now renounced him.

Through his unknowledgeable and insensitive testimony before the Senate Judiciary Committee this week, Mr. Lucas proved that his critics have been right on target all along. Civil rights groups, which have opposed the choice since it was announced early this year, said Mr. Lucas knows little about civil rights law; during testimony he admitted being "new to the law" and flubbed answers about major civil rights decisions. Opponents cited his lack of legal experience; that deficiency also became obvious when he was questioned.

But what really showed his weakness was his response to questions about the recent spate of Supreme Court decisions on affirmative action and civil rights. Mr. Lucas defended the court's actions, saying he sees no "significant change" stemming from the decisions.

One can debate the results of the decisions, but there is little question that they are significant. And change has already begun. Local governments throughout the country are rewriting their affirmative action plans and major civil rights organizations are mobilizing to ask for congressional relief.

Mr. Lucas, who has a strong background in law enforcement as a former FBI agent, sheriff and Michigan politician, may be highly qualified for other government service jobs. But this position should go to one who knows the law, who will fight fiercely to preserve it and who can be an outspoken champion of the cause. Those attributes are particularly necessary during a time when public confidence in the department is at an all-time low, when racial and ethnic violence is increasing, when minority communities are reeling from eight years of civil rights retrenchment.

The Bush administration does a disservice to itself and cancels out its claims of concern for minorities and women by pushing such a candidate.

Based on Mr. Lucas' testimony, even supporters and friends like Rep. John Conyers, D-Mich., felt forced to withdraw their endorsements. President Bush should follow their lead and rescind the nomination. Failing that, the Senate should refuse to confirm.

THE ARIZONA REPUBLIC
Phoenix, Arizona, July 25, 1989

S· OMETHING happened after the landmark 1964 Civil Rights Act was passed. The U.S. Supreme Court said as much in seven recent decisions involving civil rights law.

The court affirmed that non-discrimination, the cornerstone of the 1964 act and the civil rights movement before it, applies to all citizens regardless of race. Preferential treatment accorded one racial group over others is discriminatory. Affirmative action plans, quotas, minority set-asides and other remedial programs that favor some at the expense of others, the court reasoned, can become new forms of discrimination.

To be sure, not everyone, including most of the civil rights establishment, agrees with the high court. The prevailing orthodoxy measures civil rights commitment on the basis of unqualified support for race-based favoritism. Those who subscribe to the ideal of a colorblind society — advocated, it should be remembered, by Dr. Martin Luther King Jr. — are branded "insensitive."

Such is the backdrop to the Senate confirmation process now under way for President Bush's nominee to head the Justice Department's office of civil rights. The nomination of William Lucas, a black attorney who once worked on civil rights issues for Robert Kennedy, is in trouble.

Before the Judiciary Committee hearings opened, the rap against Mr. Lucas was that he had a demonstrated "insensitivity" to civil rights. In other words, like William Bradford Reynolds, who held the post in the Reagan administration, Mr. Lucas does not toe the accepted line. He favors instead a non-preferential approach to the enforcement of equal opportunity laws.

Questioned by the committee about the Supreme Court's recent turnaround, Mr. Lucas said that he thought the decisions were "sound," but would need more time to assess their impact, a moderate response roundly condemned by the professional civil righters.

But Mr. Lucas's problems do not stop there. Among the 80,000 pages of documents ordered up by the Senate panel, it was found that the nominee fudged on his resume. He did not include that he had once failed a bar exam, but, then, who would include such an embarrassing fact?

More troubling, however, was the discovery that he was fined by the Customs Service in 1985 for failing to report $8,800 in goods purchased during a family trip abroad.

If the Senate finds that Mr. Lucas's resume lapse or his breach of Customs rules disqualify him as the chief enforcer of civil rights laws, so be it. As far as his civil rights philosophy goes, however, Mr. Lucas deserves to be credited for what he believes in — a colorblind society with equal opportunity for all.

The Hartford Courant
Hartford, Connecticut, July 31, 1989

Republican senators attempting to save the nomination of William C. Lucas to be the assistant attorney general for civil rights argue that he has the experience to do the job. As the former county executive for Wayne County in Michigan, Mr. Lucas held a job equivalent to that of governor in many states — 2 million people live in Wayne County. But experience at administration is not the issue; knowledge of the law is.

In the nominee's defense, it is said that much of the antagonism toward him rests on his opposition to affirmative action. This may be true, but even juridical conservatism is not the issue here; depth of knowledge and commitment are the issues.

Mr. Lucas is woefully inexperienced in civil-rights law. "I am new to the law," he said after his nomination. The government's top civil-rights enforcer must have more than a passing acquaintance with the law, regardless of where the nominee stands on affirmative action.

There is reason to believe that Mr. Lucas's commitment or enthusiasm for civil rights has been dampened by his personal history. When Democratic Sen. Paul Simon of Illinois asked if Mr. Lucas would be firmly committed to civil rights, he answered "yes," but qualified his response by observing that he was angry and saddened at the lack of support he had received from black leaders. Mr. Lucas said he would do his job, but made

clear that he is bitter.

Bitterness toward Mr. Lucas, on his opponents' part, goes back to his switch of political parties in order to be the Republican candidate for governor of Michigan. That is not the issue either, but it does illustrate the fact that Mr. Lucas is not a political innocent and it does indicate that he has been nominated for this job primarily to pay off a political debt.

There is nothing wrong with appointing some officials on the basis of patronage. But this particular post should be above patronage, like the CIA and FBI directorships.

Mr. Lucas made it easier for his critics by not being entirely truthful. He had exaggerated his government service in job applications and was not truthful about his bar exam failures. He still has to explain convincingly the circumstances that led to the U.S. Customs Service's penalizing him for attempting to slip $8,900 in jewelry into the United States.

These questions, if nothing else, should rule him out for a top job in the Department of Justice. Sen. Joseph P. Biden Jr. was run out of the presidential race for exaggerating his background.

It is true that Mr. Lucas is a victim of pressure politics in Washington. But that's not the entire story. There are patronage jobs in Washington that suit his administrative qualifications. But he is not the right man to be assistant attorney general for civil rights.

PORTLAND EVENING EXPRESS
Portland, Maine, August 8, 1989

The president and the Senate are at sword's point these days over the confirmation process. Each accuses the other side of playing politics with top governmental appointments.

So what else is new? Political battles stemming from the competing responsibilities of the executive and legislative branches with respect to top governmental appointments has a long and sometimes dishonorable history.

In this case, the president says Congress has been moving far too slowly when it comes to confirming some of his key appointments. At the same time, Capitol Hill has done a lot of grumbling over the quality of many White House nominations.

Both sides have a point. On Friday, Congress headed out of Washington for its summer recess leaving about 120 presidential nominations dangling.

Meanwhile, the Senate has been forced to swallow an inordinate number of ambassadorial appointees whose principal qualifications appear to be the size of their contributions to the Bush presidential campaign. And just a week ago, Democrats on the Senate Judiciary Committee found themselves in the embarrassing position of rejecting as unqualified a black nominee, William C. Lucas, for the top civil rights post in the Justice Department.

Some Republican strategists have suggested that the president appoint Lucas to the post anyway on an interim basis, then simply neglect to send a new name to the Senate.

That might be smart politics but it's also lousy government. The American people are the big losers in this political wrestling match.

Both sides ought to stop manhandling the confirmation process and get down to the business of filling some of the nation's top governmental offices with the best qualified persons.

Arizona Defeats King Holiday

In Arizona, voters Nov. 6, 1990 defeated two initiatives that would have established a paid holiday for state workers in honor of slain civil rights leader Rev. Martin Luther King Jr.

The holiday had been a contentious issue in the state since former Gov. Bruce Babbitt (D) set the holiday by executive order in 1986, only to see that order rescinded in January 1987 by his successor, Evan Mecham (R).

The state legislature had passed a bill in May 1990 reestablishing the King holiday in January 1991, but two citizen's initiatives put the question on the November ballot. Arizona Initiative 301, which would have substituted a King holiday for the current Columbus Day holiday, was defeated by a margin of 3 to 1. Initiative 302, establishing a King holiday while maintaining Columbus Day, fell to a surprise defeat by about 15,000 votes out of one million cast.

In response to the vote, the National Football League Commissioner Paul Tagliabue Nov. 7 said he would recommend to league owners that Super Bowl XXVII, scheduled to be played in Phoenix in 1993, be moved to another site. (Montana and New Hampshire were the other two states where there was no state holiday marking King's birthday.)

Previously, President-elect George Bush marked the anniversary of the birth of slain civil rights leader King Jan. 16, 1989 by pledging that his administration would pursue equality for black Americans. Bush made the remarks at a prayer breakfast in Washington, D.C.

Bush praised King as a man who had "destroyed segregation, transformed a nation's history...and realized a great people's promise."

His remarks contrasted sharply with those of outgoing President Ronald Reagan. In an interview taped Jan. 13 and broadcast Jan. 15 on the TV program "60 Minutes," Reagan accused civil rights leaders of dishonesty in their motives.

Black leaders immediately condemned Reagan's remarks and blasted his record on civil rights.

THE RICHMOND NEWS LEADER
Richmond, Virginia, November 12, 1990

The world dismays. Politics *is* everywhere.

There was a time you could say with fair certainty that religion and sports stood secure from political things. The past generation has changed that for much of religion, whose organized types seemingly spend more of their energy pronouncing on abortion, the budget, federal housing policy, and Iraq than on the salvation of souls.

Which left sports. But not anymore.

The weekend has brought us the spectacle of Arizona and the Fiesta Bowl — verily, even the Super Bowl.

Because Arizona's voters on Tuesday rejected the celebration of Martin Luther King's birthday as a state holiday, UVa evidently decided not to accept a bid to play in the Tempe-based Fiesta Bowl. And the National Football League's commissioner made clear his inclination to move the 1993 Super Bowl from Tempe unless Arizona wanders back onto the King-holiday reservation.

We have, now, college football in the van of political purity. We have professional football right out there, too. They may protest. They may say,

Oh, no. This is not politics but economics.

We're talking hundreds of millions of dollars here, so very well: Whether economics drives politics or vice-versa matters not at all. The effect is the same. Economics makes us feel good about our politics toward South Africa. And the economic threat brought us (for instance) Drive 55 and Drink 21.

We can attest that Arizona is not South Africa: We've been to both places. Arizona's voters simply do not think they ought to devote a state holiday to celebrating the birthday of an individual — despite the demonstrable good he accomplished — who has been revealed as a philanderer, in thrall to certain Leninist associates, and (last week) a plagiarist.

So we await with interest the NFL's decision to scrub the Phoenix Cardinals' schedule pending a reversal of last week's vote. And we await UVa's decision not to play in Carolina because last week the voters there re-elected Jesse Helms.

Now sports — even college sports — are into political posturing. It almost would be enough to make one go to church and pray — if the pew hadn't become as politicized as the stadium seat.

St. Petersburg Times
St. Petersburg, Florida, November 13, 1990

It seems a bit unusual coming from the National Football League (NFL), a sports bastion that still can claim only one black coach and no black general managers, but the message is serious.

NFL Commissioner Paul Tagliabue made a statement last week that confronted discrimination in a way Tampa's Ye Mystic Krewe of Gasparilla and many other exclusively white male organizations have so far refused: The only way to rid society of racism and other discriminatory practices is to spurn their perpetuators. The commissioner reasoned that if voters in the state of Arizona saw fit to cancel its holiday honoring Martin Luther King, the city of Phoenix is no place for the 1993 Super Bowl.

"I do not believe that playing Super Bowl XXVII in Arizona is in the best interests of the National Football League," Tagliabue said in recommending to the NFL owners, who have to vote on such a move, that the game be played elsewhere.

Moving the game is an appropriate action, as is the decision by University of Virginia to refuse an invitation to the Fiesta Bowl in Tempe, Ariz., because of the King holiday vote, which as of late Monday had officials puzzling over the bowl's fate. Such insensitivity to the black community deserves bold repercussion on the level of losing the championship game's economic benefits.

Anything less would merely anger the guilty parties, not inspire real reforms. That was exactly the case with Tampa's Ye Mystic Krewe which, under pressure to add black members before the Super Bowl version of its annual Gasparilla parade in January, canceled the parade instead. It didn't want to tarnish Tampa's image with a racial controversy while the city was under the national Super Bowl spotlight. In other words, it's okay to keep discriminating as long as no one is watching.

The Krewe says it will get around to inviting black members, eventually, but it still balks at admitting women. Neither stance constitutes an acceptable attitude for any group that reflects a community, let alone one that represents a community's power. Since the Krewe won't be taking any steps soon as a whole to denounce discrimination, individual members ought to take the high ground by resigning.

As Tampa civic leaders rush to put together Bamboleo, the replacement festival and parade meant to include all segments of the Tampa Bay community during Super Bowl weekend, they are attempting to mend what Ye Mystic Krewe has torn. The damage would be easier to repair if the Krewe embraced the idea that a healthy society no longer tolerates racism and sexism.

The problem in Arizona goes beyond a private club brimming with movers and shakers, but it is born of the same ill. Phoenix still has a chance to keep the Super Bowl two years from now, if the Arizona Legislature restores the Martin Luther King holiday, joining the 47 other states that so recognize his contribution to our nation. Of course there would still be a lot of Arizona residents who might think that was a bad idea.

The NFL's action, however, should help them think twice.

THE BUFFALO NEWS

Buffalo, New York, November 13, 1990

IN 1955, Boston University granted a doctor of divinity degree to an obscure 36-year-old Alabama pastor. If the pastor's name had not been the Rev. Martin Luther King Jr., his doctoral dissertation would probably still be gathering dust. But as a result of the close scrutiny in the years since then, it has now become the center of a minor controversy.

Apparent plagiarism in the thesis was discovered by a friendly observer, Clayborne Carson, the Stanford professor chosen by King's widow to edit her late husband's papers. He found passages that had been taken from other sources without any attribution.

Passages or paraphrases from other works are commonly used in academic writing, but meticulous footnotes are supposed to give credit to the source of the quotation or thought. In King's dissertation, many footnotes were missing. Carson said he believed King's lapse was unintentional. If it hadn't been, it is doubtful that King would have donated the thesis to university scholars, who were sure to give it a working over.

It is also a safe bet that if other doctoral theses were examined with the same close scrutiny, many would be found to have similar lapses.

The controversy is, in itself, a footnote — and should be understood as such. It means little next to King's subsequent career as a national civil rights leader and winner of the Nobel Peace Prize. It is not the first time that a great historical figure has been found to have human flaws.

The revelation of such flaws may give insight into King as a human being, but they have little to do with his courage and greatness in leading a vast national civil rights movement. He remains a meaningful symbol of the great movement toward racial justice in this nation in the 1950s and 1960s.

As the Rev. Joseph Lowery, current head of King's rights organization, put it: "History is caught up in his footprints and will be hardly disturbed by the absence of some footnotes."

It is because King is a national symbol that in another recent controversy, the National Football League has announced that it wants the Super Bowl to be held in a state that recognizes Martin Luther King Day as a state holiday. Arizona voters rejected the holiday in a referendum last week, and so the NFL commissioner is appropriately proposing to move the 1993 Super Bowl from Phoenix.

Phoenix was chosen as the Super Bowl site by the NFL last March, but only if the state recognized Martin Luther King Day. Only three states do not recognize the holiday. The other two are Montana and New Hampshire.

Arizona, of course, can do what it wants, and the NFL, as a private organization, can do what it wants. But it is not surprising that the holiday issue should be an especially sensitive one for professional football, a sport that once barred black athletes but that now has a majority of black players.

The holiday issue is not a racial one. Martin Luther King Day was made a national holiday in 1986 not as a gesture to black Americans, but as symbol of the transformation of the meaning of justice and equality that occurred under the leadership of Martin Luther King Jr. If more Americans made the effort to understand its true meaning, as applicable to all races as the concept of justice itself, it is hard to imagine that it would be controversial anywhere.

THE KANSAS CITY STAR

Kansas City, Missouri, November 14, 1990

Arizona voters decided last week that they didn't want a Martin Luther King Jr. holiday. The National Football League and some college football teams are retaliating the only way they know how, with a swift kick at the state's coffers and reputation.

NFL Commissioner Paul Tagliabue says the league is likely to move the 1993 Super Bowl out of Phoenix to a state that honors King. Meanwhile, several top college squads have told the Fiesta Bowl that they won't play in this year's game unless it is moved from Arizona.

Blacks make up around 60 percent of the players in the NFL. Black players often dominate play at the college level as well. The opening pages of the Nov. 12 issue of *Sports Illustrated* contained 10 photographs of three different college games. Blacks were the featured players in all 10 pictures.

Not just black athletes are upset about Arizona's action. Other cities and states have shown concern about the issue. Owners of professional football teams have plenty of places to choose from when it comes time to put on the Super Bowl.

The more primitive elements of the sports industry can't understand such an act based on principle any more than they can see what's really so bad about tampering with transcripts or the outright purchase of college players. Pay no attention to them.

THE TENNESSEAN

Nashville, Tennessee, November 11, 1990

MR. Paul Tagliabue, the commissioner of the National Football League, did an honorable thing last week.

Mr. Tagliabue said he will recommend to the NFL owners that the league withdraw the 1993 Super Bowl from Phoenix, after Arizona voters rejected proposals that would have made Martin Luther King's birthday a state holiday.

The state voted on two proposals concerning the issue. One, which would have replaced a Columbus Day holiday for state workers with a King Day holiday, was defeated by a 3-1 margin. Another would have given state workers both days off. It lost by about 15,000 votes.

Some members of the Phoenix Cardinals, an NFL team, had supported the proposals and expressed their disfavor with the outcome. "It's disheartening to me to live in a state that's behind the times," said Mr. Luis Sharpe, a tackle and the squad's player representative.

Now some elected officials in Arizona are concerned — and rightly so — for the state's image in the wake of the rejection of the King holiday.

The Super Bowl can be a financial bonanza for a city, bringing in an estimated $200 million in revenue. Mr. Tagliabue knows his league carries a great amount of clout in that regard. He knows his league is in a position to send a powerful message of its own to Arizona.

The NFL may not be alone. The National Basketball Association has voiced a similar stand. It is considering an all-star game in Phoenix for 1993 or 1994 but has said it doesn't intend to put events there without the King holiday.

The Arizona voters have spoken on the issue. The state can conduct its affairs in the way it chooses. But Mr. Tagliabue has shown that not everyone else is willing to play the game. Arizona can act as it wishes, but it should know that its action may have its cost. ■

Houston Chronicle

Houston, Texas, November 9, 1990

The NFL is engaged in perfectly proper play calling in its move to withdraw the 1993 Super Bowl from Phoenix after Arizona voters turned down a proposal to make Martin Luther King Jr.'s birthday a state holiday. Those who claim it is corporate blackmail or undue interference with what should be only the business of the Arizona electorate are wrong.

In the first place, the Super Bowl was awarded to Phoenix with the understanding that it would be contingent on passage of the King holiday proposal. When the voters said "no" to that on Tuesday, no one should have been surprised by NFL Commissioner Paul Tagliabue's subsequent call for the league's team owners to vote on moving the game. And no one should be surprised if the owners, as expected, agree.

Second — and far more important — the National Football League has a legitimate right to use its fiscal clout to make a statement. Americans have long been willing and supportive of free enterprise using such pressures to sway public opinion and influence social change — even when those pressures are aimed across international borders. Consider sanctions and boycotts against South Africa, Iran and Iraq, to name a few.

The NFL is far from a perfect arbiter of social justice. It needs, for example, to look much closer at its lack of opportunity for the advancement of minorities and at its policies on drug abuse. But if the league feels a sense of responsibility on behalf of its minority fans, players and coaches to speak out on this issue, it should be encouraged. It's a worthy sentiment.

It is a sad irony that although the King holiday proposal failed statewide, it passed by a substantial majority in Phoenix. Thus, Phoenix will, perhaps unfairly, pay the substantial economic price for loss of the Super Bowl.

But the Arizona electorate did have its say. The NFL now has its say. That's part of what Martin Luther King Jr. stood for. That's the way we play the game in America.

The Gazette

Cedar Rapids, Iowa, November 11, 1990

WHERE NEXT does the National Football League plan to dictate public policy? Where next are the people of this country going to humbly accept their punishment from the NFL — or any other professional sports organization — for wrong thinking?

We, too, believe the voters of Arizona made a mistake Tuesday in refusing to approve a state holiday commemorating the late Dr. Martin Luther King Jr. It was, however, THEIR mistake to make and theirs are the consciences that must answer to the propriety of their decision.

That's not good enough, however, for the NFL. It is threatening to inflict on Phoenix a penalty that, were it not being anticipated with such dread, would border on being juvenile. Rejection of a King observance, intoned NFL Commissioner Paul Tagliabue, means it is not "in the best interests of the NFL" to hold the 1993 Super Bowl in Phoenix. He will seek to move it to another city.

That shows the power of money, but then we already knew how much clout professional sports have, especially when they collaborate with the great god television. Even as they pay millions to just one athlete, they are so brazen as to ask taxpayers to finance stadiums. Dire consequences (such as moving the team) are predicted in the event voters refuse to knuckle under.

Now the specter of economic sanctions (and losing the Super Bowl truly would be costly to Phoenix) is imposed because the powers that be in professional football disagree with a decision reached by free citizens exercising their constitutional right to vote.

Indications are Arizonans will have a chance to redeem themselves before 1993, as lawmakers there promised to reintroduce the King holiday proposal. The decision, however, should be made because it's the right thing to do, and not because the NFL has been offended.

Where will it end?

Newsday

New York City, New York,
November 10, 1990

Now it's the NFL's turn to vote.

And it should, quickly, by exercising its economic power — an estimated $200 million for Super Bowl XXVII in 1993 — now that Arizona voters have refused to join 47 other states and the federal government in declaring Martin Luther King Jr.'s birthday a holiday.

The game is scheduled for Tempe, outside Phoenix. But league officials warned they'd move elsewhere if voters sustained the bigotry of former Gov. Evan Mecham, who first banned the holiday three years ago.

Sure, the issue is symbolic. But that's precisely the point: The NFL doesn't like symbols of bias and fighting them is important to the league's owners, players and fans. Bigotry is bad for the football business and counter to the values that sustain all sport.

The NFL has it right. Go, team, go.

Richmond Times-Dispatch

Richmond, Virginia, November 11, 1990

On Tuesday the voters of Arizona declined, by a narrow margin, to enact a Martin Luther King Jr. holiday. The National Football League, which had offered Phoenix the 1993 Super Bowl, had threatened to move the game if the holiday was not approved. NFL Commissioner Pete Tagliabue, the beautiful liberal autocrat who fined the coach of the Cincinnati Bengals $30,000 for excluding women from the locker room, announced he would make the threat good.

By Friday, Times-Dispatch sportswriter Jerry Lindquist, and no doubt others across the land, were wondering whether the Fiesta Bowl, a major post-season collegiate game played annually in Tempe, Ariz., might be shunned by likely invitee Virginia, or by the NBC network, which has contracted for the Jan. 1 telecast. But another story broke on Friday, too, on the front page of The Wall Street Journal. There readers learned how Dr. King had essentially plagiarized his doctoral dissertation at Boston University, and how in several more famous writings he had relied heavily on "voice merging," a euphemism for lifting whole passages of others' work and delivering them as one's own. A bit of voice merging, you will recall, forced Delaware Sen. Joseph Biden right out of the 1988 presidential campaign.

The story of Dr. King's academic license has been quietly spreading for some months, and it is interesting that The Wall Street Journal chose to hold it until after the Arizona referendum. The disclosure of course does not diminish the moral force of the American civil rights movement, nor does it demean Dr. King's place as a leader and to some degree a martyr in that just cause. But put alongside other revelations about Dr. King's private character, it raises legitimate questions as to whether he is an unassailable human symbol for the civil rights struggle. Can the people of Arizona be fairly cast as bigots because a majority resists placing Dr. King alongside Washington and Lincoln and creating yet another paid state holiday to honor him?

Indeed, had the NFL not threatened to pull its $200 million Super Bowl, thereby creating an atmosphere of extortion among an independent Western people, it is quite possible the holiday would have been approved. And in any case we fail to see how anyone is honored when the public is induced or blackmailed to pay the desired tribute. Even had the holiday passed the NFL's threat would have left the inference that Arizonans voted for the holiday merely to avoid the threatened financial loss. Whether or not one thinks a Martin Luther King Jr. holiday is a necessary condition of a just society, the NFL and the others threatening boycotts gave Arizona a chance to do something admirable in standing up to the mob.

Racial politics in modern America is made treacherous by people like Paul Tagliabue. For one thing, he is hip-deep in hypocrisy; the NFL played its Pro Bowl all-star game in Hawaii for years when that state had no King holiday, and if Arizona is not good enough for the Super Bowl then it cannot be good enough for an NFL franchise, which it holds in the Phoenix Cardinals. Presumably the NFL will order the Cardinals out soon, and for that matter, how did it ever let them go to such racist climes in the first place? Why did all the black members of the team consent to go?

More than this, though, Mr. Tagliabue fans a fire, like some social pyromaniac, simply because he likes to watch what he's done. Any wise person who truly seeks racial justice and harmony would not pursue those ends by browbeating an entire state over such an issue as this. There is a good deal less racial discord in Arizona than in any eastern state, and certainly no more racial injustice. Does anyone suppose that Mr. Tagliabue's posturing will help rather than hinder Arizona race relations? Even the commissioner himself has more brains than that.

History has yet to take Dr. King's final measure, but as the current controversy makes clear he has long since become another secular idol, to which all must bow or face angry charges of racism. Our commitment to racial justice and a colorblind society stands with or without Martin Luther King Jr., even as we recognize the leadership he offered and the meanness of his assassination. Arizonans were asked to vote and they voted; the idea that the state ought to be punished for its decision springs from arrogant minds too ready to think the worst of others. That sort of outlook never brought peace to any people or to anyone's heart.

Omaha World-Herald

Omaha, Nebraska,
November 14, 1990

The longer the battle over Martin Luther King Day goes on in Arizona, the sillier the battle looks.

The NAACP and others are making Arizona out to be a racist state because the voters narrowly defeated a measure to establish a paid King holiday for state workers. The National Football League is threatening to pull the 1993 Super Bowl out of Phoenix. College football teams are coming under NAACP pressure to snub an invitation from the Fiesta Bowl. And the civil rights group has condemned the University of California at Berkeley's decision to appear in the Copper Bowl in Tucson.

Talk about overreaction. The City of Phoenix, it turns out, already has a King holiday for city workers. So does Tempe, the home of the Fiesta Bowl. The State of Arizona designated a day on which to honor King.

But the voters turned down a paid day off for state workers. The margin of defeat was less than 1 percent of the vote. Now an entire state stands condemned.

King's memory has been tarnished by posthumous disclosures of his unfaithfulness to his wife and recent evidence of plagiarism as a doctoral student in the 1950s. To many Americans, however, he remains a leading symbol of the struggle for civil rights. Some way of recognizing his role is appropriate.

The NAACP and the NFL, however, have taken a position suggesting, in effect, that King will be dishonored unless a few thousand Arizona highway workers, Revenue Department secretaries and social workers are allowed to get a paid day off from work. The monumental illogic of that detracts from the credibility of those organizations.

25th Anniversary of King's "I Have a Dream" Speech Noted

Twenty-five years after Rev. Martin Luther King's famous "I have a dream" speech at the momentous August 1963 civil rights march on Washington, D.C., newspaper editorialists from across the U.S. commented on the significance of the event's anniversary.

More than 200,000 persons, mostly blacks but including thousands of whites, held a massive peaceful demonstration Aug. 28, 1963 to focus attention on black demands for immediate equality in jobs and civil rights.

The marchers came from throughout the nation. They included large delegations from churches and unions, but by and large the demonstrators were average black Americans from country areas. It was estimated that about 200 religious leaders – Protestant, Roman Catholic and Jewish – took part in the march and 40,000 persons participated as representatives of churches and synagogues.

Observers remarked on the purposefulness and good nature of the marchers and the orderly atmosphere that prevailed throughout their demonstration. Before arriving in the capital, many of the participants had attended orientation meetings held by sponsoring Negro organizations that stressed the non-violent nature of the march.

The Salt Lake Tribune
Salt Lake City, Utah, August 30, 1988

Saturday's commemoration was smaller in audience but no less significant in the exorcising of this country's racial disharmony. As an estimated 55,000 people gathered in Washington, D.C., to celebrate a similar congregation memorably addressed by the late Rev. Martin Luther King on Aug. 28, 1963, they effectively renewed an on-going crusade against bigotry and intolerance.

Analysis and interpretation of last weekend's anniversary in the nation's capital tended to dwell on the gains, actual and still needed, for the country's black minority. As apt as that may be, it threatens to obscure a central theme in the Rev. King's stirring message.

The United States civil rights movement of the late 1950s and early '60s was very much about breaking the pernicious hold that racial inequality had fastened on this country for much too long. There was a recognition that clear and conspicuous emphasis must hammer on opening both the political and economic avenues previously closed to blacks strictly because of skin color.

Action then provoked incidents, and notoriety generated by the incidents compelled changes, in laws, by institutions, of attitudes. Equal opportunity became a pursuit of law, a deliberate, determined purpose of formalized public policy.

The 1963 "March on Washington" was actually conceived as another event through which "people power," demonstrated noticeably enough to put more impact on political pressure points, would keep the anti-segregation and anti-discrimination momentum rolling. It was originally designated the March for Jobs and Freedom.

The Rev. King, however, lifted the episode to a higher level. Facing what was a surprisingly large throng of 250,000 enthusiasts, the country's most prominent civil rights orator, in his seminal "I have a dream" address, verbally envisioned the fulfillment of his fondest ideals.

Commenting on the 25-year reenactment Saturday, observers aptly pointed out that while black America has made strides politically during the past two and one-half decades — the most obvious example being the near success by Jesse Jackson to become this year's Democratic presidential nominee — economic progress has not kept pace; income for blacks generally still trails earnings enjoyed by whites.

As pertinent as that may be, it does not capture and revivify the essence of the King eloquence. His words still echo and lead because they spoke to an incomparably sanctifying aspiration of the human spirit, the belief in a genuinely functioning brotherhood.

In fervently proclaiming that his dream encompassed the day when his four young children would be judged not by the color of their skin, but by the content of their character, Dr. King wasn't talking about vote-getting or employment rewards, as crucial to the evaluation of a truly just and fair community as these manifestations are. He was, however, challenging this nation, people everywhere, to move permanently away from the poisonous distraction of racism so that more accurate, honest and decent standards for evaluating human worth can reign.

It's so much easier to scan the passage of time and measure numerical differences in public offices won, education levels achieved and kinds of jobs held. But that alone will not disclose how much of Dr. King's dream has become reality.

His vision at its most inspirational was of a time when racism is purged from the land, heart and soul, as well as politically and economically. Until it is, Saturday's revival should be repeated at least annually, not only as a point of statistical reference, but also as a prominent renewal for the understanding that racial distinctions have no standing in the ennobling of human relations.

The Record
Hackensack, New Jersey, August 11, 1988

Twenty-five years ago this month, some 200,000 people marched from the Washington Monument to the Lincoln Memorial to dramatize the drive for racial equality in this country. Dr. Martin Luther King Jr. electrified those marchers — and the millions who have heard and read his words since — with his vision of a just and harmonious America.

"I have a dream," he said, "that my four little children will one day live in a nation where they will not be judged by the color of their skin but by the content of their character."

How close have we come to fulfilling Dr. King's legacy? A recent national poll commissioned by The Associated Press and Media General Inc. asked 1,223 Americans and received some answers that surely would have disappointed the civil-rights leader. Fifty-five percent of the respondents, including 68 percent of blacks, said that American society is racist. And while 71 percent of those asked said that racial equality was achievable, 40 percent said it would not come in their lifetimes.

While they saw society's inequalities, most poll participants were opposed to giving special treatment to minories in hiring and college admission. Close to 80 percent of all repondents opposed such preference; blacks were evenly divided on the question.

There were some bright spots in the poll results. Eighty-four percent of those questioned said that the nation has moved closer to equality in the years since Dr. King's speech. Nearly all the blacks surveyed, 94 percent, said they have close friends who are white; 67 percent of the whites said their close friends included blacks.

That's progress. But it's hardly enough. As the poll shows, our society remains largely divided. A child's future — his access to education and a career — is still determined all too often by the color of his skin, not the content of his character. If, as most Americans say, the answer is not special treatment in college admission and hiring, then the nation must make sure that everyone reaches the classroom and the employment office with the kinds of skills that allow for fair competition.

In the years since his murder, Dr. King has been honored as a national hero. His birthday has become a holiday. Schoolchildren recite the facts of his life. But we will not have provided sufficient honor to him — and to all the Americans for whom he spoke — until we have made his dream of true equality a reality.

The Duluth News-Tribune
Duluth, Minnesota, August 27, 1988

"Everything has changed, and nothing has changed. We have come a long, long way, but we still have a terribly long way to go."
                    The Rev. Joseph Lowery

A quarter century ago, the Rev. Martin Luther King Jr. captured the nation's soul with his compelling call, "I have a dream . . ." On Aug. 28, 1963, King led a march on Washington of a quarter-million strong to rally support for federal civil rights legislation. The march and King's speech were a turning point in the civil rights campaign, a point at which the general population came into the movement.

Civil rights marchers return to Washington today to commemorate their campaign's flash point. And Lowery, who now heads the Southern Christian Leadership Conference which King led to Washington, knows so well that while many of King's dreams have come to pass, many more remain but dreams.

As a nation, we have made tremendous strides in 25 years to dismantle institutional and governmental barriers to equality for all citizens. Racial as well as sexual equality — along with avenues to assure such equality — is now the law of the land in all fields of public policy. And that is indeed a laudatory national accomplishment.

Yet laws which prohibit discriminatory treatment should be the baseline, not the upper limit, of our ongoing drive to attain and maintain equality. And not even the strongest of laws can force individual citizens to alter or abandon personal discriminatory attitudes. We must as individuals work to overcome those human barriers.

In 25 years, we've come a long way. We still have far to go.

THE SAGINAW NEWS
Saginaw, Michigan, September 6, 1988

A quarter million people gathered in the nation's capital 25 years ago and heard Martin Luther King Jr.'s renowned "I have a dream" speech.

Many of the lines are committed to memory — the passages about "sons of former slaves and sons of former slave owners" living in harmony, about children being judged "not by the color of their skin but by the content of their character."

And there was a social impact. Congress passed the Civil Rights Act of 1964, the Voting Rights Act of 1965, the Fair Housing Act of 1968. The separate toilets and lunch counters are all but gone.

Remember, though, this was billed the "March for *Jobs* and Freedom." Organizers wanted not only civil rights, but also economic gains. One hundred years after the emancipation proclamation, King declared, "the Negro lives on a lone island of poverty in the midst of a vast ocean of material prosperity."

There are still such islands in the mainstream.

It is on the economic side that little progress has been made in achieving the dream of racial harmony.

In 1963, the average income for black families was roughly half the typical wage for white families. The same holds true in 1988.

The poverty rate for blacks is 33.1 percent; for black children under 18, it is 45.6 percent.

In 1963, the unemployment percentage for blacks was twice as high as for whites. The gap since then has grown. The rate for whites is 4.7 percent, compared to 11.4 percent for blacks.

Those facts are shocking to many, because the black middle class — even the upper class — has expanded dramatically during the past 25 years. Unfortunately, however, the number of blacks at the bottom of the economic scale also has grown, and social activists have created a new term — underclass — to describe them.

It is true that if non-cash benefits such as food stamps, housing subsidies and health care were figured in, the overall poverty statistics would not be so dismal. It is also true, though, that there is a depressing permanency to the underclass. Mere spending is no solution; the Great Society helped not at all. Sociology has not succeeded in strengthening the poor-family structure.

If King were alive today, we are certain he would stand at the forefront in trying to uplift the downtrodden. He would continue his social themes, no doubt, but we suspect he would sharpen his economic focus. He would talk about upper-income executives and minimum-wage custodians living in harmony. He would talk about children being judged not by the designer labels on their clothes but by the depth and daring and desire of their own dreams.

Blacks' struggle for civil rights is far from over, but the progress since 1963 is tremendous. The same cannot be said about the dream of hewing "out of the mountain of despair a stone of hope." As those King inspired continue their work, education and employment and self-esteem should serve as their vision and their goal.

THE SUN HERALD
Biloxi, Mississippi, August 29, 1988

Once in a great while, someone makes a speech that stirs the soul and is permanently imbedded in the national consciousness. Martin Luther King's "I have a dream" speech was one of these. It was arguably the best speech in modern American history.

Thousands gathered over the weekend to commemorate the 25th anniversary of the speech, given before 200,000 people who had marched on the nation's capital in support of civil rights legislation.

King was an orator of immense talents, and those talents were put to maximum use that hot August day in Washington. But the memory of his speech would not have endured on style alone.

The substantive message was a vision of a new America devoid of racial injustice, an America that would "live out the true meaning of its creeds." King believed deeply in the American promise, and his dream was of a time when all would be free to pursue it. He dreamed, King said, of a day "when my four little children will live in a nation where they will not be judged by the color of their skin but by the content of their character."

How can anyone argue with that sentiment? And yet it was impossible to argue with King that the nation that would judge his children on character alone had not arrived in 1963.

It is closer today, thanks to King and others, but it is not yet fully here. The legal barriers to full citizenship are gone, but the barriers of the heart have not all been removed. Race, unfortunately, still matters in America.

Unlike some of the would-be heirs to his legacy today, King's rhetoric was anything but divisive. He preached unity, not division; his call was for a color-blind society, not one preoccupied with past injustices to the detriment of future progress. He preached hope and opportunity, not fear and despondency.

King's "I have a dream" speech, like most of his rhetoric, was hard for white Southerners to confront without some unease because it met them on their own turf, on the common religious ground shared by blacks and whites in the South. He spoke of "all of God's children" being able to sit at "the table of brotherhood." It is still a powerful idea for those who believe in the equality of all people before their Maker.

The vision, the dream, that King articulated for America 25 years ago is as relevant today as it was then. It asks only that all have freedom and opportunity.

That is the American dream.

Controversy Overshadows Signing of Job-Bias Bill

President George Bush Nov. 21, 1991 signed the Civil Rights Act of 1991. The legislation was a compromise between Bush and congressional leaders that would make it easier for workers to sue in job-discrimination cases. However, the signing ceremony for the long-awaited law was dominated by a controversy over a proposed presidential directive that had tried to impose a conservative interpretation on the new legislation.

White House Counsel C. Boyden Gray Nov. 20 had circulated to all federal agencies and departments a draft of a presidential directive on the Civil Rights Act that was intended to end the use of affirmative action policies in hiring by federal agencies. The controversial draft, written by two White House lawyers under Gray's direction, tried to reverse federal regulations authorizing the use of certain racial preferences and "set-asides" in hiring and promotions. The regulations had been established in 1965.

In an effort to defuse a mounting controversy over the draft directive, White House Press Secretary Marlin Fitzwater Nov. 21 said Gray had written and circulated the document without Bush's knowledge. The White House retracted the draft directive, which was to have been part of Bush's signing statement accompanying the new law.

(Signing statements described the legislative history of a law and emphasized any point the president wanted to amplify. The tradition of attaching presidential signing statements to new laws began during the Reagan administration.)

Some political observers and those who had doubted Bush's commitment to the civil rights compromise suggested that Bush, through Gray, had been trying to undo by executive action parts of the law that he had been unable to change in congressional negotiations.

(Under Gray, the White House Counsel's office had become a center for conservatism and had taken over many duties that had previously been carried out by the Justice Department. Those duties included screening judicial nominations and crafting civil rights policies and the related enforcement regulations.)

Immediately after the draft was circulated Nov. 20, civil rights leaders and others, including senators and cabinet members, condemned it as an assault on decades of civil rights progress. Objections to Gray's draft reportedly came from Labor Secretary Lynn Martin, Health and Human Services Secretary Louis W. Sullivan and Transportation Secretary Samuel K. Skinner. Sen. John C. Danforth (R, Mo.), the architect of the compromise bill, called Gray's draft "a serious mistake."

Also Nov. 21, the White House called civil rights leaders who had been invited to a Rose Garden signing ceremony for the Civil Rights Act, to assure them that federal affirmative action regulations were not being reversed.

In his speech at the signing ceremony, Bush repudiated Gray's statements on affirmative action. Although he did not mention Gray's proposal, Bush said, "This administration is committed to action that is truly affirmative, positive action in every sense, to strike down all barriers to advancement of every kind for all people." He added, "I say again today that I support affirmative action. Nothing in this bill overturns the government's affirmative action programs."

Despite Bush's statements, the final written version of the signing statement attached to the bill Nov. 21 did include one controversial segment of Gray's directive. The statement said an analysis of the legislation submitted by Senate Minority Leader Robert J. Dole (R, Kan.) "will be treated as the authoritative interpretive guidance by all officials" in the federal government in enforcing the law.

The Dole memorandum described the bill as "an affirmation of existing law," including—according to the *New York Times*—Supreme Court rulings that it was designed to override. Danforth and others maintained that the memorandum, seen to favor business interests over minority and female workers attempting to sue for job discrimination, went against the intent of the law's drafters.

The Washington Post

Washington, D.C., November 22, 1991

IN THE MIDST of a muddle after a chaotic 20 hours of backing and filling, President Bush signed the civil rights bill yesterday. For weeks there has been skirmishing about what this new law really means, with congressional sponsors claiming to have gotten a compromise from the White House and the president's counsel insisting that the victory belonged to his end of Pennsylvania Avenue. But these exchanges paled in comparison with the furor that arose Wednesday evening and has not really abated. In a draft circulated to senior White House staff and federal agencies on the eve of the scheduled signing ceremony, counsel C. Boyden Gray sought to seal his alleged legislative victory by having the president proclaim that the new bill required the termination of 25 years of government affirmative action and set-aside programs. The backlash was so forceful that the statement was later amended, but there are still no guarantees that the suggested policy will not be resurrected later.

The action was both politically inept and substantively indefensible. The White House looks absolutely ridiculous. The impression has been created once again—an earlier indication was the credit card interest rate fiasco—that staffers are winging it, making decisions on behalf of the president without any understanding of the ramifications of their pronouncements or any consultation with the people working in the relevant fields within the administration who might have forestalled the action. Moreover, the president does not give the impression that he either understands all the implications of what political-minded staffers suggest that he say—or cares. It is spectacularly inconsistent to pledge support for affirmative action, as the president has done, and then allow a document to be sent out, supposedly with presidential imprimatur, that calls for what the original memo did.

As the president surely knows, the government has, over the years, adopted dozens of programs that would be cancelled by the Boyden Gray fiat, programs involving federal contractors, FCC licensees, small-business applicants and a host of others. These efforts have always been controversial, and people of good will have been grappling for years over the fairness of preferences. There has been litigation, lobbying and debate about them for decades. But so far they have been accepted on grounds that for a certain period of time special steps must be taken to overcome the effects of centuries of discrimination. The idea that civil rights groups would have compromised away these programs in exchange for the new civil rights bill is ludicrous. Yet this week the White House has created the impression of ignoring the historic foundations of this policy—and indeed President Bush's own previously stated support for affirmative action—in order to placate those on the right who have fought the new civil rights law. Wednesday's memorandum is an embarrassment to the White House, and while the revised version finally used at the signing ceremony deletes some of the more off-the-wall rhetoric, it is not reassuring.

The Philadelphia Inquirer
Philadelphia, Pennsylvania, November 22, 1991

In an astonishing feat of political contortionism, President Bush extracted his foot from his mouth long enough yesterday to give a little homily on black and white togetherness in America. The scene was the Rose Garden. The occasion? Well, we'd thought that it was to be the ceremonial burial of the hatchet on the civil rights bill that Congress (including key Republicans) and the White House have dickered over for the last 18 months. You remember — *The Quota Bill.*

The President had agreed to sign the darn thing a few weeks ago, after it became clear that its anti-bias provisions were playing well enough in the Senate to override a veto. One big clue that the tide was turning was when Sen. John Danforth, the Missouri Republican who was shepherding the nation's second black Supreme Court nominee, came down on the White House for playing "racial politics" on civil rights.

But if one side of the President's brain got the message, apparently the other side didn't. So the nation has been treated to the twisted spectacle of Mr. Bush working out on David Duke with every epithet in the thesaurus, while his personal counsel, C. Boyden Gray, was penning a churlish, spit-in-your-eye piece for the Washington Post, "Civil Rights: We Won, They Capitulated."

The administration's split personality was still in evidence the evening before the signing. Mr. Gray fired off a directive to federal agencies ordering them to review any rule backing racial quotas, preferences or set-asides. Then, hours later, the President stood in the garden, promising a fight against the evil of discrimination, pledging that "nothing in this bill overturns the government's affirmative action program."

How he was able, after his inept performance, to utter the phrase, "Today we celebrate ... building bridges of harmony among all the races," is beyond us. He has been doing for bridges between races what he did for the bridges of Iraq. Only, this time the White House hasn't given one hoot in hell about collateral damage.

The Tennessean
Nashville, Tennessee, November 22, 1991

YESTERDAY'S signing of hard-fought civil rights legislation should have been recorded as a great moment for this nation.

Instead, the event was bitterly marred by an indication of President Bush's own ambivalence — or contempt — for civil rights programs that have existed for years.

On Wednesday — the day before the signing — the media obtained a copy of a statement written by White House counsel C. Boyden Gray that Bush was supposed to issue on Thursday at the signing of the civil rights bill. The statement said any regulation or practice that "mandates, encourages or otherwise involves the use of quotas, preferences, set-asides" or other devices on the basis of sex, religion, race or national origin is "to be terminated as soon as legally feasible."

An administration official said that Bush wanted to underscore his opposition to affirmative action programs that give "unfair advantage" to minorities and women.

But when civil rights leaders and attorneys read the proposed statement, they flipped — and for good reasons. The directive would have wiped out all instruments and guidelines that have helped women and minorities get a chance in the workplace. And the order would have applied to all companies as well as the federal government.

By Thursday morning, the White House backed off. In his remarks yesterday, Bush underscored his support for affirmative action. But White House spokesman Marlin Fitzwater specifically said that Bush might issue a order ending employment preferences at some later date.

This whole thing is mighty curious. It's also mighty scary.

Perhaps the flap was just an internal White House screwup. Gray, who wrote the statement, is one of Bush's more conservative insiders. Reports indicated that he wrote the memo and sent it to federal agencies before the President read it.

Or perhaps the flap was an attempt at political jockeying. Clearly, Bush is feeling heat from Republican right-wingers. Ultra-conservative commentator Pat Buchanan and former Klansman David Duke are both considering White House bids, saying that right-wing Republicans feel abandoned by Bush.

The proposed statement could have been leaked as a way of saying to ultra-conservatives: Bush's signature may be on a civil rights law, but his heart is with you.

The President has repeatedly asserted his support for civil rights and equality. He did so again yesterday. But after the White House's 20-month opposition to the civil rights bill — including a veto for a previous version — he should know that he is not viewed as a civil rights advocate.

If the proposed statement was evidence of a White House staff that if divided on civil rights, then Bush should know that his administration looks ambivalent about a major domestic concern. If the statement was leaked to placate the right wing of his party, then Bush has let politics get in the way of his convictions.

But in the end, Bush, not Boyden Gray or anyone else, bears the responsibility for the incident and for White House policy on civil rights. After all, he is the President. ■

The Boston Globe
Boston, Massachusetts, November 22, 1991

The Civil Rights Act of 1991 has finally been passed and signed, but not without one final effort from inside the White House to turn back the clock on civil rights.

The law, enacted after a two-year bipartisan effort to find language President Bush would grudgingly accept, negates six Supreme Court decisions that made it more difficult for workers to fight discrimination. It provides added protection for working women and includes remedies for victims of sexual harassment. It protects against discrimination in Congress and instructs the Equal Employment Opportunity Commission to conduct education and outreach programs to inform employees about their rights.

The law, signed by Bush in a Rose Garden ceremony yesterday, still has flaws that some find troubling. For instance, workers in one of the Supreme Court cases that the law is meant to negate are not covered by it.

Although the law will allow female victims of discrimination to collect punitive damages for the first time, it places a cap on those damages. No such cap has been established for victims of racial discrimination.

The most unfortunate aspect of the law, however, involves not its content but the atmosphere that surrounded its drafting and signing. The president's perfidious contention for nearly two years that the legislation was a "quota bill" – a contention members of his own party denied – fostered a divisiveness that even the most moving Rose Garden speech could not erase.

And most troubling of all was the action of C. Boyden Gray, the White House counsel. The night before the signing ceremony, Gray circulated a statement announcing the president's plans to abolish affirmative action guidelines, a move that by some assessments would set back the executive branch's policy on civil rights 25 years.

Bush wisely distanced himself from the directive and expressed his commitment to affirmative action during the ceremony.

Still, he must accept responsibility for statements that created an atmosphere within the White House that would allow his staff to even consider that such an action would be acceptable.

As John Lewis, a veteran of the civil rights movement and a US representative from Georgia, said: "Mr. Bush, you ought to be ashamed. To have this mentality, this mind-set, in the White House dramatizes the fact that the scars and stains of racism are embedded in every corner, in every section, in every institution of our country."

The new civil rights law will serve as an antidote for the racism that exists in America's workplace. But even as it was being signed, the nation received a chilling reminder of the racial poison that is still pervasive.

THE RICHMOND NEWS LEADER

Richmond, Virginia,
November 18, 1991

The Senate was so anxious to pass the Civil Rights Bill of 1991 that it overlooked some fine points. A solid majority of the Senate agreed to an amendment that was not included in the final text.

Doesn't the Senate read the final versions of the legislation it approves? No. Should it? Of course. But when the Senate acts to satisfy a high-pressure lobby like the civil rights industry, it can ride roughshod over niceties such as reconciling the language of its bills with its votes.

The amendment in question is one of those special exemptions that crops up in almost every measure. This one exempted the Wards Cove Packing Company from the bill's provisions. The exemption seemed only fair: Wards Cove has spent millions of dollars fighting a "disparate impact" job bias suit for 17 years. The Supreme Court rewarded the company's persistence when the court ruled in 1989 that those who launch job-bias suits must prove intentional discrimination on the part of the employer.

The *Wards Cove* opinion was among the several high court rulings the new civil rights law seeks to reverse. By not exempting the company from the measure, the Senate would have said to Wards Cove: You won by working within the system, but now we say you lose. We're changing the rules once more.

A few days later, the Senate voted to restore the exemption in one of those sessions devoted to tidying up oversights — that is to say, in a rewrite session rectifying its sins of omission and commission. Those procedures used to be rare, because the Senate (and the House) once insisted on clean final versions of bills brought to a vote. Nowadays, the only thing that matters is a vote that will get the special-interest harpies off the lawmakers' backs. A clean version of the bill always can come later — provided anyone takes the time to spot what was added or subtracted, of course.

The Des Moines Register

Des Moines, Iowa, November 23, 1991

The timing couldn't have been worse. Even as President Bush was getting ready to sign a long-awaited civil-rights bill this week, the administration's antipathy to the concept of civil rights was making itself obvious.

First, a directive circulating around the White House expressly forbade the use of affirmative action for minorities and women in federal hiring. Later, the president used language in a statement accompanying his signing of the civil-rights bill that would have the effect of undermining the very intent of the legislation.

The president has sought to distance himself from the directive on federal hiring, passing it off as the work of White House Counsel C. Boyden Gray and ordering a review of the policy. But his insistence that affirmative-action regulations dating back to 1965 are not being wiped out is far from reassuring, given the language he used in signing the civil-rights law.

The new law is intended partly to reverse recent Supreme Court decisions that have eroded earlier civil-rights gains, such as the ability to sue for workplace discrimination. And it goes further by enabling women to sue for damages, rather than merely for back pay, for sexual discrimination or harassment. But legal language inserted into Bush's signing statement seems to undercut those provisions, with references to "business necessity" as a justification for discrimination in hiring. And the statement endorses a memo by Senate Republican leader Bob Dole calling the bill "an affirmation of existing law" — thereby undercutting its role in reversing Supreme Court decisions.

Bush's longstanding antipathy to affirmative action is no secret. His veto of the Civil Rights Act of 1990 was defended on the erroneous grounds that the bill would promote the use of quotas in hiring.

Last spring, it was reported that Bush staffers had tried to sabotage negotiations between the Business Roundtable — a consortium of corporate leaders — and civil-rights leaders trying to reach independent agreement on civil-rights legislation.

Now, all of a sudden, the talk of quotas has ceased. It's hard not to view Bush's new embrace of the legislation — though welcome — as somehow linked to the advancing election season, in which racial issues are certain to figure prominently.

Regardless of who authored these policy statements, the president's top staff is expected to be aware of his perspective on major issues. It's his job to set the agenda and theirs to implement it. These actions suggest a hidden agenda that undercuts much of Bush's civil-rights rhetoric.

The New York Times

New York City, New York, November 22, 1991

In a festive Rose Garden ceremony yesterday, President Bush embraced the Civil Rights Act of 1991 and signed it into law. But he did his best, in the fine print of a formal signing statement, to undermine that law and appease its opponents. What counts more, fortunately, is what the law says and not what the White House says it says.

The act is a signal legislative achievement, restoring and strengthening laws against job discrimination that the Supreme Court gutted with a series of recent misinterpretations. If the Justices appointed by Presidents Reagan and Bush will read the new law's plain language and its message of reaffirmation of civil rights, there will be more justice in the workplace for minorities, women, the disabled and other victims of bias.

Mr. Bush was dragged to the signing table by an overwhelming, bipartisan Congressional majority. Republican moderates led the way, fearing that continued White House racial politics would backfire.

After insisting for two years that the measure was a "quota bill," Mr. Bush suddenly discovered that a new draft, barely distinguishable from old ones, was not a quota bill. His instant revision of history fooled nobody, least of all the bill's angry, die-hard opponents on the Republican right.

On the eve of the signing, Boyden Gray, the President's counsel and chief commando of the White House resistance, circulated a proposed signing statement that would have tried to do by fiat what Congress had just ruled out. It directed all executive agencies to terminate any Federal affirmative action program within their control, like longstanding guidelines for the Equal Employment Opportunity Commission and Government contract officials.

This sneak attack met with immediate resistance in and out of Government, prompting the President to call for modifications. He dropped the termination orders but retained what he called a "highly technical" directive. He told executive officials to treat as "authoritative interpretive guidance" a view of the law written by Mr. Gray and entered in the Congressional Record by a dozen Republican opponents of the bill.

In other words, the E.E.O.C., the Labor Department and other agencies that must obey and enforce the civil rights laws should act as though Congress had not overruled the Supreme Court in the most controversial of the cases. But the law is clear on its face. It requires that when employment practices screen out minorities, women and the disabled, employers must demonstrate that those practices are both "job-related to the position in question" and justified by business necessity.

Presidents often try to put their spin on legislation but courts are rarely impressed. Judges will look to the law's language and, if necessary, the arguments of its sponsors in Congress, not Congressional opponents — and certainly not the Administration that lost the battle with Congress. The mischief of President Bush's decree is thus limited to the agencies that are supposed to be on the cutting edge of law enforcement. Its impact is mainly political, telling right-wingers that they still have a friend in the White House.

For all the sore losers' last-minute efforts to undermine this hard-fought act of Congress, it now stands. The bill is now the Civil Rights Act of 1991, a triumphant command to maintain and increase the gains made over a generation for justice in the workplace.

The Record

Hackensack, New Jersey, November 25, 1991

JUST WHEN the nation is crying out for calm, confident leadership, President Bush and his administration appear in disarray.

Last week's fiasco on civil rights and affirmative action was only the latest example of erratic action and sudden reverses that suggest a White House that is out of control. The picture might actually be amusing if it were not that Americans, suffering under a miserable economy, desperately need some competent presidential leadership to overcome these bad times.

Only hours before Mr. Bush was to sign the compromise civil rights bill last week, White House Counsel C. Boyden Gray circulated a draft of a directive ending the use of minority hiring preferences for federal employment that had been in effect since 1965. Reports indicated the president would announce this end of affirmative action at the bill signing on Thursday.

Civil rights leaders cried foul. Many Republicans protested vehemently. The administration held frantic overnight meetings. And at Thursday's bill signing ceremony, the president made no mention of the directive and spoke instead of his support for affirmative action. White House officials said Mr. Gray had circulated the draft on his own, without Mr. Bush's knowledge.

> ## The White House disarray might be amusing if the nation weren't in bad shape.

Still, it is unclear whether the president has permanently shelved the directive, or simply postponed its issuance to a less sensitive occasion. Further confusion was provided by language in the president's signing statement that, in effect, contradicted much of the civil rights bill he signed. The statement was drafted by Mr. Gray and his subordinates.

•

Earlier last week, the president conveyed a similarly erratic impression of his feelings about the economy. He first indicated the economy was in overall good shape and deplored his inability to convince the nation that his economic programs were working. Later, he backed down somewhat, saying he sympathized with Americans who were suffering under the economy. Still unclear, however, is what Mr. Bush plans to do, if anything, to help these people.

Some days ago, Mr. Bush urged banks to reduce interest rates on credit cards as a means of encouraging consumer spending. Some Republicans in Congress went a step further, calling for legislation to set a cap on such interest rates. In what some economists saw as a reaction to these moves, the stock market took a drastic drop on Nov. 15. The talk of credit card interest rates stopped.

Even the administration's foreign policy, a bright spot throughout the Bush presidency, is suffering. Responding to criticism that he has been preoccupied with international travel and events, Mr. Bush suddenly canceled his long-planned trip to Japan. Many officials viewed the trip as essential because of Japan's influence on the U.S. economy. Now, there's talk of rescheduling the trip.

•

At least part of Mr. Bush's problem has been his failure to spell out exactly what he believes on civil rights, the economy, and even on the importance of international policy and travel. If Mr. Bush were to proclaim his unequivocal support of affirmative action, Mr. Gray would never have circulated the statement rescinding the policy. If Mr. Bush were unalterably opposed to affirmative action, he would have announced Mr. Gray's directive, regardless of the flak. If Mr. Bush were convinced his economic programs were the right course to follow, he would push on with them without reversing himself. If he really believes his international travel is essential, he should continue it, regardless of the criticism.

This is not the time for indecisiveness at the White House. Mr. Bush should tell us what he believes — and act accordingly.

St. Petersburg Times

St. Petersburg, Florida, November 22, 1991

It would have been a triumph of mean-spiritedness and cynicism, but in the end it didn't happen — at least not yet.

The president had planned to use Thursday's signing of the civil rights bill to launch a sneak attack on affirmative action, ordering an end to 20-year-old federal hiring policies that at least try to correct some of the effects of centuries of bias and exclusion. But he backed down at the last minute, amid a growing furor in the civil rights community and within his own administration. Instead, upon signing the measure strengthening job protections for minorities and women, Mr. Bush reiterated his commitment to affirmative action.

Had the president issued the tougher order, it would have been tantamount to signing the bill while simultaneously rescinding the rules implementing it; the result would have been chaos. But the damage was done anyway. His spokesman still refuses to rule out such an order later, leaving employers and the federal agencies that regulate them waiting for the ax to fall.

It was a totally baffling performance by a White House that seems adrift without a helmsman. The list of domestic-policy issues Mr. Bush has backtracked on is growing at an alarming rate: unemployment benefits, civil rights, taxes, trips abroad, financing for black colleges, minority scholarships.

The statement purging so-called racial preference policies apparently was crafted by political aides alarmed about Mr. Bush's growing vulnerability to challenges from the right. Since the president's only morality seems to consist of getting re-elected, it's not surprising that he still is willing to let them lead him and the country down the primrose path of race-baiting politics, but even he should have appreciated the poor timing: Race relations are at their lowest ebb in a generation, after the polarizing David Duke campaign.

Worse still was his choice of settings. Issuing such an order at the signing ceremony would have been a display of utter contempt for the kind of real suffering the bill is designed to address. It would have amounted to thumbing his nose at every victim of racism and sexism in the workplace.

Just when you thought he'd learned something, in one lapse Mr. Bush has virtually destroyed any good will gained by his cooperation on the civil rights bill. And it's all a con. The grand conspiracy he's fighting — to steal jobs from deserving people and give a free ride to the undeserving — simply doesn't exist. On the contrary, brave people have faced all manner of terror and even died to win the meager advances the White House now proposes to trade away for votes.

Either Mr. Bush really doesn't understand the magnitude and volatility of the issues he's playing with, or he just doesn't care. A troubled country can ill afford either explanation.

Mandela Visits U.S., Receives Hero's Welcome

South African black nationalist leader Nelson Mandela arrived in the U.S. June 20, 1990 for an 11-day, eight-city tour that attracted enormous public attention and during which he was widely hailed as a hero. The visit's highlights included a June 20 ticker-tape parade in New York City, a June 25 meeting at the White House with President George Bush and a June 26 address to a joint session of Congress.

Mandela's U.S. visit came in the middle of a six-week, 13-nation world tour that began with a sweep through Western Europe and a stop in Canada.

Mandela, 71, was the deputy president and preeminent leader of the African National Congress (ANC), which had recently been legalized after decades of armed struggle to overthrow the apartheid system of racial separation. Mandela had been released in February after more than 27 years in prison and had immediately plunged into the South African political maelstrom, trying to pave the way for negotiations from white minority to black majority rule.

The major aims of Mandela's tour were to urge Western governments to maintain economic sanctions against the South African regime, despite President F.W. de Klerk's moves toward reform; to raise funds to help the ANC function as an above-ground political party in South Africa; and to thank and encourage those who had been active in the international antiapartheid movement. The major slogan of the trip was, "Keep the Pressure On."

In particular, many black Americans said they viewed him as a much-needed inspirational figure, as a charismatic African hero and as an international symbol of resistance to oppression who had emerged from prison unbroken and yet without apparent bitterness. His presence was widely described as having brought an unaccustomed feeling of public euphoria to many blacks in American cities that were often divided by racial animosities and beset by poverty and drugs.

Many blacks said Mandela had sparked a renewed pride in their African roots. At many of his stops, the aging revolutionary and his wife were met by groups of black women, young men and children wearing traditional African dress and celebrating with African songs, chants and dance.

Mandela also won the acclaim of mainstream white America and was treated to massive, positive coverage in the U.S. news media. The only real notes of controversy resulted from his refusal to distance himself from some of the ANC's more radical international supporters. Winnie Mandela also won a mostly glowing reception, and there was little mention of her troubles in South Africa, where her bodyguards had been convicted of murder.

Mandela June 22 went to the United Nations headquarters, where he addressed the Special Committee Against Apartheid. The General Assembly was not in session, but most delegates attended the meeting, along with Secretary General Javier Perez de Cuellar, and gave Mandela several standing ovations. "Victory for a united, democratic, non-racial South Africa is within our grasp," Mandela declared.

Throughout his visit, Mandela had avoided being drawn into discussions of U.S. racial and other domestic issues. But in his June 30 Oakland, Calif. speech, he referred specifically to the problems faced by "the first American nation, the American Indians," and promised to return to the U.S. in the fall to investigate them.

Arkansas Gazette
Little Rock, Arkansas, June 20, 1990

Tomorrow, Nelson Mandela, only four months out of a South African prison, will arrive in New York to the traditional hero's welcome, a ticker-tape parade, and begin 12 days of pomp that is ordinarily reserved for the most celebrated heads of state. He will address the United Nations, meet with the president, receive hundreds of honorary degrees, be feted at concerts, favor scores of politicians with photo opportunities and, in kinship with Churchill, de Gaulle and MacArthur, address a joint session of Congress.

There is nothing unfitting about the attention given to this aging resistance fighter, who was hardly known in this country five years ago but who at the moment arguably is the most admired person in the world. We are out to impress this man, and the world too, that our principles aren't flagging and that the United States is an agent of and not a barrier to change.

Little else the country can achieve. Unlike the other foreign celebrities who have addressed Congress recently — Lech Walesa, Mikhail Gorbachev and Vaclav Havel — Mandela isn't beseeching the U.S. for lucrative trade and financial favors. He wants the opposite: continued sanctions against his country.

Every sign is that he will get what he wants. Despite astonishing changes wrought by its new president, F. W. de Klerk, South Africa is a long way from meeting the conditions for ending sanctions that were established by Congress in 1986. The ban against Mandela's African National Congress has been lifted, but other conditions — freeing thousands of political prisoners, ending the requirement of segregated living areas and making substantial progress toward dismembering apartheid — have not been met. The Bush administration seemed to signal early this month that it was re-evaluating the sanctions, but Bush, whose priority is strengthening his position with American minorities, will not do it. Lifting the sanctions has little support in Congress, and after Mandela's visit there may be none save Sen. Jesse Helms'.

The United States may have less influence on the pace and configuration of reforms in South Africa than does Europe, including the old colonial powers and even Eastern Europe, but Mandela's welcome and his impressions in the U.S. and other Western countries may shape more than subtly the kind of government and society the new South African leaders embrace.

Mandela has praised, with an evenhandedness that upsets many in the West, both Marxist and democratic help for the cause of black South Africans. Shabby protocol has played a bad role before in the shaping of nations. By feting Nelson Mandela, the U.S. can be principled and shrewd in its self-interest, too.

Miami, Florida, June 29, 1990

With respect to the reaction of the Cuban exiles against the ideological stand of mister Nelson Mandela, it is fitting to clarify —because reality so demands— that there is no disagreement whatsoever with Mandela's fight against racial segregation (apartheid), but against his ideological identification with Fidel Castro and the communist system.

The Cuban people —whites and blacks— are against racial segregation, which in Cuba was not practiced and was condemned. We must remember that in the Nineteenth Century, the Cuban slaves were freed before their counterparts in the United States of America.

With or without racial segregation, the Cubans in exile would be against the stand taken by the black South African leader, Nelson Mandela, in all that concerning his defense of Fidel Castro and being identified with his political ideology and his system of government. The Cubans, who have suffered communism, who know it because they have lived it, do not want for the people of South Africa the substitution of their present regime with a communist tyranny. The Cubans in exile want for that people the elimination of racial segregation and all the injustice that this implies, wishing for that nation the full prevalence of human rights and of political freedom.

During a long coexistence of thirty-one years in Dade County, the Cubans never have had any type of confrontation with the black community. Their spirit of human solidarity and their custom of living in their fatherland with peoples of different races, especially of the black race which was represented there in a significant and positive way in different circles of human endeavor, has inspired a civilized and cordial behavior in their relations with all sectors in this County, among them, of course, the important black sector.

This clarifying explanation should be made constantly about the stand of the Cubans in the face of mister Mandela's statements, to prevent that the Anglo population, or that of any other origin, in this jurisdiction and in the rest of the country, because television goes everywhere, might get the impression that there was a racial or capricious intransigence based on mere political empathy. There has been a division of profound ideological meaning between Mr. Mandela's ties with and support of the Castro communist tyranny, and what constitutes —on the part of the Cuban population— rejection of everything that intentionally, doctrinally, might favor the type of dictatorship that for thirty-one years has been oppressing the Cuban nation.

CHICAGO Sun-Times

Chicago, Illinois, June 24, 1990

Nelson Mandela, staunch and steadfast symbol of black African liberation, deserves the hero's welcome he has been accorded in the early days of his eight-city U.S. tour.

We add our own welcome to and respect for this 71-year-old warrior in the cause of human dignity and racial justice.

While the chief purpose of his tour here is to win political and financial support for the fight against apartheid in South Africa, his trip transcends politics. The survivor of 27 years in South African jails has become living legend.

He is also "real," said Ann Lamar, an accountant from Philadelphia who traveled to New York to see him, "There is no pretension, no politics."

Mandela attracts people of all races and faiths in his call for equality. His words cross borders, continents, oceans: "As we enter the last decade of the 20th century, it is intolerable, unacceptable, that the cancer of racism is still eating away at the fabric of societies in different parts of our planet."

We understand his feelings of comradeship for three controversial figures who have supported the "liberation movement" of South African blacks—Yasser Arafat, Moammar Gadhafi and Fidel Castro. It is a mistake, he says, for people to "think their enemies should be our enemies." We are not bound to, though, and we don't, share his view of that trio. It is also a mistake to think that his allies need be our allies.

Such disagreements in no way diminish him or his cause.

DAILY ◼ NEWS

New York City, New York, June 20, 1990

'HERO" IS AN OVERUSED WORD. But its definition — a person of great strength and courage — is the perfect description of Nelson Mandela, whose visit to New York is the first stop on a historic U.S. tour.

Mandela arrives at a troubled time in this city's history. Ethnic and racial differences threaten to divide a great metropolis that was built on a foundation of diversity. Ideally, his visit will be a grand celebration that uplifts New Yorkers. And reminds them that *amandla* — power — comes not only from individual heroism, but from collective tolerance and cooperation.

Who is Mandela? A tireless fighter against racism. A black man who repeatedly says his enemy is apartheid, not white people.

He is a radical and a revolutionary who must show greater care in choosing his companions. World leaders — and Mandela is certainly that — cannot praise the likes of Yasser Arafat, Moammar Khadafy, Fidel Castro and Ethiopian dictator Mengistu Haile-Mariam without losing a lot of credibility. Alliances with these thugs can only hurt Mandela and his cause. His American friends should stress that to him during this tour.

Mandela also is a man of great dignity and personal grace. After 27 years of hellish imprisonment, he walked out talking about respect, progress and compromise. Lesser men would have spit venom and hate. It says a lot about a man who blames his imprisonment not on other men, but on a racist system.

Mandela's U.S. visit is not a victory lap. His mission is to persuade the U.S. to retain its economic sanctions against South Africa. He's right. South Africa has a long way to go before the nightmare of apartheid is over. Before the U.S. can ease sanctions, the South African government must end apartheid and meet all the criteria established in the 1986 Comprehensive Anti-Apartheid Act, which established U.S. sanction policy.

SOUTH AFRICAN PRESIDENT F.W. de Klerk has met some of the act's goals. Mandela has been released. Yesterday, the Separate Amenities Act, which allowed legal discrimination, was repealed. The state of emergency, which among other things limited freedom of the press, has been lifted in all but one violence-scarred province. Bans against 36 political parties — including Mandela's African National Congress — have been lifted. And de Klerk has agreed to enter negotiations with the ANC. A good start, but more is needed:

◼ *Release all political prisoners.* About 3,000 men, women and children — some under the age of 12 — continue to languish in South African prisons.

◼ *End all restrictive apartheid laws.* The Group Areas Act, which permits separate and unequal education, must be wiped off the books. Also the Population Registration Act, which pigeonholes every South African by race.

◼ *Take positive steps to erase apartheid's harms.* Improve the quality of education for black children. Open the political process to *all* South Africans. End human rights violations.

Mandela's visit should also spur Washington to think about South Africa's future. Sanctions are America's stick. But encouraging progress will require some carrots, too. When and if de Klerk takes constructive steps, he should be rewarded in trade and aid. He'll need the help to revive his faltering economy — and to fend off hard-line white opponents.

Mandela's visit will be an emotional time for New York. But emotion cannot blind anyone to the work that remains. Apartheid is still the law of South Africa. It will take more than one man to change it.

Rockford Register Star
Rockford, Illinois, June 26, 1990

In an enormously fitting tableau, Nelson Mandela stood in Yankee Stadium showing off his gift New York Yankees' baseball warmup jacket and cap and said, "Now you know who I am. I am a Yankee."

Thus he recognized the special ties between many Americans and his own fight for racial equality in South Africa.

But Mandela, of course, is much more. Mandela is a true hero.

In an era when we make heroes of our athletes and entertainers and politicians, Nelson Mandela is so much more. That's why millions of Americans of all colors are thrilled by this South African.

Mandela is not an athlete. Nor is he an entertainer or orator, although he is wonderfully articulate and candid in his speech. Instead, Mandela is a 71-year-old hero who emerged from 27 years in prison to be instantly acclaimed leader of South Africa.

Mandela's heroism is by virtue of speaking the truth about man's inhumanity to man. Such inhumanity is manifest in the "shameful blot" of South African apartheid, in which a minority white population holds in bondage a majority black population.

Mandela came to America to say that while he can "see the light at the end of the tunnel" in his struggle for African freedom, final victory depends on continued pressure from the United States. He makes it clear his priority is equality for the blacks of Africa and an end to racism there.

He acknowledges that the cancer of racism still gnaws at the fabric of freedom in America. But he properly reminds American blacks they already have won one battle, the fight for legal equal rights — rights black Africans still only dream of.

What Mandela has brought to Americans of all colors is an urgently needed role model of a man for whom truth has prevailed over hate.

The Philadelphia Inquirer
Philadelphia, Pennsylvania, June 27, 1990

To destroy racism in the world, we together must expunge apartheid racism in South Africa. Justice and liberty must be our tools, prosperity and happiness our weapon. . . . Peace will not come to our country and region until the apartheid system is ended.

— Nelson Mandela, speaking to a joint session of Congress yesterday

In his meeting with President Bush, and in his stirring message to the Congress, Nelson Mandela made the case that economic sanctions should remain in place as a lever to pressure South Africa to end apartheid. There was little doubt before, and less now, that his advice will be taken.

So the question arises: If not now, when? What would be the right moment to lift the sanctions? What would constitute proof positive that South Africa is serious about changing from a racist society to an open, genuinely democratic one?

No one, not even Mr. Mandela, has given definitive answers to these questions. But some guidelines may be defined by examining the U.S. response to the changes that have occurred in Eastern Europe. This country had imposed economic sanctions on Poland for its suppression of Solidarity. In the initial stages of negotiations between Solidarity and the communists, the United States was properly cautious. But once it was clear that democratic forces were in the ascendancy, the Bush administration moved swiftly to ease those sanctions.

Despite the release of Mr. Mandela from his long period of incarceration, the legalization of the African National Congress and the lifting of the state of emergency, the first clear sign that South Africa's black population will be given political power has yet to be seen. It is almost certain that the impact of the sanctions, and the isolation of South Africa by the international community, played an important part in pressuring the white government to make the changes it has already made. And it would be wrong to remove that pressure before it is certain that there will be serious, sustained and meaningful negotiations between the white government and black leaders.

Lifting the sanctions now would send a message to the South African government, and to any country against which the United States might impose sanctions in the future, that symbolic changes are sufficient.

The success of Mr. Mandela's tour of Europe and the United States is likely to enhance his strength and authority in South Africa, where blacks themselves are bitterly divided. At present he is clearly the man who is best equipped to lead the struggle of South Africa's majority for democratic rights. He deserves whatever support the United States can offer him in pursuit of that goal.

The Des Moines Register

Des Moines, Iowa, June 20, 1990

One of the world's best known political prisoners begins a visit to the United States today. Nelson Mandela's U.S. tour, part of a six-week foreign trip, is cause for celebration and reflection.

For more than 27 years Mandela was held in a South African prison, his only crime having been his service as a leader in the fight against the cruel and repressive system of apartheid. He was released last February. His current tour is an opportunity for him to address the throngs of people worldwide who have supported his cause, and to promote a better appreciation for how much still needs to be done in his country — and our own as well — in building equal opportunities for people of all races.

Mandela, speaking in Toronto the other night, acknowledged that South Africa is on the "threshold of major change." But dramatic as some government actions have seemed — Mandela's release, the unbanning of his African National Congress, the freeing of other political prisoners and the desegregation of public facilities — the country's 5 million whites still control South Africa's government and the economy, and the lives of 28 million non-whites.

The government has been meeting with black leaders, but only to talk about talks. Serious discussions about a new non-racial government have yet to take place.

Leaders of Britain and some officials within the Bush administration argue that a relaxation of sanctions against South Africa would encourage the government to move ahead with change. Theirs is not a persuasive postion.

The sanctions have hurt South Africa's economy and have been essential in forcing the government to change. Why should the Pretoria government be rewarded for some easing of laws regarding political dissent and racial separation when blacks still cannot vote, when blacks are educated in inferior government schools, when a majority of the land is reserved for whites, and when a person's race still must be registered at birth?

Mandela is asking his audiences to "walk the last mile with us" through the final and most difficult stages in the dismantling of apartheid. His plea was heard in Canada, where Prime Minister Brian Mulroney pledged to maintain his country's trade and economic sanctions against South Africa. It deserves to be heard in Washington, as well.

AKRON BEACON JOURNAL

Akron, Ohio, June 29, 1990

IN THE ROOM where Congress has squabbled often and bitterly over domestic civil rights issues, members scrambled to shake the hand of an African leader.

Nelson Mandela's address to Congress on Tuesday was at once a demonstration of how far this nation has come and a reminder of how America's revolutionary heritage and ideals, though we sometimes conveniently forget them, still inspire others.

Mandela invoked the names of his influences, including Jefferson, Lincoln and Martin Luther King Jr. It was a moving moment, a high point in a remarkable week.

Virtually everyone knows the story of Mandela's 27-year imprisonment in South Africa as head of the African National Congress and of his recent release. In his determination and his dignity, Mandela has become an important symbol for oppressed people everywhere.

But he also is finding support, even celebrity status, among white Americans. The nation has a shortage of heroes at the moment and Americans frequently embrace a heroic underdog who has triumphed — in spirit if not yet in fact — over an evil system. There is discord. Some members of

Congress boycotted the session to protest what they called the Marxism of the ANC.

It is troubling for Westerners to see Mandela continue to speak of Castro, Arafat and Gadhafi as friends.

It's no justification, but the United States also has taken up with some pretty unsavory and violent characters in pursuit of higher policy goals. In any case, it is hard to judge the motives and experience of a movement fighting for simple human rights in the context of our history as a powerful nation.

Likewise, it is disturbing to hear Mandela speak of political manipulation of the economy after apartheid. But it should be remembered the South African economy is not free and open now, and Mandela is committed to private sector vitality.

What Washington and the West should do is focus on the positive momentum of the movement that Mandela represents, and be willing to work with him, and the man who freed him, President F.W. de Klerk, toward a peaceful end to apartheid.

Mandela represents hope. The excitement over him is justified. So is the need to support his vision of human dignity.

The Houston Post

Houston, Texas, June 27, 1990

NELSON MANDELA'S current American tour is consolidating support for his campaign against South Africa's deplorable system of apartheid. But some of his views have not met with universal approval.

President Bush assured Mandela on Monday that the United States will not repeal sanctions against his homeland until all the conditions for lifting them have been met. He received similar assurances from congressional leaders, as well as a warm welcome, when he addressed a joint session of Congress Tuesday.

New York gave this personification of the struggle against apartheid a ticker tape parade. He has had saturation media coverage. And enthusiastic audiences have greeted him wherever he has appeared.

By any measure, Mandela is a remarkable man. He spent 27 years in prison for his defiance of his country's racial-separation policies. Throughout his imprisonment, he continued to be recognized as the head of the African National Congress, the anti-apartheid guerrilla movement outlawed until recently by the South African government.

After being freed in February at the age of 71 and in poor health, Mandela plunged into talks with South Africa's reform president, F.W. de Klerk. Their aim was to write a new constitution, a document that would end white-minority rule and give the black majority political representation and a share of power.

Yet despite the fact that the vast majority of Americans support Mandela's goal of dismantling apartheid, some of his remarks have been disturbing. His militancy is understandable, given the behavior of South Africa's white rulers for the past four decades. A defense may even be made for his refusal — when pressed by President Bush — to renounce violence, though he says he opposes it as long as the government negotiates in good faith.

But his praise for Libya's Col. Moammar Gadhafi, Cuba's Fidel Castro and Yasser Arafat and his Palestine Liberation Organization sticks in the American craw.

Mandela's explanation is that these leaders, their countries and causes supported the ANC's struggle when it found no help among the Western democracies. The terrorist affiliations of his benefactors don't seem to bother him. Nor does the motive behind their aid — sowing trouble. Mandela also has had kind words for the South African Communist Party, which has been an influential force in his ANC.

Telling Congress in his Tuesday speech, "Our people demand democracy," Mandela said black South Africans were following the examples of Washington, Jefferson, Lincoln and the Rev. Martin Luther King.

Let us hope so. They set far sounder examples than a Gadhafi, a Castro or an Arafat.

20th Anniversary of Kerner Report Marked

Newspaper editorial writers from across the U.S. noted the 20th anniversary of the President's National Advisory Commission on Civil Disorders, commonly known as the Kerner Commission.

The President's National Advisory Commission on Civil Disorders warned Feb. 29, 1968 that America "is moving toward two societies, one black, one white – separate and unequal." Reporting after a seven-month study of the racial disorders of the summer of 1967, the commission asserted that "this deepening racial division is not inevitable." With adequate action, it said, "the movement apart can be reversed."

The summer of 1967 brought racial disorders to U.S. cities, and with them shock, fear and bewilderment to the nation. The worst came during a two-week period that July in Newark, New Jersey and then in Detroit, Michigan. Each set off a chain reaction in neighboring communities.

"White racism," the commission charged, was chiefly responsible for the "explosive mixture" of discrimination, poverty and frustrations in the Negro ghetto that was vented in violence. The report said: "What white Americans have never fully understood – what the Negro can never forget – is that white society is deeply implicated in the ghetto. White institutions created it, white institutions maintain it, and white society condones it."

The commission called for a "massive and sustained" national commitment to action. It recommended sweeping reforms in federal and local law enforcement, welfare, employment, housing, education and the news media. While the programs would require "unprecedented levels of funding and performance," the commission said, "there can be no higher priority for national action and no higher claim on the nation's conscience."

THE SACRAMENTO BEE
Sacramento, California, March 13, 1988

In 1968, in the wake of urban riots that set American cities ablaze, the Kerner Commission warned that "our nation is moving toward two societies, one black, one white — separate and unequal." Today, 20 years later, the commission's worst fears have not materialized. In most areas of U.S. life, doors to advancement and opportunity, once barred by discrimination, have swung open to black Americans. But even as America has avoided the commission's worst fears, it has not lived up to its hopes of "common opportunities for all within a single society."

For black Americans, the last two decades have laid down two diverging paths. On one path, millions of middle-class blacks have pushed past the old color line to move into the mainstream of American life. Since 1968, the percentage of blacks graduating from high schools has risen by half, the percentage of young blacks completing college has doubled and the number of blacks in managerial, professional and technical occupations has soared. Black families with both husband and wife in the work force now earn, on average, 82 percent as much as similar white families. In big cities where black youths, frustrated and powerless, torched buildings in 1967, black mayors now control city hall; the number of black elected officials in the United States has increased fivefold in the last two decades.

But there is another black path, which has led downward into even worse misery than the Kerner Commission portrayed. As millions of blacks have advanced out of the ghettoes into decent jobs and orderly suburbs, they have left behind in inner cities a black underclass plagued by joblessness, crime, drugs and broken families. Rising skill requirements in the job market, the dispersal of factories and offices into the suburbs and the disappearance of older heavy manufacturing jobs have stranded inner-city youth — not just black, but white and brown as well — with fewer opportunities and less social support than two decades ago.

The Kerner Commission's report pricked the conscience of the nation and gave a push to efforts to break down racial barriers in American life. Rereading the report in the light of today's conditions, however, one cannot escape the conclusion that the United States has yet to take its policy recommendations — for expanded early childhood education, year-round schools, improved vocational training, more public housing dispersed outside of inner-city neighborhoods, welfare reforms linking work with higher benefit standards — seriously to heart.

Today, as in 1968, America is two societies, separate and unequal, though not so much divided between black and white as between haves and have-nots. "Only a commitment to national action on an unprecedented scale can shape a future compatible with the historic ideals of American society," the commission said then. It is still right.

ST. LOUIS POST-DISPATCH
St. Louis, Missouri, March 3, 1988

Even though the Kerner Commission's final report was issued 20 years ago, on Feb. 29, a wise presidential candidate could still use that document as a takeoff for spelling out his program for urban America. The report also offers a way to call attention to the special needs of the type of inner-city resident who hasn't shared in Michael Dukakis' "Massachusetts Miracle" and couldn't afford one of Richard Gephardt's K-cars or even one of Jesse Jackson's VCRs.

The subjects of the Kerner study into civil disorder that swept through U.S. cities in 1967 haven't been completely forgotten, however. Among those taking note of the document was a group of scholars who met last weekend in Racine, Wis. Some of them concluded that the problems confronting inner-city residents are probably more economic than racial. To an extent, this is correct. The type of jobs that many inner-city residents held in the 1960s have vanished. One study says manufacturing jobs in 12 major cities have declined by 1.6 million since 1967.

The loss of these jobs may explain the slow pace of economic progress made by certain segments of the nation's black community in the 20 years since Kerner. About 9.6 percent of the nation's black population earned less than $5,000 a year in 1970; that figure jumped to 14 percent by 1986. Those earning between $10,000 and $35,000 dropped to nearly 47 percent by 1986, down from 58 percent in 1970.

But something else has hurt blacks, according to those at the Racine conference. In previous decades, the scholars noted, poor inner-city youngsters seeking a sense of direction had a larger pool of role models, employed acquaintances and institutions from which to draw inspiration — not just churches, but self-help groups, business owners, community organizations and employed neighbors.

The movement of manufacturing jobs from central cities, rising crime and expanded suburban housing opportunities have all enticed middle-class blacks in particular to move out of their old neighborhoods and leave behind an underclass that lacks a support system so important to stability in any community.

Moreover, federal policies are doing little to reverse this trend, except to blame these victims for resorting to welfare and criminal activities in order to survive. This situation only causes racist feelings among those who don't understand why this group can't move up the economic ladder on its own initiative, according to sociologist Julius Wilson, one of those who participated in the Racine conference.

"This image of a dangerous inner city is generalized to the entire black population. Until we deal with the underclass, it will be impossible to have healthy race relations in this country," Mr. Wilson said.

This means the next president must have a new agenda for urban America and for reviving hope in the nation's inner cities, where those locked in poverty have been virtually written off as lazy, untrainable and generally unneeded for productive work in the larger society.

THE DAILY OKLAHOMAN
Oklahoma City, Oklahoma, March 3, 1988

TWENTY years ago, social reformers were blaming racial prejudice for poor living conditions for inner-city blacks. Now they're pointing the finger at economic causes.

But their proposed remedy is still the same: pour more federal money into the ghettos.

Still a strong advocate of big government programs to solve people problems, former Oklahoma Sen. Fred Harris is on the stump citing the overall lack of progress made since the Kerner commission issued its 1968 report on urban riots. Harris, a commission member, organized an academic discussion of the state of black America two decades later.

He and black leader Roger Wilkins acknowledge that great strides have been made in race relations and that racism is not now a key cause of urban poverty. They also recognize the emergence of a black middle class, major gains in the number of black elected officials and significant inroads into the professions by blacks and other minorities.

But that doesn't deter them from unfairly attacking the Reagan administration for being "hostile" to civil rights measures.

They call for doubling the amount of government spending on anti-poverty efforts.

It sounds as if Harris and his liberal friends are suffering from an attack of "Great Society" nostalgia.

AKRON BEACON JOURNAL
Akron, Ohio, March 4, 1988

TWENTY YEARS have passed since Martin Luther King's death, since whole blocks burned in riots in Chicago and Washington, and since President Johnson's Kerner commission finished its report on the causes of racial tensions. Today, the race riots are mentioned in schools during Black History Week. Martin Luther King is remembered on his birthday. And the Kerner report gets occasional attention, as it did this week on the 20th anniversary of its release.

So on special occasions, black America gets a turn in the spotlight.

Some might think that racial injustice has passed now, that it is enough to reflect on special occasions on the kind of discrimination that seems unthinkable today, and to marvel over how far the nation has come.

Anyone could draw examples from personal experience to make the point about progress. Just look at the workplace. Or look at government, and see how many blacks hold elected offices — 7,000 nationwide by the last count.

Yes, how easy it is note progress from the worst days of racial injustice. But beware. Racial injustice is a stubborn affliction. And to the nation's misfortune, it's still here in America.

Yes, the black middle class has grown and prospered, to the credit of the civil-rights movement. By 1980, about 56 percent of the black wage earners belonged to this group. That, of course, is encouraging.

But poor blacks are as bad off as they've ever been, trapped in poverty with little hope for decent jobs and a better future. More frightening, their numbers are growing. The statistics tell a bleak story:

● By 1986, the black poverty rate has risen to 31 percent.

● Three times as many blacks as whites live in poverty.

● The median income of blacks is 57 percent that of whites.

● About 55 percent of black families are headed by females.

Making matters worse, many factory jobs have left the big cities, compounding economic problems there. Moreover, the government has done less, reducing housing subsidies, for example, and college aid.

Blacks in poverty, many of them high school dropouts, make up what's called a permanent underclass, since little suggests their plight is temporary. They also make up a segment of society that the nation is overlooking, except on special occasions.

But how long can the nation afford to exclude such a large segment of society from the hope of prosperity? And is the nation willing to wait passively to learn the consequences of permitting this underclass to exist?

Indeed, the nation is moving toward two societies, as the Kerner commission warned. The commission feared one black society, and one white. Increasingly, the nation is becoming a society of haves and have-nots, reflecting the widening gap between the rich and the poor. And increasingly, blacks are finding themselves as have-nots.

For its own good, the nation needs direction, a realistic blueprint on how to make the underclass a not-so-permanent social fixture. So far, leadership from the Reagan administration has been sorely missing. The President could change that by appointing another commission, as forceful as the Kerner commission, to start working on answers.

THE ARIZONA REPUBLIC
Phoenix, Arizona, March 3, 1988

THE words are familiar: the government should create 1 million new jobs and raise the minimum wage significantly. Massive federal initiatives are needed to increase welfare benefits, school spending and funding for housing programs for the nation's poor.

The Democratic Party's 1988 platform? A stump speech by Jesse Jackson? No, these are among the proposals of the Kerner Commission, a presidential panel established in August 1967 in the aftermath of widespread urban rioting — Watts, then Chicago and Cleveland followed by Newark and Detroit. The long, hot summers of the 1960s suggested that something was fundamentally wrong in America.

The Kerner Commission was charged with investigating the causes of urban racial unrest and suggesting remedies. Its final report, issued two decades ago last month, recommended a massive infusion of federal social programs and spending to head off what the panel saw as an America "moving toward two societies, one black, one white — separate and unequal."

It found that "prostitution, dope addiction, casual sex affairs and crime create an environmental jungle characterized by personal insecurity and tension." Coming at a time of a growing conviction that the social programs of the Johnson administration had failed, the report's conclusions gave the Great Society's enlightened liberalism" a much-needed lift.

But it accomplished little else. As Thomas Bray of the *Detroit News* points out in a recent article for *Policy Review*, "the Kerner Commission had a splendid opportunity to jolt the country into thinking about fresh approaches to some old problems. Instead, it settled for conventional wisdom" — an expensive wish list of federal programs.

Twenty years and billions of dollars later, the commission's "dewy-eyed faith in government's ability to 'solve' problems," as Bray puts it, has yielded more crime, more unemployment, more poverty, and more welfare dependency in the inner cities. Today a third of Detroit's population is on welfare.

And although institutionalized racism has declined appreciably, Detroit and many other large cities are as segregated in 1988 as they were nearly a generation ago when the Kerner panel's recommendations were considered the high-water mark of liberal thinking.

Yet despite overwhelming evidence that the government's well-intentioned programs actually have increased the alienation of poor people, and particularly blacks, from the mainstream, some presidential contenders and congressional advocates are touting the same bromides.

If anything can be gained from revisiting the Kerner Commission's findings, it is the understanding that 20 years of failure should not be repeated.

There's a thin silver lining in last week's otherwise dismal update of the 1968 Kerner commission report: The black middle class has grown somewhat in 20 years, and blacks have made significant gains in the political arena.

It's precisely because of these successes — the result of legislative initiatives to bring about equality of opportunity — that America must now redouble its commitment to bring blacks into America's mainstream.

THE ANN ARBOR NEWS
Ann Arbor, Michigan, March 1, 1988

A generation of Americans has grown up since the Kerner Commission, appointed by President Johnson to investigate the causes of racial riots in the cities, issued its findings.

The report pulled no punches. The country was "moving toward two societies, one black, one white — separate and unequal." That startling conclusion shook America out of any complacency it might have had over several years' successes in civil rights legislation.

The characterization of America as two separate, unequal societies was supported by a stinging diagnosis of the cause. "White racism," the report stated, "is essentially responsible for the explosive mixture which has been accumulating in our cities since the end of World War II."

The report went on to say, "White society is deeply implicated in the (black) ghetto. White institutions created it, white institutions maintain it, and white society condones it."

Two decades later, America is having to look in the mirror again. Racial tensions seem on the rise, especially on college campuses among young people who weren't even born when the Kerner Commission issued its report. Legal segregation and Jim Crow are long gone, but American society is still divided along racial lines.

Generally speaking, black and white communities are often uncomfortable with each other. Suspicion and fear have taken the place of trust and friendliness. There are obvious exceptions, of course, all across America.

But as Richard Bernstein wrote in The New York Times, even though the division of America into separate but unequal societies has not come about, "The general direction predicted by the report and the stubborn persistence of the race problem in America have endured."

For example, to remedy the ills it identified, Kerner made numerous recommendations, including job creation, welfare reform and provision of housing for low-income family units.

After 20 years, what issues are still being discussed today? The need for jobs, reform of the welfare system and affordable housing.

The picture after 20 years isn't all one of despair. An integrated society hasn't arrived yet, but progress has been made toward racial equality. A black middle class, educated and economically secure, has expanded as earning power has increased.

William Julius Wilson, a University of Chicago sociologist and author of two works on race, believes there are three different groups. "There's a black middle class that has experienced gradual progress. There's a black working class that has had difficulty holding its economic position because it's been vulnerable to de-industrialization. And there's a black underclass that's slipping further and further behind the rest of society."

As for the "black power" slogan which terrified so many whites in the sixties, power has taken the form of political ownership of seats in Congress and other parts of the federal government and especially of big city mayorships.

But even as more blacks have moved into positions of genuine economic and political power, some black leaders and analysts are worried that progress is slowing or even reversing. Public enthusiasm for sustaining sixties-era black gains has waned. The Reagan administration has not distinguished itself in the area of race relations; federal programs which have helped to nurture black progress in such areas as affirmative action have been cut back.

The mixed picture 20 years after Kerner shows how far America has to go before blacks and whites commingle harmoniously in board rooms, city halls, industry workplaces, social settings, schools, power positions and the like. Now more than ever, education is the hope on which all else depends.

Newsday
New York City, New York, March 6, 1988

But signs of apparent progress, such as increased numbers of black elected officials cannot mask reality. The Commission on the Cities says that, just as forewarned by the National Advisory Commission on Civil Disorders in 1968, America is again becoming two societies, one black (and Hispanic), one white; separate and unequal.

Meeting last week to review progress toward economic and social justice since the urban riots of the 1960s, the new commission found very little change from 20 years ago. Black median income is now 57 percent of the median income for whites, lower, slightly, than in 1968; black unemployment remains double that of whites.

Life for many blacks is markedly worse. Those who live in city pockets abandoned by whites and blue-collar manufacturing jobs form an underclass. They are poorer and even less able to escape; they are afflicted by the quiet riots of family disintegration, social disorganization and crime.

The most discouraging finding is that segregation in housing and public education has actually *increased* since 1968, further fueling inequality by increasing the likelihood of inferior education and lessening opportunities for employment.

How to fix it? The laws are already on the books. We need a renewed commitment to fair housing, more vigorous enforcement of equal employment laws and redoubled efforts to desegregate the schools. These are the tools. Now we need the will to wield them.

The Courier-Journal
Louisville, Kentucky, March 1, 1988

OUR NATION is moving toward two societies, one black, one white — separate and unequal." That warning by the Kerner Commission, 20 years ago this week, was only partly accurate. The divisions in America are more numerous and complex than the two societies described by the commission.

Still, the advisory panel was basically right about the persistent problem of racial inequality. Today, the median income of black households is 57.6 percent of that of white households, slightly lower than in 1968. And while the percentage of black families earning more than $35,000 a year (adjusted for inflation) has grown, so have the ranks of those earning less than $10,000.

To some extent, then, blacks in America have been moving toward two societies: an expanding middle class composed mostly of two-parent, dual-income families, and an urban underclass in which a disproportionately large number of households are headed by women with low-paying jobs, or with no jobs at all.

The Kerner Commission blamed white racism for the economic and social inequality that fueled the urban riots of the 1960s. One would have to be willfully ignorant to deny that racism continues to poison American society today.

But it would be equally foolish to ignore the enormous progress that has occurred over the past 20 years. Anti-discrimination laws, which were still new in 1968, have greatly expanded job opportunities for blacks. More and more white Americans have grown accustomed to working and going to school with blacks. Desegregation of apartments and residential subdivisions has come more slowly, but here, too, there has been progress.

Paradoxically, the very success of some blacks in escaping poverty has exacerbated the problems of the inner-city neighborhoods they left behind. This is in no way an argument against the mobility of middle-class blacks. But it suggests that the problems of the economic underclass are too stubborn to be solved solely by expanded job and educational opportunities.

Many conservatives sneer at the idea of "throwing money" at these problems. They may be partly right — though the United States has never thrown as much money, per capita, at domestic needs as most other industrialized nations have. But if big new social programs aren't the answer, our political leaders should be looking much, much harder for less costly solutions. One that's overdue is a change in welfare rules so that recipients would no longer be penalized financially for finding jobs, or for living together as husband and wife.

ILLUSTRATION BY ELEANOR MILL

President Reagan has provided little political or moral leadership in this area. In fact, he seems cheerfully oblivious to conditions in our cities that breed crime and despair. In choosing their next president, Americans should look for someone who is at least aware of the problem and willing to talk about it. Otherwise, a commission may one day write about the urban riots of the 1990s — and how nobody heeded the warning signs.

The News and Observer
Raleigh, North Carolina, March 5, 1988

HOW DISTANT seem the flames of the nation's 1967 riots. How even farther away seem Jim Crow, "colored" seats on buses, and "separate but equal" schools.

After all, things are so much better now, aren't they, with equal opportunity, affirmative action, poverty programs, and black office holders? Yes, some things are better — but some are worse.

It has been 20 years since the National Advisory Commission on Civil Disorders, headed by Illinois Gov. Otto Kerner, issued its report on a nation of two societies. Now, say scholars updating that report, society has divided even further. Some black Americans have made strides forward. But for others, poverty and isolation have deepened.

The underclass — a permanent stratum of hard-core unemployed plagued by epidemic teen pregnancy, illiteracy, drug use, and violent crime — swells in every major inner city. It is alienated from society, fallen so deep through the cracks that it seems unreachable.

Before it is sucked down the vortex, society must interrupt that spiral. Government can and must redouble its efforts for the poor. Those efforts can and must focus on helping rebuild a once-strong tradition of family life in the black community. That includes welfare reform that encourages, not discourages, intact families; decent housing; and crime-free neighborhoods. Help also is needed to halt the precipitous decline in the number of blacks going to college, a traditional path to economic well-being.

Local government no longer can push the problem off onto Washington. Nor can it depend so heavily on the renewed efforts of voluntary organizations such as the Urban League, no matter how conscientious those efforts are.

This nation has an emergency, a real emergency, when crime holds its black neighborhoods hostage, when three times as many blacks as whites are poverty-stricken, and when black families earn 57 cents for every dollar made by white families. It shouldn't take the flames of a riot to illuminate that emergency.

The Miami Herald
Miami, Florida, March 7, 1988

Twenty years ago, a commission appointed by President Lyndon B. Johnson and headed by Illinois Gov. Otto Kerner concluded chillingly that the United States was "moving toward two societies, one black, one white — separate and unequal." And since then, even though some of the barriers dividing the races have come down, blacks have made only modest gains. In some respects they have even fallen farther behind.

Enormous problems thus remain if blacks are to achieve a truly equal standing in American society — problems that can only be addressed through better education.

In 1988, politics is one of the bright spots. About 300 cities have black mayors, and such North Carolina cities as Raleigh and Charlotte have elected blacks as their chief executives. The Rev. Jesse Jackson is a serious presidential candidate. But blacks still are under-represented in state legislatures, and statewide black candidates are a rarity.

In terms of material wealth, gloom is the word. The average income of blacks has increased, but the gap between family incomes of blacks and whites is widening. Three times as many blacks as whites live in poverty.

Crime statistics are equally bleak. More than a million black Americans are behind bars or on probation or parole. Black arrest rates exceed the national averages for every offense except drunken driving.

But it is in education that the outlook is, paradoxically, both depressing and hopeful, offering what indeed may be the last, best hope.

On the down side, the percentage of black high school graduates starting college has dropped from 34 to 26 since 1976, and only 42 percent of the blacks entering college go on to graduate. Blacks lag behind Asians, whites, Puerto Ricans and Mexican-Americans in scores on Scholastic Aptitude Tests, even when the students come from families with comparable incomes.

Yet, education can break the cycle in all these areas — politics, income, crime. Education is a way for disadvantaged blacks to move into the mainstream of American life, mastering the common language — standard English — and learning the modes of behavior of the majority culture.

Inevitably, that will mean a dilution of the black cultural heritage. But that is the price that has been paid by other ethnic groups, from the Germans and Scotch-Irish to the more recently arrived Koreans and Vietnamese.

Whether the trends can be reversed is by no means certain. But on this 20th anniversary of the Kerner Commission report, a time for looking back, education at least offers hope. The alternative — giving up, doing nothing — is an invitation to disaster.

THE PLAIN DEALER
Cleveland, Ohio, March 3, 1988

The underlying premise of the 1968 Kerner Commission report was that white racism accounted for two "separate and unequal" societies in America—one black and one white. Although progress has been made, the poignant finding of the Kerner panel, formally called the National Advisory Commission on Civil Disorders, continues to be an American reality.

While opportunity in many significant areas, including income, education, politics, employment and housing, has improved for many blacks, those are areas in which other blacks have not kept pace with other Americans and, in fact, have fallen further behind. The Kerner report charged the government with being the nucleus of the solution. But despite government actions, separate societies have survived, resulting in more blacks remaining among the "have-nots" than among the "haves." Some examples:

■ There are more blacks earning more than $50,000 than ever before, but three times as many blacks as whites live in poverty.

■ Fair-housing legislation has enabled scores of black families entree into previously all-white suburbia, but the plight of inner-city blacks has worsened.

■ There are more black mayors of big cities than ever before, but many of those mayors, especially in the North, gained power as population decreased, poverty increased and industry no longer could accommodate a growing work force.

■ Employment opportunities have brought more blacks into the professional marketplace, but black median income still is 57% that of whites, according to a New York Times report reprinted on today's first Forum Page.

The question, then, is this: If white racism accounted for the findings of the Kerner report, what is responsible for the above discrepancies? Many persons correctly have concluded that the answer continues to be racism, an accusation that has been cited frequently in Cleveland—from the City Council president's charges against Cleveland State University last year, to the predominance of segregated housing patterns in the city.

But racism is not by itself at the core of racial unrest. Urban problems have been exacerbated by an unanticipated decline of the economy of older cities. Employment opportunities opened in the professions, but for skilled and unskilled workers, the jobs began to disappear, leaving whites and black competing for fewer places on the assembly line. Additionally, the racism charge too often has become a convenient and disingenuous excuse for other problems, many of which never get explored.

The Kerner report provided a prescription for improved race relations. But that prescription dealt mostly with racism. The problem has become much larger than that, and so must the solutions.

Plight of Young Blacks
Draws Nationwide Concern

The homicide rate among black males between the ages of 15 and 24 had risen by 68% between 1984 and 1988, according to figures released Dec. 6, 1990 by the federal Centers for Disease Control. Homicide was the leading cause of death among black men in that age group, the CDC reported.

Dr. Robert G. Froehlke, the principal author of the CDC report, noted, "In some areas of the country it is now more likely for a black male between his 15th and 25th birthday to die from homicide than it was for a United States soldier to be killed on a tour of duty during Vietnam."

According to the CDC report, black males age 15-24 had a homicide death rate of 101.1 per 100,000 population, or one in a thousand – nine times greater than the rate for white males, and six times greater than the rate for black females. The problem was particularly acute for black males age 15-19, whose homicide death rate had nearly doubled between 1984 and 1988.

Increases in homicide rates among young black males had been highest in Florida (up 88% over the four-year span), New York (up 84%), Michigan (78%), California (71%), the District of Columbia (40%) and Missouri (22%).

The CDC report stated that 95% of the increase in homicide deaths among young black males between 1984 and 1987 had been caused by shootings. In addition to greater access to firearms, the CDC blamed "alcohol and substance abuse, drug trafficking, poverty, racial discrimination and cultural acceptance of violent behavior" for the increase in homicide deaths. Separately, the center reported that deaths from homicide and the fatal disease AIDS had both increased in 1988.

The life expectancy gap between blacks and whites had widened in 1988, according to figures released by the National Center for Health Statistics Nov. 28, 1989.

For babies born in 1988, the center estimated that the average life expectancy for blacks was 69.2 years, down from 69.4 in 1987. For whites, the average was 75.6 years – unchanged from 1987.

In a related development, most children living below the poverty line had wage-earning parents, according to a report released June 3, 1991 by the Children's Defense Fund, a child advocacy group. The federal poverty line was defined as an annual income of $12,675 for a family of four.

According to the report, 63% of families with poor children had at least one wage-earning member. Almost half of poor children were in families that received no welfare, and 55% lived in rural or suburban environments, the study said. About half of poor children had mothers who were out of their teens when they were born. Of the total number of poor children, according to the study, 41% were non-Hispanic whites, 35% were non-Hispanic blacks and 21% were Hispanic.

Previously, the American Council on Higher Education had released a study stating that the number of black men enrolled in U.S. colleges and universities had declined over the past decade. The report, which was released Jan. 15, 1989, noted that black male enrollment had dropped to 436,000 in 1986 from 470,000 in 1976. At the same time, the enrollment of black women had risen to 645,000 from 563,000. Overall, black enrollment had decreased to 8.6% of the 1986 undergraduate and graduate student population, down from 9.4% in 1976. Some educators blamed the decline on federal policies that had shifted financial aid away from grants in favor of increased loans.

The Star-Ledger

Newark, New Jersey, October 6, 1990

In the past two or three years, disturbing statistics about young black males have been repeatedly cited from various sources. These data are all the more disturbing because in too many cases they are irrefutable. And while some use this information as the basis for a resurgent racism, others view them in a positive context as a reaffirmation of the need to address these very real problems.

Among the negative circumstances involving young black males are homicide rates, involvement with the criminal justice system, declining educational achievement and incidence of heart attacks, cancer, AIDS and other ailments at levels far exceeding their white counterparts.

On a recent visit to New Jersey, the sole black member of President Bush's Cabinet, Health and Human Services Secretary Dr. Louis Sullivan, called upon black business and professional leaders to make a more diligent effort to address what he termed "the crisis of the black male" in America.

Dr. Sullivan, speaking to the national convention of 100 Black Men of America, called for a shift of emphasis from negative stereotyping to "the many positive role models that grace our community." He suggested the time has come to begin "an open, frank, comprehensive national dialogue on the crisis of the black male"—one he asserted will leave young black males believing they are part of the solution, rather than part of the problem.

While charging that prevailing media images of young blacks are negative and stereotypical, Dr. Sullivan maintained it is necessary that troubled black youth be "saved by the example of the vast majority of our men who have thrived in spite of adverse circumstances, because of the determination of their wills and the integrity of their souls."

He urged the gathering of black professionals to "sound the call" against drug abuse and other negative factors, and to encourage educational excellence, as well as developing a "face-to-face, man-to-man" relationship with a young black man.

Much of what Dr. Sullivan said is unarguable. There is a need for successful black men to take an active part in overcoming the problems faced by young black males. On the other hand, there is a role to be played by government to eradicate some of the social roadblocks.

The needs are great and, in Dr. Sullivan's words, represent "a crisis for America." There are many roles to be played, and a void can be filled by the black professionals. There is also a role for Dr. Sullivan, which is to use his Cabinet-level status to persuade President Bush to support federal policies that can serve as life-rafts to save young black males from the tempest to which society still subjects far too many.

St. Paul Pioneer Press & Dispatch
St. Paul, Minnesota, October 13, 1990

The African American community in Minneapolis is tired of losing so many of its people to violent crime. It is tired, angry and frustrated. That frustration has given birth to a noteworthy community effort.

African American community tired of losing so many to violent crime.

By the end of this year, 9,000 African American people will die of gunshot wounds in the United States. In his lifetime, an African American man has a one in 21 chance of being murdered by an unlicensed gun. (That compares to one in 131 for white males.) In Minneapolis, so far this year, 26 of 37 homicide victims were black — most have been men. Too many have been young men or teen-agers.

Those horrifying statistics — the tragic loss of so many sons, husbands and fathers — and their effects upon neighborhoods have mobilized a coalition of youth, community and church organizations in Minneapolis. This week, a group of more than 30 Minneapolis agencies announced a "Stop the Violence" campaign against murders and other violent crimes, especially in black neighborhoods. Among the organizations backing the effort are the NAACP, Urban League, Urban Coalition, YMCA, YWCA and the Boys and Girls Clubs.

"Stop the Violence" illustrates what "power to the people" can really mean. Certainly, those neighborhoods that are plagued with crime and violence need law enforcement, housing and other government assistance. Of course efforts must continue to provide support services to neighborhoods that are more vulnerable to crime. But people empowering themselves can work wonders.

A group of leaders within Minneapolis' black community very wisely turned inward. They asked themselves what could be done to stop the escalating black-on-black violence that is paralyzing some African American neighborhoods. And they came up with answers that are a good start.

The Minneapolis area agencies will establish parent support networks, citizen foot patrols and a telephone hot line. Another component of the campaign effort is traveling trauma teams to counsel teen-agers in schools who have witnessed or been involved in violence. The counseling is designed to help them avoid or head off similar violent situations.

Today the campaign kicks off with a march on Minneapolis' North Side and a memorial service for those who were killed.

Self-help crusades like "Stop the Violence" deserve the support and encouragement from all Twin Citians. Reducing violent crime benefits everyone.

TULSA WORLD
Tulsa, Oklahoma, August 10, 1991

ECONOMICALLY, there are two "communities" of blacks in the United States, according to the Population Reference Bureau a non-profit organization that reports on population trends.

One group made up of middle-class and affluent blacks, "took advantage of the increased opportunities provided by the civil rights movement; the other of poor, largely urban blacks who remain socially and economically isolated from the American mainstream," the report notes.

Since the 1960s, the number of affluent blacks doubled in percentage terms. In that accomplishment, blacks matched the performance of whites who also doubled the number of affluent families with an income of $50,000 or more.

But poor blacks, if anything, congregate more in the ghettoes of the inner cities and little progress was made in breaking down housing segregation.

In comparing salaries, blacks averaged about 56 percent of the whites' income. But among the young, two-income families, blacks earned almost as much (93 percent) as their white counterparts.

The population bureau report shows black progress in the sense that opportunity is there for increasing numbers of black citizens. But it also shows there is a distressing situation in which too many black citizens are overwhelmed in their efforts to break out of the ghetto and poverty.

The Chattanooga Times
Chattanooga, Tennessee, March 25, 1990

The leading killers of teen-age boys are not natural causes — cancer, heart attacks, infectious diseases — but gunshots. That's the depressing news from Health and Human Services Secretary Louis Sullivan, but it gets worse. A black male teen-ager, he said last week, is *11 times* more likely to be murdered with a gun than a white counterpart. That's not just depressing; it's a statistic that demands society's attention at all levels.

In a speech that linked firearms, race and family breakdown, Mr. Sullivan disclosed the results of a study that is both chilling in its conclusions and challenging in outlining the scope of the problem.

The leading killer of young black males, Mr. Sullivan said, is young black males. As a black man and a father of three, he said, "this reality shakes me to the core of my being." All of us should share that sentiment because these statistics cannot be considered in isolation. The carnage that stalks young black males — indeed, all young American males — will eventually stalk us all.

The study by HHS's National Center for Health Statistics showed that the firearm death rate among teen-agers increased by more than 40 percent between 1984 and 1988. That means firearms killed more black and white male teen-agers than all natural causes. In 1988, the study reported, a white male age 15 to 19 was 11 percent more likely to die from a bullet than a disease. A black male teen-ager was nearly three times more likely.

In that same year, 1,641 Americans in the 15-19 age bracket died in homicides by firearms. When firearm deaths from accidents and suicides are added, the toll rises to 3,226. In the last two years, the situation has gotten much worse.

Statistics can be mind-numbing, but Mr. Sullivan sought to illustrate the problem in more understandable terms.

"During every 100 hours on our streets," he said, "we lose three times more young men than were killed in 100 hours of ground war in the Persian Gulf. Where are the yellow ribbons of hope and remembrance? . . . Where is the concerted, heartfelt commitment to supporting the children of this war?"

Where indeed? In a telling omission, Mr. Sullivan declined to discuss any attempt at gun control, even the relatively innocuous proposal to mandate waiting periods for handgun purchases. Rep. Edward Feighan, D-Ohio, said he hoped the information in the secretary's speech "will persuade some in his administration to support handgun control."

Good luck. Mr. Feighan is the lead sponsor of waiting-period legislation, but the Bush administration, as usual, opposes it.

Obviously that legislation, while helpful, will not cure the deadly "disease" of handgun deaths that is wreaking havoc among our teen-age population, not to mention older Americans as well. The root causes of the carnage are social, economic, racial, moral; they can only be defeated, or at least contained, by a far-reaching commitment at all levels of society.

Just as obviously the federal government has to commit more than words to the battle. Mr. Sullivan said he believed the federal government's role "should be to encourage and assist the spread of local indigenous" community organizations that combat crime and try to restore families. That's good, but not good enough. Those organizations lack the resources and the expertise to try to control the vast traffic in handguns and automatic weapons that are easily available — and easily used — on our streets today. Until the administration gets serious about that, speeches by its officials will remain simply "sound and fury, signifying nothing."

The Des Moines Register

Des Moines, Iowa,
May 14, 1987

President Reagan told a group of college students that blacks in the United States have made "great strides" in the last two decades and that focus should be on black successes rather than problems.

But the president did not mention that those success stories are largely a result of policies enacted by previous administrations and severely undermined by his own.

Reagan applauded civil-rights legislation, but failed to mention that his administration has consistently opposed affirmative-action cases in the Supreme Court. He endorsed statutes that "outlawed" racism, but did not mention his opposition to imposing sanctions against the apartheid government in South Africa.

Reagan then praised the Rev. Martin Luther King Jr. but did not talk about his own efforts to prevent a holiday from being named in honor of King.

These inconsistencies may only be examples of Reagan's propensity to ignore bad news. But they also indicate the Reagan administration's failure to deal with the systemic problems faced by poor, inner-city blacks.

Of course, great strides have been made in the last two decades, evidenced by the growing black middle and upper classes. But there are millions more who remain trapped in poverty, with little chance of climbing out.

Census figures show that the number of poor whites declined in the last decade by 18 percent to around 2 million, while the number of poor blacks rose 18 percent to more than 3 million. Unemployment among blacks is twice that of whites, and more than one million blacks live in extreme poverty, compared to 260,000 whites.

Meanwhile, federal welfare assistance to the working poor and to poor students has declined or been eliminated by the Reagan administration.

These are not statistics anyone expects a president to cite during a commencement speech. But for the millions of black youths living in poverty with little opportunity to attend college, they are a daily reality that cannot be ignored.

Lincoln Journal

Lincoln, Nebraska, August 18, 1991

President Bush's nomination of Clarence Thomas to the U.S. Supreme Court has divided the nation's black citizens. In that division can be read a number of telling subtexts.

One with large relevance but only modestly understood is how the nation's black population is being stretched apart and segmented.

As never before, socioeconomic divisions are tearing at the African-American community. Particularly is this so when racial discrimination is a declining factor limiting or barring educational, employment and housing opportunities.

Recently the Population Reference Bureau, a private organization, drew a statistical profile of "African Americans in the 1990s." What that etching reveals is a rapidly increasing diversity, and a polarization along the lines of class, as has long existed in the majority white population.

During the 1980s, the number of black Americans living in urban poverty soared by 49 percent. The stories of black hopelessness in metropolitan centers span the continent. Homicide is the leading cause of death of young African-American males. They also have the highest unemployment and school dropout rates.

But in the same decade, the number of black families in the $50,000 and above classification doubled. Average earnings for college-educated black married couples, the study projects, is now 93 percent of what it is for comparable white college-educated married couples.

The critical elements, obviously, are a solid martial status and educational attainments. Median income for single, female-headed (and poverty-afflicted) black households was found to be about $9,500, contrasted with $32,000 for two-parent black households with children.

Which kids have the heaviest clouds weighting their future? The question hardly has to be asked.

The gloomy news of stratification is summarized in the report: "These stark differences [in income, education, home ownership] highlight the two separate worlds inhabited by poor and middle-class black children, and suggest that the African-American population will become more polarized as these children mature."

That prospect cannot be seen, in any way, as in the national interest for Americans of all racial backgrounds.

Post-Tribune

Gary, Indiana, August 14, 1991

A recent study on black Americans paints a picture that is both encouraging and disheartening.

More than 1 million black families now earn more than $50,000. That's 14 percent of all black families and nearly triple the number that were in that rarefied income stratum in 1970.

Yet, the number of black families living in the poorest sections of the inner city rose by 49 percent during the same 20-year period. The number of black families earning less than $10,000 per year — one in every four — also increased.

It's obvious that some blacks with education and technical skills are being permitted to sup at the table on which is spread the American Dream. Too many others, though, are still being fed the scraps from the table. Others, still, aren't even allowed into the kitchen.

> **Our opinion**
>
> **Some blacks with education and technical skills are being permitted to sup at the table on which is spread the American Dream; others aren't.**

The disparity that led the Kerner Commission to report in 1968 that America was becoming two societies — one black, one white, separate and unequal — still exists. Now though, like a giant amoeba, one of those societies has split in two and created its own disparate society.

Myriad reasons exist for this frightful — and the situation is nothing less than frightful — trend: corporate mercenaries who transferred tens of thousands of industrial jobs from the cities to suburbs or to other countries to exploit cheap labor, racism, an inadequate educational system and a welfare system that too often encourages and rewards slothfulness.

The consequences of having an entire generation of people locked out of a society in any meaningful way — with scarcely a dream of rising — are too dire to ignore.

People without a stake in society have no reason to care.

As Langston Hughes asked, "What happens to a dream deferred? Does it dry up like a raisin in the sun or fester like a sore — and then run? Does it stink like rotten meat or crust and sugar over like a syrupy sweet? Maybe it just sags like a heavy load? Or does it explode?"

Yes, eventually.

The Miami Herald

Miami, Florida, October 9, 1990

NOW THAT there is empirical evidence as to the dire economic status of blacks living in the Miami-Fort Lauderdale area, who's going to do what about it? A recent study by the University of Michigan's Population Studies Center says that blacks here are excruciatingly poorer than their counterparts in nine other urban centers with sizable black populations.

Keep in mind, of course, that the statistics from across the country are nothing to crow about either: In Detroit, blacks' per-capita income of $8,460 is just 55 percent that of whites; in Washington, D.C., blacks' $13,153 is 63 percent of whites' income.

But the $6,154 that blacks in the Miami-Fort Lauderdale area earn — a basement-level 40 percent of whites' $15,322 — delivers a particularly galling, but not too surprising, sting. Blacks and nonblacks alike who plan to stay in the area — and a lot don't — can continue to blame racism, immigrants, and lack of self-determination.

These things all go into the mix, but none is the sole reason.

Progress isn't made by looking for blame, anyway. Progress is made by declaring what is to be achieved and going for it. And rarely is that kind of progress made without a fight on the part of blacks seeking access, and hardly ever because nonblacks think that it's the right thing to do.

When the persistent ethnic fissures widen into major, earth-grinding faults, the cry for racial and ethnic unity resounds from the pulpits, the boardrooms, and the newsrooms of this community. Always on our lips, never achieved. It is not the worst of track records, though. Is there a major urban area in this country that actually can claim that true unity reigns?

Perhaps the call for unity needs replacing by a call for a commitment to achieving parity. It suggests more than feel-good sentiments. It suggests the determination — which is parent to the ability — to achieve tangible results despite daunting odds.

DAYTON DAILY NEWS

Dayton, Ohio, August 16, 1991

If Dayton's 1,000 Black Males Summit can become a national model, good for the local organizers and participants.

Local activists know that the educational, social and employment problems many black men face are enormous. One challenge is tied to another. In the thicket of problems, it is hard sometimes to know where to start chopping.

On Wednesday, the chairman of the local effort, Ricky Boyd, discussed Dayton's black males' summit before the national convention of the Southern Christian Leadership Conference in Birmingham, Ala. Dayton's summit began with a community-wide conference at UD Arena on July 13. About 1,600 people showed up, and Dick Gregory took hold of the audience.

Now the summit — as the organization is called — is having hearings to listen, get ideas and work up an agenda before the next summit Oct. 12. The focus is sound: that black males locally have to organize and work to overcome the heightened risks they face.

Dayton's black community several years ago started Parity 2000, which had hundreds of people brainstorm and ended up focusing on a strategy for economic development and self-sufficiency.

In time, it will be clearer whether the summit can actually make headway against a problem that is serious, and do it in a way that Parity 2000 does not. Still, the acceptance of responsibility is the way to start.

ST. LOUIS POST-DISPATCH

St. Louis, Missouri, January 15, 1991

The National Urban League's latest review of problems affecting African-Americans couldn't be more timely. It comes as the nation slides into a recession, when the consequences are likely to be more devastating for blacks than they are for others, mainly because black communities in general tend to experience recession-level unemployment even during the best of economic times.

That's why the Urban League's director, John E. Jacob, has sounded the alarm. He pointed out that in this recession, blacks are certain to be among the first to face hardships because they were among the last to enter the labor force. In that sense, the downturn will widen the already yawning gap between the incomes of blacks and whites.

The Urban League's review points out that no major initiatives have been undertaken in more than a decade to bridge that gap. It adds that the neglect has allowed a host of social problems, including homelessness, drug abuse, inadequate

health care and crime, to continue to inflict deeper wounds on blacks than on other Americans.

Some type of anti-recessionary program, Mr. Jacob argues, will be needed to bring jobs to communities hurt most by the economic downturn. Meanwhile, the head of the local Urban League, James H. Buford, points out that a nation that can bail out S&Ls ought to be able to rescue economically hard-pressed urban communities.

The recession heightens public awareness that inner cities still are the first to catch pneumonia whenever the economy sneezes. This results because of the lingering disparity in the black-white income and employment rates.

Such a disparity means the nation must do more, through public works programs, job training and affirmative action, to prevent blacks from falling further behind during this recession — and after it is over.

THE ROANOKE TIMES

Roanoke, Virginia, March 3, 1991

BLACK and, sometimes, Hispanic children in America are far more likely than white kids to be born at low weights, or to lack health insurance, or to die young, or to live in poverty.

Such results, from a study by The Center for the Study of Social Policy, come perhaps as no surprise to most people. But don't assume too much. The study explodes a few myths, too.

■ Myth: Black and Hispanic babies are likelier than white babies to die before their first birthday.

Fact: This is true for blacks, whose 1988 infant-mortality rate (17.6 per 1,000 live births) was more than double the rate for whites (8.5). But the rate for Hispanics (8.1) was better than for whites.

■ Myth: The chief cause in the rise of out-of-wedlock births in America is that more babies are being born to unwed black teens.

Fact: During the '80s, out-of-wedlock teen births as a percentage of all births declined among blacks. The increase occurred among whites (up 25 percent) and Hispanics (up 20 percent). By decade's end, however, the percentage of out-of-wedlock teen births among blacks was still nearly four times that of whites.

■ Myth: Black teen-agers always have been likelier to die from violence or an accident than white teen-agers.

Fact: This has become true only in recent years. In 1989, black teens were 25 percent more likely to meet such an end than white teens. But as late as 1984, black teen-agers were less likely than white teen-agers to die of non-natural causes.

■ Myth: The growth in the number of impoverished children during the '80s occurred principally among minorities.

Fact: While black and Hispanic children at the end of the '80s were far more likely than white children to live in poverty, as was also the case at the beginning of the decade, white kids during the '80s slipped into poverty at about the same rate as black and Hispanic kids.

The truly sobering statistic is the growth in the number of impoverished children of all ethnic backgrounds. At the beginning of the '80s, fewer than one in six children lived in poverty; 10 years later, the number had grown to more than one in five.

While the economy as a whole was growing and some were growing richer, children became the most impoverished population in our society. And why not? They're the most vulnerable. They don't vote. They're natural victims of a decade's skewed priorities.

Congress Upholds Bush's Civil Rights Bill Veto

The House Oct. 17, 1990 gave final approval to a major civil rights bill that was designed to modify or reverse several recent Supreme Court rulings that had made it more difficult for women and minorities to win job discrimination suits. The Senate had given its approval to the measure Oct. 16.

The vote in the House was 273 to 154, and in the Senate, 62 to 34. Both votes were short of the two-thirds majority needed to overcome a veto. President George Bush had threatened to veto the bill, arguing that it could force employers to adopt hiring "quotas" for minority employees.

Both houses approved a version of the bill that had been worked out by a conference committee after each house had passed its own version. The conference committee had sought to overcome some of President Bush's objections to the bill by easing the burden of proof on employers who were sued for job discrimination. In the final legislation, workers who sued for discrimination would be required to cite specific practices that excluded women and minorities. Employers who could prove that the practices were not intended to discriminate would not be liable for damages.

Despite the changes, President Bush said Oct. 16 that the bill was "neither sound nor practical" and added, "I will be compelled to veto it."

President Bush Oct. 22 vetoed the Civil Rights Act of 1990, saying it would "introduce the destructive force of quotas" in the workplace. The legislation had cleared Congress five days earlier.

An attempt to override the veto in the Senate Oct. 24 fell one short of the necessary two-thirds majority. In the vote, 66-34, all 55 Democrats in the Senate were joined by 11 Republicans to override the veto. Supporters of the legislation picked up one more vote than had been cast in approval of the measure in July. Sen. Rudy Boschwitz (R, Minn.), who voted against the bill originally, switched sides and voted to overturn the veto.

"I deeply regret having to take this action with respect to a bill bearing such a title," Bush said in casting the 15th veto of his presidency, "especially since it contains provisions that I strongly endorse."

But the measure "employs a maze of highly legalistic language to introduce the destructive force of quotas into our national employment system," he said.

Equal opportunity, he said, was "thwarted," not served, by quotas, and "the very commitment to justice and equality that is offered as the reason why this bill should be signed requires me to veto it."

Bush said the "incentives" for quotas in the legislation were "created by [its] new and very technical rules of litigation, which will make it difficult for employers to defend legitimate employment practices."

Senate Minority Leader Robert Dole (R, Kan.) stressed the issue Oct. 24 in urging the chamber to uphold the veto. The bill, Dole said, would result in "quotas, quotas and more employment quotas."

Sen. Orrin G. Hatch (R, Utah), leading the fight to uphold the veto, said the civil rights bill would cause "tension and discord in the workplace" by promising "preferential treatment on the basis of race, ethnicity, color, religion and gender for some Americans."

Democrats saw it otherwise. Sen. Brock Adams (D, Wash.), in urging an override, Oct. 24 called the veto "a cold political decision" made in an attempt to curry favor with "conservative, Democratic blue-collar workers."

President Bush proposed Oct. 20 an alternative bill that put the burden on the individual to prove discrimination and allowed more leeway for companies to defend their employment practices.

In addition, the administration bill put a ceiling of $150,000 on compensatory and punitive damages, and restricted the awarding of damages only to deter an employer from discrimination in the future.

Civil rights leaders rejected Bush's alternative bill as a "sham."

The Des Moines Register

Des Moines, Iowa, October 8, 1990

President Bush used a veto threat to force changes in important civil-rights legislation, yet despite Congress' willingness to make those changes, Bush continues to hold out the threat. That leaves lawmakers with one choice — pass the Civil Rights Restoration Act of 1990 over the president's head if necessary.

The act would reverse five U.S. Supreme Court rulings issued in 1989, in which the court grievously misread the meaning of landmark civil-rights legislation and years of previous court decisions.

Critics have attacked provisions in the legislation aimed at the court's 1989 Wards Cove Packing Co. vs. Antonio ruling, which made a subtle yet important change in how Title VII of the Civil Rights Act is enforced. They say the new law is a "Quota Bill."

That's unfair. The bill would restore the law to be read as the courts had read it for nearly 20 years before the Wards Cove decision, which shifted to employees the burden of proving that an employer's practices have a "disparate impact" on minority groups.

The new legislation would shift the burden back to the employer. The president and business groups characterize that as forcing employers to hire a certain percentage of minority employees to equate with their numbers in the general population.

That's a gross oversimplification. A straight demographic comparison is not used, but a comparison of employment figures with the *pool of qualified applicants*. Moreover, a statistical imbalance by itself proves nothing: The bill gives the employer great latitude to defend any imbalance as a business necessity.

Administration critics and business groups suggest that the legislation is somehow an effort to open the door to whole new generations of costly and unnecessary discrimination lawsuits. That is just not true. The bill merely restores the congressional intent, as expressed 25 years ago.

If Congress believes now as it did then in the importance of legislation to make the workplace fair and open to all Americans, it will pass this act to make sure those laws are properly enforced.

THE CHRISTIAN SCIENCE MONITOR
Boston, Massachusetts, October 26, 1990

PERHAPS President Bush truly does want, as he says, to sign a bill attacking discrimination in the workplace; and maybe he vetoed the Civil Rights Act of 1990 with genuine reluctance in hopes that an even better bill would be forthcoming from Congress. Maybe he honestly thinks that the bill would result in jobs quotas for minorities and women and therefore would itself be discriminatory.

It's troubling, though, that the White House has put forth no credible evidence in support of its professed objections to the bill that passed both houses of Congress by wide margins. Besides labeling the act a quotas bill, the administration contends that it would set off an avalanche of opportunistic litigation by fee-mad lawyers. But where's the proof?

The bill reverses or modifies six Supreme Court decisions that made it harder for plaintiffs to win lawsuits claiming discrimination in hiring or promotions. It also expands compensatory and punitive damages available to victims of job discrimination.

President Bush contends that the bill unfairly stacks the deck against employers defending such suits, and that to avoid costly litigation companies will quietly adopt quotas ensuring that their workforces mirror the surrounding population.

A key section of the bill would reinstate a 1971 ruling by the Supreme Court that placed the burden on employers to prove that seemingly discriminatory hiring practices were justified by business necessity. If quotas are the inevitable result, there should be a pattern of quotas in the wake of the 1971 decision. The administration has been unable to identify such a pattern, however. The same is true of provisions Bush says would detonate a litigation explosion: Similar anti-bias provisions in other statutes have not had the bugabooed effect.

With the Senate's failure Wednesday to override the veto, this useful corrective legislation is dead, for now. Too bad. The president acted on either faulty advice or faulty instincts. He may pay a political price.

THE TENNESSEAN
Nashville, Tennessee, October 24, 1990

WHEN does a law become a quota? The sad answer this week: whenever President Bush says it does.

Claiming that the legislation established quotas, President Bush became the third president of the United States to veto civil rights legislation. The previous two presidents, Mr. Ronald Reagan and Mr. Andrew Johnson, had their vetoes overridden. Mr. Bush's veto won't be — and he's going to have to live with it throughout his political career.

From the beginning, the intent of the Civil Rights Act of 1990 was to undo the damage done by six recent Supreme Court decisions that made it easier for an employer to get away with job discrimination.

One of the decisions says that it wasn't enough for employees to prove that discrimination had occurred, they had to be able to document each act of discrimination. Another decision shifts the burden of proof on discrimination from the employer to the employee. If a business, for example, claims it can't hire women for a job because they aren't strong enough, the business used to have to prove it needed those qualifications. The Supreme Court last year said that the employee charging discrimination had to prove the qualifications weren't necessary.

This year's civil rights legislation revoked those decisions by adding details to the Civil Rights Act of 1964. It would ban racial harassment. It would extend job protections now given blacks to women and other racial and religious minorities. In the worse cases, it would allow for a jury trial to determine if punitive damages were in order.

Nothing in the six lawsuits before the U.S. Supreme Court had anything to do with quotas. The Supreme Court, in reaching its decisions, had no reason to bring up quotas.

And the bill that Mr. Bush vetoed doesn't call for quotas. In fact, it expressly says that it is not calling for quotas.

But Mr. Bush argues otherwise. He says that the language in the legislation would make it so easy for an employee to sue a business for discrimination that all businesses would initiate hiring quotas to protect themselves.

That may sound logical — until you look at the past. The Civil Rights Act of 1964 didn't result in a slew of businesses initiating quotas. And earlier Supreme Court rulings that interpreted the law didn't result in quotas.

If the 1964 law and the subsequent court decisions didn't magically result in scores of companies initiating quotas to protect themselves, why should the Civil Rights Act of 1990? It wouldn't, and the White House knows it.

This bill's sponsors were aware of Mr. Bush's concerns about the legislation all along. They wanted it passed so badly that they revised it, amended it, compromised on it, and rewrote parts of it, just so Mr. Bush would sign it.

Why he didn't is a mystery. Mr. Bush has conferred with many civil rights leaders on this and other matters. He has also tried to win over more minorities to Republican ranks.

Perhaps he is still trying to woo back Reagan Republicans who were so displeased with his appointment of Mr. David Souter.

Only President Bush knows his motive. But try as he may, this veto won't be remembered as quota veto, but as a civil rights veto. And on that score, Andrew Johnson and Ronald Reagan aren't such good company to share. ■

THE SACRAMENTO BEE
Sacramento, California, October 26, 1990

TUESDAY's headlines went to President Bush's veto of the civil rights bill, which the Senate on Wednesday failed to override by one vote. That one crucial vote for justice could have been Sen. Pete Wilson's, but Wilson voted for fear rather than hope.

Still, the real news on civil rights may be coming from North Carolina, where Sen. Jesse Helms, running for his third term, is trailing his black opponent, Harvey Gantt, by 4 to 8 points, and from Oregon, where a jury ordered a bunch of racists to pay $12.5 million in civil damages for inciting the fatal beating of a black man.

Neither of those things proves anything conclusively. Helms may yet win, in part because of covert racism, and the judgment in Oregon is on an act so heinous that the sum awarded, however large, doesn't testify to any particular degree of racial tolerance. Yet both events suggest, as did last year's election of Douglas Wilder in Virginia and David Dinkins in New York, that in vetoing a civil rights bill that would have done no more than restore legal employment rights to where they had been for nearly 20 years, Bush is behind, not ahead, of the times.

There is a lot of confusion about the civil rights bill. Its prime purpose was to nullify six Supreme Court rulings that had made it far harder and, in some cases, impossible to prove racial or gender discrimination in employment and promotion and, in one outrageous decision, seemed to tolerate racial harassment on the job. The vetoed bill also would have made it possible for juries to award compensatory and punitive damages in cases of intentional discrimination based on gender or religion.

The White House wants to limit such damages to $150,000; it also wants to allow discrimination prompted by "legitimate community or consumer relationship efforts." That means that a company can refuse to hire blacks or Catholics on no ground other than that customers don't like dealing with them, which, of course, is precisely the argument that Southern employers, including school districts, once used to justify whites-only hiring policies.

The president is entirely justified in opposing quotas in hiring and promotion, but this bill no more imposes quotas than did the laws and decisions, going back to 1970, that the Reagan Supreme Court overturned. Indeed, it contains a set of protections written specifically in response to White House demands. But each accommodation, according to congressional negotiators, brought new demands from the president.

A considerable number of congressional Republicans supported the bill, as did the senior black members of Bush's own administration, who pleaded with the president not to veto it. Bush wants credit for leadership on civil rights, but when it comes to action, he is pathetically behind the parade.

The Wichita Eagle-Beacon

Wichita, Kansas, October 24, 1990

From the very beginning, cynicism tainted the debate over the Civil Rights Act of 1990, which President Bush vetoed on Monday. The bill's supporters offered a vision of an American workplace so hostile to minorities that only the heavy hand of the federal government could ensure that jobs are allocated fairly. Its opponents offered a vision of a workplace so receptive to minorities that the heavy hand of the federal government could only be counterproductive.

Each side cared only about forcing the other to accept its version of reality, and not about bargaining in good faith. So the civil rights debate somehow never got around to defining exactly what job-discrimination problems exist in the American workplace, let alone to crafting workable remedies. The proponents and opponents of the bill became so wrapped up in bashing and discrediting each other that the poor ordinary citizen, watching from the sidelines, didn't know who or what to believe.

Certainly, there was merit in the bill's original objective of overturning six U.S. Supreme Court decisions that had the net effect of reducing minority workers' rights to win damages for job discrimination. But the coalition of senators and representatives led by Sen. Edward Kennedy, D-Mass., and Rep. Augustus Hawkins, D-Calif., who wrote the bill and guided it through Congress, wanted to go much farther than restoring the legal status quo ante. They insisted on new language that would have had the net effect of making it even easier for minority workers to win discrimination lawsuits than it had been before the Supreme Court decisions.

This, in turn, caused opponents to charge that the Kennedy-Hawkins faction was trying to force American employers to adopt minority hiring quotas. Rightly, they pointed out that most American employers have come to understand that sex and race discrimination in hiring is bad business. How can it be otherwise when white males are a minority in the national labor market, when women and minorities are just as likely to have the skills employers need?

However, the opponents, led by the national business community, never acknowledged that pockets of job discrimination remain, and that as a matter of simple justice, discrimination victims deserve due process — a chance to fight back. They, too, claimed to want to undo the damage done by the Supreme Court. But based on the way they lobbied against the bill, one can't help suspecting they're not sorry that Mr. Bush sent the whole bill down in flames. They seemed to want that all along.

Mr. Bush's veto, then, is probably for the good. Let the 102nd Congress start over in January, and let the 1991 civil rights debate be conducted honestly instead of cynically.

Herald News

Fall River, Massachusetts, October 26, 1990

The Civil Rights Act of 1990 seems bound to fail as Congress winds down to adjournment in this session.

Last week, the bill was approved by the House, 273-154, and the Senate, 62-34. But proponents of the bill were doubtful that they could muster votes to override the veto that President Bush, true to his warning, imposed Monday.

Actually, the purpose of the measure is consistent with the long-evolving progress of anti-discrimination legislation. It would modify or negate six recent Supreme Court decisions that made it harder for minorities to file and win lawsuits that allege workplace discrimination.

The bill was sponsored in the Senate by our own Sen. Edward Kennedy, and in the House by Rep. Augustus Hawkins (D-Calif.)

Bush has been under fire for vacillation in the federal budget stalemate. He whiffled, compromised, declared "Enough is enough," and then signed a new extension.

But at least Bush kept the hot potato bouncing back to his Democratic adversaries. The U.S. Government stayed in business while the wearisome budget game dragged into the longest overtime since World War II.

In contrast, the civil rights legislation was blocked because Bush, returning to what Emerson would have called 'a foolish consistency,' harped on a single word: "Quota." Bush said he regretted the veto, but "When our efforts, however well-intentioned, result in quotas, equal opportunity is not advanced, but thwarted." He meant that the proposed civil rights measure would make employers so subject to discrimination suits that they would hire by quotas in defense.

Many observers, including *The New York Times* and *The Boston Globe,* reproached Bush for quibbling on the so-called quota issue, and trying to affix a false label.

The measure, attempting to correct what activists had regarded as civil rights setbacks implied in the Court's 1989 decisions, clearly bans racial harrassment in the workplace and provides for punitive damages in extreme cases of discrimination.

Bush had an alternative bill to offer, giving businesses a broader base of defense in suits involving unintentional discrimination against women and religious minorities. Such vague categories as "customer relations" could be used to maintain questionable hiring practices; total damages any employee could win in a job discrimination suit would be capped at $150,000. Democrats regarded Bush's proposal as retrogressive even in terms of current law.

Democrats would show better strategy if they did not exploit the image of Bush as a foe of civil rights just before the elections, thus polarizing a debate that might have had a dim possibility of becoming a compromise.

Bush proclaims his support of civil rights with more credibility than Ronald Reagan did. Yet in any laissez-faire view of the free market system, business can't flourish under too many laws, or too many lawsuits. However, if basic principles of justice were mutually observed, neither would be necessary.

Even some Republicans are rebuking Bush for being stubborn on a major civil rights bill, and tarnishing his "kinder, gentler" image. On Tuesday, when Bush was stumping in Vermont for GOP candidates, Republican Rep. Peter Smith underscored "specific disagreements" on civil rights and taxes.

And Sen. Paul Simon, (D-Ill.) expressed the thoughts of many working-class Americans when he he called the president's veto "disturbing and difficult to understand."

The Record

Hackensack, New Jersey, October 24, 1990

Now that President Bush has vetoed the Civil Rights Act of 1990, he should take a little time to reassure the nation that he and his administration are firmly behind civil rights for all Americans, and that he finds racism in all forms unacceptable.

Mr. Bush vetoed the civil rights measure because, he said, it would have forced business to establish hiring quotas for minorities. In doing so, however, he failed to make it clear that the veto in no way signifies a retreat for the federal government's advocacy of equal rights for all people, regardless of race, sex, or religious affiliation.

Mr. Bush should make that point in the days ahead. He should also announce that he will work immediately on compromise legislation assuring equal rights in the workplace.

The Seattle Times

Seattle, Washington, October 4, 1990

PRESIDENT Bush talks a good line about civil rights; he
just isn't prepared to enforce them. His threatened veto of
the Civil Rights Act of 1990 defies reason and the will of
most Americans.

The House and Senate are now prepared to pass the
legislation after making some tough compromises. In particular, the conference committee agreed to cap punitive damages
at $150,000 in cases where intentional job discrimination is
proven. The cap, resisted by some Democrats, should erase
employer fears of multimillion-dollar awards for wrongdoing.

With that issue resolved, the act is expected to pass both
houses easily. Its purpose is to restore the laws that governed
the workplace for 18 years before the U.S. Supreme Court
struck them down in a handful of 5-4 votes in 1989.
Specifically, the act shifts the burden back to employers (where
it has been since 1971) to show that employment practices
which deny jobs to women or minorities have a "significant
relationship" to successful job performance.

Bush insists the act will promote racial quotas. He has no
evidence that businesses created quotas in the past or had
trouble coping with civil-rights standards throughout the 1970s
and 1980s. Yet he is willing to allow long-standing protections
to be dismantled.

To reassure Bush, the act has been drafted with specific
language that rejects any quota requirements, makes clear
mere statistical imbalance in a workforce is not sufficient
evidence of a violation, and allows punitive damages only in
intentional discrimination cases.

What more does Bush want? It's time he joined civil-rights
advocates and enlightened business leaders to support,
essentially, the previous status quo.

"Conservatism" at times means retaining policies that work.
A mindless, stubborn veto by Bush on the Civil Rights Act will
betray the support he's enjoyed among minorities and his own
party's ideals.

The News Journal

Wilmington, Delaware, October 24, 1990

Supporters of the failed Civil Rights Act of 1990
pledge to return in January with an anti-bias package even tougher than the one spiked by President
Bush and the Senate last week. All the better.

The way things have been going for Mr. Bush and
his Republican Party, there might be enough turn-
over among civil rights opponents next week to ensure passage of a stronger civil rights bill.

That would be just what the David Dukes of the
world deserve — a civil rights bill that, if flawed, was
flawed on the side of fairness, dignity and human decency.

Plain and simple, Mr. Bush's veto last week of the
1990 bill was nothing more than paper-thin demagoguery in its worst incarnation.

He painted the measure as a "quota bill" — short-
hand for "handout to unqualified minorities" —
when it clearly wasn't. Compromise had produced
clear language specifically rejecting quotas.

He painted the bill as some bonanza for lawyers,
when it was no such thing. Ever see a lawyer's advertisement — soliciting civil rights suits? You don't because such cases are very labor intensive, seldom accompanied by big cash awards, and can drag on for
years. This bill wouldn't have changed that.

Unfortunately, though, a Republican-led contingent in the Senate, given ample cover by the president's mischaracterizations, upheld his veto. The effort to override failed by a single vote.

So we'll have to wait to close loopholes that weakened anti-bias measures already on the books; wait to
raise the ante for those who discriminate; wait before
making discrimination a less attractive proposition.

Supreme Court Act Limits
'65 Voting Rights Act

The Supreme Court Jan. 27, 1992 ruled, 6-3, that county commissions in two Alabama counties did not need federal court approval under the 1965 Voting Rights Act to reorganize or diminish the authorities of individual commissioners. It was the first time the high court had adopted a narrow interpretation of the 1965 law.

The court's decision came in cases against two separate counties. The cases, which had been consolidated, were *Presley v. Etowah County Commission* and *Mack v. Russell County Commission*.

The Voting Rights Act was designed to protect against voting rights inequities in historically segregated areas. Section 5 of the law required nine states, including Alabama, and parts of several other states to obtain approval from a federal court or the Justice Department before adopting any new "practice or procedure with respect to voting."

In the case before the court, blacks had been elected to previously all-white county boards. Following the elections, white incumbents on the boards had voted to reorganize their structures and strip individual commissioners of their historic budgetary authority over roads. (In both counties, the commissioners' main function had been to supervise and control road maintenance, repair and construction.)

The reorganizations had been carried out without prior federal approval. The Justice Department and the Bush administration had argued that federal approval of the shifts of power was necessary. The U.S. District Court for the Middle District of Alabama had ruled that such approval was not needed.

In an opinion written by Justice Anthony M. Kennedy, the court affirmed the district court's ruling and offered a narrow interpretation of the Voting Rights Act. The high court ruled that measures that curtailed the authority of elected officials but did not affect voting or the creation or abolition of elective offices were not subject to federal supervision.

The court's decision did not overturn any of its voting-rights precedents, but it marked a retreat from its previous position. In its 1969 *Allen v. State Board of Elections* ruling, the court had said the Voting Rights Act "should be given the broadest possible scope."

THE PLAIN DEALER

Cleveland, Ohio, February 2, 1992

The Supreme Court has provoked alarming new doubts about its commitment to civil rights, now that it has retreated from its traditional, principled interpretation of the federal Voting Rights Act of 1965. All voters who value racial fairness must be astonished by the Rehnquist Court's latest misjudgment: By adopting a crabbed view of the voting-rights law — a view that had been rejected even by the Bush administration — the Rehnquist Court last week may have opened the way for abuses of minority rights in white-majority districts.

The Voting Rights Act, which covers most states in the South and many urban areas in the North, forbids local governments from adopting any "practice or procedure with respect to voting" without receiving prior federal approval. But two counties in Alabama, where white majorities have deplorable histories of ignoring minority rights, have evaded the law.

After voters elected the first black county commissioners in Etowah and Russell counties, the departing all-white boards suddenly changed the county's rules. Without federal approval, the white lawmakers shifted part of the county's budget-making authority, removing it from the new black lawmakers' jurisdiction.

Bush's Justice Department joined the black officials in denouncing the white lawmakers' ploy. But a 6-3 majority of the Supreme Court upheld the white lawmakers' obvious effort to strip some power from the black officials.

Ruling that "the Voting Rights Act is not an all-purpose anti-discrimination statute," the Rehnquist majority scorned the federal government's "intrusive mechanisms" that enforce the law. Justice Anthony M. Kennedy insisted that the law applies to any kind of local change "with respect to voting," whereas the Alabama ploy was an abuse "with respect to governance." Quibbling with that phrase, the court reversed its voting-rights precedents.

The court's dissenters flayed the Rehnquist bloc's ruling for allowing a blatant voting-rights abuse to continue. Without federal oversight, "recalcitrant white majorities could be expected to devise new strategems to maintain their political power," wrote Justice John Paul Stevens. That, he wrote, is "indistinguishable from, and just as unacceptable as, gerrymandering boundary lines" or using other schemes to subvert the will of the majority of voters.

The narrow-minded decision saw the all-too-predictable split on the court. All six justices who weakened the Voting Rights Act were appointees of Ronald Reagan and George Bush; the three who held to the traditional view were appointees from the Kennedy, Nixon and Ford eras. Sadly, the newest justice, Clarence Thomas, disappointed many members of the black community by joining the Rehnquist bloc.

For all Americans, of all races, who believe in vigorous federal support for civil rights, the Rehnquist Court's anti-voting-rights ruling is a deplorable assault on an idealistic law.

Lincoln Journal

Lincoln, Nebraska, February 3, 1992

All six members of the U.S. Supreme Court who owe their exalted position to appointment by President Reagan or President Bush arguably didn't deliberately intend it but they landed a substantive, heavy blow last week to the political vitality of minority groups.

On a 6-3 division, the court approved the ability of state or local governments to redistribute political authority among elected officials so as to limit the power of minority elected officials.

Inferentially, that also means limiting the representation of minority voters.

In a pinched technical sense, the majority likely can defend itself saying that "changes which affect only the distribution of power among officials are not subject (to the act) because such changes have no direct relation to, or impact on, voting."

So the white majority in two Alabama counties will not be reversed for rewriting the ground rules on historic spending authority of their individual commissioners shortly after blacks finally were elected to the board for the first time.

But the rebuttal of Justice John Paul Stevens, speaking for himself and Justices Byron R. White and Harry A. Blackmun in dissent, rings true to editorial ears:

The majority's decision really means states and local government now are "free to . . . undermine the purpose of the (voting rights) act simply by transferring the authority of an elected official, who happens to be black, to another official or group controlled by the (white) majority."

In this fashion can the underlying foundation spirit behind the words of the civil rights law be ambushed. Remember, this was a law shaped in 1965 to attack the injustices of racial segregation.

Even the Bush administration's Justice Department held what had been the nationally accepted view, only to be rejected by the aggressively "strict-constructionist" jurists.

The Rehnquist Court already has issued more troubling decisions than this. Undoubtedly it will produce additional heartbreaks in the future. But the Alabama rulings are cause for sadness, clouding as they do a better vision of racial cooperation.

Pittsburgh Post-Gazette

Pittsburgh, Pennsylvania, February 6, 1992

The 1965 Voting Rights Act has transformed the politics of the American South by empowering black voters and black candidates for office. But can the law also serve as a check on the alleged mistreatment of black officials by their colleagues once they take office? Last week the U.S. Supreme Court said no. The decision was right as a matter of law and probably also as a matter of policy.

The case originated in two Alabama counties that had switched from at-large elections for county commissioners to a district-election system that fostered greater black representation. (Pittsburgh switched from at-large to district elections for City Council for the same reason.)

Under the at-large system, the counties paradoxically had divided their road-maintenance operations into individual districts, each supervised by a single commissioner. Recently, however, the counties switched to a system in which road projects were handled on a county-wide basis. In one county the change preceded the election of two black commissioners by seven years; in the other, the new approach followed the election of a black commissioner.

The black commissioners challenged the change in highway administration, citing a provision of the Voting Rights Act that requires most Southern states to "pre-clear" with the Justice Department or a federal court any new "practice or procedure with respect to voting."

But the Supreme Court, in a 6-3 decision, held that the pre-clearance provision didn't apply to an internal reorganization of local-government procedures. Speaking for the court, Justice Anthony Kennedy said that "the Voting Rights Act is not an all-purpose anti-discrimination statute." In other words, the law protects the rights of voters, not those of "votees."

As an exercise in legal interpretation, the court's conclusion is indisputable. "Voting" means "voting." But there is also a policy argument against using the Voting Rights Act to second-guess decisions made by a representative body about how it will conduct its business.

It is possible that the changes the two Alabama counties made in their highway programs were motivated by a spiteful desire to dilute the influence of present or future black commissioners. But a countywide approach to roads also makes sense from the perspective of efficiency and economy. It would be bizarre if the Voting Rights Act were used to lock in an administrative system that encouraged waste, duplication or excessive patronage.

Because of the legacy of racism in American public life, and not only in the South, Congress and the courts rightly have subjected election laws and procedures to special scrutiny to ensure that minorities have a fair chance of electing the representatives of their choice. But once those officials take office, the federal government should tread lightly.

Los Angeles Times

Los Angeles, California, February 1, 1992

The U.S. Supreme Court majority has once again shown its myopia when it comes to civil rights protections. With its decision earlier this week, six justices—including the only black, Clarence Thomas—have come up with an interpretation of the Voting Rights Act of 1965 that severely narrows the protections of the law.

Consider what the court's ruling endorsed: In Alabama, three black county commissioners were elected in two counties after at-large elections had been found to violate the Voting Rights Act. They were the first blacks elected to those posts since Reconstruction.

Before the election of the black commissioner in one county, each white commissioner had control over funds to maintain or build county roads in his or her district. Those duties represented significant political power and patronage. After his election, the four white incumbents transferred that authority to the group and imposed majority rule on new funding decisions.

In the second county, a corruption indictment prompted the transfer of authority for road maintenance to an appointed county engineer well before the election of two black commissioners. They argued that decision had been made on the basis of race.

The court ruled—in opposition to the Bush Administration—that local governments could reorganize, even in a manner that stripped authority from newly elected black officials, without the advance federal approval known as "preclearance." The preclearance requirement applies to nine states, and parts of seven others, including California.

The court's decision sends a dangerous signal to other elected officials who have no intention of sharing power with blacks or Latinos despite their gains in population. The incumbents apparently need only to change the political structure to maintain the status quo, despite any past history of discrimination.

Before the Voting Rights Act, fewer than 1,000 minority members held public office; now, there are more than 7,500 African-Americans and 4,000 Latino elected officials.

Just as Congress passed new legislation to remedy the court's weakening of protections against job discrimination, it must strengthen the Voting Rights Act.

THE CHRISTIAN SCIENCE MONITOR

Boston, Massachusetts, February 6, 1990

DESPITE its rather stingy record on civil rights during the Reagan-Bush era, the Supreme Court has unwaveringly protected the voting rights of blacks, Hispanics, and other minorities. In particular, the high court has generously interpreted and strongly enforced the 1965 Voting Rights Act.

Thus it's disappointing that the justices last week sent a message to whites in the South: You can't keep blacks from voting, but you can devalue their votes.

In two cases from Alabama, the Supreme Court ruled that governments in historically segregated areas could reallocate powers away from black officeholders without the prior approval of the federal government. The court refused to apply Section 5 of the Voting Rights Act, which requires officials in nine Southern states and designated jurisdictions in seven other states to obtain federal approval for any new "standard, practice, or procedure with respect to voting."

In both cases, black county commissioners were, as a result of government "reorganizations," stripped of commissioners' traditional control over street paving and maintenance in their districts – an important power in rural areas where many blacks still live along dirt roads.

In Russell County, Ala., soon after two blacks were elected to the county commission for the first time, the commission abolished separate road districts and gave road responsibilities to a county engineer appointed by the commission's white majority. In Etowah County, road maintenance funds previously distributed among the county commissioners were put into a common fund to be disbursed by majority vote; the change was challenged by two black commissioners elected several years later.

(It should be noted that in both counties, blacks were elected to the governing boards only after court-ordered redistricting.)

The Supreme Court ruled 6-3 that the Voting Rights Act's prior-approval requirement does not apply to local-government reorganizations like those being contested. Reallocation of authority among officials, said Justice Anthony Kennedy in his majority opinion, are not changes "with respect to voting," but rather with respect to "governance."

It's true that most practices challenged under the Voting Rights Act have related more directly to voting, such as procedures that inhibited blacks from registering or voting, or that diluted black voting power through gerrymanders and at-large districts. Even so, given all the circumstances of these two "reorganization" cases, it would not have been much of a stretch for the justices to find that the reshuffling effectively nullified black votes for commissioners.

If such blatantly evasive tactics are widespread in historically segregated communities, Congress should amend the Voting Rights Act to cover them.

Thurgood Marshall Retires; Justice Blasts Conservative Majority

Justice Thurgood Marshall June 27, 1991 announced his retirement from the Supreme Court after 24 years of service. Marshall, the first black American to sit on the Supreme Court, cited his "advancing age and medical condition" as reasons for his decision to retire. In his final dissent on the Supreme Court, Marshall blasted the court's conservative majority for what he said was recklessly overturning court precedents in the case *Payne v. Tennessee.*

In a statement issued June 27, Bush thanked Marshall for his "extraordinary and distinguished service to his country." Marshall, 82, who had repeatedly promised to remain on the court until he died, was a stalwart liberal and staunch defender of civil rights and personal liberties on the Supreme Court.

In his resignation letter, Marshall said his retirement was contingent on the confirmation of a successor. His retirement came almost exactly one year after his close friend and ideological ally Justice William J. Brennan Jr. had left the court.

Appointed to the high court in 1967 by President Lyndon B. Johnson, Marshall had a distinguished career – both before and after joining the court – that virtually traced the development of the civil rights movement in the U.S. As the chief counsel for the National Association for the Advancement of Colored People's Legal Defense and Education Fund, Marshall had argued and won the 1954 landmark school desegregation case, *Brown v. Board of Education of Topeka, Kansas,* before the Supreme Court. (Overall, Marshall had won 29 of the 32 cases he had argued before the Supreme Court.) His nomination to the Supreme Court had aroused strong objections from Republican Sen. Strom Thurmond of South Carolina and other Southern senators, but had been confirmed by a 69-11 vote of the full Senate.

After joining the court, Marshall became known for his strongly worded opinions and dissents on a range of issues. He fervently believed that the death penalty, in all cases, was wrong and should be considered cruel and unusual punishment. Marshall concurred with the majority on the 1972 decision *Furman v. Georgia* that ruled state capital punishment statutes to be unconstitutional. He dissented in the 1976 decision *Jurek v. Texas* that ruled that capital punishment was not a per se violation of the Eighth Amendment and that reinstated the death penalty as a means of punishment.

He was a strong supporter of affirmative action and an advocate of free-speech rights. He wrote the majority opinion in the 1968 *Amalgamated Food Employees Union v. Logan Valley* decision that said striking employees had the right to picket on private property that was normally open to the public.

At a news conference June 28, Marshall answered questions about his plans for the future and his decision to retire, but repeatedly avoided comments on cases or judges. He said the most important factor for deciding on a successor should be "choosing the best person for the job, not on the basis of race one way or another."

Thurgood Marshall, born in Baltimore, Md. on July 2, 1908, was the great-grandson of a slave and the son of a steward at an exclusive whites-only club. He worked his way through college at Lincoln University in Chester, Pa., and graduated first in his class from Howard University Law School in 1933.

After three years of private legal practice in Baltimore, Marshall was hired as an assistant to the national counsel of the National Association for the Advancement of Colored People (NAACP) in 1936. He became chief counsel for the NAACP Legal Defense and Education Fund in 1938.

Marshall played a major role in U.S. legal history long before his appointment to the Supreme Court, winning hundreds of civil-rights victories in 23 years as the NAACP's chief counsel.

THE KANSAS CITY STAR
Kansas City, Missouri, June 29, 1991

The best successor to Justice Thurgood Marshall on the Supreme Court would be a young, vigorous Thurgood Marshall. That is not possible. But President Bush surely can find an outstanding individual of color to reflect America's minorities on what should be the court of last resort for all Americans.

That would be both a tribute to Marshall, the only African American ever to serve on the court, and recognition of the minorities' place in this society.

Marshall had a distinctive place in history even before he was appointed to the court by President Lyndon Johnson in 1967. Marshall will be remembered as a founding father of this century's civil rights revolution.

It was the Baltimore-born lawyer who won the landmark 1954 Brown vs. Topeka Board of Education case. That Supreme Court ruling ended the "separate but equal" doctrine that had justified racial segregation in public schools.

The decision provided the legal basis for subsequent efforts to desegregate the schools, a job that remains far from finished today. But the ruling opened to the door to education, a basic requirement in the struggle for equal rights. It inspired supporters of civil rights to new expectations and goals. It showed that the system, weighted as it is for the majority, could sometimes respond favorably to the minority.

The seeds for change had been sown.

The Brown triumph won Marshall acclaim as the leading civil rights lawyer in the nation. He had devoted his career to that cause, using the legal system to break down barriers of discrimination in many areas, including housing and voting. A measure of his skill: He won 29 of 32 lawsuits he took to the Supreme Court.

Marshall's early years on the bench of the nation's highest tribunal represented a high point in American liberalism. As a member of the liberal wing of the court, Marshall helped to further the causes of individual liberty and civil rights. Many of the court's decisions during this period brought minorities closer to an equitable position in our society.

The liberal dominance on the court began to melt away in the 1970s. Marshall votes in recent years had fallen into the minority. The retirement a year ago of William J. Brennan Jr. left Marshall without the support of a valued colleague.

A conservative majority on the court is now eroding many of the gains Marshall had helped to achieve. The retirement of Marshall, 82, is distressful for those who look to the court for an advocate and defender of human rights.

Thurgood Marshall is the only member of the court who ever experienced racial discrimination. His presence brought to the court's deliberations a crucial viewpoint that is all too rare in the upper circles of the country's legal system.

President Bush should recognize this essential role as he chooses a nominee to fill the Marshall vacancy.

LEXINGTON HERALD-LEADER
Lexington, Kentucky, June 30, 1991

The retirement of Thurgood Marshall leaves more than a vacancy on the Supreme Court. It also removes an inspiring presence from the national scene.

For more than half a century, Marshall played a leading role in advocating an end to segregation and racial discrimination. As a lawyer, he argued cases that made integration possible, including the 1954 case that outlawed segregated schools. As solicitor general of the United States, he pushed forward the next generation of anti-discrimination cases. As a Supreme Court justice, he was an unwavering believer in fairness, a harsh critic of discrimination, a compassionate advocate of the idea that the law should go out of its way to render justice to the poor.

In each of these roles, Marshall stood as an example of fairness and equal opportunity. As a lawyer for the NAACP at a time when black attorneys were a rarity, he won 29 of 32 cases before the Supreme Court. He was the first black American to hold the post of solicitor general, the first to be named to the Supreme Court.

His career put the lie to racist stereotypes. And his success offered a model to the generations of black Americans who came after him.

With his retirement, the attention now shifts to questions about whom President Bush will appoint to replace him. Arguments about that can wait for another day. But it is doubtful that anyone can replace Thurgood Marshall as an advocate of justice and an inspiration to all Americans who believe in it.

THE ARIZONA REPUBLIC
Phoenix, Arizona, June 30, 1991

WHEN the complete history of 20th century America is compiled, it will require no more than a footnote to summarize the judicial accomplishments of Thurgood Marshall, the first black to sit on the U.S. Supreme Court. Yet many pages will be needed to relate how, as chief counsel for the National Association for the Advancement of Colored People, he devised the strategy and led the legal assault that ended centuries of racial segregation in the United States.

Even without Mr. Marshall's skillful and persistent efforts, Jim Crow in time would have met an inevitable, inglorious end. But segregation would have survived a while longer, with evil consequences impossible to assess. As Yale Professor Paul Gewirtz put it, Thurgood Marshall "really changed the world" — and vastly for the better.

It is a pity that such a record should have been dimmed by service on the nation's highest court. Now that he is stepping down, much ink will be spilt extolling his virtues as a justice, but such plaudits are pro forma — the kind of mindlessness that issues spontaneously from liberal law school deans and editorial writers for The Washington Post. Among those who follow the court it is scarcely a secret that Thurgood Marshall, for all his stunning qualities as a trial lawyer, was, to push charity to the limit, a mediocre justice.

Perhaps he did not, as was whispered, hole up in chambers reading comic books and watching the television soaps. But it is undeniable that, in nearly a quarter-century on the bench, he produced little of consequence. His opinions were the meanest boilerplate, offering scant insight even in those areas of the law where he was expert. To his liberal colleagues he was a mere appendage — useful not because of his intellectual power or the force of his arguments, but only because his vote could always be relied on. Most of the time

he was content to keep a close eye on Justice William J. Brennan, his polestar. During the 1980s, when Mr. Brennan dominated the court's liberal wing, Mr. Marshall voted with him no less than 94 percent of the time.

Mr. Marshall's career ought to have unfolded in reverse, because as a trial lawyer he had few equals. He was knowledgeable in the law, compellingly articulate, burning with a controlled zeal for the causes he undertook, conspicuously the repeal of segregation. On the bench, in contrast, his life approached suspended animation; he seemed to lack entirely the scholarly interest so essential on a court whose primary responsibility is to balance legal niceties and enunciate the Constitution.

He lacked other judicial qualities as well, including restraint. He declared publicly that he considered George Bush "a dead person" and that he "wouldn't do the job of dog-catcher for Ronald Reagan." He told Life magazine that "if it's a dope case, I won't even read the petition. I ain't giving no break to no drug dealer." He even disparaged the Constitution, viewing it retrospectively and pronouncing it "defective from the start" because its imperfect Framers, struggling to invent democracy, had sanctioned slavery and denied women the vote.

Yet in the long view his shortcomings as a justice will be offset by his stature as a lawyer, his weakness for the intemperate remark balanced by an appealing lack of pomposity and a self-deprecating wit. Chief Justice Warren Burger, a man ever mindful of his own standing, he once startled with, "What's shakin', Chiefie baby?" One another occasion, when a group of visitors mistook him for an elevator operator, he played along with polite amusement, giving no hint of his real identity.

George Bush will search the nation over without finding Thurgood Marshall's equal at the bar, but he should have no difficulty finding his superior on the bench.

The Evening Gazette
Worcester, Massachusetts, June 30, 1991

When President Lyndon B. Johnson nominated Thurgood Marshall for the Supreme Court in 1967, he said his nominee had already earned his place in history as the legal champion of the rights of the individual.

Justice Marshall's 24 years on the highest court have transformed that place into a monument.

The great-grandson of a slave, Marshall made his mark as director of the NAACP Legal Defense Fund, federal judge and solicitor general before becoming the first and only justice from a minority group and a powerful advocate of civil rights.

Perhaps his most memorable achievement came in 1954 when as a lawyer he successfully argued the case against school segregation. The Supreme Court decision in Brown vs. Board of Education opened a new chapter in racial progress.

The last justice appointed by a Democrat in the White House, Marshall remained a passionate defender of liberal causes. In recent years, he grew disenchanted with a court that has increasingly sided with government authority, and his frustration may have prompted his abrupt decision to retire.

His departure has a greater symbolic impact than a practical one; the court's conservative majority was effectively established with the retirement of another liberal, Justice William Brennan, last year.

But Marshall's legacy as America's legal architect of racial justice will prevail. The country is indebted to him.

The News Journal

Wilmington, Delaware, June 28, 1991

The retirement of Supreme Court Justice Thurgood Marshall, although it has been expected for some time because of his deteriorating health, inevitably wobbles a court that for 24 years has had him as an anchor holding from the left. Even though many of his opinions have come from the minority side of the high court in the past decade, his influence continues to be felt in legal circles.

Thurgood Marshall is one of the nation's great lawyers. He won 29 of 32 civil rights cases before the Supreme Court before President Lyndon B. Johnson put him on it in 1967. He has never waivered on issues of the rights of individuals, an ideology that has more and more often set him against the court's majority.

His record as a champion of individual rights made him important to the cause of abortion rights. They will view his departure with sadness and alarm. A court that may have already tilted toward striking down abortion rights in America now seems poised to tip sharply in that direction, depending on President Bush's choice of a successor.

The question of who should succeed Justice Marshall has been debated since near the end of President Jimmy Carter's tenure in office, when, with the only black justice's health already in decline, there was a short-lived boomlet to have Justice Marshall resign so that Mr. Carter could nominate another younger, and equally liberal, black jurist to replace him. Marshall would have none of it. Despite questions about his capacity to function at full steam, he hung on, thundering dissents to the rising conservatism of the court.

Although he will continue to serve until his successor is chosen, for practical purposes, yesterday was his last day on the bench. The Supreme Court will not begin to hear cases again until fall.

President Bush is now faced with the opportunity to fill the shoes of a legal lion. We urge him to look first among the many qualified minority jurists who can bring balance, fairness and substance to the court. Our top court should continue to reflect the diversity of the nation.

THE SUN HERALD

Biloxi, Mississippi, June 28, 1991

As the closing bell echoed on a U.S. Supreme Court term that issued some of the most conservative rulings in decades, the court's most liberal justice is turning in his robe.

Thurgood Marshall cited age and health reasons in his letter of resignation to President George Bush, but it is not improbable that the 82-year-old champion of civil rights has grown weary of pulling the reins to the left as the nine-member court has turned more sharply and strongly to the right.

Marshall was appointed in 1967 to a Supreme Court that was liberal and more inclined to judicial activism than to strict interpretation of the Constitution. His hand was felt as the court guided the nation through an era of landmark civil-rights decisions.

Successive Supreme Court appointees have steadily weighted the bench on the conservative side, and, more and more in recent years, the court's only black justice has filed dissenting opinions.

Marshall disagreed so vehemently with the leanings of the three high-court appointees of Ronald Reagan that he vowed to remain on the bench as long as Reagan was alive — or long enough to prevent Reagan from filling his seat on the bench. But with Bush's appointee David Souter siding more often with the conservatives, and the strong possibility of Bush holding the power to make Supreme Court appointments until Thurgood Marshall is almost 90 years old, Marshall may have reckoned that the ride would be uncomfortably long.

Few actions of an acting president of the United States touch the lives of each citizen as directly, and for as long, as the appointment of a justice to the U.S. Supreme Court. Serving until death or retirement, the justices set the precedents used as arguments in every level of our judicial system, often for many decades.

Less than a year after filling the post of another retiring justice, President Bush must look for another candidate to serve on the Supreme Court, knowing that this nominee may be making decisions long after his own term in office is history.

ARGUS-LEADER

Sioux Falls, South Dakota, June 30, 1991

In the midst of troubled times for liberals in their quest for rights on issues such as abortion, civil rights and openness in government, Thurgood Marshall on Thursday announced his retirement from the Supreme Court.

The decision by Marshall, 82, was no surprise. The only black who has served on the high court cited age and poor health as reasons for his decision.

Marshall has been a liberal's liberal on the bench, championing individual rights such as privacy and abolition of the death penalty, and defending a woman's right to an abortion.

The decision by Marshall fulfills the prophecy of judicial domination hoped for by conservatives as they elected George Bush to the presidency. The decision ignites the worst fears of liberals who warned without a listening ear in 1988 that Bush's election would mean a conservative-controlled court for generations to come.

That seemed readily apparent long before the Marshall decision.

The decision facing Bush now seems relatively easy and predictable. Yet there needs to be an obligation on the part of the president to understand this appointment far beyond the lines of liberalism and conservatism.

Marshall's role as a minority on this highest court cannot be diminished. The challenge here for Bush is to acknowledge that minority constituency in replacing Marshall.

In this nation of millions, there are many qualified minorities who should be given priority as a replacement.

This is an opportunity for the president to make good on his commitment to represent all of the people.

It is not necessary for Bush to fill Marshall's role as the embattled dissenter. It will always be acknowledged that sitting presidents shall have the option of appointing people of their philosophy. The concern here is that Bush's perception of minority problems is not as good as it could be. He needs to exercise care in this appointment so as to fill the demographic void that has been created.

A body such as the Supreme Court, charged with a responsibility to be fair and impartial, needs to have seated in its midst someone who is a voice for minorities.

This appointment, then, should not be about liberals and conservatives. It should be about fairness in representation.

That can only be achieved if the president appoints a racial minority to court. Please don't tell us there are no blacks, Hispanics, American Indians or Asians qualified for the U.S. Supreme Court.

The Seattle Times

Seattle, Washington, June 28, 1991

AN ERA passes away with the announced retirement of Justice Thurgood Marshall, the lone liberal left on the conservative Supreme Court.

As much as any single person can symbolize the expansion of human rights in America, Marshall does so. When he graduated from law school in 1933, Americans lived under a system of racial apartheid. His lawyering forced a reluctant, morally troubled nation to change.

His judicial opinions were like him: straightforward, passionate, impatient with legalese. Yet history may judge him a greater lawyer than a judge.

Marshall's reputation was built long before he donned a black robe. As chief counsel of the NAACP Legal Defense and Education Fund, he argued the 1954 Brown v. Board of Education case, which dismantled segregated school systems. In all, he argued 32 cases before the Supreme Court and won 29. He remained a powerful civil-rights advocate on the bench.

Since the Reagan era, Marshall has been a dissenter on the court, though it wasn't always this way. In the late 1960s and early 1970s, he was part of the court majority that ordered desegregation of schools and housing, declared the right of women to choose abortion, and struck down capricious state death-penalty laws.

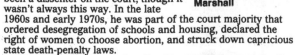

Marshall

Marshall's retirement gives President Bush the opportunity to appoint another justice. The stakes involved for human rights are immeasurably high, since Bush's first appointee, Justice David Souter, has become part of the conservative pack.

In this term alone, the court has restricted due-process rights in nearly every criminal appeal that has come before it; allowed cities to limit the right of free expression, and weakened privacy rights just short of overturning abortion rights.

It's now up to the Senate to make certain that a new nominee will champion racial equality, women's rights, and the right of the individual to be left alone by government, as Marshall has done for the past 24 years.

CHICAGO Sun-Times

Chicago, Illinois, June 30, 1991

Retiring Supreme Court Justice Thurgood Marshall says he would like his epitaph to read, "He did what he could with what he had." That too modestly describes a career that shone brilliantly over half a century.

Marshall early on developed a passionate zeal for civil rights while practicing in the courtrooms of the segregated South. By the time President Lyndon B. Johnson appointed him to the high court in 1967, Marshall had long been recognized as the most influential black lawyer in the country's history.

He had earned that distinction most signally in arguing the case that led to the 1954 Supreme Court decision outlawing racial segregation in public schools.

The first and only black ever named to the high court, Marshall wrote few majority decisions of significance, but his frequent dissents were eloquent in behalf of the poor and unprivileged.

Discussing how crucial for some could be a savings of even $2 a week or less, he wrote, "No one who has had close contact with poor people can fail to understand how close to the margin of survival many of them are." In another dissent, he argued that a majority of justices did not understand that many Americans could not afford to go to an occasional movie or buy a pack of cigarettes. He wrote: "It is perfectly proper for judges to disagree about what the Constitution requires. But it is disgraceful for an interpretation of the Constitution to be premised upon unfounded assumptions about how people live."

Within hours of Marshall's announced retirement the media became littered with demands, conditions, suggestions and whatnot about whom President Bush should appoint to his place. There were forecasts of catastrophic consequences if Bush failed to appoint someone whom this or that faction found worthy of occupying the same space Marshall has in the halls of justice.

Those interested parties now so busy speculating on and maneuvering for influence in the choice of his successor might do well to heed the example set in Marshall's own words as he announced his retirement last week.

Acknowledging that race could not be ignored altogether, he said, "The most important factor is to pick the best person for the job not on the basis of race, one way or the other." He refused to discuss the succession, saying "It is none of my business . . . I am not trying to run the country."

Justice Marshall did have a wise way of putting things into perspective. "Roosevelt and Churchill died," he said, "and the world went on." And as the world goes on, none will ever doubt the fullness of the justice's courage and effectiveness. In every way, he did what he could with what he had.

Bush Names Conservative Black Judge as Marshall Successor

President George Bush July 1, 1991 nominated conservative Judge Clarence Thomas, 43, of the U.S. District of Columbia Court of Appeals to fill the seat on the U.S. Supreme Court vacated by retiring Justice Thurgood Marshall. Bush had named Thomas, who like Marshall was black, to the appeals court in 1990. If confirmed, he would be only the second black justice to sit on the Supreme Court.

In announcing his nomination of Judge Thomas at a July 1 news conference in Kennebunkport, Me., Bush repeatedly denied that race had been a factor in the selection. Thomas, Bush said, had been a strong candidate in 1990, when Bush had nominated Justice David H. Souter to the Supreme Court.

Bush said Thomas's life and achievements made him a qualified candidate for the high court. "The fact that he's a minority, you heard his testimony, the kind of life he's had, and I think that speaks eloquently for itself. But I kept my word to the American people and to the Senate by picking the best man for the job on the merits. And the fact that he's a minority, so much the better," Bush said.

Before being appointed to the appellate bench, Thomas had headed the federal Equal Employment Opportunity Commission from 1982 to 1990. He had been appointed by President Ronald Reagan. As EEOC chief, Thomas had challenged civil rights measures, such as busing for school desegregation and workplace preferences for minorities or women.

Critics said Thomas had not vigorously attacked civil rights violations while at EEOC. Nan Aron, of the liberal Alliance for Justice, was reported July 1 as saying he had "failed to demonstrate a commitment to civil rights and liberties." In 1989, sixteen prominent House Democrats had accused him of having "demonstrated an overall disdain for the rule of law" as EEOC chairman.

Thomas's opinions on other issues that the court would likely consider in the 1991–92 term, such as abortion, church–state relations and constitutional due process, were largely unknown.

Thomas was born in Savannah, Ga. June 23, 1948. Abandoned by his father, he was raised by his mother and grandparents in the poor, predominantly black hamlet of Pinpoint, Ga. and was educated in an all-black Roman Catholic school run by white nuns. After abandoning studies for the priesthood, he graduated with honors from Holy Cross College, in Worcester, Mass., in 1971.

Thomas graduated from Yale Law School in 1974 and spent two and a half years trying cases in the Missouri attorney general's office under then–Attorney General John Danforth.

In 1990, Bush appointed Thomas to the U.S. Court of Appeals for the District of Columbia Circuit.

Thomas's nomination drew praise from conservatives who saw him as a strong choice who would add to the Supreme Court's conservative majority. Liberals and Democrats questioned his positions on key issues, especially civil rights and women's right to abortion.

On the abortion issue, Kate Michelman, executive director of the National Abortion Rights Action League, in a statement July 1, said, "The 'Souter model' of silence and evasion that we saw last year is absolutely unacceptable."

The National Organization for Women (NOW) and a number of influential liberal groups July 5 announced their opposition to the confirmation of Supreme Court nominee Clarence Thomas.

Leaders of the country's largest civil rights organization, the National Association for the Advancement of Colored People (NAACP), July 8 announced that their group would take no position on Thomas's nomination until they could meet with him and review his record as a public official.

THE SUN

Baltimore, Maryland, July 2, 1991

In nominating Judge Clarence Thomas for the Supreme Court, President Bush has chosen the most widely experienced black conservative on the short list of prospective justices who have been considered by this administration. It is a controversial choice, one that will challenge the liberal civil rights philosophy that has long prevailed among African Americans and has been articulated on the court by Justice Thurgood Marshall, whose resignation cleared the way for the Thomas selection.

Whatever the outcome of the coming Senate confirmation battle, it will provide insight into the current state of race relations and attitudes in America. Not least will be the clear contrast between Justice Marshall and the man who would succeed him. While both men experienced the wounds of segregation — Justice Marshall in the Baltimore of the 1930s, Judge Thomas in the Savannah of the 1950s — they came to different conclusions, remedies and philosophies.

Justice Marshall has long stood for integration and for group benefits and preferences to help black Americans overcome historic disadvantages. Judge Thomas has been described by a sympathetic interviewer as something of a black nationalist — a man skeptical that blacks will ever be fully accepted by whites and, therefore, a believer that blacks have to make it on their own.

The Senate will have ample opportunity to examine just how this line of thinking has affected Judge Thomas' record as a judge of the U.S. Court of Appeals and might affect his future Supreme Court opinions. As chairman in the 1980s of the Equal Employment Opportunity Commission — an agency, ironically, that grew out of the mainstream civil rights movement so closely associated with Justice Marshall — Mr. Thomas displayed vigor in prosecuting cases where individuals were victims of discrimination but drew liberal criticism for his reluctance to push group action cases.

Often before his elevation for the U.S. Court of Appeal in Washington a year ago, he displayed a conservative distaste for welfare (which he felt encourages dependency), for affirmative action (which he felt implied that blacks could not help themselves) and for black-and-white-togetherness (which he considered unrealistic). Judge Thomas is closer in approach to Booker T. Washington than to W.E.B. Dubois, to Malcolm X than to Martin Luther King Jr. He believes in black businesses, black colleges and has even been described as dubious about Brown vs. Board of Education, the landmark Supreme Court decision that ordered the desegregation of public schools.

Should Judge Thomas be confirmed, he would be joining a Supreme Court that has become solidly conservative through a barrage of Reagan-Bush nominees. Presumably he would add to the trend, but justices are hard to predict. He would also be maintaining a "black seat" on the court, though the very thought runs against his grain, and he would be restoring a "southern seat" on the court that has been vacant since the resignation of Justice Lewis F. Powell.

THE ARIZONA REPUBLIC
Phoenix, Arizona, July 11, 1991

ONE of the key questions being asked of U.S. Supreme Court nominee Clarence Thomas concerns his regard for *stare decisis*, a legal term meaning "to stand by that which has been decided." The court under this doctrine is expected to honor precedent and resist overturning earlier rulings in the absence of compelling reasons.

In recent weeks the doctrine has been elevated nearly to the status of holy writ. The wail has gone up that the Rehnquist court has embarked on a binge of precedent repeal and that Judge Thomas probably harbors scant respect for *stare decisis*.

This lament notwithstanding, constitutional law has never been characterized by homeostasis. As pointed out in yesterday's *Wall Street Journal* by former Justice Department spokesman Terry Eastland, the Supreme Court has overturned precedents, explicitly and implicitly, no fewer than 260 times since 1810. More than half of those reversals have occurred since 1953, the year Earl Warren became chief justice.

Although some have accused the Rehnquist court of "recklessly reversing precedents," Mr. Eastland demonstrates that this court has been no more prone to overturn precedent than either the Warren or Burger courts. Since 1953, he notes, the court has averaged four precedent reversals a year.

During the sessions just ended the court overturned five earlier rulings, well within the norm. In 1964 the Warren court overturned 11 precedents. Seven precedents were overturned in 1967 and six in 1968. The Burger court reversed six decisions in 1970, nine in 1976 and 11 in 1978. Strange to relate, liberal devotion to *stare decisis* was nowhere to be seen when the liberal Warren court was "recklessly" at work.

While it is true that the court should respect the wisdom of the past, declining to reverse previous rulings willy-nilly, the law is by no means static. Law must be predictable and not capricious, but it also must be flexible. Constitutional law is always being refined, clarified, modified. Mindless adherence to precedent would mean that not just accumulated wisdom would be preserved, but errors and excesses as well. Surely the court was right in 1954 to overturn the 1896 decision in *Plessy* vs. *Ferguson*, which affirmed the constitutionality of racial segregation.

One's view on *stare decisis* clearly depends on the precedents being overturned. Liberals were untroubled as long as a like-minded court was rewriting conservative decisions. Even such admired members of the court as Thurgood Marshall and retired Justice William Brennan were unwilling to support capital punishment, though it is clearly established in precedent.

Cutting through the blather about the importance of respecting precedents, what critics of the Rehnquist court and Judge Thomas are really saying is that the immutable order of the legal universe requires that the Supreme Court tilt perpetually to the left.

The Washington Times
Washington, D.C., July 3, 1991

In tapping Clarence Thomas to fill the Supreme Court seat of Thurgood Marshall, President Bush has chosen one of the most promising jurists in the nation. Despite his relatively youthful 43 years, Mr. Thomas already has shown that he possesses a brilliant legal mind and a commitment to public service in the best sense of that term.

Mr. Thomas' origins are humble. His family worked hard to enable him to go to college, and he worked hard as well. In his statement to the press after Mr. Bush announced his nomination, he choked with emotion as he thanked his grandparents, his parents and the nuns from his Catholic school days, "all of whom were adamant that I grow up to make something of myself."

That he did. He graduated from Holy Cross and went on to Yale Law School, and when finished he went to work for the Missouri attorney general, now Sen. John Danforth. He made a lasting impression. "I know him to be an absolutely first-rate lawyer, and beyond that, I know him to be a first-rate human being," Mr. Danforth has said. In 1977, Mr. Thomas left government to practice law in the private sector, for Monsanto Corp., before rejoining Mr. Danforth as a legislative assistant in Washington in 1979.

In 1981, the Reagan administration named Mr. Thomas to head the civil rights division of the Education Department. In 1982, he went on to head the Equal Employment Opportunity Commission, where in the course of eight years he compiled a distinguished record of aggressive enforcement of anti-discrimination laws in the workplace. In those years, he also developed a reputation as a forceful proponent of equality of opportunity. He championed the idea of a colorblind Constitution and opposed racial quotas and other devices that gave legal status to groups rather than individuals. He also forcefully opposed the intellectually fashionable 1980s doctrine of equal pay for "comparable worth," a notion that, had it prevailed, would have had judges setting pay scales for private and public enterprises throughout the United States.

In 1990, President Bush named Mr. Thomas to the Court of Appeals of the District of Columbia. He was widely seen at the time as a rising star and a likely contender for a Supreme Court seat. That, combined with his commitment to a colorblind society, meant he was subjected to an unusually high degree of scrutiny by political opponents. The American Bar Association twice undertook full background investigations and pronounced him "qualified." Senate Judiciary Committee Chairman Joseph Biden issued a demand for him to produce thousands of pages of documents from his EEOC years. If any of the senators were hoping to find something to derail his confirmation, they failed to do so.

Meanwhile, Democratic Sens. Sam Nunn and Charles Robb, convinced of his abilities, introduced him to the Judiciary Committee and endorsed his nomination. Mr. Thomas forcefully defended his record at the hearing, and the only Judiciary Committee member who opposed him was Sen. Howard Metzenbaum.

In his year and a half as an appeals court judge, Mr. Thomas has further distinguished himself. He has written firm opinions on criminal justice matters and is obviously sensitive to the proper role of the federal courts.

President Bush has picked the right person. The Senate should move quickly to confirm Clarence Thomas.

THE CHRISTIAN SCIENCE MONITOR
Boston, Massachusetts, July 5, 1991

DIVERSITY, it seems, is in the eye of the beholder. Conservatives view Judge Clarence Thomas as someone whose background, growing up poor and black in the rural South, distinguishes him from any past nominee to the Supreme Court.

Liberals don't deny that, but say the diversity that counts is philosophical. Judge Thomas, they suspect, will be almost indistinguishable from his conservative white colleagues on the court.

There's truth in both perspectives. No nominee to the high court has had a life experience that parallels Thomas's. He has known poverty first-hand. But he's also a model of the self-made man. His qualities of courage and drive appeal to Americans of whatever political persuasion.

Regarding judicial persuasion, Thomas's record is fuzzier. After only a year on a lower federal bench, he has no trail of rulings on issues like abortion and church-state separation. But his stand against affirmative action, his statements on judicial restraint, his agreement with criticism of the court's 1973 abortion decision – all speak clearly enough of underlying philosophy. If confirmed, he's likely to cement the conservative majority.

Is Thomas, as President Bush proclaims, the candidate "best qualified at this time"? That's for political consumption. The nominee's ability and intelligence are undoubted, but in neither his case nor that of David Souter has Mr. Bush opted for heavyweights in constitutional law. These men could grow significantly on the job. Both are young; they'll almost certainly have many decades on the court to hone their thinking.

Meanwhile, the terms immediately ahead are likely to be dominated by the thinking of Chief Justice Rehnquist and Associate Justice Scalia, the court's intellectual powerhouses.

Thomas will almost surely be confirmed, but his confirmation hearings should be unstinting in their effort to provide a clearer insight into this nominee's vision of American justice.

THE BUFFALO NEWS
Buffalo, New York, July 3, 1991

IN NOMINATING Judge Clarence Thomas, President Bush signals a commendable intent to continue a presence for minority groups on the Supreme Court. But Thomas' conservatism and past record in federal office are sure to spark a spirited fight over his confirmation in the Senate.

Particularly should the controversial eight-year tenure of Thomas as chair of the U.S. Equal Employment Opportunity Commission undergo searching scrutiny in the forthcoming confirmation hearings before the Senate Judiciary Committee.

In Thomas, Bush chose a black, thus preserving a useful measure of diversity on the nation's highest court.

The president also selected the grandson of a sharecropper who fought his way up in public life. At 43, Thomas is one of the youngest of high-court nominees and a man who once studied for the priesthood. He champions rugged individualism.

The Bush administration gains politically from his selection. It advertises the readiness of Republicans to place blacks in high national office. It counters any suspicions of racism in this administration.

Philosophically, Thomas is more conservative than we would wish. His ideas, so far as we are aware, apparently would reinforce an increasing uniformity of deep conservatism that dominates this court majority.

Certainly, Thomas' views differ dramatically from the consistent liberalism of the judge he is nominated to succeed, Thurgood Marshall. Apparently, too, Thomas is less activist than Marshall sometimes was and has no inclination, if Bush's comments prove correct, to legislate from the bench.

Ahead loom especially important hearings on the Thomas nomination before the Senate Judiciary Committee. Its chairman, Sen. Joseph Biden, D-Del., rightly promises a "thorough and fair review."

Such hearings construct one part of a vital two-phase constitutional process for placing judges in a lifetime tenure on the federal bench: Presidents nominate, or recommend, their choices, which the Senate then must approve after a review of that nominee's qualifications.

The Senate committee should delve into Thomas' general philosophy and his brief record as a federal appellate judge. The Constitution must "be interpreted in a colorblind fashion," he has written, and condemned affirmative action as "social engineering" that stands "the principle of non-discrimination on its head." His preferences in other constitutionally sensitive areas, such as a free speech and church-state relations, are less widely known.

Senators need to probe determinedly for answers to sharp criticisms of Thomas' work as chairman of the Equal Employment Opportunity Commission.

Liberal House members a few years ago accused Thomas of demonstrating "an overall disdain for the rule of law" at the EEOC. Others charge lax enforcement of age-discrimination complaints, or efforts to weaken some basic civil rights the EEOC was empowered to protect.

Just as Thomas needs a full, fair opportunity to explain and expand on his own ideas, so the Congress and the country need a chance to learn more about him and his thinking. That is what the Senate hearings are constitutionally designed to do and, properly conducted, will do.

Once they have ended, Americans should know a good deal more about Judge Thomas and what he stands for than they do now. Then will be time enough for decision.

The Providence Journal
Providence, Rhode Island, July 3, 1991

We do know that (Justice-designate Clarence Thomas) is very heavily influenced by the Catholic Church, and we are very concerned about that. The indications are very, very frightening to us.

Those are the words of Ellen Convisser, president of the Massachusetts branch of the National Organization for Women.

It is insulting to choose a black who thinks like a white.

And those are the words of Derrick Bell, professor of law at Harvard.

If these are the opening shots in any campaign to deny Judge Clarence Thomas a seat on the Supreme Court, this 43-year-old grandson of a Georgia sharecropper should have little difficulty passing muster in the Senate. Indeed, it is probably a measure of President Bush's wise choice that Judge Thomas' detractors have found it necessary to resort so quickly to religious and racial bigotry in pressing their arguments.

By selecting Clarence Thomas, President Bush makes a number of important statements. By pointedly choosing a black jurist to succeed Thurgood Marshall, the President has affirmed his personal commitment to justice and equality in American life. Judge Thomas is no doubt well qualified to sit on the Court — more about that in a minute — but make no mistake: This is a political appointment in the best sense of the word. For not only does Clarence Thomas' life symbolize the meaning of freedom and the promise of opportunity, his perspective on the long road from a rural shack in the segregated South to the nation's highest court confounds conventional wisdom about civil rights and the substance of equality.

As an advocate for fundamental values of fairness and democracy, Judge Thomas is an eloquent opponent of affirmative action: "I firmly insist," he has written, "that the Constitution be interpreted in a colorblind fashion. It is futile to talk of a colorblind society unless this constitutional principle is first established. Hence, I emphasize black self-help, as opposed to racial quotas and other race-conscious legal devices that only further and deepen the original problem."

As a scholar, litigant, government official, architect of public policy and federal appeals court judge, Justice-designate Thomas has accomplished much in his 43 years. He has overcome obstacles most Americans can't imagine, and expressed his thoughts on issues with clarity and vigor. We welcome his appointment. It will be interesting to see how the Senate contends with this remarkable nominee — and tragic if his journey from Pinpoint, Georgia is disrupted by politics in Washington, D.C.

I'M AGAINST RACIAL QUOTAS AS A SOLUTION TO INEQUALITY... BUT I'LL TAKE THE JOB ANYWAY.

LAS VEGAS SUN

Las Vegas, Nevada, July 3, 1991

*I*n establishing Article III of the Constitution that judges "shall hold their offices in time of good behavior," the Founding Fathers tried to preclude politics from entering the judicial branch of our government.

That hope long gone, the question now becomes whether an even more hallowed set of principles in the Constitution – the Bill of Rights – is in peril as well.

We are not in a position to pass judgment on President Bush's nominee for the Supreme Court, Clarence Thomas. We will be watching the Senate Judiciary Committee's confirmation hearings with interest to learn more about the federal court of appeals judge and his qualifications and views.

We can believe Bush when he says Thomas was not nominated because he was black.

However, it is much harder to believe Bush when he says, "We're not trying to put a philosophical balance on this court."

Obviously, Thomas was nominated because of his conservative views. Which is ironic when considering that the Supreme Court vacancy was created by the retirement of Thurgood Marshall, the only black ever to sit on the court

and, along with William Brennan, the court's greatest champion of civil rights over the past quarter-century.

Republican president, conservative nominee. Democratic president, liberal nominee. That seems to be the pattern.

In an ideal world – one the Founding Fathers envisioned – President Bush would look at a Supreme Court leaning decidedly to the right and conclude that balance is the key.

Not liberalism over conservatism, or vice versa. Just balance. For the long-term health of the union.

No one can accurately predict exactly how a nominee will act after he's on the bench.

But it's possible there will be only one or two dissenting voices for the foreseeable future.

There has been a definite shift on the court. Just look at decisions such as those just handed down (government employees can't speak the truth to a woman about her legal abortion option; police can raid a bus and search you on demand; a signed, specific warrant is no longer needed to search your home).

The trend of the court is one that continues to chip away at the Bill of Rights.

MILWAUKEE SENTINEL

Milwaukee, Wisconsin, July 3, 1991

One would have thought that liberal Democrats in the US Senate would be elated with the prospect of confirming as the next appointee to the US Supreme Court the grandson of a black sharecropper who worked his way up to the position of federal appeals court judge.

This is the kind of American success story that was in a "whites only" category back in the 1960s. Indeed, that didn't even happen in fairy tales.

But, lo and behold, it appears that when Judge Clarence Thomas appears before the Senate Judiciary Committee with that resume, he will be in for some tough grilling by committee members.

Concerns about Thomas involve his refusal to accept such programs as affirmative action and job quotas as panaceas for black unemployment.

That does not mean, however, that he won't bring to the court a fresh and perhaps fairer approach to discrimination cases. Certainly, he will be one heck of a role model.

Another criticism of Thomas is that his position on abortion is unknown.

The hope here is that he will side with the liberals on this issue. The fact is, however, that there already are five to six votes on the so-called pro-life

side, and Thomas' vote won't make much of a difference.

Aside from Thomas' professional credentials, Democrats are making much of Bush's alleged duplicity in first saying that he didn't believe in quotas as far as the court was concerned and, after the nomination was made, saying that Thomas' race didn't enter into the decision.

Indeed, it is hard to believe that the political implications of not appointing a black to replace Thurgood Marshall, the first man of his race to serve on the court, was not taken into consideration by the president.

But, if it didn't, Bush only could have proved his critics wrong by not appointing a black, even if he believed that individual were the best qualified. It is a classic Catch 22.

All that being said, it should be noted that it is the Senate, and not the president, that is on the hot spot now.

The criticism being leveled at Thomas is not unlike that which resulted in the rejection of former Federal Judge Robert H. Bork in October 1987.

Yet, most analysts feel that, unless there are some surprise disclosures about the nominee, Thomas' nomination will be approved by a wide margin. How many who vote aye, we wonder, will admit that race was a consideration?

The Des Moines Register

Des Moines, Iowa, July 2, 1991

Was Clarence Thomas picked to replace retiring Supreme Court Justice Thurgood Marshall because of his color? The question must have been expected, and President Bush's retort was aimed at putting the idea to rest: "The fact that he is black — a minority — has nothing to do with this. He is the best qualified."

The statement is ridiculous on its face. Of all the potential candidates for a seat on the U.S. Supreme Court there are many others who are more qualified. Obviously Thomas' race had something to do with his selection. That's not a bad thing unless you are a president who misses no chance to bad-mouth "quotas."

Bush is to be credited for bringing a minority jurist to the court. But if he truly believed in colorblind hiring he could have found any number of white candidates who could pass the conservative litmus test. The fact that he chose a black could be seen as an effort to placate black voters who may have seen the Marshall seat as "theirs."

If Thomas turns out to be a good choice, it may not be for the reasons Bush had in mind. The nominee would bring the one thing to the court that the other eight justices desperately lack. That is a sense of what it is like to have been on the bottom half of society, and to be black in America.

That experience is perhaps the greatest loss for the court in Marshall's retirement. Where Marshall is a product of pre-civil-rights America, Thomas is a product of the post-civil-rights era. For a black growing up in poverty in Pinpoint, Ga., raised by grandparents in a tenement without indoor plumbing, there may not have been a lot of difference. As a student at an otherwise all-white seminary high school, and later at Holy Cross and Yale Law School, Thomas undoubtedly experienced the vestiges of the same institutional racism that influenced Marshall.

Make no mistake, though, Thomas is a political conservative. As chairman of the Equal Employment Opportunity Commission in the Reagan administration he earned a reputation for being unsympathetic to the ideals of federal equal-protection legislation. He flatly opposes affirmative action.

It's not clear how Thomas will address the many other issues dealt with by the court. It's the task of the Senate, which must confirm his appointment, to find out. Senators have a duty to ask Thomas to explain how he views the core principles articulated in the Constitution. It has a duty to challenge the fitness of a candidate who has only brief judicial experience. If Thomas comes up wanting in either case, the Senate has every right to reject his nomination.

NAACP, AFL-CIO Oppose Thomas Supreme Court Nomination

The nation's largest civil-rights organization, the National Association for the Advancement of Colored People (NAACP), July 31, 1991 announced its decision to oppose the nomination of Judge Clarence Thomas to the Supreme Court. Earlier in July, the group had deferred comment on the nomination of Thomas, who was black, to allow time to more closely consider his position on civil rights and affirmative action.

Other liberal groups, critical of Thomas's stances on affirmative action and women's issues, had earlier opposed his nomination to succeed Thurgood Marshall, who had been the first black Supreme Court justice.

After waiting to hear the NAACP's decision on Thomas, the nation's largest labor organization, the AFL-CIO, July 31 also announced its opposition to Thomas's nomination.

At a news conference in Washington, D.C., NAACP Chairman William F. Gibson July 31 said, "In the final analysis, Judge Clarence Thomas's judicial philosophy is simply inconsistent with the historical positions taken by the NAACP. We have concluded that Judge Thomas's confirmation would be inimical to the best interests of African-Americans."

In particular, Gibson said Thomas's position on civil rights policy was "inconsistent" and that he would be an "unpredictable member of an increasingly radical conservative court."

The *New York Times,* in a story datelined July 31, quoted an unidentified NAACP official as saying Thomas had met with NAACP leaders on July 19. The unidentified official said the leaders had found Thomas to be evasive when answering questions on several issues.

Two hours after the NAACP announcement, the AFL-CIO executive council, meeting in Chicago, issued a statement calling Thomas's nomination a "disgraceful" move by President Bush to pack the Supreme Court with conservatives. AFL-CIO President Lane Kirkland July 31 said, "As with the nomination of Robert Bork, the president's apparent resolve to make the court the preserve of the far right wing leaves us no other choice but to oppose Judge Thomas."

The White House July 31 expressed disappointment with the opposition to Thomas. Spokesman Gary Foster said, however, "Judge Thomas continues to enjoy diverse and growing support, and we are confident he will be confirmed" following Senate Judiciary Committee confirmation hearings set to begin Sept. 10.

Before the NAACP announcement of its opposition to Thomas's nomination, support for Thomas had grown in moderate circles. Arthur A. Fletcher, head of the U.S. Commission on Civil Rights, July 26 announced his backing. Fletcher stressed that his support for Thomas came as a private citizen and not as a civil-rights official.

Sen. Sam Nunn (D, Ga.), an influential senator who would formally introduce Thomas to the Senate Judiciary Committee at the start of his hearings, July 16 said he would have "warm words of support" for Thomas.

Other groups, including the Women's Legal Defense Fund, the National Women's Political Caucus and the People for the American Way, also opposed Thomas's nomination.

Jewish groups July 12 expressed concern over Thomas's support for controversial Black Muslim leader Rev. Louis Farrakhan. According to a July 12 story in the *Dallas Times Herald,* Thomas had praised Farrakhan in two speeches in 1983. Farrakhan had been criticized in 1984 for anti-Semitic comments.

Thomas reacted immediately, denying July 12 that he was an anti-Semite. He said, "I cannot leave standing any suggestion that I am anti-Semitic. I am, and have always been, unalterably and adamantly opposed to anti-Semitism and bigotry of any kind, including by Louis Farrakhan."

The National Urban League, a predominantly black civil-rights group, July 21 announced that it would take a neutral position on Judge Thomas's nomination.

The Forum
Fargo, North Dakota, August 5, 1991

To its credit, the National Association for the Advancement of Colored People bases its opposition to U.S. Supreme Court nominee Clarence Thomas on ideology, not race.

Thomas would understand that. It is disappointing, however, that the NAACP opts to ignore race *only* in regard to Thomas, one of the most successful black jurists in the nation.

More than any other representative of blacks in America, Thomas seems to understand what Martin Luther King Jr. meant when he talked about a color-blind society. Unlike the NAACP, however, Thomas rejects the fashionable "group rights" ideology in favor of adherence to a racially sensitve understanding of individual rights.

The NAACP (and the AFL-CIO which also opposes Thomas) has a liberal agenda. It's so liberal, in fact, that the oldest and most influential black organization in the country could not bring itself to support a conservative black. Conservatism — as understood by the NAACP's leadership — is anathema to blacks.

But is it?

Public opinion polls show support for Thomas among blacks (and whites) has actually increased since his nomination was announced by the president. As more and more is learned about this man who knew rural, southern poverty, his stature increases. He *is* the kind of example all Americans — black, white, brown, whatever — admire. Even his detractors admit grudgingly that he overcame the circumstances of his birth by hard work and strength of character.

But that's not good enough for the leaders of the NAACP, AFL-CIO and other liberal organizations who are more interested in securing group rights and privileges based on race or income, rather than recognition of individual initiative and ability.

In announcing opposition to Thomas, an NAACP spokesman said the nominee's record on civil rights was "inconsistent," and that Thomas would be "unpredictable" on the Supreme Court.

We certainly hope so.

Thomas calls himself a conservative, but so did the late Chief Justice Earl Warren, who presided over the most liberal court in the nation's history.

Thomas likely will be confirmed, despite the opposition of extreme liberals who (like radical conservatives) tend to put people in ideological pigeonholes. Thomas's brand of conservatism makes liberals nervous because it incorporates into traditional American values his personal sensitivity to poverty and racism.

We think that's an excellent combination in a Supreme Court justice.

The Boston Globe

Boston, Massachusetts, August 1, 1991

Keeping faith with the highest purpose of the NAACP, the nation's oldest and largest civil rights organization has put principle ahead of expediency in opposing black jurist Clarence Thomas as a nominee to the Supreme Court.

In an agonizing but courageous decision, the NAACP denied Thomas its backing. Without it, the prospects for his confirmation are notably dimmed – as they should be – and his nomination by President Bush has been shorn of its political slickness.

The NAACP's stance is particularly bold, considering its efforts to maintain cordial relations with the Bush administration, which has been far more accessible than the previous administration. But the organization's integrity was on the line. And in the end it came through.

The NAACP had three options. It could have supported a nominee who derided its most fundamental tenets, simply because that nominee was an African-American. It could have taken the middle path, as the National Urban League chose to do, and not supported or opposed the nomination. Or it could have taken a stand, as it did, setting its full weight behind the opposition.

Race alone was not enough to sway the NAACP to Thomas' side. Dr. William Gibson, NAACP board chairman, said, "We have concluded that Judge Thomas' confirmation would be inimical to the best interests of African-Americans."

More than that, Thomas does not reflect the best interests of all Americans. Thomas' record, said Benjamin Hooks, NAACP president, was deficient beyond the issue of civil rights; his sense of the larger role of government is flawed. His failure to uphold the law during his tenure at the EEOC suggests that he is not only insensitive but also mean-spirited on the issues of women's rights and age discrimination.

Despite that record, without the NAACP's stance, the Senate Judiciary Committee would have been hard pressed to frame its opposition. The Senate's rejection of Robert Bork as a nominee to the court illustrated the NAACP's strength. Its position is key to garnering votes of Southern Democrats to oppose Thomas' confirmation.

President Bush will predictably assert that the NAACP is out of touch with the black community. He will likely cite a poll showing that a majority – however slim that majority – of blacks support Thomas' nomination.

Yet Bush cannot ignore the NAACP's considerable influence in reversing black public opinion. Nor can he dismiss the now-strengthened coalition of civil rights, women's and abortion rights groups lined up to press for Senate disapproval.

Bush's cynical efforts to use race as a red herring have now backfired. He should withdraw his nomination of Thomas and find a more suitable nominee.

St. Petersburg Times

St. Petersburg, Florida, August 3, 1991

The NAACP's decision to oppose Clarence Thomas' nomination to the Supreme Court marks a turning point in the confirmation process. The odds still favor Thomas' confirmation, but when the nation's largest, oldest and most influential civil rights group declares a black nominee "inimical to the best interests of African-Americans," everyone notices.

The NAACP did not reach that conclusion lightly, since Thomas' rejection could well mean a return to an all-white court after 25 years of Thurgood Marshall's imposing presence. That Thomas himself didn't take the group's decision lightly was evidenced by the fact that he had met personally with an NAACP delegation, a rare private-sector departure from his current smile-and-shrug strategy. Whatever he told them, it obviously wasn't persuasive.

Thus far the nominee has benefited from the lack of consensus about him in the civil rights community. Now that consensus — if not unanimity — appears to be emerging. The NAACP's assent or even abdication would have virtually assured Thomas' confirmation. Instead, the NAACP now joins the Congressional Black Caucus in almost unanimously opposing him, and there's little reason to think that they won't soon be joined by the Leadership Conference on Civil Rights, an umbrella group for 180 organizations. Meanwhile, the closest thing to major-league black support that Thomas can point to is the National Urban League's studied neutrality and its leader's rather forlorn hope that at least he's a better bet for understanding black grievances than any white conservative nominee who replaces him.

That's support by default, and focused civil rights opposition may well lead to an exodus among the 57 percent of blacks who tell pollsters Thomas should get the job. Add to that the opposition of the largest labor union, groups representing the elderly, Hispanics and women, and he faces the specter of a revival of the coalition that toppled Robert Bork's perceived sure-fire nomination in 1987.

To head that off, the pressure is now on the White House and Thomas himself to provide answers to more than the NAACP. Thomas can't keep relying on others to fend off the questions. The Souter-silence strategy may not work for Thomas, because Souter enjoyed the advantage of no visceral opposition of the sort that eventually toppled Bork.

Much depends on how strongly the NAACP and the other opposition attack Thomas. At the very least, he should be required to make a strong personal defense during confirmation hearings before the Senate Judiciary Committee next month. Ideally, he would stand or fall on his own qualifications, but clearly political considerations have come to dominate the nomination process to a highly politicized, reactionary court. So far the debate has focused on his disdain for affirmative action, but key questions remain unanswered about his inclinations on other constitutional issues, such as school integration, the extent of the intrusive and coercive powers of the state, individual privacy rights and abortion.

The latter may be the key. With *Roe vs. Wade* hanging by a thread, if Thomas' abortion answers wind up alarming even women not normally in the activist camp, that could well turn out to be one too many strident constituents for some senators to ignore.

The Phoenix Gazette

Phoenix, Arizona, August 3, 1991

Supreme Court nominee Clarence Thomas has been judged and found wanting by the leadership of the NAACP and the AFL-CIO. Both organizations have announced that they will oppose his being seated on the highest court in the land.

The grandson of impoverished Georgia sharecroppers, only the second black chosen for a spot on the high court, is unacceptable because he doesn't subscribe to the orthodoxy required of blacks who aspire to high office.

Thomas' endorsement of a color blind society, though consistent with the Constitution, is not acceptable in the view of the liberal leadership of the black civil rights organization.

However, as Republican Leader Bob Dole pointed out, "It's not Judge Thomas who is out of the mainstream, it's the NAACP leadership." A recent Gallup poll reveals that 57 percent of the blacks in this country support his nomination, with only 18 percent in opposition.

The mugging of Clarence Thomas will now begin. Despite what will be alleged, neither his abilities nor his credentials are at issue. It is his belief in judicial restraint and his departure from the civil rights orthodoxy of quotas and government handouts that offend his opponents.

The reaction was predictable. It doesn't take a rocket scientist to figure out how paternalistic white liberals would react. The discouraging part of the attack on Thomas is that black leaders have failed to recognize that he is exactly the role model that they should embrace.

Thomas is the embodiment of the virtues of individual responsibility, hard work and self help that have contributed to the rise of generations of immigrants and others who begin life in the poorest ranks of society.

Mr. Thomas appointment to the court is not a betrayal of black aspirations but a fulfillment of the American dream.

The Honolulu Advertiser

Honolulu, Hawaii, August 3, 1991

The decision of the NAACP and AFL-CIO to oppose the Supreme Court nomination of Clarence Thomas means his hearings will be a major battle.

The National Association for the Advancement of Colored People, the oldest and largest civil rights organization, is also a key part of the 185-member Leadership Conference on Civil Rights which will decide on Thomas next week.

The NAACP staff reportedly compiled a highly critical report on Thomas, citing his opposition to affirmative action and willingness to tolerate discrimination as seven-year head of the Equal Employment Opportunity Commission.

The 50-member NAACP board of directors' opposition was a tough call because if Thomas is rejected, the chances for another black are small. Bush denies Thomas was chosen because he is black. His protests would be even less believable were he to pick yet another black to replace Justice Thurgood Marshall, the court's first black and a civil-rights hero. So a Hispanic or a woman is said to be more likely.

The 35-member AFL-CIO executive council's decision is not surprising but it is the largest of many labor, liberal and women's groups to oppose Thomas. The major group for Thomas so far is the U.S. Chamber of Commerce.

The NAACP action makes it easier for Democratic senators to vote against Thomas. But only seven Democrats are needed to confirm Thomas, if all GOP senators stick by Bush.

Bush has the right to nominate to the Supreme Court whomever he wants, based on political ideology, color, gender or other factors. But while there is a disposition to let the president have his choices for Cabinet jobs, a high court justice demands a different, deeper scrutiny.

THE ARIZONA REPUBLIC

Phoenix, Arizona, August 4, 1991

A recent cartoon by Mike Shelton of the *Orange County Register* shows Edward Kennedy, Howard Metzenbaum and Joseph Biden of the Senate Judiciary Committee conferring on George Bush's embattled nominee for Thurgood Marshall's seat on the Supreme Court. "Back in '89 when we confirmed Clarence Thomas to the Appeals Court," an agitated Sen. Biden is asking his colleagues, "didn't we specifically warn him not to get uppity?"

The cartoon assumes special cogency in the light of last week's blast of Judge Thomas by the NAACP and its Big Labor confederates. Both groups repudiated the nomination, in the words of NAACP Chairman William F. Gibson, because "Judge Thomas's inconsistent views on civil rights policy make him an unpredictable element on an increasingly radical conservative court."

Skittish senators, some of whom previously had looked with favor on the Thomas nomination, at once began to vacillate. Observing the shift, Arizona's Sen. Dennis DeConcini declared that the nomination was "moving in a direction that is detrimental to the nominee." Judge Thomas, he added, now would be obliged to dispel suspicions that he was a "radical conservative," though in fact the suspicions are mostly smoke.

Actual objections to Judge Thomas have nothing at all to do with his "inconsistent views on civil rights policy," to quote the NAACP's Dr. Gibson. It is precisely the consistency of his views that has aroused the opposition. A man of independent intellect, Judge Thomas has alarmed and angered civil rights professionals by habitually refusing to fall in behind them on the issue of affirmative action and preferential treatment for minorities. They are offended, it might be said, because Judge Thomas takes literally the "equal protection" clause.

As for his being a "radical conservative," the slur is so rubbery and so ideologically loaded as to be useless as a gauge of his temperament and judicial philosophy. Dr. Gibson — and perhaps Sen. DeConcini as well — is of the opinion that the Rehnquist court is "increasingly radical conservative," whatever this means, and that Judge Thomas would either be compatible with this drift (Dr. Gibson's view) or must show that he would not be (Sen. DeConcini's).

Meanwhile, the executive council of the AFL-CIO, predictably left wing, has denounced as "disgraceful" George Bush's unremarkable effort to do as all presidents do and pick Supreme Court nominees with whose philosophy he is comfortable. Yet what is truly disgraceful is the deplorable level to which some of Judge Thomas's critics have lowered the debate on his nomination.

Newsweek quotes Spike Lee, the Hollywood producer, as calling Judge Thomas "a handkerchief-head, chicken-and-biscuit-eating Uncle Tom" — this about a man who overcame grinding poverty and racial prejudice to become a distinguished appeals court judge. The insult is contemptible. No other word will do. And where, it must be asked, are Dr. Gibson and other high-minded detractors of Judge Thomas when such loathsome bigotry is being unloosed?

Sen. DeConcini has yet to declare himself one way or the other on the Thomas nomination. But many of the senator's constituents will be more than a little disappointed if he does not stand firm against the rabble-rousing stratagems to which many of Judge Thomas's avowed enemies, despairing of honorable opposition, have sunk.

The San Diego Union

San Diego, California, August 2, 1991

"When it comes to individual discrimination, his record is pretty clear. If a black or a woman has been discriminated against, he'll go to the ends of the earth to correct it."

This testimony to Supreme Court nominee Clarence Thomas was offered last week by no less a figure than Benjamin Hooks, executive director of the National Association for the Advancement of Colored People. In light of Hooks' comment, many might find it odd that the NAACP has just announced it opposes Judge Thomas' nomination. The NAACP's announcement was timed to coincide with the AFL-CIO's declaration that it too will work to block Thomas's elevation to the Supreme Court.

Despite Rev. Hooks' earlier statement, NAACP chairman William Gibson declared this week: "We have concluded that Judge Thomas' confirmation would be inimical to the best interests of African-Americans."

Yet, according to recent polls, the majority of African-Americans, for whom Gibson presumes to speak, do not share his dim view of Judge Thomas.

A poll conducted for *USA Today* showed that blacks approved of the Thomas nomination by a 3-to-1 margin. Moreover, nearly 7 of 10 blacks expressed confidence he would be fair in protecting the rights of minorities. Thus, by coming down against Judge Thomas, the NAACP leadership has shown itself to be out of step with its constituency.

It is not surprising, of course, that the NAACP and the AFL-CIO would prefer a Supreme Court nominee who would reflect their own liberal agendas. Both organizations plainly would prefer someone whose thinking mirrors that of retiring Justice Thurgood Marshall. But it is merely fanciful to demand, as the NAACP does, that President Bush nominate a person with liberal views that are diametrically opposed to his own conservative philosophy.

Moreover, Judge Thomas' views on matters of race are hardly "reactionary," as Gibson has charged. Rather, they reflect the thinking of the mainstream of America. Like most Americans, Thomas believes in the primacy of individual rights, rather than group rights and racial preferences.

RAPID CITY JOURNAL—
Rapid City, South Dakota, August 1, 1991

The nomination of Clarence Thomas to the United States Supreme Court ran into a major stumbling block Wednesday when the National Association for the Advancement of Colored People urged the Senate to reject Thomas.

Essentially, that means the largest and oldest black organization's leadership feels that despite Thomas' color, his views are in such opposition to the best interests of minorities that he should be denied membership to the highest court in the land.

That is particularly significant considering the NAACP leadership can have no doubt that whoever would replace Thomas would hold similarly conservative views and probably not be a black. Despite that fact, the NAACP has chosen to actively oppose Thomas.

The NAACP is widely considered to be the organization that must spearhead any successful drive to deny Thomas the seat. Now that the group has decided to act, Thomas' other potential weaknesses — his reported belief in so-called "natural law" as a principle by which judges should be guided above and beyond contents of the Constitution, for example — are more open to debate. Politically, white liberal politicians can actively oppose the nomination on ideological grounds since the NAACP blunted the race issue.

Many other minority groups have chosen to be silent on the nomination, neither supporting nor opposing Thomas. But that silence speaks loudly. Momentum is working against Thomas.

The NAACP is taking a stand where principle and belief matter more than race and background. Whether right or wrong, that's a courageous stand with potentially far-reaching consequences.

Until yesterday, Thomas' confirmation by the Senate seemed certain. Today, it is not.

The Register-Guard
Eugene, Oregon, August 14, 1991

The National Association for the Advancement of Colored People has papered over its differences with the Compton, Calif., chapter. But it cannot erase the surprise of public discovery that the organization is so hostile to internal dissent.

The controversy arose when the NAACP board announced its opposition to the nomination of Clarence Thomas to the U.S. Supreme Court. That happened July 30. Ten days earlier, the Compton branch had already voted to endorse Thomas' nomination.

For a while, the national office publicly threatened to expel the officers of the Compton branch unless they rescinded the resolution of support for Thomas. Eventually, a deal was made: No action would be taken against the Compton branch as long as it was willing to describe its endorsement of Thomas as a non-binding expression of the sentiment of the individuals who voted for it, rather than the official position of the branch.

This is a semantic charade. The Compton branch's resolution was approved by majority vote at a general meeting presumably in the same manner as other comparable official actions. Of course it represented the sentiment of those who voted for it. It also represented at the time enough votes to constitute a formal, official position that has now been downgraded by fiat to the status of an informal, unofficial, non-position.

Benjamin Hooks, executive director of the NAACP, and Royce Esters, president of the Compton branch, issued a joint statement saying: "The national NAACP has no reservations about individual members of the Compton branch, or any branch, expressing their opinions as individuals. Membership does not require conformity."

Thank goodness for that, but it isn't much. NAACP officials acknowledged that the group's formal bylaws prohibit any branch from adopting a position contrary to that taken by the national group. So if 299 of the 300 members of NAACP branch X think one way about an issue they can say so out loud. But if their view runs contrary to the position adopted by the national body, they must either remain officially silent or adopt a branch position that reflects the views of one member rather than the 299.

An extreme and hypothetical example, of course. But it illustrates the point. The conformity imposed by the national organization is so rigid as to cast doubt on the actual level of support for national positions among the constituent chapters. It would be far better — and more democratic — to loosen up the bylaws, let chapters vote their consciences and let the world know that every now and then a few local branches disagree with headquarters.

Chicago Tribune
Chicago, Illinois, August 5, 1991

The NAACP and the AFL-CIO decided last week that they had seen and heard enough. Judge Clarence Thomas, the two groups said in coordinated announcements, is not fit to sit on the Supreme Court, and so they will oppose his confirmation.

Given the ideological casts of the two organizations and their result-oriented approach to Supreme Court appointments, their actions were not surprising.

Many other Americans, however, probably will reserve judgment on Thomas, at least until he has testified before the Senate Judiciary Committee.

Nevertheless, there has been a steady drip, drip, drip of journalistic "disclosures" about the nominee: that he knowingly held his sister up to undeserved public ridicule as welfare-dependent; that he opposes affirmative action even though he benefited from it in gaining admission to Yale Law School; that he administered the law badly or, worse, ignored it altogether while serving as head of the Equal Employment Opportunity Commission; that he is "strange" because he believes in natural law.

How much do any of these things matter? What should a conscientious citizen want to know about the man who would be Mr. Justice Thomas?

None of the "disclosures" is completely unrelated to Thomas' fitness for the Supreme Court. But some are more important than others.

It would say something troubling—though not necessarily disqualifying—about Thomas if he cynically used his sister as an example of welfare-dependency. But it is far from clear that he did. And anyone who has ever been a member of a family ought to know that, for an outsider making judgments about family relationships, modesty is the best policy.

As for affirmative action, is Thomas or anyone else to be barred from criticizing an existing social arrangement because he benefited from it in his youth? Must every white male who benefited from policies skewed in favor of white males therefore refrain from criticizing them? More important than the fact that Thomas now considers affirmative action unwise is how he reached that conviction.

Thomas' record at the EEOC is critical. He does not deny that he consciously set out to change the agency's approach from one of seeking large-scale, class-action settlements to seeking justice for individual victims of bias. That was in keeping with his philosophical conviction that justice is a matter of fairness for individuals, not groups.

Assuming both approaches are allowable, can an administrator be accused of ignoring the law when he chooses one rather than another? Is such a policy difference a criminal offense?

For many people, Thomas' affinity for natural law may be the most problematic issue. The problem lies in whether the nation can be comfortable with a justice who derives laws from sources other than the Constitution and the statute books, which are available to everyone in the society.

The nation certainly is not unaccustomed to such thinking on the Supreme Court. Justice Thurgood Marshall, for example, apprehended from some source that capital punishment is unconstitutional, even though the Constitution approves it in several places.

Those interested only in what results he'll deliver may already have heard all they want to about Judge Thomas. Those who genuinely want to take the man's measure will keep their ears—and minds—open.

Thomas Accused of Sexual Harassment; Confirmation Vote Delayed Amid Debate

A former aide to Supreme Court nominee Judge Clarence Thomas Oct. 6, 1991 publicly accused him of sexually harassing her over a period from 1981 to 1983.

The charge sparked an emotional and contentious national debate over the issue of sexual harassment, particularly after the woman, Anita F. Hill, a tenured law professor at the University of Oklahoma, Oct. 7 accused the Senate Judiciary Committee of not fully investigating her complaint. Amidst the growing controversy over the charges and the committee's handling of them, the Senate Oct. 8 agreed to postpone until Oct. 15 the vote on Thomas's confirmation to the Supreme Court. The vote had originally been scheduled for 6:00 p.m., Oct. 8.

The controversy surrounding Hill's charges erupted into a political mudfight as Republican legislators accused Democrats of illegally leaking reports of Hill's charges to the press. A battle of the sexes also developed as female legislators and lobbyists accused their male counterparts of simply not comprehending the seriousness of sexual harassment in the work place.

Until Hill's charges were publicized, Thomas's confirmation had appeared guaranteed. Most Senate Republicans and several Senate Democrats had announced their support for the nominee.

The specifics of Hill's charges were contained in an affidavit submitted to the committee in September, which was later leaked to the press. In the affidavit, Hill charged that beginning in 1981, when she had worked as Thomas's assistant at the Education Department, Thomas had repeatedly asked her out and after she had refused to date him, had begun telling her about his sexual interests. Hill described Thomas's remarks as explicit, saying he had discussed sexual acts he had seen in pornographic movies. She said the comments had stopped for a time and she had moved with Thomas to the Equal Employment Opportunity Commission, where the harassment had begun again. Hill had quit her job at the EEOC in 1983.

According to reports Oct. 6 in New York *Newsday* and on National Public Radio, the Senate Judiciary Committee staff had first heard of Hill's charges the week of Sept. 10. However, the Federal Bureau of Investigation did not begin to investigate the charges until Sept. 23. An FBI report was completed on Sept. 25 and made available to the committee one day before its Sept. 27 tie vote, 7–7, on Thomas's nomination.

Sen. John C. Danforth (R, Mo.), Thomas's main Senate patron, Oct. 6 said Thomas "forcefully denies" Hill's charges. Thomas Oct. 8 released an affidavit that said, "I totally and unequivocally deny Anita Hill's allegations of misconduct of any kind toward her, sexual or otherwise. These allegations are untrue." In the same statement, Thomas asked the Senate to delay the vote on his confirmation to give him a chance to clear his name.

Professor Hill, speaking at a news conference at the University of Oklahoma, Oct. 7 explained her reasons for coming forward with the charges against Thomas and accused the Senate Judiciary Committee of not fully examining the accusations.

Although Hill had denied socializing with Thomas outside the office, Thomas said that while they worked together, he had occasionally driven Hill home after work and that Hill had invited him in for "a Coke or a beer or something."

Hill Oct. 11 had testified under oath before the Senate Judiciary Committee that at the Department of Education in 1981 and extending until she left her job at the EEOC in 1983, Thomas had repeatedly verbally harassed her, asking her out, telling her of his sexual prowess and relating to her sexually explicit scenes he had seen in pornographic movies.

During testimony that lasted for nearly seven hours, Hill was questioned often harshly by committee Republicans and more gently by committee Democrats.

The Star-Ledger

Newark, New Jersey, October 11, 1991

Perhaps more disturbing than the allegation charging Supreme Court nominee Clarence Thomas with sexual harassment of a former employee was the bumbling manner in which the nearly all-male Senate dealt with it. The events leading to the postponement of a confirmation vote did not produce a flattering image of that legislative body.

The delay appears to be more an act of damage control, a furtive effort to contain a growing controversy, than an act of statesmanship. Political pragmatism seemed to play more of a role in the Senate's decision than any sense of conviction.

It was only after senators were deluged with telephone and fax messages from irate female constituents that they opted to put the confirmation vote on hold for a week to investigate the allegation made by University of Oklahoma law professor Anita Hill.

Professor Hill has charged that Judge Thomas made lewd and intimidating comments to her while she worked for him in two different federal jobs in the early 1980s—one at the Equal Employment Opportunity Commission which handles sexual harassment complaints. Judge Thomas has "totally and unequivocally" denied the accusation.

The extra week is not expected to uncork any information that will settle the matter of the nominee's guilt or innocence or Professor Hill's credibility. At best, it will be an opportunity for both parties to respond to direct questioning about the alleged incidents—his word against hers.

Sen. Joseph Biden (D-Del.), who was privy to the charges nearly a month before they became public, said additional hearings are necessary "because we cannot fail to take seriously such a charge." But Sen. Biden, who chairs the Senate Judiciary Committee which grilled the nominee, apparently felt otherwise about the importance of the charge prior to feeling the heat of public opinion.

The committee's action—or inaction—on the allegation seems to lend credence to angry women who charge that the Senate is an exclusive "old boys' club" that chose to wave away what could be a serious charge. Even those who disbelieve Professor Hill's charge are nonetheless appalled at its handling by the Senate committee.

If the senators thought there was insufficient cause to address the allegation—which the Judiciary Committee certainly failed to do—then that should have been clearly stated, and there would have been no need for a delay and additional hearings. But to admit that at this point would mean facing the wrath of angry women who view the Senate as insensitive to their gender, which would be politically unwise.

Whatever the outcome, the Senate has not done itself or the country proud in this matter, and whatever the ultimate decision, the Senate's "advise and consent" role will be tainted by its old boys' blunder.

THE ANN ARBOR NEWS
Ann Arbor, Michigan, October 9, 1991

The U.S. Senate was correct Tuesday in postponing a vote on the Clarence Thomas nomination in the interest of fairness as well as the integrity of the Senate and Supreme Court.

Had a decision been made without having seriously considered the sexual harassment accusations made against the judge, it would been unfair to Thomas and to Anita F. Hill, the law professor who made the charges. It would have ignored the seriousness of the issue and implied that the Senate places expediency above justice. If nominated, it could have cast a permanent shadow over Thomas' effectiveness as a justice and his role on the Supreme Court.

The vote, delayed for a week, gives Thomas a chance to defend himself before the Senate and gives Hill the opportunity to testify under oath. It is the only just way to handle the case.

At the same time, it should be remembered that the Senate is not a court of law. This is not a trial, and the outcome is to determine Thomas' fitness to serve on the Supreme Court, not his innocence or guilt on sexual harassment charges.

> **If there is a "trial" during these next days of testimony, it will involve the Senate and its capability of handling a sensitive issue in a dignified manner.**

If there is a "trial" during these next days of testimony, it will involve the Senate and its capability of handling a sensitive issue in a dignified manner. So far, in the Hill case, it has not performed well.

Hill has rightfully questioned the way the Judiciary Committee handled her accusations. Thomas ought to be asking similar questions. These charges were serious enough to have delayed the committee's vote to send the nomination to the full floor. No excuses can justify the committee's decision not to give Thomas and Hill full hearings after they received the FBI report on Sept. 25 regarding the professor's charges.

Unfortunately, senators did not find it important to air Hill's charges until the last minute. It signals indifference, ineptitude or rotten politics, all of which are deeply disturbing.

DAILY NEWS
New York City, New York, October 9, 1991

THE SENATE'S REACTION to Anita Hill's explosive allegations against Clarence Thomas has made one thing absolutely clear: There's a distressing degree of confusion and discomfort around the issue of sexual harassment, even at the highest levels of government.

The Equal Employment Opportunity Commission defines sexual harassment as any behavior that has the "purpose or effect of unreasonably interfering with an individual's work performance or creating an intimidating or hostile or offensive environment."

Disturbingly, some members of that mostly men's club, the Senate, have revealed that they didn't know even that basic legal fact. Nor, as Hill correctly contends, did most senators react to the issue at hand. Instead of seriously examining her charges of harassment — and their implications for a prospective Supreme Court justice — the politicians largely saw Hill as an interloper in their confirmation process.

Arguably, the law is uncomfortably vague. Perceptions of a "hostile" or "offensive" environment can vary widely. Still, this incident illustrates why women must move beyond fear and vigorously assert their right not to be verbally assaulted in the workplace. Saying "this offends me and it must stop" is part of the battle. But only part of it.

Most important, men must learn that a supervisor's power is not a tool of seduction, that a "no" (even an unclear one) must be heeded, and that sexual harassment is a serious crime. If nothing else, the Thomas-Hill episode should lead to a more educated population — including the members of the Senate.

The Hutchinson News
Hutchinson, Kansas, October 10, 1991

How much more will the process of selecting a Supreme Court Justice endure?

How many more 11th-hour surprises are in store for Judge Clarence Thomas?

It is not surprising that senators were pressured to postpone their scheduled vote Tuesday on Thomas' confirmation. The charge against him, if true, would make him unsuitable for holding a seat on the nation's highest court.

But how credible is the charge of sexual harassment by Thomas of his former aide, Anita Hill, and why has it been issued so late in the process?

The dilemma pits one honorable reputation against another, a no-win situation, but even more importantly, it delivers a severe blow to the nomination process, a system that already has proven itself less than satisfactory.

Now the issue before the nation is not just the question of who will assume the post to the high court. It has suddenly become broader than that, now including the issue of male insensitivity in matters of sexual harassment.

Surely, Clarence Thomas, who already has been given his day in court on numerous occasions, now will get one more, but this time to defend himself against the charge. Anita Hill, an attorney and a law professor, will also get an opportunity to make her case.

Senator Bob Dole says the postponement of the vote on Thomas and the subsequent hearing will be "a test of (Thomas') character."

That is baloney.

What the nation now faces is a test of the nation's paltry leadership, which plays politics with the nation's future, and special interest opportunists who know when to pounce, having dithered for years without the courage to attempt to fix asserted problems.

Any American ever having contact with Thomas has had dozens of past opportunities to discredit him. He held a high-profile government job before assuming his position on the federal court, both posts highly visible, and one of which was determined by a senate confirmation process.

Judge Thomas' "character" has already been tested under the repetitious and redundant questioning by senators. He has displayed his calm under pressure. He is a decent man who would give service to his country, though the despicable actions of vast numbers of public officials have now ensured that nobody will win this debacle.

FORT WORTH STAR-TELEGRAM
Fort Worth, Texas, October 8, 1991

Allegations that Supreme Court nominee Clarence Thomas was guilty of sexual harassment of a former female aide a decade ago raise sufficient questions to justify a delay in the Senate's confirmation vote, scheduled for later today.

Anita Hill, a law professor at the University of Oklahoma, told Senate committee members in early September that Thomas had harassed her while she was employed as his assistant in the Education Department in 1981 and again after both had transferred to the Equal Employment Opportunities Commission.

According to Hill, Thomas, separated from his first wife at the time, frequently asked her out and, when she refused, described his sexual interests and scenes from pornographic movies. Senate Judiciary Committee Chairman Joseph Biden, D-Del., said he and his fellow committee members knew of Hill's allegations when they voted 7-7 to send Thomas' nomination to the full Senate without recommendation.

Hill has made some troubling accusations, and we are disturbed by the fact that committee members chose not to acknowledge them publicly, thus depriving the full Senate of information it needs to make a sound decision.

The confirmation vote should be delayed long enough for a full investigation. Without it, the allegations will leave a cloud of suspicion over the nominee and, ultimately, the Supreme Court that can do far more damage than a delayed vote could ever do.

The Houston Post

Houston, Texas, October 10, 1991

ANITA HILL and Clarence Thomas will have their day in court Friday.

Will Hill be able to convince the Senate Judiciary Committee that she was the unwilling target of lewd remarks allegedly made by Thomas several years ago?

Can Thomas clear his name and win Senate confirmation as President Bush's choice for a seat on the U.S. Supreme Court?

Will the male-dominated Senate be able to overcome the impression, especially among women, that it has little understanding of what constitutes sexual harassment and less inclination to investigate such charges?

The Senate decision to delay for a week Tuesday's scheduled vote on Judge Thomas' confirmation seemed to stem more from political expediency than a genuine desire by senators to air the controversy. After Hill's accusations were made public over the weekend, the nominee's support began to erode so precipitously that his backers feared they didn't have enough votes to confirm him.

Whatever the outcome, the drama to be played out before Chairman Joseph Biden's Judiciary Committee Friday is a tragedy. In the balance are the reputations of two people of attested-to high character and integrity. What happens now could not only doom Thomas' chances to sit on the nation's highest court but wreck the 43-year-old conservative black jurist's remarkable poverty-to-success career. It could also be devastating for Hill, a black University of Oklahoma law professor, who also has struggled to succeed professionally.

In a sworn affidavit, Thomas denies "totally and unequivocally" Hill's claims that he tried to date her and, when she declined, he talked to her about his sexual interests and graphically described scenes from pornographic movies.

She charges he first made such remarks 10 years ago when she was his assistant at the Department of Education. He later ceased, she says, and when he became chairman of the Equal Employment Opportunity Commission she went with him as his aide, only to be subjected to a repetition of the dirty talk.

Hill defends her decision to accompany Thomas to the EEOC on the grounds that she wouldhave been without a job had she not done so, that she was young, and felt she had something to contribute to civil rights. But does this explain why, since she left the agency, she has kept in touch with a man whose behavior she claims to have sometimes found offensive?

Thomas' supporters angrily cry that he is the victim of a last-minute smear attempt by one or more of his opponents on the Judiciary Committee who leaked the panel's confidential report on the law professor's story to a reporter.

The fact remains that the committee should have pursued Hill's allegations more vigorously than it did. The FBI questioned her, but did not reach a conclusion on the veracity of her claims. She says she did not volunteer it until asked about it by the committee.

To put it bluntly, either Hill or Thomas is lying. The Judiciary Committee will have to decide which to believe. Unfortunately, nobody is likely to emerge from this experience unscathed. But the overriding concern must be to fill the empty high court seat with a justice who can interpret the Constitution and the laws of the land fairly for all Americans.

THE EMPORIA GAZETTE

Emporia, Kansas, October 9, 1991

THE recent charges of sexual harassment against Clarence Thomas cause us to pause and think about what constitutes sexual harassment.

The Equal Opportunity Commission defines sexual harassment as any unwelcome sexual advance or request for sexual favors, or verbal or physical actions of a sexual nature that affect the victim's employment or create a hostile environment.

The problem is that it is often unclear what constitutes an intimidating or hostile environment for the employee. Obviously, blatant sexual proposals are harassment, as are displays of suggestive pictures or graphic or degrading comments about a person's dress, appearance or anatomy.

Unfortunately, we are not all vulnerable to the same things, and our reactions and sensitivity levels vary according to our personalities and experiences of life. This often leaves a fuzzy area when it comes to individual definitions of harassment. What may seem to be a slight to one person may not elicit a negative response in another.

The majority of sexual-harassment victims are women, and many men find that they do not understand the law or are confused by it. Women are sometimes confused by it too, but they can easily identify that uncomfortable feeling that comes from unwanted advances or innuendoes. Fun and harassment are two different things. Harassment is almost always a hostile act, even when it comes from learned behavior, and it usually elicits some sort of fear or anger in a woman. The male who is having fun with a woman will usually stop when the woman asks him to, but a harasser does not stop. Flirting is not harassment, nor is exchanging bawdy stories, if both parties are having fun.

Harassment is not fun!

Women can help men understand harassment by communicating to them what they like and do not like. And, men can help women by listening to them and respecting what they have to say.

In the end, when it comes to relationships between men and women, it is still, *Vive la difference!*

The Union Leader

Manchester, New Hampshire, October 11, 1991

"How can Ted Kennedy possibly sit in judgment over someone who is accused of sexual harassment? It's outrageous."

Thus sayeth state Senator Thomas Colantuono of Londonderry, speaking the unspoken thought that has been on many people's minds ever since it was decided that U.S. Supreme Court nominee Clarence Thomas will be hauled back before the U.S. Senate Judiciary Committee to answer charges that he sexually harassed an employee ten years ago.

Only those lacking in a sense of the bizarre will dissent.

Kudos and paeans to Colantuono. Aesop would be proud of him. Truly, King Ted has no clothes on.

Seriously, anyone who doesn't think that it requires a measure of courage for someone in public life to speak less than flatteringly of a member of America's only royal family is not aware of the true situation. Attorney Colantuono will receive from his professional and political peers knowing nods and assenting winks for what he has said.

But he will get no outspoken *public* support.

Strange, isn't it? If it wasn't for the courage of a sturdy people who possessed the intellectual integrity to challenge royalty run rampant, America would not exist.

"SAME HERE—I'VE NEVER BEEN SEXUALLY HARASSED EITHER"

U.S. SENATE

©1991 HERBLOCK

TULSA WORLD

Tulsa, Oklahoma, October 11, 1991

WHO'S telling the truth, Judge Thomas or Anita Hill? The question has America buzzing, and members of the Senate Judiciary Committee will attempt to resolve it when they resume hearings Friday on Judge Clarence Thomas' fitness to serve on the U.S. Supreme Court.

Is it possible that each of them is telling the truth?

Anita Hill, now a law professor at the University of Oklahoma, says Thomas made remarks to her nearly 10 years ago, when he was her boss at one federal agency and then another, that constituted sexual harassment. Thomas says no such thing happened.

Based on a number of reactions and comments, both published and on-the-street, many men apparently wonder what the big deal is. Thomas is alleged to have asked Hill for a date and, when she turned him down, attempted to engage in some banter of a sexual nature. If it was so bad, why didn't she say something earlier?

Conversely, many women apparently believe that Hill's accusations merely point up a behavior that women in the workplace have had to face far too often and for far too long. Nor are they bothered by the fact that Hill waited so long to come forward — part of the problem is that despite the law and regulations, there really is little women can do to protect themselves and still preserve their career prospects.

Hill and Thomas both appear to be people of exemplary character — people to be believed. Perhaps the "truth" is that men and women perceive things differently and react to things differently, and that solid definitions of what is sexual harassment remain to be worked out.

The situation has sparked a national debate on what men and women in the workplace can expect of one another, and what is acceptable and unacceptable behavior. In the long run that might be more important than Judge Thomas' fate as a Supreme Court nominee, and the Senate's sorry handling of the confirmation process.

The Gazette

Cedar Rapids, Iowa, October 10, 1991

CLARENCE THOMAS, it is said, "will look the American people in the eye" over the next six days and repeat, frequently we suspect, his "total and unequivocal" denial of allegations that forced the United States Senate to postpone Tuesday's scheduled vote on his suitability to serve on the Supreme Court.

Thomas, of course, is the one with the most at stake, having been accused\of sexually harassing a woman a decade ago. Already unpopular with those who disapprove of his silence on the question of reproductive freedom and abortion, Thomas has seen his stock go downhill even more since the allegations by Anita Hill, a University of Oklahoma law professor, were leaked. The next week is intended to give his inquisitors time to determine whether Thomas is guilty, although once again the ideological forces in Congress were quick to pass judgment — one way or the other.

Our sense is that regardless of the ultimate verdict, Thomas is damaged merchandise. Even if he is vindicated, nothing can erase the nagging doubt that surely will surface whenever the issue of sexual harassment crosses his desk, as inevitably it must. If allegations are verified, of course, Thomas need not worry about confirmation. He will remain a jurist in the federal court system, however.

Painful as rejection obviously would be for Thomas at the end of this week of additional probing, we see a potentially bigger loser in this unhappy scenario. If any individual or group is obliged to explain its misdeeds, it is members of the United States Senate in general, and its Judiciary Committee in particular.

From the outset, the examination of Thomas has been marked by pettiness and personal agendas, rather than a thoughtful analysis of attributes most of us find important, indeed essential, qualifications for a member of the United States Supreme Court: education, experience, personality, physical and emotional health, personal background, character. Yes, *character*. Charges brought by a former colleague raise questions about Thomas' moral strength. The Judiciary Committee, too intent on pursuing its political agenda, seems to have swept an important character question under the rug.

We haven't been impressed the last four years with the committee's increasingly hostile attitude toward nominees or the narrowness of its agenda. By giving short-shrift to the Hill accusations, though, the subcommittee has been judged guilty of being insensitive to a concern that is very real to American women. We can't anticipate what will occur next week when the Senate finally votes on the Thomas nomination. Whatever else happens, however, he will have served the nation well if his confirmation hearing was the catalyst that forced an overhaul of this sadly abused hearing process.

Hill Testifies as Nation is Riveted by Harassment Hearings

The country was mesmerized Oct. 11, 1991 as Anita Hill, a tenured law professor at the University of Oklahoma, calmly described what she said were Supreme Court nominee Judge Clarence Thomas's sexually harassing comments and actions over a period from 1981 to 1983. During that period, Hill, who, like Thomas, was black, had worked as his assistant at the Department of Education's Office of Civil Rights and then at the Equal Employment Opportunity Commission, where Thomas was chairman.

Thomas, in testimony beginning Oct. 11, emphatically denied ever harassing Hill. He attacked the Judiciary Committee and the confirmation process. He called the process "Kafkaesque" and repeatedly compared it to a "lynching."

Thomas's defense focused on testimonials to his character and attempts to discredit Hill and to paint her accusations as part of a political plot. Some Republicans on the Judiciary Committee and members of panels of witnesses for Thomas attacked Hill's character, her mental stability and her motives.

The hearings, which were broadcast live on television and radio, drew more public attention than any political incident in recent memory. They captured the attention of the country and scored highly in television ratings. The Senate was swamped with phone calls and telegrams both for and against Thomas.

A poll conducted Oct. 13 by the *New York Times* and CBS News showed that as the hearings ended, 45% of Americans favored Thomas's confirmation, while 20% opposed it. Asked whom they believed more about the charges of sexual harassment, 58% backed Thomas and 24% backed Hill.

Beginning with his opening statement Oct. 11 and continuing throughout his sworn testimony Oct. 12, Thomas voiced outrage at being questioned on charges he called "lies," "sleaze," "dirt," and "gossip."

Thomas invoked the issues of race and racial hatred during his testimony, saying that the country still had "underlying racial attitudes about black men and their views of sex."

Thomas made his opening statement Oct. 11, before Hill addressed the committee, and then returned Oct. 11 and 12, after she testified, to rebut her allegations. At all times he denied ever having harassed Hill, and he angrily attacked the confirmation process. "This is a circus. It's a national disgrace. From my standpoint as a black American, it is a high-tech lynching for uppity blacks who in any way deign to think for themselves, to do for themselves," Thomas raged at the committee.

Thomas told the committee, "No job is worth what I've been through—no job. No horror in my life has been so debilitating. Confirm me if you want. Don't confirm me if you have been so led. But let this process end. Let me and my family regain our lives."

In an effort to undermine Hill's testimony, Thomas Oct. 12 raised questions about Hill's account of their working relationship. His statements came in response to questions from Utah Republican Orrin G. Hatch, one of Thomas's staunchest defenders on the committee.

The Boston Globe
Boston, Massachusetts, October 12, 1991

On her office door at the University of Oklahoma, Anita Hill has placed a poster of Eleanor Roosevelt. It reads: "You gain strength, courage and confidence by every experience in which you really stop to look fear in the face.... You must do the thing that you cannot do."

For Hill, fear was 14 senators, every one of them white and male. Fear was Judge Clarence Thomas, her former employer and alleged harasser. Fear was the embarrassing recollection of verbal humiliation. Fear was the American public tuned in to watch as she sank or swam.

But the power of unadorned truth barreled across the nation as she told her story. After a week of tormenting doubt, all the myths about her allegations of sexual harassment were dispelled one by one.

■ No longer can her view of the situation be dismissed as a misinterpretation of a misstep by Thomas when he was her boss. The harassment she described was far removed from a girlish over-reaction to some offhand remark or gesture on his part – an exaggerated response to the equivalent of a casual arm across a subordinate's shoulder.

■ No longer can anyone question whether Hill's allegations constituted genuine sexual harassment. Her youth and strict upbringing were assaulted repeatedly by Thomas' obscene – and singularly cruel – sexual commentary; her intelligence and professional ability were insulted and demeaned.

■ No longer is there any question of the stupidity of the Senate Judiciary Committee for putting Hill's affidavit aside without so much as interviewing her. Members of the committee can decry the leak to the press into eternity. They cannot, however, get away from the hideous prospect that were it not for the leak, Thomas would be sitting on the Supreme Court without having to respond publicly to Hill's charges.

■ No longer can President Bush hide behind a mask of loyalty to his nominee. No longer can he, in good conscience, deride the credibility of Thomas' accuser.

■ No longer can Thomas' cries of victimization be taken seriously. His denial was powerful, but it proved no match for Hill's clarity, her composure, or her pain.

■ No longer, in our view, is there much room for the argument that this was a he-said-she-said standoff, in which the question of who was telling the truth would be to difficult to discern. It seems clear – all too clear. She was.

With every question, Anita Hill became stronger, more courageous, and more confident. She did the thing she could not do.

FORT WORTH STAR-TELEGRAM
Fort Worth, Texas, October 12, 1991

When the Senate Judiciary Committee agreed to hear Professor Anita Hill's tale of sexual harassment at the hands of Judge Clarence Thomas, the ax was poised over Thomas' neck.

When the hearings were televised into millions of American homes and offices, the blade fell.

It is always dangerous to speculate on what a group of senators may find believable or compelling or politically expedient, but the televising of Hill's statement and the committee's questions made the American public the real jury.

It is a far-fetched notion that a young woman of Hill's background — manipulated into coming forth though she may have been — would appear before a Senate committee, on national television, with her octogenarian mother and father in the room, and *invent* the shocking details and graphic descriptions to which she testified.

And it is equally difficult to see how Thomas can be confirmed to the Supreme Court now. Indeed, it may be difficult for him and his sponsors to manage even a graceful withdrawal of Thomas' nomination. There are too many questions that would follow him to the court.

Yesterday's were among the least-orchestrated Senate hearings the public is likely to see. Because the stage was hastily set and the order of business decided on the wing, it was great theater. But it was also honest theater.

Hill, telling her story, was attacking Thomas. Republicans on the committee, by pulling and tugging at Hill's rendition of events, were defending Thomas — but they were really acting as defense counsel for George Bush, whose White House staff somehow failed to detect the bombshell in Thomas' closet, just as the senators seemed to brush it off.

The White House and the Senate, as much as Thomas, need damage control.

If he is not confirmed, Thomas can retreat, for a while at least, to his present appellate court position. He will be remembered as a victim of his president's hit-and-run warfare with a Democratic Congress as well as a victim of alleged character flaws.

Hill can try to resume her relative anonymity. Remember, she is not a guileful, ambitious politician, but a rather private person engaged in teaching law.

The Senate can take a long, embarrassed look at itself, and, with the White House, perhaps begin seeking a more sure-handed and less injurious way of choosing and examining Supreme Court justices.

THE TENNESSEAN
Nashville, Tennessee, October 13, 1991

WHEN seven congresswomen marched to a Senate Democratic caucus room last week to voice concern about Clarence Thomas and sexual harassment, they met a closed door.

Would an delegation of congressmen have received such a cold reception? Only the senators can say. But one thing is clear. Despite years of progress, a closed door still symbolizes the plight of women in government.

And that is embarrassing.

The controversy over Anita Hill and Thomas brought the issue into focus. How can Congress hope to adequately address women's issues when its membership is virtually all men? Representation in Congress is nowhere close to reflecting the nation's population.

Many males in Congress have excellent track records in upholding women's rights. But even the best of those men cannot begin to have the personal understanding of women's issues that women can. That point was brought home painfully by the flap over Thomas and Hill.

The number of American women in high-level elected offices is shameful. Only two U.S. senators are women. Only 29 of the 435 members of the House are women. There are only three female governors.

If half of the Democratic senators in that caucus room last week had been women, there would have been no need for the congresswomen's march up the Capitol steps. And if half the nation's senators were female, the Senate would have known from the beginning that the statements by Anita Hill were extremely serious and could not be ignored.

A Congress that is 95% male deserves the kind of scrutiny it has gotten over the sexual harassment issue.

But the problem goes deeper. Congress has exempted itself from all major civil rights bills, including laws prohibiting discrimination on the basis of sex, race, religion and physical impairment. It claimed the doctrine of separation of powers prohibits any executive branch agency from telling those in the legislative branch what to do.

How horridly ironic! It means that members of Congress — primarily white men — have passed laws that dictate how every other employer acts, but they don't have to answer to anyone. If a congressional employee believes she has been sexually harassed by a congressman, she can't take him to court. She can only take him to the House Ethics Committee — and we all know how that operates.

Women's perspective must be heard on everything — on sexual harassment, on child care, on arms control, on health care, on transportation, on education, on everything. Until the makeup of Congress reflects the nation's sexual, racial and ethnic diversity, its members carry an added responsibility to be totally sensitive and totally receptive to the concerns of all Americans. Last week's event demonstrate painfully how far Congress has to go. ■

The Wichita
Eagle-Beacon
Wichita, Kansas, October 15, 1991

Americans have been mesmerized by the Senate Judiciary Committee's hearings into allegations that Supreme Court nominee Clarence Thomas sexually harassed a former colleague.

Most Americans wanted to see a clear-cut resolution, some unequivocal evidence to prove or disprove Professor Anita Hill's allegations. None was forthcoming.

In the Thomas case, there was no third-party witness to support Professor Hill's charges. There was no pattern of harassment shown. That doesn't mean Judge Thomas is guilty or innocent. It means only that the Senate proceedings did not resolve the issue conclusively. It boiled down to his word against hers.

By any measure of fairness it is wrong to destroy Judge Thomas' career and ruin his reputation based on unsubstantiated accusations. In previous appearances before the Senate Judiciary Committee, Judge Thomas proved to be a man of strong moral beliefs, a man who had overcome poverty and racial discrimination, a competent jurist who was qualified to sit on the Supreme Court. It would be tragic for the Senate to refuse to confirm him based solely on unproven sexual harassment allegations.

However, it would also be tragic if the Thomas case were used to disparage the very real problem of sexual harassment in the workplace. Likewise, it would be tragic if women interpreted the Thomas case as evidence that Americans don't take the problem of sexual harassment seriously.

Indeed, Judge Thomas' confirmation process may prove of greater value in making America a more just nation than any decision he may render on the Supreme Court. Reaction to the case has raised the nation's consciousness about sexual harassment. For the past week, the issue has been the No. 1 topic across the country. It's safe to say that the Thomas case has educated millions of Americans about sexual harassment.

Out of that should come a greater awareness of sexual politics in the workplace — of the potential for abuse and unequal power relationships between male bosses and female employees, of the varying senses of propriety men and women bring to the job. The ultimate goal is mutual respect among professional colleagues, and a work environment where no one faces sexual humiliation, where each person is free from unwanted sexual advances.

Each American has his or her own theory as to why Anita Hill stepped forward and whether Clarence Thomas was convincing. Yet, based on the Senate Judiciary Committee hearing, all is conjecture and personal opinion.

The issue of sexual harassment will continue long past today when the Senate makes its decision on Judge Thomas. There simply was not compelling evidence to disqualify him from the Supreme Court.

THE ☼ SUN

Baltimore, Maryland, October 15, 1991

This evening the Senate will vote on Judge Clarence Thomas to be an associate justice of the Supreme Court. On Sept. 22 *The Sun* recommended his confirmation in what we conceded may have been "a triumph of hope over realistic assessment" of his judicial qualifications. Today we again recommend that he be confirmed, in what we must concede is the hope that he has not been guilty of sexual harassment and of lying about it.

Three days of hearings into the charges against Judge Thomas by a former aide, law professor Anita F. Hill, provided no grounds for a realistic assessment of the charges either way. We predicted that on Oct. 9. Senators are right back where they started. They know more details than they did last week. They have heard more character witnesses for both principals. They have heard witnesses and principals skillfully cross-examined. But they are no surer of the truth.

Even Thomas opponents admit the case against him was not proved. Some argue that nevertheless he should not be confirmed because a Supreme Court justice should not have to labor under a cloud of suspicion and notoriety. Judge Thomas' supporters agree he is under such a cloud. It is perhaps a permanent one, as he himself said.

However, the argument that he therefore be disqualified is revolting. Liberal Democrats and liberal special-interest groups created this cloud (against the expressed wishes of Professor Hill, we would note, resulting in the creation of a cloud of suspected dishonesty over *her*). For these advocates then to suggest that he must be defeated because of the accusation against him is a call for validating a standard operating procedure that encourages character assassins and gives them veto power over nominees.

Ugly as the weekend spectacle was, in some ways Judge Thomas was a more attractive candidate than the first time around. In the first hearings, several senators said they did not find in his bland, evasive, White House-prepared testimony "the real Clarence Thomas." This time, with "no handlers, no advisers," as he put it, a passionate, human Clarence Thomas was on view.

The real Clarence Thomas is still a movement conservative. He is still a black man from a poor, segregated background. He is still young, relatively inexperienced, relatively undistinguished. He is different from the Clarence Thomas we endorsed last month only by having gone through this ordeal. The ordeal may have created a bitter, vindictive personality, which is the last thing a Supreme Court justice should be. It may have created a man with a more acute understanding of the pain of victimization and the horror of invasion of privacy, which would be valuable assets for a justice.

We hope that Judge Thomas has been made stronger and wiser by this weekend. So hoping, we recommend again that the Senate confirm him.

THE DAILY OKLAHOMAN

Oklahoma City, Oklahoma, October 13, 1991

THOSE who watched this weekend's nightmarish Senate Judiciary Committee hearings saw one witness after another counter University of Oklahoma professor Anita Hill's charges against Supreme Court nominee Clarence Thomas. Several called Hill's stability into question, describing her abrupt mood shifts, leading them to discount her testimony.

Back in Oklahoma, Tulsa attorney Larry Shiles, a former student in Hill's legal research classes at Oral Roberts University, says he has submitted to senators a sworn deposition with shocking assertions, the least of which is that she was not respected as a teacher and could not handle her teaching load at the school.

Looking back on his experiences with professor Hill, Shiles described behavior which appears to support charges by other witnesses. At the least, Shiles and others describe Hill in ways that make her sound mercurial. Shiles even described class papers returned to him containing certain extraneous material — an echo of one of Hill's assertions about Thomas. Shiles told *The Oklahoman* he believes Hill is "unreliable" and that he "wouldn't believe a thing she said."

One way or the other, the tribulations of Clarence Thomas and Anita Hill may ease after today's vote in the U.S. Senate. After that, the staffer or senator responsible for the most reprehensible leak in Senate history must be identified and punished.

Wisconsin ⚖ State Journal

Madison, Wisconsin, October 15, 1991

For those who stayed up late on Sunday night to watch Washington's live soap opera, "As the Worm Turns," one of the most telling episodes came when Sen. Howard Metzenbaum, the doddering disgrace from Ohio, tried to assassinate the character of a Clarence Thomas character witness, John Doggett. Isn't it true, the senator asked, that a woman had just come forth to say that 10 years ago, Doggett kissed her square on the lips on her first day on the job at the firm where both worked?

The Yale law and Harvard business graduate waited until Metzenbaum had fumbled his way through a transcript of an investigator's telephone interview, and then proceeded to dress down the senator in a way that made one wish there were more John Doggetts in the upper house of Congress (and, at least, one less Howard Metzenbaum).

Doggett first explained that he expected that someone would crawl out from under a rock as soon as it became known he would testify against Anita Hill, who has accused Clarence Thomas of sexual harassment, because that's the way Washington works. "I debated with my wife whether to start this process . . . because I knew it would be vicious," but went ahead in hopes of taking "the public process back into the pale of propriety."

Then he demanded to know under what legal rule, what code of fairness, would a member of the Judiciary Committee bring into the record a transcript of unsworn telephone conversations? Chairman Joseph Biden, who had left the room for a few minutes, came back and seemed genuinely stunned by what Metzenbaum had done. He cleared the committee record and ordered that it show there was "no evidence" that Doggett had ever done anything of the kind. Indeed, there was no such evidence, it smelled of an utter fabrication. But the forces driving the likes of Metzenbaum, not content to destroy the character of Clarence Thomas, had now taken to abusing the rights of ordinary citizens.

The Senate has gone so far beyond its "advise and consent" role in this affair that it may not be possible to repair the damage. The Senate's role was not to substitute its own judgment for that of George Bush, who as president is entitled to send forth a nominee of his choice, but to assess the nominee's basic qualifications for the job.

When it seemed that Thomas would survive the 7-7 "no recommendation" vote of the Judiciary Committee, someone leaked portions of the FBI report involving Anita Hill, and the televised circus began. The very committee that ought to stand for fairness in our legal system became an instrument of raw politics.

Who is telling the truth? Perhaps we'll never know for sure, but there is no more reason to believe Hill than to doubt her. Witnesses on all sides seemed credible. If anything, she comes across as a woman scorned, not sexually, but institutionally.

Even if some version of Hill's story is to be believed, are incidents that took place 10 years ago in a different time and context enough to disqualify Thomas? If purity is now the standard, Washington would be a ghost town.

Thomas has suffered beyond the limits of what a seat on the Supreme Court is worth. Like John Doggett, many Americans are appalled at the actions of the Senate, as much as they abhor the offenses of which Thomas stands accused. Senators may judge the judge based on his judicial experience, background and elements of his character that they know to be true, but not on the basis of a hatchet job.

THE DENVER POST
Denver, Colorado, October 13, 1991

JUDGE Clarence Thomas cannot serve honorably on the Supreme Court of the United States, and his nomination should not be confirmed by the Senate next week.

The accusations against him — which seemingly cannot be proved or disproved — have so tarnished his reputation that he cannot effectively sit in judgment of others on the most important court in this land.

The entire Thomas confirmation process is an American tragedy. Had the Senate Judiciary Committee taken Anita Hill's accusations seriously, it's possible they could have been handled in a more dignified manner. As it occurred, the spectacle not only irreparably damaged the reputations of two people — Thomas and Hill — but further tarnished the institution of the Senate itself.

In her early statement to Senate staff members and the FBI,

Miss Hill described persistent, personally offensive behavior by Thomas while she worked for him 10 years ago. But those statements apparently were not considered critical enough by the judiciary committee to merit a role in its deliberations — until they were made public.

Regardless, what has happened has happened. Miss Hill's accusations — denied by Judge Thomas but not clearly refuted by evidence — have indelibly stained the nominee's professional reputation. Although he still enjoys the support and respect of many, he cannot recover the confidence of millions of Americans.

Rightly or wrongly, the hearing has ruined Judge Thomas's distinguished career. This newspaper, which originally endorsed his nomination, recommends that he voluntarily withdraw his name to avoid being rejected by the Senate next Tuesday.

THE ATLANTA CONSTITUTION
Atlanta, Georgia, October 14, 1991

The U.S. Senate is in the unenviable position of wrestling with a decidedly discomfiting case involving sordid charges of sexual harassment and the diametrically opposed testimony of two compelling figures, Judge Clarence Thomas and law Professor Anita F. Hill.

As powerful as Judge Thomas's denials have been, the greater credibility finally rests in the case presented by Ms. Hill.

Why would Ms. Hill lie? She has nothing to gain by subjecting herself to the intense scrutiny she now faces. Her discomfort discussing explicit sexual language was evident during her testimony, and her reluctance to come forward is clear in the chronology of events leading up to her public appearance.

She has friends who support her testimony. At various times, she spoke to several people about the sexual harassment she endured from her former superior, Clarence Thomas. They recall she spoke of the ordeal reluctantly and in evident distress, reinforcing her account and adding insight about her failure to file formal charges against him.

Judge Thomas has angrily denounced the hearings on the allegations of sexual harassment, charging that groups opposed to his nomination have scoured the countryside to dig up information to smear him. Sadly, the judge is right. Low-road tactics threaten to pervert the entire political process.

But the resort to gutter politics is not confined to groups who oppose him. In fact, it was Judge Thomas's supporters who aired a nasty commercial viciously attacking liberal members of the Senate Judiciary Committee, shortly after the judge was nominated.

At any rate, Ms. Hill is no part of a liberal conspiracy to trash Judge Thomas. She was comfortable working in the Reagan administration and an enthusiastic supporter of the

nomination to the Supreme Court of Robert Bork, a doctrinaire conservative.

There were always reasons to doubt Judge Thomas's fitness. When he was nominated, he had only his honorable rise from poverty, his character and his integrity to commend him. He lacks judicial experience.

Nor did the earlier portion of the confirmation hearings shore up a sense of trust in his integrity. He so distanced himself from every strong political position he had taken as to seem to have no beliefs worth defending. When he declared he had never discussed Roe v. Wade, the case that established a woman's right to a legal abortion, he went beyond mere evasiveness to utter implausibility.

Yet, it still seemed possible at the end of the first set of hearings that Judge Thomas could be an asset to the court. Reluctant supporters hoped he might add compassion to political conservatism, and there were indications that he was no rigid ideologue.

But this second set of hearings has shifted the pattern of perceptions of the judge in a different direction. It now seems he lacks the character and the moral compass required to serve on the Supreme Court.

The nation's highest court could survive a justice who has had the poor judgment to ask a subordinate for a date. It might even survive a justice so crude as to view pornographic details as a tactic for seduction. The court ennobles some, such as former Klansman Hugo Black. But the foundations of the court would be rocked by a justice whose veracity cannot be trusted.

Since Judge Thomas has declared that he "would rather die" than withdraw, it is the duty of President Bush to withdraw his name from consideration. The nation deserves a nominee who would bring to the court both the integrity and the experience it demands.

THE BLADE
Toledo, Ohio, October 15, 1991

PRESIDENT Bush is said to have a short list of potential Supreme Court nominees ready should Clarence Thomas be rejected by the Senate in a vote tentatively scheduled for this evening.

But if Judge Thomas is rejected, and the President has to turn to his list, he may find it even shorter than he thought.

For if Clarence Thomas has now decided that a Supreme Court nomination is just not worth the personal pain and sacrifice of a Senate Judiciary Committee "high-tech lynching," it's a safe bet that the men and women on Mr. Bush's replacement list are beginning to wonder the same thing.

No matter what happens in the Senate vote, the real casualty of this whole mess could be the willingness of future prospective nominees to wade into the process. If America now insists that its Supreme Court consists of men and women whose character is as pure as the driven snow, America will have a Supreme Court so out of touch with the real world that its decisions will be meaningless and irrelevant.

Judge Thomas' accuser, Prof. Anita Hill, apparently passed a lie detector test on Sunday, adding yet another bizarre act to an already bizarre theater of the absurd. The pressure grew immediately for Judge Thomas to take a lie detector test of his own, one more glob of mud on a proceeding that is knee-deep in it already.

If Judge Thomas were to pass such a test, nothing would be proven. If he were to fail, the same would be true, yet he would be finished. How fair is that?

Fairness, of course, went out the window when Ms. Hill came forward 10 years after she first claimed Judge Thomas harassed her.

Consequently, one wonders what is going through the minds these days of the individuals most likely to get a long look from Mr. Bush as his new choice, should Judge Thomas fall.

All of the most commonly mentioned prospective nominees are in their 40s and 50s, which means that all of them have actually gone about living their lives, making friends and making enemies and perhaps even entertaining a lustful thought now and then. Can the Republic possibly survive if one of *them* joins the court?

Some members of the Senate will face a difficult political dilemma when they vote up or down on Judge Thomas's confirmation. Those who come from conservative districts may like the judge's philosophical predilections but fret about the fallout of backing a nominee seen by some back home as morally suspect. At the same time, there is no denying that public opinion polls show more support for Judge Thomas than Ms. Hill.

The Senate Judiciary Committee has brought this embarrassment upon itself, and just as Clarence Thomas and Anita Hill are forever scarred by the events of the past few weeks, so is the U.S. Senate.

Thomas Narrowly Confirmed as 106th Supreme Court Justice

After one of the most bitter and divisive confirmation battles in the 202-year history of the Supreme Court, the Senate Oct. 15, 1991 confirmed Judge Clarence Thomas as the court's 106th associate justice. The 52–48 vote came after three days of televised Senate Judiciary Committee hearings Oct. 11–14 on charges of sexual harassment made against Thomas by a former aide, Anita F. Hill.

The vote was the closest for a Supreme Court justice in the 20th century. Thomas, who would replace retired Justice Thurgood Marshall, would be the second black to sit on the high court.

After the hearings, the Senate had one full day of debate Oct. 15 before the vote on Thomas's confirmation was held. The Bush administration tried to retain behind Thomas the coalition of Republicans and Southern Democrats who had supported the nominee before Hill's charges arose.

Three Democrats who had openly supported Thomas in September— Joseph Lieberman of Connecticut and Richard H. Bryan and Harry Reid, both of Nevada—switched their votes and opposed his confirmation Oct. 15. They were joined by three other Democrats who had hinted their early support for Thomas. Those were Bob Graham of Florida, Daniel Patrick Moynihan of New York and Robert C. Byrd of West Virginia.

Byrd Oct. 15 took the Senate floor in an impassioned speech on the importance of protecting the judicial process from any cloud of doubt over Thomas's fitness for the Supreme Court. He criticized his fellow Democrats for being intimidated by Thomas's charges of racism and said, "I think it was blatant intimidation and, I'm sorry to say, it worked. I sat there thinking, Who's going to ask him some tough questions? Are they afraid of him?"

He added, "I believe Anita Hill. I did not see on that face the knotted brow of satanic revenge."

Other senators, however, said Thomas deserved the benefit of the doubt. Sen. Alan J. Dixon (D, Ill.) cited criminal court precedent when he explained his decision to back Thomas. He said, "The accused gets the benefit of the doubt."

Sen. Nancy Landon Kassebaum (Kan.), the only woman Republican in the Senate, voted for Thomas, but she chastised the Judiciary Committee for subjecting Hill to an "intellectual witch hunt." She said Thomas would "live under a cloud of suspicion he can never fully escape."

The two Republicans who voted against Thomas, Sens. Bob Packwood of Oregon and James M. Jeffords of Vermont, both said they had made their decision before the hearings on Hill's charges.

Senate Majority leader Sen. George Mitchell (D, Maine) Oct. 15 announced that he would order an investigation of the leaks to the news media of Hill's affidavit to the committee and possibly of copies of the FBI report on her charges.

The six Republican senators on the Judiciary Committee, led by Strom Thurmond of South Carolina, had called for an Federal Bureau of Investigation (FBI) investigation to determine who was responsible for the leak. Throughout the hearings, Republicans charged that Democratic senators' staff members had given confidential committee documents to the media to force hearings on Hill's charges.

The Senate Oct. 16 began a reappraisal of the Supreme Court confirmation process after public criticism swelled in the wake of Thomas's confirmation.

Sens. Sam Nunn (D, Ga.) and Paul Simon (D, Ill.) made proposals for alterations to the process. Both proposals called for more Senate involvement in selecting candidates for confirmation.

President Bush Oct. 16 said all sides agreed that "the present process is simply not fair." He said he was working on suggestions for improvements.

Some observers said women were better off in the wake of the hearings because sexual harassment had been clearly defined and explained to the public. Others said because of the treatment Hill received, the burden of proof was put on women, making it harder to prove harassment claims.

The Times-Picayune

New Orleans, Louisiana, October 16, 1991

Now that the vote is over, Clarence Thomas and Anita Hill can begin to rebuild their lives and reputations.

They have plenty of time to do it. Both young, both secure in the support of their family and friends, they have years to mold their careers, to make their marks.

But the biggest mark already has been left on us.

The most savage confirmation hearing in memory has left a nation of men and women wrestling with their consciences and their memories. It has caused us to remember and to wonder about what we've done and what has been done to us. It has shaped the debate over sexual harassment in the workplace for years to come.

No one knows what form that debate will take. Some columnists have written, in all apparent seriousness, that the Thomas hearings have created a climate in which men and women will be too fearful to make social contact with the opposite sex. They won't be able to flirt, they will never get together, with drastic consequences for the propagation of the human race.

Others worry that Judge Thomas' confirmation hearings send a clear signal to women that it will do no good to complain about the way men treat them on the job. If someone as professional and well spoken as Anita Hill was not believed, what are the chances of an ordinary woman being believed?

They worry that the Thomas hearings — and the outcome of those hearings — only reinforce the code of silence with which women have long met unwelcome sexual attention from men.

We subscribe to a third, more optimistic theory. It holds that what has happened in the Senate hearing room over the past week has for the first time forced the nation to attend to a very real problem that has never been dealt with openly before.

People who never thought about sexual harassment before are thinking about it. People who never talked about it before are talking and arguing and sometimes even communicating.

U.S. Senators were confronted with their own embarrassing lack of understanding and foresight, and sometimes, their own embarrassing pasts.

As a nation, we have had an education in the sometimes difficult relations between men and women in the workplace. Our consciousness, whether we like it or not, has been raised.

There are many questions left to be answered, many disagreements to overcome.

But at least we're talking.

Calgary Herald

Calgary, Alberta, October 16, 1991

The confirmation of Clarence Thomas to the United States Supreme Court was the most profound challenge the Senate review process has ever faced.

Allegations of sexual harassment against Thomas, brought forward by law professor Anita Hill, tested but did not destroy the method by which the United States picks the members of its top court.

There were many who criticized the process for victimizing Thomas or Hill or both, depending on who was believed, but the real problem revealed by the show in Washington was more profound.

The bitterness and animosity unleashed at the hearings are troubling signs of a political system in deep trouble. The 52-48 Senate vote in favor of Thomas reveals a deeply divided Senate. The credibility of Thomas' future judgments has more than likely been seriously undermined.

The issue revealed a nation divided along sexual and racial lines espousing unreconcilable polarized positions.

The system itself, with one party ensconced in the White House while the only other party in the land enjoys perennial sway in Congress, dictates that Supreme Court appointments become the focus of political infighting.

The problem for American voters, already disillusioned as shown by ever lower voter turnouts, is to decide when infighting has transformed into meltdown. The Thomas hearings revealed a stagnant system slouching toward that dark political abyss.

Las Vegas Review-Journal

Las Vegas, Nevada, October 16, 1991

There will be no shortage of political fallout from the riveting final week of the Thomas nomination hearings. Some of it, surprisingly enough, will be positive.

Widespread in the country's largest dailies this weekend, for instance, were earnest expressions of concern on the part of black Americans that the spectacle of a black man and a black woman sniping at each other over matters sexual might only perpetuate evil stereotypes of the past.

In fact, a television audience whose images of black Americans are all too often limited to the amoral and illiterate drug dealers, pimps, and prostitutes of the evening police dramas got a chance this weekend to hear from a singular array of concerned, articulate Americans of color from both sides of the political spectrum. Robert L. Steinback, writing Monday for The Miami Herald, may have best summarized this unintended benefit of the unique spectacle when he declared "African-Americans in general" to be among the "winners" of the hearing process:

"It might not seem obvious at first, what with two African-Americans slinging slime at each other in front of a panel of white male senators. But the controversy has shown that blackness isn't the only issue in the lives of black people," Steinback writes.

"It has shown that blacks are willing to disagree publicly with each other — meaning we are maturing politically. And most of all, America got a chance to see a series of confident, courageous, eloquent, successful and highly intelligent African-Americans — especially males — testifying forcefully and persuasively. There wasn't a stereotype in the bunch. And not one black witness embarrassed himself or herself in the national spotlight."

America has a long way to go to realize the goal of legal color-blindness. But perhaps a nation that exceeds all others in self-criticism can be forgiven for pausing in this moment of confusion to note that gathering together such an array of obviously well-educated, well-paid professionals from the fields of law and government, all of African descent, would have been nigh on impossible only 40 years ago. However painfully, progress is being made.

Times~Colonist

Victoria, British Columbia, October 17, 1991

For crass political gamesmanship, racial conflict, sexual titillation and old-fashioned mystery, American network television has never offered anything remotely like the Clarence Thomas saga. Which is probably no bad thing because it was an unedifying spotlight on a flawed process which tarnished all who participated.

On a very basic level, the televised confirmation hearings of President George Bush's Supreme Court nominee provided riveting drama, even for Canadians. Someone *had* to be lying. Was it Anita Hill, the calm and plausible University of Oklahoma law professor, with her graphic accounts of sexual harassment by Thomas when she worked for him at two agencies in the 1980s? Or Judge Thomas, with his vehement denials and his impassioned invocation of Ku Klux Klan imagery?

Was the whole Hill testimony a machiavellian plot to carry out — in Thomas's own words — a "high-tech lynching for uppity blacks"?

A narrow majority of senators chose to believe him rather than her, and Thomas now can claim his seat on the Supreme Court. But at what price to himself, the integrity of the court, the confirmation process and the whole tangled area of sexual politics in the 1990s?

One obvious danger is that this bizarre episode will discourage capable men and women from agreeing to be nominated if they have any reason to expect the kind of exposure Thomas has been subjected to. Any incident from a nominee's past, no matter how long ago, is apparently fair game for the snipers, with few of the protections offered by a full judicial process.

The Americans' confirmation process in theory is a model of democratic openness, but in practice it has become a three-ring circus rather than a sober review of a nominee's views and record.

However, the hearings have produced at least one positive benefit, in forcing millions of Americans and others to confront the whole question of sexual harassment and inappropriate behavior in the workplace. This is a grey area with no ground rules, where male and female viewpoints on what is and what is not acceptable seldom find any common ground. It is surely healthy that the subject is now being discussed so openly.

As for Thomas, who insisted he would rather die than withdraw, the cloud over his head is certain to linger because many Americans will refuse to accord him the presumption of innocence. How can that not diminish the credibility of the court and render future decisions on women's issues suspect?

A candidate for a position as important as the highest court in the land must be proved innocent beyond a reasonable doubt. Thomas remains a question mark.

Some have argued that our system of appointing Supreme Court of Canada judges — at the prime minster's discretion, usually with expert advice including consultation with provincial bar associations — leaves the public too much in the dark about appointees' biases, leanings and fitness for office. Perhaps so. But by and large the system works; all of those appointed by Prime Minister Brian Mulroney have proved worthy of the honor. If Canadians feel the need to have an open review of government appointees, we should reject the idea of having MPs doing the reviewing. The inevitable partisanship is simply too bruising, too destructive.

THE SPOKESMAN-REVIEW

Spokane, Washington, October 16, 1991

The confirmation of Clarence Thomas was an ugly spectacle but the country is better off for having beheld it.

Ugly in the same sense that a throat culture is ugly but nevertheless valuable to a physician who needs to diagnose illness before he can prescribe treatment.

Thomas moves on to the U.S. Supreme Court, where eight colleagues at present are working around a vacant seat. His less than ringing 52-48 endorsement by the Senate Tuesday is said to be the weakest Supreme Court confirmation vote in history, but it might as well have been 100-0 for all the limitations it will have on his influence.

He is appointed for life and can be expected to serve for years, decades. He brings to the court the valuable perspectives of one who has felt the sting of bigotry and, more recently, one who has been the target of vicious attack. And judging by his career to date, the odds he has overcome, the tenacity he has shown, he will serve ably.

Meanwhile back at the Senate, cleaning up the rubble that the confirmation process left behind will be a long and demanding effort. Thomas' foes went to such extremes to besmirch him that they compelled a normally apathetic public to watch the legislative body do its dirtiest work.

It was clear that when anti-Thomas members of the Judiciary Committee could not shoot him down on the ideological differences that were foremost in their minds, they grasped at any issue that might suffice.

Along came Anita Hill. We're left to follow our individual hunches about whether she or Thomas, if either, was being totally honest in the dramatic weekend examination of her sexual harassment accusations against him. But it really doesn't matter at this point as much as how the whole bizarre showdown came to pass.

The role of faceless staffers in a partisan witchhunt; the desperate lengths to which seemingly honorable politicians will go to win a fight; the willingness of the Senate to let itself be manipulated by select special-interest organizations — all these phenomena have scarred the Senate itself and require attention.

There is reason to hope, based on some members' own words, that the Senate is sufficiently chastened that it will make internal reforms. There is even greater reason to believe that this riveting event has forced some new governmental insights upon a once-disinterested public.

In both cases, the interests of future nominees and of the nation will be better served.

THE KANSAS CITY STAR

Kansas City, Missouri, October 17, 1991

Congress was not exactly riding a wave of public support as it headed into the sexual harassment controversy involving Judge Clarence Thomas.

Resentment continues to smolder across the country over congressional pay. News of check-bouncing in the House left many taxpayers angry at the idea that their political representatives lived in another world, one in which they were not subject to the ordinary rules and concerns of everybody else. Reports that some lawmakers had unpaid restaurant bills at congressional dining rooms didn't help, either.

Then came the sexual harassment charges against Thomas, which were mishandled from the start. The significance of these charges was ignored, the preliminary investigation was botched, and the latest round of hypocritical debate over Washington's favored form of communication — leaks to the press — began.

Sen. Joseph Biden, chairman of the Senate Judiciary Committee, denied that his committee — he was referring basically to himself — had messed up.

Things went downhill from there as the special hearing on Anita Hill's charges against Thomas got under way. A fascinated public tuned in to watch the Judiciary Committee at work. It was not a pretty sight. It was, no doubt, quite an education for millions of people who do not regularly watch their congressional representatives in action.

The hypocrisy was overwhelming. The pontificating was unbearable. The proceedings were unnecessarily repetitious. Senators sometimes fought over trivial issues while ignoring central ones. Democrats and Republicans alike contributed to the spectacle.

The Democrats, of course, had Sen. Ted Kennedy sitting in judgment of a man accused of sexual misconduct. They also had

Biden, who once plagiarized a British politician's life story, discussing the credibility of witnesses.

Sen. Howard Metzenbaum defined the term "sleazy" by introducing unsworn allegations against one witness by reading a transcript of that witness's denial of those allegations. Biden eventually denounced this as improper, but by then, of course, Metzenbaum had done what he set out to do.

On the Republican side, Sen. Arlen Specter began by politely assuring Hill that she was not in an adversarial situation. By the end he had charged her with perjury and challenged her sanity.

For reasons that were not exactly clear, Sen. Orrin Hatch, apologizing profusely, felt compelled to return again and again to the excruciating specifics of Hill's allegations. At another point Specter couldn't seem to get his mind off the subject of female breast size long enough to understand what Hill repeatedly tried to tell him.

The explanations of some Senate votes are likely to further anger many people. Some senators, for example, complained that Hill was not emotional enough during her appearance before the committee. What, no tears? She's a woman, isn't she?

There are some mitigating factors. Investigators sometimes ask the same questions in several different ways, for example, to probe for discrepancies in someone's story. It should also be noted that some senators offered some thoughtful remarks and logical arguments on the controversy.

But the overriding impression is that the Senate did a poor job of handling this matter. Once the dust settles from the confirmation debate, voters will still be asking questions about congressional pay, check-bouncing and unpaid restaurant tabs. The further erosion of public confidence in Congress should concern everyone on Capitol Hill.

MILWAUKEE SENTINEL

Milwaukee, Wisconsin, October 16, 1991

With the exception of sending American troops to war, the anguish that attended the Senate vote to confirm the appointment of Clarence Thomas to the US Supreme Court has rarely been exceeded.

And it may be some time before the bitterness subsides. The bad feelings that resulted from the clashes between proponents and supporters of the nominee as to the issue of whether Thomas was guilty of allegations of sexual harassment can hardly be put aside.

To the extent that this controversy may lead to clearer standards of what is sexual harassment, there may be a positive result from the weird weekend that preceded Tuesday's vote.

The best measure of the washed-out feeling of the lawmakers who wrestled with the charges by Thomas' former assistant, Anita F. Hill, probably was summed up by Sen. James Exon, one of 11 Democrats who voted for Thomas.

"I intend to vote for confirmation but without enthusiasm," Exon said.

And that should not make either supporters or opponents of Thomas very happy. Indeed, it is a sorry day when an appointment to the highest court in the land is approved with such tepid backing.

Despite this consternation, however, all need not be lost. Indeed, the nominee can rescue a blemished reputation by applying himself to the task at hand

and vowing to carve a niche for himself in the category of respected jurists by his performance on the bench.

As Sen. Herbert H. Kohl (D-Wis.) suggested, it is time to put aside any bitterness about a racial society, and, we might add, the entire confirmation debacle. Thomas' call for healing is a good sign he is ready to embark on that course.

And the Senate surely must reckon with the high priority the public obviously gave the issue of sexual harassment through its intense interest in the proceedings. When the television ratings of a Senate hearing top those of all the Sunday sports events, the public has issued a wake-up call that must be answered.

Certainly, employers in both the private and public sectors have a fresh motivation to start taking seriously laws prohibiting sexual discrimination in the workplace.

At the same time, senators must look to their own conduct and motives and the role they played in turning this important duty into a fiasco.

Finally, a word about Hill, who turned what probably would have been a relatively pro forma approval of the Thomas nomination into a national morality play.

Dealing with her new notoriety may be difficult, but Hill obviously has the poise and courage to cope with any fallout, good or bad. If nothing else, she has proved that.

THE BILLINGS GAZETTE
Billings, Montana, October 16, 1991

The Senate has confirmed Clarence Thomas for a seat as an associate justice of the United States Supreme Court, and it doesn't matter a whit what anyone thinks now about the appointment because

GAZETTE OPINION

Americans have no choice but to accept it.

That does not mean there are no lessons to be learned from this painful episode in American history.

The first is one for people such as Anita Hill — people who bring serious charges against a person chosen by the president to perform important duties for the government. The lesson is that the burden of proof falls squarely on the shoulders of the person making the accusations. That person must prove beyond a reasonable doubt the guilt of the nominee. If there is no direct evidence, then enough circumstantial evidence must be produced to assure that there is no question about the wrongdoing by the nominee. Without clear and compelling evidence, charges such as those brought by Hill are not worth the paper they are written on — no matter how true.

Both Thomas and Hill gave testimony that was credible, or incredible, depending on your viewpoint. A juror in a court of law would have had a terrible time deciding on a verdict in this case.

Another lesson is that victims of sexual harassment must not be indignant accusers on the one hand and fawning subordinates on the other. Testimony showed Hill to be both. If there is sexual harassment in the work place, victims must speak out immediately, clearly, forcefully and unequivocally or be silent. And victims must not wait for a decade before telling all.

A lesson for Thomas backers is that they must be consistent. On the one hand, we have the Bush administration and conservatives depending on lie-detector tests in drug trafficking cases and then, on the other hand, we have those same people ignoring the results of such tests taken by political foes when the results clearly do not favor the supporters.

And senators must learn that their jobs go far beyond rubber-stamping every nominee. They should not complain when asked to scrutinize the backgrounds of people nominated for high government offices. It should be in their job descriptions that they are expected to experience some pain in their work. After all, more than 250 million of us must live with the results of their actions — and, in this case, for many years. That's a heavy responsibility, and we supervisors — the American people — must not allow senators to shrink from it. We pay them dearly to look after our interests.

"THEY MUST HAVE EXEMPTED THEMSELVES FROM THE ENVIRONMENTAL LAWS, TOO...."

Rap Singers Arrested, Acquitted in Florida Obscenity Controversy

Two members of the popular rap group 2 Live Crew were arrested on obscenity charges early June 10, 1990 following a performance at a nightclub in Hollywood, Fla. The arrests came four days after a federal district judge in Florida had ruled that the group's album *As Nasty as They Wanna Be* was obscene.

The two band members – producer and lead singer Luther Campbell and singer Chris Wongwon – were arrested on misdemeanor charges of violating state laws. If convicted, they each faced up to a year in prison and a $1,000 fine.

Legal experts said the arrests were an unusual occurrence in that they had apparently been made only in response to the band's lyrics, whereas most obscenity prosecutions in the U.S. were for nudity or indecent acts. 2 Live Crew's lyrics frequently used profanity to describe a variety of sexual acts. Some critics had also complained that the band's songs were demeaning to women.

U.S. District Judge Jose Gonzalez ruled June 6 in Fort Lauderdale, Fla. that *As Nasty as They Wanna Be* was obscene under state law.

Florida's obscenity law followed the guidelines set down in a 1973 U.S. Supreme Court ruling, *Miller v. California*, that deemed a work to be obscene if it appealed to prurient interests, lacked serious artistic value and patently offended local community standards.

In an immediate response to the ruling, law enforcement officials from Broward County, Fla. June 8 arrested a Fort Lauderdale record store owner, Charles Freeman, who sold a copy of *As Nasty as They Wanna Be* to an undercover police officer. Freeman was charged with distributing obscene material, a misdemeanor that carried a maximum penalty of one year in prison and a $1,000 fine.

Civil liberties groups expressed outrage over Gonzalez's ruling and vowed to fight on behalf of Freeman and the 2 Live Crew members. Some charged that the prosecution of 2 Live Crew was racially motivated, since the band's members were black. No similar action had been taken against any white performers such as comedian Andrew Dice Clay, whose work was also the target of obscenity opponents, they noted.

Members of 2 Live Crew were acquitted of obscenity charges Oct. 20, 1990 by a jury in Fort Lauderdale, Fla. The three were Luther Campbell, Mark Ross and Christopher Wongwon. A fourth band member had not been at the concert and was not charged.

The band maintained that its lyrics were deliberately exaggerated and were intended as humor or parody. A literature professor from Duke University who testified on behalf of the group, Henry Louis Gates Jr., argued that the songs carried on a black tradition known as "signifying," which involved teasing or insulting rhymes. "It was the way blacks would fight against the oppression of their slave masters," Gates said. "And rapping is a contemporary form of signifying."

In their case against the group, prosecutors relied heavily on a microcassette recording of the concert that had been made by undercover detectives. The tape was of poor quality and difficult to understand, however. Prosecutors' efforts to recite the lyrics in court were frequently met with embarrassment and laughter. At one point, Judge June Johnston told the court that jurors had requested permission to laugh out loud. Noting that "some of them are having physical pain" from holding in their laughter, Johnston Oct. 17 agreed to the request.

The video to the song "By the Time I Get to Arizona" by Public Enemy sparked a controversy following its debut Jan. 8, 1992. The video, which had been created by the group's lead singer, Chuck D., showed a group of black terrorists assassinating Arizona government officials, in revenge for the state's failure to adopt a holiday honoring slain civil-rights leader Rev. Martin Luther King Jr.

The TENNESSEAN
Nashville, Tennessee, June 12, 1990

THE music group 2 Live Crew should thank law authorities in Broward County, Florida.

Broward County sheriff's deputies, by arresting members of the group on obscenity charges, have brought more publicity to 2 Live Crew's music than the group could have ever attained by conventional means.

The rap on 2 Live Crew is that their lyrics are dirty. There seems to be little argument about that. Their expression of freedom of speech is an "X"-pression.

After U.S. District Judge Jose Gonzalez declared the group's album *As Nasty As They Wanna Be* obscene, the Broward County sheriff sent an undercover detective to arrest a record store owner for selling the album. Later deputies arrested members of the group after a concert.

Crew's cuts off the album went unheard in Nashville recently when the group failed to show for a concert April 15 at the National Guard Armory. But the rap session in Florida got plenty of attention.

How comforting it must be to the citizens in Broward County that law officers there chose to spend their crime-fighting efforts by targeting a group of men who talk dirty. One assumes you would never hear a dirty word in a patrol car.

"This city has a lot greater problems to deal with than who is performing at Club Nu," said City Commissioner Bruce Singer before the recent show.

Thus far, 2 Live Crew has sold more than 1.7 million copies of the album. Thanks to the publicity generated by Broward County law authorities, that number might climb.

"Until this trial, we never could have booked this group on such short notice, with no time [to advertise] and still expect a full house," said Mr. Bob Slade, Club Nu promoter. "They're more popular than ever now."

The definition of obscenity has long been open to debate. But perhaps Mr. Bruce Rogow, an attorney for 2 Live Crew, has a good one. "To have a dozen sheriff's officers spending all this time over some dirty lyrics seems to me to be obscene," he said.

This case might be a bad rap, in more ways than one. ■

The Miami Herald

Miami, Florida, June 9, 1990

'THIS IS a case," the troubling opinion began, "between two ancient enemies: Anything Goes and Enough Already." With those words, Federal Judge Jose A. Gonzalez began a 62-page ruling that the 2 Live Crew rap album *As Nasty As They Wanna Be* is obscene. Thus is escalated a First Amendment free-speech battle that is by no means as nasty as it's gonna get.

The judge's finding is a reasonable application of the U.S. Supreme Court's obscenity rule — *whatever one thinks of that rule.* What's not reasonable, what's indeed odiously intrusive, is the Florida obscenity law that makes the state a morals squad to "protect" adults from their right to read, or see, or hear sexually explicit works that the thought police deem "bad for a person."

Judge Gonzalez's ruling means that anyone selling the album in South Florida faces criminal prosecution. Even so, the judge also found that Broward County Sheriff Nick Navarro committed unconstitutional prior restraint by threatening earlier to arrest record dealers if they sold the album.

Though Skyywalker Records, Inc.'s suit against Sheriff Navarro involved the album producer's rights under the U.S. Constitution, it required Judge Gonzalez to interpret a Florida obscenity law. He held that the album meets all three tests for obscenity set by the U.S. Supreme Court in 1973.

That is, the average person, applying the community's contemporary standards, would find that the work "appeals to the prurient interest"; "the work depicts or describes, in a patently offensive way, sexual conduct" deemed obscene; and the work "taken as a whole, lacks serious literary, artistic, political, or scientific value."

At several points, his ruling's language evidences Judge Gonzalez's discomfiture at having to be the arbiter of such a prickly issue. "The absolutists and other members of the party of Anything Goes should address their petitions to the Florida Legislature, not to this court," he wrote. "If they are sincere, let them say what they actually mean — Let's Legalize Obscenity."

In sum, Judge Gonzalez said, "obscenity is not a protected form of speech under the U.S. Constitution, with or without voluntary labeling. *It is a crime* [his emphasis]. If the people of Florida want to legalize obscenity, they have every right to do so. It is much easier to criticize the law, however, than it is to work to repeal it. . . . "

That's an understatement. Yet if Judge Gonzalez's ruling is affirmed on appeal, Floridians who value free speech have a clear challenge. It is to make indelible the state's clear right to protect minors from smut, and to tell the state to butt out of adults' choices of what they prefer to see, hear, or read.

Clearly the law should protect minors from smut. Clearly it should prosecute fully those who produce or sell sexual materials involving children. Equally clearly, the law should allow adults free access to sexually explicit works, whether in their own homes or in commercial establishments where the customer unmistakably knows the entertainment's nature before entering.

All of that requires changing the law. Which undeniably is harder than criticizing a judge's interpretation of existing law.

Miami, Florida, June 14, 1990

NOW PLAYING nationwide, yet another enlightening act from South Florida: Sheriff Nick Versus 2 Live Crew. Both are getting air time on network television that they never could buy, and for reasons hardly uplifting. Sheriff Navarro is boosting his political fortunes at the expense of more-pressing priorities in Broward law enforcement, while 2 Live Crew is netting a bankroll far beyond expectations for its meager talent.

That always has been the side effect of censorship. It gives more currency to the ideas of those who are censored, thus confirming some young people's specious notion that outrageousness bears rewards.

It is the young who now should be the focus in this case. Legal arguments aside, the album *As Nasty As They Wanna Be* is obscene as most people would define it. And while adults should have free access to *anything* that they wish to read, hear, or view, no parent should have to tolerate the ready availability of obscenity to children.

That issue is being skirted. The sheriff invested a huge amount of police power — some 30 officers — to attend an after-midnight 2 Live Crew performance that admitted only adults who wished to attend.

Also extraneous to this core issue is the argument that 2 Live Crew was singled out because of race, that the group is black, and that it is being heard by middle-class white youths. For society to tolerate obscenity because it is directed to black youths would be the epitome of irresponsibility.

Indeed, children loom large in legal discussions of obscenity. Writing for the majority in the key U.S. Supreme Court decision on obscenity, Chief Justice Warren Burger said: "States have a legitimate interest in prohibiting dissemination of obscene material when the mode of dissemination carries with it a significant danger of offending the sensibilities of unwilling recipients or of exposure to juveniles."

The movie industry's rating system tries to address that issue. Imperfect as that system is, it is an honest effort, and it does convey to children a sense of demarcation and levels of acceptance. The record industry promised cooperation in voluntary labeling but has done so only in fits and starts. Some producers argue that labeling merely attracts the local morals police.

In fact, that is one of the ironies in this case. 2 Live Crew does label its albums, and it makes "clean" versions. Still, there is no bar — except in South Florida now and other scattered areas — to a 13-year-old buying the "nasty" version.

The fact that the idea of labeling has sprung from the political Right and self-righteous does not make it wrong. What would make it right would be an effort that focused carefully on controlling what *children* buy. That is, if children, rather than making a national splash, truly are the issue.

Chicago Tribune

Chicago, Illinois, June 14, 1990

Chicago's mettle is about to be tested in the war against raunchy rappers.

The controversial 2 Live Crew is scheduled to perform its rap music, if that is not a contradiction in terms, with several other rappers at the Chicago Amphitheater on Friday night.

Here's hoping cool heads prevail.

The Miami-based group has performed twice in Chicago without incident in the last eight months. But that was before two members' arrest Sunday in south Florida on charges of giving an obscene performance in an adults-only night club. It was before its album, "As Nasty As They Wanna Be," was ruled obscene by a federal district judge in Ft. Lauderdale, and before authorities there arrested a record store owner who refused to stop selling the album.

In San Antonio, Tex., police have warned store owners to stop selling the album or face obscenity charges. And the city council in Huntsville, Ala., where 2 Live Crew is to perform Sunday, expanded its obscenity ordinance to include live performances.

All of which should have founder Luther Campbell and the other members of 2 Live Crew crying all the way to the bank. Relatively unknown outside rap music circles before, they certainly are well known now—and they have booming record sales to prove it. No one is more responsible for their windfall than the man spearheading the drive to ban them, Miami anti-porn lawyer Jack Thompson.

That's what happens when you try to bring down the weight of America's criminal justice system on a set of words and ideas, no matter how vile or otherwise objectionable they may be.

And make no mistake about it: The uncensored lyrics of "As Nasty As They Wanna Be" are quite vile, graphically describing loathsome acts of degradation and brutality against women—an audio version of the video porn that many Americans routinely see on late-night cable television.

That's why the album has an adults-only label on its jacket, a signal to parents that it contains material they may not want little Johnny or Susie to hear. Some defenders of boundless freedom for recording artists have decried such labeling, charging that it smacks of censorship. Quite the contrary. It can effectively remedy parental concerns without trampling over the constitutional rights of performers.

That's why major record producers have decided to follow the movie industry's lead and implement a voluntary labeling program, if only to avoid the heavy hand of state governments that have threatened to impose labeling systems of their own.

Record labeling gives parents a fighting chance to keep filth out of their homes without subverting our Constitution. Clapping 2 Live Crew in irons is a remedy worthy of a totalitarian state, not the United States, a nation too good and strong to be shaken by a few raunchy rappers.

The Pittsburgh PRESS

Pittsburgh, Pennsylvania, June 15, 1990

Things must be pretty quiet down there in south Florida. No cocaine traffic, no kids toting assault weapons, no muggings or rapes or burglaries. How else to explain the man-hours spent by the Broward County Sheriff's Department to pursue a group of unsavory rap singers?

When a federal judge found "As Nasty as They Wanna Be," an album by 2 Live Crew, to be obscene, Sheriff Nick Navarro got the excuse to do what he clearly wanted to do anyway.

Members of the group performed the offending songs before an adults-only audience in his jurisdiction, so Sheriff Navarro dispatched deputies to arrest them. They were booked on obscenity charges.

No doubt the songs are as repulsive as sheriff and judge allege. And the singers' complaints of persecution sound hollow, considering that they designed their music to be offensive. Sure enough, people were offended, and it's no surprise that they flexed the long arm of the law to remove the offenders.

But can't the sheriff find better crimes to fight? Law enforcement everywhere suffers from meager resources. Busting pop singers should rank far down on its list of priorities.

THE SAGINAW NEWS
Saginaw, Michigan, June 14, 1990

A group called 2 Live Crew, which performs rap music — we're aware that may be a contradiction in terms — has run afoul, literally, of the law in Florida.

If it were only the Florida law, its legal problems would not hold much significance. That state has a checkered history of attention to legal niceties.

But the arrest of a record-store owner for selling 2 Live Crew albums, and of members of the group itself, had the sanction of a federal judge. That places the crackdown on nasty words on a national plane — meaning it could happen here.

It's hard to imagine Saginaw County sheriff's deputies pulling over a rock group outside the Civic Center because somebody didn't like the words or music. That's like arresting bookstore clerks or librarians because one person didn't think others should read "that type of material."

Well, now. As it happens, Michigan bookstores and libraries are worried. The Legislature is considering giving police the power, based on a single complaint, to not only arrest those selling "offensive" books, magazines or tapes, but also to destroy the whole business — before prosecution, never mind conviction. That would set the Supreme Court's "community standards" rule at the lowest Puritanical viewpoint of the Morality Police.

But wouldn't the authorities act reluctantly on such complaints? Not in Florida, where the sheriff in Fort Lauderdale dispatched six deputies to nab that dangerous record-seller, and then multiplied the absurdity by sending 30 officers against some performers armed with nothing more than lyrics.

The brutal anti-woman message of 2 Live Crew stinks. But the Bill of Rights does not protect only the words that uplift and edify. Obviously a lot of people want to hear that message; the group's current album has sold 1.7 million copies. That says something dismal about today's standards, but it's still an awfully large "community" for any judge, or any number of deputies, to disregard.

South Florida, like Mid-Michigan, has some problems considerably more serious than policing what someone says, on tape or on stage, to a willing, paying adult audience. 2 Live Crew's street language may come from the gutter. But these arrests reflect a system with priorities that are not much higher — and far more offensive to liberty.

MILWAUKEE SENTINEL
Milwaukee, Wisconsin, June 12, 1990

"Look around."

We've used that beginning to several editorials lately dealing with American values. We've mourned their decline; we've raged at their corrupters.

Now, the spotlight's glare must expose the newest evidence of decline:

An album — filthy and degrading — put out by a rap group called 2 Live Crew.

They couldn't get a date in Milwaukee last year because promoters couldn't sell enough tickets. But that was only a stop in the crew's vault to national notoriety.

The group has reached its apogee: The album — "As Nasty As They Wanna Be" — has been declared obscene in a Florida case, a Florida record dealer has been arrested for selling the record and two crew members have been arrested for singing lyrics from the album in defiance of the ruling.

First Amendment lawyers are beating a path to Florida to challenge the ruling on constitutional grounds. And liberals are wringing their hands, mourning the federal court's intrusion onto hallowed ground.

The liberals are right in this case.

There is the adult right to hear and see anything. There is a First Amendment right to produce those things that offend and shock. There is even the right to publish or produce those things that twist minds and propel someone into an act of mindless cruelty.

But there also is the principle that some things, though constitutionally protected, make a mockery of free speech and open access to ideas.

There is nothing redeeming about the album in question. It's lyrics are foul, offensive to women and, worse, encourage attacks upon them.

It took no genius to devise the words or the melody. Melody? Pardon the choice of words.

All it took was a few dirty minds and a convenient excuse that this was an album with deep social and ethnic messages that could only be properly expressed with obscenity.

Oops. There we go, using the word "obscenity." Not even the courts know what it is, it seems. They've tried for years to come up with a definition that meets constitutional muster and have essentially failed.

But some things are "obscene." The word is in the dictionary, free to be used.

What 2 Live Crew and other purveyors of smut have done takes no great talent. They have taken taste and turned it into a constitutional issue. In the end, they probably will prevail. A free society demands it.

Still, there is the implicit understanding by a civilized people that some things are taboo.

That means the First Amendment does not protect groups such as 2 Live Crew from the contempt of others, or from the kind of consumer aversion that will make their careers "As Brief As They Wanna Be."

THE TAMPA TRIBUNE
Tampa, Florida, June 12, 1990

You have to wonder about Broward County Sheriff Nick Navarro, who has charged members of the rap group 2 Live Crew with obscenity. He had intended to arrest all the members of the controversial quartet but the several deputies attending the group's Fort Lauderdale concert managed to snag only two.

In any event, Navarro's action succeeded only in getting yet more publicity for the squalid entertainers.

2 Live Crew's sole talent, such as it is, is devoted to debasing women. Their lyrics are filth, but does such filth threaten the Republic? And why the concentration on black rap bands? There are white punk-rock bands whose songs are equally lewd.

Without all the fanfare, wouldn't interest in 2 Live Crew soon wither? After all, there are talented rap groups that offer more than just obscenity, groups that capture something of the anger and vitality of the inner-city environment.

But Sheriff Navarro appears intent on keeping 2 Live Crew in the headlines. Last week, he won a ruling from a U.S. district judge that one of their albums was obscene. Sheriff's deputies made arrests when the band sang songs from that album at a concert to which only adults were admitted.

Children, to be sure, should be protected from this foulest smut, and that's the job of parents. It would help, perhaps, if the record industry adopted a rating system similar to that for movies.

But grown-ups don't need Sheriff Navarro to decide what music they can listen to. And 2 Live Crew doesn't deserve any more valuable publicity. Exploitive, anti-social entertainers should be permitted to vanish into a well-earned oblivion.

St. Petersburg Times
St. Petersburg, Florida, June 9, 1990

Assuming the First Amendment hasn't yet been eroded as badly as the Fourth, it won't take long for an appeals court to overturn U.S. District Court Judge Jose Gonzalez's ruling that an album by the rap group 2 Live Crew is obscene.

Is *As Nasty As They Wanna Be* vulgar and artless? Most people probably would think so, but when vulgarity and artlessness are made illegal, our jails will be 10 times more overcrowded than they already are. The definition of obscenity is much stricter and narrower than that, unless Gonzalez and other pandering judges succeed in changing it.

In ignoring 100 percent of the expert testimony offered in the case, Gonzalez ruled that the album *As Nasty As They Wanna Be* meets the 1973 U.S. Supreme Court standard for obscenity. Among other things, those guidelines say that the material in question must be outside of contemporary community standards. Any album that sells 2-million copies, despite intense official efforts to make it hard to find, is by definition within the mainstream of a large segment of American communities. In this case, the community in question is Fort Lauderdale, where the standards historically have been far laxer than in the great majority of communities where 2 Live Crew and other rap groups haven't been subjected to harassment.

The court's 1973 guidelines also say that an obscene work must lack serious artistic, literary or political value. *As Nasty As They Wanna Be's* artistic merits are dubious, although several sociologists and music critics have extolled them.

However, the album's political value is undeniable. This trumped-up case has already proved its political value for politically ambitious Broward County Sheriff Nick Navarro and politically desperate Florida Gov. Bob Martinez.

On the list of serious crimes that should be commanding Navarro's and Martinez's attention, nasty rap lyrics surely rank near the bottom. The issue does make a handy diversion, though, for politicians who would prefer to keep the public from giving too much scrutiny to their success in controlling the infinitely more serious issues of murder, robbery, drug trafficking and organized crime. No wonder, then, that Martinez and Navarro are at the vanguard of the anti-2 Live Crew crusade.

There's always a whiff of political expediency at the center of our periodic blue-nosed obscenity hunts. In this case, there's a whiff of racism as well.

If judges, governors and sheriffs are going to be hypocrites, at least let them be equal-opportunity hypocrites, harassing the respectable middle-aged suburban consumers of X-rated films as well as the less respectable young urban consumers of rap music.

The New York Times
New York City, New York, June 18, 1990

The rap music group 2 Live Crew, one of the raunchiest in the trade, is in the toils of Florida law for its record album "Nasty as They Wanna Be." If mere offensive talk were a crime, the record's self-styled vulgar lyrics would be criminal. But the charge is obscenity, which has two other independent elements: an appeal to prurient interests and lack of serious artistic value.

It's hard to see how this record can fail all three tests at once, but Judge Jose Gonzalez, sitting in Fort Lauderdale, finds obscenity. The musicians sought refuge in his Federal Court from the county sheriff, who is trying to stop sales of the record deviously, by threatening retailers with arrest. The judge found the sheriff's tactics reprehensible, but his obscenity finding left authorities free to try to stop sales directly, by prosecuting in County Court.

That's much harder. Conviction of crime requires proof beyond a reasonable doubt that this recording incites prurient interest or lust in the average person. It is not easy to imagine that jurors would detect anything sexually arousing in this album's vile references to sex, insults to women and dirty nursery rhymes. Judge Gonzalez delivered a 62-page opinion that wholly failed to show how sexual references, countlessly repeated to a rap beat, could stir much lust, as opposed to anger, boredom or perhaps a giggle or groan of disgust.

If constables and prosecutors want to use resources on such recordings, they could more sensibly concentrate on keeping them out of the hands of minors, letting adults take them or leave them. And they could do so more honorably than by continuing to intimidate merchants with new, devious threats.

As for artistic value, those officials, like this newspaper, are mainstream and middle class. The history of music is the story of innovative, even outrageous styles that interacted, adapted and became mainstream. Officials should hesitate before striking down, directly or indirectly, a cultural phenomenon they do not fully understand.

copyright © The New York Times 1990

The Honolulu Advertiser
Honolulu, Hawaii, June 17, 1990

The first, completely predictable result of the police crackdown on 2 Live Crew has been to boost sales of the raunchy rap group's controversial album.

Some Honolulu shops have taken the recording off their shelves, and major stores still selling it are sold out. So, we confess to not having heard it, only to having read a paraphrase of its contents.

By all accounts, it is vulgar and offensive. Even critics who appreciate rap say it is an undistinguished relative of bawdy "stag party" comedy. But there's nothing amusing about a barrage of expletives, moaning and lyrics that celebrate sadistic disrespect for women.

The hard part in defending the First Amendment right of expression (and the right of adults to choose what to read, watch or listen to) is standing up for things that are purposefully distasteful and base.

But the unsanitized versions of 2 Live Crew's songs are not performed over public airwaves. Members of the group were arrested for words sung in the privacy of an adults-only club; a store owner was jailed for selling a record with a voluntary label describing its contents as explicit.

That seems to us the wrong way to use the government's police powers.

The broad principle is relatively simple. Is anything so offensive that it should be forbidden to consenting adults in our diverse society? Yes. Child porn and so-called "snuff movies" come to mind. But what else? Agreement on what's "obscene" is elusive. Like the public, members of

The Advertiser Editorial Board disagree among themselves.

But our rule is: When in doubt, opt against censorship. We wonder whether a legal ban on 2 Live Crew, or judicial intimidation, will make it easier the next time to expand the law's definition of "obscenity" to other performers who rub the majority, or a vocal minority, the wrong way.

It's utterly galling to see people profit from purposeful bad taste. But in this, 2 Live Crew is hardly alone. Entertainers Andrew Dice Clay, Eddie Murphy, Richard Pryor, Redd Foxx, the late Lenny Bruce and others have used calculated vulgarity.

What about exposure to kids? That's a tougher one, we agree.

Label the albums? Restrict sales? Good luck. The way pop music is passed around, keeping it out of the earphones of curious and determined youngsters is impossible.

What's to be done? This is easier said than done, but:

■ Adults must monitor youngsters' activities. Parents must discourage listening to this material and, most important, explain to their kids why it is bad stuff.

■ Record stores have the right not to stock objectionable material, just as consumers have the right not to buy it and not to patronize stores that sell it. Responsible music dealers should do what they can to keep trash out of the hands of minors. That's better than government censorship.

■ On a larger level, we must ask ourselves what it says about our society that 2 Live Crew and their ilk find any audience — white or black, male or female — outside the locker room.

The Seattle Times
Seattle, Washington, June 22, 1990

IF YOU want to be shocked and appalled, buy a copy of the 2 Live Crew tape filled with vulgar lyrics, if you can find it.

Seattle music stores can't keep it in stock. So much for community standards.

The controversial recording has sold 1.7 million copies nationwide, and sales are booming.

Blame the federal judge in Florida who banned the record in his jurisdiction. Labeling the record as obscene was money in the bank for the prospering and properly outraged rap group.

A sheriff got into the act with a televised arrest of a record-store owner who dared sell the contraband. Some of Broward County's finest hauled two of the band's four members off to the hoosegow after a nightclub performance.

After these encounters with the law, 2 Live Crew has a rare opportunity to change its name. We'd suggest "Arrested Adolescence," because it's perfect match for the extravagantly foul mouths and puerile sexual attitudes.

Exaggerated language about male sexual prowess prevades our entertainment, from Sam Malone, the bartender on "Cheers," to Eddie Murphy's films and comedy concerts.

Sexuality for 2 Live Crew is a teen-ager's preoccupation with self-gratification. A partner is incidental to personal pleasure. Dr. Ruth hears that all the time.

As for bragging about sexual exploits, this rap album has given a beat to generations of locker-room hyperbole. Emotional maturity stunted at the zipper crosses race and cultural lines.

A warning: 2 Live Crew might make you smile. The nasty rappers are guilty of creating one song that will become a fraternity-party standard, and another one that puts a new twist on a familiar debate: Tastes Great vs. Less Filling.

Instead of a record review, what the wayward judge needs is a civics lesson, a refresher course in American values — values that create lines around the block for movies filled with the F word, and soaring ratings for family sit-coms rife with sexual snickers and bathroom jokes.

Beyond the hypocrisy, this country is rooted in ideas and revels in competition among them. Individuals are free to embrace or avoid words and ideas.

Chaste nations that inhibit personal expression are the greatest official moralizers. China and Cuba are not burdened with debates about obscenity. Or political diversity, or religious freedom.

This contentious, ribald democracy will survive 2 Live Crew.

Lincoln Journal
Lincoln, Nebraska, February 9, 1992

Of the mass of Dr. Martin Luther King Jr.'s adolescent and young adult writings to be published later this month, one attained national publicity late last week. That is an essay the future Nobel Peace Prize winner wrote at age 21, in 1951, while a student at Crozer Theological Seminary in Pennsylvania.

King

Looking back on a searing childhood experience of racial bias, followed by subsequent personal spiritual and intellectual growth, King found he could surmount and discard an early hatred of "every white person."

But not until his college life did King "conquer this anti-white feeling." Association with like-minded white students who joined in interracial organizations offered a wider, more promising vision. It helped King permanently move to embrace and promote the possibility of racial cooperation. "All of God's children," as he said in the most inspiring address of the 20th century by any American.

Disclosure of young King's affirming essay was juxtaposed with Black History and Black Homecoming observances on many American college campuses. One may wonder how the slain human rights champion would have reacted to several of the more strident observances.

At Penn State University, a black columnist for the student newspaper asserted "white people are devils." Writer Chino Wilson declared "white people are the most violent race ever to inhabit the earth. . . . To protect ourselves we should bear arms immediately and form a militia . . ."

At the University of Nebraska-Lincoln, Sister Souljah, a member of the popular, deliberately confrontational rap group Public Enemy, was cheered last week contending there is no such thing as reverse racism.

Racism is practiced exclusively by whites, she implied. And with them, "we [African-Americans] are at war." If not personally racist, Souljah acknowledged she certainly is prejudiced against whites, representing as they do, in her opinion, "a long line of lying, stealing cheats" and hence, collectively and individually untrustworthy.

A fair guess is that for the Sister Souljahs of our time, Martin Luther King Jr. probably was an Uncle Tom who debased his own racial integrity. His cross-racial message of inclusion falls off the edge of cultural fracture lines that groups, white and black widen, often unintentionally.

Nevertheless, the furor cloaks quiet improvements. Progress toward racial live-and-let-live attitudes in the United States since King's college days 40 years ago, if jerky and inadequate, is still undeniable. It has even reached such an advanced level that black organizations felt sufficiently confident to split on Judge Clarence Thomas' successful appointment to the Supreme Court. Some supporters swallowed the symbolism line, endorsing purely on the basis of the man's skin color.

As the sun rises in the east, the gravity of that mistake for true minority interests will become clear with the passing years. Then will it be interesting to hear Thomas' original defenders — on or off college campuses.

The Phoenix Gazette
Phoenix, Arizona, January 9, 1992

Arizona civil rights leaders would do the responsible thing by condemning a new music video by the group Public Enemy in which the rap group kills make-believe Arizona officials for refusing to make Martin Luther King Jr. Day a state holiday.

Public officials should not hesitate to be equally outspoken. The video portrays a senator falling to the floor after eating poisoned candy and the governor's car being blown up. The killings are interspersed with re-enactments of King's assassination.

A press release from the rap group left no confusion about the message the video is intended to convey, describing it as a "riveting revenge scenario intercut with black-and-white footage re-creating certain events from the segregation struggle of the 1960s — a struggle that, given the state of mind if certain higher-ups in Arizona, continues today."

Beside being wildly inaccurate — the governor, legislative leaders and the business community are all in favor of reinstating the holiday — the so-called "revenge fantasy" attempts to use the valid objectives of civil rights to justify violence.

The message sent by the video could not be more at odds with the philosophy of the man the group seeks to honor. The state's civil rights leaders need to speak out forcefully and say so.

THE ARIZONA REPUBLIC
Phoenix, Arizona, January 9, 1992

THE simmering anger in some quarters over Arizona's failure to enact a Martin Luther King holiday, delivered in the form of an intense rap music video, has stirred the ire of more than a few Arizonans. But the latest graphic and controversial work from the group Public Enemy should not be taken so seriously that we forget the true issue before us.

Public Enemy's *By the Time I Get to Arizona* video has enraged many who already had their dander up over the unfortunate setbacks in the ongoing effort to establish a King Day in this state. However, this video, which blends a depiction of Arizona politicians who oppose the holiday with re-enactments of the civil rights movement of the 1960s, is simply one politically active music group's view of things. Nothing more.

"It's a trip into the fantasy world of Public Enemy. You know, the big payback," says Chuck D, the lead rapper, whose angry persona fuels the group's raw emotional appeal. Traveling through the collective consciousness of Public Enemy — a group that attributes virtually everything it dislikes to racism — is rarely without bizarre twists and turns. Far from eschewing violence, the group embraces and exploits it, even as it preaches peace and harmony. Other inconsistencies are evident as well. Public Enemy questions the agenda of the education system, but encourages young people to stay in school.

The dichotomy shown in the video — Chuck D pushes a button, setting off a car bomb and killing an Arizona governor who had vowed that there would never be a King holiday — is hardly unusual for this group. It is unlikely, however, to advance the cause of honoring a man who championed non-violence and passive resistance to injustice.

Public Enemy's message is extreme and exaggerated. It is difficult to ignore the repugnant portrayals of our state leaders being assassinated for their philosophical or political views — just as it is difficult to overlook the murder of Dr. King for his leadership in the movement to establish equal rights and a better life for all Americans.

The rational reaction to the video would be to accept it for what it is — as a piece of popular "art," the worth of which ultimately will be determined in the eye and mind of the beholder. Any other response would suggest that Arizonans are a little too sensitive to this poking at our state's gaping wound.

Arizonans should not withdraw tortoise-like into a defensive shell over the video, thereby giving credence to Public Enemy's fatuous allegation that this is a racist state. Moreover, they should resist citing this video — a minor blip in the history of Arizona's King Day controversy — as an excuse to vote against the holiday. In all probability, by November the video and Public Enemy will be long forgotten.

Black Film Openings Spark Violence

The opening of the film *New Jack City* sparked violence in several cities across the U.S. March 8-9, 1991. The film, directed by Mario Van Peebles and starring Van Peebles and rap singer Ice T, was based on a true story about the rise and fall of a drug dealer in the Harlem section of New York City. In New York's Brooklyn Heights area, a 19-year-old man was shot to death March 8 during a fight that broke out inside the movie theater and spilled onto the street. In Los Angeles, a crowd estimated by police at between 1,000 and 1,500 went on a two-and-half-hour rampage March 8-9, looting stores and injuring several people, after a theater showing the film oversold tickets. Other incidents were reported in Las Vegas, Boston and Sayersville, N.J.

The film *Boyz in the Hood* sparked violence in several cities across the U.S. following its opening July 12, 1991. The film, written and directed by 23-year-old John Singleton, was about a young man growing up in a drug- and gang-infested black neighborhood in south-central Los Angeles. It had an upbeat, anti-drug, anti-violence message. In the riots, which in many instances involved gang members, one man was shot to death in Riverdale, Ill., near Chicago, and more that 20 others were injured in such cities as Los Angeles, Minneapolis, Seattle, Jersey City, N.J., and Tuscaloosa, Ala.

The Orlando Sentinel
Orlando, Florida, July 16, 1991

Violence is nothing but a dead-end street. That's supposed to be the message of the film *Boyz N the Hood*, which had its national debut last weekend marred by a murder, shootings and property damage in several cities, including Orlando.

But you would never know that non-violent message from most of the previews that Columbia Pictures has been using to promote the film in theaters and on television. Instead, Columbia dangerously emphasizes the film's violence, apparently to seduce people to see the film.

That's a shame, because *Boyz N the Hood* is a worthwhile movie, which stresses the responsibilities parents have to their children and young black men have to themselves, their neighborhoods and each other.

Instead of simply pushing the film's violence, which Columbia euphemistically calls the film's "entertainment value," the public deserves a more accurate preview of what the film is about.

After all, Columbia officials must have known there could be a problem with the previews emphasizing violence — they had discussed security concerns with theater operators before the film was sent out. So why did they do it? Are they simply capitulating to the idea that violence sells, no matter what the bloody consequences?

No one wants to go to the movies to be in a riot. Unless a more thoughtful marketing campaign is introduced to defuse the violent expectations of some moviegoers, Columbia may learn the hard way that sometimes violence doesn't pay off in the movie box office.

Minneapolis Star and Tribune
Minneapolis, Minnesota, July 17, 1991

A true story of anger, bullets and fear erupted Friday night outside a downtown Minneapolis movie theater after "Boyz N the Hood" played inside on the screen. Outside, six people were wounded, one critically. This week city officials and neighborhood representatives are trading frustration and recriminations on why it happened and who's going to do something about it. Perhaps all should watch the movie.

It's a gritty film with a point of view. Writer/director John Singleton, 23, tells the story of the Los Angeles neighborhood of his youth, where young people's lives are populated with easy sex, drugs (mostly booze, in this case), guns, random gang violence and a constant whine of sirens, helicopters and bullets.

Take away the helicopters and these scenes could have been shot in Minneapolis' toughest neighborhoods as well. So the values Singleton tries to convey should be instructive here — the importance of the father in raising children, honest discussion about sex including the virtue of abstinence (a Catholic girl wins in the end), the wasted potential of those who do not escape the cycle of aimlessness and violence.

Singleton's movie not only deplores violence, but publishes a message of responsibility as urgent in the Twin Cities as in Los Angeles: There can be no excuses from any individual or community for this deadly game of gangs and guns and mindlessness.

Some have suggested closing down "Boyz N the Hood." Minneapolis officials have wisely refused. Better yet, urge young people to see it over and over again, until the rough excitement of the flash of guns and macho sex talk wears off and the message of education, abstinence and hope bleeds through.

By all accounts the movie did not incite Friday night's violence, but was only the catalyst that brought together the incendiary friction of two Minneapolis gangs, and all has been quiet since then. No one should be deterred from attending tonight's Aquatennial torchlight parade. To be deterred is to miss just the kind of proud community festival that has uplifted citizens for years, and celebrates many of the values that Singleton — and all of us — want to preserve.

Los Angeles Times
Los Angeles, California, July 16, 1991

"Boyz N the Hood," a strong anti-gang movie, should not be blamed for the shooting and fights that broke out at several area theaters and at movie houses in other cities. The violence is more of a reflection of what's wrong in urban America.

The film's young director, John Singleton, acknowledges the common carnage with a statement that many will not find startling: "One out of every 21 black American males will be murdered in their lifetime." Singleton, who is black, also points out in the movie that these deaths come primarily at the hands of other young black men.

Young black men kill and get killed in the film. But the movie does not validate murders, drive-by shootings or revenge. Instead it salutes parental guidance, friendship and respect. It exalts a demanding and responsible black father who is there for his son. It captures the friendship of young black men, including two who are determined to escape the gangs, the crack and the killings.

Eight exhibitors canceled the movie after one murder and 33 injuries at 20 movie theaters in several cities. But about 830 theaters—including some in Los Angeles—have taken additional precautions and continue to screen the movie. Columbia Pictures has offered to pay for increased security and has remained committed to the movie. That is a reasonable and responsible stance.

Banning "Boyz N the Hood" won't stop the shooting. The film's message—that gang-banging is senseless—deserves widespread play. The violence is regrettable; the film is not.

THE DENVER POST

Denver, Colorado, July 16, 1991

USUALLY, IT'S violence *in* the movies that bothers people. This week, Americans are concerned about violence *at* the movies.

Fortunately, theater owners in the Denver area have reacted with restraint in the wake of the fights and shootings that marred the opening of the film "Boyz N the Hood" at numerous theaters around the country last weekend.

While the movie has been pulled from the schedule at two theaters where disturbances broke out Friday night — a Mann outlet near the Aurora Mall and another in the Cherry Creek shopping center — it's still playing at three other Mann theaters in the metro area, plus two AMC houses and a United Artists outlet.

Their managers appear to have recognized that, here and else-where, the violence was probably not triggered by anything shown on the screen. Rather, it grew out of confrontations afterward between rival gang members or other trouble-seeking youths who happened to be present in the same place at the same time.

Indeed, the message of the movie — set in gang-torn south central Los Angeles — is one of peace and hope, not hostility and despair.

It may be advisable in some situations to post extra security guards or cancel late-night showings of the film, as a way of discouraging disorderly behavior. But it would be tragic indeed if moviegoers nationwide were cheated out of a chance to see this thought-provoking work because of the actions of a few troublemakers at a small percentage of the more than 800 theaters where it's showing.

THE CHRISTIAN SCIENCE MONITOR
Boston, Massachusetts, March 21, 1991

A SAGA about inner-city drug culture, "New Jack City," is the latest movie to be greeted with violence by young theater-goers. In Los Angeles, New York, and Boston the film's scenes of killing and degradation were matched by real-life stabbings, shootings, and rioting.

"New Jack City" has also been greeted by millions of dollars in ticket sales.

It would be a mistake, however, to simply write off this film as another example of mindless Hollywood gore designed to make a quick buck. The blood, gutter language, sex, and frenetic action are certainly present, and concerns that such material sparks emulation from youthful viewers are warranted. The steady stream of viciousness coming out of studios today is deeply worrying.

Still, director Mario Van Peebles clearly intended "New Jack City" to be a movie with a message: that the excitement and money of cocaine dealing leads, quite literally, to a dead end.

In case the message is missed as the "Godfather"-like tale of gangster/drug entrepreneur Nino Brown is spun out, a sociological epitaph ends the film, warning that there are "Nino Browns in every city" – and unless something is done to alleviate the hopelessness that feeds drug use, there will continue to be.

The members of the National League of Cities who recently called for an "Operation Urban Storm" to address the needs of America's deteriorating urban hubs would agree with that message. So would Health and Human Services Secretary Louis W. Sullivan. Last week he announced ghastly statistics showing that death by gunshot among young black men rose 100 percent between 1984 and 1988. It rose by 40 percent among all teenagers. Policemen know only too well how accurate the movie's portrayal of heavily armed young drug dealers really is.

None of this, however, can offset the film's relentless violence. It's questionable, at best, whether the movie's social messages will register with young viewers. There's little doubt its scenes of cruelty will.

If moviemakers really want to counter the drug culture, they might try themes of caring and redemption instead of hatred and vengeance.

The Washington Times
Washington, D.C., July 17, 1991

John Singleton's new movie, "Boyz N the Hood," is a portrait of street life and attempts to escape it in South Central Los Angeles. The movie centers on Tre Styles, whom we meet in an opening sequence as an 11-year-old and watch in most of the movie as a senior in high school, and his friends, who are either resigned to the violence and drugs of their environment or hunting for a way out of it. Needless to say, some will die by the end of it. "Boyz N the Hood" (the "hood" is slang for neighborhood) is profane, smutty and brutal, usually convincingly so. Though it is no polished piece of moviemaking (Mr. Singleton is 23), and though it is marred by an intermittently preachy tone and a conspiratorial view of whites, it has a number of superb performances and packs some punch.

It is also, alas, getting a bum rap. There have been a number of violent incidents in and around movie theaters where it is playing — a fatal shooting in the suburbs of Chicago; shots fired in a theater in Universal City, near Los Angeles; an unruly crowd in Glen Burnie Monday night.

Do movies about street violence cause street violence? That seems to be a question on the minds of a number of people as they think about "Boyz N the Hood" and other movies — "New Jack City" and "Colors," for example. The sociologists have been after this issue for years, and despite their best efforts to make a connection, the answer is no. Trouble is caused by troublemakers — even to the point of murder, which is caused by murderers — not movies.

It is no more surprising that tough and violent young men with attitudes are going to see "Boyz N the Hood" than that firefighters went to see "Backdraft." The movie purports in part to be about people like them. They are going to be a part of the audience, and people are mistaken if they expect them to check their attitudes at the door.

But they are going to be only a small part of the audience. "Boyz N the Hood" is playing utterly peacefully in most places, and where it has not been, theaters are trying to make sure that their security is up to the challenge. Nor is "Boyz N the Hood" only about violent people; it is also, pre-eminently, about people trying to escape the violence. They will be in the audience too.

AKRON BEACON JOURNAL
Akron, Ohio, July 23, 1991

Psychologists say it's no surprise that gang members have shown up at movie theaters featuring *Boyz N The Hood*, John Singleton's thoughtful and powerful film about a young man's coming of age in the inner-city of Los Angeles.

Offer a realistic film about the world of gangs, apparently, and thugs will be there, no matter how critically they're portrayed.

Unfortunately, the gangs all too often have stayed in character, causing violence and the closing of several screenings, including two in the Akron area.

The closings haven't exactly hurt *Boyz* at the box office. It made $10 million in its first week. But the troubles have been a reminder of how tough it can be in city neighborhoods.

In a way, it makes perfect, if disturbing, sense that in places *Boyz* has been the victim of gangs. Indeed, that's the drama Singleton so poignantly captures, the choice between the world of violence and crime and the world of hard work, school and discipline.

As Singleton knows, far too many times the world of violence prevails.

We hope Hollywood resists buckling, saying 'no' to similar films in the future; the earlier release of *New Jack City*, a less accomplished gang film, attracted violence, too.

Gangs wreak much, much greater harm than closing a movie or two. When a mind such as Singleton's is discouraged from telling, so compellingly, the story of how destructive gang life can be, the gangs win one more time.

THE TENNESSEAN
Nashville, Tennessee, July 22, 1991

IT would be unfair to blame incidents of violence that have left one dead and 33 injured over the showing of the film *Boyz N the Hood* on the film itself.

The movie takes great pains to stress non-violence and to "increase the peace," as its final on-screen message to the audience says. The film opened last weekend to critical acclaim but to violent reaction in cities across the country.

Those acts of violence may be more a reflection of the very frustrations felt by young people living in the world the film depicts than anger provoked by the movie. Many of the incidents have occurred before the movie even started or just after the lights went down.

Boyz N the Hood tells the story of life in a violent inner city neighborhood. It shows the importance of proper parenting, responsible decision-making, how good kids can fall into trouble and how hard it can be to avoid it.

But it consistently preaches the right message, to avoid temptations that lead to hardship and trouble. That is why it's particularly distressing to see its distribution end in bloodshed throughout the country. Fortunately, by all accounts, showings of the film in Nashville have been calm.

The movie does not provoke anger. It promotes peace. Controversy has, no doubt, contributed to its major box office appeal thus far. But it would be a shame if publicity surrounding the movie frightened some potential movie-goers from seeing the film. ∎

Part III: Minorities in America

America has been the destination of peoples from every country in the world. The U.S. is unique among countries created by immigrants in its conscious decision to become a diverse society, where, ideally, people of all nationalities would be judged by their abilities, not their backgrounds.

In the century following the American Revolution, the door to the country was wide open: people could enter and leave as they pleased. However, starting in the mid-1800s, official U.S. immigration policy began to tighten. Rather than being welcomed to the labor pool, immigrants, first from Europe and later from Asia, were increasingly viewed as competitors for jobs and land. By the turn of the century, the federal government had imposed strict immigration regulations: health standards were set and certain forms of contract labor were prohibited.

Ellis Island in New York harbor was designated as the processing center for European immigrants and became a symbol of America's tougher policy. Not everyone could get in anymore and, in fact, one-third of all arrivals were sent back. Angel Island in San Francisco Bay performed the same function on the West Coast and had the same symbolic significance to Asian immigrants. In 1882 Congress passed the Chinese Exclusion Act and set a precedent not only for exclusion of Asians but for exclusion in general. A sentiment in favor of restrictive immigration continued to grow throughout the decades and culminated in the 1924 National Origins Act which established a quota system heavily favoring western European immigrants and stalling Asian immigration.

By the time the quota system went into effect, ethnicity was already a fact of U.S. life as ethnic minorities of all kinds dotted the American landscape. But the idea that they might assimilate was hoped for by some and dreaded by others. The conflict generated by the dispute between that hope and that dread has shaped the history of American race relations for more than a century.

In the early 1900s the term "melting pot" came into popular use. According to the vision of the melting pot, America was a great crucible in which cultural and genetic blending would inevitably take place and engender something unique among the peoples of the earth. Though many accepted the inevitability of the process they didn't necessarily welcome it. Assimilation, they worried, would debase and weaken the American "character."

Antiethnic furor used to be relatively straightforward. There was a "Negro problem," a "Chinese problem" and a "Mexican problem," for example, and the response from the dominant group was directed at each minority group separately and regionally.

Today, a new wave of immigrants has once again revived old fears. Hispanics from Central and South America are this country's fastest-growing immigrant group and are forecast to become our largest minority group in the near future. Unlike past immigrants, who left the "old country" beyond the ocean, Hispanics are very close to their homelands in the Western Hemisphere. The psychological and cultural distances that former immigrants had to travel do not exist for Hispanics, whose native countries are a relatively short distance away. Such proximity hinders the pull of assimilation and increases the pressure for bilingualism.

Complicating the issue is the fact that the different minorities have emerged at a time when sensitivity to ethnic and racial issues is at a record – and when hostilities appear to be on the rise. Part of the current tension can be seen in economic terms: many large proportions of recent immigrants come from the upper social levels of their societies at the same time that the manufacturing jobs that previously absorbed immigrants are disappearing. The new immigrants have been grafted on to extant minority communities with varying degrees of friction, with the conflict between blacks and Koreans being the most acute.

Complicating the situation further has been the emergence of nonethnic special interest groups demanding varying kinds of attention. A dramatic change in personal lifestyles and traditional sex roles has taken place during the last generation. Cutting across backgrounds and beliefs, a new social structure has been created. The women's movement, the gay rights movement and the fight for the rights of the disabled are perhaps the most significant and successful galvinizing U.S. activist forces in the last generation. Although still evolving these changes have been the basis of controversial campaigns for equality.

Reagan's Comments on Native Americans Stir Controversy

President Ronald Reagan May 31, 1988 created an uproar with comments made about Native Americans. The comments were made during Reagan's first visit to the Soviet Union. On the third day of that visit Reagan addressed the students of the Lenin Hills campus of Moscow State University, Soviet leader Mikhail S. Gorbachev's alma mater. Speaking beneath a large bust of V.I. Lenin, the founder of Soviet communism, the president said: "Today the world looks expectantly to signs of change, steps toward greater freedom in the Soviet Union. We watch and we hope as we see positive changes taking place. There are some I know in your society who fear that change will bring only disruption and discontinuity, who fear to embrace the hope of the future...Sometimes it takes faith."

The president later answered questions from the students. One of them asked Reagan if he would meet with the Native American activists visiting Moscow. An organization called the Soviet Peace Committee May 30 had sponsored a Moscow press conference at which American Indian Movement members accused the Reagan administration of fostering racism. Reagan replied that he would be happy to meet with the activists. He then went on to discourse about Native Americans in general: "They from the beginning announced that they wanted to maintain their way of life...And we set up these reservations so they could, and have the [U.S.] Bureau of Indian Affairs take care of them...."

He continued: "Maybe we made a mistake. Maybe we should not have humored them in that wanting to stay in that kind of primitive lifestyle. Maybe we should have said, 'No, come join us. Be American citizens along with the rest of us.' And many do." The president said that some Indians had become "very wealthy from oil on their reservations. And so I don't know what their complaint might be."

Organizations representing Native Americans May 31 expressed outrage over Reagan's remarks.

The Kansas City Times
Kansas City, Missouri, June 7, 1988

This time the Reagan apologists are trying to explain the president's insulting remarks about American Indians. Clearly, Ronald Reagan is a man who doesn't know when to quit talking.

By the time Reagan realizes that he has said more than enough, it is too late, the damage has been done and a rescue team is sent in to tend to the injured.

Reagan may as well have stood at Moscow State University and read from the script of "The Santa Fe Trail," the 1940 movie in which he played Gen. George Custer.

The administration's relationship with Indian organizations was poor before the summit due to its consistent recommendations for budget cuts for the Bureau of Indian Affairs and other apparent anti-Indian activities. This tense relationship has been worsened by the president's inaccurate portrayal of America's past and present while in the Soviet Union.

If the president had only answered directly the question about some Indians' trip to Moscow to meet with him, his aides probably would be tying a neat bow around Reagan's summitry. Instead, many of them are having to push all the demons back into the Pandora's box opened by their boss in this matter.

The president's description of some Indians as oil barons was absurd and embarrassing, especially before the Russians. The bigger insult, however, was Reagan's belief that reservations were one of the many ways in which the U.S. government "humored" millions of displaced Indian tribes, the survivors of years of massacre.

"Maybe we should not have humored them in that way, wanting to stay in that primitive lifestyle." It got worse, but no need to repeat the episode in its entirety here.

Peter McDonald, chairman of the Navajo Nation, the largest Indian tribe in the U.S., told a Washington Rotary Club gathering just how wrong Reagan was about the petroleum-rich Indians. "Maybe some on-site inspection of our reservation is needed to see that Navajos . . . are hardly oil-pumping barons. When you have a per capita income of $2,400 and an unemployment rate of 40 percent, you're talking poverty."

Reagan ought not recite American history, but read it for a change. If there's no time for that, he ought to meet with any of the nation's knowledgable 1.4 million Indians. A meeting with the president, after all, is one reason some of them went all the way to Moscow.

Roanoke Times & World-News
Roanoke, Virginia, June 2, 1988

WELL, THERE GOES the red vote.

And President Reagan was doing so well in Moscow. He had toured the city, beaming and waving to enthusiastic crowds; he had embraced Mikhail Gorbachev while thousands of Russians looked on approvingly; he had spoken ringingly of human rights to dozens of Soviet dissidents gathered at the U.S. ambassador's residence.

Then he found himself surrounded by Injuns.

Only figuratively. A group of American Indians had followed the president to the Soviet capital; knowing that he intended to make human rights a theme of his summit visit, they figured to head him off at the pass. They couldn't quite reach him — U.S. cavalry and all — but in a session at Moscow State University, a Soviet student asked him about the Indian delegation and their grievances.

Reagan said he'd be willing to meet with them. He should have stopped there. But he rambled on about how generous the government had been in allocating millions of acres for reservations so these native Americans could maintain tribal ways.

Through no fault of Uncle Sam, part of that blighted terrain turned out to have oil on it. As a result, the president pointed out, some latter-day Indians had become rich; so what was their complaint, he wondered. "We've done everything to meet their demands as to how they want to live. Maybe we made a mistake. Maybe we should not have humored them in that wanting to stay in that kind of primitive lifestyle."

Ugh.

This is a strange-smelling peace pipe for the Great White Father to extend to his red children. If they choose instead to go on the warpath, nobody in Washington should claim ambush.

Ronald Reagan has always done admirably with the right script. This time he didn't have a fresh one, so he had to fall back on U.S. history as written by Hollywood during his acting days. One may hope that the Soviet dissidents he so inspired on Monday did not hear his vapid, condescending remarks on Tuesday.

The Boston Herald

Boston, Massachusetts, June 4, 1988

HIS REMARKS, admittedly, were klutzy. Asked in Moscow about the problems of American Indians, President Reagan began by remarking that they live on "preservations" and suggested witlessly that oil wells have made "some of them" rich.

For all that, he was essentially right. "Maybe we made a mistake," he said, referring to the reservation system. "Maybe we should not have humored them in that. ... Maybe we should have said: 'No, come join us. Be citizens along with the rest of us.'"

It is true, as Reagan-bashers leaped to point out, that American Indians have been U.S. citizens since 1924. But for those who choose to live on reservations, it is a miserable kind of citizenship.

Tribal leaders rule the reservations mercilessly, and the constitutional liberties we take for granted do not apply there. Leaders may deny freedom of speech and assembly, and can bar residents from starting new businesses. Indians on reservations can be prosecuted for "defaming tribal sovereignty" — the one place in America where you can be punished for criticizing the government.

For more than a century, federal law has treated Indians as "wards of the state." We supply Indians with $3 billion — in cash and social programs — every year. Reservation Indians can count on cradle-to-grave medical care. They get free legal counsel and free education. Most of their property and income is tax-free. They are exempt from most hunting, fishing and environmental laws, and those who want to kill and sell endangered animals are free to do so.

Lucky sons-of-guns? Hardly. This system of pure welfare-statism has left reservation Indians a pathetic lot. Conditioned to be utterly dependent on taxpayer charity, Indians have become the quintessential American underclass. Indian affairs expert Ted Williams dubs the reservation system "America's apartheid," and calculates that Indians "have the nation's highest infant-mortality rate, the shortest life span, the poorest housing, the poorest transportation, the lowest per-capita income, and the lowest level of education in the nation. ... No ethnic group in America has lower average income than the Indians. Suicide and alcoholism are epidemic."

Nothing more perfectly epitomizes the way in which lavish, well-intentioned generosity can end up wrecking the very recipients it is meant to help.

Indians need to be weaned away from a reservation system that is politically repressive and personally destructive. Decades ago, President Eisenhower proposed such a change. But tribal leaders — addicted to their power — fought the move bitterly, and rank-and-file Indians continued to sink into despair.

It is time to try again. Reagan should repeat his call to America's Indians: "Come join us. Be citizens along with the rest of us." One century of Indian policy failures is surely long enough.

FORT WORTH STAR-TELEGRAM

Fort Worth, Texas, June 2, 1988

Even with the touchy topic of human rights as one of his priorities at the Moscow summit, President Reagan has managed generally to charm Soviet audiences — and to offend American Indians.

Reagan demonstrated an ignorance of both American history and current conditions among American Indians with his response to a question from a Moscow University student.

He seemed unaware that Indians are U.S. citizens — by act of Congress. He seemed to think that reservations were a matter of choice for Indians who wished to preserve their way of life. In reality, most Plains and Desert Indians saw their culture destroyed by an expanding nation in the 19th century and wound up confined on reservations where bare survival was a major success.

They weren't "humored" into maintaining their "primitive" lifestyle. They were made dependents of an all-too-often neglectful government, a policy that has resulted in widespread poverty and health problems for the majority of today's Indians.

The president's performance in Moscow suffered from his unscripted insensitivity about American Indians, but perhaps it will serve to focus greater attention in this country on what has been a less-than-glowing chapter in our own human rights development.

THE ATLANTA CONSTITUTION

Atlanta, Georgia, June 3, 1988

President Reagan's misstatements in Moscow on the subject of American Indians are more than a mere gaffe and more than an innocent garbling of facts. They bespeak a fundamental ignorance of the nation he was elected to govern.

Asked if he would meet with a group of American Indians that was in Moscow to spell out human rights violations, Reagan replied that the United States has given them plenty of land for reservations.

"We've done everything we can to meet their demands as to how they want to live," he said. "Maybe we made a mistake. Maybe we should not have humored them in ... wanting to stay in that kind of primitive lifestyle. Maybe we should have said, 'No, come join us. Be citizens along with the rest of us.'" Not surprisingly, these comments have brought a bitter outcry.

Maybe we should not have humored them? Americans have had many policies toward the continent's indigenous peoples. Humoring was not prominent among them.

From the beginning, European settlers could not have lasted in this strange new land without Indian help in everything from hunting to planting corn. At one point, Thomas Jefferson hoped to make tribes in the West and Midwest our trading partners.

When coexistence was inconvenient, we resorted to uglier tactics. Andrew Jackson moved the Southeastern tribes to Oklahoma along the deadly Trail of Tears. Federal troops battled and subdued the Plains tribes in the latter half of the 1800s.

Whatever our policy, this fact remains: In barely more than a century, we wiped out the major part of our native American population. Bullets did some of the work. European diseases, to which the Indians had no resistance, did the rest. We all but destroyed hundreds of indigenous cultures.

The result of that crime is evident even now. On some reservations, unemployment exceeds 60 percent. The poverty rate on reservations is 41 percent. Young Indians kill themselves at a rate six times that for other young Americans.

Primitive? That word best describes the president's view of American history.

ALBUQUERQUE JOURNAL

Albuquerque, New Mexico, June 2, 1988

President Reagan should keep his ad lib remarks to himself to avoid mischaracterizing history and incurring the anger of thousands of Americans. His recent contretemps in Moscow was downright insulting to 1.3 million American Indians.

In response to a question at Moscow State University, the president said that the U.S. government had "humored" Indians by putting them on reservations. He left the erroneous impression that American Indians are less than full citizens of the United States when he said, "Maybe we made a mistake in trying to maintain Indian culture. . . . Maybe we should not have humored them in that, wanting to stay in that kind of primitive life style. Maybe we should have said, 'No, come join us. Be citizens along with the rest of us.'"

The president is not a particularly astute student of American history. Indian reservations were set aside more than a century ago under terms of treaties signed by U.S. presidents and Indian tribal representatives. They were set aside to end white encroachment on Indian land. They are enforceable in the courts. In the decades since, government policies toward Indians have vacillated between paternal supervision and benign neglect, the latter prevailing during the Reagan administration. The president's recent remarks, however, were both paternalistic and condescending.

The Seattle Times

Seattle, Washington, June 1, 1988

EMBARRASSING: That's the only word to describe President Reagan's rambling discourse on American Indians in Moscow yesterday.

He sounded like a comic satirist doing a Reagan impression. But, in fact, it was the president himself speaking during a question-answer session at Moscow University. A Russian questioner, trying to put a twist on the human-rights issue, asked about native Americans.

"Let me tell you just a little something about the American Indian in our land," Reagan began (sounding a little like he was doing a guest shot on "Sesame Street"). "We have provided millions of acres of land for what are called preservations . . . or the reservations, I should say."

It went downhill from there. The president described all the good things done for Indians: "We've done everything we can to meet their demands as to . . . how they want to live.

"Maybe we made a mistake. Maybe we should not have humored them in that, wanting to stay in that kind of primitive lifestyle. Maybe we should have said, 'No, come join us. Be citizens along with the rest of us.'"

Reagan told the Russian students how some American Indians became wealthy, because "some of those reservations were overlaying great pools of oil. And you can get very rich pumping oil. And so I don't know what their complaint might be."

Howls promptly went up on both sides of the Atlantic. There was the rush to correct the facts. Indians are indeed citizens — American citizens whose ancestors were victimized by violations of treaties. They're Americans who happen today to have a disastrously — and inexcusably — high incidence of disease, infant mortality, alcoholism and unemployment.

Of course, the game now is to discover which old cowboys-'n'-Indians movie provided the basis for the president's view of today's American Indian. Comics can milk laughs out of that. But it's saddening to think of the president being so out of touch with a segment of America's people so beset by problems.

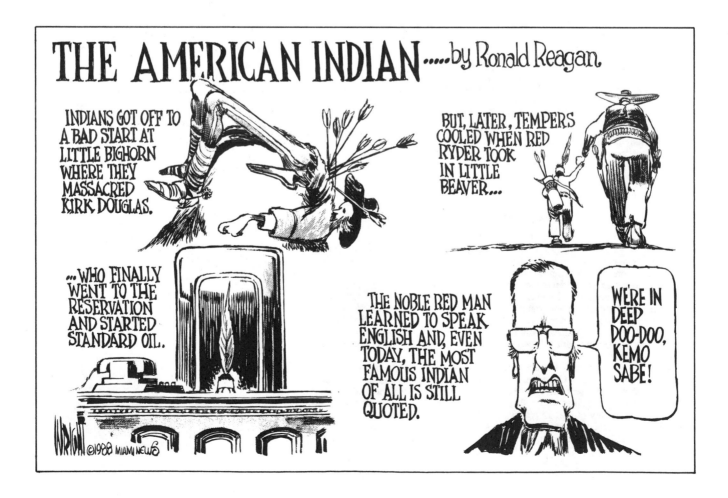

THE ANN ARBOR NEWS
Ann Arbor, Michigan, June 3, 1988

President Reagan obviously could benefit from remedial instruction in the history of Native Americans. Judging from his poorly chosen remarks in Moscow, the president's views seem to have been formed from celluloid Westerns.

No, Indians weren't "humored" into living on reservations — the land which they hold sacred was taken from them and they had no choice. No, Indians don't prefer to live a "primitive" life-style — as full American citizens, they want to share in the good life, too.

Life on the reservations is not, as President Reagan seems to think, one of general prosperity because of oil wealth. Native Americans on reservations in the West are typically poor and lacking good medical care. In northern Michigan, life among the Bay Mills and Chippewa tribes is no different.

The history of Native Americans and the white man is one of exploitation, treaty abrogation and injustice. It is a chapter in America's human rights history which reflects poorly on what this country stands for. It is embarrassing to have to explain to our friends overseas that "Kemo sabe" Reagan needs an education in history and current life on the reservation.

RAPID CITY JOURNAL—
Rapid City, South Dakota, June 2, 1988

There's no reason to bash Ronald Reagan over the statement he made in Moscow that the American people "humored" Indians by allowing them to remain on reservations.

While Reagan's words were ill-chosen, his concern was not. He regards reservation social problems as the inescapable consequences of the reservation system.

Behind the offhand lack of understanding of the special relationship between Indian nations and the United States — a relationship recognized in the U.S. Constitution — Reagan was struggling with the same social issues that so strongly affect South Dakota and other states with large Indian reservation populations. Creating a nation within a nation exacerbates social problems, creates barriers and sets people apart through a public policy of separate and unequal treatment on the basis of race.

Yes, his approach was unfortunate. Reagan has never been a details man. He tends to be hazy on historic precision.

Reagan misspoke when he said that Indians are not citizens of the United States. Of course they are. At the same time, many Indians are members of sovereign nations — reservations — within the United States.

In some superficial ways the United States Indian policy resembles South Africa's apartheid system. South Africa has created reservations of its own to create the illusion that blacks enjoy self rule there, although they are deprived meaningful participation in government of the larger white republic, and not allowed to live, travel, work and seek education on the same basis as whites.

That's not true in the United States. Indians are not officially denied the rights of citizenship. Indians vote, hold office, are free to assemble, speak out, live, work and travel where they desire. They are subject to discrimination and racism, but that is not government policy.

Compare this to the plight of Jews, or union organizers, or those who want to form a new political party within the Soviet Union. The social plight of Indians often is cited by Soviet leaders as an example of American injustice. Such Soviet criticism is intended to direct attention away from the greater injustices of that nation's domestic policies.

But the view from the reservation is much different from the view from the White House, or from the Main Street offices of the Rapid City Journal.

Reagan, and many others, do not fully appreciate that differing perspective. His statement was insensitive. But he is correct in recognizing that there are major social problems that are being worsened by setting one race apart from others.

St. Petersburg Times
St. Petersburg, Florida, June 2, 1988

Americans who know their history resigned themselves long ago to the fact that President Reagan doesn't. All the same, the latest embarrassment is especially hard to take.

The truth about the American Indians is that this land was seized from them by force of arms and overwhelming numbers. Dishonesty was the one constant of federal policy. Treaties solemnly made were casually broken whenever white settlers craved more room or found something valuable, such as gold, on Indian land. Osceola, the great Florida warrior, was captured in violation of a flag of truce. Southeastern tribes were forcibly deported beyond the Mississippi under conditions of such hardship that of the 13,000 Cherokees who set out on the infamous "Trail of Tears," 4,000 died. The lands that now comprise Indian reservations are almost invariably the barest, meanest and most unproductive — the lands no one else wanted. Poverty, disease and suicide continue to take a dreadful toll.

This is the sad and shameful history that Mr. Reagan trivialized with his offhand remark in Moscow that perhaps the government should not have "humored" the Indians by establishing the reservations.

The ignorance he expressed speaks for itself. Indians are, of course, U.S. citizens — a point he seemed not to know — regardless of whether they live in cities or on reservations. Most, in fact, live off the reservations. Very few have become "very wealthy" from oil. To the contrary, the 1980 census found that the poverty rate among Indians ranged from 22 percent off reservations to 41 percent on reservations, compared to 12 percent among society as a whole. Except for one fortunate small tribe, Indian royalties never averaged more than $107 a year per person, and they are less now.

It would be too simple to dismiss Mr. Reagan's fantasies as the consequence of too many Hollywood scripts. (Yes, he once did play a youthful George Armstrong Custer.) The problem is that these, like all his other misperceptions, are widely held among uninformed citizens. A president is supposed to know better. When he doesn't, that makes leadership that much harder for those who do.

Chicago Tribune
Chicago, Illinois, June 3, 1988

In considering President Reagan's remarks about American Indians in Moscow, it helps to remember that in his days as a Western actor, he always played a cowboy or a cavalryman.

When asked by a Russian student about a group of American Indians who had gone to Moscow to dramatize their complaints about their treatment at home, Mr. Reagan managed, apparently inadvertently, to insult Indians several times. He questioned the wisdom of the reservation system, saying "maybe we should not have humored them in wanting that kind of primitive life style. Maybe we should have said, 'No, come join us. Be citizens along with the rest of us.'" He also said some Indians had gotten rich from tribal oil rights, "so I don't know what their complaint might be."

Most American Indians will be surprised to learn that the President thinks they still live in teepees and subsist on buffalo meat. Because their income generally falls well below the national average, they may have some trouble getting used to thinking of themselves as oil barons—though, come to think of it, they may not be doing worse than a lot of oil barons are doing these days. And what are American citizens supposed to do when their highest elected official informs the world that they are not, in fact citizens?

It's too bad the President muffed the question so badly, because there is a serious issue in the right government policy toward Indians. But Mr. Reagan won't advance the debate there by saying things that hark back to "Death Valley Days."

Native American Issues Remain Controversial

The Supreme Court April 19, 1988 upheld the right to build a road across a site used for at least 200 years by Native Americans for religious rituals.

The court, in a 5-3, decision, said the roadway did not prohibit the free exercise of religion. "Government simply could not operate if it were required to satisfy every citizen's religious needs and desires," Justice Sandra Day O'Connor wrote for the majority, in *Lyng v. Northwest Indian Cemetery Assn.*

Three dissenters – Justices William J. Brennan Jr., Thurgood Marshall and Harry A. Blackmun – protested the majority's "surreal" reasoning that "governmental action that will virtually destroy a religion is nevertheless deemed not to 'burden' that religion."

Justice Anthony M. Kennedy did not participate in the case, which concerned the Chimney Rock section of the Six Rivers National Forest in northwestern California.

In another American Indian development, the Navajo Tribal Council, meeting in Window Rock, Ariz., voted Feb. 17, 1989 to strip tribal chairman Peter MacDonald Sr. of his administrative power and place him on leave in the wake of bribery accusations revealed in Senate subcommittee testimony.

MacDonald Feb. 16 had offered to take a paid leave of absence but had rescinded his offer the following day when the tribal council refused to pay for his legal effort to defend himself against what he termed "slurs and slander."

A panel of the Senate Select Committee on Indian Affairs had begun hearing testimony Jan. 30 concerning allegations of corruption on Indian reservations. The panel, which was chaired by Sen. Dennis DeConcini (D, Ariz.), had been established by the Senate in 1988 to investigate published charges of fraud and other abuses on federally funded programs for Indians, which totaled about $3 billion annually.

On Feb. 2, three contractors (two whites and a Navajo) testified that they had given MacDonald thousands of dollars, free airplane travel and other gifts in order to win construction contracts on Indian land. The three said they had set up dummy corporations in order to qualify for work reserved for Native Americans.

But the controversial testimony concerned a 491,000-acre ranch in northern Arizona that had been sold to MacDonald and the Navajo tribe on July 9, 1987. According to official documents, MacDonald had bought the land from Tracy Oil & Gas Co. of Scottsdale, Ariz. for $33.4 million. Tracy Oil had formally purchased the same property just five minutes earlier for $26.5 million.

Witnesses, including MacDonald's son Peter MacDonald Jr. and Phoenix businessman Byron T. (Bud) Brown, the middleman in the deal, testified that the tribal chief had received $50,000 in cash and a BMW automobile, and had expected to be paid an additional $500,000 in exchange for purchasing the land at the inflated price on behalf of the Navajos.

MacDonald defended his actions in a radio interview Feb. 9. he said that his acceptance of gifts was not a crime, and he blasted the investigation as a "concerted effort to undermine tribal sovereignty."

The suspended leader of the Navajo Nation, the U.S.'s largest Indian tribe, was convicted in Navajo Tribal Court in Window Rock, Ariz. Oct. 17, 1990 of bribery, conspiracy and violating the tribe's ethics laws.

The suspended chairman, Peter MacDonald Sr., 62, was found guilty of 41 of 42 counts against him. Also convicted was his son, Peter (Rocky) MacDonald, 32, who was guilty on all 23 counts against him.

The Supreme Court April 17, 1990 ruled, 6-3, that government may prohibit the use of drugs as part of religious rituals and said a ban against use of peyote by American Indians did not violate their constitutional right to free exercise of religion.

Pittsburgh Post-Gazette
Pittsburgh, Pennsylvania,
January 10, 1987

The Indian tribes of America are following the old political bromide, "As Maine goes, so goes the nation" — but in business terms.

Ten years ago two tribes in Maine won a landmark $81.5 million suit they had lodged against the state over huge areas of land and townsites they said still were theirs by treaty, even though long since occupied by others. Numerous such suits have been won by other Indian tribes in the past, and the usual procedure has been to distribute the money among tribal members in a single per-capita payment. That cautious path had been followed because tribal members had been burned in the past when the money was kept for the tribe as a whole but somehow slipped away through the hands of tribal leaders with no visible benefits for the tribe.

But the Passamaquoddies and Penobscots decided to do things differently and reserved a portion of the award for a series of economic development projects. The tribes purchased a cement factory, a radio station and a blueberry farm, started a line of products called Native American Foods and launched a venture with a Finnish firm to produce prefabricated houses. Unemployment has dropped to 10 percent from 60 percent in the early 1980s.

The lesson has not been lost on others.

According to The New York Times, tribes in Oregon, Maine, Arizona and Mississippi have started or acquired local companies and experimented with joint ventures and other investments from which they once shied away. In Oregon a group of tribes jointly own a utility, the Warm Springs dam and hydroelectric plant on the Deschutes River, an investment that cost the tribes $30 million but now brings in $2 million a year.

The tribes also have been nudged into action by cuts in federal programs aiding Indians, a drop to about $2.5 billion from the $3.5 billion allocated annually when President Reagan took office in 1981.

A key factor in the tribes' turn to business has been the return to the reservations of well-educated young people with financial expertise. This has given tribal members confidence that they won't be the victims of ineptitude or worse at the hands of their tribal council leaders or fast-buck operators from the outside.

Some reservations are on land so resource-starved that outside help always will be necessary. But the trend started in Maine is a light on the horizon for some of the most blighted areas in America — the Indian reservations.

THE
DENVER POST
Denver, Colorado, October 1, 1990

THE BUSH administration's plan to revamp the Bureau of Indian Affairs appears to be yet another attempt to address Native American problems by reshuffling the bureaucracy, rather than empowering the people. it's supposed to serve.

The proposal, outlined by Interior Secretary Manuel Lujan at a meeting of tribal leaders in Albuquerque on Friday, would split the BIA into three divisions. One would be responsible for Indian education, one would oversee other services to Indians, and one would enforce the numerous treaty obligations to the tribes.

In addition, the agency would take steps to give the tribes more control over the way in which federal dollars may be spent on the reservations, as recommended a year ago by a Senate committee that found widespread "fraud, mismanagement and waste" in the current system.

Such an expansion in tribal autonomy — already being tested under a pilot program involving six tribes — would certainly be welcome. But it might well prove pointless in the long run unless a host of pressing legal, political and jurisdictional problems can be solved.

A tribe that wanted to use federal funds to open a coal mine, for example, might be thwarted if it couldn't exercise some authority over water supplies, power lines and rail service — all issues that typically come under state or federal jurisdiction.

Similar obstacles to economic development also have cropped up in such areas as dual authority over taxation, zoning, law enforcement, resource management, and hunting and fishing rights.

In short, the question of who controls what in Indian country is a lot more complicated than it appears at first glance.

As Sen. Daniel Inouye, chairman of the Senate Indian Affairs Committee, said in a Boulder appearance earlier this month, the sovereign status of Indian tribes is a subject of much concern — and much confusion — in Washington and around the country these days.

Some of the biggest, strongest and most resourceful tribes may be well-prepared to accept Lujan's invitation to take over the programs traditionally administered by the BIA. But others — small, poor and politically vulnerable — must continue to look to Uncle Sam just to survive.

Without the BIA standing by to serve as an advocate and lobby against wholesale cuts in the $3 billion budgeted annually for Indian needs, some tribes might slip through the cracks entirely. This would surely violate the nation's constitutional commitment to act as a steward for the indigenous Americans in perpetuity.

The Interior secretary is right to be pushing for further tribal self-determination, which has been the goal of federal Indian policy since the grand experiment in assimilation was abandoned in the 1970s. And he's on the right track in proposing a separate BIA division to deal with sovereignty issues, with a supervisor reporting directly to the secretary.

But if Congress — with the help of the Indians themselves — can't find a way to resolve the complex issues that hinder the tribes' progress on other fronts, then all their so-called autonomy in economic decision-making won't be of much benefit.

Birmingham Post-Herald
Birmingham, Alabama, October 1, 1990

Lt. Col. George Custer, probably would have been astonished to think, back on June 25, 1876, that the nation whose standard he bore would one day build a monument to the Indian warriors who would soon be tying his troopers' scalps to their lodge poles.

Even today, some might think it strange to honor the side that enjoyed a 10-to-1 — perhaps a 20-to-1 — advantage over the doomed 7th Calvary column of 210 soldiers at the Battle of the Little Bighorn. But the Sioux and Cheyenne, if they fought savagely, also fought smartly and boldly, and no doubt many a brave spilled his lifeblood on the plains before the sun set. Congress is poised to approve a battlefield memorial to the Indians, which is as it should be.

Such action is squarely in the nation's tradition: Monuments at Gettysburg and Manassas remember both Billy Yank and Johnny Reb, although only one's cause prevailed. To this day, Southerners tend the graves of Massachusetts boys who fell in Dixie, a grace reciprocated by their Northern cousins. Thus do Americans treat Americans with whom they have warred. Who is more American than the Native American?

The Phoenix Gazette
Phoeniz, Arizona, October 1, 1990

Sen. Dennis DeConcini, D-Ariz., might have jumped the gun when he criticized the Bush administration's sweeping reform proposals for the federal Bureau of Indian Affairs.

But then again, probably not.

DeConcini, the legislative co-sponsor of a much more radical plan to phase out the BIA, worries that the new plan merely moves boxes on the BIA's organizational charts without real reform.

Under a plan unveiled Friday by U.S. Interior Secretary Manuel Lujan, the $1 billion BIA would be divided into three parts. A Bureau of Indian Education would operate boarding schools. A trimmed BIA would oversee economic development, welfare, law enforcement and other programs. A third agency, the Office of Indian Trust, would supervise the protection and exploitation of Indian natural resources, an area where the BIA has failed miserably in the past. All three agencies would be under the direction of the current BIA director, Eddie Brown, a former Arizonan.

DeConcini blasted the plan even before Lujan had formally announced it. The Arizona senator suggested the proposal would not give Indian tribes increased control of their own destinies; would keep the BIA's 14,000-person bureaucracy in place; and might result in fewer, not more, dollars to the tribes.

He has a point. Both DeConcini and U.S. Sen. John McCain, R-Ariz., the two lawmakers from the state with the largest Indian population, have lamented the BIA's performance and called for sweeping changes. McCain has not yet commented on the newest plan from the Republican administration.

But both understand the well-documented mess at BIA. The modest shuffling Lujan proposes appears to be nothing more dramatic than rearranging the deck chairs of a sinking ship.

Arkansas Gazette

Little Rock, Arkansas, January 8, 1991

American Indians never have so many white "friends" as when some other minority is trying to pull itself upward. In the early years of the civil rights movement, segregationists tried to justify injustice against blacks by noting that Indians had been mistreated too, and earlier. They seemed to believe that one crime excused the other.

More Indian-lovers came out of the closet during the recent debate over the payment of reparations to Japanese-Americans who were held in concentration camps during World War II. Opponents asked piously how the country could even consider paying reparations to Japanese-Americans after all that the Indians had suffered. (These people never suggest doing *more* for the Indians. They just want to do *less* for other victims.)

The tired ploy is being used again in Montana, one of only three states that don't celebrate Martin Luther King Jr. Day. State Sen. Jerry Noble, who says that King was a Communist, has introduced legislation to honor Chief Joseph of the Nez Perce on the third Monday in January, the day observed as King Day by 47 other states and the federal government. The senator pointed out that there are more Indians than blacks in Montana. "If minorities want to rally around a day, they could rally around Chief Joseph's holiday," he said.

Chief Joseph was a great leader, worth a holiday in Montana. But if Noble was really interested in honoring Joseph, he'd have picked another date. His interest is in *not* honoring King.

King lived and died for civil rights for everyone — black, white, Indian, Montanan. That is why he is honored, not simply as a representative of minorities. King Day reminds us that he achieved much. The Jerry Nobles, who would play one oppressed minority against another, remind us that there is still work for King's successors.

The Duluth News-Tribune

Duluth, Minnesota, February 19, 1991

Claims that Cloquet Community Memorial Hospital has displayed racism in its treatment of Indian patients must be addressed if that institution is to properly serve the residents in its service area.

Members of the Fond du Lac Band of Chippewa depend on the Cloquet hospital to serve those living on the nearby reservation. An article in Sunday's News-Tribune focused on two cases in which Indian patients received improper treatment (one of which has been settled through litigation) and presented the perceptions of several people, both Indians and white hospital personnel, on whether Indian patients are treated differently than whites.

Both sides can present strong arguments, but racism is a difficult thing to isolate since it, and its opposite, racial tolerance, reside in the hearts of individuals. All racism is wrong, but institutional racism can be more readily addressed.

If members of Cloquet's Indian community believe the hospital practices institutional racism or that individuals on the staff at the hospital display bias in their treatment of Indians, the hospital should address those concerns.

For years, members of the Fond du Lac Band have urged that the band be represented on the hospital's board of directors. We don't know why no band member has ever been selected, but now is the time to do so. The large percentage of Indian people living in the logical service range of the Cloquet hospital calls for it. The problems Indians see in the relationship make it imperative.

Furthermore, the hospital needs to reach out to the Indian community with better communications. Representatives should meet with Fond du Lac members — on the reservation — to discuss these concerns. The hospital should institute internal sensitivity training for all staff members, and both sides should relate their concerns on the issue.

There is no excuse for unequal treatment of patients on any basis — whether ability to pay, race or reputation — at any hospital. As long as the perception of unequal treatment exists, it must be addressed.

THE BUFFALO NEWS

Buffalo, New York, March 4, 1991

THE U.S. Supreme Court has made a sensible distinction. Unanimously ruling that states may tax goods sold on Indian reservations to outsiders, but not those sold to tribal members, it contributes some clarity to the confusing web of laws about Indian sovereignty.

The case centered on a dispute between Oklahoma and the Potawatomi Tribe, but it has promising implications for New York's efforts to collect millions of dollars in sales taxes on cigarettes, gasoline and other items sold on Indian reservations here.

The court's ruling that "states may of course collect the sales tax from cigarette wholesalers" should breathe new life into the Cuomo administration's appeal of a 1988 state Court of Appeals decision that the state could not tax those who trade with the Indians.

Levying a tax at the wholesale level would let the state avoid questions dealing with sovereign Indian land or identification of non-Indian customers. It also would help officials tax what they suspect are products ostensibly for sale to Indians, but which wholesalers divert elsewhere.

The state would like to levy taxes on the wholesalers based on population and consumption estimates at the reservations, with generous room for allowances.

In seeming to allow such a system — as well as other alternatives ranging from negotiated settlements to taxing individual Indian businessmen, as opposed to a tribe — the Supreme Court recognizes both the sovereignty rights of Indians as well as the state's legitimate interests in collecting taxes.

New York has until March 9 to appeal the state court ruling, and tax spokesmen indicated they will do so, armed with the Supreme Court's apparent endorsement. Even if that fails, the high court has left other options.

One is the negotiated settlement, which New York unsuccessfully tried with the Seneca Nation two years ago. A deal was worked out under which the tribe would levy a tax and keep all revenues up to a certain amount, with the rest going to the state.

But though the tribal council agreed at one point, the proposal never got the required support in the State Legislature, and the council later rescinded its approval.

However, the Supreme Court ruling may provide new impetus for a settlement.

The justices have at least made it clear that non-Indians do not merit the same protection against sales tax payments that Indians enjoy. While neither Indian business owners nor the wholesalers who sell to them are thrilled with the ruling — some have even vowed to ignore it — it is a reasonable one.

The state estimates it lost more than $10 million annually in taxes on cigarettes because of reservation sales — and that was before the tax was hiked last year. Officials have no estimate of the revenues lost through sales of gasoline on the reservations, but that undoubtedly runs into the millions as well.

THE RICHMOND NEWS LEADER
Richmond, Virginia, April 17, 1991

The Oscar-showered flick, "Dances With Wolves," gives a popular — if somewhat inaccurate and overly sentimentalized — view of the American Indian. Ignored, exploited, massacred, short-changed — all of these accusations about the nation's treatment of the Indian play strongly to the guilt-trippers who constantly seek new reasons for *mea culpa* whimpers.

The dangers of this renewed hand-wringing over the plight of the Indian are that (1) all Indians will be regarded as a downtrodden group, and (2) the misimpression will prevail that the U.S. has done nothing, and does nothing, to help the Indian.

Certainly many Indians live in pitiable conditions — but not all Indians do. Some tribes have grown wealthy from oil leases in the Southwest, and Mohawks still earn top wages — and due respect — for their high-rise steel work in the Northeast. Others have joined the professional classes in law, medicine, accounting, and many demanding occupations. Still others run small businesses. It would be inaccurate to deny that a solid Indian middle-class exists and grows.

Nor is the prevalence of squalor on many of the nation's 291 reservations owing to a lack of taxpayer commitment. It is, rather, the fault of a federal bureaucracy so entrenched, so inefficient, and so intractable as to constitute a long-standing, major scandal. The government spends some $3 billion a year on Indian programs, but by the time the money is siphoned through the Bureau of Indian Affairs and other agencies, only about 10 per cent of the money actually reaches the reservations.

This is not a new story. Today some 13,000 BIA employees serve 1.5 million Indians — an almost unheard-of ratio of bureaucrats-to-constituents. (It's not quite so bad as one of Ronald Reagan's favorite jokes implies: "Why is the BIA employee crying? His Indian just died." But it's bad.) Yet that ratio has made little impact in improving the lot of the average Indian on the average reservation.

Study after study damns the BIA operations, but no one ever does anything to remedy the problems. The BIA once lost more than $250 million in supplies; to this day no one has been held accountable. Last year the BIA misplaced $95 million — and no one knows where it went. Reports on the BIA's ineptitude over the years no doubt would fill a good-sized room, but the BIA just bumbles on.

Renewed interest in reservation Indians and their problems could have a positive effect if Congress feels more heat to make the BIA and other Indian programs work. But maudlin guilt trips and frantic breast-beating will not change history — although revisionists are hard at work to transform all Indians into noble savages and all New World settlers and visitors (even Columbus) into cold-blooded murderers. That wasn't the way it was. It would be better instead to demand more accountability from the government's efforts to help the Indian, and to keep that $3 billion a year from vanishing into a bureaucratic sinkhole.

The Duluth News-Tribune
Duluth, Minnesota, February 17, 1991

From time to time, we've lauded trade and cultural exchanges between the Soviet Union and America as a way to tie our two peoples together. If the people are linked through common interests and needs, we reasoned, their governments will be hard put to be enemies.

Though we hope Wisconsin's Indian and non-Indian communities have never thought of themselves as enemies, trade and cultural ties between those groups are certainly an important way to lower tensions and increase cooperation.

It is particularly good to see signs of trade and cultural cooperation as the Indians' spring spearfishing season draws near — and with it the unfortunate prospect of spearfishing protests at boat landings.

When the Wisconsin Governor's Conference on Tourism was held at Telemark Lodge in Cable last week, Indian tourism and business representatives were present — as they should have been in the past.

When Chippewa Indian reservations were created in northern Wisconsin last century, they were put in some of the most scenic spots in a scenic state. Thus they are likely contributors to and beneficiaries of the Wisconsin tourism industry.

Besides scenic offerings, Indian country in Wisconsin offers extra attractions due to the tribes' special legal status. Tax breaks available on reservations should appeal to non-Indian businesses and legal gambling can be both a tourist lure and an important local business.

But more important than any specific economic gains to come from cooperation between Indians and non-Indians are the gains in mutual respect and understanding. It may not put a stop to the spearfishing protests this year, but it should mean only good things for future relations.

ARGUS-LEADER
Sioux Falls, South Dakota, June 28, 1991

The intentions of South Dakota's Indian and government leaders to achieve reconciliation between Indians and whites is being put to the greatest test.

First Gov. George Mickelson declared 1990 as the Year of Reconciliation for the purpose of improving the relationship between both races.

Then Rep. Tim Johnson introduced a measure in Congress calling for a national year of reconciliation.

There was an era of good feeling between Indians and white people in 1990 as both sides sought a common base to **Editorial** understand the pain of the Indian people 100 years after the Wounded Knee Massacre.

As new differences arise that separate Indian hopes from white man's law, the good feeling seems to be subsiding.

The issue is about casinos and jurisdiction.

The first evidence of decay came when Mickelson stood in the path of Indian hopes for a casino at Lower Brule.

Mickelson refused to allow a plan to build the casino on property it had purchased near Interstate 90 outside of the reservation boundaries.

That stand brought angry reaction from Indian people, including Mike Jandreau, Lower Brule Sioux Tribal chairman.

Jandreau withdrew from the Reconciliation Council set up to advance the cause to improve relations between the two peoples.

The criticism didn't stop there. Indian leaders, including Clarence Skye, executive director of the United Sioux Tribe of South Dakota, pointed fingers at Francis Whitebird, coordinator of Indian Affairs for the governor.

Skye says Whitebird is too critical of reservations and has a personal agenda in his job. Mickelson defended Whitebird as an effective promoter of reconciliation.

On the issue of the casino, Mickelson and the tribe compromised. The casino will be built on the reservation rather than outside its boundaries.

While there is an agreement of sorts, the damage done by this is reason for concern.

Mickelson deserves a good deal of credit for pushing reconciliation as a high priority. Politics has often bred hypocrites in South Dakota. Many political officers have subscribed to the strategy of doing well by the Indian people, but doing it quietly so as not to alienate the white constituency. Mickelson carried his crusade openly.

The Indian people in return deserve credit for reciprocating with the governor's gestures of reconciliation.

Amid the good intentions and ceremonial handshakes, there may have been some oversights.

Sen. Ron Valandra, D-Rosebud, says the flaw is simple. The rhetoric did not address the issue of tribal sovereignty sincerely.

"Tribal sovereignty is a very serious issue that the state of South Dakota needs to recognize," Valandra says. "During the year of reconciliation, it was probably one of the issues that we failed to come to the table and talk seriously about."

There may be some truth to that.

It is unfortunate that this era of good feeling is now jeopardized.

It took a team effort to build it to this point and it will take a team effort to retain it.

The events in recent days are troublesome. They have provided satisfaction for those who love to say, "I told you so."

Both sides now need to recommit their priorities to restore the hope.

Census Bureau Reports on Hispanic-Americans

The income of Hispanics had risen relative to that of other Americans, but was still about one-third below that of non-Hispanics, according to a Census Bureau report released April 10, 1991.

The figures were based on a Census Bureau survey taken in 1990, before the completion of the 1990 census.

The median income of Hispanic families was $23,400, according to the study. The median income of non-Hispanic families was $35,200. The bureau said 23.4% of Hispanic families lived below the poverty line, an improvement over the 1982 figure of 27.2%. Of non-Hispanic families, 9.2% were below the poverty line. The poverty line was defined as a $12,675 annual income for a family of four.

The survey found that 82% of Hispanic households were families, while only 70% of non-Hispanic households were families. Nonfamily households consisted of unrelated people living together or an individual living alone.

The survey found that more than 90% of Hispanic families lived in cities. Unemployment among Hispanics was 8.2%, down from 16.5% in 1982.

A survey of political attitudes conducted by the Latino National Political Survey and presented Aug. 29, 1991 found that more Hispanics than non-Hispanic whites identified themselves as conservative. According to the poll, 39.1% of non-Hispanic whites said they were conservative, compared with 51% of Cubans, 47% of Puerto Ricans and 39.3% of Mexicans.

The Times-Picayune

New Orleans, Louisiana, August 28, 1991

According to the 1990 U.S. Census, there are 53,816 Hispanics in the seven-parish New Orleans metropolitan area. But some members of the relatively small census-certified community contend that the official count is not a true picture. They argue that the actual number is two to three times greater.

Those who question the accuracy of the census say the Hispanic undercount was largely the result of fear of immigration authorities among both legal and illegal residents, language difficulties and memories of political repression.

During the 1980s, New Orleans' Hispanic count declined by 10 percent, roughly mirroring the city's overall population loss. Jefferson's Hispanic populace showed an increase of 22 percent. And St. Bernard's Latin community suffered a decline of 19 percent as Islenos left the parish or intermarried with other ethnic groups, leaving fewer to claim Hispanic origin.

The 6 percent growth in the number of Hispanics in the metropolitan area pales alongside the 53 percent growth rate among Hispanics nationwide, an increase driven by high birth rates and steady immigration.

The government's figures are a sore spot with area Hispanics who are struggling to develop unity and gain political influence. They claim that even with the 1980s out-migration due to Louisiana's long economic slump, the area's Hispanic community saw healthy gains and that its size far exceeds 100,000.

But there is no dispute about census findings that our area's Latin community is one of the most diverse in the United States. While one group tends to dominate Hispanic colonies in other large American cities — Cubans in Miami, Mexicans in Houston, Puerto Ricans in New York — New Orleans is home to a varied blend of expatriates. New Orleans' ties to Latin America, particularly to Central America, go back many generations.

Regardless of their actual numbers, people who have come here over the years from such places as the Canary Islands (the Islenos), Mexico, Puerto Rico, Honduras, Guatemala, Panama, Nicaragua and El Salvador have made an important contribution to the rich cultural life of Orleans and neighboring parishes.

Hondurans hold the distinction of being New Orleans' largest Hispanic community. They number in the tens of thousands.

Concentrated in Mid-City, east Kenner, a dense strip of apartments near Lakeside Shopping Center in Metairie and in St. Bernard Parish, the Hispanics' influence can been seen throughout the area's social, business, professional and religious affairs.

Their love of food, music, family gatherings and public pageantry is well suited to New Orleans' celebrated joie de vivre.

The Miami Herald

Miami, Florida, September 6, 1991

THE NUMBER of Hispanic children living in poverty is up sharply during the past decade. That reflects not just the influx of immigrants, nor is it the increase in divorce among Hispanics.

Poverty among Hispanic families differs in significant ways from that of non-Hispanic whites and blacks. A Children's Defense Fund study says that a poor Hispanic family is likely to be headed by a working man, with the mother at home. The family is more likely to be younger than others, the wage-earner's hourly pay is less likely to propel the family above the poverty line, and the head of household is less likely to have a high-school diploma.

The study also found job discrimination against Hispanics increasing as a result of the Immigration Reform and Control Act of 1986. That law penalizes employers who hire illegal aliens; some have responded by not hiring persons with limited English.

The highest Hispanic poverty is found among families of Puerto Rican origin, some 48.4 percent. The lowest is among Cubans, 23.8 percent. Those numbers contrast with a non-Hispanic poverty rate of 43.7 percent among blacks and 11.5 among whites.

The Children's Defense Fund sees the study as ammunition for its drive for more direct aid to children through tax credits or other public benefits. It notes that the purchasing power of government aid to families and of the minimum wage has declined.

More money in the wallet no doubt would help, but it does not address the long-term needs of these families or of the wider society. The numbers show that these families have many ingredients for success save one — high-school diplomas.

In 1989, only 56 percent of Hispanics between 18 and 24 had graduated, compared with 76 percent of blacks and 82 percent of whites. A Dade study that followed students over four years reflected better numbers: 76.5 percent of Hispanics graduated in 1989 versus 70.6 percent of blacks and 81 percent of whites.

Drawing young adults back to school for diplomas and for better job skills is a mission that must be broadened beyond today's adult-education efforts and promising experiments. More direct economic aid for families indeed is a must for poor children, but so are self-sufficient parents.

The Star-Ledger

Newark, New Jersey, August 18, 1991

It is always heartening when New Jersey goes against negative trends gripping most of the nation in a stranglehold. And so it is pleasing to note that the state reached an all-time high last year in minority enrollments at its colleges and universities.

Following a decline in the number of black and Hispanic undergraduates enrolled in New Jersey schools between 1983 and 1987, a new report found those numbers exceeded 48,000 in the past year.

The record numbers were taken from fall 1990 figures compiled by the Department of Higher Education. The previous record of 44,500 students was set in 1989, according to the New Jersey State College Governing Boards Association.

What those figures indicate is that, following what appeared to be a declining trend, New Jersey has increased its minority enrollment in record numbers over the past two years. But even with that good news, the author of the study, "Turning Challenges into Opportunites for Minority Students at New Jersey State Colleges," acknowledges that more must be done to encourage minorities to seek advanced degrees.

At a time when there is national debate about affirmative action initiatives, the report found that the increase was primarily the result of aggressive outreach efforts that colleges across the country have aimed at minority students. It also said that increasing minority enrollment will be essential to ensure the future of America's work force.

However, information on higher education opportunites isn't being effectively distributed to the students who need it most, especially those in poorer, urban districts. Churches, community groups and minority advocacy organizations are some of those who can help spread the message that college is necessary and affordable.

While recognizing that more needs to be done to encourage minority enrollment in the state's colleges and universities, the higher education community in New Jersey is to be commended for its aggressive and successful recruitment efforts. The continuation of those efforts should result in another record year, and a further opening of the doors of opportunity for its minority residents.

The Seattle Times

Seattle, Washington, July 28, 1991

A COMBINATION of supportive court rulings and a savvy reading of political demographics by the Bush administration is giving Hispanic voters clout to match their growing numbers.

This month Justice Department officials refused to accept a redistricting plan for the New York City Council because federal attorneys said the new lines were detrimental to Hispanic voters in Brooklyn and the Bronx.

These city boroughs, with Manhattan, are required by the Voting Rights Act to have any changes in their election laws or procedures prescreened by the Justice Department.

All or portions of 16 states must submit to prior review because of a history of discrimination against minority voters.

States and cities throughout the nation are redrawing political maps to reflect demographic changes found in the 1990 Census. In the 10 years since the last previous statistical profile, the number of citizens of Hispanic origins increased 53 percent, from 6.4 percent to 9 percent of the nation.

By contrast, the African American population grew by 13.2 percent, from 11.7 to 12.1.

Gerrymandering districts to minimize the influence of minority voters is timeless, but court challenges are forcing honest reassessments.

Early this year the U.S. Supreme Court left intact a redistricting plan that two weeks later helped elect the first

Newark, New Jersey, October 19, 1991

A new trend, predicted more than a decade ago, is now becoming a reality that could change the politics of America, or at least have an impact on the way politicians look at America. The new demography shows minority groups are actually a majority of the population in the nation's big cities.

The latest census figures show that heavy Hispanic and Asian immigration has tipped the demographic scales in favor of minority groups in 22 big U.S. cities during the last decade. Most of the cities where minority groups together attained the majority status are in the South and West, but four of them are in urban areas of New Jersey.

Even with an acknowledged undercount of minority populations in the country, the growth pattern of non-whites in large cities continues to go unabated. In New Jersey, Newark topped the list — going from 76.7 percent minorities in 1980 to 83.1 percent in 1990. In Paterson, the minority population rose from 62.7 percent to 75.1 percent; in Elizabeth, from 45.6 percent to 60 percent, and in Jersey City, from 50.1 percent to 63.1 percent.

The figures, which represent minority growth in cities of more than 100,000 people, may not indicate a new political group strength, since there is much diversity involved in the members classified as minorities. The category includes African-Americans, Hispanics, Native Americans and people of Asian and Pacific Island origin. Some of those broad groupings were further divided by national origin, such as Hispanics from Mexico and Cuba, and by language, such as Asian-Americans from Korea, Vietnam and China.

The change points up some potentially interesting ramifications. Although big-city minorities are culturally diverse, the National Urban League believes that poverty is an issue that binds them together. "To the extent that common circumstances are recognized, especially by the leadership, there could be a tremendous opportunity for disadvantaged minority groups to make real progress to benefit them all," a League spokesman said.

The growth in big-city ethnic and racial populations comes at a time when central cities have become less important to the economic and social life of their region — with such activities as residential life, shopping, entertainment and employment moving outside the urban cores. Some believe that is the reason for a failure by government to address the growing problems of the cities.

But the new demographics represent an opportunity to foster a political change based on minority coalitions who now occupy the center cities. If they recognize their common concerns, this new political trend could represent a new melting pot approach that could bode well for depressed urban areas.

Hispanic to the Los Angeles County Board of Supervisors in 115 years. One-third of the county is Latino.

"During the 1981 redistricting process," a federal judge wrote, "the supervisors' primary objective was to protect their incumbencies and that of their allies. This objective, however, was inescapably linked to the continued fragmentation of the Hispanic population core."

The Bush admininstration seeks to woo Hispanics to the Republican Party by making localities live up to the law. Transparent, perhaps, but hardly dirty politics.

Given a fair shake at the polls, and the right to be represented according to their numbers, Hispanic voters are a growing power for the 1990s.

Arab-Americans Interviewed by FBI During Gulf Crisis

The U.S. Federal Bureau of Investigation Jan. 7, 1991 ordered its agents to interview more than 200 Arab-American business and community leaders, in order to gather information about possible terrorism in the U.S.

The interviews were vehemently protested by some Arab-Americans. Albert Mokhiber, president of the American-Arab Anti-Discrimination Committee, denounced the measure, saying it was reminiscent of the internment of 120,000 Japanese-Americans during World War II. Kate Martin, an attorney for the American Civil Liberties Union, said the "presumption" behind the FBI activity was "outrageous" and "clearly unconstitutional."

But the FBI and the U.S. Justice Department defended their decision as a precautionary measure, and said that the interviews would also spread the word that the FBI wanted to protect the Arab-American community from any backlash resulting from a war. "These interviews are not meant to intimidate," said Deputy Attorney General William F. Barr.

In related moves, the Justice Department Jan. 10 ordered Immigration and Naturalization Service officials to begin photographing and finger-printing anyone entering the U.S. with an Iraqi or Kuwaiti passport. On the same day, security was increased at the U.S. Capitol building, as Congress began debate on the Persian Gulf crisis.

The FBI had concluded its "interviews" with hundreds of Arab-American leaders across the country, it was reported Jan. 31. The FBI refused to release any information on the results of its inquiries. FBI Director William Sessions had responded to criticism of the bureau's tactics by noting that participation in the interviews had been strictly voluntary, it was reported Jan. 31. Session insisted that anyone who did not wish to answer the FBI's questions had been free to say, "I prefer not to, thank you" without repercussions.

THE ⟨⟨⟨ SUN

Baltimore, Maryland, January 15, 1991

We're stunned and embarrassed the Federal Bureau of Investigation's plans to interview U.S. Arab business and community leaders about Iraqi terrorism.

The agency's obvious assumption is that Arabs, no matter where they live or who they are, are somehow connected into Middle Eastern terrorists' pipeline. Therefore, all Arabs are suspect.

How insulting and racist. The FBI ought to be ashamed of itself. Equally to blame is the Bush administration for allowing stereotyping to become a part of official U.S. policy.

We thought the government learned something from the World War II, when 110,000 Japanese Americans were rounded up and placed in detention camps. The assumption then was that their heritage made them enemies of America — and therefore potential traitors. Never mind the majority were U.S. citizens. Never mind they had committed no crimes — except the one in the government's mind: being born in or having ancestors from Japan.

The same is true for Arab Americans. Why should they know anything about Iraqi terrorism? It would be one thing if the FBI had cause to believe certain individuals or groups were agents of the Iraqis. But that is not the case here.

The FBI is basing its "interviews" on the fact that when Iraq seized Kuwait, it also took Kuwaiti passports. The agency thinks that Iraqi citizens may be using the passports to enter the United States.

It's a legitimate concern. But assuming that all Arabs are suspicious is unfair. It would be the same as assuming that all Italians are connected in some way to the Mafia. The FBI's actions run the risk of whipping up anti-Arab sentiment and making Arabs targets of verbal and physical attacks.

It's scary to think what the FBI will do if it finds Arabs who oppose the U.S. gulf policy. Will the agency detain them or put them on a special watch list? Will their names end up in special files that will prevent them from getting government jobs? Will they be afraid to express opinions about the gulf for fear of being singled out?

They shouldn't be. Non-Arab Americans can say anything they want about U.S. involvement in the gulf, or even about President Bush, without fear of reprisal. Arabs should have the same protections.

After all, this is still a democracy. And in a democracy, a government does not, without cause, target ethnic groups for scrutiny. It made that mistake in 1942; it shouldn't make it again in 1991.

The Honolulu Advertiser

Honolulu, Hawaii, January 12, 1991

With war in the Persian Gulf a growing likelihood, Americans are justly concerned about terrorism. Attacks could be sponsored by Iraq or undertaken by independent groups or even unbalanced individuals upset by the crisis.

Attacks are most likely in the Middle East or Europe. But incidents at home cannot be ruled out. Precautions are needed at military bases, airports and other strategic sites.

Understandably, federal authorities are watchful of Iraqi citizens in this country, and of anyone carrying a possibly false Kuwaiti passport.

But word that the Federal Bureau of Investigation is seeking "interviews" with more than 200 Arab-American business and community leaders raises troubling recollections of the way Japanese Americans were treated (or mistreated) at the start of World War II.

The American-Arab Anti-Discrimination Committee says hate crimes jumped just after Iraq's invasion and have tapered off since. But they fear a resurgence if war comes.

The FBI says it wants to keep channels open and to gather information. That sounds fine. But care must be taken not to reinforce prejudices that all Arab Americans are disloyal or support terrorism.

A new study, begun before the invasion, finds the 2.5 million Arabs and Arab Americans here are better educated and better off than other major immigrant groups, except perhaps Pacific-Asians. Nearly half are Lebanese, followed by Syrians (16 percent), Egyptians (6 percent) and Palestinians (3 percent). Iraqis are only 2.2 percent.

Passions run high in times of war. But let's not forget the ugly mistakes of our past and confuse people who live and work honestly and loyally here with our enemies abroad.

THE KANSAS CITY STAR
Kansas City, Missouri, January 15, 1991

The crisis in the Persian Gulf has left the Federal Bureau of Investigation and other law enforcement agencies with two distinct jobs. First, they must protect Arab-Americans from the racists who will try to use the crisis as an excuse to harass and harm others. Such protection can be a large task by itself, as the experiences of previous crises in the Middle East have shown.

In addition, however, authorities must keep informed on the possibility of terrorist attacks sponsored by certain regimes and organizations in the Middle East. Doing this job right involves asking some delicate questions, inquiries that by their very nature can easily give offense.

Assigning FBI agents to tackle these two jobs simultaneously in individual interviews doesn't seem like the best approach, regardless of how polite the agents might be. *Hello, just stopped by to make sure no racists are bothering you. Good, good. Oh, say —*

you're not a big fan of Saddam Hussein, are you?

The impression such an approach leaves is that the agent's initial questions concerning harassment were merely designed to serve as some sort of conversational ice-breaker.

Authorities must be careful not to rely heavily on ethnic background in deciding whether someone might be involved in terrorism. That simply isn't appropriate.

Americans who cheer terrorist organizations and regimes in the Middle East, however, should not be surprised to discover that the FBI has at least some mild interest in them.

Being questioned by law enforcement officials can be an unpleasant experience, but sometimes certain questions are necessary. People must be careful about leveling charges of harassment and prejudice merely on the basis of these questions being asked.

RAPID CITY JOURNAL—
Rapid City, South Dakota, January 13, 1991

There are so many ugly aspects about war that have nothing to do with combat.

One of them is being highlighted by former senator James Abourezk right now — the issue of law enforcement officials treating Arab Americans as a special subclass of Americans.

As America poises at the brink of war with Iraq, the Federal Bureau of Investigation is stepping up interrogation of Americans of Arab descent. Abourezk, founder of the American-Arab Anti-Discrimination Committee and himself of Lebanese ancestry, is particularly sensitive to such tactics.

Abourezk believes the FBI operation is intended to stifle dissent and debate on the part of Arab Americans by making them afraid to speak out. Considering the documented occasional excesses of the FBI — as in the case of its activities against the Black Panther Party in the 1960s and early 1970s, for example — it is easy to understand and share Abourezk's concern.

However, there is also a legitimate concern involved here. Unquestionably, terrorism is a tactic sponsored and fomented by Iraq's Saddam Hussein and his few supporters in the present Mideast crisis — the Palestinian Liberation Organization and Libya's leadership. Therefore, it is not only proper but necessary that the security forces of the United States watch more closely for evidence of emerging terrorism. It is natural that the burden of suspicion falls most heavily on Arab Americans. That doesn't make it right.

Officials feel it necessary to interview people who may have some glimmering of potential problems. That is understandable and proper, but in their zeal they must not trample on constitutional protections. That has happened too many times in the past.

It is true that the United States is no stranger to terrorism in pursuit of its interests. It is true that Arab ancestry or origin is no proof of malicious intent against the United States. It is true that the United States has acted badly in the past to deprive basic citizenship rights to obvious minorities — Japanese Americans during World War II, German Americans in some places during World War I, blacks and Indians throughout much of our history. It is true that this polyglot country too easily forgets we are many peoples making one great nation. It is also true that in times of war we must be more vigilant than in times of peace.

So, once again, fear leads to one group of Americans being isolated from others, set aside by unjust suspicion from others who have different backgrounds. This is an ugly face of war. We must do all we can to counteract its negative effects.

Abourezk is correct when he says it is wrong to single out people for special treatment just because they are of Arab origin. The FBI should interview people only when it has bonafide reasons to believe they know something significant about national security. Separating one person from another merely on the basis of race, national origin or religion is an evil we should have abandoned long ago.

CHICAGO Sun-Times
Chicago, Illinois, January 13, 1991

There's a knock on your door at 7 a.m. Groggy, you open it and you're surprised to see an FBI agent. You're surprised, because you've done nothing wrong. Nor does the FBI have any evidence that you've done anything wrong or that you know anyone who has done something wrong.

You quickly discover that the FBI is on a fishing expedition, that the only reason the FBI is on your doorstep is that you happen to be a member of a particular ethnic group. And the assumption is made that because you are a member of that group you may be guilty of something or know someone who is.

It is the most outrageous, most un-American kind of presumption to make. But it is exactly the kind of absurd, insulting and dangerous conduct engaged in by the FBI last week when it started ringing the doorbells of Arab-Americans. Sure, the FBI said it was asking Arab-Americans if they had experienced any harassment as the result of the growing Persian Gulf tensions. FBI concern about such harassment is warranted and appreciated.

But it ought not be part of a blanket attempt to question Arab-Americans about feared, but not proven or perhaps not even identified, conspiracies and treasonous activities with no shred of evidence that these people as *individuals* are involved.

It has taken decades for this country to come to try to make up for the shameful treatment of Japanese-Americans during World War II. On the threshold of another war, let us not open a similar chapter with Arab-Americans.

Chicago, Illinois, March 28, 1991

Sick, sick, sick. There is no other way to describe the harassment of Arab-Americans by people with grudges against Saddam Hussein. But such incidents are up sharply in Chicago, according to a spokesman for Chicago's Arab community, who says that people with Arab surnames are becoming scapegoats of those with strong feelings about the war.

Several dozen complaints have been filed with the Chicago office of the Arab-American Anti-Discrimination Committee this month by people who claim to have been taunted or made the butt of cruel jokes, compared with five in all of last year.

These include a security guard who was told he was being laid off because the company no longer trusted him, and, incredibly, the father of a second-grader whose teacher had been "making fun" of Arabs.

Appalling as any of these incidents are, there is nothing quite so repugnant as the teaching of bigotry in a public-school classroom—or so bewildering as the slowness of school officials to condemn it. There can be no hint of ethnic intimidation in the curriculum and no quarter for mindless bigotry in the schools.

Japanese-American Internment Apology, Reparations Set

President Ronald Reagan, in a White House ceremony, signed into law Aug. 10, 1988 a bill offering the nation's apology and reparations to Japanese-Americans interned during World War II.

The final version of the measure had been adopted by the Senate July 27, by a voice vote, and by the House Aug. 4, by a vote of 257-156.

It offered cash payments of $20,000 to each internee still living, estimated to number 60,000, out of the 120,000 detained in camps established 46 years earlier following Japan's attack on Pearl Harbor.

The measure acknowledged that the nation committed a "grave injustice" by the action. The relocation and internment program was undertaken, it said, "without adequate security reasons and without any act of espionage or sabotage" being recorded.

"Yes, the nation was then at war, struggling for its survival," President Reagan said at the signing ceremony. "And it's not for us today to pass judgment upon those who may have made mistakes while engaged in that great struggle. Yet we must recognize that the internment of Japanese-Americans was just that, a mistake."

The legislation also acknowledged that the nation was remiss in relocating several hundred Aleuts in Alaska, for their own safety, following a Japanese attack on the island of Attu in 1942. The government "failed to provide reasonable care" for the Aleuts, who were removed from their native villages to southeast Alaska, and the relocation "resulted in widespread illness, disease and death among the residents of the camps," the bill recounted.

Survivors were eligible under the legislation for $12,000 payments to compensate for loss of property in that episode.

The Salt Lake Tribune
Salt Lake City, Utah, June 3, 1987

Justice delayed, it has long been recognized, is justice denied. Japanese-American citizens interned during World War II, in the wake of the U.S. Supreme Court's latest ruling, are surely about to see justice delayed, at least one more time.

Whether justice will be finally denied will depend on how the U.S. Circuit Court of Appeals for the Federal Circuit views — once again — a lawsuit seeking compensation from the government. In the meantime there is no reason to doubt the accuracy of the prediction of Justice Harry A. Blackmun, who said the controversy "will be back in this court once again months or years hence."

The justices unanimously decided that the wrong appeals court had ruled in a 1983 suit. In the 8-0 decision the Supreme Court said the U.S. Circuit Court of Appeals for the District of Columbia should not have heard the case.

In sending the case to the Circuit Court of Appeals for the Federal Circuit, which has exclusive appellate jurisdiction is such cases, the justices have kept alive the issue of whether uncompensated survivors of the World War II banishment of some 120,000 Japanese-Americans and resident aliens of Japanese ancestry from their homes in California, Oregon, Washington and Arizona are entitled to compensation for their lost property.

The Reagan administration in appealing the 1983 suit, in which the District of Columbia appeals court overruled the trial judge who said the suit was barred by a six-year statute of limitations, wanted the Supreme Court to either kill the suit outright or to send it to another appeals court.

Of those interned, about 60,000 are believed alive today. Of those, about 28,000 had already been compensated under the American-Japanese Evacuation Claims Act of 1948. The appeals court decision, set aside by the Supreme Court, said the government may have to pay "just compensation" for property losses suffered by those internees who weren't compensated under the 1948 act. Also, in that decision the government was told it would have to defend the suit brought in 1983.

Now the issue will be reviewed once more, over the "months or years" Justice Blackmun envisioned. Perhaps, through this long agony of litigation, some U.S. citizens will receive a modicum of justice for the misery they endured in what the Reagan administration has acknowledged was "a deplorable episode" and what the Ford administration characterized as one "of our national mistakes" and a "sad day in American history."

If such is the result, then delayed justice will not have been justice denied, at least not totally.

The Grand Rapids Press
Gary, Indiana, August 16, 1988

Forty-three years after the end of World War II, the United States is facing up to one of its most grievous wartime mistakes — one of the most shameful acts, in fact, in the nation's history.

Congress has passed and President Reagan has signed a bill which acknowledges the injustice done to 120,000 people of Japanese descent who were rounded up in 1942 and held for up to three years in internment camps. Each of the 60,000 internees who are still living will receive a tax-free payment of $20,000, amounting to a total federal cost of $1.2 million. The sums are trifles in comparison with the offense committed, but they are large enough to signify a serious attitude toward what happened. In that way, they are necessary companions to the more important element in this legislation: the apology given to those who were detained. "For here we admit wrong," President Reagan said in signing the bill. The admission has been awaited for 46 years by Japanese-Americans, many of whom have felt disgraced at having been feared and collectively accused of disloyalty.

The internment was ordered in 1942 by President Franklin Roosevelt, acting on the advice of his secretary of war, Henry L. Stimson. The 120,000 Japanese-Americans — about 77,000 American citizens and 43,000 resident aliens — were routed from their homes on the West Coast and taken to 10 barbed-wire camps scattered in desolate areas of seven western states. They could take with them only what they could carry in their hands. Homes, businesses, cars and farms were lost.

The camps themselves were bleak. Families lived in single rooms in tar-paper barracks. Eating and bathing were done en masse. Privacy was scarce to nonexistent. Wages were held to $19 a month.

A stinging irony is that while these unfortunates were being held in dishonor, other Japanese-Americans — soldiers in the U.S. armed forces — were abroad defending the liberties their relatives were being denied. In a final indignity, release of the internees in 1944 was blocked for political reasons in that presidential election year. The last camp was not closed until five months after the end of the war.

The fact that nothing similar befell Americans of German or Italian descent underscored the racism in the policy.

The nation has been slow to confront and answer for this outrage. Not until 1972 did Congress act on a bill to repay personal savings that were confiscated. In 1983, a federal commission concluded a two-year investigation — finding no military necessity for the internment — and recommended the $20,000 payments. Five more years passed before the present legislation cleared Congress.

The act, however, mustn't be misunderstood. This is an apology to Japanese-Americans, not to the government of Japan. Nothing excuses the atrocities committed by Japan in wartime or diminishes the sacrifices of U.S. servicemen. An important aspect of that war was the confirmation it gave of American values and moral strength. This legislation, in a very different way, does the same thing.

ST. LOUIS POST-DISPATCH
St. Louis, Missouri, August 12, 1988

When President Reagan signed the bill to pay $20,000 in reparations to each surviving Japanese-American who was wrongfully interned during World War II, he correctly characterized the legislation as ending a "civil rights disaster."

In the weeks following the Japanese bombing of Pearl Harbor in December 1941, a wave of anti-Japanese emotion swept the West Coast and was aimed at the 120,000 Japanese-Americans, 64 percent of them American citizens. Local politicians and top military officers in the region demanded that they be rounded up and sent to concentration camps. The standard argument was that spies and saboteurs were among them. That was total nonsense, and the FBI and military intelligence knew so at the time and told officials so.

But these intelligence reports were ignored, and in a shameful violation of civil rights, innocent civilians were sent off to internment camps for the rest of the war, with most them losing their homes, businesses and farms in the process. The payments to the 60,000 survivors represent only a small percentage of the value of their lost property.

It is also heartening to see that President Reagan is now endorsing this $1.2 billion reparations bill. The White House had initially opposed the bill on the grounds of its cost. But the president has come around, and he was right when he said, "This bill has less to do with property than with honor, for here we admit a wrong." It is an admission that has been too long in coming.

The Register-Guard
Eugene, Oregon, August 23, 1988

"What is important in this bill has less to do with property than with honor, for here we admit a wrong." With those words, President Reagan signed into law a bill that seeks to remove a 46-year-old blight from the national conscience.

The legislation offers a modest payment of $20,000 and the apology of the nation to each of about 60,000 Japanese-Americans who were taken from their homes, deprived of their property and placed in detention camps for the duration of World War II. Their only "crime" was their race. More than 120,000 Japanese-Americans — two-thirds of them *American citizens* — were sent to internment camps under a presidential wartime order that was upheld by the U.S. Supreme Court. The estimated 60,000 recipients of the cash payments are the surviving internees.

Because Congress may not approve funds to begin the $1.25 billion reparation program until next year, no payments are expected to be made until 1990 at the earliest. The delay is attributable in part to the fact that Congress limited the total amount of payments annually to $500 million, meaning that it will take at least three years to complete distribution of the $1.25 billion. Anticipating difficulty in locating all of the former internees, Congress authorized a 10-year period for making the payments.

Also adding to the delay is the new law's requirement that the attorney general "locate and identify each eligible individual." That will take time and a considerable staff, although former internees can help speed up the process by submitting documentation of their wartime detention. Also, the U.S. archives contains extensive records on the relocation camps, which existed in several Western states from 1942 to 1946. Help in finding former internees also will come from various organizations, especially the Japanese-American Citizens League.

The $20,000 is admittedly a token payment. No amount of money can adequately compensate the Japanese-American internees for being deprived of their civil rights, their property, their freedom and their dignity. But the payment and the nation's apology represent an attempt to acknowledge the injustice. The president was right. This law is about honor — national honor.

THE LAST INTERNEE

Chicago Tribune
Chicago, Illinois, August 20, 1988

Now that it's over, what defies belief is that it took so long. But Ronald Reagan, 42 years after the last of 120,000 Japanese-Americans were released from our World War II internment camps, has signed legislation that finally apologizes for their forced relocation and sets up a trust fund for reparations.

The internments were ordered in 1942 in an executive order by President Roosevelt. The last camp was closed in January, 1946, five months after Japan surrendered, ending the war. In signing the law, President Reagan, a New Deal Democrat in Roosevelt's day but America's leading Republican today, remarked with some generosity that "it's not for us today to pass judgment upon those who may have made mistakes while engaged in that great struggle."

But he added what was perhaps more important to camp survivors than the $20,000 tax-free payments that will come to each from the $1.25 billion trust fund: "Yet we must recognize that the internment of Japanese-Americans was just that, a mistake."

Earlier, President Reagan had threatened to veto the bill—because of its cost, said his spokesman, Marlin Fitzwater. Critics quickly attributed his late embracing of the position George Bush took in the California primary to the political importance of that state, which has many Japanese-Americans. Fitzwater insisted such considerations "were not a factor in any way."

No matter. Sen. Spark Matsunaga, the Hawaii Democrat and Japanese-American who led an impassioned fight for the bill, said it all at the signing. A one-time detainee who was twice wounded after the Anzio landing in Italy in World War II, he decried the internment as a "blot on our nation's constitutional history which had to be removed." But now, he said, the law not only will leave a legacy for the children of Japanese-Americans who fought for the bill, but also "for all immigrant minorities who continue to migrate to this great country of ours, founded not on race but on ideals."

Finally, the bill is law. And now the burden is upon us all to hold as truth the words Spark Matsunaga spoke. Chicago would be a good place to start.

AIDS & Homophobia Cause Vast Turmoil in Gay Community

The federal Centers for Disease Control (CDC) Jan. 24, 1991 said that of 161,073 persons in the U.S. reported to have develope .IDS since June 1981, a total of 100,777 had died by the end of December 1990.

In 1990, the CDC said, 31,916 Americans had died of AIDS. In 1989, the number had been 24,264. The death toll for both years, 55,460, was greater than the death toll between 1981, when the disease was discovered, and 1986.

Approximately 90% of AIDS victims were male, and nearly 75% were between the ages 25 and 44, according to the CDC. AIDS was the second-leading cause of death among men in that age bracket, after fatal injuries. It was also the leading cause of death among men in that age group in San Francisco, Los Angeles and New York City, and also among black women 15 to 44 years old in New York State and New Jersey.

"The epidemic is here," said Ruth Berkelman, chief of the CDC's AIDS surveillance branch. "We see from these numbers alone that AIDS has already taken an incredibly heavy toll, and there's no letup in sight."

The CDC Jan. 10, 1991 abandoned plans to conduct a $32 million nationwide survey of households to determine the prevalence of AIDS infection.

In 1989, the CDC had initiated two pilot surveys involving questionnaires and blood tests in Dallas County, Texas, and in Pittsburgh and Allegheny counties, Pa. The CDC found that people who engaged in high-risk behavior tended not to cooperate, making it impossible to garner accurate statistics.

In another development, CBS News Feb. 8, 1990 suspended satirical commentator Andy Rooney of the popular news magazine program "60 Minutes" for three months without pay. The suspension came in response to remarks that Rooney allegedly made that were derogatory to blacks and homosexuals. Rooney was quoted in the Feb. 27 issue of the *Advocate*, a gay newspaper based in Los Angeles, as saying, "I've believed all along that most people are born with equal intelligence, but blacks have watered down their genes because the less intelligent ones are the ones that have the most children. They drop out of school early, do drugs and get pregnant." The *Advocate* did not tape Rooney's comments. The paper had sought an interview with Rooney after he made what many homosexuals considered to be offensive remarks in a television special, "The Year End with Andy Rooney," broadcast on Dec. 28, 1989. In the program, Rooney said, "Too much alcohol, too much food, drugs, homosexual unions, cigarettes. They're all known to lead quite often to premature death." Rooney denied making the comments quoted in the *Advocate* and said he "abhorred" the racist sentiment expressed.

CBS News announced March 1 that it was ending Rooney's three-month suspension from the news show "60 Minutes" after only a month. CBS officials said the network was concerned that the show's ratings would be hurt by Rooney's absence. Since the suspension began, CBS had received thousands of letters and telephone calls supporting Rooney. Rooney returned to "60 Minutes" March 4 and said he "felt terrible" about the incident and had "learned a lot." His return helped lift the show's ratings, putting it in fourth place among all television programs broadcast that week. A week earlier, it had been in 18th place.

The Supreme Court Feb. 26, 1990 declined to review challenges to the military's policy of barring homosexuals from service.

Without comment, the court refused to hear two appeals, one from a Navy reserve officer dismissed from active duty after saying he was gay and another from an Army sergeant denied reenlistment after she announced that she was a lesbian.

A federal district judge in Washington, D.C. Dec. 9, 1991 asserted that the military's ban on homosexuals was justifiable to prevent the spread of AIDS.

The assertion was made by U.S. District Judge Oliver Gasch in dismissing a bias suit by a gay man, Joseph C. Steffan, against the U.S. Naval Academy in Annapolis, Md.

THE ATLANTA CONSTITUTION
Atlanta, Georgia, October 1, 1990

Two Atlanta men who have been life partners for 32 years are suing Continental Airlines for refusing to issue them a frequent-flier companion ticket. The airline says the men aren't "family" to each other because they aren't legally married.

Now in their fourth decade together, the couple's interwoven social life and emotional commitment to each other count for nothing in the airline's rule book because the men cannot establish a legal relationship to one another. While the frequent-flier policy clearly is unfair to the couple, the airline's difficulty with this situation is understandable.

Increasingly, airlines, personnel offices, hospitals and insurance companies are struggling to sort out issues involving longtime families that aren't "families" under the law. So far, they have received little guidance from lawmakers to help settle matters.

But even as politicians continue to duck the issue, real life problems keep piling up in the courts.

Currently in New York, the surviving lesbian partner of a deceased AT&T employee is suing that company for the death benefits it would have paid to a surviving husband. The woman says that even though the couple was married in a 1977 ceremony for friends and relatives, AT&T refuses to recognize her as the deceased woman's partner.

In probate courts, judges grapple with disputes over the wishes of deceased gay people whose blood relatives refuse to recognize the validity of their wills.

Other judges grope for ways to settle custody battles when gay families break up. Gay parents who reared children together for years have no way to address custody and visitation disputes because the laws don't spell out formulas for such matters.

Hospital administrators don't know whether to allow gay partners to visit patients in intensive care units reserved for family members. Health clubs can't decide whether to extend family rates to gay couples.

The time has come for lawmakers to accept that gay families are not going to disappear — and that corporations and courts need guidance in addressing the rights of these social units.

Laws are needed to recognize gay marriages, or at least, to establish legal bonds. Several cities now recognize "domestic partnerships," which create ties between gay partners or heterosexual couples living together. Pretending such relationships don't exist won't make them go away; it will only clog up the courts and confuse corporations.

The Oregonian

Portland, Oregon, December 14, 1991

It's not easy to defend the U.S. military's irrational policy of excluding homosexuals from service. That's why a federal judge this week had to move from the ridiculous to the absurd to find justification for the Navy's expulsion of a gay midshipman from the U.S. Naval Academy.

U.S. District Judge Oliver Gasch ruled that the military's ban on homosexuals is a legitimate weapon in the fight against AIDS.

It is nothing of the kind.

The way to fight the spread of AIDS is through education and safer sexual practices. Singling out an entire group of people for discriminatory treatment because they are at higher risk of contracting the disease does little good.

Besides, Gasch's ruling ignores the fact that in other parts of the world, heterosexual sex is the leading means by which AIDS is spread. He also ignores the fact that the no-homosexual rule also bans lesbians, whose risk of spreading AIDS is lower than that of heterosexual men and women.

The military is finding it increasingly difficult to justify its policy on homosexuals. The often-cited but never proven argument that homosexuals are targets for blackmail and, thus, a security risk was described as "a bit of an old chestnut" even by Defense Secretary Dick Cheney.

The argument that allowing homosexuals in the military would undermine discipline, destroy morale and hurt enlistment efforts was attacked by the 9th U.S. Circuit Court of Appeals this year. That court ruled that the anti-homosexual intolerance of military personnel does not on its own justify excluding homosexuals.

That leaves the military clutching at straws, including the straw that Gasch so injudiciously handed it this this week. Although AIDS has never been an issue in this or other lawsuits challenging the military's policy, Gasch made it one. This is, by the way, the same judge who called the plaintiff a "homo" during court proceedings, but insisted that did not mean he was biased.

When it comes to homosexuals, the military services' actions speak louder than their words. Commanders sent avowed homosexuals to serve in the Persian Gulf, preferring to wait until after the war ended to begin dismissal procedures. Apparently, during wartime their contribution counted for more than the imagined morale and security problems their presence might cause.

The military's anti-homosexual policy is no way to run an army — and certainly no way to win a war against AIDS.

THE BUFFALO NEWS

Buffalo, New York, December 11, 1991

IT TOOK SOME tortured reasoning to uphold the Pentagon's absolute ban on homosexuals in the military, but federal Judge Oliver Gasch was up to the challenge. His strange linking of the ban to AIDS makes us wonder both how well he understands the traditional anti-gay policy and how well he understands AIDS — not to mention how well he understands how a free society ought to operate.

The Pentagon, meanwhile, continues to play the fool with its irrational ban. Whether the court ruling stands or not, it's a Pyrrhic victory.

Gasch may well be right that "implicit in the power to support armies is the power to make rules concerning their health and welfare." But that doesn't answer the question of whether gays in the services threaten that, which they don't.

Or, on the other side, whether the absence of gays could actually undermine military strength and a sense of fair treatment, which it might.

No one contests the military's right to screen prospective applicants for illnesses and reject those who fail the tests. But to equate testing for venereal diseases with an absolute ban on all homosexuals, which the judge appears to have done, boggles the mind.

Why ban all homosexuals, including the disease-free? And hasn't the judge heard that AIDS is spreading in the heterosexual community, too?

The military's distaste for homosexuals has little to do with AIDS, anyway. It was around long before the disease was.

One by one, the arguments the military has advanced for its ban have fallen on their faces. No studies prove homosexuals are greater security risks because of threats that they might be exposed. On the contrary, one study called this fiction. And by penalizing homosexuals who are open and honest about their sexual orientation, the Pentagon ban actually promotes what it fears.

Currently the Pentagon contends that homosexuality "is incompatible with military service" because it weakens discipline, good order and morale. Again, no evidence. Indeed, one high-ranking Naval officer conceded last year that gay women in uniform often were "hard-working, career-oriented, willing to put in long hours on the job and among the command's best performers." *That's* incompatible with military service?

Then, of course, there is the Pentagon's open double standard. It doesn't apply the ban to its civilian employees. Are we to seriously believe that homosexuality is incompatible with the military for those of its members in uniform but not for those in civilian dress? The arguments grow sillier and sillier.

This case arose from the resignation of a young midshipman, Joseph C. Steffen, from the Naval Academy just days after he admitted to homosexuality and was told he could not, because of that fact, graduate.

The loss to the Pentagon of his talents and those of other homosexuals may hurt the effectiveness of America's national defense. However the courts rule on this ban, it distorts reason and dishonors the military. It mistreats patriotic Americans simply because of prejudice and myth.

Chicago Tribune

Chicago, Illinois, December 14, 1991

U.S. District Judge Oliver Gasch is hardly the first judge to uphold the ban against homosexuals in the military ranks, but he has broken new ground in justifying it. The ban is necessary, Gasch ruled this week, to protect soldiers and sailors from AIDS.

That's novel and innovative because the issue of AIDS had not been raised by either the Defense Department or Joseph Steffan, the former midshipman whose suit against the Naval Academy was the occasion for the ruling. But it is based more on ignorance than science, military need or common sense.

In dealing with AIDS, the Defense Department already is way ahead of the judge. It has been screening recruits since 1985 for the virus that causes AIDS and, by a year ago, had rejected more than 3,000 of 2.9 million applicants for that reason.

When active-duty members test positive, they are allowed to remain in the service until they are too ill to serve. As of September, 1,888 were still on duty.

Why, then, reject all members of a particular group whether they have the virus or not, in order to control the spread of AIDS, yet allow people who have tested positive for AIDS to remain on duty? Judge Gasch, who three times referred to the plaintiff as a "homo," does not say.

Unfortunately, the military's stated policy does not hold up much better than the judge's logic in light of new information. About 1,400 men and women are discharged annually under a directive that says "homosexuality is incompatible with military service" because it undermines the armed forces' ability "to maintain discipline, good order and morale."

Yet, as more and more gays and lesbians challenge the directive in court, evidence mounts that homosexuals have been performing better in uniform than military leaders have been willing to acknowledge.

Sgt. Perry Watkins, a Vietnam veteran ousted after 16 years of exemplary service, was reinstated by the Supreme Court last year. It upheld an appeals court ruling that the Army had no right to discharge Watkins after having allowed him to re-enlist three times previously, knowing he was a homosexual.

Steffan was ordered in April 1987 to resign from the Naval Academy or be discharged after he told officials there that he was a homosexual. At the time, he was in good standing and six weeks from graduation.

A traditional reason for the ban on homosexuals—that they are security risks subject to blackmail—has been abandoned even by Defense Secretary Dick Cheney, who called it "an old chestnut."

It may be that the issue will come down not to whether homosexuals should be allowed to enlist in and receive full benefits from the military, but whether they should be allowed while in uniform to practice an "openly gay" lifestyle.

The military always has set strict limits on behavior through rules and regulations that ban various forms of inappropriate "fraternization." It is not unimaginable that there could be rules that would allow homosexuals to continue their service while also requiring them to keep their private sexual lives private.

If Judge Gasch's ruling has any merit, it is as one more reminder to the military that it must ultimately face this issue squarely and rationally.

St. Petersburg Times
St. Petersburg, Florida, April 27, 1991

Condoning homosexuality is not the issue facing Tampa and Hillsborough elected officials.

Discrimination is.

The Tampa City Council and the Hillsborough County Commission will meet May 28 to decide whether homosexuals should be included in their human rights ordinances prohibiting discrimination in employment, housing and public accommodations. The question before them: Do you approve of discrimination or not?

It's that simple.

Some ministers and self-proclaimed conservatives in the community have tried to make it difficult. Fear and misinformation are their weapons. Pass this amendment and transvestites, dressed one day as a man, the next as a woman, will be teaching our children, they say. Employees will be pressured by homosexual co-workers to share their "aberrant, immoral" lifestyle.

Hogwash.

The proposed amendments to the ordinances simply perpetuate one of the noblest concepts upon which this country was built: equal rights for all. They simply say that being different is not grounds for denying a person's rights.

Homosexuals are certainly in need of that protection. According to the National Institute of Justice, they are among the most frequent victims of bias and hate crimes in this country. Although-government officials likely can't change the attitudes of the people who commit those crimes or the vocal, intolerant group of ministers and activists in their community, they can send a message. They can declare that discrimination of any kind won't be tolerated.

That's what the ordinance changes are all about. Elected officials — especially County Commissioners Ed Turanchik and Phyllis Busansky — should keep that in mind.

San Francisco Chronicle
San Francisco, California, March 12, 1991

EVEN AS greater gay visibility has begun to crack old stereotypes of prejudice and hate, that new activism can be held partially responsible for an average 42 percent increase in the number of incidents of violence against gay men and lesbians last year in six American cities.

Nationally, there were 1,588 such attacks recorded by agencies that monitor anti-gay violence. Their study, in addition, showed an increasing number of cases reflecting more severe physical injuries.

Locally, Community United Against Violence listed 425 anti-gay physical assaults, threats, verbal harassment and other incidents in 1990 for a 28 percent increase over 1989. The growing homosexual visibility here includes the successful election bids of several lesbians and the vocal support of the local gay community for gay rights legislation in Congress.

AT A NEWS conference in New York, the only city to surpass San Francisco in the number of reported cases with 507, a spokesman for the National Gay and Lesbian Task Force proudly referred to the added acceptance and understanding that have been achieved with greater gay visibility and activism. But he recognized that the unapologetic openness of many gays has bred hostility and created a more identifiable target for harassment and other attacks.

Anti-gay violence has, deplorably, become one of the country's fastest growing hate crimes. One proper reaction is imposition of stiff penalties for perpetrators of this type of reprehensible offense.

The Miami Herald
Miami, Florida, December 14, 1991

IMAGINE the uproar if a judge in a civil-rights case called a black the N-word. Such an epithet is repulsive anywhere; in a court of law, it's unforgivable.

But there were no legal repercussions earlier this year when U.S. District Judge Oliver Gasch in Washington, D.C., thrice called Joseph C. Steffan — kicked out of the U.S. Naval Academy for being a homosexual — a "homo." The judge refused plaintiff's request that he recuse himself.

Thus it was Judge Gasch, who this week reaffirmed the military's exclusion of homosexuals. He not only upheld it, he found a new reason: AIDS. He found the policy "rational in that it is directed, in part, at preventing those who are at the greatest risk of dying of AIDS from serving."

This reasoning is specious. Since 1985 the military has been testing recruits for HIV, the virus that causes AIDS. About 3,500 of 2.9 million prospects tested positive. They were excluded, and properly so. The military's health *is* a valid concern. That's no reason for the military to discriminate against homosexuals as a class.

Granted, there's a higher-than-average incidence of HIV among homosexuals — although the disparity is gradually lessening as AIDS's spread escalates among heterosexuals. The same bogus logic, however, could exclude unmarried persons, blacks, Hispanics, or low-income recruits. Those groups, after all, also have a higher-than-average incidence of AIDS.

Equally specious are Judge Gasch's other stated reasons for upholding the policy. The fear of sexual harassment — long used to exclude females — has been discredited.

The notion that homosexuals are especially vulnerable to blackmail and thus are security risks is an argument that Defense Secretary Dick Cheney calls "that old chestnut." It's a reminder that the phrase "Catch-22" was born of military illogic. If homosexual GIs were not forced to hide their sexual preference, blackmailers would have no leverage.

More is at stake here, however, than the future of homosexuals in the military. To condone such a policy consigns an estimated 10 percent of Americans to a second-class status. On such a large issue, this small-minded ruling must not be the last word.

THE BUFFALO NEWS
Buffalo, New York, December 9, 1991

THE ALFRED University faculty's warning shot against the Pentagon's outdated ban on homosexuals gives the military's top brass plenty of lead time to drop the discriminatory prohibition.

The Pentagon should use that time wisely and get rid of the ridiculous ban.

In voting the other day to deny academic credit for Reserve Officer Training Corps classes unless the ban on homosexuals is rescinded, Alfred's faculty may well have been the first in the nation to try to take such action.

But that does not mean instructors at the small private university are the only ones to recognize that there is no longer any logical reason to keep homosexuals out of any part of the military establishment — if, indeed, there ever was.

The State University at Buffalo had tried to bar military recruiters because of the Pentagon's policy of discriminating on the basis of sexual orientation. That effort was stymied by a state law mandating equal access to all recruiters at the public university, as well as by the absence of any New York law that makes discrimination against homosexuals illegal.

But UB's sentiment was on target, as are policies at Harvard, Yale, the University of Wisconsin and other schools that bar military recruiters.

In voting to deny ROTC credit, Alfred's faculty would add that school's voice to the outcry against policies that overtly discriminate for no good reason.

The Pentagon has yet to say exactly what makes homosexuality "incompatible" with military service. It's not surprising that the generals have been silent on that point, because they would be hard-pressed to offer persuasive reasons. They've never presented any evidence that sexual orientation makes a soldier a security risk subject to blackmail. And with attitudes toward homosexuals changing, that red herring holds even less legitimacy than it ever did.

The Alfred faculty's vote still could be overturned by the board of trustees, but that body would be wise to follow the lead of its instructors. The proposal to take away credit by the fall of 1996 if the Pentagon doesn't change course next year is fair to those currently enrolled in ROTC, because it allows them to finish what they have started.

It also gives the Pentagon enough lead time to drop its institutionalized bias, which undoubtedly is what the instructors really would like to see happen.

But if it doesn't, there is no reason that Alfred must abet the military's discrimination. Universities add and drop courses all of the time. It could teach a valuable lesson by dropping credit for this one.

Minneapolis Star and Tribune
Minneapolis, Minnesota, February 22, 1991

Organizers of the new drive to repeal St. Paul's gay-rights ordinance have hit upon a shrewd strategy: Instead of carrying on about homosexual depravity, they're calmly questioning the wisdom of granting "special status" to gays and lesbians. That approach sounds momentarily reasonable, which makes it all the more dangerous. Whether high-pitched or low-key, any campaign against gay rights resonates with intolerance.

The quest for gay rights in St. Paul has been rocky from the start. A gay-rights ordinance was derailed in 1978 after a vituperative crusade by clergy who invoked the Bible in assailing homosexuality. In 1988, voters rejected a charter amendment that would have prohibited the use of initiative and referendum to enact or repeal laws dealing with human rights. The new ordinance was approved 6-1 by the City Council last summer. It bars discrimination on the basis of "sexual or affectional orientation" in housing, employment and public accommodations.

That step inspired a replay of the 1978 repeal effort — with a '90s twist. A group called Citizens Alert is gearing up to collect the 5,000-plus signatures needed to put a repeal measure on the Nov. 5 ballot. But the group doesn't plan to stress the moral issues that caused so much rancor a dozen years back. Instead opponents will argue that the ordinance improperly extends special rights to gays and lesbians, and thereby limits the power of religious groups and parents. It could force religious organizations to hire people with objectionable lifestyles, Citizens Alert will warn, and keep parents from discovering the sexual orientation of teachers and others who care for children.

St. Paul voters should look hard before they swallow the Citizens Alert appeal. Though it is less strident, at its core is the same intolerance that for years has kept gays and lesbians from enjoying full human rights. Its claim that the ordinance grants special rights to homosexual citizens is false. The provision merely adds gays and lesbians to other groups who need a legal shield from public scorn.

Offering that protection takes no powers from parents. And it need not be seen as an infringement on religious freedom. No such conflicts have arisen in the months since the law's enactment; if they do, religious groups can press for their First Amendment rights in court.

Even with the volume turned down, a call to repeal gay rights sounds shrill. It contradicts the root premise of a democratic society, that all people are created equal. Its effect would be to subject innocent citizens to humiliating exclusion. Whatever its marching tune, St. Paul citizens should turn a deaf ear.

THE ATLANTA CONSTITUTION
Atlanta, Georgia, December 15, 1991

The ruling by a federal judge barring a homosexual Naval Academy midshipman from armed service just might turn out to be a reverse-spin victory for groups trying to stop the military from automatically rejecting gays and lesbians.

The logic of the decision is such obvious nonsense that it is difficult to imagine it surviving appeal, though, of course, there's finally the Reagan-Bush Supreme Court, committed to reactionary activism.

Joseph C. Steffan was bounced from the academy when he acknowledged his homosexuality. U.S. District Judge Oliver Gasch sustained the expulsion in substantial part on the grounds that the policy is appropriate because gay men "are at the greatest risk of dying of AIDS."

True enough currently, but that is only an excuse, not a reason for barring gay men as a class. There is no evidence that Mr. Steffan has AIDS or even that he has had sex with anyone, male or female. Nor does it follow that his future behavior would put him or anyone else at heightened risk.

If AIDS is now the reason to bar homosexual men — the military's rationale tends to float with the times — what of all the heterosexual members of the armed services with other sexually transmitted diseases?

And some communicable diseases tend to occur with greater frequency in low-income groups or in certain parts of the country. Is economic class, then, or region a reason for forbidding service in the military?

If Judge Gasch's logic is to be honored, then the armed services must be cleared of heterosexual women. The incidence of AIDS in that population, though less than among gay men, is far higher than among lesbians.

The military once argued that homosexuals were security risks per se; it has pretty much given up that line. Then it claimed they would be disruptive, though disruption mostly occurs when the services find one out and expel her or him. Now AIDS. Isn't it time just to let willing men and women serve and to judge them on their military performance, not their private sex lives?

The Pittsburgh PRESS
Pittsburgh, Pennsylvania, February 25, 1991

A petition drive aimed at nullifying a gay-rights amendment to Pittsburgh's Human Relations Act has provoked little visible response from the Masloff administration. That's unfortunate. Unless City Hall quickly rouses itself to fight this campaign, a hate-filled, name-calling spring could develop.

The petition-signing was instigated by a group called Citizens for Pittsburgh. Last week, it presented more than 9,300 signatures to the Allegheny County Elections Bureau, seeking a referendum in the May primary on the city's gay-rights law.

That law, approved last March, expanded the longstanding Human Relations Act to prohibit discrimination in matters of housing, employment or public accommodation based on "sexual orientation." Similar legal protections already existed to cover race, color, religion, ancestry, national origin, sex, age or non-work-related handicap.

The gay-rights legislation provoked a storm of controversy, much of it filled with venom and fear and aimed at Pittsburgh's gay residents. Critics claimed the new law would promote this lifestyle and corrupt everybody else's morals.

There's been no evidence this has been the case. In the past 11 months, seven complaints have been filed by gay persons with the Human Relations Commission. The only one to receive public attention does not appear to involve a significant issue; none has been settled.

Although the apprehensions of the critics have not been realized, they have not given up their fight against the gay-rights law. Their latest strategy, however, raises serious legal questions.

The proposed referendum aims at amending the City Charter in such a way as to strip the gay-rights language from the Human Relations Act. But the Human Relations Act is not part of the charter. Taking this route could be compared to changing the state Constitution to get rid of a littering law. It's a legally-flawed approach, and the city should seek to block it.

It's possible the county Law Department, which is now reviewing the petition, may decide not to allow the referendum to go on the ballot. But the city shouldn't wait and hope for that outcome; it needs to get into the fight to stop this end-run maneuver without further delay.

If it doesn't, the public wrangling and campaigning could turn ugly — with more divisive and hurtful results than the gay-rights law ever produced.

'Moment of Silence' Debated Across U.S.

The Supreme Court Dec. 1, 1987 refused to rule on a New Jersey law requiring a daily "moment of silence" in public school classrooms "for quiet and private contemplation and introspection."

A federal district court in Philadelphia found the law unconstitutional, a violation of the First Amendment requirement for separation of church and state. Although the law did not mention prayer, the courts detected a veiled purpose behind it to facilitate student prayer.

The law, enacted over the governor's veto, was challenged by a teacher and several students and parents. The governor, Thomas H. Kean, refused to defend it. The state Assembly speaker, Alan J. Karcher, and Senate President Carmen A. Orechio stepped in, on behalf of the legislation. But they lost their leadership posts before the Supreme Court appeal was filed and the new leaders did not pursue the case.

Justice Sandra Day O'Connor, writing for a unanimous court in *Karcher v. May*, said the former leaders lacked legal standing to appeal.

The court did not consider the issue of whether the law, and by implication, at least, similar laws in about two dozen other states, was constitutional.

The action left intact, however, the appellate court ruling that the New Jersey law was unconstitutional.

The Duluth News-Tribune
Duluth, Minnesota, March 20, 1991

It's too bad that all public school administrators can't seem to learn what should be a basic principle for them (and other government officials): Religious ceremonies must not be part of public school life, whether in the classroom or at graduation ceremonies.

It's also too bad the U.S. Supreme Court can't find its way this year to restate this principle, which it has upheld many times before.

It is further too bad President George Bush seems to have no philosophical understanding of America's Constitution even though he took a pledge to uphold it. His administration supports efforts of school officials in Providence, R.I., to have group prayers at school graduation.

The constititional principle is simple: Church and state shall be separate. That doesn't mean students can't study religion as an academic topic; it means government, including public schools, can't advance religion.

Most people can easily see when a ceremony or practice is religious in nature. All school officials — and others in government — need do is avoid such ceremonies or practices.

We don't want to seem to be picking on schools. They do better than many other units of government at avoiding the problem. Prayers that begin meetings of governing bodies violate the spirit and letter of the constitutional ban — but they go on in too many cases.

This ban exists not to hurt religion, but to protect its exercise without government interference. The high court agreed this week to consider the latest challenge to the ban. It's too bad justices won't rule on it until next year. But we hope that, when they do, it will resolve this simple but important matter forever.

Arkansas Gazette
Little Rock, Arkansas, March 19, 1991

The Gravette case has come to its predictable end. The Constitution is upheld. Church and state remain separate.

Without comment, the United States Supreme Court on Monday let stand lower court decisions prohibiting Bible classes in Gravette public schools during regular school hours.

The Gravette Bible classes were an anachronism. They were taught for more than 50 years, continuing long after courts had ruled that inclusion of such classes in a public-school curriculum violated the constitutional separation of church and state. Finally, a suit was filed by a couple whose child attended the Gravette schools.

Federal District Judge Morris Arnold of Fort Smith ruled that the classes were unconstitutional, rejecting the school district's argument that the classes passed muster because they were voluntary and non-denominational. The classes were clearly sectarian, Arnold said, and indeed they were.

(A volunteer instructor of the classes testified that she taught songs that included phrases such as "Jesus is God's son," "Jesus died for me" and "Great in heaven is my reward." She said those statements were factual, not religious.)

The 8th Circuit Court of Appeals at St. Louis upheld Judge Arnold's decision in October. Now the Supreme Court has upheld it, and obstinate Gravette school authorities have no place else to go.

Students at Gravette have learned a lesson in government from all this. We hope as well that they and their elders have gained a greater appreciation of the freedom of religion.

THE DAILY OKLAHOMAN
Oklahoma City, Oklahoma, February 25, 1991

CURIOUS indeed is the logic of Norman school officials who put a halt to students meeting on the playground during recess to read Bible verses and say prayers.

Presumably, in this brave new world, 11-year-olds are allowed to gather and sing the latest rock music hits. But religious hymns are no-nos.

Shakespeare or even Teen Magazine are permitted reading materials. However, the Bible and other religious literature are bad business.

Expressions of political opinion are hunky dory unless they advocate violent overthrow of the government, genocide or organized religion.

Perhaps the wearing of crosses or crescents or Stars of David should be forbidden. Of course, a New Kids on the Block T-shirt is proper dress.

It obviously is proper to invite friends to a rock concert. But invitations to a church school are proselytizing.

If Norman 11-year-olds are like others, there is an occasional dirty joke told on the playground. Kids will be kids, but psalms and prayers are too offensive to be tolerated.

Playground debates on abortion, teen sex, drug use, birth control or smoking are harmless unless, of course, religious values enter the discussion.

Like smoking and drinking, religious beliefs are much too harmful to young minds and should be practiced only behind the barn. School property must be reserved for important educational pursuits.

The TENNESSEAN
Nashville, Tennessee, March 27, 1991

IN 1962, the Supreme Court ruled that teachers should not lead organized prayer in public schools.

In 1971, that ruling was enhanced with a guideline — a three-pronged "test" by which to judge whether formal conduct at school functions advanced religious beliefs. That standard has served the judicial system well, standing as the measure on church and state arguments.

But now the Supreme Court has decided to open the issue again. The very fact that the court is hearing a case that could weaken the church/state division is a troubling development for those who thought the issue had been wisely settled.

This case started at a Rhode Island middle school when the parents of a student sued the school board after a rabbi offered prayers at the graduation ceremony. The family objected that the prayers could be offensive to non-Jewish students, although they themselves were Jewish.

After two lower courts ruled against the school board, the city appealed the case to the Supreme Court.

Under the 1971 guidelines, the court said that to pass as constitutional, a practice must have "a secular purpose," that "its principal or primary effect must be one that neither advances nor inhibits religion," and it must not involve an "excessive entanglement" with religion.

The current standards should not be weakened. Long before the 1971 standards, or the 1962 ruling on the issue, the Constitution stipulated that there should be separation between the church and state institutions.

There is nothing at all in the Constitution that prohibits a student from praying. Students can offer their individual prayers before a test, before a football game, at commencement or anywhere else.

What is prohibited by the Constitution is organized prayer so that young students who are being taught one religion at home won't be confused by the prayer of a different religion.

Sixteen-year-old Deborah Weisman, the student whose parents first brought the suit, seems to have a firm grasp of the issue. "It is against the law," she has stated. "This is a basic First Amendment right and I think they are wasting a lot of money on something that should be an opened and closed case."

Perhaps the wisened judges of the Supreme Court should hear the arguments of this 16-year-old girl. ■

The Miami Herald
Miami, Florida, March 23, 1991

SOME ISSUES just don't want to stay closed, and the role of organized religion in public schools is one of them. Consequently, the U.S. Supreme Court has agreed to hear an appeal by the Providence, R.I., School Board of lower-court rulings against a prayer by a rabbi at a middle-school graduation.

The lower courts, citing the 1971 *Lemon vs. Kurtzman,* said that the rabbi's prayer violated the First Amendment's prohibition against state establishment of religion. The nonsectarian prayer invoked God's blessing and ended with "Amen."

The *Lemon* standard imposed three tests for satisfying the "establishment" clause: The practice "must have a secular purpose"; its "principal or primary effect must be one that neither advances nor inhibits religion"; and it may not encourage "excessive entanglement" with religion. A former Reagan Administration assistant Attorney General represents the Providence School Board, and the Bush Administration has entered the case on the board's side.

In previous cases, Justice Anthony Kennedy has complained of "an unjustified hostility toward religion" in the *Lemon* standards. Justice Sandra Day O'Connor has said that a more-permissive "endorse-

IMPOSITION IS STILL WRONG

ment"-of-religion standard might be better. The views of the newest Justice, David Souter, are untested. Thus it is likely that the Court will examine the issue broadly.

That's fine. An honest examination will show that inviting a cleric to invoke God's blessing upon underage public-school students indeed *is* an "establishment of religion." There is no mistaking the aura of the clergy in asking the Deity to act, or in thanking Him for acting, in human affairs. That is the very essence of organized religion, at least in Western societies.

Even so, there is something to Justice Kennedy's concern about an "unjustified hostility toward religion." Some history textbooks, for example, have omitted the religious motivations of the Pilgrims and other early colonists and explorers. Some school officials censor students' own valedictory addresses to purge religious references. These acts are wrong.

The state may not impose its religious views or its view of religion on students — period. That's the point that the Court should reaffirm.

Rockford Register Star
Rockford, Illinois, June 9, 1991

■ **Change proposed:** Rockford schools would expand their focus on religion.

As we gauge it, the knee-jerk reaction to a proposed change in Rockford School District policy concerning religion amounts to this mournful cry: Once again, the atheists and humanists are trying to kick God out of the public-school classroom.

Nothing could be further from the truth in this case. In reality, the proposed policy is one of inclusion, not exclusion. The intention is to broaden, not diminish, the exposure of students to religious customs. The policy would bring more, not less, focus on the role of religion in this and other societies.

Yet, here comes Jim Mays, a Rockford police lieutenant and former mayoral candidate, complaining that the new policy would end up "totally destroying our traditional values ... I don't think this is what our Constitution says. I think school leaders are taking this too far."

Taking what too far? Is it going too far to supplement Christmas and Easter programs in the schools with programs that acknowledge special observances of non-Christian faiths? Is it going too far for tax-supported schools to make the focus on the trappings of, say, Christmas an academic focus rather than a devotional one? Is it going too far to adopt a policy that actually would *increase* classroom attention to the influences of religion on secular life?

Mays, like so many others, seems to labor under a popular misreading of Supreme Court rulings barring public-school sponsorship of prayer. The court never said that God or religion couldn't be mentioned in schools. It merely prohibited schools from pushing religious worship, as in prayer. The ruling didn't reflect a philosophy that religion must be kept out of government; rather, it said that government must be kept out of religion. Public schools are governmental units, and as such they have no business sponsoring religious exercises.

Nor did the high court ban the study of religion in public schools. On the contrary, the court explicitly *encouraged* the study of how religion has so greatly influenced the long history of the world, including the history of this country.

The proposed policy change for the Rockford schools is a good one, and long overdue. It would bring more emphasis on religion in the curriculum. It would show greater respect for the religious sensibilities of all students, Christian and non-Christian alike.

And it would help put the lie to the durable fiction that the courts are trying to keep religion out of public schools.

Immigration Law Signed; Issues Remain Divisive

President George Bush Nov. 29, 1990 signed the Immigration Act of 1990, calling it the "most comprehensive reform of our immigration laws in 66 years."

"Immigration is not just a link to America's past, it is also a bridge to America's future," Bush said at a White House signing ceremony.

Among its provisions, the bill provided a "safe haven" for 18 months to Salvadorans who had entered the U.S. illegally. The measure was considered an ambiguous gesture to Salvadorans fleeing military strife in their country because they would have to register with the government in the first half of 1991 and would return to their previous status after 18 months had passed. During that time they would be granted all the benefits of legal citizens.

The Senate Foreign Relations Committee with State Department backing, June 12, 1991 voted, 18-0, to require the department to remove almost all names from a list of foreigners considered ideologically unacceptable for entrance to the U.S.

The action was largely symbolic because a 1990 change to the 1952 Immigration and Nationality Act, known as the McCarron-Walter Act, had barred the State Department from excluding any person from the U.S. for any beliefs, statements or political associations for which U.S. citizens would be protected by the Constitution.

Civil rights officials estimated that the Foreign Relations Committee's action would force the State Department to remove 69% of the 367,000 names on the secret list. The State Department would still be permitted to keep a list of individuals to be excluded from the U.S. for national-security or foreign-policy reasons. Another three million people were barred because of criminal actions, drug trafficking or immigration violations.

The State Department received at least 12 million applications for 40,000 permanent-resident visas available by lottery on a first-come, first-served basis. The lottery, which was open Oct. 14-20, 1991, had been established by the Immigration Act of 1990 and was to be held annually through 1994.

The visas, known as green cards, allowed immigrants to live and work legally in the U.S. The lottery was limited to nationals of 34 countries and territories, 28 of them in Europe. It was designed to aid nationals of countries that had experienced a decline in legal immigration to the U.S. since the passage of a sweeping immigration reform law in 1965.

The 1965 law had lifted strict quotas that had limited immigration to the U.S. from Latin America and Asia, and it had given strong preference to immigrants who already had relatives in the U.S. The 1990 law was designed to "diversify" the immigrant population in the U.S.

Forty percent of the visas available in the lottery were reserved for immigrants from the Republic of Ireland. Sen. Edward M. Kennedy (D, Mass.), a cosponsor of the 1990 law, defended the Irish preference program, saying it was designed to correct past discrimination against Irish immigrants. (Natives of Northern Ireland were considered British citizens, and were not included in the Irish set-aside provision.)

Response to the lottery was overwhelming, with many entrants mailing hundreds and often thousands of applications. Many hopefuls who hand-delivered their applications to the Merrifield Post Office in Fairfax County, Va. that was designated to receive the applications were disqualified from the lottery because the applications were received before the 12:01 a.m. Oct. 14 start of the application period.

The Wichita
Eagle-Beacon
Wichita, Kansas, March 16, 1991

At the recently opened Ellis Island museum in New York City there is a display focusing on the rough welcome some immigrants received when they arrived in the United States at the turn of the century.

To put it mildly, many native-born Americans didn't appreciate the newcomers, most of whom were from southern and eastern Europe and thus different from the country's then-dominant northern-European stock. Union leaders, for example, opposed the immigrant wave because they feared cheap labor. Some Protestants objected to the Catholic or Jewish faith of many of the immigrants. Conservatives worried that the new "huddled masses" would bring radical political ideas.

Nevertheless, the period between 1901-1910 was the greatest period of immigration in the nation's history, as 8.8 million people entered the country.

While many of the first generation of immigrants kept their native customs and clung to their old ways, their children eagerly adapted to the United States. Now, three generations later, Americans of all ethnic backgrounds admire the people who sought a new life in the United States.

That same process is being repeated in today's United States. According to Census Bureau figures released this week, the decade of the 1980s recorded the largest number of immigrants since the turn of the century. Eight million foreigners have joined American society over the past 10 years, accounting for more than one-third of the nation's population growth.

Although the new immigrants represent every part of the world, 85 percent of them came from Latin America or Asia. Their numbers dramatically alter the racial composition of the United States. Americans of European ancestry now constitute 75 percent of the country, down from 80 percent in 1980 and even higher percentages in earlier decades.

That means the United States faces major cultural, political and intellectual changes as the new arrivals seek their role in American society. Similar to what happened in the Ellis-Island era, some people are warning that the immigrants represent a threat to social unity, that they will retain their old customs and languages and turn parts of the country into U.S. versions of Quebec or Belgium.

More likely, as did earlier immigrants, the newest Americans will enhance the diversity and rich cultural mix that has made the United States one of history's greatest experiments in human relations. They will maintain pride in their heritage, but seek the opportunities that the larger U.S. society offers.

Sociologists argue whether the United States is a "melting pot" or a "mosaic." The point, however, is that millions of people still leave their old lives in distant lands to commit their fate and those of their children to an American future. If it were otherwise, this would not be America.

The Record
Hackensack, New Jersey, June 17, 1991

IT IS FITTING that one of the last vestiges of the McCarthy era is being done away with this year, as we celebrate the bicentennial of the Bill of Rights. Up to now, the State Department has kept a secret list of the names of 250,000 people barred from entering this country simply because of the beliefs they hold. That should be offensive to anyone who cherishes the freedoms guaranteed under the Bill of Rights.

Now, thanks to Congressional action, the list is about to be done away with. The State Department has been ordered by Congress to remove the names on its roster of "political undesirables."

The list, which has been in existence for almost 40 years, was created during a time of paranoia to protect American citizens from "subversive" ideas. But the Bill of Rights is based on the premise that American citizens need no such protection. Exposure to all kinds of political beliefs and ideologies — and the freedom to express them — is exactly what gives our democracy its vitality and strength.

The State Department was forbidden last year from excluding anyone from another country strictly because of their beliefs or political associations. But people on the list had to apply to have their names removed. Since the list was secret, many people didn't know they were on it. A measure just passed by Congress, and supported by the White House, changes that.

Among those on the list were author Gabriel García Márquez and poet Pablo Neruda, both Nobel prize winners, the late novelist Graham Greene, and actor Yves Montand, as well as assorted political leaders, from Daniel Ortega of Nicaragua on the left to Roberto d'Aubuisson of El Salvador on the right. A Canadian labor leader was on the list because he once played on a Little League team sponsored by the Communist Party.

Truly dangerous people — such as criminals, drug traffickers, and national security risks — will still be kept out of the country. But it's time the United States affirmed that we have nothing to fear from those with differing opinions, and much to gain from hearing their views.

> **"Americans don't need protection from 'subversive' ideas."**

Detroit Free Press
Detroit, Michigan, June 13, 1991

Detention without telling the detained what the charges are. Secret trials in which evidence never released to the defendant or examined or questioned by the defense is admitted. Secret verdicts that could lead to the defendant's indefinite imprisonment, torture or death. Possible, you think, in only some backward country but never in the United States of America?

Well, such could be the results of a process that the Bush administration is proposing to deal with aliens branded by the government as undesirables. The "terrorist alien removal" provision is part of the administration's crime bill and is supported by Attorney General Dick Thornburgh.

The proposal profanes the Bill of Rights — which applies to all persons on U.S. soil, not just to citizens — and 200 years of proud legal tradition. Even if Congress let this outrage pass, it is improbable that the courts would let it stand.

The secret hearings and expedient deportation rules could apply to legal and illegal aliens, including long-term permanent residents and persons married to U.S. citizens. Terrorism is defined so broadly in the bill that not only violent acts would be covered, but also political activities that the present U.S. government dislikes. Aliens who, for example, raise money for the African National Congress, the Irish Republican Army, or Palestinians in the Israeli-occupied territories, or Chinese students who organized rallies in Washington against the anti-democratic regime in Beijing could conceivably be deported. And if the foreign regimes refused to admit the deportees, they could be detained indefinitely in the United States.

It is a cynical ploy for the Bush administration to try to acquire such extraordinary, unchecked power over individuals by invoking the dreaded word "terrorism." There is scant evidence that a new deportation process is needed to combat terrorist acts. The Persian Gulf War hysteria notwithstanding, terrorism has never been a major problem in the United States, and its incidence actually has declined in the last decade. The government does not need secret trials to defend our security.

The executive branch ought to be embarrassed for even submitting this sort of a proposal. Congress should repudiate it firmly and loudly. This nation has thrived for two centuries because of fierce protection of due process and individual rights; it does not need authoritarian measures now.

The Washington Post
Washington, D.C., June 19, 1991

THE SENATE is about to consider a terrible proposal that would allow the government to hold secret trials leading to the deportation of certain noncitizens. It will come up as part of an assorted crime package moving to the floor this week. On the agenda are two crime bills, one supported by Sen. Joseph Biden and the Democrats, the other the administration's proposal sponsored by Sen. Strom Thurmond. Because the major features of both bills—the death penalty, habeas corpus revisions and changes in the exclusionary rule—have been considered in both houses recently, the Senate Judiciary Committee held only three perfunctory hearings this year—one on habeas, another on rural crime and a third to hear Attorney General Dick Thornburgh.

Incredibly, no hearings were held on the deportation proposal, which is new this year. Moreover, because the committee didn't even vote on these bills but simply sent both to the floor without recommendation, there is not even a committee report that evaluates this section of the president's bill.

The proposal is directed against aliens the government believes are engaged in "terrorist activity." It applies to all noncitizens, even those who have entered legally, lived here for decades and have children and other close relatives who are citizens. The bill uses a definition of "terrorist activity" that is broad and includes raising money for or urging others to join "terrorist organizations," though it does not define the latter term. That is a political decision left to the government, and presumably it could include groups such as Kurdish nationalists, Afghan rebels, Sikh separatists and the IRA. Spokesmen for the PLO are singled out in the statute as engaging in terrorist activity.

The administration bill would allow the Justice Department to go to a secret court and get an order for a special proceeding to deport such people. Targeted individuals would have no notice of this hearing and no opportunity to attend or be represented. They could be arrested and detained as soon as this petition was filed. At the special proceeding that followed, the government could present secret evidence—outside the presence of the alien and his lawyer—and could even withhold a summary of that evidence from the accused. Theoretically, appeals would be allowed, but again, the evidence used at the trial could be kept under seal and the appeal argued in secret.

Does this sound like a proceeding in an American court? It is a nightmare that could allow the worst kind of injustice. Though not a criminal trial, a deportation hearing involves severe penalties and must afford due process. There is not much that is good in either of the crime bills coming up for consideration—gun control is the exception—but this blueprint for a kangaroo court stands out. It's hard to see how anyone with any respect for the American idea of justice could support it.

Chicago Tribune
Chicago, Illinois, June 20, 1991

Americans take it for granted that the federal government may not discriminate against them because it disagrees with their political opinions. Freedom of speech is the cornerstone of our democratic system.

But for 38 years the government defied the spirit of the Bill of Rights by treating foreigners in a way it would never be allowed to treat its own citizens—refusing them admission to this country on the basis of their ideologies.

Last year, the offending provision of the 1952 McCarran-Walter act was scrapped. And now, after a battle between Congress and the State Department over how to implement the law, one of the unsavory relics of the McCarthy era will finally be destroyed.

Originally aimed at communists, the law has served to bar a diverse group of "political undesirables," including novelist Graham Greene, Rhodesian Prime Minister Ian Smith, Salvadoran rightist Roberto d'Aubisson, actor Yves Montand, Northern Irish Protestant leader Ian Paisley and nature writer Farley Mowat. Successive administrations have expanded the list, which now contains some 250,000 names.

The law was presumably as useless as it was offensive. The weird result was that although the dangerous opinions were not kept out—Americans could read Greene's novels or see d'Aubisson on the evening news or listen to Paisley speak live on a telephone hookup—the human vessels of those opinions were.

As part of an overhaul of immigration laws, Congress last year barred the State Department from excluding foreigners for holding views that would be pro-tected if they were held by U.S. citizens. The Bush administration insisted on retaining the list, requiring the excluded to petition individually to have their names removed—a burden they should not have to bear. But under threat of congressional action, the State Department now has agreed to purge the list of all but a few names.

This change of policy presents no national security threat: Some 3 million criminals will remain on the list. It merely tells the world that this country's receptivity to open debate doesn't stop at the border.

THE CHRISTIAN SCIENCE MONITOR
Boston, Massachusetts, June 21, 1991

SO long to a cold-war dodo. Under bipartisan urging from Congress, the State Department has agreed to remove some 250,000 names from a list of foreigners who are denied entry into the United States because of their political views. The list, created under the 1952 McCarran-Walter Act, is a relic of the anticommunist frenzy of the early post-war years.

It's easy to wax indignant over this international blacklist, one of the corrupt fruits of McCarthyism. But in those days of Soviet betrayals in Eastern Europe, of the Korean War and the Rosenbergs, a lot of Americans besides the senator from Wisconsin were worried about communist threats to American security. President Truman's courageous veto of the act was resoundingly overturned.

Yet the misguided keep-out list was overly broad right from the start. It barred few spies or saboteurs, and lots of politicians, labor leaders, writers, and entertainers whose ideology didn't mesh with the patriotic orthodoxy. Even more appalling has been the list's endurance decades beyond the dangers, however implausible, that gave rise to it.

How many Americans were still in the grip of the Red scare by the 1980s? Yet the McCarran-Walter blacklist ballooned under Reagan from 100,000 names to 367,000, as the administration stepped up efforts to keep left-wingers away from America's shores. The government stopped blocking the door for ideological reasons a couple of years ago, but the list still existed.

Now the State Department will purge most of the names. An alien will remain listed for political reasons only if the department certifies that there are compelling reasons for the blackball. (The names of foreigners denied entry on national-security grounds, as opposed to ideological, will remain on the list, and other people are prevented from entering the US under criminal or immigration laws.) McCarran-Walter has been a blot on America's commitment to civil liberties and human rights for too long. It's past time to bleach that stain.

The News and Observer
Raleigh, North Carolina, June 16, 1991

Though the action was long overdue, it was still good timing last week when the U.S. State Department agreed to begin purging a secret list of aliens to remove the names of a quarter of a million people whom somebody, somewhere had branded "ideologically unacceptable" and thus unfit to enter this country.

On a day that the Russian republic was picking Boris Yeltsin as its first popularly elected leader, it was especially fitting for Americans to start dismantling a blacklist that grew out of paranoid fears about communist subversion in the 1950s.

Millions of Americans are too young to have seen the 1950s spectacle when the late Sen. Joseph McCarthy of Wisconsin waved aloft a piece of paper, declaring it to be a list of subversives in the State Department. Mr. McCarthy didn't have to name any names or show any proof to keep his political enemies in check.

All he had to do was use the tactics of smear. He spread the idea of guilt by association and even forced people out of government because of fear he would brand them as communists or communist sympathizers.

Although his colleagues in the Senate eventually censured Mr. McCarthy for his tactics, fears and suspicion of the kind he spread got reflected in such laws as the Immigration and Nationality Act of 1952 (the McCarran-Walter Act), which was passed over President Truman's veto. The argument was broadly made that the law would protect Americans against subversive ideas.

Almost without exception, the people on the secret list have been barred from even visiting the United States. Over a 40-year period, State Department officials and U.S. embassies and consulates around the world have supplied the names — often on the basis of information provided by other governments.

Today, the list includes foreigners whose political ideologies run from the far left to the far right. But the number of names apparently grew rapidly in the 1980s because of the Reagan administration's hostility to people with left-wing views. Among those banned from American shores are Nobel laureates, actors, writers and naturalists who don't come bearing explosives but philosophy and ideas.

The State Department has agreed to purge the list of the "ideologically unacceptable" over a three-year period. This is part of a compromise with the Senate Foreign Relations Committee on a bill that will permit the department to retain the names of some aliens by certifying there are "compelling reasons" to do so. Indeed, there will continue to be lists of known or suspected terrorists, criminals and immigration-law violators — as there should be.

But the agreement is in keeping with coveted American freedoms of speech and association. It is also in keeping with the spirit of last year's revision of law that bars exclusion of an alien because of beliefs, statements or associations that would be protected under the Constitution for Americans.

May Boris Yeltsin and the Russians go forth and do likewise.

ALBUQUERQUE JOURNAL
Albuquerque, New Mexico, June 3, 1991

It seems the Immigration and Naturalization Service is seeking to branch out into the business of artistic quality and quantity control.

INS has proposed regulations that would arbitrarily limit the number of foreign performers permitted to visit this country for the purpose of entertaining in U.S. concert halls and theaters. The INS seeks to deny millions of Americans the chance to hear and enjoy live entertainment from other nations.

The proposed regulations were drafted in response to a little-noticed change in a law passed by Congress last fall that established a new non-immigration class for artists and entertainers. It's difficult to hypothesize any beneficiaries for it; its main losers would be American audiences.

Under existing visa rules, 78,000 entertainers visited the United States in 1988. Many of them were members of orchestras, opera and ballet companies. Under the proposed rules, the number of performers would be limited to 25,000 a year. Visas would be issued on a first-come, first-served basis. Such limitations could discourage cultural and ethnic performing groups from obtaining visas that let them expose Americans to their national performing heritage. What would the regulations do to cultural exchange programs now so popular?

Equally onerous is a proposed regulation that would prohibit visiting opera and ballet companies and orchestras from applying for visas until 90 days or less before their scheduled performances. What national purpose would be served? Most major touring groups and sponsors plan schedules more than a year in advance. They complain the provision would make it impossible to set bookings.

INS also would set stricter standards for soloists, requiring them to provide evidence of having won major awards or to have evidence of large box-office receipts or strong television ratings to qualify for entry. The INS also would require members of ballet and opera companies and orchestras to prove they had been continuously associated with the group at least a year.

The INS, in short, is proposing to become taste and proficiency police over foreign performers. In its own inimitable way, the INS seems to be charging ahead with a plan assured to constrict the cultural environment of the United States — and, through retaliation, limit the opportunities of American performers abroad.

The proposed INS rules have the feel of artistic protective tariffs. They fly in the face of U.S. policy encouraging free trade for goods and services.

All the world would be the loser. Music and dance are universal languages that foster understanding among nations and peoples. Congress should amend the law and force INS to reconsider its restrictions.

The Record
Hackensack, New Jersey, June 17, 1991

IT'S ONLY fair and humane that immigrants who have applied for permanent residence be eligible for unemployment benefits. That's just how the New Jersey Supreme Court ruled last week when it said the benefits apply to immigrants covered by the 1986 amnesty program.

The ruling means some 2,000 alien workers in New Jersey, mostly agricultural workers, will receive the benefits if they are laid off from their jobs, even if they have not yet received a green card.

Justice Gary Stein, who wrote the decision, said these workers are entitled to the unemployment benefits, since they have been given legal permission to work while they are waiting for their green cards. He noted that they have paid unemployment taxes. "To authorize certain aliens to perform jobs vital to the economy while denying them the right to collect unemployment benefits . . . would be unfair and incongruous," Justice Stein wrote.

An application for a green card can take up to four years to process. That's far too long to wait for unemployment assistance. The benefits are needed most when the person is laid off, as Mr. Stein pointed out.

Agricultural workers are vital to the economy, and as the 1986 amnesty program for illegal aliens recognized, there is a national need to have an adequate supply of such workers. However, these workers have traditionally had little protection when it comes to housing, health care, or even sanitary conditions in the field. The work is usually seasonal, and they sometimes move from place to place looking for jobs.

The New Jersey Supreme Court's ruling is significant because it guarantees the workers some financial security if they are laid off from their jobs.

The United States has welcomed these immigrants by granting them amnesty. Now New Jersey can see to it that they are protected if they become unemployed.

U.S. Begins Haitian Repatriations, Eases Economic Embargo

The U.S. Feb. 1, 1992 began forcibly returning to Haiti thousands of Haitians who had been picked up at sea while trying to flee their homeland. The move came after the U.S. Supreme Court Jan. 31 ruled, 6–3, without comment, to lift a December 1991 U.S. District Court injunction that had barred repatriations.

The first 381 refugees arrived Feb. 3 aboard two U.S. Coast Guard cutters at Port-au-Prince, Haiti's capital. The Haitian Red Cross gave each returned refugee $15 and food vouchers upon arrival. Most of the returnees were expected to go home to villages across the island from Port-au-Prince.

Since a coup that had ousted President Jean-Bertrand Aristide Sept. 30, 1991, more than 14,000 Haitians had been picked up at sea by the U.S., it was reported Feb. 1. Most were being held in a tent city at the Guantanamo Bay U.S. Naval Base in Cuba and on Coast Guard cutters in the area.

Some 3,400 refugees, about 30% of those interviewed by U.S. Immigration and Naturalization Service officials, had been found to have plausible claims for political asylum in the U.S. Of that group, some 1,400 had been moved to Florida to pursue their asylum claims. The remaining 2,000 were being held in a separate tent camp at Guantanamo, waiting to be taken to the U.S.

The U.S. maintained that the majority of the refugees leaving Haiti were fleeing for economic, not political, reasons. Under a 1981 agreement with Haiti, the U.S. had returned most Haitians picked up at sea as economic migrants. The U.S. said there was no evidence that returnees were mistreated.

However, on Jan. 27, a week before the current repatriations began, the Bush administration had protested the growing political violence in Haiti and recalled U.S. Ambassador Alvin P. Adams Jr.

The Bush administration said the repatriations were designed to discourage other Haitians from attempting the risky boat trip from Haiti to the U.S. In another effort to discourage the boat trips, the U.S. Jan. 30 announced that the U.S. embassy in Port-au-Prince would accept Haitians' applications for asylum in the U.S. The U.S. had similar asylum programs in Cuba, Vietnam and the former Soviet Union.

Opposition to the new refugee policy was strong both in the U.S. and abroad. U.N. High Commissioner for Refugees Sadako Ogata had voiced doubts about the safety of the returnees and called for a delay of the repatriations, it was reported Feb. 4.

The U.S. House Judiciary Subcommittee on International Law, Immigration and Refugees Feb. 5 voted, 5–3, to approve a six-month moratorium on the forced repatriation of Haitian refugees. However, the measure was not acted on by the full House before it recessed late Feb. 5.

The U.S. Jan. 27 recalled Ambassador Adams to protest a Haitian police attack on a meeting led by Rene Theodore, Haiti's Communist Party leader. Theodore had been designated as premier in a proposed negotiated solution designed to ultimately restore ousted President Aristide to power.

Uniformed and plainclothes police officers suspected of opposing Aristide's return Jan. 25 had attacked Theodore's headquarters, killing a bodyguard, Yves St.-Pierre, and beating several others. It was the second attack on Theodore's office in a week. No deaths were reported in the earlier attack, on Jan. 18.

The Haitian army Jan. 27 arrested a police corporal and accused him of the murder and beatings. (In Haiti, the police were under the command of the armed forces.)

The Bush administration Feb. 4 announced plans to modify its trade embargo against Haiti in an effort to increase pressure on the de facto government and restore some jobs for impoverished Haitians. In October 1991, the U.S. had begun a strict embargo on all but humanitarian aid to Haiti in response to the military-led coup.

The Washington Times
Washington, D.C., February 6, 1992

The United States has begun its repatriation of some 10,000 refugees to Haiti. The reputation of the United States as a safe haven had beckoned the Haitians, as it has beckoned freedom-seekers throughout this country's history. The Haitian refugees struck out for the Florida shores, risking their lives in rickety boats on a treacherous journey they knew had taken the lives of scores before them. But after weeks and months of being held at bay in makeshift camps, they were told there will be no asylum for them here. Over the weekend, authorites began sending several hundred on their way, having determined they were not, as they claimed, political refugees — those with a well-founded fear of persecution in their homeland, as official designation of refugee status demands — but rather seekers of economic sanctuary.

Just how one makes a distinction between economics and politics for people living in a country like Haiti is puzzling. It is recognized as the poorest in the Western Hemisphere. But it also has a reputation for violence and intolerance (to put it mildly) of divergent political views.

A few months ago, the military overthrew the country's democratically elected president Jean-Bertrand Aristide, pushing him into exile and threatening his death if he returns. About 1,500 people have been killed since the coup, among them some of Mr. Aristide's political supporters. The Organization of American States had worked out an agreement that would allow Mr. Aristide to return to office with a political critic, Rene Theodore, serving as his prime minister. Two weeks ago, armed police under the direction of the military raided one of his meetings, randomly beat those in attendance and machine-gunned one of his bodyguards to death.

There is a clear pattern of oppression that includes arbitrary arrests and random violence. The murderous Ton Ton Macoutes have re-emerged. Mere suspicion has resulted in widespread slaughter in areas that are believed to have supported the ousted president. Simple possession of his photograph or supportive literature can mark one for death. It is a country in which carnage is standard operating procedure for changing governments. The bloodshed has recurred nearly every six months since the military's ouster of Jean Claude Duvalier in 1986. Forcing people to return to these conditions is unconscionable.

Negotiating with the rebels has been futile. Haiti's neighboring governments have tried to pressure the army with an economic embargo. But the resilience of the army, which is skilled at running drugs and smuggling, was underestimated. Instead, the embargo is hurting the people and enhancing the smuggling trade. The Bush administration has now decided to reconsider it. The administration will allow the export of raw goods that factories in Haiti finish for re-export. The embargo had disrupted some 40,000 jobs, which supported nearly a quarter of a million Haitians. The State Department has said it will not issue export licenses to firms that support the military government, however. So what all this means is something that remains to be seen.

Meanwhile, in a development that would be farcical were it not tragic, the Haitian government has asked the United States for a temporary halt in repatriations, and the United States has agreed. Haiti says it is unable to reabsorb its citizens as quickly as the United States is dispatching them. Why that should be so is a good question. One hopes it is not because the coup government is looking to make good on the "well-founded fear of persecution" that returnees have been feeling.

The world has seen enough of people adrift on boats with nowhere to go. The United States has no business contributing to the phenomenon. The decision to discount the vast majority of Haitian refugees for political asylum is based on the Refugee Act of 1980, which recognizes an individual's fear of persecution based on race, religion or political beliefs but does not address "unrest." That, too, is something in need of reconsideration.

The Oregonian
Portland, Oregon, February 5, 1992

If there were a way to throw a whole country into involuntary bankruptcy, Haiti would be a prime candidate.

When a business gets into bad enough trouble, a court can put it in the hands of a trustee to straighten out its affairs. But there is no recognized system for declaring a government too cruel, corrupt and incompetent to continue, and to intervene in behalf of that country's suffering citizens. If there were, Haiti would qualify on all three counts.

The Bush administration's decision to return Haitian boat people forcibly to Haiti is harsh but justified. Doing nothing to discourage Haitians from trying to make the risky 500-mile crossing from their island to Florida puts their lives at risk.

If the United States were to throw open its gates to every Haitian threatened with either political violence or bitter poverty, most of the 6 million would be eligible.

Haiti is the poorest country in the Western Hemisphere, with an annual per capita income of about $300. It raises only about 25 percent of the food needed to feed itself. Haiti has been surviving on public and private foreign aid, mostly from the United States.

Encouraging a stream of refugees would do nothing to cure Haiti's problems. The solutions have to be found in Haiti itself, if they can be found at all.

The Organization of American States has been enforcing an embargo against Haiti in an attempt to restore President Jean-Bertrand Aristide, who was driven into exile by a military coup Sept. 30. So far the main effect of the embargo has been to increase the misery of Haiti's poor, who supported Aristide, without much affecting the military and economic elite who overthrew him.

Haiti never has had good government, and cannot hope to until the power of the army and of the shadowy Tonton Macoute militia gang left over from the regimes of the Duvalier family is broken.

The OAS has a clause in its charter prohibiting interference in the internal affairs of any state. In Haiti's case that is becoming a cop-out. All of the countries in the hemisphere share the responsibility of deciding how much longer to tolerate misrule in Haiti.

The OAS should face that responsibility and act. If intervention sounds too harsh, call it a rescue mission. But act.

The Register-Guard
Eugene, Oregon, February 6, 1992

Denying asylum to Haitian refugees places the Bush administration in an awkward position while putting the refugees in a potentially deadly spot. The refugees should be sheltered until a legitimate government returns to Haiti.

Last week the U.S. Supreme Court lifted an injunction on the repatriation of Haitian refugees, and on Monday the first of 12,000 were sent home. The court's decision permits the U.S. government to follow its policy of regarding the Haitians as seekers of economic opportunity rather than as people fleeing political persecution.

The distinction has always been vulnerable to cynical application, permitting, for instance, Cuban boat people to enter the United States while closing the door to refugees from violence in El Salvador. Labeling the Haitians as economic refugees is especially hypocritical because it runs counter to the rest of U.S. policy toward Haiti.

Since the Sept. 30 coup that deposed Haiti's first freely elected president, Jean-Bertrand Aristide, the United States has joined with other members of the Organization of American States to press for a restoration of democratic rule. The United States has participated in an economic embargo of Haiti and has supported efforts to negotiate Aristide's return.

Haitians' desperate attempts to escape their country are direct consequences of the coup and the embargo. Amnesty International estimates that 1,500 people have been killed since the armed forces overthrew Aristide. The embargo has hit poor Haitians the hardest, while some elements of the armed forces that now run the country are enriching themselves through smuggling operations.

There was no flood of refugees before the coup. It's obvious that the sudden flight of thousands of refugees is directly related to political events in Haiti and other nations' response to them. To insist otherwise, as the Bush administration does, implies that Haitians have no reason to fear or oppose their new government.

The United States cannot open its borders to all who would seek work here; strong immigration controls must be maintained. But the Haitians can't be classed with economic opportunity-seekers from other poor countries. They have other reasons for leaving Haiti, and they have good reasons to fear going back.

Congress is considering a bill that would grant Haitians "temporary protected status" until a democratically elected government is restored. The legislation deserves prompt approval. If the government of Haiti is bad enough to deserve condemnation and an embargo by the United States, its people's desire to escape should be recognized as legitimate.

THE SACRAMENTO BEE
Sacramento, California, February 4, 1992

U.S. Coast Guard cutters have begun ferrying refugee Haitians by the hundreds, soon to be thousands, from the U.S. naval base at Guantanamo Bay, Cuba, back to their homeland and an uncertain fate.

This follows a Supreme Court decision lifting a lower court ban on repatriating Haitians who tried to flee to this country since the military seized power last September and launched a wave of terror. Two-thirds or more of the 15,000 Haitians who have been intercepted may be sent back. Why?

The Bush administration's fatuous answer, given by Defense Secretary Dick Cheney, is that most of them are economic refugees, not political refugees with a legitimate fear of persecution, and therefore can go home "without fear of their lives."

Surely Cheney knows that that's not true, as human rights groups, the United Nations refugee agency and others knowledgeable about Haiti have said in denouncing the U.S. decision. Haitian police and immigration officers are sitting at the dock in Port-au-Prince as the refugees land, taking names. Given the lawless behavior of Haiti's so-called security forces, can anyone doubt that the returnees have legitimate fears?

The administration does not deny the hellish situation in Haiti. After the bodyguard of the new prime minister-designate was killed and others beaten by plainclothes police at a political rally, Washington recalled its ambassador. Both the United States and the Organization of American States, which are trying to mediate a return to democratic government, have threatened to use force if the regime remains unyielding.

That threat is justified as a last resort. Before that, the international embargo imposed after the Sept. 30 coup needs to be tightened, and quickly, to bring the junta to its senses before the embargo's effects do intolerable damage to the population generally. The alternative to such tough action is for the world to turn its back, which is unacceptable.

U.S. fears that not to repatriate refugees would bring a tide of thousands more may be valid, but other factors must have influenced the administration. About 10 percent of those intercepted are infected with the AIDS virus — and Haitians are black, unlike most Cubans, who are taken in without question under a 1966 law. A 1981 accord with the Duvalier dictatorship allows Washington to engage in legal hair-splitting and claim that it's not violating both U.S. and international law with respect to political refugees.

Whatever the legality of the repatriation, it's irresponsible for U.S. officials to pretend that Haitians, whatever their motives for fleeing, have no reason to fear for their lives at home. U.S. law allows the government to provide temporary protected status to national groups whose homelands are in a state of chaos. On that score, Haiti clearly qualifies.

MILWAUKEE SENTINEL

Milwaukee, Wisconsin, February 4, 1992

By every moral standard available, the United States is obligated to accept refugees who have fled, or who are about to flee, the illegal government in Haiti. But realistically, the situation in Haiti has created a potential refugee crisis in the U.S.

Short of concrete evidence that every refugee returned to Haiti will face repression and perhaps death, the U.S. has little choice but to force the return of those unable to prove that their flight from Haiti had political rather than economic reasons.

Nevertheless, returning the refugees to Haiti — with the possibility of harassment by the military regime, or worse from roving bands of the feared secret police, Tonton Macoutes — requires a commitment from the U.S. and other regional powers to the refugees' safety and well-being after their return.

The new world order — a much overused, catch-all phrase for a vision of the globe after the fall of communism in Europe — must apply to those areas of the world where tyranny and disregard for democratic processes still exist.

Haiti clearly qualifies as such a nation, among the poorest on earth, where the powerless are most in jeopardy.

Since the Supreme Court lifted an injunction that prohibited repatriation of the refugees, it has been reported that another 20,000 Haitians are preparing to make the dangerous voyage from Haiti to Cuba, where the U.S. is housing thousands of Haitians at Guantanamo Bay.

Strangely, not a single candidate for U.S. president from either major party has taken up their cause, or the cause of the 10,000 or more already at Guantanamo Bay.

Why not? Because even Democrats recognize the tremendous impact that 30,000 Haitians, many unskilled and destined for the welfare rolls in a recessionary economy, could have upon domestic political fortunes.

But that should not prevent any American who believes in freedom and democracy to insist that those refugees returned to Haiti be guaranteed safety, within the power of the U.S. and its partners in the hemisphere to guarantee it.

Safe conduct is what the U.S., the United Nations and the Organization of American States must insist upon — and then be prepared to back it up with more than a debilitating economic embargo, which ironically is forcing much of the flight from Haiti.

That may mean the use of observer forces as guarantors. But what better way to assure that the new world order is more than just an empty catch-phrase?

DAILY NEWS

New York City, New York, February 4, 1992

On Saturday, after the Supreme Court lifted an injunction that barred the forced return of Haitian boat people, the Bush administration quickly began to ship them back. Many will no doubt end up dead.

As the Organization of American States' embargo squeezes Haiti, and as the blood of those murdered by the army flows through Haiti's streets, it's hard to accept the administration's attitude. Even if many boat people are economic migrants — as the White House argues — they are also human beings. Their lives are imperiled. And they saw America as a place of refuge.

The Supreme Court decision has dealt that notion a serious blow. But Congress can still take action. Representatives Charles Rangel and Charles Schumer are working now to get an emergency nonbinding resolution to the floor that would urge the President to grant Haitian refugees temporary protected status until the crisis is resolved. The bill number is H. Con. Res. 220. Contact your congressman to urge quick action. Or write President Bush — The White House, Washington, D.C. 20500 — and let him know that somebody out there believes America should live up to its ideals.

TULSA WORLD

Tulsa, Oklahoma, February 4, 1992

U.S. IMMIGRATION laws are full of heartbreaks, most of them unavoidable unless this country wants to simply open its door to all comers.

The pathetic case of the Haitian "boat people" now being shipped home from the U.S. naval base in Guantanamo Bay, Cuba, is a case in point.

The U.S. Supreme Court has held that the 10,000 fugitives from the troubled Caribbean island nation are not refugees from political oppression but from poverty. Under U.S. law, those endangered by oppression are eligible for visas; those fleeing from starvation are not.

On the face, it is a cruel law. But it is based on a hard practicality. The United States is unable — or unwilling — to take over the care and feeding of millions who would rather live here than in their impoverished homelands. Many, perhaps most, legal immigrants to this country do very well. Because of the standards for entry, they are usually employable, educated people. Many others, including most of the Haitians, are not educated and skilled in the ways of an industrial society. The refugees in Cuba were mostly people intercepted by the U.S. Coast Guard in Cuban waters as they tried to reach the United States in small boats.

When the United States had plenty of free land and needed manual labor to build railroads and cities, these people would have been welcome. But no more.

Whether the fugitives from Haiti were fleeing oppression or poverty or both is not an easy question. Haiti has a history of dictatorship and, more recently, political disorder. But the legal definition of oppression is strictly written, and it was strictly interpreted by the U.S. Supreme Court.

The best America can offer the poor and hungry today is help at arms length — foreign aid, technical assistance and investment. It is no substitute for the welcome sign that once hung on the Golden Door.

The Salt Lake Tribune

Salt Lake City, Utah, February 5, 1992

As distressing as it is, the U.S. government's returning of desperate Haitians to their disheveled island home is consistent with necessary national policy. What's urgently needed is a policy that can restore some law, order and stability to a Haiti so chaotic that it terrifies its own population.

In rejecting many of those hapless "refugees" found on the open sea between Haiti and Florida, the United States maintains its formal distinction of granting sanctuary to legitimate political escapees while barring illegal immigration by foreigners seeking economic security. The doctrine can be debated but not arbitrarily suspended.

Clearly, interviews confirm that most of the 15,000 Haitians plucked from the Caribbean were merely fleeing their country's latest political upheaval — the overthrow by the military of a popularly elected government. Enough random killing accompanied the coup to convince an already frightened people that everyone was endangered.

Unfortunately for most of the "boat people" intercepted by U.S. patrol ships, few could demonstrate that they were actually menaced. In fact, 3,379 did provide that justification and were given U.S. asylum, so the repatriation policy is not completely callous.

The United States, like most countries worldwide, attempts to control its own borders against criminal traffic, against subversive threats, against illegal immigration. Since Latin America and the Caribbean account for an estimated 118,950 refugees, the potential for illegal alien flow from this source alone is immensely and continuously troublesome.

Haiti under the best of circumstances prompts thoughts of emigration among the general population. Violence such as that provoked during last year's eviction of the leftist Jean-Bertrand Aristide government, compounded with an economic embargo slapped on Haiti by the Organization of American States, converted the thinking into doing. But it's not the answer.

The OAS, the United Nations, various governments individually, especially the United States, correctly demand that Haiti's usurpers restore the island nation's democratic institutions, including a permanent respect for honest election results. But trade and aid restrictions are hurting not the oligarchy, but, rather, unemployed and underemployed Haitians, causing the seaward departures that ensnare the United States in a recurring tragedy.

The State Department may be correct to assert that the repatriated Haitians aren't punished after reaching Haiti, but that misses the point. What they are returned to is the same political tyranny and even worse economic deprivation, conditions they understandably try to escape.

Some progress has been made in moving the coup-makers away from dictatorial power. Not nearly enough, however. The effort must continue, with redoubled persistence and resourcefulness. Haiti and its people need help, not through eased emigration but by a restored self-government capable of ending fear and hopelessness.

Calgary Herald

Calgary, Alberta, February 5, 1992

By deciding to send home 10,000 Haitian asylum seekers the United States has acted with undue haste.

It has failed to show that the Haitians who fled their Caribbean island homeland after the military coup last September were not legitimate refugees — people with genuine fear of persecution if they stayed home.

Blandly deciding that anyone from poverty-stricken Haiti who washed up on American shores was necessarily an economic, as opposed to a political, refugee is callous in the extreme.

There is significant evidence to indicate that the soldiers who toppled democratically elected president Jean-Bertrand Aristide are not behaving with much regard for the human, let alone democratic, rights of Haitians.

There are even suggestions of deals made with the old tonton macoute state terrorists who have dominated Haitian society since the early days of the former Duvalier dictatorship.

An alliance between the junta and the macoutes would serve to re-establish the old exploitive elite which looted Haiti and helped make it the poorest nation in the Western Hemisphere.

Aristide's election, the first time democracy had achieved apparent success in Haiti, raised hopes that the scourge of totalitarian terror and its necessary absolute corruption would at last be purged from Haitian politics.

Many people spoke up and began to exercise newfound political and social freedoms.

But this did not last long. Many of these same outspoken new democrats were placed at risk by the forces which overthrew Aristide. Some were executed while many fled or drowned trying to get away after Aristide was forced out.

Now the United States, which made a great noise along with Canada and other members of the Organization of American States about the loss of democracy in Haiti at the time of the coup, has decided that these refugees along with all those defined as Haitians seeking a better economic way of life will be sent back to poverty and probable persecution.

It would be gratuitous to point out that any Cuban who escaped from Castro's land would be greeted with open arms in the U.S.A.

Why is the same welcome not extended to Haitians who are fleeing a regime with a track record much more appalling than anything communism has done or not done to Cuba?

LAS VEGAS REVIEW-JOURNAL

Las Vegas, Nevada, February 4, 1992

Reporter Robert Glass described it as a "poignant scene" as dozens of Haitians crowded the rail of the U.S. Coast Guard cutter Mohawk on Sunday to watch 250 of their countrymen climb aboard the Mohawk's sistership, the Bear, for the journey home.

The U.S. Supreme Court has ruled the bulk of the would-be emigrants crowding the detention camp at Guantanamo Bay, Cuba, can indeed be classified as "economic" rather than "political" refugees, and thus properly deported to the island they have fled by the thousands since the military coup there last fall.

Under the circumstances, it's small comfort to note that — despite President Bush's overzealous admission that America is in an economic "free-fall" — America is still the promised land for these people.

Problem is, it's the promised land for millions more on a thousand foreign shores. That's why it's important that this nation, like any other, retain the right to control its borders. If any Haitian who can buy or build a boat can row ashore here unquestioned, what are we to tell the thousands who wait patiently in Hungary, Pakistan, Zimbabwe and Guatemala in hopes of receiving a legal visa?

The more important question: Does our turning back of the Haitian tide, while we grant political asylum to any Cuban who can make it to Florida, constitute prejudice?

Almost as though to deny that charge of racism, the high court last week also denied political asylum to Guatemalan Jairo Zacarias, who fled to this country after his life was threatened by armed guerrillas who said they would kill him unless he took up arms for their cause. Since Zacarias' plight had nothing to do with his previous public political statements, that persecution was no more "political" than the random murders of black citizens in Port-au-Prince, according to the logic of Justice Antonin Scalia, writing for the majority.

To charges that this is hair-splitting, Justice Scalia could presumably respond that someone has to split the hairs, lest we wake up to find every one of the world's unfortunates living in vast tent cities around our international ports of entry, jobless and clamoring for food.

Nonetheless, immigration quotas for Northern Europeans routinely go unfilled, while the latest attempt by Congress to ban racial preferences with a "lottery" turned out to be just the opposite of what that term implies, with thousands of slots set aside for Irish immigrants.

We have nothing against the Irish, but neither do we buy Patrick Buchanan's transparently racist assumption that they necessarily have a better chance of success here than "Zulus."

We don't know how many Zulus want to come to America. However many they are, we think the ratio of hopeful Zulus — or Haitians for that matter — admitted should be the same as the percentage of those named Pompa and O'Rourke. After all, it's the American way.

Newsday

New York City, New York, February 5, 1992

The Bush administration has given the bum's rush to many of the 15,000 refugees who've fled Haiti since a military coup there last fall. True, most of the refugees appear to be fleeing for *economic* reasons and not because of personal dangers from the military junta that would qualify them for political asylum within the narrow definition of U.S. law. But that shouldn't deprive them of due process and a safe haven while their permanent status is being sorted out.

The United States has acted too precipitously to repatriate the refugees, sending some back to Haiti without fair hearings.

Ultimately, U.S. policy toward the Haitians and their Caribbean country must evolve as part of a coordinated effort by the Organization of American States. The goal is to restore deposed President Jean-Bertrand Aristide, Haiti's first democratically elected president. Whether by increased diplomatic pressure, adjustment of the U.S. embargo or even armed intervention remains unsettled.

But while the OAS debates a long-term solution, this country should behave with compassion to Haitians plucked from refugee boats in the Caribbean. An informal way is simply to proceed more deliberately with refugee processing while providing temporary haven at the U.S. base at Guantanamo Bay, Cuba. Another would be to grant temporary protected status to Haitians under legisla-

tion sponsored by Rep. Romano Mazzoli (D-Ky). Both ways risk creating permanent camps with their attendant health and safety problems. But that is better than sending people into a milieu of methodical violence under a junta that America opposes.

The administration's assertion that repatriated Haitians face no persecution must be weighed against its own statements, following the coup, denouncing widespread killing and other atrocities there.

The Supreme Court's lifting of a lower court's injunction against repatriation last week was not a license to trample on American principles of humanity and equal protection for would-be immigrants under our laws.

Affirmative Action Curbed by Supreme Court Ruling

The Supreme Court Jan. 23, 1989 invalidated a Richmond, Va. program that required setting aside 30% of the city's public works funds for minority-owned construction companies. In a 6-3 ruling, written by Justice Sandra Day O'Connor, the court said such programs could be justified only if they served the "compelling state interest" of redressing "identified discrimination." Otherwise, the court said, the set-aside programs were a form of reverse discrimination against nonminority contractors and violated their constitutional right to equal protection under the law.

Justice Thurgood Marshall, in a biting dissent, protested the ruling as sounding "a full-scale retreat from the court's longstanding solicitude to race-conscious remedial efforts directed toward deliverance of the century-old promise of equality of economic opportunity."

Redressing specific instances of bias, to justify an affirmative-action program, was known in constitutional doctrine as "strict scrutiny." Marshall called this a "daunting standard." In practical terms, it was considered difficult for governments to meet. Marshall favored a more flexible standard in such cases, one that allowed justification for "important governmental objectives." In seeking to help blacks and other minorities to overcome past discrimination, he said, a government should be allowed to take the country's racial history into account.

But O'Connor ruled this out. "An amorphous claim that there has been past discrimination in a particular industry cannot justify the use of an unyielding racial quota," she said.

"Racial classifications are suspect," she declared. "The standard of review under the Equal Protection Clause is not dependent on the race of those burdened or benefitted by a particular classification." Any "rigid numerical quota," no matter how small, she said, was suspect in such cases.

The ruling could have a wide repercussion, in that affirmative-action programs of the same kind as Richmond's had been adopted by 36 states and 190 local governments across the country. Presumably, these would now have to be reviewed by the governments concerned to see if they were in compliance, or could be brought into compliance, with the "strict scrutiny" rule required by the court.

The ruling was a belated victory for the outgoing Reagan administration, which had vigorously opposed affirmative-action programs and had filed a friend-of-the court brief against the Richmond plan.

Portland Press Herald
Portland, Maine, January 26, 1989

The Supreme Court this week hardly brushed off affirmative action programs as casually as the justices might brush a speck of lint from their robes. But from now on, laws which set aside a percentage of public works construction money to minority-owned companies must reach rigid tests to assure they are constitutional.

The decision is a reasonable one. Affirmative action programs were undertaken as a means, first, of redressing decade upon decade of racial injustice and, second, to give blacks a helping hand into the nation's economic mainstream. But, inevitably, programs that guarantee blacks preferential treatment produce reverse discrimination.

They remain a paradox. The Civil Rights Act of 1964 specifically bars discrimination because of race. Yet affirmation action programs specifically require race to be a factor in hiring in order to eliminate racial imbalance.

The Supreme Court has been backing away from affirmative action programs for the past 10 years. It struck down, in the case of Allan Bakke, a rigid quota system that denied a qualified white admission to medical school in favor of less qualified blacks. But at the same time the court said race could continue to be used as one of many factors in determining college admissions.

Ditto in the latest case, involving Richmond, Va. "Set-aside" laws may be legal, but only if they are used to redress clearly identified discrimination, the majority argued. The effect will be to make the imposition of such quotas more difficult.

Slowly moving away from affirmative action programs is an eventual necessity if the nation is ever to finally end racial discrimination and achieve the goal of a colorblind society. The Supreme Court is right in nudging us along that path.

The Charlotte Observer
Charlotte, North Carolina, January 30, 1989

In a 6-3 ruling involving the City of Richmond, Va., the U.S. Supreme Court made it harder for local governments to help their communities overcome the legacy of racial discrimination. How much harder is difficult to tell.

The case involved a Richmond program that required public contractors to set aside 30% of their subcontracts for minority businesses. Though the justices in the majority differed on some aspects of the plan and on the acceptability of some forms of affirmative action, they agreed on this:

A quota system is acceptable only if there is a "strong basis in evidence" that minorities were purposely excluded from doing business with the city. Statistical evidence, such as the fact that minority businesses had won less than 1% of Richmond's $124 million in construction contracts over a five-year period, isn't enough — even when it is buttressed by repeated findings by the Richmond City Council, the U.S. Labor Department and Congress of discrimination against blacks in the construction business.

On the central point, the court's ruling was justified: The Richmond plan was unacceptably rigid. Beyond that point, the court went astray.

Though justices may dwell in theory, the rest of us must live with fact. In asserting a color-blind America, the justices ignored what is plainly true: The segregated South long denied blacks many economic opportunities; local governments were part of that racist system; and the burdens of that racist history remain with us. Governments, as well as private firms, need the flexibility to find reasonable ways to remove those burdens.

A look at the federal set-aside program shows how difficult it is to legislate fairness. A by-product of the program, for example, has been the creation of sham firms that exist solely to take advantage of the set-asides. A rigid system is likely to create its own varieties of injustice.

A worthwhile set-aside program should have reasonable goals, not unrealistic quotas; it should require honest effort, not success at any cost; and it should require competence as well as minority ownership.

If the court's decision rules out programs that pass those tests, Congress needs to change the law.

SYRACUSE
HERALD-JOURNAL
Syracuse, New York, January 25, 1989

Assuming that what the Supreme Court ultimately seeks is justice, not merely legal correctness, Monday's ruling against "set-asides" for minority contractors is a bad one.

For justice is not some intellectual exercise for a jurist in chambers. It is not something for legal scholars to ponder at their ease in the years to come. It is not small talk at the Bar Association cocktail party.

Justice — or the absence of it — is what happens to people's lives. And the effect of this ruling — intended or not — will be to deny economic justice to people, to lessen the quality of their lives. Dissenting Justice Thurgood Marshall is correct in calling the ruling "a deliberate and giant step backward" in achieving equality among the races.

In a 6-3 decision, the court ruled that a Richmond, Va., program earmarking 30 percent of the city's construction contract funds for minority firms violated the Equal Protection Clause of the 14th Amendment. Justice Sandra Day O'Connor, writing for the majority, said: "While there is no doubt that the sorry history of both private and public discrimination in this country has contributed to a lack of opportunities for black entrepreneurs, this observation, standing alone, cannot justify a rigid racial quota in the awarding of public contracts . . .

"While the states and their subdivisions may take remedial action when they possess evidence that their own spending practices are exacerbating a pattern of prior discrimination, they must identify that discrimination, public or private, with some specificity before they may use race-conscious relief."

In other words, no action may be taken before the fact to ensure minorities a fair shot at winning government business. Only after a specific injustice has been identified can the injured parties seek redress.

It almost sounds reasonable in theory. Everybody gets an equal chance to prosper. No one has a contrived advantage over anyone else.

But bitter experience has shown that in real life it just doesn't work that way. Unless special arrangements are made beforehand — such as with set-asides — minorities often are effectively shut out.

Not that those awarding government contracts are necessarily motivated by racism — although that surely happens. But the people in charge tend to favor their friends, the people they know, the people they've done business with before. Cracking that tight little circle can be impossible — or next to impossible — for a minority entrepreneur trying to get a business off the ground.

There's nothing wrong with free enterprise and a level playing field. It's the best economic system yet devised. But there are capable, worthy people who before affirmative action had no hope of even getting into the game. The upshot of the Supreme Court ruling will be to put many of them back on the sidelines. That is not justice.

THE ATLANTA CONSTITUTION
Atlanta, Georgia, January 24, 1989

Last Wednesday, the U.S. Supreme Court made the right call but ratified a bad law. The justices decided, 8-1, that a tough new system for sentencing federal criminals is constitutional.

Well, yes. The system is a product of some strange constitutional cross-breeding. It was produced by the U.S. Sentencing Commission, a creature that was conceived by Congress, appointed by the president and chaired by a federal judge. But — as Justice Harry A. Blackmun pointed out — the framers of the U.S. Constitution never prohibited such a co-mingling of powers.

The decision is even efficacious in one sense. It settles doubts about the validity of criminal sentences imposed since late 1987, when the system went into effect. Some 150 trial judges had declared the new sentences unconstitutional, while a greater number had ruled in their favor. Result: The new sentences could be legal in one courtroom but illegal in another one down the hall. Now they are legal everywhere.

Heaven help us.

While constitutional, this new system of sentencing is anything but smart. It takes discretion from judges and turns criminal sentencing into a by-the-numbers exercise.

Yet this mechanistic scheme does not take the leeway out of the justice system. It only transfers it — from open court to behind the closed doors of prosecutors' offices. "Look," prosecutors may tell defendants, "the judge has little choice but to give you a tough sentence if you're convicted. But if you cooperate with us, we'll reduce your charges and that will lighten your time."

Moreover, the new system is guaranteed to pack overcrowded federal prisons even tighter — with little attempt to distinguish between hapless and dangerous felons. With a red-ink federal budget, Washington will be hard-put to increase prison bedspace. We're left with a formula for disaster.

For years, the feds ran a prison system that was a model for state administrators. Now, it seems, the feds are looking to the states for inspiration. Georgia's system is dangerously overcrowded, and no one has the will to fix it. We hand out hard time to too many not-so-dangerous people, then use crisis management and impromptu releases to keep the burgeoning inmate population under control. This is an awful way to do business, as the feds will soon discover.

The dictates of the U.S. Sentencing Commission are not unconstitutional — just stupid.

THE
DENVER POST
Denver, Colorado,
January 24, 1989

NOW THAT the U.S. Supreme Court has given its blessing to a rigid new set of rules for sentencing federal prisoners, the nation's overloaded federal courts seem likely to be burdened by even heavier dockets.

The rules, mandated by Congress five years ago, were intended to reduce the disparities in punishment meted out by different judges for similar crimes — and thus to improve the administration of justice. But ironically, the guidelines may end up impeding the process by vastly increasing the number of requests for time-consuming and expensive jury trials.

With prison terms to be determined by an arbitrary and impersonal "point" system, rather than by flesh-and-blood judges, plea-bargaining will be all but pointless. Hence the drug pushers, bank robbers and tax evaders who make up the bulk of the federal caseload will be more inclined to take their chances on a plea of "not guilty."

Another possible result of the new sentencing system may be an eventual decline in the quality of federal judges, as their opportunities for exercising discretion are curtailed. The most talented lawyers are hardly likely to seek appointments to the bench when the role of a federal judge is being reduced to that of a mere numbers-cruncher.

Fortunately, the Sentencing Reform Act of 1984 — which gave rise to the new system — contains one merciful loophole. It allows judges to depart from the guidelines when they find aggravating or mitigating factors that the rules don't adequately consider. But if they decide to be more lenient — or more punitive — than normal, such judges must explain their reasoning in writing.

Three federal district judges in Denver — Jim Carrigan, Richard Matsch and Zita Weinshienk, as well as John Kane, who has since retired — threw out the new sentencing setup as unconstitutional before the Supreme Court issued its 8-1 ruling affirming the law last week. We encourage these jurists to take full advantage of the tiny opening the law gives them to act like thinking judges instead of computers.

Meanwhile, Congress should consider rewriting the law itself to restore more human judgment to the federal courts. Just because a law is constitutional doesn't mean it's wise public policy — and this one causes more problems than it solves.

DAILY ☒ NEWS

New York City, New York, January 25, 1989

MINORITIES HAVE GOTTEN the shaft in hiring—and firing—throughout American history. But unfair employment practices won't go away because a bunch of high-minded bureaucrats say so. They must be ripped out of American life root and branch. One responsible way to do that is with affirmative-action programs.

On Monday, the U.S. Supreme Court outlawed a Richmond, Va., program that set aside 30% of the city's public-works subcontracts for minority-owned companies. That decision was not an attack on the broad concept of affirmative action. The Supreme Court has already ruled that affirmative-action programs are constitutional. Now it has set limits—proper ones—on how far such programs can go.

From now on, any government program that singles out members of minority groups for preferential treatment must undergo the strictest form of judicial scrutiny. Justice Sandra O'Connor, writing for a 6-to-3 majority, ruled that set-aside programs, in order to pass constitutional muster, must be designed in response to *specific* acts of discrimination. "An amorphous claim that there has been past discrimination in a particular industry," she wrote, "cannot justify the use of an unyielding racial quota."

THAT'S SIMPLE COMMON SENSE. Numerical quotas imposed without reference to specific and actual acts of discrimination—or to the availability of qualified minority workers—are gilt-edged invitations to corruption. In addition, as Justice O'Connor pointed out, "they may in fact promote notions of racial inferiority and lead to a politics of racial hostility."

The Supreme Court has not declared an end to affirmative action. Indeed, its decision has no effect whatsoever on private-sector affirmative-action initiatives—and is not likely to have any effect on New York's set-aside programs, which do not impose numerical quotas.

What it *has* done is draw a legal line that should have been laid down long ago. Affirmative-action programs are right and responsible. But to insure fairness to all Americans—regardless of color—they must be subject to reasonable limits. The Supreme Court has taken a major step towards establishing those limits.

Omaha World-Herald

Omaha, Nebraska, January 25, 1989

A six-member majority on the U.S. Supreme Court dealt sensibly with a lawsuit in which a good cause — helping minority groups enter the work force — was carried to extremes. The decision in a Virginia case should supply some of the balance that was missing from some earlier decisions dealing with affirmative action and racial quotas.

Racial discrimination in the work place is illegal, as it ought to be. Congress, since the mid-1960s, has forbidden a number of discriminatory practices that had been used to deny opportunities to racial minorities. It also prohibited the use of preferential treatment to address racial imbalances in the composition of the work force.

The City of Richmond, like a number of other U.S. cities and states, has reserved a portion of its municipal contract work — 30 percent — for minority contractors. The argument has been that preferences correct the effects of past discrimination. Similar arguments have been accepted by the courts in other kinds of affirmative action cases.

Some people, even though they hate racial discrimination, have been troubled by the inherent inconsistencies in the use of what amounts to reverse discrimination to correct the "effects of past discrimination."

Preferences give special treatment to an individual without regard to whether he has been the victim of past discrimination. Other individuals are penalized, by being passed over, without regard to whether they have discriminated illegally against anyone.

To demand preferential treatment, in effect, is to imply that minorities can't compete and succeed on their merits.

The "past discrimination" argument is sometimes carried to ludicrous extremes. The City of Richmond included Eskimos in its program — a group that, as Justice Sandra Day O'Connor noted in the majority opinion, is hardly likely to have a history of being discriminated against in Richmond.

Justice O'Connor's opinion said that state and local governments must almost always avoid the use of quotas. Instances of past discrimination, when used to justify an affirmative action program, must be documented, she wrote.

The decision dealt specifically with state and local minority contracting preferences. It doesn't affect federal minority hiring programs. Nor does it affect a number of other efforts, both private and public, to help minority groups participate more fully in the opportunities of the marketplace through voluntary goals and targets.

A construction industry spokesman told The Wall Street Journal that the outcome of the Richmond case places "an obligation on the construction industry to now make special efforts to demonstrate that fair play and decency will be extended all the time to minority business enterprises." His statement reflects an attitude that ought to be shared wherever minority groups remain outside the economic mainstream.

Chicago Defender

Chicago, Illinois, January 25, 1989

The Supreme Court made a serious error in striking down a law requiring construction companies bidding for city contracts in Richmond, Virginia to set aside a share of the jobs for minority subcontractors. The high court's decision was approved 6-3.

Set-asides are affirmative action programs calling for a percentage of government contracts at all levels to be awarded to minority- or female-owned firms. The ruling was established mainly to stop the traditional exclusion of these groups from such business. For years, the set-aside program has worked to correct past injustices and to lessen the economic impact from any present form of racial or sex discrimination.

Justice Sandra Day O'Connor wrote in the majority decision: "While there is no doubt that the sorry history of both private and public discrimination in this country has contributed to a lack of opportunities for Black entrepreneurs, the observation, standing alone, cannot justify a rigid racial quota in the awarding of public contracts in Richmond." In so ruling, O'Connor is exhibiting the same kind of thinking when she served on California's Supreme Court.

But her words are extremely limited, in that they make no reference to the private and public discrimination which for centuries has assailed female entrepreneurs in

this country's construction industry. Even though the Richmond case specifically involved African Americans, the ramifications of the ruling will definitely impact negatively on the nation's minorities *and women.* That should have been taken into consideration and made a part of the court's majority ruling. But perhaps it was but just ignored.

Also, the "observation" of past racial abuse limiting opportunities for Blacks is not, as Justice O'Connor mentioned, "standing alone." It stands right alongside the reality of present racial bias and sexism in the construction industry across America.

It is rather obvious that O'Connor and the five justices who voted with her simply refused to observe or acknowledge that racism and sexism still are potent barriers to minority and female entrepreneurs. The six justices, in effect, are telling these groups: in each and every case, before set-aside levels can be established, you must prove that racism and sexism truly are keeping you out of the construction industry.

Worst of all, those justices, in effect, are saying: "Look, we know that your opportunities have been severely restricted by racism in the past, but we can't recommend that anything be done to right that wrong or to make sure that it does not happen again. We realize that you've been severely wronged, but we can't

even offer you a small bandaid. And even if you are still being attacked, you are going to have to categorically prove that the assault is taking place before you can even get an aspirin." And this is coming from the highest court in America, the body that has the prime directive of distributing *justice,* the organization that is the supreme law of the land.

The *Defender* thinks Justice Thurgood Marshall, who voted against the ruling, was right when he said it was a "giant step backward" because it discourages local and state governments "from acting to rectify the scourge of past discrimination." The *Defender* must stress that the Richmond City Council chose to establish the set aside program in 1983. Therefore, Marshall correctly said, "I find deep irony in second-guessing Richmond's judgment on this point. As much as any municipality in the United States, Richmond knows what racial discrimination is..." If anyone doubts the wisdom of those words, that person should remember that Richmond was the capital of the Confederacy and, according to Marshall, "...a century of decisions by this and other federal courts has richly documented the city's disgraceful history of public and private racial discrimination."

What makes O'Connor and company think the situation in Richmond has changed?

Supreme Court Widens Ban on Juror Race-Exclusion

The U.S. Supreme Court June 3, 1991 ruled, 6-3, that potential jurors in civil cases could not be excluded on the basis of race. The case was *Edmondson v. Leesville Concrete Co.*

U.S. legal tradition allowed attorneys to bar potential jurors without explanation, using peremptory challenges. State laws granted an equal number of challenges to each side. The number varied from state to state.

A Supreme Court ban on race-based juror exclusions, set in the 1986 case *Batson v. Kentucky* and extended in the 1991 case *Powers v. Ohio*, had previously applied only to criminal cases. The court's June 3 ruling overturned a decision by the U.S. 5th Circuit Court of Appeals in New Orleans.

In the case before the court, Thaddeus Edmonson, a black man, had sued his employer, Leesville Concrete Co., in Louisiana, after he had been injured at work. The company's lawyer had used two peremptory challenges to remove black potential jurors from the case. The appeals court had allowed the challenges because the *Batson* precedent had not included civil cases.

The Constitution's guarantee of equal protection under the law could be applied only to action by the government, not to action by private individuals. Civil cases had not been considered government action. In this decision, the court held that a jury was "a quintessential governmental body" and was thus bound by constitutional guarantees.

Writing for the majority, Justice Anthony M. Kennedy said the ban should be extended to civil cases because the process of jury selection took place with the "overt, significant assistance of the court."

Kennedy added, "Racial discrimination has no place in the courtroom, whether the proceeding is civil or criminal." Justices Byron R. White, Thurgood Marshall, Harry A. Blackmun, John Paul Stevens and David H. Souter joined the majority.

The dissenters, in an opinion written by Justice Sandra Day O'Connor, said jury selection by private lawyers in a civil case "is fundamentally a matter of private choice and not state action."

The Atlanta Journal
THE ATLANTA CONSTITUTION
Atlanta, Georgia, June 10, 1991

Two decisions issued last week show the Rehnquist Supreme Court at its most enlightened.

In *Edmonson v. Leesville Concrete Co.*, the court decided by a 6-3 margin that race is not a legitimate basis for excluding jurors from serving in civil cases. Previously the court had forbidden prosecutors from using their peremptory challenges to exclude jurors from criminal cases on the basis of race.

To extend the principle to cases where the government is not a party is to say civil litigation is a fundamentally governmental affair that is properly subject to the public goal of creating a non-discriminatory society. As Justice Anthony M. Kennedy, writing for court, declared, "If our society is to continue to progress as a multiracial democracy, it must recognize that the automatic invocation of race stereotypes retards that progress and causes continued hurt and injury."

Meanwhile, in a unanimous decision, the court ruled that elections to fill 12 judicial vacancies in Louisiana were invalid because the U.S. Justice Department had not approved, "pre-cleared," changes in voting procedures for the ·icts in question. Reversing a three-judge a pellate panel, the justices made it crystal clear that judicial elections must comply with the pre-clearance section of the federal Voting Rights Act.

In so deciding, the court may also have telegraphed its views on the standard used to decide what the act requires in the case of judicial elections. These views, which are forthcoming, will likely determine the outcome of Rep. Tyrone Brooks's (D-Atlanta) suit contesting the elections of a large number of Georgia's Superior Court judges. If the court requires judicial elections to be free of discriminatory intent and effect, the state of Georgia will have some heavy work to do.

Gov. Zell Miller has abandoned efforts to settle the Brooks suit. He will regret that if the Supreme Court is in fact moving in the direction suggested by its ruling in the Louisiana case. The state would have been wise to read *Clark v. Roemer* as indicating a little more flexibility on its part, not an end to negotitions.

The Des Moines Register
Des Moines, Iowa, June 5, 1991

The U.S. Supreme Court's holding that blacks cannot arbitrarily be excluded from juries in civil trials turned on a seemingly minor point: whether the court should even concern itself with suits between private parties. More important, though, the court made it clear that the courtroom cannot become a forum for racism.

At issue was whether attorneys representing a Louisiana concrete company could, without cause, use race alone to exclude potential jurors hearing a case brought by a black employee suing the company for negligence.

Dissenting justices argued the case was not properly before the high court because the Constitution addresses government actions. Civil trials, they said, are private matters between pr ate parties. A six-justice majority held otherwise.

Writing for the court, Justice Anthony Kennedy argued that parties to private litigation become "state actors" for purposes of constitutional law once they enter the courtroom. The courts operate under the auspices of states and the federal government. Jury selection is supervised by judges under rules set out under the Constitution and state and federal law, and the process must not be corrupted by racial discrimination.

If jury selection is tainted by racism, Kennedy wrote, the "injury is made more severe because the government permits it to occur within the courthouse itself. Few places are a more real expression of the constitutional authority of the government than a courtroom where the law itself unfolds."

It should be obvious that the courtroom is the last place that racism should be permitted, whether the parties are arguing a civil suit or a criminal case. In making the obvious ruling, the Supreme Court expanded the principle of fairness in the jury system and buttressed the integrity of the courts.

The State
Columbia, South Carolina, June 7, 1991

THE U.S. Supreme Court has almost completed a step-by-step journey toward a discrimination-free jury-selection process.

Monday, a 6-3 majority of the court said the lawyers in civil cases can no longer exclude jurors because of race. Since 1986, prosecutors in criminal courts have been required to give race-neutral reasons when they used peremptory challenges to prevent the seating of jurors of the same race as the defendant — normally to excuse black jurors from a case with a black defendant.

"Racial discrimination has no place in the courtroom, whether the proceeding is civil or criminal," said Justice Anthony M. Kennedy for a majority that included both liberals and conservatives.

Since the Constitution binds the government more than private parties, the court had to address the question of whether the process of selecting the jury in a purely private suit is "state action" subject to the equal protection of the laws. Justice Kennedy said yes, that a jury is "a quintessential government body" set up to decide private disputes.

That strikes us as being logical, but it struck Justice Antonin Scalia as being an excessively burdensome additional requirement to place on the courts. In a strongly worded dissent, he said, "We have now added to the duties of already-submerged state and federal trial courts the obligation to insure that race is not included among the other factors (sex, age, religion, political views, economic status) used by private parties in exercising their peremptory challenges.... Thus another complexity is added to an increasingly Byzantine system of justice that devotes more and more of its energy to sideshows and less and less to the merits of the case...."

Justice Scalia predicted the next step in this progression when he said that, in treating jury selection as state action, the majority opinion "logically must apply" to criminal defendants as well as parties to a civil suit.

South Carolina saw an example of the current criminal procedure in practice last week during the jury selection in the trial of Circuit Judge Tee Ferguson, a black, on bribery charges. His lawyer argued the prosecutor couldn't give racially neutral reasons for excusing three blacks. At the same time, the prosecutor, seeking "tit for tat," urged the defense attorney to give race-neutral reasons for striking 13 whites.

The trial judge then ordered the defense also to provide race-neutral reasons for strikes. He found grounds for that position, but it does not appear to be settled law. But as Justice Scalia hinted, that is the logical final step in removing race from jury selection.

The New York Times
New York City, New York, June 4, 1991

The Supreme Court has rightly extended its attack on covert racial discrimination in the selection of juries.

Five years ago the Court empowered judges in criminal cases to examine whether prosecutors were using peremptory challenges to exclude jurors of the same race as a defendant. It was a breakthrough because normally such challenges are not questioned. Two months ago the Court broadened the attack, allowing even white defendants to trigger an inquiry when blacks were being excluded.

Yesterday the high court carried the principle a dramatic step further. Even in civil cases, when private attorneys are striking jury candidates, judges must step in to make sure that racial discrimination is not at work, a 6-to-3 majority ruled.

Dissenters on the Court sought to limit the equal protection guarantee of the Constitution to situations in which a government officer, such as a prosecutor, appears to be systematically striking jurors of one race. But Justice Anthony Kennedy, writing for the majority, saw clearly that the very process of jury selection is a government activity. Government, which gives the courts their power, is responsible for blocking this discrimination, no matter where the bias originates.

"Few places are a more real expression of the constitutional authority of the government than a courtroom, where the law itself unfolds," Justice Kennedy said. What a welcome recognition that equal justice at the courthouse serves both equality and justice.   copyright © The New York Times 1991

THE TENNESSEAN
Nashville, Tennessee, June 6, 1991

THE Supreme Court took a significant step this week to ensure that race is not a factor in the selection of jurors in civil cases.

The court, in a 6-3 decision, ruled that jurors in civil cases can't be excluded from that duty because of their race. It extended earlier rulings that kept prosecutors in criminal trials from excluding potential jurors because of race.

In writing the majority opinion, Justice Anthony Kennedy made a simple argument that should be self-evident. "Racial discrimination has no place in the courtroom, whether the proceeding is civil or criminal," he said.

That is fundamental reasoning that should never have been put to the test. Fortunately, the Supreme Court has seen to it that the practice is forbidden.

The case involved a black man who sued his employer after an injury on the job. Two blacks were removed from the jury by the company lawyer using peremptory challenges. This week's ruling sides with the employee.

Part of the decision by the court involved the question of whether jury selection is a state action. In the dissenting opinion, justices said that the selection of jurors by private lawyers was "fundamentally a matter of private choice and not state action." That's wrong. The selection of a jury comes under the auspices of the court and cannot be viewed as strictly a private undertaking.

The ramifications of the ruling may reach Tennessee in the bank fraud case of Rep. Harold Ford, in which an effort has been made to bus in a jury to Memphis from Madison County.

A juror should not be selected on the basis of race. And no juror should be excluded for reasons of race either. The Supreme Court sees this and made the proper ruling this week.

The search for a fair jury in any case should be priority. But as Kennedy points out, "If race stereotypes are the price for acceptance of a jury panel as fair, the price is too high to meet the standard of the Constitution."

There should be no disagreement. Jury selection according to race is wrong. The court is wise not to allow it. ■

Rockford Register Star
Rockford, Illinois, June 9, 1991

"Race discrimination within the courtroom raises serious questions as to the fairness of the proceedings conducted there." — U.S. Supreme Court Justice Anthony M. Kennedy.

If Kennedy seems to be stating the obvious, why has it taken until now for the high court to issue such a declaration? He said it last week in a 6-3 decision prohibiting racial bias in the selection of juries for civil trials. That properly extends the same prohibition already in effect for criminal trials.

It's about time.

In selecting jury members in criminal and civil cases, lawyers are given a limited number of peremptory challenges — generally invoked without explanation.

Surprisingly, it wasn't until 1986 that the procedure was challenged on racial grounds in criminal cases. Then the High Court said that when such automatic challenges of jury candidates appear to be based on race, the burden shifts to the prosecutor using that power to prove there is no racial motive.

Now, finally, the same rule applies in civil cases.

"The ruling is a good idea," says a former public defender. "A jury of one's peers should include all minorities."

Amen.

The Record

Hackensack, New Jersey, June 5, 1991

AN IMPORTANT principle of racial fairness underlies this week's U.S. Supreme Court ruling that jurors may not be barred in non-criminal trials because of their race. Racial discrimination, abhorrent everywhere, is particularly out of place in a courtroom — a setting that is supposed to serve as a symbol of impartial justice.

The outcome of the court's decision wasn't as obvious as it might seem. The Constitution bars racial bias by government bodies, but not, in most cases, in dealings between private citizens. A prosecutor could not bar a prospective juror because of his race in a criminal trial, for example, because prosecutors are agents of the government. In the case decided this week, the court had been asked to extend the principle to civil trials, which are disputes between private parties. Attorneys sometimes seek to bar blacks from a jury because of possible prejudice in favor of a black defendant or plaintiff. Using what is known as a peremptory challenge, lawyers can exclude a potential juror without giving a reason.

Justice Anthony M. Kennedy reasoned that the system of civil trials itself is a creation of government, and therefore protected by the Constitution. "Racial discrimination has no place in the courtroom, whether the proceeding is civil or criminal," he wrote. Giving litigants a say in jury selection is important, he noted. "But if race stereotypes are the price for acceptance of a jury panel as fair, the price is too high to meet the standard of the Constitution."

In a dissent, Justice Antonin Scalia worried that disputes over juror exclusion will impose new burdens on an already overstrained justice system.

Even if that's true, it is a small price to pay if the result is courtrooms that are free of the stain of racial bias.

> "It is a small price to pay if the result is courtrooms free of racial bias."

ST. LOUIS POST-DISPATCH

St. Louis, Missouri, June 7, 1991

Because jury duty is the closest contact that many Americans will ever have with the courts, emphasizing fairness and barring racial discrimination are particularly important in selecting juries. The U.S. Supreme Court has taken several steps to ensure that fairness; Monday's decision extending the ban on discrimination to civil cases as well as criminal ones is an important, welcome addition.

In a 6-3 decision written eloquently by Justice Anthony Kennedy, the court said lawyers in civil cases cannot use their peremptory challenges — ones for which they do not have to give reasons — to exclude jurors on racial grounds. Such protection had been granted in criminal cases by a landmark ruling in 1986, but Justice Kennedy made it clear that because the courts are an important arm of the government, all dealings there should conform to the constitutional requirements of colorblind justice:

"Race discrimination within the courtroom raises serious questions as to the fairness of the proceedings conducted there. Racial bias mars the integrity of the judicial system and prevents the idea of democratic government from becoming a reality."

The case involved a black man from Louisiana, Thaddeus Edmonson, who sought damages after being injured on the job. Lawyers for his employer used peremptory challenges to strike two blacks from the jury; the subsequent jurors, 11 white and one black, decided Mr. Edmonson's suffered damages of $90,000 but awarded him only $18,000 because they felt his own negligence contributed to the accident.

He pursued the case all the way to the Supreme Court, where he got the support he deserved. Justice Sandra Day O'Connor dissented, saying that the Constitution does not sweep as broadly against racial discrimination as Justice Kennedy said; in a separate dissent, Justice Antonin Scalia complained of the "sideshows" such rulings cause. But racial justice is not a sideshow that should escape the protection of the Constitution. It is a central principle, calling for everyone to be treated fairly, regardless of race. Justice Kennedy's decision made that clear.

THE DALLAS TIMES HERALD

Dallas, Texas, June 10, 1991

The ruling by the U.S. Supreme Court that makes it illegal to bar a juror based on race goes a long way toward ensuring that criminal and civil trials are not decided based on a person's skin color.

The court began making this change in 1986 when it ruled 7-2 in Batson vs. Kentucky that prosecutors never may disqualify potential jurors because of race. Over the next five years, the court strengthened the position against race-based pre-emptive dismissals.

In April 1986, the court made the application retroactive. Last April, the ruling was extended to white criminal defendants.

In last Monday's decision, Justice Anthony M. Kennedy said racism cannot be allowed to infect the jury-selection process. The ruling says neither side may discriminate when using its automatic challenges to remove potential jurors.

"Race discrimination within the courtroom raises serious questions as to the fairness of the proceedings conducted there," Justice Kennedy said. "Racial bias mars the integrity of the judicial system and prevents the idea of democratic government from becoming a reality."

In the case under consideration, Thaddeus Edmonson, a black construction worker, was injured in an on-the-job accident at a Louisiana concrete company. During jury selection in the case, the company used two of its three peremptory challenges to remove blacks from the jury panel.

The jury that ultimately was selected, consisting of 11 whites and one black, awarded Edmonson only $18,000, saying his own negligence was largely responsible for the accident. The federal appeals court in New Orleans concurred.

The high court reversed that decision, questioning whether the company attorney in fact used his peremptory challenges in a discriminatory way.

The court's message in these landmark cases is very clear — race should not and will not be a factor when prosecutors or civil litigants pick a jury. It's been proven over and over again that decisions can be skewed by racial biases. These decisions help balance the scales of justice.

Arkansas Gazette
Little Rock, Arkansas, June 5, 1991

"Racial discrimination has no place in the courtroom, whether the proceeding is civil or criminal," the Supreme Court ruled Monday, and American courts have become fairer.

In a 6-3 decision, the court said that barring jurors because of race is impermissible in civil cases. The court thus extended its 1986 ruling that prosecutors in criminal cases cannot bar jurors because of race.

The argument against banning discrimination in civil trials, made by Justice Sandra Day O'Connor in a dissenting opinion, is that while a prosecuting attorney represents the state, civil trials are private affairs. A private litigant who wants to strike a juror because of race is not bound by prohibitions against government bias, O'Connor said.

But all trials, civil and criminal, are part of the governmental process. Justice Anthony M. Kennedy wrote discerningly for the majority:

"Although the conduct of private parties lies beyond the Constitution's scope in most instances, governmental authority may dominate an activity to such an extent that its participants must be deemed to act with the authority of the government and, as a result, be subject to constitutional restraints. ... It cannot be disputed that, without the overt, significant participation of the government, the peremptory challenge system, as well as the jury trial system of which it is a part, simply could not exist."

The case was appealed from Louisiana. A black man sued his employer after he was injured on the job. The employer's lawyer used peremptory challenges to remove two blacks from the jury. Each side in a trial has the right to reject a given number of jurors without stating a reason. The jury found the plaintiff, Thaddeus D. Edmondson, 80 percent at fault in the accident and awarded him only 20 percent of the damages he sought. Edmondson can now seek a new trial.

The Supreme Court has not yet answered the question of whether a defendant in a criminal trial, as well as the prosecutor, is barred from removing jurors peremptorily because of race. The court's ruling Monday suggests that the answer to this question, when it comes before the court, will be yes.

THE PLAIN DEALER
Cleveland, Ohio, June 13, 1991

In a wise defense of racial fairness in the courtroom, the Supreme Court last week issued a ruling that should help expunge any taint of racism from jury selection. In civil cases as well as criminal trials, said a 6-3 majority of the Rehnquist Court, lawyers cannot use their peremptory challenges to exclude potential jurors solely on the basis of their race. Such a race-neutral standard had been in effect in criminal trials since 1986.

"Racial discrimination has no place in the courtroom, whether the proceeding is civil or criminal. The Constitution demands nothing less," asserted Justice Anthony M. Kennedy's opinion. For the second time in this year's session, Kennedy assembled a strong majority — uniting the court's liberals with most of its conservatives — supporting racial fairness in jury selection. In April, he wrote the opinion for a 7-2 majority that struck down race-based peremptory challenges in an unusual criminal case, in which blacks had been excluded from the jury of a white defendant.

Regrettably, Justice Sandra Day O'Connor joined the court's most narrow-minded members, Chief Justice William H. Rehnquist and Justice Antonin Scalia, in dissenting from Kennedy's logic. O'Connor found that a civil suit (unlike a criminal trial) is a proceeding among private parties, not a "state action" where the Constitution's due-process clauses might be violated. "As much as we would like to eliminate completely from the courtroom the specter of racial discrimination," she wrote, "the Constitution does not sweep that broadly."

O'Connor's legalistic argument found fewer sympathizers than Kennedy's broader view of the courts' role: "Few places are a more real expression of the constitutional authority of the government than a courtroom, where the law itself unfolds." The ideal of "equal justice under law" has been promoted by Kennedy's rejection of racial bias in America's courts.

THE KANSAS CITY STAR
Kansas City, Missouri, June 11, 1991

The Supreme Court has taken a logical step in its 6-3 ruling on juror challenges in civil cases. If jurors cannot be excluded from criminal cases because of race, they should not be barred from civil lawsuits for that reason.

Last week's decision expands on a 1986 ruling that prohibits prosecutors in criminal trials from using peremptory challenges to reject prospective jurors because of race. Writing for the majority, Justice Anthony Kennedy summed up the matter this way: "Racial discrimination has no place in the courtroom, whether the proceeding is civil or criminal. The Constitution demands nothing less."

In reaching this finding, the court determined that jury selection in private lawsuits has constitutional protection as a "state action" similar to criminal cases. That is a basic change in the law.

Of late the court has ruled adversely on the rights of criminal defendants. It is encouraging that the court has reached an equitable decision.

The Courier-Journal
Louisville, Kentucky, June 5, 1991

By limiting the ability of lawyers to exclude jurors without cause, the U. S. Supreme Court is making trial by jury fairer. But that leaves questions hanging: Are peremptory challenges inherently biased? Is it time to mothball them?

Beginning with a Kentucky case five years ago, the court has regularly visited an important but confusing area of law. In *Batson v. Kentucky* it held that defendants are denied equal protection of the law when prosecutors use peremptory challenges to exclude jurors because they belong to the same race as the defendant. Two months ago it broadened that initiative, and this week it extended it to prohibit the exclusion of jurors on the basis of race in *civil* trials.

The decision is significant, in part because the Constitution often is considered binding on the government, not individuals. But even in a civil trial, a jury is essentially a governmental body, the majority said. And, as Justice Anthony M. Kennedy declared in his majority opinion, "Racial discrimination has no place in the courtroom, whether the proceeding is civil or criminal."

To be inclusive, the principle ought to be extended even farther to bar the use of peremptory challenges to exclude people solely because of their gender, race, religion or ethnic origin. But that's unlikely because the court has been reluctant to extend bans on racial discrimination to gender when the ban is based upon equal protection or due process.

The use of peremptory challenges is, as Justice Thurgood Marshall argued in *Batson*, generally based upon seat-of-the-pants instincts, which are often hopelessly biased and badly mistaken. Peremptory challenges aimed at eliminating women, Hispanics, Asians, Jews or Irish people are as discriminatory as those directed at blacks. Why, then, should one be banned while the others remain permissible?

1990 Census Count Revision Barred; Minorities Undercount Acknowledged

Commerce Secretary Robert A. Mosbacher July 15, 1991 announced that the 1990 census would not be statistically adjusted to account for persons missed in the original survey.

The Census Bureau had agreed to consider an adjustment as part of the settlement of a 1988 lawsuit by state and local governments convinced that their full populations were not being counted.

The adjustment, supported by census officials, would have been based on the results of a "post-enumeration" survey of 165,000 households released April 18. That survey estimated that the 1990 census had missed 5.3 million people. (A General Accounting Office report released June 27 concluded that at least 9.7 million people had been overlooked.)

Mosbacher had been under court order to announce a decision by July 15. His decision had been eagerly awaited because the census figures were used to determine the size of each state's delegation to Congress, to draw state legislative district maps and to allocate the flow of federal aid to cities and other localities.

In announcing his decision, Mosbacher acknowledged that there had been an undercount and that a disproportionate number of minority-group members had been missed. However, he said he was reluctant "to abandon a 200-year tradition of how we actually count people."

In addition, Mosbacher said he was "deeply concerned that adjustment would open the door to political tampering with the census in the future." The unadjusted count "cannot be directly affected in such a way," he said.

Mosbacher also cited questions concerning the accuracy of an adjustment. Experts had agreed that the adjustment would improve the accuracy of the count nationally and for local areas containing almost two-thirds of the population. However, opponents had pointed out that the smaller the community, the more statistically unreliable the results of an adjustment would be. "We cannot proceed on unstable ground in such an important matter of public policy," the commerce secretary said.

(A larger post-enumeration survey would have increased the reliability of an adjustment. The plaintiffs in the 1988 lawsuit originally had sought a sample size of 300,000 households, according to a *New York Times* story datelined April 18. However, the Commerce Department, citing factors of time and cost, had argued for a smaller sample size. A 165,000-home survey was agreed upon as a compromise.)

Mosbacher also argued that "an adjusted set of numbers will certainly disrupt the political process and may create paralysis in the states that are working on redistricting or have completed it."

In rejecting the adjustment, Mosbacher overruled Census Bureau Director Barbara Everitt Bryant, as well as a nine-member panel of Census Bureau experts, which had recommended it, 7–2. An eight-member panel made up of experts from outside the government had split on the issue, with four members appointed by the Commerce Department voting against adjustment and four appointed by the plaintiffs in the 1988 lawsuit voting in favor of it.

"The improvement in counts on the average for the nation, states and places over 100,000 population outweighs the risk that the accuracy of adjusted counts might be less for some smaller areas," wrote the Census Bureau panel, according to the *Washington Post* July 17.

Mosbacher's announcement July 15 was swiftly and angrily condemned by congressional proponents of an adjustment and by the plaintiffs in the 1988 lawsuit, who said they would take the Commerce Department back to court.

Analysts said that an adjustment would have slowed the flow of political power from the predominantly Democratic big cities to the more Republican suburbs, since the largest number of residents missed by the census lived in cities. Particularly affected would be battles for the control of state legislatures.

The Philadelphia Inquirer
*Philadelphia, Pennsylvania,
July 17, 1991*

The 1990 census is now official even though it appears to have missed about five million people — and many of the missing were poor blacks and Hispanics. By deciding not to expertly massage the numbers to undo this "undercount," the Bush administration has ensured that ailing cities will be shortchanged financially and underrepresented politically. This is a bad decision, a blow to the nation's cities, but a mixed bag for Philadelphia.

Ideally, this complicated, high-stakes issue would have been decided by experts. Most of the key people at the Census Bureau, including its director, concluded that their techniques have reached the point that most of the adjusted statistics on population would be more accurate than the actual count was. But Secretary of Commerce Robert A. Mosbacher disagreed. While this may be his honest judgment on the merits, it is especially distasteful coming from a political operative who ran fundraising for the Bush campaign in 1988 and may soon take a key role in the re-election campaign.

Thanks to this policy, money and power will be distributed in a way that generally helps Republicans and hurts Democrats. For one thing, the census figures are a factor in divvying up nearly $60 billion per year in federal and state aid to lower levels of government. That's a major reason why urbanized states such as New Jersey and major cities including Philadelphia went to court in the late 1980s in an effort (futile thus far but now being revived) to force the Census Bureau to adjust for the undercount. The second basic impact is on how legislative districts are drawn. Within each state, the tendency to undercount the urban poor leaves cities with less power than they should have in the House of Representatives and in state legislatures.

Still, because the Census Bureau estimated that it had failed to count only about 20,000 people in Philadelphia, this city had less money and legislative power at stake than lots of others. What's more, a nationwide adjustment in census figures would have cost Pennsylvania an additional seat in the House, on top of the two everyone has been expecting it to lose.

Thus there's some consolation from the saved House seat, and from Mr. Mosbacher's plan to start making corrective adjustments in population estimates within the next few years. With his half-measure, tax dollars would be allocated more fairly sometime in this decade, but legislative power will not.

Rockford Register Star
Rockford, Illinois, August 24, 1990

Faced with a firestorm of criticism for objecting to a white actor in the role of a Eurasian in a Broadway production, Actors Equity has wisely reversed its decision — and perhaps also has learned a lesson about racism. That lesson would be that you can't fight racism with racism.

The controversy arose when plans were made to bring the hit London musical, *Miss Saigon*, to Broadway with British actor Jonathan Pryce in the lead role of a pimp who is half Asian and half European. Actors Equity, the union of 39,000 stage performers, turned thumbs down on Pryce, arguing that the role should go to an actor of entirely Asian extraction.

That position seemed preposterous on its face. Racially speaking, a pure Asian would fit only half the role, just as Pryce would. Why did the union seem to recognize only the Asian half of the character? The implied answer to that question is that too often in the past Asian roles have been played by white actors, just as whites long ago used to play black roles in blackface, (which clearly would be unacceptable today).

That point might be valid if the role in *Miss Saigon* were that of a pure Asian. But it isn't. Besides, there is a long and admirable history of certain lead roles in stage productions being played by persons of other races who are made-up to look the part — Laurence Olivier in *Othello*, for example. These cases seem to be valid exceptions to the worthy principle of hiring only minority actors to play minority roles.

In a sense, the marketplace should make the determination. Audiences seem to buy Jonathan Pryce as a Eurasian. It isn't likely, however, that they would buy, say, Joel Gray as the male lead in *Porgy and Bess*.

THE RICHMOND NEWS LEADER
Richmond, Virginia, August 15, 1990

In the growing animus generated by a racial spoils system, Actors Equity has lent a whole new dimension to hypocrisy parading as moral superiority. The actors union has forbidden a British actor, Jonathan Pryce, from starring in the hit musical, "Miss Saigon," scheduled to open on Broadway in April. The union says an Asian should be cast in the role of the Eurasian pimp that Pryce has been playing for two years in London.

And how, you may ask, does a union have a final say over what should be a purely artistic decision by the musical's director and producer? After all, with America's *artistes* in a snit over restrictions in funding by the National Endowment for the Arts, much is being made of artistic "integrity." If Pryce were a U.S. citizen, Actors Equity could do nothing. Because he is British, however, the union had to certify that he is a "star," so he could qualify for a visa. Equity had no trouble in finding Pryce "a star" for visa purposes in 1984 when he appeared on Broadway. But in 1990, he has become a non-star to satisfy Equity's egalitarian — some say racist — cravings.

To his credit, Cameron Mackintosh, the British producer of "Miss Saigon," promptly cancelled the musical's opening on Broadway. Said he, Equity's stand is "irresponsible and a disturbing violation of the principles of artistic integrity and freedom." Mackintosh thus rejects $50 million in advance sales and takes a loss of $600,000 that already had been spent on the Broadway production. Gone, too, are 34 supporting roles in which Asians would be cast and 125 other jobs in the production.

A mutiny in the rank-and-file has forced Equity to call a special meeting tomorrow to reconsider its decision — and well it should. If Equity wants to get technical, an Eurasian is half-Caucasian, and certainly Pryce half-qualifies for the role under Equity's suddenly pristine notion of typecasting. The union did not squawk when Morgan Freeman played Petruccio, nor did it raise questions about Yul Brynner as the King of Siam, Ben Kingsley as Gandhi, Robert Hooks as Henry V, or Laurence Olivier as Othello. It has been reported, by the way, that Equity president Colleen Dewhurst — who bleated that "this is the time. The time has arrived" to start racial stereotyping in Pryce's case — played the role of an Asian in a 1970 production.

For years, minorities complained of being excluded from many entertainment jobs. Anyone who follows the entertainment world today, from the popular to the sublime, would find that claim ludicrous. In fact, non-traditional casting has put minorities in many starring roles they would not get under Equity's new rule. If Equity's foolish experiment in social engineering stands, the play no longer will be the thing, but the least of it.

St. Louis, Missouri, August 19, 1990

Actors' Equity has acknowledged that it erred in trying to prevent British actor Jonathan Pryce from recreating his role as the Eurasian "Engineer" in the New York production of "Miss Saigon." Stung by the adverse reaction to its decision, the actors' union reversed its earlier vote barring Mr. Pryce from appearing. Now the producer of "Miss Saigon," Cameron Mackintosh, should return the favor by rescinding his cancellation of the show.

All's well that ends well? Not quite. Certainly, Actors' Equity made a major blunder in how it handled the "Miss Saigon" controversy, and it was savant to recognize — and correct — its mistake. But the union's points about the dearth of roles for minorities should not be ignored. Non-traditional casting is meant to open the doors for all actors, not to provide a new name for the old practice of reserving leading ethnic roles for whites.

DAILY NEWS
New York City, New York, August 11, 1990

BEFORE THE FINAL CURTAIN goes down on "Miss Saigon," Cameron Mackintosh should know one thing: Broadway needs you. Broadway wants you. Actors' Equity is rethinking its misguided decision to ban Jonathan Pryce from appearing as the star of your show. If it backs down, you should bring "Miss Saigon" to New York — with Pryce.

Mackintosh, the producer of "Miss Saigon," did make some mistakes. Right from the start, he should have announced that he planned to bring Pryce, the star of the London production, to play the lead in the New York version. Period. Nothing wrong with that. It's been done a million times before.

Instead, he claimed that he had searched the world over for an Asian actor but "couldn't find one that was qualified." That statement was demeaning and insulting to Asian actors and the entire Asian community. It did much to trigger the present controversy. Mackintosh should apologize for it.

At the same time, Actors' Equity also owes Mackintosh an apology. Its hysterical reaction to the casting of Pryce has been an international embarrassment.

Equity is part of an arts community that is dead set against the government dictating which artists it will and won't fund by placing content restrictions on the National Endowment for the Arts. For months, artists have been crying: "Artistic freedom!" "No censorship!" "No outside control!"

But Equity is practicing exactly the same censorship it decries when it won't grant Pryce and Mackintosh the right to practice *their* artistic freedom in "Miss Saigon." The shameful irony of that position appears to be lost on the members of the Equity council who voted to bar Pryce.

THE ARGUMENT OVER WHO SHOULD STAR in "Miss Saigon" has been muddied by frequent comparisons of the casting of a white man to play a Eurasian with the casting of a black man (like Morgan Freeman in this summer's Joseph Papp production of Shakespeare's "Taming of the Shrew") to play a role usually reserved for whites.

These comparisons may sound plausible on the surface. But they ignore the once-common practice of using white actors, with makeup to darken their skins, to play people of color — at the same time that other actors and actresses were barred from roles *because* of the color of their skin. And it remains disgracefully difficult for people of color to find work on the stage. Yes, a growing number of plays make use of "non-traditional" casting. But such productions are few and far between.

The one good thing to be said for Actors' Equity's heavy-handed conduct in the "Miss Saigon" controversy is that it may well have helped sensitize Mackintosh, as well as the general public, to the complexities surrounding ethnic casting decisions.

But now that the point has been made, it is essential that Equity get firmly behind the principle of truly color-blind casting. Equity's decision on Thursday to reconsider the ban on Pryce provides a perfect opportunity to let Mackintosh bring his production to Broadway with Pryce as the star. Jobs and livelihoods depend on it. Let the show go on.

The Record

Hackensack, New Jersey, August 9, 1990

Long before the scheduled opening of "Miss Saigon" on Broadway next year, it looked like a sure-fire smash. Rave reviews in London, a producer with "Cats," "Les Miserables," and "The Phantom of the Opera" among his credits, and a lavish $10-million production all made "Miss Saigon" the hottest ticket of the coming season. That is, until the heavies from Actors Equity, the actors' union, came galumphing onto the stage and threatened to kill all the fun.

The leading character in the musical, a remake of "Madame Butterfly" set in Vietnam in the Seventies, is a Eurasian pimp. The union's executive secretary, Alan Eisenberg, complains that the part is played by an English actor named Jonathan Pryce, a Caucasian. And that's impermissible in New York, the union's council has decided.

"The casting of a Caucasian actor made up to appear Asian is an affront to the Asian community," Mr. Eisenberg said this week. "The casting choice is especially disturbing when the casting of an Asian actor, in this role, would be an important and significant opportunity to break the usual pattern of casting Asians in minor roles."

It's hard to know whether the actors' union is pursuing a kind of affirmative action gone mad, or just trying to keep out foreign talent to make life easier for its own members. Whatever the motive, the union is wrong.

Actors Equity has no right to be making delicate moral judgments about who is suitable for leading roles in "Miss Saigon" or any other play. An agreement between the British and American actors' unions clearly allows stars to perform in either country. Mr. Pryce's credentials as a star are impeccable. He won a Tony Award in 1976 as best actor for his performance in "The Comedians," and in England he has won an Olivier Award as best actor for his appearance in "Miss Saigon." Actors Equity has no legal grounds for blocking his appearance on Broadway.

In addition, Actors Equity's stand is an embarrassment that will undermine better-thought-out efforts to increase job opportunities for minority members on Broadway or anywhere else. The union, usually an advocate of non-traditional casting that emphasizes talent rather than race, certainly can't argue that characters of a particular race can only be played by actors of the same race. That would keep black or Asian actors from winning many desirable parts. Morgan Freeman never could have played Petruchio in "The Taming of the Shrew" in Central Park, for example. The union says it is just trying to increase employment opportunities for its minority members. That's an eminently worthy goal, but knocking an established star out of a hit production is the wrong way to pursue it.

Cameron Mackintosh, the producer of "Miss Saigon," canceled the New York production on Wednesday, saying he preferred to have no show at all rather than give in to the union's demand. So unless a compromise is reached, some 50 actors will lose jobs — including 34 minority union members already signed up for the production. And Broadway will lose the excitement of an international hit such as "Miss Saigon."

Actors Equity should reconsider and find a graceful way to back down. Broadway needs "Miss Saigon," and it needs a production in which the actors union doesn't interfere with casting decisions. That's also exactly what's needed by minority members that Actors Equity is trying to help.

The Washington Post

Washington, D.C., August 15, 1990

IT LOOKS as if Actors Equity, the New York-based actors' union, will have a chance to reverse itself tomorrow on last week's ludicrous decision to prevent the Caucasian actor Jonathan Pryce from playing the Eurasian lead character in the musical "Miss Saigon." The decision, which brought a prompt flood of ridicule, seems to have startled everyone involved; it demonstrated the silliness of taking an initially well-intentioned sentiment to absurd and legalistic extremes. The long-ago original motive of the union's policy is clear enough: ethnic minority actors have long suffered from the widespread refusal of directors to cast them in any but specifically minority roles. When specifically minority starring roles *are* written into musicals—such as the "Miss Saigon" character or, for that matter, his Asian female co-star—pressure mounts to give them to Asian actors. Casting more minority actors is a laudable purpose. But held rigidly, Equity's position would prohibit casting non-white actors in white roles, the very solution to the problem it addresses.

That solution, to which more and more directors are now turning, is the so-called "nontraditional casting": ignore the race of actors, cast the best ones and rely on their talent at creating illusion. Washingtonians have seen great successes in this vein at the Arena Stage, the Shakespeare Theater at the Folger and elsewhere; and Shakespeare in general has been a fruitful field for such efforts. (This is only fitting for plays whose female roles were written to be played by male Elizabethan actors and whose minorities, such as Othello, almost certainly were played by white ones.) The acclaimed British musical "Miss Saigon" is not in this league, but it fell afoul of the "protective" policies of the union, which also, for example, opposes any actors' appearing in blackface for any reason. The union, which admitted to "long and emotional debate" on the matter of Mr. Pryce, said in a statement last Thursday that it could not "appear to condone the casting of a Caucasian actor in the role of a Eurasian." Rather than back down, the British director, Cameron Mackintosh, canceled the show, turning an instance of mere silly thinking into one that would cost 50 actors jobs (including 34 minorities), forfeit $25 million in advance ticket sales and bite into the always precarious New York theater industry.

Mr. Mackintosh and Equity in fact have a history of friction, the director having threatened before to close shows when the union tried to keep him from importing his London stars rather than replace them with Americans. The union has also complained about his general record on casting minorities, especially in the large ensembles of his "Les Miserables" and "Phantom of the Opera"; but in the case of "Miss Saigon," with an Asian co-star and largely Asian ensemble, the showdown would seem misplaced even if it were not so wrongheaded. The union, to top it off, had also certified Mr. Pryce a "star" when he wished to recreate an Italian role in 1984. Equity's "long and emotional debates" evidently didn't cover much ground. Maybe it will straighten things out in this second run-through.

Los Angeles Times

Los Angeles, California, August 17, 1990

Actors' Equity did the right thing. The union reversed its monstrous decision that would have barred the English star Jonathan Pryce from taking a role on Broadway because he allegedly wasn't the right race for the part. That move outraged theater lovers everywhere—and threatened to kill the show.

In now approving Pryce to play a Eurasian pimp in the U.S. version of the London hit musical "Miss Saigon," the union's council said the actor qualifies as a "star." Under an agreement between American and British unions, a star billing allows a foreign actor such as Pryce to perform in the United States.

The union had originally voted against Pryce in an effort to dramatize its campaign to open up more roles to Asian actors. This is a laudable and inarguable goal, and Asians have long struggled with the limited number of roles—and a great deal of stereotyping—in the entertainment industry.

But Actors' Equity's cure was worse than the disease. It was an assault on freedom of artistic expression and choice. It triggered widespread criticism and objections from within and outside entertainment circles. "Miss Saigon's" producer retaliated by canceling plans to bring the musical to New York. But now "Miss Saigon" could be back on track and headed for Broadway's lights. A decision will be made in a few days.

That's good. But let us not forget the very real and troublesome problem that the incident brought to light: continued racism in the entertainment industry against Asian actors.

TULSA WORLD

Tulsa, Oklahoma, August 18, 1990

ACTORS' Equity reversed its decision that forbade a prize-winning British actor to recreate his role in the smash hit "Miss Saigon" on Broadway. But not before the American stage actors' union made itself look foolish.

Jonathan Pryce portrayed a Eurasian character in the British stage production of "Miss Saigon," but Equity said he couldn't do it here. The union said it couldn't "appear to condone the casting of a Caucasian in the role of a Eurasian," and insisted the role be filled by an Asian.

The ruling, of course, was reverse racism at its worst. Further, it ignored the fact that the very nature of acting is to play someone who the actor is not.

Producer Cameron Mackintosh balked at the union's attempt to dictate who he could or couldn't cast in his play — an obvious infringement on his artistic freedom — and canceled the $10 million Broadway production. Thus the union's attempt to make work for an Asian actor led to 50 actors, including 34 minorities, losing their jobs.

Union board members voted to reverse their decision and announced that they had "applied an honest and moral principle in an inappropriate manner." The board members were too kind to themselves. The rule that minority characters must be played by appropriate minority actors is unfair. Would the union object if an Asian actor played a Caucasian role? Not likely.

Producer Mackintosh said he would decide over the weekend whether plans to stage "Miss Saigon" on Broadway can be resumed. Let's hope B'Wayites aren't denied the opportunity to see a popular show because of Equity's foolishness.

WHERE WERE YOU, ACTORS' EQUITY, WHEN WE NEEDED YOU?

St. Petersburg Times

St. Petersburg, Florida, August 27, 1990

If black actors want to play English kings, and whites want to play Moors, and women want to portray boozing male blowhards, so be it. Let producers cast plays and movies, and let critics and audiences decide what works and what doesn't.

That's clearly the lesson that Actors' Equity should learn from the whole *Miss Saigon* debacle, wherein the 39,000-member union ran into a public relations buzzsaw over its refusal to permit English actor Jonathan Pryce to recreate on Broadway his lead role as a Eurasian pimp in the hit London musical. It was an unwise and potentially costly decision, and the union was right to reconsider and reverse itself.

But let's be clear about *what's* being reversed.

The union cannot presume to decide who gets to play what based on whose racial sensibilities might be offended; that is misguided and could backfire against the very people it's trying to help. But the union has every right to continue its efforts to see that Asians, blacks, women and other minority groups get better treatment and more opportunities in show business. Anyone who truly thinks such efforts aren't needed just isn't paying attention.

The union does need to get its equality act together, though. Its characterization of a white actor playing a Eurasian as "an affront to the Asian community" only drove a painful racial wedge between its membership. Worse, it created an opening for cheap shots from the kind of people who seem to resent any attempt at fairness for any minority group under any circumstances.

Columnist George Will lost no time denouncing "the union's weaselly position" as "the usual one of liberals running a racial spoils system;" he even managed to tag it to the "legacy" of retired Supreme Court Justice William Brennan. "Obscenely racist," harrumphed right-wing dilettante Charlton Heston, declaring his intention to resign from the union.

To hear them howl, you'd think white males were persecuted pariahs instead of the undisputed controllers of Broadway, television, movies or any other medium. That doesn't make any instance of unfairness to a white male performer any less unfair, but it hardly signals the end of Western civilization.

These same critics have been remarkably silent about the well-documented tradition of meaningless, demeaning or nonexistent roles for minority performers that Actors' Equity is at least trying to address. How those who pooh-pooh racism charges can so readily acknowledge the existence of "reverse" racism seems to be one of those unfathomable mysteries of the right-wing mind.

Actors' Equity erred, but only in an attempt to include the people who some seem to wish would just shut up and go away. That gives the union a lot more credibility than some of its critics.

Part IV: Minority & Multicultural Education in America

Since the importation of the first blacks to the U.S. into the Jamestown colony in the 1600s, the issue of minority education in the U.S. has generated controversy. During the Colonial period, education was recognized as a threat to slavery.

During Reconstruction, the South's policies toward the education of freedmen were determined not only by the traditional attitudes toward blacks, but also by the outlook and interests of the various groups that emerged with the collapse of the traditional class and economic structure. Historically, the South had always been opposed to education of children at public expense. Slavery and its concomitant historical, cultural, social and economic value systems were contrary to the notion of education at public expense and this feeling carried over to the education of blacks during and after Reconstruction.

However, though the establishment of public tax-supported education was an achievement, the education of whites and blacks in the same school was not attempted on a meaningful scale.

The famous Supreme Court case of *Plessy v. Ferguson* in 1896 had an important influence on blacks until it was overturned in 1954. Though the case involved a challenge to a Louisiana statute requiring segregation on interstate railroads, the "separate but equal" doctrine set forth in the ruling also applied to education. The court actually went out of its way to recognize that segregation in education was a general American practice, not a uniquely southern one. Thus, the court firmly placed its authority behind school segregation.

From 1896 to 1954, the dual system of education was developed and expanded in the South while permissive segregation was maintained in the border states.

Under the leadership of Thurgood Marshall, chief counsel for the National Association for the Advancement of Colored People (NAACP), the celebrated case of *Brown v. Board of Education of Topeka*, was brought before the Supreme Court. On the basis of testimony that segregated education damaged the personality of black children, lowered their motivation and contributed to their development of negative self-images, the Supreme Court May 17, 1954 ruled unanimously and unequivocally that segregation of the races in public education was unconstitutional.

During the two decades following *Brown*, various methods were employed to eliminate racial segregation in schools. Busing became one method. Black children were sent to predominantly white schools away from their own neighborhoods and white children to predominantly black schools, also in other neighborhoods.

Few issues in the movement towards desegregation in education generated as much divisiveness as busing. In some communities, both northern and southern, emotions erupted into rage and violence. Supporters of busing argue that history and experience have taught black Americans that it is impossible to have equal opportunities when facilities and institutions are segregated. Since education is of such great significance in the improvement of the quality of life for any individual, many blacks view desegregation as the most compelling issue confronting them today.

Closely related to the issue of desegregation is the nature of the education recieved in public and private institutions, particularly the issue of black or multicultural studies. Roscoe C. Brown, director of New York University's Institute of Afro-American Affairs, has defined black studies as a scholarly examination of the culture and the history of black people, and of the social, economic and political influences on black people in Africa, the Caribbean and the United States.

Unprecedented in its dramatic and rapid implementation, the idea of teaching black history was ushered into higher education in the U.S. during the period of turmoil on college campuses in the late 1960s, although some black colleges had taught such topics a generation earlier. Driving the growth of the new discipline were black students who felt that college personnel were insensitive to their particular needs, especially the teaching of their own history. Some advocates maintained that the programs should be purely educational in its goals and should not be used as forums for the advancement of a political agenda. Others held that a thorough and well-organized black studies curiculum was an indispensable part of the cultural liberation of black people.

Whatever the approach, black and minority studies programs survived the 1960s, 1970s and 1980s, though the permanent survival of these programs has been threatened at some colleges and universities because of low enrollments and lack of financial support.

The entrenchment of black studies in academia has become part of the national debate over "political correctness" and the notion that liberal ideas, particularly those involving the rights of minorities, women and homosexuals were being coercively enforced in academia. Virtually every known ideology has been invoked in this debate, making it difficult to determine exactly what was under dispute.

The first to engage in the debate were conservatives, who complained that a new postmodern generation from the 1960s has come into power in university humanities departments and central administrations to promote a radical ideology that unfairly denegrates the United States and the West as hopeless oppressive. The conservatives were joined by many liberals, who objected to steps such as speech codes barring racist or sexist speech. As the debate intensifies, there seems little doubt that these issues and will be with us well into the 21st Century.

Columbus Day and Quincentennial Marked by Heated Historical Debate

In recent years Christopher Columbus's voyage to the New World has come under increasingly heated historical and cultural debate. Central to the discussion is both the validity of the claim that the explorer "discovered" America in 1492 and the legacy of violence and slavery he left as a result of his adventure.

In 1991 and 1992, as groups in North America prepared to celebrate the quincentennial of Columbus's landing, the arguments became more acute, prompting newspaper editorials across the nation to address the educational, historical and cultural issues surrounding Columbus Day.

ST. LOUIS POST-DISPATCH
St. Louis, Missouri, January 1, 1992

When a coalition of Indians, blacks and Hispanics tries to prevent a descendant of Christopher Columbus from appearing in the Tournament of Roses parade, the quincentenary is off to an ominous start. The discovery of the Western Hemisphere was a watershed event in the history of humankind and deserves to be celebrated — without apology. To be sure, the celebration should include an examination of the effect of European settlement on the native cultures and the environment, but it is absurd to regard the Europeans' arrival as an unmitigated disaster or to argue that the hemisphere would be better off if they had not come. So, here is a New Year's resolution for all those scolds who would convert the quincentenary into a guilt-edged remembrance: Let Christopher Columbus rest in peace.

THE SPOKESMAN-REVIEW
Spokane, Washington, January 1, 1992

To hear poet-humorist Ogden Nash tell it, Christopher Columbus was a regular 15th-century Rodney Dangerfield:

So Columbus said, somebody show me the sunset and somebody did and he set sail for it,
And he discovered America and they put him in jail for it,
And the fetters gave him welts,
And they named America after somebody else.

So now, after waiting 500 years for a little respect, the Admiral of the Ocean Sea is under more fire than ever. The latest assault comes in conjunction with today's 103rd Tournament of Roses parade in Pasadena, where a direct descendant, one Cristobal Colon (the same name Columbus took for himself when he settled in Spain), was to be grand marshal.

Native American groups object to such an honor being bestowed on one whose ancestor not only exploited the Arawak people who were waiting when the ancestor first stumbled upon the West Indies, but also opened the Western Hemisphere to European settlement and development, and all the evils that followed. A group called the Los Angeles Indigenous Peoples Alliance threatened to disrupt the parade.

On the surface, the selection of Colon, described by tournament officials as a Spanish aristocrat, seems fitting enough.

After all, 1992 does mark the 500th anniversary of Columbus's expedition, which the pageant theme — "Voyages of Discovery 1992" — commemorates.

This is a new age, however. History is being examined more closely and figures from the past are being held accountable not only for their deeds but for their misdeeds. And while Christopher Columbus may have been a fine navigator, he was not exactly a New Age-sensitive guy.

He used force and trickery on the natives. He took some of them as captives back to Spain to be shown off at court. He allowed the Spaniards under his authority to enslave them to work their own land after the Spaniards had stolen it.

If Columbus were around today and tournament officials invited him to be grand marshal of their parade, such a resume would brew up enough of a PR storm to swamp the Nina, the Pinta *and* the Santa Maria.

But he is not around and if every adversity that has occurred in the Western Hemisphere in the past 500 years is going to be laid at his feet — let alone the feet of his descendants, or the Tournament of Roses — the new year is going to get old in a hurry.

Besides, the Arawaks got even. Columbus introduced them to disease and forced labor. They introduced him to tobacco.

Pittsburgh Post-Gazette
Pittsburgh, Pennsylvania, January 14, 1992

No longer will Oct. 12 date be celebrated as Columbus Day in Berkeley, Calif.; now it will be "Indigenous Peoples Day."

We mention this fact not as another example of California craziness or even as further proof that Columbus is taking his lumps during the 500th anniversary of his landing in the Western Hemisphere. We're more interested in the semantics of Berkeley's post-Columbus holiday.

In expressing the city's desire to honor "indigenous people," Berkeley Mayor Loni Hancock spoke in the present tense of "the important place that indigenous people hold in this country." The dictionary defines "indigenous" as "native." "Native," in turn, means "belonging to a particular place by birth."

But the descendants of the people who greeted Columbus are not the only people born in what is now the United States. The "indigenous" peoples of 20th-century America come in all colors and races.

Of course, the city parents of Berkeley aren't using the term "indigenous people" literally, any more than people who prefer "Native American" to "American Indian" deny that whites and blacks born in this country are native to it in the dictionary sense of the word.

Something else is obviously intended: an implication that one's identification with this country depends on how early one's ancestors lived here. This sort of nativism is not new, but its invocation by "progressives" is. It is more customary to associate this line of thinking with self-important descendants of passengers on the Mayflower.

Present-day "Native Americans" have roots in North America that go back further than those of black and white Americans — but not all the way. Anthropologists believe that the ancestors of American Indians came to this continent from Asia anywhere from 15,000 to 30,000 years ago. That's right, even these "indigenous people" aren't truly indigenous.

There was nothing wrong with Berkeley praising the descendants of the people who beat Columbus to America. But instead of calling them "indigenous peoples," the city should have used the form of address bestowed on the Daughters of the American Revolution by Franklin D. Roosevelt: "Fellow immigrants."

DESERET NEWS
Salt Lake City, Utah, October 13, 1991

As Columbus Day approaches, the country already is preparing for next year's holiday — a quincentenary commemorating 500 years since the fabled 1492, when Columbus "sailed the ocean blue." That celebration has focused attention on Columbus as never before.

PBS this week began a seven-part documentary series, "Columbus and the Age of Discovery," and in the year ahead nearly half a dozen more television series and films will run Columbus and conquistadors through a gauntlet of revisionist history.

There will be a Philip Glass opera, three dozen books, several big museum exhibits and an album of Columbus calypso music. Some of these may concentrate on a human hero and others may take the view that he was a greedy, violent kook who deserves to be castigated.

In an era that frowns on many of the practices of Columbus, some historical revisionists unfortunately are trying to judge the explorer out of the context of his times, which is neither fair nor accurate.

Most of us understand by now that Columbus was a less than perfect individual. Historian Samuel Eliot Morison's acclaimed 1942 opus, "Admiral of the Ocean Sea: A Life of Christopher Columbus," still the best book on the man, did not hesitate to note that Columbus enslaved and exploited the natives he encountered. Yet Morison's greater fascination was with what he considered Columbus's nautical achievement.

Until recently, the biggest Columbus controversy was over whether he was really the first. Obviously, he wasn't. It has been well-established, that nearly 500 years before Columbus's voyage, Vikings settled for a few years on what is now Newfoundland.

What Columbus really discovered was a new world of the mind — in which the human mind did not need to be limited by the barriers of geography, a world in which all human knowledge, experience and inventiveness could be put together and be available to any human being.

Columbus was a dramatic, engaging young redhead who dreamed of sailing west to India. He had "presence," the quality that commands attention and respect.

He was captivated by his own dream and he captivated others. He was an ambitious adventurer who knew thoroughly what he planned to do. He was an expert chartmaker who learned the science of geography.

If he had been content to be a discoverer, he might have been happier. But he also aspired to be a developer and administrator. His second, third and fourth voyages to America were anticlimactic and bred trouble. He had undertaken too much. In the end he became an embarrassment to Spanish royalty, and in 1506 he died, a lonely, unhappy man.

All his life he thought he had sailed around the world and reached Asia. In fact, he had found a new continent beyond which lay still another great sea. Though a flawed man — as are all men — the amazing Columbus still deserves the accolades of history.

THE ATLANTA CONSTITUTION
Atlanta, Georgia, October 13, 1991

Somewhere in between the traditional and the revisionist depictions of Christopher Columbus is a real-life representation of the storied 15th-century sailor. After all these years — 499 since he set foot in the Western Hemisphere, to be exact — he still doesn't seem to be in clear focus in the public mind.

How fitting then that the National Council of Social Studies is "just trying to be honest with the kids" in teaching about Columbus with a new emphasis on the historical consequences, good and bad, of his encounter with a world whose existence he never fully grasped.

The idealized Columbus, a byproduct of the early colonists' quest for appropriate Americanizing symbols, is a cardboard hero. Yet the view of Columbus-as-monster advanced by some American Indian activists and academics is no less one-dimensional.

To Columbus's credit, he was an enterprising, visionary adventurer, not to mention a phenomenally persistent seeker after King Ferdinand and Queen Isabella's loose change to pay for his far-flung expeditions.

On the debit side, he was a man of his times, when the dignity of alien races wasn't much valued, to say the least. Fairly enough, he can be judged a plunderer and exploiter. Though he admired the simple, generous folk he first encountered, he showed no qualms about hauling them back to Spain as slaves.

Still, it takes a leap of illogic to hold him responsible, as some do, for what followed in the wake of the Nina, Pinta and Santa Maria — rapacious Spaniards, to be sure, but greedy Britons, Frenchmen and Portuguese, as well. All told, they managed by conquest and spread of disease to decimate the native populations of North and South America, estimated to have been *about 70 million* in 1492.

It is time Euro-Americans recognized that systematic depopulation of native peoples, primitive or advanced, for what it was: in part an accident of history but, at times, genocidal, too. The council on social studies doesn't intend to gloss that over, nor should it.

The lesson to be taught about Columbus is that he embodied all the contradictions of those who followed him across the Western Sea — base qualities, yes, but noble ones, too. It makes for a more complex history but also a more genuinely human and believable one.

Lincoln Journal
Lincoln, Nebraska, October 13, 1991

It happens every century in the year whose last two digits are 92. People on both sides of the Atlantic display an unusual interest in Chrisopher Columbus' first voyage to the other side of the Earth.

Flowers are strewn around his various statues. Towns named after him celebrate. There are parades. Would you believe, even national holidays. Two communities once more renew their ancient claims of hosting the great admiral's remains.

Next year's 500th anniversary of the epic sailing risk already has brought an unprecedented volume of hostile reaction. This is ginned by the memory of monumental calamities visited on the indigenous populations in South, Central and North America in Columbus' wake.

Cruelty, exploitation, slavery, genocide. The fate for the survivors — some even down unto this very day — has been generations of degradation and poverty. All of that is in the historical record. Nor can any overview miss how the extracted, seized wealth of western lands, mineral and botanical, reshaped the globe; some for the better, some for the worse.

Another reality: If the Italian venture-capitalist Columbus and his Spanish associates had not played oceanic pointmen, other Europeans later would have done so. That inevitability must be realized.

Close your eyes and think about the misnamed "New World" had those very first Europeans been sponsored by the crowns of England, or Norway, not Spain.

Would those imaginary 15th or 16th century adventurers have equally lusted for gold, personal gain and, religiously speaking, souls? Would their body-borne European diseases also have doomed never-exposed millions of natives? What would be the dominant, non-native languages of today's Latin-America? In what way would the fused cultures, even styles of government, be different?

Playing "what if" is an amusing exercise. Harmless, too. It doesn't, however, come close to a better-rounded knowledge of the turbulent, awakening world 500 years ago as it actually existed, the role filled by Columbus and the mighty, unforseen events triggered by the Spanish conquest. The truth is more than a little astonishing.

Such as Columbus' flagship, the Santa Maria, hitting a reef on Christmas Eve, 1492, and sinking. As an example of cosmic symbolism, what more could anyone want?

The Washington Post

Washington, D.C., October 12, 1991

FIRST OF ALL, it *isn't* the 500th anniversary—not yet. This Columbus Day will mark only the 499th year since Columbus did his thing in 1492 (miraculously, this is still considered the right date) or, if you want to maximize the drumroll potential, it's the start of the full-year anniversary commemoration of the voyage that had such thunderous consequences. At least no one has to lament this year that Columbus Day, like some presidents' birthdays, is observed solely as the occasion for department store sales and extra sleep. Rarely in this country has a holiday been subject to such prolonged and furious revisionism.

Passions have flamed high this year over Columbus and his blessed or cursed landfall, not just in academic circles but also among curriculum-makers and ethnic interest groups. Can we "celebrate" an event that led to so much violence and the near total eradication of native American cultures? On the other hand, is it plausible to omit recognition of something on which so much later history turns? Should the word "discovery" and the expression "New World" be purged? Is it "Eurocentric" to honor Columbus? Or, perhaps, anti-Italian to attack him? (If he was Italian. One scholar proposed apropos of Leif Ericson Day, Oct. 9, that Columbus was, in fact, Norwegian.) What is the politically correct stance for Hispanic organizations?

As these queries suggest, the debate has ranged from serious and soul-searching to pretty trivial at times. And yet, for all that, we'd say it has been healthy, even bracing. Admitting that one's national heritage is problematic in parts is a sign of cultural coming-of-age. Every national, ethnic or religious heritage includes unsavory stretches, ugly deeds, times when a nation's values were not adhered to and times when those values themselves were misguided or benighted. Understanding that is simply achieving historical maturity. And demanding that it be taken into account is not the same thing as rejecting the culture out of hand.

In Columbus's case, both reevaluation and commemoration now move into a higher gear with the start of formal quincentennial events—for instance, this weekend's opening of the National Gallery blockbuster show "Circa 1492" and the slightly tongue-in-cheek arrival last week of three replica Viking ships on the Potomac, intended, they said, to steal Columbus's thunder by recalling the 1,000-year-old Viking landfall. Positive, negative, contemplative or incidental, it all adds up to serious respect for the occasion and, yes, celebration.

The Phoenix Gazette

Phoenix, Arizona, October 11, 1991

Well, now we have somebody to blame for every tragedy, war and social problem in the last five centuries: Christopher Columbus.

The quincentennial celebration of Columbus' "discovery" of America wasn't supposed to be like this. But the long anticipated 500th anniversary party celebrating Columbus' voyage has broken out into a food fight.

The new revisionists want to demonize Columbus as the first of the Europeans to rape and pillage the Western Hemisphere. But Europeans didn't invent murder, greed and racism. Rousseau's Noble Savage is as illusory and ethnocentric a lie as Kipling's "White Man's Burden." And if American history too long ignored the native peoples who first settled our continent, it does historical accuracy no service to belittle those who linked the New and Old Worlds 500 years ago.

As for Columbus' character, like the rest of us, he was not a perfect person. Ambitious and driven, he stands accused of inflexibility, greed and inflated egoism.

But the man who convinced Queen Isabella you could sail west to go east is a remarkable man of history. His voyage to America in 1492 ranks among history's most important events, arguably the turning point in world history. Though he didn't realize it at the time, Columbus discovered a whole new world, opening up opportunities for billions of people who followed him. He is considered by many as the greatest seaman ever, a captain of moral and physical courage, strong and confident, loyal to his mission and his convictions. On his trips, Columbus faced mutinous sailors, tempestuous storms, armed rebels and fierce Indians. His story inspires those who would explore the universe, soar among the stars, navigate the oceans, rise above humble beginnings.

His name will be invoked whenever and wherever boldness, faith, courage and determination are honored. 500 years from now, they will be celebrating Columbus Day.

The Wichita Eagle-Beacon

Wichita, Kansas, October 12, 1991

Almost 500 years after the fact, many Americans haven't decided whether Christopher Columbus' "discovery" of the New World was a good thing.

For Native Americans, Columbus' arrival in the Caribbean meant the end of a way of life. For blacks, the Nina, Pinta and Santa Maria could be seen as the harbinger of the fleets of ships that would bring slaves from Africa. For some environmentalists, Columbus and his fellow Europeans were the despoilers of a pristine wilderness.

Americans will have all next year to fight over Columbus when the hemisphere commemorates the quincentennial of his famous voyage. But today, the 499th anniversary of his arrival on San Salvador Island, is a chance to put away the rightness or wrongness of Columbus and salute the first Europeans to visit North America.

The expert on the subject is the late historian and sailor, Samuel Eliot Morison, author of the monumental work, "The European Discovery of America."

An Irishman was probably the first European to see the New World. As Mr. Morison relates, St. Brendan the Navigator sailed from Ireland in the 6th century, certainly getting as far as Iceland, and possibly, though doubtfully, getting to America.

In the early 8th century, several hundred monks left Ireland and settled in Iceland because they didn't want to join the Church of Rome. In about 870, the Icelandic Irish were attacked by Vikings. Many of the monks escaped in crude boats, and some of them likely landed in North America.

The saga picks up with the most intrepid seamen of the Medieval era, the Scandinavians. By the year 1000, Norsemen had arrived in Greenland, and shortly afterward they discovered "Vinland," which now is thought to be Newfoundland.

Mr. Morison says Leif Ericsson spent one winter in Vinland and his family founded a short-lived colony there.

The earliest chronicle of Ericsson's discovery comes from Adam of Bremen, who in about 1075 reported on a meeting with the king of Denmark: "He spoke of an island in that (northern) ocean, discovered by many, which is called 'Winland,' for the reason that vines yielding the best of wine grow there wild."

Vinland disappeared from recorded history shortly afterward.

Legends also credit Welsh, Portugese and other Europeans as beating Columbus to the New World.

Of course, what now are called Native Americans, who originally came from Asia, are the true discoverers of America.

The point is that the ancestors of all Americans were immigrants. That's something to remember as the "Columbus controversy" heats up between now and the next Columbus Day.

THE BLADE
Toledo, Ohio, October 13, 1991

CHRISTOPHER Columbus, the explorer who introduced the New World to the Europeans, has suffered many changes of images in the 499 years since he and his three ships made their landfall on a Caribbean island — from intrepid navigator to brutal colonizer and symbol of genocide.

The debate over what kind of commemoration of the Columbus voyage should be staged has more relevance to today's society

> *Columbus' voyage was an extension of Europe's intellectual, commercial, and political ferment. By no means was it unique in world history*

than it does to the one that existed at the end of the 15th century.

Today a sour mood exists among many native peoples of the Americas as well as the descendants of the Africans who were brought here as slaves, and few would deny they have a valid case. Most of the indigenous civilization was wiped out. Even the clerics who on a number of occasions tried to limit the excesses of conquerors bent on plunder and exploitation committed their share of cultural sins, wiping out writings and cultural artifacts that would have preserved the heritage of the advanced Mayan, Aztec, and Inca civilizations.

Disease, slave labor, and warfare decimated the Indian populations, though their descendants remain, often living in misery and poverty even to this day. Leaders of these societies are in no mood to sing the praises of Columbus, even though he died virtually unaware of the fateful forces of history for which he had been an important agent.

Euro-American civilization has spread across the world, and has become the defining standard by which people measure progress. Even so, many individuals find that an aberration, a kind of sickness on the part of the West. They note that the Chinese, with the longest *continuing* record of civilization in the world, exercised hegemony in their own region, but saw no need to set sail to conquer peoples on distant shores. And for a century or more after Columbus' voyage, they were the richest country on earth.

All that notwithstanding, Columbus' voyage was but an extension of the intellectual, commercial, and political ferment that marked Europe after it emerged from feudalism and formed national states. By no means was this invasion of the New World unique in world history. The forces of Islam marched east as far as what is now Indonesia and west as far as Spain before they were checked. The Tartar hordes swept Russia and rolled back the modernizing influences from the rest of Europe. Some say that is even today the most traumatic event in the history of the Russian nation.

Obviously, Columbus cannot be regarded with mindless reverence; neither can he be ignored. There is a good deal of intolerance afoot in our own country now. Many individuals asserting their rightful place in history would, in effect, deny free expression to others.

The world is to have a whole year of Columbus celebrations. Why it is starting a year early is one of those things best explained by a public-relations functionary. But in that year, and beyond, it ought to be possible to lower the rhetoric and elevate the level of discourse.

Perhaps all of us will emerge with a greater appreciation for both the accomplishments of western man symbolized by the scientists, explorers, and others and the residual values espoused by the best that was in the traditional societies which the Europeans encountered.

Reading a book about Columbus' era and his voyage is still the shortest cut to knowledge and the best way to separate fact from myth — even though it might take some of the fun out of the debate over whether Columbus was a hero or heel.

FORT WORTH STAR-TELEGRAM
Fort Worth, Texas, October 12, 1991

In the wee hours of the morning on this date 499 years ago, a Spanish sailor aboard the caravel Pinta sighted land, and human history lurched in a new direction at an accelerating speed.

That sailor, who was the first European to lay eyes on the Island of Guanahani in the Bahamas, was supposed to have received a sizable monetary reward from the king and queen of Spain for the sighting. His admiral, Chrisopher Columbus, claimed the prize instead.

That incident speaks volumes about the character of Columbus, who was as vain, greedy and autocratic as he was brilliant, resourceful and courageous.

Whatever his failings as a human being and as an administrator of the new lands he found and claimed for Spain, Columbus' place of towering importance in the advance of human civilization is anchored firmly by the outgrowths of his explorations in the Western Hemisphere.

It is fitting, therefore, that today marks the start of a yearlong celebration of the 500th anniversary of the small fleet's landfall at what Columbus thought was one of the fringe islands of Asia.

The celebration, however, has generated some criticism and outright opposition. There are those who contend that Columbus' voyages blazed the trail for European exploitation, brutalization, enslavement and, in some cases, the virtual extinction of indigenous populations.

Those assertions are undeniable. It may even be added that but for Columbus' explorations in the new world and those that came after him, there would have been no massive African slave trade.

Such observations add a needed perspective to a proper understanding of world history. They do not, however, provide justification for raining on the Columbus quincentennial parade.

The unavoidable truth is that Columbus' voyages set in motion a frenzy of exploration, discovery, migration, economic development, trade and war that laid the foundations of the modern world.

No historical grievance, however valid, can justify distorting history by denying Columbus' pivotal role in the evolution of human civilization.

Columbus deserves his day and his year, and so does the nameless, farsighted sailor whose reward he took.

Minneapolis Star and Tribune
Minneapolis, Minnesota, October 14, 1991

The countdown to the 1992 Columbus quincentenary takes full sail this Columbus Day. Some argue that current recognition of the negative as well as positive effects of that encounter is trendy political correctness. In fact, it is an encounter with rediscovered truths.

The significance of Columbus' voyage must be explored and reevaluated every century. Chicago's famous Columbian Exposition of 1893 celebrated the explosion of American economic growth, particularly the opening of the vast Great Plains and the beginning of the economic revolution caused by petroleum and electricity. At the end of the Indian wars, no significant Indian presence was sought or wanted.

Now we know that such development — which created the current prosperity of most Americans — had costs, both ecological and human.

In 1893, American Indian ideas, interests and contributions had no voice. Today Americans must listen.

Yet the Christopher Columbus Quincentenary Jubilee Commission, authorized by Congress in 1985, still has no Indian members. Although one will soon be added, this is not just an oversight, but an insult to all Americans who believe that the nation must learn from its own experience.

The 500th anniversary of Columbus' remarkable voyage represents an opportunity for America to reexamine itself, and to commit itself to a more inclusive future. It's not yet clear that the nation will take full advantage of the opportunity.

CHICAGO Sun-Times

Chicago, Illinois, October 13, 1991

As the yearlong observance of the 500th anniversary of Columbus' landfall in the "New World" begins this weekend, teaching about the great explorer has gotten caught up in what has become a broad and touchy controversy.

Should his arrival here, for instance, be described as a "discovery" or an "encounter"? He may have found riches for Spain, but what about the people who were here before he got here?

Appropriately and usefully, the National Council for the Social Studies is taking the lead in encouraging teachers to be honest with kids about Columbus and other European explorers.

Good for them. Like the compromise between Italian-Americans and Native Americans over this year's Columbus Day parade in Chicago, no one expects both sides in the debate over Columbus' place in history to have identical views of the same historical events.

That isn't what the study of history is all about. The real point isn't to choose between a sanitized version of his deeds and one that accuses him of genocide, but to tell the whole story of Columbus' life and to ask questions about what happened.

One of the best observances has been the public television special, "Columbus and the Age of Discovery," which chronicled his search for funding, the shipbuilding industry, the process of navigation that made Columbus' journey possible, his problems as a governor and the adverse effects on the Indians already on the continent.

The seven-part series even showed the continuing effects today of that encounter around the world—on people, animals and even plants like the potato and tobacco.

What many Americans learned about Columbus in school came in nutshell form—1492, the Nina, Pinta and Santa Maria, set sail from Spain. But so much more happened beyond the list of dates and essential facts that used to make up the first lessons of American history.

In celebrating Columbus, those facts from 499 years ago need to be linked to a rediscovery of history today.

San Francisco Chronicle

San Francisco, California, October 14, 1991

THE MISCHIEVOUS question 50-odd years ago before the Oxford Union, the debating society of Oxford University, was: "Resolved, that Christopher Columbus went too far in 1492."

It has been long argued that Columbus did not discover America. The descendants of the first settlers who crossed a then-existing land bridge from Siberia to Alaska were on hand to welcome Columbus, as they had earlier greeted Leif Ericson and perhaps other voyagers.

BUT IT WAS the arrival of Columbus that opened up the New World to European settlement and, in the process, inaugurated the great age of discovery. Only five years later, John Cabot (known in his Italian birthplace as Giovanni Caboto) landed in North America. A scant 20 years after Columbus set foot on an island in the West Indies, the survivors of Ferdinand Magellan's crew completed the first round-the-world voyage.

Christopher Columbus, whose explorations are being honored today, did far more than complete a courageous, perilous voyage 499 years ago. The consequences could not be foreseen in 1492, but Columbus began the extraordinary process that resulted in the society we know today in the Americas, North and South.

That's no small accomplishment.

The Des Moines Register

Des Moines, Iowa, October 15, 1991

What's all this uproar about Christopher Columbus? The quincentennial of the 1492 voyage still is a year away, and it looks as if the whole year will be a shouting match about whether he was a great explorer or a terrible guy.

Why must he be portrayed as either all of one or all of the other? Why can he be both? Or something in between?

People have a tendency to overglorify historical figures, then to overdenigrate them when it is revealed they had human

imperfections. When it comes to understanding history, neither hero-making nor vilification is very helpful. Why can't people just accept historical figures as human beings not much different from people like themselves?

Take Columbus. He was an ambitious and bold mariner out to make a buck. Lots of bucks. And he did what entrepreneurs are still doing today: He needed financing, so he went to the government for a handout. He didn't live up to his promises. Columbus never found the Orient, never brought home much gold, and his first colonies flopped.

Unintentionally, Columbus opened contact between two land masses that had been separated since the Ice Age. That led to some terrible consequences. It also led to some great advances. For better and worse, it changed the course of history more than any event before or since.

But Columbus died embittered and in broken health. In his own time, he was nearly forgotten. He was so obscure and out of favor that the New World he discovered bears the name of an explorer who came after him. Amerigo Vespucci was a lesser sailor than Columbus, but better at self-promotion.

That's the way it goes.

The Union Leader

Manchester, New Hampshire, October 14, 1991

Citizens who are appalled by the continual drumbeat of vilification of Christopher Columbus by leftist character assassins in the news media and academe should not give in to tunnel vision.

Columbus, white, Christian, European, male, is simply a convenient **symbol** of what the Left in American political life despises.

COLUMBUS

The larger target of the Left — Western culture itself — will come into even clearer focus next year during the Quincentennial Celebration of the first of Columbus' four voyages to the new continent. The opening shots have been fired, but they have not yet attained the frenzy and intensity that can be expected next year.

"What some historians have termed a 'discovery,' " the National Council of Churches huffed in a document issued in May of last year, *"in reality was an invasion and colonization with legalized occupation, genocide, economic exploitation, and a deep level of institutional racism and moral decadence."*

Other groups, propagandizing taxpayers with the taxpayers' own money, are using their federal grants to peddle much the same line: The voyage of the man from Genoa brought evil to a happy people who lived tranquil lives, at peace with both nature and neighbors.

The self-destruction of the magnificent Mayan civilization occurred nearly **seven centuries before** the arrival of Columbus and other Europeans in the Western Hemisphere? The peddlers of one-sided, Politically Correct "history" don't want to hear about it.

Nor is it Politically Correct to point out that the Aztecs, for all their other admirable qualities, practiced human sacrifice on a grand scale. An estimated 20,000 to 80,000 people

were slaughtered at one temple dedication **five years before** the voyage of Cristóbal Colón (the Spanish name adopted by Colombo — Latin name "Columbus" — after he settled in Spain) presaged the arrival of the Europeans.

And fie to anyone who would cite the fact that the Incas, for all their modern advances, lived under a totalitarian despotism that, in the words of Peruvian novelist Mario Vargas Llosa, included *"a state religion that took away the individual's free will and crowned the authority's decision with the aura of a divine mandate."*

The Incas' and Aztecs' versions of a state religion would cause even the ACLU to blanch, and pacifists didn't last long in those days during times of tribal warfare. Moreover, it simply is not true that Europeans brought slavery to America. It was already here, a fact verified, for example, in the current issue of National Geographic, which features interesting articles about pre-Columbus culture written by modern-day inheritors of that culure.

The point of it all, of course, is that there is good and bad in all cultures and the latter frequently is accentuated when cultures clash. Previous cultures should be judged more by the standards of their time than by modern perspectives.

To revile Columbus, one of the greatest seamen and navigators of all time, or to belittle his contribution to life in America today is to be guilty of the most grotesque kind of historical revisionism.

That contribution, which brought science and other knowledge westward, was summed up magnificently and succinctly, we thought, by William Norman Grigg, a columnist with the Provo (Utah) Daily Herald, who wrote in the August 27th edition of The New American magazine:

"Without Columbus, modern America would not have been possible. There would have been no place of refuge for those who fled from religious and political tyrannies. America has drawn from the best of all cultures by attracting those who seek religious liberty and the blessings of ordered liberty . . . "

The New York Times

New York City, New York, October 14, 1991

Whether Christopher Columbus is viewed as a hero or a scoundrel, he can also be viewed on more New York City pedestals than anyone else who never even paid a visit. Only George Washington, who lived in the city as President, is exalted by more statuary.

Best known of the six New York Columbuses is the one in Columbus Circle. But there are two more in Manhattan, one each in Brooklyn and Queens, and a Depression-era bust in the Bronx, sculpted as a W.P.A. Art Project.

The Columbus Circle Columbus, dedicated in 1892, marked the 400th anniversary of his discovery. Now freshly refurbished under the privately funded Adopt-a-Monument program, he stands atop a narrow column in the classical style that raised heroes so high you can't see their faces. No matter. No one knows what Columbus looked like anyhow.

In the contest between rival Spanish and Italian claims to his fame, this statue is pure Italian. It was the gift of Italian-Americans through a public fund-raising campaign by the city's Italian-language newspaper, Il Progresso. An Italian, Gaetano Russo, sculpted it in Carrara marble. And its inscriptions are in Italian and English. In Italian, the identification is Cristoforo Colombo.

For Hispano-Columbians, who call him Cristóbal Colón, there is another image, barely a half-mile away inside Central Park, by a Spaniard, Jeronimo Suñol, and cast in bronze in Barcelona.

The oldest statue, dating from 1869, was done by an American, Emma Stebbins — in Rome. Like Columbus, it has wandered. It stood originally in Central Park, then downtown in Little Italy, and now in Brooklyn. The newest statue, from 1925, is in Queens. And the hardest to find is perched on a sixth-story ledge of the old Custom House at Manhattan's Bowling Green.

Though mute, they all speak the same message. Revere him or not, this man made history. In the words of the inscription in Columbus Circle: "To the world he gave a world."

The Des Moines Register

Des Moines, August 19, 1991

In this age of political correctness, it can be touchy to celebrate too enthusiastically some historical landmarks such as the discovery of the New World.

When a replica of a Viking longship arrived this summer in Canada to commemorate the 1,000th anniversary of Leif Eriksson's voyage, Norwegian officials took pains to deny any attempt to upstage next year's 500th-anniversary of Columbus' first voyage.

There was no intent to belittle the Italian-born Columbus, they insisted. It was only a celebration of the Norse heritage and of the feats of adventurers who sailed without compass or chart through the foggy North Atlantic.

The Norwegians' worry about possible hurt Italian feelings is only a hint of the sensitivity booby-traps ready to explode at next year's Columbian observance. Be careful how you celebrate.

Here's the first lesson: Avoid the mistake made in the first paragraph of this editorial. Don't use the word "discover." The politically correct point out, correctly, that America couldn't be discovered because it wasn't lost. The people who already lived here knew perfectly well it existed. To say it was discovered is an example of Eurocentrism. That's a no-no.

So how do you cheer the anniversary of 1492, when Columbus sailed the ocean blue, without appearing to have a Eurocentric bias? How do you celebrate Columbus' accomplishments without seeming insensitive to the fact that his arrival didn't lead to good things for the people who already lived here?

Considering the way European settlers and their offspring plundered two pristine continents in the last 499 years, is there really anything to celebrate at all?

Yes, but a thoughtless rejoicing over the Western notion of "progress" won't do. Using the occasion for a deeper, all-inclusive reflection on 500 years of human history and where we're headed from here would be appropriate.

The Detroit News

Detroit, Michigan, October 13, 1991

Rare is the nation that declares a national holiday in the name of an individual who not only was not a citizen of that country, but who never set foot in it. The national holiday for Christopher Columbus, instituted in 1934, was a recognition by the people of the United States of the grandeur of his achievement in defying the conventions of his times and setting out on his great voyage of exploration and discovery.

This Columbus Day marks the beginning of the yearlong period leading up to next year's 500th anniversary of the sighting of land on Oct. 12, 1492. Already, the public has been treated in the press to a very different Columbus than the brave, resourceful man portrayed in most Americans' grade school history books.

The debunkers are determined to portray him as a racist, slaver, perpetrator of genocide against the native Indian populations and guilty of "ecocide." There is nothing wrong with debate about the reputations of historical personalities. But the amount of attention the Columbus debunkers have received recently threatens to obscure the very real substance of what he wrought.

Columbus was merely part of a time that became known as the "Age of Discovery." Famous voyages of discovery preceded his, primarily down the coast of Africa and around the Horn to India. Rapidly advancing technology produced the magnetic compass and the first crude navigation instruments, which made it possible to fix position when out of sight of land. It also produced the cara-

Christopher Columbus

vel, a light, fast ship that could sail into the wind.

Leif Erikson probably reached North America centuries earlier. But Columbus' "Enterprise of the Indies," as he called it, electrified Europe. It was one of the catalysts for the explosion of learning that animated the Renaissance, which in turn paved the way for humanistic ideas that profoundly affected political and economic institutions. Unlike earlier voyages, it gave people an idea of worlds yet to be discovered.

Would this be a better world if Columbus had never lived, or America had been developed by some other culture? It's hard to see how. If the Arabs, who also had excellent maritime abilities, had gotten here first, the whole hemisphere might now be a fundamentalist theocracy. Would discovery by the Chinese, who at one point led the world in technology, have been an improvement? Would an unchecked Aztec empire, with its tradition of human sacrifice and slavery, be better than what Columbus wrought?

Columbus' discovery led to a raising of living standards that is incomparable in human history. It allowed the establishment of a country, the United States, whose ideals even today serve as a beacon for the newly free peoples of Eastern Europe and Russia. It gave to the world an unparalleled example of personal bravery and initiative that have offered valuable lessons to generations of school children.

Columbus Day is indeed something worth celebrating.

THE SPOKESMAN-REVIEW
Spokane, Washington, October 12, 1991

Poor Christopher Columbus. On this, the 499th anniversary of his voyage across the ocean blue, he has fallen resoundingly from political favor.

The National Council of Churches has pronounced him a scapegoat for "genocide ... exploitation ... racism ... moral decadence" and has called on the Western world to spend 1992 repenting the explorer's sins as invader of the Americas. Indian activist Russell Means says Columbus "makes Hitler look like a juvenile delinquent."

Upon hearing such babble one wonders if the year-long commemoration of Columbus, which begins today, should culminate in exhuming his corpse and nailing it to a cross, there to hang for the considerable sins of Western imperialism.

However, the venom being spat on this long-dead sailor's grave reveals more about the spitters than it does about their target.

Unresolved anger and guilt over the appalling treatment of Native Americans have combined with the current political correctness movement to make an ideological circus of what ought to be an educational observance, the Columbus quincentenary.

The fuss pits revisionist history against the steady evolution of historical understanding. The difference must be understood, if any of us are to glean something worthwhile from the quincentenary.

Revisionist history imposes political judgment upon prominent figures, judgment reflecting the prejudice of those who impose it, and resting upon current values rather than those which guided the people under study. In Soviet classrooms Joseph Stalin alternately has been lionized and vilified depending on who controlled the country.

During Columbus' day, a controlling religious orthodoxy interpreted the world for its inhabitants and placed clamps upon thought, speech and inquiry. In our day, the emerging secular orthodoxy of the political correctness movement seeks to control academic inquiry and to recast history as a simplistic struggle between an evil establishment and groupings of oppressed but noble victims.

The steady evolution of history, on the other hand, presses for the growth of knowledge. It aims to shed the light of broader understanding rather than the heat of contemporary political reinterpretation.

There is much to be gained — for those of us who are living out the pages of tomorrow's history books — from an expanded body of historical knowledge.

To learn more of Native American cultures is a worthwhile exercise indeed, and the Columbus quincentenary could make it happen.

To learn about other cultures including their imperfections is to confront imperfections in our own culture. To recognize past wrongs, intended or not, is to recognize that the admirable pursuits of discovery require sensitivity on the part of the Christopher Columbuses of today.

It is absurd to blame one sailor for an inevitable tide of world exploration and settlement, ugly as it sometimes was.

The most important issue isn't who committed which wrongs against whom a few centuries ago and how guilty or victimized we ought to feel about it now.

The issue is what sensitivities we might be overlooking now as our own generation's explorers and risk takers continue the initiative to expand boundaries of human knowledge and achievement. Civilization needs Columbuses and their daring deserves emulation. Civilization also needs broader vision than it sometimes has shown during moments of dramatic progress.

The Pittsburgh
PRESS
Pittsburgh, Pennsylvania, October 12, 1991

As we plunge deeper into the dark age of political correctness, Columbus Day seems increasingly an anachronism, a quaint contrivance, a celebration with nothing to celebrate. It was originally intended to commemorate a national, and at the time uncontentious, belief — that the great explorer Christopher Columbus discovered America, thereby preparing the advance of a noble civilization.

Among sophisticates today, however, that statement is unbearably crude — akin to a belief in pixies or phrenology. To them Columbus was a vulgar merchant, a glory hound not an explorer, a fop who didn't even know where was he going; and by no definition could such a blood-soaked imperialist be considered "great." Nor did he "discover" anything, the continent having been populated for thousands of years before he blundered into it.

And can the European civilization that Columbus embodied and that followed him to the New World really be called "noble"? The more generous of today's sophisticates will concede that this is a subject still open for debate — although, they will add, the consensus is almost complete. (Hint to admirers of European civilization: You won't like the "consensus.")

At the risk of heresy, we can't help thinking that the old faith in Columbus has been shrugged off a bit too easily. In the most literal sense, of course, Columbus didn't discover America. Viking enthusiasts have pushed this literalism for years. And now comes the National Council for the Social Studies, a teachers group, which in a new report instructs that in discussing Columbus children must not use the dreaded "d" word at all.

But discover means more than "find"; it also connotes exploiting a thing's potential, envisioning its possibilities and drawing them out. It is in this sense that Columbus discovered America, along with the brave men and women who followed him. Technology, industry, the institutions of individual freedom, both political and economic — these gifts beyond price flowed from Columbus' discovery, the 499th anniversary of which is today.

That is why most Americans either today or Monday will celebrate Columbus Day, and are right to do so.

The Gazette
Cedar Rapids, Iowa, October 12, 1991

TODAY BEGINS the Columbus quincentennial, the year-long observance leading up to the 500th anniversary of the Great Navigator's Oct. 12, 1492, landing in the West Indies.

It wasn't a "discovery," because Indians had inhabited North and South America for thousands of years. And Norsemen had explored the coast of North America some 500 years earlier. But it was Columbus' footfall that connected Europe with the New World, opened new windows of knowledge and started our section of North America toward development of the greatest democracy ever.

To hear his detractors tell the tale, though, you would think Columbus was the scourge of two continents — an exponent of disease, rapine and death as only his cruel Spanish partners could deliver it. Columbus bashing is all the rage these days. On some points, the critics are correct. Unlike his noble screen persona, Fredric March in "Christopher Columbus" (1949), Christobal Colon (as the Genoese sailor called himself) was a braggart who never tired of crowing "I told you so!" He had a lousy sense of geography, thinking Japan was where the Virgin Islands are; educated men of the day told him he was wrong. And he was so greedy — seeking ships, honors, titles, percentage of trade — that he could have made it today as a major league baseball player, or, at least, a player's agent.

It's unfair, though, to blame Columbus for the depredations of the Spanish conquest. As Time magazine (Oct. 7) observed, "For too long, the American myth demonized or ignored the people whom Columbus encountered on these shores. Must people now replace this with a new myth that simply demonizes Columbus?"

Let's stow the revisionist myth and view Columbus in the 1490s context. It took an ambitious businessman to organize a three-ship expedition in search of a new trade route to the Orient. It took a bold sailor to venture out of land's sight for more than a month. And it took a great navigator — an unparalleled practitioner of "dead reckoning" — to make it back to Spain. Christopher Columbus was all three — shrewd businessman, intrepid sailor, peerless navigator.

It was his "accidental discovery" that began the Western Hemisphere's transformation. We owe a great debt to Christopher Columbus.

Bush Deplores 'Political Correctness'

President George Bush, in a commencement address at the University of Michigan in Ann Arbor, May 4, 1991 took issue with what he saw as a growing intolerance on American college campuses.

The phenomenon to which President Bush referred had become known as "political correctness." The term embraced a wide range of generally liberal attitudes, particularly in regard to expanded rights for women, minorities and homosexuals.

The movement had generated controversy on many college campuses. Some schools had adopted speech codes barring the use of language that insulted or demeaned anyone on the basis of gender, race, ethnic origin or sexual orientation. At Brown University in Providence, Rhode Island, one student had been expelled for shouting racial slurs.

In his address, Bush focused on freedom of speech, saying it "may be the most fundamental and deeply revered of all our liberties."

"Ironically," Bush continued, "on the 200th anniversary of our Bill of Rights, we find free speech under assault throughout the United States, including on some college campuses. The notion of political correctness has ignited controversy across the land. And although the movement arises from the laudable desire to sweep away the debris of racism and sexism and hatred, it replaces old prejudices with new ones. It declares certain topics off-limits, certain expressions off-limits, even certain gestures off-limits.

"What began as a crusade for civility has soured into a cause of conflict and even censorship. Disputants treat sheer force – getting their foes punished or expelled, for instance – as a substitute for the powers of ideas.

"We should all be alarmed at the rise of intolerance in our land and by the growing tendency to use intimidation rather than reason in settling disputes," Bush added.

"But you see, such bullying is outrageous. It's not worthy of a great nation grounded in the values of tolerance and respect," he continued. "We must conquer the temptation to assign bad motives to people who disagree with us...We must build a society in which people can join in common cause without having to surrender their identities."

Although Bush was heckled by a small group of students protesting the U.S.'s involvement in the Persian Gulf war, his speech was reportedly well received.

Students at predominantly black Hampton University in Virginia May 12 staged a silent protest against a commencement address by Bush. An estimated two-thirds of the 1,023 graduating seniors sat down and remained silent as Bush took the stage to give his address and receive an honorary Doctor of Laws degree.

Student leaders said they had staged the demonstration as a subtle protest against Bush's civil rights policies. (The Bush administration was opposed to a civil rights job-discrimination bill proposed by congressional Democrats.)

Bush made little mention of civil rights in his address. He expressed his support for a free-trade pact with Mexico, educational reform and a housing program that would enable public-housing residents to buy their homes.

Minneapolis Star and Tribune
Minneapolis, Minnesota, May 12, 1991

Shortly before President Bush's heart went aflutter May 4, he gave a speech at the University of Michigan in which he took after the phenomenon of "politically correct" speech that is being felt on college campuses. It was an easy target — too easy.

Much of what Bush said was on the mark, as when he observed that although the political correctness movement "arises from the laudable desire to sweep away the debris of racism, sexism and hatred, it replaces old prejudices with new ones. It declares certain topics off-limits, certain expressions off-limits, even certain gestures off-limits. What began as a cause for civility has soured into a cause of conflict and even censorship."

"Political correctness" is a label — intended as derogatory — that loosely applies to a number of influences affecting life and learning on college campuses. Those influences range from efforts to leaven traditional emphasis on Western civilization with information on African and Asian culture and thought, to rules imposed by college administrations that prohibit faculty and students from expressing sexism, racism or other hateful ideologies — on pain of censure or expulsion.

Bush argued properly that free speech can't be subordinated to civility. People have the right to be boors, and on college campuses they should have the right to examine all ideas and expound all philosophies. It is especially dangerous that requirements for political correctness are being imposed from above — by faculty councils, deans and college presidents.

But there is more to this issue than a clean and easy call for free speech and against enforced civility. As with the civil and women's rights movements, critics who focus only on overzealous behavior and extremist statements risk missing the intellectual substance that undergirds the movement. Both the civil rights movement and feminism have been powerfully beneficial forces in American culture — because people were able to get past the discomfort and dissonance they initially felt from these new ways of viewing the world.

The same can be true of the political correctness movement. Its advocates seek to change American consciousness of the world and those who live in it. They are unfortunately being judged by the consciousness they seek to change. They are labeled fascistic, silly, overbearing and self-righteous. Some of them are all of those things and less. But so were some feminists and some of this nation's most prominent civil-rights advocates.

Critics decry the political correctness movement's efforts to impose orthodoxies of thought, speech and behavior. The implication is that no such orthodoxies now exist. But they certainly do exist, and many are narrow and intolerant. Advocates of political correctness need to learn from other Americans that new orthodoxies can't be imposed. Other Americans need to learn from advocates of political correctness that old orthodoxies need to be challenged.

The Hutchinson News
Hutchinson, Kansas, May 11, 1991

President Bush has hit the nail on the head in questioning the growing intolerance that threatens the free expression of Americans.

Speaking at the University of Michigan, Bush told graduating students that American society is becoming less tolerant of dissent and free speech for those citizens who voice unpopular views.

While he did not present any examples, surely the recent Persian Gulf war is a case in point. Citizens could not voice their opposition to the war in their own neighborhoods. Reports indicated that dissenting views were subdued for fear of repercussions from war supporters.

The dissenters, mind you, were no less American, no less patriotic. They were merely made to feel less so because supporting the war became the litmus test in grading one's love of country. These are, of course, dangerous waters for a nation to sail, especially a nation that celebrates diversity of opinion and open debate.

The president called for reason and tolerance, good advice for these awkward times.

Attacks on free speech and free expression are staining the Bill of Rights. When Sen. Bob Dole once criticized Israel, he was labeled anti-Jewish, an ugly and indecent charge that was hurled without a shred of truth.

The true test of America is the strength of the embrace in which liberty is held. The president was reminding all Americans to give freedom of expression a wide berth, especially on college campuses, where diversity of opinion ought to be ambitiously and enthusiastically explored, not silenced under the dead weight of intolerance.

The president's speech was a triumph of moral leadership. He portrayed a captain guiding his ship away from the awkward shoals of narrow-mindedness and back out into the open seas of free expression.

The Salt Lake Tribune
Salt Lake City, Utah, May 9, 1991

American college campuses are awash in a debate over how academia can best rid itself of racism, sexism and various other isms. Unfortunately, most of the treatments developed for these diseases create complicating side effects.

For example, some universities have adopted codes of conduct that ban "hate speech" — usually racial, ethnic, religious or sexual epithets. The intent is laudable. Civility and mutual respect are essential to reasoned dialogue, if not to society itself, and it's hard to defend ugly slurs against people as worthwhile expressions of thought.

Yet any censorship curbs free expression, and such limits run contrary to the unbridled intellectual inquiry that is the heart of the academy. Critics worry that in an effort to avoid offending anyone, such policies may foster a system in which only "politically correct" opinions are allowed.

Language can be extremely tricky. "Indian" offends some people when it is used as a general term to mean members of aboriginal American tribes, but "Native American" isn't accurate or universally accepted either. A sociology professor at Yale was forced to stop teaching a course because he favored the term "Indian." In his defense, the teacher cited his own studies indicating there is no consensus within the minority community as to whether the word is offensive.

"Multicultural" courses have been designed to serve as an alternative and antedote to a Western European intellectual tradition dominated by white males and their culture's racial and gender biases. These courses often focus on Asian and African cultures and intellectual traditions or women writers.

These classes filled needs that the traditional curriculum overlooked, sometimes out of cultural blindness. Ironically though, these multicultural studies often develop political orthodoxies and limited perspectives of their own.

Further, a student who delves into these fields at the expense of neglecting the Western intellectual tradition can't hope to understand the culture that is ascendant in the world today.

President Bush entered the debate the other day, calling for tolerance of divergent points of view and criticizing those who would censor speech not deemed "politically correct."

The president has got at least part of the equation right. College campuses must be open to all ideas, no matter how repugnant some people might find them.

Every thought must be subject to intellectual challenge, appeals to logic and the weighing of evidence. That's the core of education. It's not an exercise for the thin-skinned or the overly sensitive.

At the same time, however, while ideas must be open to attack, people shouldn't be. Honest argument presupposes respect. Personal assaults, either literal or verbal, must be out of bounds. Civil discourse must be the rule.

If today's college communities can't balance these rudimentary notions, higher education has failed its most basic task. Worse, it will have abdicated a responsibility it fulfills far better than politicians and government officials — defining, preserving and fostering the principles of free speech openly, vigorously and fearlessly practiced.

St. Petersburg Times
St. Petersburg, Florida, May 9, 1991

By wading into the "political correctness" controversy, President Bush has done the correct thing from his political perspective.

Adding his voice to those alleging that various campus minorities are conspiring to stifle free speech and the perpetuation of Western civilization might seem a little simplistic, but it's good for some conservative votes.

Coming from someone with better credentials in race relations and civil rights, Mr. Bush's warning might have more value. Some zealots on all sides are indeed trying to play thought police, but concern for the free flow of ideas never seemed to trouble a president who thinks it's perfectly okay to rewrite the Bill of Rights to outlaw flag burning. His real intention was to toss a wink and nod in the direction of the latest conservative code words for scapegoat politics.

What's really galling is that the president honestly sees no indictment of himself or his predecessor in the fact that Americans are at each other's throats. The truth is we might not be having this political correctness debate if leaders had the courage to tackle festering social issues and set a tone of healing for the nation instead of campaigning against welfare queens and Willie Horton. Despite dire warnings of growing racial polarization, thus far the 1992 campaign is shaping up as one over the non-issues of racial quotas and political correctness.

On the same front page that reported the president's speech, the *New York Times* carried the story of a Chicago high school whose black and white students are so divided they've returned to separate senior proms. To hear the students talk about the pain of the situation is to be haunted by the realization that a whole generation has grown up talking past each other on the subject of race and culture. Who's to blame? We adults are, for deliberately ignoring the problem; now we're reaping the bitter harvest in division that could yet erupt into ugly violence. The winner of such a clash will be the international economic competitors who'll leave us squabbling in their dust.

Ironically, history could well come to see political correctness as George Bush's greatest skill. It certainly won't be his abysmal record in bringing Americans together. Though he speaks "correctly" enough on that topic, his deeds — such as engineering the political blackmailing of businesses away from negotiations with civil rights groups — increasingly belie his shallow grasp of the complexities involved.

The Augusta Chronicle

Augusta, Georgia, May 7, 1991

The hoopla surrounding President Bush's minor heart problem overshadowed a significant weekend speech he made at University of Michigan commencement ceremonies assailing the notion of "political correctness" on college campuses.

The "PC" movement, as it has come to be called, replaces education with political indoctrination. Like an old-style Maoist campus in Communist China, those who go astray of political orthodoxy must either confess their sins and submit to "re-education" or be punished via suspension or dismissal.

In addition to assaulting free thought and speech, PC, as the president pointed out, also tries to micro-manage people's personal behavior — a sure prescription for tyranny.

What gave rise to PC was a desire to rid the campuses of stereotypical thinking regarding race, women and homosexuals — but what has resulted is a new type of stereotypical thinking that says if you're black, female or sexually perverse you can't be criticized because you can do no wrong.

Concomitant with this is an attack on Western civilization, culture and ideas as being nothing more than the product of the bigotry and oppression of "dead white males." So much for Shakespeare.

Unfortunately, this is typical at many of the nation's most prestigious universities. For instance, Dartmouth College President James Freedman is threatening and harassing a conservative student journal opposing "political correctness." And Duke University Professor Stanley Fish even sent a letter to the provost demanding that faculty members not "politically correct" be barred from participating on key committees regarding curriculum, faculty hiring and tenure.

President Bush's call for an end to such intimidation and a return to reasoned campus discourse should encourage spineless college administrators, who ought to be standing up for freedom of speech, to develop some backbone. Indeed, we are pleased to note that two prominent presidents of Ivy League schools, Benno Schmidt of Yale and Derek Bok of Harvard, are singing the Bush tune.

Rockford Register Star

Rockford, Illinois, May 7, 1991

While wishing President Bush a complete recovery from the irregular heartbeat he suffered over this past weekend, we praise here the spirit of remarks he made in a commencement address at the University of Michigan just hours before he was hospitalized with his illness.

The president devoted much of his speech in Ann Arbor to a well-warranted condemnation of "the notion of political correctness" currently in vogue on so many American college campuses.

The reference was to the wave of intolerance reflected in campus speech codes calculated to protect women and minorities from any speech or other forms of expression that might give offense on the basis of race, religion, gender or sexual orientation.

"Although the movement arises from the laudable desire to sweep away the debris of racism and hatred," said Bush, "it replaces old prejudices with new ones. It declares certain topics off-limits, certain expression off-limits, even certain gestures off-limits. What began as a cause for civility has soured into a cause of conflict and even censorship."

The president's admonition is a welcome one. It helps draw national attention to the growing problem of enforced political correctness in the same halls of academe where the spirit of unfettered inquiry and uninhibited expression are supposed to reign supreme.

Moreover, it is always good to hear a conservative Republican eschew censorship. Would that all the self-appointed guardians of decency and morality among the president's political kin heed his words.

Censorship from the political left (generally the kind President Bush criticized) and from the political right (generally the kind that would bowdlerize popular culture) have in common a moral smugness that would smother freedom in the interest of a narrow view of the overall good. Either variety should be steadfastly resisted.

We hope the president's new defense of free expression signals his abandonment of such illiberal schemes as a constitutional amendment to protect the American flag from desecration.

Or does he still harbor his own notions of mandatory political correctness?

The TENNESSEAN

Nashville, Tennessee, May 9, 1991

PRESIDENT Bush's recent defense of free speech was refreshing, particularly in light of his administration's record on the First Amendment.

In giving the commencement address at the University of Michigan last Saturday, Bush said that the right of free speech was "under assault throughout the United States, including on some college campuses." He pointed out that the movement toward "political correctness" has led to some sweeping college rules that declare "certain topics off-limits, certain expression off-limits, even certain gestures off-limits."

The President is right. Some universities have initiated speech codes that prohibit students from making racist, sexist, or ethnic slurs or comments intended to hurt another person or incite problems.

This spring, the Tennessee Board of Regents passed a regulation saying that universities in the system could adopt rules barring "hate speech." That decision — well intentioned though it was — takes Tennessee in exactly the wrong direction.

Of course, racist, sexist and ethnic epithets are disgusting. So is a lot of language. But the First Amendment doesn't protect just polite speech, or nonpolitical speech, or speech that is acceptable to the majority of people. It protects all speech.

It is particularly disturbing to see universities resorting to censorship when they have so many avenues to demonstrate an appreciation for diversity and tolerance.

Bush's choice of topics for the commencement address was most appropriate. His words reflected great wisdom. But he should remember that the freedoms guaranteed in the First Amendment aren't confined only to college campuses or only to verbal speech.

The same right of free expression that he praised in Ann Arbor is the right that protects the symbolic act of burning a flag to protest the government — and Bush personally campaigned for a constitutional amendment that would have eliminated that right.

The First Amendment also says "Congress shall make no law respecting an establishment of religion." The late Justice Hugo Black said the amendment erected a wall between church and state that "must be kept high and impregnable." But the Bush administration is now pushing for some kind of school choice plan that would put public dollars into private schools — including parochial schools that teach the Ten Commandments right beside the multiplication tables.

Bush is dead right about the dangers of speech codes on campuses. But ignoring any phrase, or skirting any freedom guaranteed in the First Amendment is just as dangerous. ■

ST. LOUIS POST-DISPATCH

St. Louis, Missouri, May 13, 1991

President Bush's defense of free speech, and his criticism of the notion of political correctness, should be required reading for all campus officials and government policy-makers — including those in his own administration. Mr. Bush's rhetoric is at odds with several of the stands taken during his own term, but his concept is sound: Free speech is under assault, and its importance as the most basic of American rights must not be jeopardized.

At the University of Michigan last weekend, Mr. Bush said that "the notion of 'political correctness' has ignited controversy across the land." Too often, on too many campuses and in too many cities and towns, people are persecuted and punished not because of what they do but because of who they are, what they think and how they express their ideas. Voicing certain ideas has become unpopular; criticizing certain groups has become forbidden. "What began as a cause for civility," Mr. Bush said, "has soured into a cause of conflict and even censorship."

Such words sound strange from a president who sought a constitutional ban on burning an American flag. That *cause celebre* may have been the quintessential case of defending unpopular sentiment: Those who chose traditional American values over the symbolic worth of a piece of cloth were painted as unpatriotic and worse by those who wanted to make free expression unconstitutional.

Increasing cultural diversity has caused widespread frustration on campus, both for members of minority groups and white male students who feel somehow threatened. Vietnam-era protesters who now are tenured faculty members too often feel their views are the only ones that should be heard, and that any sentiments critical of minority groups or cherished causes should be suppressed. But the true test of freedom of expression is tolerating dissent, from either side of the political spectrum.

"We must conquer the temptation to assign bad motives to people who disagree with us," Mr. Bush said. And Americans must be allowed to air those disagreements as widely as possible. Listening to those whose thoughts are disagreeable is a way to learn; and after all, that's what the campus is for.

The Washington Times

Washington, D.C., May 7, 1991

When the Sunday edition of the New York Times reported on Page One President Bush's Saturday speech at the University of Michigan denouncing "political correctness," it also reported on the same page that at Chicago's Brother Rice High School, black students are holding their own senior prom separate from that of the white students. The two stories are closely related. Under the slogan of fighting "racism" by means of "speech codes" and other Politically Correct devices, racism is actually flourishing. The no-whites-allowed prom in Chicago plays the same tune as some students at Virginia's historically black Hampton University. The president is expected to speak there next week, and one Hampton student whines, "Now we're going to have a white man at the podium telling us what to do."

Mr. Bush was correct — politically or not — to say what he did, and he will be correct again if he says it at Hampton next week and keeps on saying it until it sinks in. Indeed, the president was perhaps more conciliatory than he needed to be. Mr. Bush's main concern is that Political Correctness jeopardizes freedom of expression, but he also acknowledged that while "the movement arises from the laudable desire to sweep away the debris of racism and sexism and hatred, it replaces old prejudice with new ones." The president's rhetorical concession was probably necessary, but it may not be entirely true.

The genesis of speech codes, sensitivity codes and the other paraphernalia of PC for the most part did not originate with blacks or other groups that have legitimate historical grievances. Political Correctness seems to have bubbled up from the dyspeptic veterans of the New Left, many of whom are now empowered on faculties and in university administrations all over the country. PC is a more subtle but no less dangerous version of what New Left striplings in the 1960s tried to belch out on campuses by trashing buildings, disrupting classes and beating up professors, deans and students who disagreed with their line. Now that they've grown up to be college professors and deans themselves, they've decided to beat up the whole concept of academic freedom in the name of exorcising what they purport to be the demons of racial and sexual bigotry.

But the truth is that they seldom find any demons in any recognizable forms. The list of horribles that have resulted from speech codes is endless. At Michigan itself, one student made the mistake of asking a professor for proof of her assertion that lesbians make the best parents. She demanded of him, "Why are you challenging me?" At the next class he found himself barred from entering by campus police. Michigan's grotesque code was struck down by the Supreme Court as unconstitutional, but other schools have not been so lucky.

At the University of California at Los Angeles, a student editor was suspended for satirizing affirmative action — technically, for publishing "articles that perpetuate derogatory or cultural stereotypes." At Vassar, the student association dropped funding of its newspaper after the paper criticized a black who had brayed anti-semitic venom. At other schools, speakers of whom the local thought police don't approve have been banned. Smith College's student handbook warns against "lookism" and "ableism." Another college forbids "inappropriate laughter." Back during Mao Tse-tung's "cultural revolution," the Red Guards used to break the fingers of musicians who played Western music. The Red Guards on American campuses today haven't gone that far yet, but they're flexing the same ideological muscles.

What is largely missing from the annals of PC is any evidence that it has really exposed or prevented any real racism. American universities are not now and probably never have been institutions where Ku Kluxers and brownshirts congregate. The claim of PC is that universities (and American society in general) are permeated with "institutional racism," a persistently vague charge that covers just about any form of conduct, speech, glance or gesture that the Red Guards don't like. What often ensues from the obsession with "institutional racism" (or "sexism") is the further charge that whites and males are inherently racist and sexist and that blacks (women, homosexuals) are "better," more "liberated" and less encumbered with the pathologies of "white male hegemony." Hence, the racially segregated proms, the stupid claim that lesbians make the best parents, the contrived resentment at "a white man . . . telling us what to do." PC doesn't root out racism; it breeds it. As Mr. Bush said, "It replaces old prejudice with new ones."

That the PC cult endangers freedom of expression is clear, but it endangers other valuable things as well. It tries to subordinate spontaneous human thought, curiosity and emotions to preposterous legal codes enforced by campus bureaucrats. It gives power to ideologues and malcontents who use it to hammer down anyone in their way. It delivers the university itself into the hands of self-appointed minority "spokespersons" who proceed to transform institutions of learning into Trojan horses from which they can spring upon the rest of society, challenging its fundamental institutions and beliefs and carrying it off into ideological slavery. Mr. Bush is right to speak out against the insane subversion that Political Correctness represents, and the nation's colleges need to hear his speech again and again.

Multicultural Education Debated Across U.S.

New York State Education Commissioner Thomas Sobol June 20, 1991 received a report prepared by a panel of educators on the teaching of history and social studies in the state's schools. The panel recommended a "multicultural" approach that "reflects the rich cultural diversity of the nation."

The report, titled "One Nation, Many Peoples: A Declaration of Cultural Interdependence," was expected to be controversial. It argued that students should be taught U.S. history from a variety of perspectives, but acknowledged that it would be impossible to fully take into account the contribution of every national, ethnic, religious and cultural group. Instead, the panel concluded, emphasis should be shifted "from the mastery of information to the development of fundamental tools, concepts and intellectual processes that make people learners who can approach knowledge in a variety of ways and struggle with the contradictions."

Three of the 24 panel members – Arthur M. Schlesinger Jr. of the City University of New York, Kenneth T. Jackson of Columbia University and Paul Gagnon of the University of Massachusetts – issued dissents to the report. Jackson complained that the report did not have enough to say "about the things which hold us together." Referring to the official U.S. motto "E pluribus unum" (Latin for "from many, one"), he argued that in the report, "The emphasis is too much on the pluribus and not enough on the unum."

Sobol June 20 said he planned to use the report as the basis for proposed revisions to the state's history and social studies curriculum. He refused to offer specifics, however, on which aspects of the report he would accept and which he would reject.

In a related development, City College of New York professor Leonard Jeffries Jr., chairman of the school's African-American Studies department, touched off a storm of controversy at a conference in Albany, N.Y. July 20, 1991. In his address to the Empire State Black Arts and Cultural Festival Jeffries charged that Jewish and Italian executives in the entertainment industry had conspired to destroy black American culture by producing films in which "black people were totally denigrated." Jeffries declared that there was "a conspiracy, planned and plotted and programed out of Hollywood by people named Greenberg and Weisberg and Trigliani." He added, "Russian Jewry had a particular control over the movies, and their financial partners, the Mafia, put together a financial system of destruction of black people."

THE WALL STREET JOURNAL

New York City, New York, January 3, 1992

For more than a year now Americans have received a higher education in the pathology known as Political Correctness. Books and press accounts gave tutorials on how PCness taints citadels of free thought with political indoctrination masquerading as education.

This exposure has had results. A few victories in battle do not necessarily signal the end of a war, but the news from the PC front includes several sightings of creeping sanity.

There's even good news from Stanford "Hey, hey, ho, ho, Western Civ's got to go" University. The PC crowd there tried to make it harder to defend claims of rape on campus by lowering the standard of proof for conviction under campus disciplinary codes for all crimes. The Sexual Assault Task Force proferred a high-minded reason for their assault on innocent until proven guilty—that weakening the burden of proof would encourage women to press charges of rape and harassment. The proposal was defeated after opposition by stu-

dent leaders from all sides of the political spectrum.

At Wichita State University, faculty members recently voted down a proposal that students must take courses in race, gender and ethnicity. The leader of the faculty faction fighting this requirement reminded his colleagues that the issue was academic freedom. One dissenting professor declared the vote only proved that there were "a closet full of David Dukes" on the WSU faculty. The faculty at the University of Washington also recently defeated a plan to require such PC sensitivity courses.

The faculty at Drake University in Des Moines approved guidelines affirming principles of academic freedom. These included a statement opposing any university regulation that would prohibit any form of speech or communication in the classroom, however offensive. The faculty also refused to single out sexual, racial or religious harassment as crimes for especially heavy punishment.

On a related front, PCers might wish they had never defeated the nomination of Carol Iannone to the National Humanities Council. Joel Conarroe of the Guggenheim Foundation and the leaders of the Modern Language Association last summer managed to block the Senate confirmation of this conservative scholar because she didn't share their race-and gender-obsessed views of literature. Lynne Cheney, head of National Endowment for the Humanities, has a new nominee, Kenny Jackson Williams, a well-established professor of English at Duke who takes classical literature seriously. She is also highly articulate, a skill she has used to register her distaste with the faddish orthodoxy's emphasis on race and ethnic studies. Prof. Williams is black.

There is also some bad news. At the University of Wisconsin-Milwaukee, conservative radio personality Mark Belling was invited as a speaker, then attacked by objects hurled by protesters and driven off

The Honolulu Advertiser

Honolulu, Hawaii, January 7, 1992

Should all Hawaii public schools use the same social studies textbooks?

That question came up when Lynne Cheney was here recently talking about "multi-cultural education," one of her greatest challenges as chairwoman of the National Endowment for the Humanities.

Cheney likes a social studies textbook series developed for California. The books are both accurate and fair, she said. They don't try to build the esteem of some groups by being over-critical of others.

Those texts were written to correspond with California's new, statewide social studies curriculum, so it works for all schools to use the same texts.

Hawaii's Department of Education also is revising the social studies curriculum here. But the current procedure — letting Hawaii schools choose their own texts from an approved list — is more in tune with the new era of more school/community-based management.

One irony is that teachers are likely to find most social studies texts inadequate in these times of rapid-fire events and shifting historical perspectives. Or they may be just plain bland.

Publishers compensate by offering student magazines and newspapers that are exciting and more relevant. And since they're paperbacks, they're affordable. The Department of Education encourages teachers to use them.

Under SCBM, it's likely more parents will become involved in making sure the texts their schools buy are objective, appropriate and interesting. That's good.

You can start now. Take a look at your own children's textbooks. Are they clearly written? Would you want to be assigned to read them? Do they reflect the changes in the modern world, and in the way the modern world looks at history?

If you're turned off by the books, your youngsters may be, too.

the stage. The local ACLU leader criticized the assault on free speech, but rationalized the mob's action by saying the students were "justifiably frustrated"—racism and homophobia led them to violate the First Amendment rights of others. At least student newspapers, left and right, denounced the demonstrators.

It's too soon to celebrate a turning of the tide, but not too soon to say that intellectual dignity and conscience are finding their voices here and there on the campuses. We call that good news by any measure.

The New York Times
New York City, New York, July 4, 1991

Listening to all the controversy about multicultural education, the man realized how lucky he had been as an immigrant boy in America. He had his very own Uncle Sam.

Uncle Anselm, a cousin really, was born in this country but for him, foreign forebears were a source of pride. To the boy, Uncle Anselm personified America. He stalked the streets, tall, bald and correct. As a concession to summer, he sported a straw boater but wore a vest even on hot days. Though he seemed gruff, he talked easily of American wonders like scrimshaw, panning for gold and baseball.

Best of all, when the whole family gathered for July 4th, the boy knew Uncle Anselm could be cajoled into sitting down with him at the black upright piano to play from the big Yankee Doodle song book. When they got to "Put a feather in his cap and called it ma-ca-ro-ni," the boy roared in certifiably American delight.

His own Uncle Sam. That was how it felt after lunch, when Uncle Anselm took the boy to his first baseball game. What could be more American: sitting in the bleachers, gripping a heavy brown bottle of Orange Crush and giggling when the organ played "Three Blind Mice" as the umpires came out.

The thoughts came flooding back now, stirred by the angry commotion about "multiculturalism," the demand for respect and recognition from diverse groups once quick to shed their cultural identity. The agitation came to a new boil in recent days with the publication of a report urging that social studies in New York public schools be taught from multiple perspectives.

The outcry was eloquent. Champions of cultural unity rightly appealed for understanding: Common values must transcend racial and ethnic differences. Otherwise, there's no melting pot; indeed, there's no pot at all, only antagonism. Still, there's a danger of overreacting to a sometimes-exaggerated desire for recognition and thus forgetting that for many people from racial and ethnic minorities there's a deeper yearning: to find the mainstream.

•

That was true a half-century ago when the immigration tide swept in refugees from Hitler. It is true now, when the tide carries thousands of Hmong mountain people from Laos to places like Eau Claire, Wis., and when the largest group of new citizens sworn in at New York City's 1991 naturalization ceremony is from Guyana.

Of course minorities do not want to be punished for their background the way Mexican children were in Southwest schools for speaking the only language they knew. Of course immigrants wish to preserve their heritage. Of course blacks want recognition of their long oppression and its effects on the present.

But Hispanic parents know what language their children need to succeed — and press for them to become proficient in English. Korean grocers want Ivy League educations for their children. David Dinkins and Douglas Wilder triumphed as majority, not minority, candidates.

Assimilate is not a dirty word; not a denial of diversity; not a synonym for the arrogant dominion of one culture over others. Neither is *respect* an outrageous demand. The man couldn't help thinking of Uncle Anselm's pride in his American ancestry and his foreign roots. There was no need to choose, then or now, especially not today, as Americans celebrate who they were and who we are.

The Washington Times
Washington, D.C., August 22, 1991

Following a war council at a local high school last week, the tribes of multiculturalism today will unleash their attack on history, science and social studies when the Prince George's County school board sees a draft of a new curriculum. Like the multicultural curricula hunting heads at schools in Portland, Atlanta, Baltimore and the District, this one is supposed to build the "self-esteem" of minority students. In fact, it will do little more than assault them with ideology masquerading as scholarship.

As Carol Innerst of The Washington Times reported last week, the program's origins can be found in the fevered brow of Asa G. Hilliard III, author of the so-called "Baseline Essays." The program was discussed at length at last week's powwow at Eleanor Roosevelt High. The handouts were vague, but Mr. Hilliard's scholarly pursuits pretty much explain what's going on.

Among other heretofore unknown facts, he has discovered that ancient Egyptians were really black; that Africa is the birthplace of mathematics and science because it is the birthplace of the human race; and that the smallpox vaccine was invented in 1721 by a slave named Onesimus from Boston, not by Edward Jenner in 1796.

Teachings such as this will figure prominently in the new Prince George's curriculum. Nor are the Indians to be excluded. One topic students will master is how the Indians lived in harmony with nature, while the pale-faced Europeans wanted "control" and "mastery over" everything.

Other topics will include "Hispanics and the New Deal," "The Edges of Islam: Spain, India and Indonesia," "American Indians Mourn the Loss of Their Land to the White Man" and "Who Discovered America?" The "Guide to Nonsexist Language" turns "statesmanship" into "diplomacy," "maiden voyage" into "premier voyage" and "act like a gentleman" into "be polite." "Lady Luck," "Mother Nature" and "mothering" are out as well.

Not surprisingly, the conference featured whole workshops on Hispanic-, Asian-, African- and Native-American culture, while "European-American Culture" and the "American White-Male Perspective" were relegated to a workshop on "Additional Cultures Represented in the United States."

The point here is obvious, and the esteemed and highly respected Leonard Jeffries, the New York education establishment's premier bigot, has been making it quite clearly: White Christians are the wellspring of suffering and oppression, and nothing good came of Jamestown, the War for Independence, the Alamo, the 49ers, wagon trains, the 7th Calvalry, Kit Carson or anything else central to the American experience. "Ice people," as Mr. Jeffries calls the white folk, are the bitter enemies of people of color everywhere.

Well, here's a little secret: The discovery and settlement of the United States by Europeans was the best thing that ever happened here. That doesn't mean the genuine contributions of other cultures and races ought to be ignored, which in some cases they have been. But it does mean educators should impart the truth, not proselytize a weltanschauung based on myth. If people in Prince George's County care about education, teaching what's true is what they must reaffirm as the goal of its schools.

The Cincinnati Post
Cincinnati, Ohio, June 13, 1991

Forced to support forced busing, the state of Ohio has funneled hundreds of millions of taxpayer dollars into court-ordered desegregation plans that divided communities and drove masses of white families into the suburbs.

Now the Ohio Senate, to its credit, wants to take a different approach. In their version of the state's next biennial budget, senators are proposing to voluntarily spend $5 million a year to increase support for voluntary desegregation in Cincinnati schools over the next two years. A verbal agreement would extend the payments for three additional years.

There's no legal gun to state legislators' heads here. As yet at least, no federal judge is ordering the state to come up with more desegregation money for Cincinnati, which received $35 million in state funds over seven years under the terms of its 1984 settlement agreement with the NAACP.

But there are compelling reasons why the state assistance is justified. According to national desegregation expert Christine Rossell, Cincinnati is the only district in the state where integration continues to improve without significant white flight.

In contrast, as the state was spending $242 million on Cleveland's forced desegregation plan over the last decade, that district's enrollment plummeted by more than 27 percent. Cincinnati enrollment dropped by less than 8 percent over the same period.

Clearly, too, Cincinnati needs the money. Its current financial crisis threatens the future success of its desegregation efforts, which include specialized alternative or "magnet" schools. Extra state desegregation help wouldn't eliminate the district's need for a new local operating levy, but it would reduce the amount needed.

The state has its own budget problems, of course, which makes it especially important that legislators be guided by sound priorities in making spending decisions.

We believe if Gov. George V. Voinovich and lawmakers on the House-Senate conference committee place a high priority on doing what's right to support effective school desegregation, they will approve the Senate proposal in the final budget.

NEH Nominee Iannone Opposed by Congress

The nomination of a conservative literary scholar, Carol Iannone, to the advisory council of the National Endowment for the Humanities had generated a controversy among humanities scholars, the *Washington Post* reported May 10, 1991.

Iannone had been nominated to the post in the fall of 1990, but the nomination had languished in Congress. Such groups as the Modern Language Association and the American Council of Learned Societies were opposed to Iannone's nomination on the grounds that she was not sufficiently distinguished as a scholar.

Iannone supporters, including NEH Chairwoman Lynne V. Cheney, charged that much of the opposition to Iannone was politically motivated. "Perhaps it's because Carol has a very sharp eye for the follies of the left," Cheney said. Cheyney described one attack on Iannone, by Guggenheim Foundation President Joel Conarroe, as "a classic example of political correctness – to oppose someone's ideological position and then make inflammatory and irresponsible charges."

The U.S. Senate Labor and Human Resources Committee July 17 rejected, 9-8, the nomination of Carol Iannone, a literature professor from New York University, to the advisory council of the National Endowment for the Humanities. Iannone's nomination had created a controversy, with many humanities scholars charging that her academic credentials were weak. Supporters claimed that the opposition was politically motivated, because of Iannone's conservative views.

THE ARIZONA REPUBLIC
Phoenix, Arizona, July 29, 1991

THE debate in the U.S. Senate's Labor and Human Resources Committee over the nomination of a New York University professor to a seat on an unpaid National Endowment for the Humanities panel has mercifully ended. It was not a pretty sight.

After months of deliberate delay the committee, chaired by Massachusetts Sen. Edward Kennedy, finally scheduled a vote the other day. Professor Carol Iannone, the senators quickly determined by a party-line vote, was unqualified to serve as one of the 26 part-time members of the panel, which advises the endowment on federal grant proposals.

It was not Professor Iannone's credentials that scuttled her chances. After all, she is the president of the National Association of Scholars, the managing editor of the journal *Academic Questions* and has served as a member of the U.S. Commission on Civil Rights. What troubled Sen. Kennedy and like-minded cohorts was the professor's politics — more specifically, what critics in academe thought of her politics.

Professor Iannone's crime, according to the thought Gestapo, which last fall launched a letter-writing offensive against her, were her attacks on "political correctness." According to the indictments handed up by the radical-left campus set, the professor had the temerity to criticize the merits of so-called "feminist writing" and academic awards handed out to minority authors of works she deemed less than worthy of scholarly recognition.

What is more, instead of confining them within the non-read publications of academe, she aired those views in such popular intellectual journals as *Commentary*. That was enough, in the judgment of the committee's Democrats, to reject Professor Iannone's nomination, which had been pigeon-holed in the Senate for nearly 10 months.

The Senate committee's embarrassing treatment of Professor Iannone has not gone unnoticed. Sen. Daniel Patrick Moynihan took to the Senate floor to declare that his fellow-Democrats' handling of the nomination demonstrated "the further intellectual decline" of the party. "I almost said demise, but will leave bad enough alone," he added.

Professor Iannone, who remained silent during the inquisition out of respect for the Senate's confirmation process, then answered her critics with a thought-provoking article in *The Washington Post.* ". . . The real issue in the uproar over my nomination," she wrote, "is the disappearance of principled discourse from our cultural and intellectual life. Intellectual intimidation and campaigns of vilification and character assassination have replaced rational discussion of opposing views."

She went on to describe her father, a man who "had his fingers broken, twisted and permanently crippled by the fascist police in Mussolini's Italy." One of the great achievements in his life, she notes, was to have become an American. "He always reminded us of what it meant to live in a land where you could speak your mind openly and fearlessly, where all kinds of ideas could be discussed with rigor and honesty. I'm glad that he was not alive to witness this hideous episode; it would have broken his heart in more ways than one, as it has mine."

In his usually eloquent style, Sen. Moynihan said that Professor Iannone could take some comfort in knowing that she "has now been banned in the Democratic Party. What greater fortune could befall an American intellectual in this decadent *fin de siecle*?" There's a lot to be said, he could have added, for not meeting Sen. Kennedy's standards.

THE WALL STREET JOURNAL
New York City, New York, July 19, 1991

Viscount Claiborne Pell was instantly persuaded, but until the last hour it seemed that a majority of the committee would resist the slander campaign. Senator Barbara Mikulski, for example, assured the candidate that in her view the charge that Professor Iannone lacked scholarly credentials was typical academic snobbery; but later Senator Mikulski offered her regrets to Senator Orrin Hatch, explaining that Senator Kennedy had made the defeat of this nominee a personal priority. Similarly, Senators Paul Simon and Christopher Dodd voted against the nominee despite earlier inclinations, leaving Jeff Bingaman of New Mexico as the only Democratic vote to confirm.

Prior to the vote, Senator Kennedy went to some lengths to persuade Professor Iannone and her sponsors that she would be better off without a public hearing on the nomination. Such eagerness to avoid a public hearing should be a clear warning to future nominees, but this time the Senator's persuasions let him do his work in the dark. The public and press lost the opportunity to witness the Kennedy machismo in its full glory, beating up on a 43-year-old woman scholar whose sole offense was to hold politically incorrect opinions.

Senator Edward Kennedy, once expelled from Harvard for having a friend take his Spanish exam, has ruled that literary critic Carol Iannone doesn't have the academic credentials to serve on the National Council on the Humanities. Bowing to the Senator's personal leadership, his Senate committee on Labor and Human Resources turned down her nomination by a 9-8 vote.

If you believe this petty act had anything to do with academic resumes, you probably also believe the Senator made a wrong turn on Chappaquiddick Island. Professor Iannone drew opposition because she shares the political views that have consistently won presidential elections, instead of those considered acceptable in the fever swamps like the Modern Language Association. A conservative literary critic, Professor Iannone ran afoul of the guardians of political orthodoxy by daring to write about the corrupting effects of the current obsession with gender and race. Brigades of the politically correct, led by the Modern Language Association and Guggenheim Foundation Chairman Joel Conarroe, formed up to mount a campaign of vilification against her. "Racist," they screamed.

THE RICHMOND NEWS LEADER
Richmond, Virginia, July 22, 1991

They've done it again.

The Senate Labor and Human Resources Committee has rejected the nomination of Carol Iannone, the 43-year-old New York University scholar, to a post on the National Endowment for the Humanities. The committee claims that she lacked the academic qualifications.

That's the usual line from spiteful Leftists, who gang up on nominees of Republican Presidents with nauseating regularity. They did it in 1982 to the Rev. Sam Hart, President Reagan's nominee to the Civil Rights Commission. They did it to John Tower, and to William Lucas, and to Robert Bork (who ranks among the most intellectually gifted Supreme Court nominees of this century).

Now they've done it to Miss Iannone. They've done it because she dared to challenge the Liberal dogma, saying (for instance) in *Commentary* magazine that certain black authors have received awards less for the content of their works than for the color of their skin.

It's one way, we suppose, of rebelling against those awful voters who insist on returning Republicans to the presidency — a way of venting a small dribble of the seemingly-endless supply of spleen.

It's petty, of course, and — like catching someone with his trousers around his ankles — at once both revealing and embarrassing, not only to the exposed, but to unwilling witnesses as well.

Richmond Times-Dispatch
Richmond, Virginia, July 25, 1991

The Borking of Carol Iannone, whose nomination to the National Endowment for Humanities advisory council has been narrowly rejected by a narrow-minded Senate committee, at least serves one useful purpose: We now know that the left seeks an Orwellian academic dictatorship in which only Newspeak thoughts and words are permitted.

There is little question that Ms. Iannone, a widely published literary critic and an accomplished teacher at New York University's Gallatin Division, was defeated for purely political reasons. Her traditional conservative cultural views and her incisive expression of those views made her too dangerous for liberals to allow her to sit on the NED board. Thus some powerful members of the leftist academic establishment used some of the slimiest political tactics seen in recent years in opposing her nomination.

The always sober-minded Sen. Ted Kennedy and his Committee on Labor and Human Resources could come up with no legitimate reason to reject her nomination, so it counted the number of times she has been cited in footnotes of the professional humanities journals that almost no one actually reads. Ms. Iannone was cited in footnotes of such journals but eight times over the last 10 years. Of course, the pedantic essays in such journals tend to footnote other pedantic essays, and Ms. Iannone has done much of her writing for Commentary and other highly literate and accessible publications.

The Iannone nomination was less about Carol Iannone herself than the fight over freedom of inquiry and freedom of speech. The left has fired a warning shot: Those who fail to conform to politically correct academic codes can look forward to political floggings. This is a serious matter, for if the left wins, the very thing that has made the humanities worthy of study — the free exchange of ideas, inquiry and criticism that collectively are called academic freedom — will be lost.

The left has called the intellectual battle. There can be no neutrals in the war to come.

The Washington Times
Washington, D.C., July 22, 1991

The collapse of the liberal arts in the United States continued apace last week with the Senate Labor and Human Resources Committee's rejection of the nomination of Carol Iannone for a seat on the advisory panel of the National Endowment for the Humanities. Ms. Iannone is an adjunct professor at New York University, where she directs freshmen studies. But what got her into trouble was the literary criticism she has written over the years for such publications as Commentary and the New Criterion. That body of criticism left her exposed on three flanks. One is political, one is literary, the other is scholarly, and the combination is an explosive mixture whose implications extend well beyond Ms. Iannone.

Ms. Iannone has done most of her writing for conservative magazines, and indications are that she is herself conservative. Her sternest judgment on political matters is probably her view that in some cases, the awarding of literary prizes in the United States proceeds on something like a quota system, in which committees select winners not on the basis of literary distinction but on the basis of the race or sex of the author. That view (which is all too correct) has met with cries of racism.

On the literary works she has written about, Ms. Iannone has generally rendered harsh judgments. If you are a devotee of the New York Times Book Review, you have probably come to the conclusion that ours is a literary Golden Age. Novel after novel gets praised to the skies. Ms. Iannone's work has convincingly demonstrated that the praise is in most cases unwarranted. She has also noted that the praise many novels receive comes for extraliterary reasons. The standards of judgment are corrupt, and the source of the corruption is political. Authors are praised for their literary achievements, but in many cases what they have really achieved is not so much literary distinction as the adoption of a political posture that reviewers find congenial. The casualty in the process is art.

Ms. Iannone's work is not scholarly. She contributes to magazines that belong in a different category, namely intellectual periodicals. The premise of such periodicals is that there is a broad, cultured audience for serious discussion of ideas. Scholarly journals, full of jargon and extensive footnotes, are not generally accessible to such an audience. But the academic community, understandably, favors contributions to scholarly journals over contributions to intellectual magazines. So officials of the Modern Language Association were quick to brand Ms. Iannone as unqualified.

All of which takes us to the issue of what the National Endowment for the Humanities is for. No doubt, in the view of its supporters, it should fund scholarship. But they would concede that that is only part of its mission, the other part being to support serious public discussion of topics in the humanities. That is where Ms. Iannone could have made a substantial contribution.

But that was unacceptable to the academic establishment. The universities — which most people used to think of as repositories of great ideas, places to turn to for guidance on what is good art and what is not, home to the debate that links the great minds of the 20th century with those of the 19th and the 18th and so on back to Homer and the Bible — are instead narrow-minded and politicized to the core. That a Senate committee embraced this narrow-mindedness and politicization last week, however depressing, should come as no great surprise. Meanwhile, it is up to Ms. Iannone and people like her to make the case for literature and the liberal arts in general. The universities and their stooges in the U.S. Senate have abdicated.

The Cincinnati Post
Cincinnati, Ohio, July 30, 1991

Politicians and parties define themselves by the battles they deem worth fighting. Sen. Edward Kennedy used his power as chairman of the Labor and Human Resources Committee the other day to defeat a nominee for a part-time, unpaid advisory board, thus showing himself a servant of the PC agenda.

PC, as most people have registered by now, stands for "politically correct" and connotes the peculiar cultural dogma of left-wing academics.

Kennedy organized fellow Democrats to block Carol Iannone's appointment to the board of the National Endowment for the Humanities because she writes from a traditional point of view and has criticized PC sacred cows like radical feminism and affirmative action in the study of literature.

Reflecting on her rejection in The Washington Post, Dr. Iannone recalled her father, a working-class refugee from Mussolini's Italy, who taught his children "what it meant to live in a country where you could speak your mind openly and fearlessly, where all kinds of ideas could be discussed with rigor and honesty."

She was glad, she wrote, that her father was not alive to see what happened to her.

Another apt comment was that of Sen. Daniel Patrick Moynihan, who called Kennedy's performance proof of "the further intellectual decline of the Democratic Party."

Coming from a Democrat, that charge should sting.

Racism in Universities Becomes a Troubling Issue

Four white students at Dartmouth College who had been accused of harassing a black professor were punished March 10, 1988 by the school's disciplinary review board.

The four were all staffers of the *Dartmouth Review*, a politically conservative off-campus newspaper whose members had been involved in a number of racial controversies since the paper's founding in 1980.

Three of the students – John H. Sutter, a senior, Christopher L. Baldwin, a junior, and John W. Quilhot, a sophomore – were found guilty of disorderly conduct, harassment and invasion of privacy. The fourth student, Sean P. Nolan, was found guilty of disorderly conduct.

Sutter, the executive editor of the *Review*, and Baldwin, the editor-in-chief, were suspended from the college in Hanover, N.H. until the fall semester of 1989. Quilhot, the paper's photography editor, was suspended until the fall of 1988, and Nolan, a contributing writer, was placed on probation for one year.

The charges stemmed from a confrontation Feb. 25 between the four students and William S. Cole, a professor of music at the college. The students, who were not members of any of Cole's classes, had approached the professor to get his response to an article in the Feb. 24 issue of the *Dartmouth Review* in which Cole's "American Music in Oral Tradition" class was called "one of Dartmouth's most academically deficient courses."

The meeting quickly escalated into an angry shouting match and shoves were exchanged, witnesses said. One witness asserted that the *Review* students were the aggressors.

The confrontation between the white students and the black professor touched off two weeks of heightened racial tension on the campus and spawned a number of anti-racism rallies there. Only 6.2% of Dartmouth's undergraduates were black. Cole was one of only nine black faculty members on a staff of 310.

The president of Dartmouth College, James O. Freedman, March 28 accused the *Dartmouth Review* of "poisoning the intellectual environment of our campus."

A federal judge in Concord, N.H. dismissed a civil rights suit brought against Dartmouth College by three of the students in response to their suspension, it was reported March 23, 1989. Their suit claimed that Dartmouth had violated their First Amendment rights and had discriminated against them because they were white and conservative.

However, U.S. District Judge Shane Devine ruled that the three students had failed to show that the college's actions were racially motivated. In addition, Devine said that even if the students had been able to prove that Dartmouth had punished them because of their political beliefs, they were still not entitled to sue for racial discrimination.

Three staff members of the *Dartmouth Review* resigned Oct. 1-2, 1990 and criticized the paper for printing an anti-Semitic quotation from Nazi dictator Adolf Hitler on its masthead Sept. 28.

The president of Brown University in Providence, R.I., Vartan Gregorian, Jan. 25, 1991 upheld the expulsion of a student for using racist slurs in violation of a campus anti-harassment speech code. The case, which was reported in the press Feb. 12, was believed to be the first in the U.S. in which a student had been expelled for such a violation.

The student, Douglas Hann, a junior, had allegedly shouted the slurs in a dormitory courtyard on his 21st birthday in October 1990. Student witnesses said Hann had yelled an obscenity and the word "nigger." When a student complained about the noise, Hann then allegedly called the student a "faggot" and a "[expletive] Jew."

Hann was charged with violating campus rules against excessive drinking and also with violating a Brown code of speech adopted in 1989 that defined harassment as "the subjection of another person, group or class of persons to inappropriate, abusive, threatening or demeaning actions based on race, religion, gender, handicap, ethnicity, national origin or sexual orientation."

THE ⬛ SUN
Baltimore, Maryland, March 17, 1991

Do complaints about photos of lynchings, racial brawls and discipline and tracking patterns add up to racism in Anne Arundel County schools? A lot more will be known once the U.S. Department of Education wraps up an investigation prompted by complaints from parents and community groups. They allege that black students are more harshly disciplined, overrepresented in special education and low-level courses and kept out of gifted and talented programs.

Racism is too ugly and divisive a term to be tossed about lightly. Yet a growing body of anecdotal and statistical evidence makes plain the need for a deeper look. The McKenzie report, a study prepared by an outside education consultant last year, found inordinately high numbers of disciplinary actions involving black students, who make up 13.9 percent of the county's student body yet account for 20.7 percent and 18.8 percent of detentions and suspensions, respectively.

Equally troubling are statistics showing that blacks are overrepresented in special education classes — 28.4 percent — and underrepresented in gifted and talented programs — 5.2 percent. Parents also cite racial incidents. Last November, more than 100 students joined in what one administrator called a racially motivated lunchroom fracas and students have complained about graphic photographs of black lynchings on school walls. Perhaps most disturbing, say critics, is a tolerance for such actions on the part of school administrators.

Superintendent Larry L. Lorton is quick to point out that racial incidents don't necessarily suggest a problem. He's right. Taken individually, the complaints cited by parents and community groups may not be cause for undue alarm. Taken together, however, they suggest that Anne Arundel may be suffering from some of the same attitudes that led to similar allegations of unfairness in the early 1970s. That lead to a discipline code.

This is not a time for denials and defensiveness. Dr. Lorton and other officials have an important role to play and should be open to the possibility of problems, *and* solutions. Racial intolerance in Maryland is neither non-existent nor confined to any one jurisdiction. The message that Anne Arundel's public school system is a fair and equitable one should be articulated clearly and decisively from the superintendent's office to the classroom.

THE DAILY OKLAHOMAN
Oklahoma City, Oklahoma, October 10, 1990

A black student at the University of Oklahoma claims racism is "running rampant throughout the campus." That is not true, so the tendency is to reject out of hand his anger. That rejection should not feed unawareness of problems facing many Americans.

Shelby Steele observes that "the trouble between the races is seldom what it appears to be." He says the problem on many campuses is "a politics of difference, a troubling, volatile politics in which each group justifies itself, its sense of worth and its pursuit of power, through difference alone."

In "The Content of Our Character," Steele demonstrates the ways in which "black and white Americans simply have the power to make each other feel shame and guilt." His conclusions disturb advocates of the black power mentality. The "feeling of vulnerability a black may feel" in many settings such as universities, he says, "is not as serious a problem as what he or she does with it." If that sounds vaguely psychological, it's because Steele offers sensitive explorations of the ways people of different races stand apart, too ready to deal with one another as caricatures, not as individuals.

Campuses do not need more multi-cultural centers or ethnic student unions. Nor do they need more visits from the likes of ex-Klansman David Duke or Black Muslim Minister Louis Farrakhan. No. Campuses need reduced dropout rates among all students and uniform, consistently applied educational standards in a setting of civility and decency.

Some have chuckled at OU President Richard Van Horn's modest suggestion for students to "Say hello to minority students" on campus. That's a gesture, but he's on track. Respect. Diversity. Dialogue. These create an environment in which learning can occur. The words describe values which are not black, white, Hispanic, or Asian, but American.

Van Horn's committee on racial harrassment might help, if the objective is to encourage a climate where all students of all backgrounds learn successfully. They deserve that climate, which can emerge when leaders act responsibly, dealing with real problems.

The Des Moines Register
Des Moines, Iowa, February 24, 1990

Racial slurs often go unchallenged because no one has the courage, or cares, to complain. So it's news when someone prominent isn't willing to put up with such bigotry. Like Rudy Washington, the Drake University men's basketball coach, who recently told Register reporter Ron Maly that he heard the word "nigger" more than once from fans during Drake's loss Jan. 30 to Indiana State in Terre Haute. Washington, who is black, also said he heard fans direct racial slurs at him during other games.

The coach's remarks received a measured response in some quarters. Missouri Valley Commissioner Doug Elgin has said he was disappointed that Washington complained to a newspaper instead of to the conference office, which oversees the athletic competition of Drake and those schools. Others will wonder why Washington made such a big deal over the remarks of a few louts. Or they'll question whether the racist comments really were made, hinting that the coach is trumping up char-

ges because of the Bulldogs' lousy season, Washington's first as head coach of the team.

Anyone who doubts such slurs were made isn't living in the real world. They surface commonly in all too many private conversations and sometimes in very public places. Take, for example, an offhand remark by Marine Brig. General Richard Neal last week at a daily news briefing on gulf war activities, as reported by the Associated Press.

About the rescue of a downed airman in Iraqi-held territory, Neal reportedly said that Air Force helicopters made a dash into "Indian country," and lifted the airman out of the desert. Neal inadvertently made American Indians out to be the enemy by comparing them to Iraqis.

Insensitivity is part of the problem, sometimes combined with ignorance or malice. Part of the cure is for more people — and not just those who are the targets of racial slurs — to make clear their abhorrence of such remarks.

The Grand Rapids Press
Grand Rapids, Michigan, August 21, 1991

Those who wrongly opposed Jeffery Grotsky's appointment in July as superintendent of Grand Rapids' schools in favor of a black candidate had some good points. Among them, the Board of Education must work harder to hire minority teachers.

This issue goes beyond fairness in giving minorities a chance at important jobs in the community. Almost half of the district's 26,500 students are black or Hispanic, while just 312 teachers, or 18 percent, are minorities. Many of the minority children are poor and from single-parent families. They need role models as well as teachers.

Unfortunately, things won't get better without some dramatic changes. The percentage of minority teachers has remained the same for the last 20 years and threatens to get worse as a significant number of minority teachers, hired in the '60s and '70s, near retirement age. Making the problem worse, there aren't many minorities going into education. In 1988, only 9 percent of students in college education programs were black or Hispanic.

Given those problems, the Board of Education has its work cut out. One hopeful sign was a minority hiring plan adopted earlier this month by the board. The new measures include strengthening ties between the school district and colleges with high minority enrollments, as well as adopting procedures that will allow administrators to make firmer job offers to all teachers, including minorities. That's a crucial step, because so many school districts are competing for so few minorities. The black and Hispanic teachers will wind up at districts where their jobs are safe.

Efforts to bring black, Hispanic and other ethnic minority teachers to this community have not faltered out of a lack of awareness over the problem. The board has adopted some minority recruitment programs which have been marginally successful. One program — the Urban Teacher Preparation Project — was started last year to help teacher aides and other school system employees become certified teachers. Open to all, but focusing on minorities, the project currently has 41 students enrolled.

Another program is the newly formed group of local minority teachers called Third World Teachers. By serving as a support group and forum for their concerns, these teachers will be able to address issues, develop ideas and possibly work with those teachers who have shown an interest in coming to Grand Rapids.

There remains, however, a gaping hole in the district's commitment toward recruiting minority teachers. The district spends little time and money actively recruiting teachers, preferring instead a word-of-mouth effort.

And rather than sending recruiters to colleges with high minority enrollments, Grand Rapids sends applications. That approach might save the district money, but it's unlikely to lure many qualified black or Hispanic teachers to the city. Would a student who has been visited at his college job fair by humans from all around the country give serious attention to schools like Grand Rapids that send pamphlets instead?

The Board of Education also can create an aggressive program to contact minority teachers laid off by other districts. This would involve travel and expense, so the board must make allowances.

Something worth looking at is a dual seniority system, which is in place in Milwaukee where Mr. Grotsky came from. Under that system, minority teachers accrue seniority faster than other teachers. To some, such measures might seem unfair. But bringing equity to a system requires unusual, creative efforts. Such an effort also would require approval from the the Grand Rapids Education Association.

A minority hiring plan is nice, but it's a paper tiger. If the Board of Education really wants to improve on a dismal 20-year performance of attracting minority teachers, the next 20 years will require an all-out effort — and money.

THE ANN ARBOR NEWS
Ann Arbor, Michigan, January 14, 1991

Americans still have a long way to go in race relations. An opinion sampling by the General Social Survey of the National Opinion Research Center found that most whites cling to harmful racial stereotyping. At the same time, support among them for racial equality is gaining ground.

This seeming contradiction may be explained by the fact that stereotypes, racial or otherwise, die very hard. Many white Americans articulate a belief system that embraces equal rights and fair treatment for African Americans and Hispanics, but privately these whites still are shaped by negative imagery.

One definition of racism is a lack of awareness of what an ethnic group is about. Education succeeds in breaking down race stereotyping. Holding on to racist views is really ignorance on display.

It is not encouraging that well past its 200th birthday, America is still trying to come to grips with the passions that fuel race hatred. For all the barriers that have fallen in public accommodations and in laws that perpetuated discrimination, America still has promises to keep on the constitutional principle of equity among its citizens.

As always, we must begin with ourselves and look within our own hearts. We must do a mental inventory of how we define ourselves and others in the world in which we live.

FORT WORTH STAR-TELEGRAM
Fort Worth, Texas, March 16, 1991

Some things no one should be expected to grin and bear.

The racial slurs, harassment and actual physical abuse to which some African-American students at Bedford Junior High School say they have been subjected falls into that category of the intolerable.

There is no free-speech issue involved here. If the allegations made in the complaint filed by the students with the NAACP are true, something bordering on abridgement of those students' civil rights is occurring and school officials are not fulfilling their responsibility to protect them from such abuse.

The girls who brought the complaints say they have been kicked and spat upon and that a group of boys routinely directs racial slurs at them in classes and harasses them in the hallways.

They say complaints to the principal have not remedied the situation, and that teachers have told them to smile and endure the taunts as a part of growing up.

No one should have to endure such abuse. And it does a disservice also to the abusers who could grow up believing they can get away with such egregious behavior.

The principal of that school has a moral and legal responsibility to put a stop to this discipline problem, and the elected officials of the H-E-B school district must make certain this happens.

"OF COURSE, WE'LL HAVE TO DO AN EXHAUSTIVE STUDY OF CREDIT HISTORIES, APPLICANT QUALITY, DEBT SITUATIONS, WORK EXPERIENCE AND ASSET LEVELS BEFORE WE KNOW WHAT'S BEHIND THIS."

The Atlanta Journal
AND
THE ATLANTA CONSTITUTION
Atlanta, Georgia, February 26, 1991

Just how segregated can a desegregated school system be?

That's one way of posing the question the U.S. Supreme Court may answer in taking on DeKalb County's 22-year-old school desegregation suit. The court's decision could affect school districts across the country and determine the quality of education offered to millions of children.

The case that DeKalb has made thus far could be made by many school systems under court-ordered desegregation plans. DeKalb says it has made considerable progress toward eliminating segregation of its schools.

Separation of the races is no longer required by law; there are, in fact, programs in place that encourage students of one race to attend schools where the students of another race predominate. The crucial question of funding that favors majority white schools over majority black schools is being addressed.

Some vestiges of segregation that remain have causes that are beyond the school board's control, primarily housing patterns. The more drastic desegregation remedies being offered — such as mandatory busing of students — are likely to result in the long run in more segregation, not less, or so their opponents contend.

The counter-case made by the DeKalb plaintiffs also could be offered in many school districts.

While the system has moved toward desegregation, there remain schools that are clearly identifiable as black or white: about half of the system's black students attend schools that are 90 percent or more black; about a quarter of white students attend schools that are 90 percent or more white. The history of segregation has placed a stigma on black schools that has not been erased.

While school officials may claim that segregated housing patterns are beyond their control, they ignore the historical role school segregation played in forging those patterns, and the role that school desegregation can play in breaking it. Finally, other school districts have shown that aggressive desegregation plans, including the use of busing, do not necessarily cause further segregation.

In last year's split decision on an Oklahoma City case, the Supreme Court showed its willingness to give school systems a way out of court-ordered desegregation plans, even if the end result includes some racially identifiable schools.

The DeKalb County case gives the justices an opportunity to state clearly what is required to earn that way out. In doing so, the court should keep in mind the goal of its landmark Brown v. Board of Education decision: not simply the elimination of segregation laws but the offering of the equal chance at a quality education that generations of black children had been systematically denied.

THE BLADE
Toledo, Ohio, October 28, 1991

A LARGE dose of common sense and an understanding of the nature of life in America a half-century ago ought to accompany the disclosure that President Harry Truman in his time spewed out more than a few racist epithets.

William Leuchtenburg, a University of North Carolina professor and a noted historian, has reported that the 33rd president expressed strong racist sentiments before, during, and after his tenure in the White House.

Alarm bells will doubtless go off in the minds of people who cannot countenance any kind of derogatory racial comments. And, in this day and age of sensitivity toward the feelings of all Americans, Truman surely could not have gotten away with it — surely not in public and certainly not in private, either.

But before Truman is discredited in some people's minds as just another bigot and his achievements on behalf of civil rights downgraded, it's important to consider the times in which Truman moved.

Truman was known for spicy candor — a willingness to say whatever was on his mind, even if it were profane. And if the man used racial epithets, so did just about everyone during the unenlightened 1930s and 1940s, when virulent racism existed on just about every level of American life and certainly in every corner of the nation.

Today, using an epithet to describe a black man or woman in most circles would not be condoned. Forty years ago it was a conversational gambit that was taken for granted — just as racial discrimination was an accepted part of American life, with few if any questions asked.

Truman's tenure in the White House helped to promote racial progress, though not in any radical ways. He supported a committee's call for anti-lynching and anti-poll tax legislation. The President ordered desegregation of the armed forces and became the first president to campaign in Harlem, which earned him the wrath of southern Democrats.

He continues to deserve credit for his achievements in that direction and should not be discredited simply because the foul language that he used reflected the tenor of the times — as reprehensible as American racial attitudes were more than a generation ago.

The Star-Ledger

Newark, New Jersey, March 11, 1988

One would hope that the time would arrive when racism would no longer be a blight on American society. Racial prejudice, whether open or subtle, has no part in the American tradition. The civil rights battles of the 1950s and 1960s, and the legislation that evolved from them, were designed to put this social specter to rest.

But racism keeps erupting, sometimes where least expected. It is no respecter of any places or institutions in our society. Racial incidents occur from time to time in the nation's highest places as well as on the streets, in the marketplace, the workplace and the back alleys.

If there is one place in America where racism seems most inappropriate and shocking, it is on the campuses of the nation's colleges and universities. Racism and higher education are incompatible. The mind and the spirit are totally opposed to everything racism stands for.

But even here, racism can still be found. A recent Star-Ledger survey showed that racism is back on campus, both at New Jersey institutions of higher education and across the nation.

While some authorities have labeled this latest wave of racial incidents a subtler form of discrimination than the more overt incidents of the past, racism is not a subtle thing. It is offensive by its very nature.

The racial incidents that appeared on campuses recently took various forms—from simple insensitivity in conversation that gets out of hand and provokes protest, to graffiti, to offensive published comments in college newspapers, to fist fights to club-wielding violence. The causes of such incidents have left authorities puzzled and disturbed.

Some believe that racism never really left the campus. But the incidents do seem more numerous than before—so much so that authorities are apt to place racism high on the list of social problems on campus, along with drug use.

The college and university administrators in New Jersey have acted in a responsible manner in trying to put a stop to this latest round of racism. They do more than issue strong statements. There are real efforts to increase the number of minority students and to hire more minority group members at both the faculty and administrative level.

It may be that racism will never be completely stamped out, but it must be put down firmly wherever it occurs. The latest round of incidents is distressing, but it does make clear anew the need for constant vigilance. The remedies for racism are tolerance and intelligence—and these are the qualities that a university education is intended to nurture.

The Union Leader

Manchester, New Hampshire, March 10, 1988

Scott Evans, student assembly president and a graduating senior at Dartmouth College, seems to know more about the true purpose of education and whether Dartmouth fulfills that purpose than does James Freedman, president of the college.

The Freedman administration is deliberately stifling the voices of any who oppose a left-wing ideology and is cheating the students by only half-educating them.

This is the way education works in a communist society. It should not be the way at Dartmouth, a place of great tradition as a bastion of freedom of thought. Daniel Webster, who defended Dartmouth, must be turning in his grave.

Graduates, students, and alumni who are in Hanover for this weekend's college commencement ought to take note of what student president Evans has to say. We are happy to publish his thoughtful commentary on Page 1 today.

The State

Columbia, South Carolina, September 26, 1988

A QUARTER of a century has passed since South Carolina's then all-white colleges and universities were desegregated. While discrimination no longer enjoys legal sanction, racism in subtler forms persists on the campuses of predominantly white institutions of higher learning in this state and elsewhere.

An in-depth exploration of bigotry and the overall status of blacks in higher education was the subject of a national conference held at Clemson University last week. Regrettably, the consensus among participants was that deeds and genuine commitment to the interests of blacks and other minorities lag far behind words and good intentions.

"The violence that has erupted on campuses is distressing," observed Benjamin Payton, president of Tuskegee University and a former president of Benedict College in Columbia.

"We have to create a climate of acceptance and support for black students as well as others," he said.

According to one source, more than 30 consequential occurrences of racial bias and intimidation have been reported to the U.S. Justice Department in the past three years.

In 1985, for example, The Citadel suffered through a spate of negative publicity when five white cadets wearing sheets and towels entered the room of a black cadet shortly after midnight, uttered obscenities and left behind a singed paper cross.

Earlier this year, Clemson recognized the ongoing, insidious presence of prejudice when it implemented a new policy regarding racial harassment and discrimination.

Institutions of higher learning are supposed to be places of humanism and enlightenment — stimulating venues which shape minds and define codes of conduct in ways that are acceptable and productive for everyone in a pluralistic society.

According to a recent study by the Hudson Institute, minorities will make up nearly 30 percent of new entrants into the national workforce between now and the year 2000 — double their current share. This means they must be nourished intellectually and socially in a healthy, non-hostile educational environment from the primary grades through post-high school years.

The Wil Lou Gray Opportunity School has just issued a report estimating that an alarming 35 percent of students who enter South Carolina high schools don't graduate four years later. Many kids, sadly, also drop out during the elementary grades. According to the state Department of Education, the holding power over the 12-year span ending in 1987-88 was 72 percent for black students and 78 percent for white pupils.

The schools' holding power has shown progress in recent years. Still, there is room for improvement. Fortunately, state and local school officials, in cooperation with segments of the private sector, are pushing a number of innovative programs designed to turn the dropout rate around.

Our future economic and social well-being depends on keeping all youngsters — black and white — through high school and promoting them into a college climate free of racism and other pernicious influences.

THE ANN ARBOR NEWS
Ann Arbor, Michigan, August 15, 1988

Taken out of context, things may appear to be something they are not.

Such is the case of the initial cover of August's "Michigan Today," the University of Michigan magazine distributed to staff

1907 POSTER

and alumni. The cover featured a 1907 poster, a description of "hazing" on the U-M campus. It showed a giant, white upperclassman grasping a small, green freshman in his palm. A headline at the bottom of the poster labeled a hazing event as "Black Friday."

Unfortunately, in today's world, the poster's caricatures looked too much like a great white man squeezing a small black man. The coloring on the magazine's cover as well the "Black Friday" headline contributed to an association with racial violence. The decision to use the poster as cover art may have been made without realizing how it could have been misunderstood, but the damage could have been severe at a time when the university is striving to improve its race relations.

The U-M acted wisely in quickly taking 300,000 copies of the magazine out of circulation last week. Although the poster is historical and a part of the Bentley Historical Library, it's historical importance is unfortunately lost in its use as cover art.

The magazine will reappear with a cover letter of apology from U-M Interim President Robben W. Fleming. U-M's sensitivity over possible misinterpretation of the poster indicates it is serious about combating racism on campus. One of the best ways to further demonstrate its commitment is for the university to make sure that its campus is accessible to black students and black faculty.

The Sun Reporter
San Francisco, California, May 25, 1988

The younger racists have not only used racial slurs, but have engaged in physical fights, so strong that the police had to be summoned to restore the peace.

Racism on school campuses is a reflection of the larger sickness which is a part of the American folklore. It is not only directed against Blacks and Hispanics, but also against the growing Asian population. Jews are also the targets of this form of Americanism.

The NAACP, ACLU, ANTI-DEFAMATION LEAGUE, and whatever organizations which the Hispanic and Asian organizations maintain for the retention of their respect —these groups will never become a memory like the dodo bird.

The big hope of the ethnic groups in the country is that the courts of law do not become infected with the sort of racism, that the judges do not forget that the people who appear as plaintiffs are also covered by the laws of the land, and such judges' attempts to change the laws from the bench would disenfranchise all but white Americans.

In the immediate post-Civil War era, Black parents established a goal to provide an education for their children as a means of providing the path for their offspring to take their places in society as a full-fledged citizens.

It has not been an easy goal for Blacks; for they had to enter student bodies that were segregated on color lines, and those segregated schools for the most part were second- or third-class appendages of the American educational system.

There has always been resistance directed against Blacks opening the doors to institutions which would provide equal education based on the ability of students to absorb what the educational system offered to all children. In the recent past Blacks resorted to filing suits in the courts to equalize education for all of American young people; and the courts, following a historic decision by the U.S. Supreme Court, declared segregation based on race in the public, and in the private, schools was unconstitutional.

Some of us believed that the court's decision had brought changes. But alas, from news stories we have read lately, we learned that Black students on the college or university level have been exposed to all manners of racial remarks from students who let the Blacks know that they are not welcome.

There were incidents at Dartmouth College, the University of Massachusetts, University of Michigan, and the University of California at Berkeley.

Racial incidents have not been confined just to the above named institutions; but they stand out in our minds now, which is sad to us, because we were naive enough to believe that the higher education received by individuals freed them of racial differences, at least among the peer groups that students encounter on campuses.

That there have been incidents of racism at Berkeley High School, we learned from a number of stories we read in the San Francisco Examiner.

Arkansas Gazette
Little Rock, Arkansas, November 14, 1988

One of the great hopes for the George Bush administration is that it will be less hostile toward civil rights than Ronald Reagan's. The resignation of William Bradford Reynolds virtually assures this.

The Reagan administration was the first since World War II that tried to halt the nation's slow and painful progress toward racial equality. That being the goal, Reynolds was a logical choice to head the Justice Department's civil rights division.

Reynolds boldly upheld the fears and prejudices of the white majority. He led the administration's legal attacks on affirmative action and busing, two initiatives that have afforded blacks a chance to enter the American mainstream. He opposed the removal of the tax exemption of an openly racist university. But give him this, and that's all — in a perverse way, like war or serious illness, he brought out the best in some Americans. Knowing that affirmative action was not only just but practical, even some Southern white police chiefs opposed Reynolds' effort to end it. It was a long way from Bull Connor, and a long way from the days when the Justice Department was assumed to be in favor of civil rights.

Reynolds defended the rights of minorities the way James Watt defended public lands from exploitation, and he will be missed as much. In a cynical letter of resignation Wednesday, Reynolds said, "The civil rights accomplishments of this administration will be with us for years to come ..." George Bush has a duty to prove him wrong.

THE SACRAMENTO BEE
Sacramento, California, November 8, 1988

Officials at some of the best colleges in the country are trying to understand what appears to be a rise in racism, sexism and anti-Semitism on their campuses: swastikas scrawled at Yale's Afro-American Cultural Center and at New Haven's Holocaust Memorial; harassment of black students at Stanford, Dartmouth and Smith; and a variety of similar incidents on other campuses, including Berkeley and UCLA. At DePauw, they thought it would be cute to have a "ghetto party."

A number of explanations have been offered, none fully satisfactory: the general anxiety among white Americans faced with increasing economic competition from Asians and others; the indifference, if not the hostility, shown by the Reagan administration to civil rights and racial justice issues; the not-so-subtle exploitation of the racial overtones of the Willie Horton case.

Yet if national leaders help set a tone, so do the secondary schools and communities from which the bigots come, and so, of course, do the colleges they attend. Recognizing that, a group of college presidents in New England issued a statement the other day condemning the racist incidents as "cowardly acts" and calling for vigorous action to identify those responsible. At other campuses, administrators have organized workshops and committees to promote tolerance on campus. What's certain is that to the extent such bigotry thrives on the campus, the educational enterprise fails. To the extent it originates and thrives elsewhere, democracy fails.

School Busing Remains Divisive; Justice Dept. Shifts on Desegregation

The school bus became a symbol of school integration in the 1970s. As a symbol, it often simultaneously represented the emotions of integrationists (who saw it as a vehicle of escape from the ghetto and toward equality) as well as supporters of "neighborhood schools" (for whom the practical concepts of safety and property had greater meaning than the more abstract "equal opportunity"). The turn to busing as a means to achieve integrated education was prompted in the South by an array of strategies intended to maintain segregated schools: the closing of public schools; the creation of private schools; a Southern governor's "standing in the classroom door" to prevent the enrollment of two black students in a university of thousands; and the linking of integrationists with subversion. In the North it was a reaction to stubborn *de facto* residential segregation.

But since the court rulings of the 1970s loosened the legal constraints on busing, the controversy surrounding the topic has continued.

The Boston school committee December 28, 1988 agreed in principle to adopt a new plan that would allow parents to choose where to send their children from among a number of nearby schools. Agreement to the plan was the latest development in the controversy over school districting that had embroiled the city since the mid-1970s.

Under the plan, the city's school system would be divided into three zones of 14,000 students each. Parents would be free to send their children to any school within their zone, providing all schools remained racially balanced.

The Supreme Court March 26, 1989 agreed to rule on a case, *Board of Education of Oklahoma City v. Dowell*, involving the question of when court supervision of school desegregation should end.

An Oklahoma City busing program had been abandoned in favor of a neighborhood school plan in 1984, after a federal court had determined that a "unitary" school system had been established.

The Supreme Court ruled, 5-3, Jan. 15, 1991 on conditions for ending court supervision of formerly segregated school districts. The case was *Board of Education of Oklahoma City v. Dowell*.

The majority opinion, written by Chief Justice William H. Rehnquist, held that court orders for busing could end if school districts had done everything "practicable" to eliminate the "vestiges of past discrimination." Rehnquist said the reemergence of single-race schools as a result of local housing patterns was not necessarily a reason for continued busing.

The ruling did not define how lower courts could determine whether the "vestiges" of segregation had been eliminated. Nor did the ruling define "practicable."

The decision overturned a 1989 ruling by the U.S. 10th Circuit Court of Appeals that had refused to return the once-segregated Oklahoma City schools to local control. The Supreme Court said the appeals court had used too strict a standard in refusing to release the system from a 1972 desegregation decree. However, the Supreme Court refused to lift the decree. Instead, it returned the case to the U.S. District Court in Oklahoma City for a decision under the new standards.

In the dissenting opinion, Justice Thurgood Marshall wrote that the majority had overlooked the fact that single-race schools were part of the "stigmatic injury" of racial discrimination that the court's landmark 1954 decision in *Brown v. Board of Education* had tried to erase.

The Justice Department had shifted its position on challenging court-ordered desegregation plans, according to a report in the *Washington Post* Jan. 24, 1991.

Some civil rights leaders had feared that the department would mount new efforts to overturn desegregation plans, following the Supreme Court ruling on Jan. 15 that had made it easier for school districts to free themselves from court-ordered busing plans.

The *Post* noted that during the tenure of William Bradford Reynolds, who had served as assistant attorney general for civil rights under President Ronald Reagan, the Justice Department had actively approached more than 82 Southern school districts to see if they were interested in mounting legal challenges to court-ordered desegregation plans.

THE ATLANTA CONSTITUTION
Atlanta, Georgia, August 17, 1990

The cost of school segregation in this country has been incalculable, from the extra money spent to maintain dual school systems to the wasted potential of black children who were told that they were inferior and were given a second-class education to reinforce it.

But the days of state-mandated school segregation are over, and states that spent good money to maintain an evil system have long considered the ledger closed.

Well, not exactly. School systems across the country are suing state governments, claiming the states imposed school segregation and therefore should share in the cost of ending it. Georgia's largest school system, DeKalb County, has become one of the litigants.

Thirty-six years after the U.S. Supreme Court said segregation had to end, school systems are finding that ridding themselves of its last vestiges is expensive. The state of Missouri has settled on paying $500 million to help finance Kansas City's desegregation plan. DeKalb County is asking the state to help with about $25 million in costs, but that figure could grow depending on what desegregation remedies come out of a pending court case.

Such lawsuits raise an interesting historical question. Are the local boards claiming that they wanted to end school segregation but the states just wouldn't let them? In many cases, that would be revisionist history of a high order.

Georgia's obstructionist record on desegregation is clear, however. A rabidly segregationist General Assembly passed laws denying state funds to integrated schools and directing money toward segregated ones. The political atmosphere in the state was such that Ernest Vandiver, who knew better, felt compelled during his successful 1958 campaign for governor to pledge that "no, not one" black child would attend school with whites in Georgia.

The state of Georgia called for a defiant tune when the courts ordered that school segregation end. It seems only fitting that it now help pay the piper.

The Birmingham News
Birmingham, Alabama, January 1, 1988

The cost of a federal judge's ruling that Alabama's colleges and universities still bear the taint of segregation is still being figured out.

No matter what the ultimate cost is computed to be, it will be very hard to swallow for a state that has had to reduce education funding both of the last two years because tax revenues didn't meet projections.

No one should be surprised by U.S. District Judge Harold Murphy's endorsement of the long ago accepted observation that America's old separate but equal education systems, in many states besides Alabama, were very separate but hardly equal.

Only the naive would

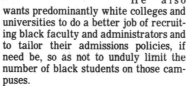

believe racial preferences were in no way a factor in the location of branch campuses of predominantly white state universities within cities that already had state universities with historically black student bodies and administrations.

It is an expensive proposition to duplicate the same educational services at two state-funded institutions within the same city. That a federal judge has had to order a stop to such an obviously unnecessary drain of tax revenue serves as commentary on the political power of some state schools.

That it took 10 years and a court decree to settle this matter is commentary on our leadership, in education and government, during that period.

The inability to get beyond partisan interests and come to agreement without a judge's order has done little other than increase the millions being paid to the lawyers involved in this case.

Murphy has not ordered the merger of institutions, as many feared the court would as the most drastic means to end program duplication. But certainly there must be greater collaboration and cooperation between campuses to meet Murphy's guidelines.

Ending program duplication will save

the state money. That's good. However, Murphy's order will have the opposite effect in most other criteria.

The judge has demanded that the Alabama Commission on Higher Education increase its funding recommendations for Alabama State and Alabama A&M universities. Although ACHE only makes recommendations, the Legislature cannot ignore that Murphy has retained the right to make his order more explicit if the lawmakers choose to ignore ACHE.

Murphy already has been explicit about the amount he wants spent on new buildings for the two historically black institutions — $10 million apiece over the next three years.

He also wants predominantly white colleges and universities to do a better job of recruiting black faculty and administrators and to tailor their admissions policies, if need be, so as not to unduly limit the number of black students on those campuses.

Gov. Hunt is right to point out Alabamians can find some solace in the court's not finding evidence of current discrimination within the higher education system. Also, some elements of Murphy's order might be appealed and the U.S. Supreme Court's pending decision on a similar Mississippi higher education case may be a factor in what eventually occurs here.

The Murphy decision, however, confirms what was known when this case began in 1981 — that the cost of righting past wrongs will be high. And no one should expect that continuing to delay a final solution to this case will decrease its cost.

Using Murphy's order as their guide, state leaders now need to come up with a comprehensive plan to ensure higher education spends its dollars wisely and in a fashion that removes all clouds of past discrimination.

The Boston Globe
Boston, Massachusetts, January 10, 1992

The resegregation of America's public schools is not simply a measure of the failure of the nation to live up to the spirit of Brown v. Board of Education. It points more directly to the failure of America's leadership to uphold the spirit of racial coexistence and equality.

A Globe series marked the 38th anniversary of the Brown decision and coincided with the release of a study by the National School Boards Association. The study showed that progress toward desegregating the nation's public schools stalled or went backward between 1986 and 1988.

The Reagan administration pointed to public resentment of busing as justification for turning back the clock. Studies show, however, that public support for integration has grown steadily over the years. According to a Globe poll, 80 percent of those surveyed support at least the notion of school integration. Fewer would put their own children on buses to achieve it, but a majority said they would if it were the only option.

Another study, conducted by the University of Chicago, shows that public support for busing has increased dramatically since 1972. Thirty-two percent of whites supported busing last year, compared with 13.5 percent who supported it 20 years ago. Yet, despite these figures, there is no groundswell of opposition to the court's abandonment of desegregation.

A Supreme Court ruling expected this spring in the Freeman v. Pitts case will serve as a guide for federal judges to determine when to extricate themselves from desegregation orders. That ruling is likely to wield a damaging blow to hundreds of other pending cases.

The onus will be on individual school districts, such as Cambridge, to develop successful controlled-choice programs. Or on groups, such as Concerned Parents for Public Schools in Mississippi, that work to persuade white parents to send their children to public schools. Or on suburban integration programs, such as Metco, that provide opportunities for inner-city and suburban students to attend school together.

These efforts, however, benefit only a small portion of students, while the majority of America's inner-city poor are abandoned in classrooms that are not only racially segregated but also ill-equipped. As long as the reliance on property taxes as the basis for school funding remains, there will exist a dual system of haves and have-nots divided largely along racial lines.

The failure to deal with social problems of the poor, segregated housing patterns made worse by redlining, and federal abandonment of public education contribute to America's return to separate and unequal schools. Without a commitment to the education of all children, the nation will find itself more divided than it was in 1954.

Supreme Court Eases
School-Desegregation Controls

The Supreme Court March 31 ruled, 8–0, that school districts operating under court-supervised desegregation orders could be released from court supervision bit by bit. Under the ruling, formerly segregated school districts could be returned gradually to local control as they achieved racial equality in each of the seven aspects of their operations that the high court had previously set out for consideration when determining whether a district had achieved desegregation. The case was *Freeman v. Pitts*.

In 1968, in the case *Green v. New Kent County School Board*, the Supreme Court had identified seven aspects of a school district's operations—student assignments, transportation, physical facilities, extracurricular activities, assignments of faculty and administrators, allocation of resources and the "quality of education"—to test whether a school system had been desegregated.

In the case before the court, the DeKalb County, Ga. School System, outside Atlanta, had been operating under a court-supervised desegregation order since 1969. Under the order, the system had closed some all-black schools and redrawn district lines. The measures had achieved integration for a short time until demographic patterns in the county shifted, changing the racial composition of the school system to 47% black in 1986 from 5% black in 1969. The shift created many schools that once again were either predominantly black or white.

In 1988, U.S. District Judge William C. O'Kelley ruled that the system had eliminated segregation in several of the required areas and released the system from court supervision in those areas. He said the resegregation that had occurred was the result not of official action but of private choices. He said the school system was not constitutionally responsible for remedying the resegregation. In 1989, the U.S. 11th Circuit Court of Appeals in Atlanta reversed the district court decision, ruling that to be released from the court order, the school system had to eliminate segregation in all the required aspects and maintain equality for at least three years.

The Supreme Court's ruling overturned the appeals court's decision. The U.S. District Court in Georgia would now apply the high court's decision to the facts of the DeKalb County case.

The Supreme Court's decision, while unanimous, included a series of concurring opinions.

The majority opinion, written by Justice Anthony M. Kennedy, held that federal courts could relinquish control over a school district "in a gradual way" as a district achieved desegregation. Kennedy also reiterated the district court's position on resegregation caused by demographic shifts. He said, "Returning schools to the control of local authorities at the earliest practicable date is essential to restore their true accountability in our governmental system."

Kennedy said, "Racial balance is not to be achieved for its own sake. Once the racial imbalance due to de jure violation has been remedied, the school district is under no duty to remedy imbalance that is caused by demographic factors."

Although he did not give the lower courts additional specific tests to show when districts had met the criteria for ending desegregation orders, Kennedy did set some loose standards for courts to use when reviewing specific court orders. He specified that a school district that had achieved equality in some areas would remain under judicial supervision unless it could demonstrate "its good faith commitment to the entirety of a desegregation plan so that parents, students and the public have assurance against further injuries or stigma."

More explicit standards were offered in a concurring opinion filed by Justice David H. Souter. Souter wrote that when gradually releasing a district from court supervision, judges must be careful the vestiges of discrimination that remained did not "act as an incubator for resegregation in others."

St. Petersburg Times
St. Petersburg, Florida, April 2, 1992

The Supreme Court's decision in the DeKalb County, Ga., school desegregation case was far from the definitive signal many had hoped for. Easing the criteria by which federal judges decide whether public schools have been adequately integrated is clearly more encouraging to foes of court-ordered integration plans than to proponents; but the only certainty seems to be that the nebulous ruling is bound to inspire even more confusion and court challenges.

In its unwillingness to confront festering questions of school integration more decisively, the court mirrors society's own ambivalence. A majority of Americans are inclined toward retreat from the current emphasis on racial balance; they simultaneously believe that a *de jure* dual system is wrong and that *de facto* segregated schools can still be equal.

There is for this court, too, a form of politically correct school segregation; it definitely sees a constitutional — if not a moral — distinction between the kind caused by actions of the state and that caused by private choices and "demographic factors." That such a distinction seems largely artificial appears to matter little, provided a "good faith effort" has been made.

The court's growing desire to wash its hands of this sticky social issue is perhaps the clearest point to emerge from the otherwise murky language of Tuesday's ruling. For varying reasons, the justices want to return control to local school boards sooner rather than later, and are opting to put even more tools in the hands of lower court judges, many of them conservative, to do so.

No one wants the courts involved in the business of running schools forever, but a retreat from the court's obligation to safeguard constitutional rights of minority children now would be unforgivable. That obligation is clearer than ever, given the poor track record of other branches of government, and the current decade-long backsliding from hard-won racial progress.

Less certain is whether racial balance — achieved mainly through busing — can or should endure as the primary tool to achieve that end. To that extent, at least, Justice Anthony Kennedy wasn't necessarily wrong in declaring that "racial balance is not to be achieved for its own sake." On the one hand it seems the most effective way found so far to blunt the tendency of white-controlled systems to shortchange minority children in resource allocation; on the other hand, those very children tend to bear the brunt of the disruption that busing causes.

But there are reasons to doubt whether the court is genuinely interested in solving such dilemmas. There's little question the nation's commitment to equal education will wither without the court's historic leadership from the top. Yet a retreat seems clearly under way, and the tone of Tuesday's opinions gives little cause to hope otherwise. Those who think a growing racial chasm will prove fatal to the nation if not attacked effectively through the schools, will simply have to keep searching for some way to reckon with this court's disengagement.

The Oregonian

Portland, Oregon, April 7, 1992

The Supreme Court ruled March 31 that a formerly segregated school district can satisfy court orders by desegregating in stages. That action resigned much of the nation to a racially divisive polarization that has dogged the country for generations.

The case of DeKalb County, Ga., including parts of Atlanta and its suburbs, mirrors some of the social problems that have occurred since the court's landmark school-desegregation ruling in Brown vs. Board of Education in 1954.

DeKalb County schools became integrated under a federal court desegregation order. After the order was lifted, the school system again became racially segregated, this time because of white flight rather than deliberate school board action.

Parents of black school students sought reinstatement of the desegregation order. School officials protested that they shouldn't be held accountable for changes in racial populations of neighborhoods.

The Supreme Court agreed that if the school board was not at fault in bringing about segregation in the population, court supervision over that area could be withdrawn.

Indeed, Justice Anthony M. Kennedy's majority opinion stated that "racial balance is not to be achieved for its own sake . . . the school district is under no duty to remedy imbalance that is caused by demographic factors."

The court's decision overturned an appeals court ruling that said a school system had to achieve racial equality in all of six criteria established in 1968 before court supervision could be withdrawn. These performance areas are desegregation of student assignment, faculty, staff, transportation, extracurricular activities and facilities.

The Supreme Court's recent ruling allows court supervision to be withdrawn from one area at a time, as a local federal judge says that desegregation caused by the school system has been remedied.

The net effect is that many school districts will be freed from federal desegregation orders while racial isolation remains as confining as ever.

The dusty old '50s justification, "separate but equal," has the comfort and support of the high court.

The court says that standard is legally sufficient. But it is not socially and ethically acceptable.

Not in Portland.

This is a multiracial, multiethnic society, composed of rich, poor and middle-income families. Our school system, as it should, encourages integration, whatever demographic patterns linger or change within our community.

This has as much to do with how we see and define ourselves as with how Portland's schools are governed.

Separate may be seen as equal by the court and some school districts. But separateness is usually as hostile to equality as isolation is to integration. That's not what Portland wants.

John E. Bierwirth, who takes over as Portland's new superintendent of schools July 1, will have to fight racial isolation as fiercely as Matthew Prophet, his fine predecessor.

The Wichita Eagle-Beacon

Wichita, Kansas, April 2, 1992

The U.S. Supreme Court's 8-0 declaration Tuesday that federal courts need no longer be concerned with school segregation resulting from housing patterns will disrupt race relations in many communities. Wichita won't be one of them.

Wichitans long ago created an equal-opportunity school system and implemented a busing plan to make it work. As a result, the school district has avoided painful and costly federal court action to force integrated schools. The city's commitment to integrated schools remains strong.

The problem here isn't avoiding resegregation, but finding a way to maintain integrated schools without exacting such a heavy burden on black youngsters. That's why the Wichita school board earlier this year approved Superintendent Stuart Berger's recommendation to establish neighborhood magnet elementary schools in or near the black community.

The board's intent was to allow black parents wishing to spare their children onerous cross-town bus trips to send them to schools near home. To make space for children whose parents choose this option, the board allowed the magnets, which are to open in the fall, a higher percentage of minority students than is allowed in standard Wichita elementaries.

Indeed, the Wichita school district has ventured far along the path that the Supreme Court justices appear to be nudging other American school districts: toward color-blindness in public education. With the prodding of Mr. Berger, Wichita school board members have recognized that the best means of establishing true color-blindness is parental choice.

If parents have an array of educational possibilities for their children, in other words, the racial makeup of the classes their children attend scarcely matters. The Supreme Court's decision is yet another signal that Wichita's schools are on the right path, and would be wise to continue.

The Washington Times

Washington, D.C., April 7, 1992

It says something about the sweeping authority of today's federal courts that the Supreme Court's decision not to play school administrator in a Georgia school district would be front-page news last week. So often have distant federal judges been turning places like DeKalb County, Ga., into long-running experiments in social engineering that many people apparently take it for granted now.

What Justice Anthony Kennedy wrote for the majority in Freeman vs. Pitts is a welcome reminder that there are indeed limits to federal intrusion. "We have said that the court's end purpose must be to remedy the violation and in addition to restore state and local authorities to the control of a school system that is operating in compliance with the Constitution. . . . Returning schools to the control of local authorities at the earliest practicable date is essential to restore their true accountability."

DeKalb schools lost their accountability in 1969 when courts ordered the county to shut down its dual school systems — one for black students, one for whites — and integrate them. DeKalb bused students hither and yon to satisfy the order. It also built so-called magnet schools to attract both black and white students on a voluntary basis.

For all these efforts, the county school system failed to meet its quota of black and white students. Busing encouraged white flight either out of the county or at least into its northern half. Meanwhile, DeKalb's black residents, who went from around 5 percent of the school population in 1969 to 47 percent by 1986, resided mostly in the southern half.

DeKalb officials complained that despite their best efforts to eliminate de jure school segregation, de facto segregation remained. How much longer, they wondered, would the courts require them to continue extensive busing operations that neither blacks nor whites wanted?

Justice Kennedy's answer is telling. Although vestiges of discrimination are "a stubborn fact of history," he said, the courts are limited to remedying those that result from a constitutional violation. Racial balance, he said, is not to be achieved for its own sake. "Where resegregation is a product not of state action but of private choices, it does not have constitutional implications," he said. "It is beyond the authority and beyond the practical ability of the federal courts to try to counteract these kinds of continuous and massive demographic shifts."

In other words, it's not a crime if school populations fail to achieve the kind of racial balance laid out by racial bean-counters in Washington. It's not a crime if parents in predominantly black communities want to send their children to neighborhood schools. It's only a problem if government actions somehow dictate all-black or all-white schools.

The DeKalb County case now goes back to the lower courts, where busing proponents and school officials will try to determine what if any government policies have led to segregation that requires federal remedies. If the courts agree there are none, DeKalb County schools and perhaps others around the country will be able to get back to the business of serving students rather than federal judges.

THE TENNESSEAN
Nashville, Tennessee, April 4, 1992

ONE thing the U.S. Supreme Court didn't agree to in the DeKalb County, Ga., desegregation case, is to free school districts from their obligations to integrate.

School districts who try to shoo the federal government from their classrooms would be premature. The unanimous decision rewards school boards that are trying, but it doesn't give them permission to quit.

Justice Anthony M. Kennedy, who wrote the majority opinion, in fact, put some important qualifications on this latest desegregation case. A school district could attain racial balance in student enrollment, for example, yet still not be freed from court order unless it can show good faith efforts to erase imbalances in other areas like teacher assignment.

Justice David Souter, who wrote the concurring opinion, warned courts to be especially careful to ensure that "the vestige of discrimination" not "act as an incubator for resegregation in others."

In short, the battle is not yet over. While some may view the court's decision as a partial retreat on desegregation, it's more remarkable because of the qualifications by a majority of justices who had been viewed as more conservative than their predecessors.

In DeKalb County's case, it was a matter of population shifts. The court ruled that the school board couldn't be held accountable for swings in the population that saw a great influx of black students to DeKalb County. An appeals court had ruled that the school district had to show equality in seven aspects of its operations before it could be freed from desegregation orders. The Supreme Court allowed only a partial showing of compliance. In any event, DeKalb County must still present its case to a federal district court once again.

The justices' decision unquestionably will tempt many districts to follow suit, but it should only be done with great care. Last fall, the Metro School Board started preliminary discussions on trying to lift the burden of desegregation orders and it wisely decided to take its time making a decision.

Mayor Phil Bredesen has much the same idea. The mayor said in his state of the city address last week that desegregation must continue to be the primary goal. Then, he proceeded to introduce a series of steps, working within that framework, to reinvigorate the school system.

As the court said, cities can release their school districts from burdensome federal oversight, but they can't ignore the problems of resegregation. Desegregation must remain the foundation on which any school system must operate. ∎

THE PLAIN DEALER
Cleveland, Ohio, April 6, 1992

The U.S. Supreme Court may have made it easier for some 800 school districts around the nation to come out from under federal courts' desegregation orders. But the guidelines are by no means certain, given the court's fragmented ruling last week in a case involving court-ordered school desegregation.

The nation's highest court left many ambiguities in its approach to court-ordered school desegregation, producing four separate legal opinions to support the justices' 8-0 ruling in a case involving DeKalb County, Ga. In last week's ruling, the justices began to apply the theory set down in a more far-reaching 1991 decision involving desegregation in Oklahoma City. In that case, the court weakened the argument for continuing busing where it had failed to eradicate every vestige of discrimination.

The court now has held that federal judges have broad discretion to end, step by step, their supervision of student assignments and transportation plans in DeKalb County, even though the county's schools are not fully integrated. Those schools had been under federal court control since 1969, when 5% of the district's pupils were black. For a brief period, soon after court intervention, a new pupil-assignment plan erased such segregation. But demographic shifts within the county caused segregation to occur again, despite the desegregation efforts.

Lawyers for the school district argued that district officials had done everything they could to end school segregation (which may have been caused, at one time, by the district's own policies). However, the lawyers said, the district could not be held accountable for demographic changes that have left the schools 90% black.

The Supreme Court's decision reaffirmed the district court's authority to incrementally remove court control over school districts under remedial orders, even though compliance with all parts of the order has not occurred. Writing for a five-member majority, Justice Anthony M. Kennedy said school districts could not be held liable for schools that are predominantly single-race because of communities' housing patterns and residents' choices.

The court did not, however, provide guidelines that district court judges could use to gauge schools' compliance with desegregation orders. It said the judge *may* lift portions of a court order; it did not *require* the judge to do so. That leaves federal district judges with tremendous discretion.

Cleveland's schools seem to be moving in the general direction set by the DeKalb County decision. A hearing last month in U.S. District Judge Frank Battisti's courtroom resulted in the lifting of 534 mainly procedural and technical portions of the desegregation order. Battisti also agreed to allow the new, more cooperative Cleveland school board majority until Aug. 1 to craft a pupil-assignment plan that could begin to move student assignments and transportation out from under court control.

That the situation in Cleveland was well-positioned for the Supreme Court ruling is a testament to Battisti and to the new board majority, which has shown an eagerness to negotiate an end to court control over Cleveland schools rather than fighting it out in court.

The Supreme Court decision, however, does not make it certain that Cleveland would have a free ride to independence from the court. The court's majority said judges should give "particular attention to the school system's record of compliance." Cleveland schools still have a way to go before reaching that stage, according to a report from the Office on School Monitoring and Community Relations. That progress has been slowed by past school officials working harder to fight the order than to comply with it.

Beyond the particulars of what the Supreme Court's decision means for DeKalb County, Ga., or Cleveland public schools, there is the question of whether a return to totally segregated schools is going to become an accepted part of the American education system. Clearly, the answer to that question must be no.

Even after the short-term device of busing has been removed by the federal courts, communities should recognize that there is long-term value in racially diverse classrooms. Busing, troublesome as it is, has been only one means to a much more important end: the goal of community harmony and greater racial understanding.

ST. LOUIS POST-DISPATCH
St. Louis, Missouri, April 5, 1992

Far from being the death knell for school desegregation that some had feared, the U.S. Supreme Court opinions on schools in DeKalb County, Ga., are reasonable analyses of thorny, longstanding problems that stubbornly defy solution. Since the court declared segregation illegal, schools nationwide have spent countless hours and dollars, but the goal of integrated classrooms remains far out of reach.

At issue in the DeKalb County case was whether federal courts can withdraw from supervision of desegregation cases gradually, as various criteria are met, or whether they must oversee cases until every vestige of segregation is erased. Despite years of court supervision, 60 percent of the county's 77,000 school students are black. More than half of them attend schools that are at least 90 percent black.

School officials argued that the current segregation was caused by changing housing patterns, not by any government law or policy, so court supervision should end. They found an ally in Justice Anthony Kennedy, who said federal judges could withdraw from desegregation plans step by step, as goals are met in various areas. But he went further, raising the nettlesome question of how far legal responsibility for segregation — and desegregation — should go. "Racial balance is not to be achieved for its own sake," he wrote. "Once the racial imbalance due to the *de jure* violation has been remedied, the school district is under no duty to remedy imbalance that is caused by demographic factors."

Under that formula, the hundreds of school districts nationwide operating under court-supervised desegregation plans — including the St. Louis area — could expect to be released from a judge's control in the next several years. The details differ from one area to the next, but in most cases housing patterns, not legal barricades, result in segregated schools.

But in a concurring opinion, Justice David Souter highlighted the obvious pitfalls of withdrawing from desegregation plans altogether. When they give up supervision of schools, he said, federal judges must make sure that they do not leave an atmosphere that acts as "an incubator for resegregation." Fulfilling that mandate will not be easy, and courts must make sure they have done everything they can to wipe out any legal justification to keep the races apart.

Detroit Free Press

Detroit, Michigan, April 2, 1992

In a deeply discouraging decision, the U.S. Supreme Court seemed to say this week that it is willing to give up on the goal of desegregating the nation's public schools.

That appears to be the thrust of its 8-0 decision in a case from the DeKalb County, Ga., school system, in Atlanta's suburbs. That system sought an end to court supervision of its pupil desegregation efforts, saying the segregation that remained was not its fault.

About 47 percent of students in the DeKalb system were black in 1986. Half attended schools more than 90 percent black; 27 percent of white students attended schools more than 90 percent white.

A federal appeals court ruled that for court supervision to end, school districts must achieve racial equality in seven areas: pupil assignments, transportation, physical plants, extracurricular activities, teacher and administrator assignments, resource allocation, and "quality of education."

No, the Supreme Court said, a federal judge "has the discretion to order an incremental or partial withdrawal of its supervision and control." Good-faith effort by the school system is one criterion for that assessment, Justice Anthony M. Kennedy wrote for the unanimous court.

That *sounds* reasonable, but in fact the high court declared that the proof need not be in the pudding. That narrow vision does not bode well for the future.

Liberal Supreme Court majorities used to be criticized for placing too great a burden on the schools for social change. And black parents have had their reservations, because their children ended up on buses more than anyone else's.

But the grim reality remains that racial attitudes probably are more polarized in this country today than they have been for many a decade, and the economic and racial segregation that afflicts many in inner cities is sharpening the gap.

If more children who live in segregated neighborhoods are not sent into the future from classrooms that look like their nation, the vision of equality that animates the Constitution will remain blurred and unreal.

This conservative court seems to have taken another step backward toward accepting the American apartheid: de facto segregation.

The Washington Post

Washington, D.C., April 2, 1992

IN AN 8-0 ruling Tuesday, the Supreme Court took another necessary step toward defining when and under what circumstances lower courts can release formerly segregated school districts from desegregation decrees. But as with its prior decisions, this one left important parts of the answer up in the air. The great issue still is what to do in urban and suburban districts where enrollment tends to be by neighborhood, and neighborhoods tend to be (or have newly become) largely segregated. How responsible is a school board for that?

Justice Anthony Kennedy's majority opinion said that it's the responsibility of the courts to return the schools to local control wherever and as soon as possible. But five of the justices, having easily subscribed to that worthy goal, then felt it necessary to file or join in three concurring opinions indicating that the court remains split on many of the next questions.

The decided case came from DeKalb County, Ga., where the school system had been operating under court order since 1969. A district court found in 1989 that the system had made exemplary progress in eliminating the residual effects of the dual school system that had been the hallmark of segregation. It released the district from court supervision with regard to student assignment, transportation services, extracurricular activities and physical facilities. Because vestiges of the old system remained in faculty assignments and allocation of resources, these two areas would remain under court supervision. An appeals court reversed, holding that all aspects of the system had to be in compliance together, for at least three years, before relief could be granted. Moreover, since the system still had racially imbalanced schools because of white flight and constantly changing residential patterns (the schools were 5 percent black when court supervision began and are 47 percent black now), major new steps, including possibly heavy busing, would have to be undertaken.

In overturning the appellate court this week, the Supreme Court said that an incremental return of responsibilities to local school boards is justified so long as they have made a good-faith effort to comply with court orders and have succeeded, in some areas, in eliminating government-sponsored segregation. But the practical as distinct from symbolic effect of that is unclear. The court also said that school districts have no obligation to overcome racial imbalance resulting from residential segregation so long as the residential segregation is itself the result of private as distinct from governmental actions. But that has always been the rule. The question is, what constitutes governmental involvement—how far back in history do you go?—and which side, school board or plaintiff, has the difficult burden of proof? It's at that level that the unanimous court still seems divided.

Our own sense is that the standard here should be a high one. Justice Kennedy is right that there are limits to both the authority and the ability of the courts to "counteract . . . demographic shifts" when, as in this case, blacks move into a district and whites flee. But Justices Harry Blackmun, John Paul Stevens and Sandra Day O'Connor warned in one of the concurrences that "an integrated school system is no less desirable because it is difficult to achieve," and districts should not be "relieved of the responsibility to desegregate" just "because such responsibility would be burdensome." It's the balance between those two points of view that the court is still struggling to define and achieve.

Rockford Register Star

Rockford, Illinois, April 3, 1992

Those who would comb the U.S. Supreme Court's ambiguous ruling this week on school desegregation in an effort to find a loophole for the Rockford School District to climb through will only be wasting their time. The high court has not retreated an inch from the established doctrine on which the pending desegregation suit here is based.

The typical headline on the court's ruling is somewhat misleading. Yes, the rules for school desegregation have been eased a bit, but all eight justices involved in this case (Clarence Thomas didn't participate) have effectively reiterated the basic principle embodied in the landmark desegregation ruling of 1954—that is, that racial segregation in public schools is unconstitutional. Even this most right-wing high court in half a century shows no inclination to turn back the clock on that score.

The court reiterated the doctrine that racial segregation in public schools is unconstitutional.

This is not to say, however, that the court made itself perfectly clear in this week's ruling. On the contrary, though the vote was 8-0 to allow school districts to win release from court control in piecemeal fashion as they achieve desegregation in their various operations, four separate written opinions attended the decision. The overall result is ambiguity, if not confusion. It seems that the court is feeling its way on this issue and will have to revisit it in the next few years to achieve greater clarity.

But, as we say, already there is clarity on the central principle that makes school segregation illegal. For the parties to the Rockford case, then, there is no choice but to continue good-faith efforts to comply with the mandates of the interim desegregation order from the federal court. Somewhere down the line, the effects of this latest Supreme Court ruling might come into play in the case here, but obviously not for now.

The Seattle Times

Seattle, Texas, April 12, 1992

SCHOOL desegregation continues to perplex school boards around the country and the Supreme Court. Thirty-eight years after Brown vs. Board of Education, the case that declared segregated school systems unconstitutional, racial imbalance in urban classrooms remains entrenched.

Yet decades of efforts to desegregate through busing have not, in most places, improved educational opportunity for minority children or created fully integrated school systems.

The changing ethnic makeup of cities makes balancing the numbers increasingly difficult. In districts where the student body is composed mostly of minority groups, the exercise is pointless. Besides, most parents and school administrators don't believe that educational equity is achieved through perfect racial balance — even if that were possible.

So the arduous search for new ways to integrate is being played out on both the national and local levels.

The recent Supreme Court decision involving DeKalb County, Ga., schools is notable for what it did not do. The conservative majority did not retreat from the goal of integration nor did it indicate that school districts are free to do as they please. However, the 8-0 decision shifts the focus away from numbers.

It allows school districts to regain local control over aspects of school life — student assignment, physical facilities and transportation, for example — that had become desegregated even though other parts of the system had not. It also states that racial imbalance which results from demographic changes and is not traceable to past illegal segregation is not unconstitutional.

The ruling suggests communities, particularly those such as Seattle that are not under court supervision, may be freer to fashion more flexible solutions.

Seattle Superintendent William Kendrick's new goals for the district's desegregation plan attempt to do that. The goals — increase student choice and maintain marginally integrated schools — clearly are achievable.

The district has asked the state Board of Education to relax state guidelines so that a Seattle school with 82 percent minority students or with more than 50 percent of a single minority would be considered integrated under the law. That change would reduce the disproportionate busing of minority students from the South End, and lessen the amount of mandatory assignments overall.

Does this mean Seattle would have an "all-voluntary" assignment plan? Probably not.

Limited capacity and transportation costs will inevitably prevent some students from attending the schools they want. Even so, creating a more voluntary system is possible with magnet programs replacing forced assignments.

A successful system assumes, of course, that there are good schools to choose from — the crux of the problem. Seattle parents, white and minority, voluntarily bus their children to good programs; in fact, 50 percent now choose *not* to attend their neighborhood school.

A generation after the Brown case, maintaining racial diversity depends on top-notch programs, not busing orders. Even if the courts allowed school districts to turn back the clock, Seattle, having grown accustomed to choice, probably wouldn't want to do so.

TULSA WORLD

Tulsa, Oklahoma, April 2, 1992

BEGINNING in the 1960s, hundreds of school districts in which racial segregation once was a matter of law or custom were required by federal courts to implement broad desegregation plans. Often those plans involved busing students to schools outside their neighborhoods to achieve racial balances.

The U.S. Supreme Court this week issued a ruling that will make it easier for judges to relinquish supervision of districts that have complied with court-ordered desegregation or are making good-faith efforts to do so.

The high court, in an 8-0 decision, specifically permitted an end to federal court supervision in DeKalb County, Ga., even though its schools have never fully been integrated.

More significant is that a five-member majority of the court held that racial imbalances are not necessarily illegal, if they result from naturally occurring housing patterns, and not as a result of law or custom. Writing for the majority, Justice Anthony M. Kennedy said that "racial balance is not to be achieved for its own sake."

The ruling could affect hundreds of school districts that bus students to achieve court-ordered desegregation. Oklahoma's large urban school districts previously have complied with desegregation orders and have been released from direct supervision by federal courts. But the court's ruling could mean that continuing desegregation programs still in effect, such as Tulsa's magnet school program, now are a matter of local choice.

More importantly, it appears to mean that racial imbalances, which might recur in schools that once were under desegregation orders, are not necessarily illegal.

THE CHRISTIAN SCIENCE MONITOR
Boston, Massachusetts, April 6, 1992

THE US Supreme Court last week unanimously gave school districts greater leeway to challenge desegregation orders. Does this mean the court is abandoning the principles laid down in its landmark 1954 case, Brown vs. Board of Education?

Not necessarily. The 1954 ruling emphasized the "feeling of inferiority" imposed on black children by officially segregated schools, and the words emanating from the high court last week showed a continuing awareness of the importance of justice in education. But today's conservative-leaning court is clearly less inclined to see all or mostly black schools, in themselves, as grounds for a lawsuit.

Writing the majority opinion for a splintered court, Justice Anthony Kennedy argued that schools which are resegregated because of changing residence patterns don't require the kinds of remedies applied where racial separation was state-sanctioned.

Even on that point, however, the court held multiple views. Three justices joined in a separate opinion calling for a closer look at what lies behind the continued racial split in the classrooms of De Kalb County, Ga.

Instead of rallying to the view that official segregation is long past and court-ordered desegregation interferes with local control, the court acted cautiously.

Desegregation plans could be dismantled piece by piece, it said, if "good faith" compliance was proven in specific areas.

The appeals court, whose ruling the high court overturned, had demanded full compliance in all areas, from student assignments to racial makeup of the faculty, over a period of years.

Dozens of school districts may seize on the court's ruling to explore their own chances of winning release from portions of their desegregation plans. But last week's decision gave little assurance of easy victories for those who would try to overturn desegregation plans by arguing that housing patterns, not official policy, underlie racially unbalanced schools.

"Separate but equal" has a different implication today than it had 38 years ago, when the court handed down the Brown decision. Segregation was then a fact of life, and "equal" was a well-exposed myth.

Yet equality is still a myth to countless youngsters in struggling schools in inner cities and poor districts elsewhere.

Absolute racial balance in public schools may elude public policy. But genuine equality of opportunity, through well-equipped and well-staffed schools, remains a right of every American child. Legislatures and the courts have plenty of work ahead in upholding that right.

The Virginian-Pilot

Norfolk, Virginia, April 3, 1992

It's late, but welcome nonetheless. The U.S. Supreme Court, in a decision that validates much of the school-desegregation approach now used in Norfolk, has put practicality ahead of ideology in dealing with school busing.

The Supreme Court, ruling Tuesday in a Georgia case, overturned a federal appeals-court order to begin massive forced busing for racial balance in De Kalb County in suburban Atlanta.

The county has been under a federal desegregation order since 1966. It went back to court in 1986 hoping to obtain a ruling that it had achieved an integrated, "unitary" system — even though some schools in the district were 90 percent black. The predominantly black schools were caused, the county said, not by segregationist school-system policies but by shifting housing patterns and "white flight." (The percentage of blacks in the county's schools had increased from 6 percent to 64 percent in 20 years.) Therefore, the county said: (a) it should not be required by the courts to use busing to create racial balance and (b) control of the school system should be returned by the court to the locality.

This was similar to the argument that the Norfolk School Board made in federal district court in 1984 when it asked that its system be declared unitary and that busing be ended in elementary grades.

Norfolk's request was approved by lower courts and never heard by the Supreme Court. But Justice Anthony Kennedy, writing for the Supreme Court in the Georgia case, endorsed the position taken by Norfolk and De Kalb County that school systems should not be ordered to constantly change busing patterns when racial imbalance results from individual, personal choices or shifting demographics.

"Racial balance is not to be achieved for its own sake," he wrote. "Once the racial imbalance due to the *de jure* [government] violation has been remedied, the school district is under no duty to remedy imbalance. . . ."

In other words, absent any evidence of a violation of the law and the Constitution, local school boards — not federal courts — should be running public schools.

This is refreshing common sense about a "remedy" — busing — that has had a negative effect on American cities for two decades. The primary result of busing has been to drive thousands of parents and students, black as well as white, from urban school systems, either to private schools or to school districts that didn't have busing. (In Norfolk, 7,000 students left the public schools in the two years after busing began.) This exodus not only damaged urban schools; it diminished urban tax bases — in Norfolk, in Richmond, in Boston and dozens of other cities.

Racial integration and equality of opportunity in public schools must remain national goals. But the methods used to reach those goals — better funding for all schools, voluntary busing programs, magnet schools — must never be as impractical and counterproductive as forced busing.

THE BUFFALO NEWS

Buffalo, New York, April 8, 1992

THE U.S. Supreme Court's decision in a Georgia school desegregation case makes it imperative that local judges — like federal Judge John Curtin here in Buffalo — look very carefully before deciding to loosen their grip on such cases.

The decision, though unanimous, is one more chip from the foundation laid by previous courts that found segregated schools to be a societal blight. Even some of those joining in the 8-0 ruling warned that federal judges should be wary of the consequences of implementing the new freedom the ruling grants them.

That caution should be taken to heart here in Buffalo, where both Mayor Griffin and a misguided faction of the School Board have sought to end the court-imposed school desegregation prematurely.

In ruling that school districts governed by desegregation orders can get out from under them bit by bit, the justices have opened the door to the possibility of federal courts ending their supervision in certain areas, only to have the progress undone by the effects of segregation in others.

It's a point Justice David Souter was quick to note, and one all judges handling school desegregation should take to heart.

In the case at hand, De Kalb County school officials had sought to shed a desegregation order handed down in 1969. A district judge ruled that the school system had indeed eliminated segregation in several categories, including student assignment. He ended court supervision in those categories.

However, an appeals court disagreed, saying court supervision should not end until equality had been achieved in all areas, ranging from assignment of teachers and students to allocation of resources. The Supreme Court overturned that decision, ruling court supervision could end in certain areas while remaining in force in others.

There is, of course, an alluring logic in the high court's verdict. Following the principle of local control, it makes a certain sense to say that schools should be freed from court supervision where they have corrected violations.

But as Souter, other justices and legal experts note, the boundaries between various forms of segregation are not impermeable. Even if a school system achieves desegregation in one category, such as enrollment, other factors — such as an unfair distribution of resources — can quickly lead to resegregated classrooms.

Unfortunately, the court's ruling opens the door to such dangers. It puts the burden on Curtin and other judges to be mindful of such pitfalls.

With this new license for judges to act comes a greater responsibility to make sure there will be no backsliding. The Supreme Court could have guarded against that; it didn't. The rest of the judiciary must as it decides whether school systems guilty of segregation are suddenly to be trusted when they correct only part of the problem.

The Cincinnati Post

Cincinnati, Ohio, April 2, 1992

The Supreme Court's latest pronouncement on school desegregation is helpful in several ways. The unanimous decision reaffirms the limited purpose of court-ordered desegregation: not racial mixing for its own sake, but redress for past illegal discrimination. And it holds out the hope that districts supervised for years by federal courts can someday regain control of their affairs.

Under court order since 1969, DeKalb County, Ga., schools were found by a lower court to have reached desegregation targets in four areas: student assignments, transportation, physical facilities and extracurricular activities. The Supreme Court held that these aspects can be freed from court control — even as the lower court continues to supervise other areas.

U.S. District Court Judge Walter Rice followed the same pattern in his ruling declaring the Cincinnati Public Schools in compliance with most of its 1984 settlement agreement with the NAACP. Rice retained jurisdiction over low-achieving schools, student discipline policies and teacher racial balance.

Justice Anthony Kennedy's opinion affirmed that courts have no business intervening to remedy racial imbalances caused by people's private choices about where to live. The complication comes in determining which present-day racial disparities, including those in residential patterns, are vestiges of long-gone legal segregation.

Yet it is to be hoped that districts demonstrating good-faith commitment to racial fairness can graduate from court supervision. In the many hundreds of districts still under court order, the need to improve racial balance dominates almost every educational decision. Sometimes racial balance is tangential to what ought to be the paramount goal: the best possible education for every child.

Black History Courses Celebrated, Debated

Until the late 1960s, most American children would have learned in school of only a few blacks who made major contributions to the nation's history. Even today, many school textbooks are still limited to references to Booker T. Washington and George Washington Carver. It was to rectify this omission that black history courses came into being, to celebrate the ignored heritage of the many black scientists, civil rights leaders, inventors, writers, artists, military leaders and other figures who helped shape American history. In 1984, the achievements of the "Father of Black History," Carter G. Woodson, were celebrated during February, designated as Black History Month in 1978. The tradition, aptly enough, was begun in 1926 as Negro History Week by Woodson himself, a historian and author who founded the Association for the Study of Afro-American Life and History, and established a publishing house to provide textbook material about black Americans.

Although black history courses have become a standard part of the curriculum at many schools and colleges, disagreement remains over whether these courses should constitute a separate discipline. Proponents of separate black courses and black studies programs argue that the added emphasis thus placed upon the subject matter is necessary to compensate for its complete omission in the past. Those who feel that the material in black history courses would be more appropriately learned in the context of other history courses maintain that such special treatment gives the subject matter more weight relative to the whole than it deserves, and that special courses could equally well be demanded by any other of the many groups – Japanese, Jews, American Indians, etc. – who have also come together to form the fabric of American history and society.

The Record

Hackensack, New Jersey, February 4, 1992

FEBRUARY is Black History Month, a time for everyone to learn more about black achievement. But how can we think about black achievement without being struck by what remains to be done?

The central question is: How many of tomorrow's black achievers continue to be thwarted, and what can be done to help them succeed?

Black children need the role models that history reminds them of — the scientists, writers, artists, musicians, teachers, and civil-rights leaders whose achievements will be honored during the next few weeks in schools and cultural programs. But black children also need a strong sense of their own promise, a sense many of them do not get from hearing about violence, bias crimes, poverty, and the grave problems with urban education.

White children also need a fuller understanding of black history, as one of the first steps toward developing tolerance and respect for minorities. Most of the string of bias crimes committed in recent weeks in New York City were the work of children. It began when a white teenage gang beat two black children in the Bronx and sprayed them with white shoe polish.

After a New York high school student was shot and killed by another student in a school hallway recently, Mayor David Dinkins decried the violence. He said the black community did not make its way from the back of the bus only to see its children in the back of an ambulance.

Education is a strong antidote to hatred. The multicultural curriculum taught in several New Jersey schools is a way to combat intolerance and to defuse the biased remarks some children may hear at home.

The great progress of the civil rights movement and all past black achievement can best be honored by finding ways to ensure that the progress continues — and that today's black children do not see, in the words of the poet Langston Hughes, their dreams deferred.

THE TAMPA TRIBUNE

Tampa, Florida, February 12, 1992

When Christopher Columbus sailed to the New World, a black man, Alonzo Pietro, navigated the flagship.

When the first settlers landed in the Tampa Bay area more than 400 years ago, a black man, Estevenico "Esteban" D'Orantes, was among them.

In 1770, Crispus Attucks, a black man, was the first person to die in the effort of American colonists to break free from Britain.

Sound like a game of black trivial pursuit? Hardly.

The mosaic of world and American history features many shades and features woven by a diversity of groups. To disregard or ignore them would be like leaving pieces out of a jigsaw puzzle.

More importantly, the more we understand about one another, the more likely we can dismantle the walls of intolerance and hatred that divide us as human beings.

That's why Black History Month weighs as such an important annual observance each February.

Young black people need to know their forefathers played a key role in shaping the past and present. The self-esteem and pride garnered from that knowledge is insurance for their future.

All of us should realize that the study of black history — or that of any people — is part of the human story and serves the pursuit of truth. As we learn more about others, we discover more about ourselves.

Everyone benefits.

This year's celebration of Black History Month in Hillsborough County perhaps offers more activities to experience than ever before.

Children can attend performances by dance troupes, films on black culture and hear stories at various public libraries. On Feb. 16, history buffs can learn about pre-Columbian journeys by Africans to the Western Hemisphere at the Museum of African-American Art. Ethnic food lovers can get their fill at the second annual African-American Cuisine taste-off on Feb. 29 at the College Hill Public Library.

Black History Month began as Negro History Week in 1926 and was founded by educator and historian Carter G. Woodson to spotlight accomplishments of blacks. The observance was expanded to a month in 1976.

But the exploration of black history shouldn't stop there. After all, we are a diverse community 365 days a year.

"I HAVE A DREAM."
—REV. MARTIN LUTHER KING, JR.

"I HAVE A NIGHTMARE."
—RODNEY KING

SYRACUSE
HERALD-JOURNAL
Syracuse, New York, February 2, 1992

This weekend launches Black History Month. If the mere mention of this special observance mixes your emotions, you qualify as a certified member of this whacky melting pot that is America. You're also typically human.

Has there been a time in the history of the world when certain groups of people didn't find reason to raise their collective blood pressure over the differing shades or ways of other groups? We doubt it. Even within culturally distinctive groups, there always has been grousing, fault-finding and some-are-more-equal-than-others posturing.

And, so it is, that we stand on the threshold of another Black History Month and knock at the door, gingerly — for we can't ignore what is. Racism is what is in this great country — which could be so much greater, were it not for that. Yet, we smile as the door opens to another February filled with African American lore and special events locally. We know the price of harmony, of all kinds, is high — but not unreachable.

It simply takes time. Centuries, perhaps. But every attempt toward closing the gap between our differences, such as Black History Month, is a step closer. You have to believe that. In a modern world of surveys, statistics and film at 11, it's a matter of faith, a belief in the ultimate good of the human race.

We wish this could be less philosophical. We wish it could just say to one and all, "It's Black History Month. Let's celebrate." But that's not facing what is.

Americans' social consciousness is very much still in transition. The contributions of African Americans mostly were ignored in United States schools until the mid-1960s. Today, multiculturalism is barely a bud. Most recently, many Italian-Americans have been angered because Christopher Columbus' role in discovering America is under attack. Those wanting history to reflect the contributions of all peoples are taking a fresh look — as they should, sensitively and respectfully.

Giving credit where credit is due is easier said than done. It requires the finest of diplomacy and honesty. Black History Month is a reasonable path toward this goal of all peoples accepting one another. We're glad it's here again. But our knock at its door remains tentative.

Despite all past Februarys have taught about African Americans, there's still so very much left to know. Lack of knowledge triggers fear like nothing else. And, like beasts that bare their teeth and attack when frightened, human beings too often do the same — in ways only sometimes more subtle.

Perhaps, Americans never will know enough about the cultural and other differences that distinguish and divide them as a population. But they always can use what they have in common to smooth the rough spots. We all need love, food, clothing, homes. We all want the best for our children. Those needs are a start toward true understanding.

Black History Month is a good reminder of those needs we share, as well as of differences that need not divide. It is a warm hand reaching out in winter's cold. It's up to each individual to return the gesture.

St. Petersburg Times
St. Petersburg, Florida, February 1, 1992

Why a black history month when there is no white history month? Why start a National Association for the Advancement of Colored People when there was no such organization for white people?

Those are the sort of leading questions David Duke loves to pose to receptive crowds, and they make sense if you accept the fairy tale of a once-perfect America brought to near-ruin by slothful minorities demanding special treatment.

Black History Month, which begins today, is one way to replace simplistic nostrums with a more realistic perspective on race relations in America.

History is not the average American's strong point. But it doesn't take a Rhodes scholar to appreciate that the tradition of singling out blacks for "special" treatment was nurtured not by blacks but by those who went to great lengths to repress and exploit them. Of course, neither a month nor a century of remedial history can satisfy those who question such efforts just to stir racial resentment. The good will must come from each of us.

But with deepening racial divisions fueled by signals from respectable political leaders and hard economic times, that message threatens to be lost in the shuffle. There is a danger that frustration with growing racial insensitivity will lead some blacks to see February as "our" month, a chance to demonstrate counterintolerance by giving forums to black merchants of hatred and racial division. That would be playing directly into the hands of those who try to distort the intent of any race-conscious remedies.

Had black history not been buried or distorted to begin with, no special emphasis would be necessary. Most blacks, including historian Carter G. Woodson, who in 1926 originated the Negro History Week that has since expanded into all of February, yearn for the time when black history is honestly woven into American and world history.

That time is still far off. The ugly truth about — and sheer volume of — black mistreatment tends to be painful for either race to hear. There is simply no way, for example, to convey in short order the magnitude of even one region's — the Mississippi Delta's — systematic post-slavery economic exploitation of black sharecroppers. Yet as Nicholas Lemann chronicled in his book *The Promised Land*, the desire to escape such treatment played a direct role in the massive black migration to what are today's troubled northern urban centers.

Those who sincerely think this month of focusing on such history creates division, forget that any relationship built on lies and omissions cannot stand. By confronting uncomfortable truths, we build a more solid foundation for the only racial harmony that endures: that based on mutual respect.

Roots Author, Alex Haley, Dies

Alex Haley, 70, Pulitzer Prize-winning author of the best-selling book *Roots: The Saga of an American Family* (1976), died of a heart attack in Seattle February 10, 1992. *Roots*, which sold over five million copies, was made into a television miniseries that became one of the most popular in U.S. history when it was broadcast in January 1977. A sequel, *Roots: The Next Generation*, followed in 1979; the original saga traced Haley's family through seven generations, back to an ancestor, Kunta Kinte, who was shipped as a slave from the Gambia region of West Africa to the U.S. in 1767. The book was hailed as helping define the black American experience. It generated controversy, however, with some historians criticizing Haley for his blending of fact and fiction. Haley also had to settle a plagiarism suit over one passage. Haley's other works included *The Autobiography of Malcom X* (1965), which he wrote in collaboration with the black nationalist leader, and which was estimated to have sold six million copies worldwide.

The Record
Hackensack, New Jersey, February 11, 1992

MORE THAN 130 million people watched the 1977 television miniseries "Roots." It told a gripping tale of black oppression and survival, beginning in the 18th century, when Kunta Kinte, a young West African, was captured, sold into slavery, and taken to America.

Much later, the story went, his great-great-great-great grandson, Alex Haley, would spend years tracing his family history to that remote ancestor, a quest that turned into a Pulitzer-prize-winning book and the hugely successful miniseries.

Millions of Americans — black and white — gained an understanding and feel for the cruel injustice suffered by blacks throughout the nation's history. The tragedies of slavery and segregation were described through real people. Readers and viewers got a feeling of the humiliation and degradation that blacks suffered.

Mr. Haley died yesterday, and Benjamin Hooks, the executive director of the NAACP, said of "Roots," "It was the story of our people. It was the story of how we came from Africa. He [Mr. Haley] was truly a gifted person who wrote a book that was monumental."

As is so often the case with heroes, the history of Mr. Haley's achievement has complications. Shortly after the book was published, evidence emerged that raised serious questions about the factual reliability of some of the "Roots" saga.

The town of Juffure, where Kunta Kinte supposedly lived in 1767, was no remote Eden untouched by Western civilization. To the contrary, it was a white trading post surrounded by white civilization.

Further, it appeared that Kunta Kinte was not, after all, an ancestor of Mr. Haley's. A man by that name may have lived, but much later than Mr. Haley described.

In addition, the author of another book, published a decade earlier, sued for plagiarism, and won an apology from Mr. Haley and a settlement of $500,000. Mr. Haley's explanation was weak. From time to time, he said, people gave him slips of paper with various information, and some excerpts from the earlier book apparently made their way into "Roots."

As unfortunate as all this was, "Roots" is an important book, integral to understanding what blacks endured. Its basic message remains clear, despite the serious questions about authenticity. No one has questioned the sections of "Roots" dealing with the experiences of American blacks living in slavery and its malignant successor, segregation.

Mr. Haley enabled Americans to see that blacks had a vast heritage in Africa long before the days of slavery. Real people, black people, were indeed captured in western Africa, sent down the rivers to stockades on the coasts, and from there shipped in the holds of sailing vessels to America.

Mr. Haley's legacy is that he put human faces on this American tragedy.

> **Its message remains clear, despite the serious questions about authenticity.**

The Washington Post
Washington, D.C., February 11, 1992

"EARLY IN *the spring of 1750, in the village of Juffure, four days upriver from the coast of The Gambia, West Africa, a manchild was born to Omoro and Binta Kinte.*" And thus began the 1974 epic "Roots," a Pulitzer Prize-winning story about the family ancestry of author Alex Haley. "Roots" was quickly transformed into a symbolic chronicle of the odyssey of African Americans from the continent of Africa to a land not of their choosing. Alex Haley, a descendant of Kunta Kinte—the 1750 baby boy and Mr. Haley's six times removed grandfather—died yesterday at the age of 70.

"Roots" sold in the millions and as a record-setting television miniseries attracted an estimated 130 million viewers around the world. As history and as an original work, "Roots" was not without its critics, nor was Mr. Haley immune from lawsuits charging plagiarism. The work and Mr. Haley, however, survived both. "If somebody comes up and says something good about you, that is never taken as an adhesive thing like something negative about you," he told The Post in an interview three years ago. "I don't think I've had but a handful of reporters in all these years say, 'Tell me about the nine years that you trekked all over everywhere researching.'" But "Roots" endures as a life story. Mr. Haley's work remains a stirring metaphor of the heritage of generations of African Americans and their struggle to survive a shameful American legacy of kidnapping and enslavement, and a history of legally enforced racism.

In fact Alex Haley's mark was made on this country several years before the appearance of "Roots" with the publication of his first book, "The Autobiography of Malcolm X," which grew out of lengthy interviews he conducted with Malcolm. Through all the years of praise and celebrity he remained what he always was: a writer and teller of stories, traveling widely to recount tales of African-American history.

Not too long ago, Mr. Haley returned to the sea, his own literary roots of sorts, to continue work on a book about his hometown of Henning, Tenn. It was during his years in the Coast Guard, in which he served until his retirement in 1959, that he had developed his taste for writing. To escape the pressures that came with his fame, Mr. Haley often booked passage on cargo ships, where he could enjoy the solitude necessary for his writing. He often said he thought he had it in him to write better books than either "Roots" or Malcolm X's autobiography. "The problem," said Mr. Haley, "is to find the time to write. That's why I go to sea. I couldn't be happier than when at sea." Those books will never be written now. But Alex Haley's legacy will continue to be deeply felt by generations of all races, both here and far beyond the seas he loved.

The Evening Gazette

Worcester, Massachusetts, February 13, 1992

The death of writer Alex Haley this week is certain to rekindle interest in his monumental novel "Roots" and the television miniseries it inspired. The re-examination is appropriate, for they mark a watershed in American race relations.

It would be difficult to overstate their combined influence. Like nothing before, "Roots" sparked the growing black pride movement in the country. Black history, previously approached as a recitation of generations of bondage and degradation, suddenly was transformed into a saga of nobility and courage of biblical proportions.

Haley's novel also marked a turning point in the civil rights movement. Seemingly overnight, what many had viewed as a struggle against racial discrimination took on a new, forward-looking dimension: a celebration of the black experience.

For many white Americans, the impact was comparable to that of "Uncle Tom's Cabin," Harriet Beecher Stowe's abolitionist novel. Haley's fictionalized history provided the majority culture with a new, more enlightened perspective on the nation's racial history.

The "Roots" legacy continues today in the heightened appreciation of people of all ethnic backgrounds for their own cultural heritages. The current multiculturalism movement also is part of its legacy.

There is, however, a certain irony in the fact that promoters of multiculturalism choose to focus on the differences among races.

While Haley celebrated the unique history of African-Americans, "Roots" was far more: It was a celebration of the common humanity that unites all cultures and races.

THE SAGINAW NEWS

Saginaw, Michigan, February 14, 1992

When Alex Haley wrote "Roots," he produced not only a book, but also a movement.

In a way, Haley, who died Monday at 70, might have helped release the latent forces of ethnic pride that contributed to freedom in Eastern Europe and the breakup of the Soviet Union.

On its face, "Roots" was the story of one black man's odyssey in search of his own history.

Inspired by the storytelling of his grandmother and great-aunts, Haley spent 12 years tracing his family back six generations, finally finding his ancestral home in a village in Gambia, in West Africa.

The book became a 12-hour television miniseries. Amazingly, given its sometimes disturbing nature, it drew an audience of 130 million, then the largest ever.

That made it a universal cultural phenomenon. Here was a deeply personal drama — and also one that touched the human side of us all that yearns to know where we came from, so that we might better understand who we are.

In particular, Haley's work contributed mightily to an increased African-American sense of personhood and place.

It gave scholarly testimony to the fact that the slaves, sold and shipped as chattel to America, preserved within them, against the brutality and the horror of

displacement, the sense of a rich culture and a real homeland.

Today, the nation faces a dual challenge: To respect and nurture those important differences, while bringing black Americans into full citizenship in a country with which they have scant historic affinity, and that has committed multiple grave offenses against them.

On a wider scale, the late-1970s period of "Roots" prompted a fresh fascination with the concepts of nationhood and heritage.

People of many backgrounds, here and abroad, looked anew at themselves, at their family — and at the map. They thought more deeply and carefully about their defining identity, and about the pain of its potential loss.

Did Haley simply, even unwittingly, tap into an emerging nationalism? Or did he somehow seed an ethnic assertiveness and resistance that has cut through Communism and Columbus alike?

The sequence doesn't really matter. It happened, and Haley was part of it.

He deserves honor for a body of work; in 1965, for example, he wrote "The Autobiography of Malcolm X," based on Playboy magazine interviews with that leader.

But "Roots," with its inspiring, true-to-life story, will endure as long as families carry their traditions over the generations.

The Oregonian

Portland, Oregon, February 11, 1992

Alex Haley's contributions to American history and literature often have confused his critics. He never claimed to be a great historian. He was a great story teller with an ability to inspire masses of people to contemplate their own heritage and the heritages of others.

Haley, 70, died early Monday in a Seattle hospital from an apparent heart attack. He should be remembered most for his invaluable contributions to improved race relations through better public understanding of Afro-American history.

His personalized treatment of his own family history in the 1977 Pulitzer Prize-winning book, "Roots: The Saga of an American Family," enlightened a nation. It was an entertaining mix of meticulously researched fact and fictional detail that traced his ancestors back to the village in Gambia, West Africa, where they originated.

The 12-hour TV miniseries adapted from the book drew 130 million viewers, and it motivated people of all races to to think about who they are and search for their ancestors.

Haley had a profound impact on instilling a heightened sense of black pride in America. Moreover, his powerful personal story sensitized white Americans to feel the frustration that identification crises can cause. And it forced them to ask themselves, "What would it be like not to know who I am?"

While "Roots" was the work that reached the greatest number of people, "The Autobiography of Malcolm X," his first book, may be Haley's longer-lasting legacy. It is being used in schools throughout the nation. It fosters a greater understanding among whites of black people's struggle for equality.

For the last five years, Haley toured the nation telling stories of Afro-American heritage at black family reunion celebrations sponsored by the Washington, D.C.-based National Council of Negro Women.

Just last month, Haley announced he was giving up life on his Tennessee farm to devote more time to writing, including a planned book on C.J. Walker, the first black woman in America to earn $1 million.

Projects such as these enlarge the public's knowledge of the obscured contributions of black people to America's greatness. They also define the essence of Alex Haley's value to this nation's history.

Entertainer Bill Cosby Gives $20 Million to College

Entertainer Bill Cosby Nov. 4, 1988 announced that he and his wife, Camille, would donate $20 million to Spelman College in Atlanta, a predominantly black women's institution. The gift was the largest individual contribution ever made to a historically black school. The announcement came at an inagural ceremony in Atlanta for Johnetta B. Cole, the college's first black woman president.

Sixty percent of the money would be used to build the Camille Olivia Hanks Cosby Academic Center, which would house classrooms, a women's center, an audio-visual center and faculty offices. The remaining funds would be used to endow chairs in the fine arts, social sciences and humanities,

One of Cosby's daughters had graduated from Spelman, and he had occasionally used the school's campus in shooting scenes for the television series *A Different World*, which he produced.

THE ATLANTA CONSTITUTION
Atlanta, Georgia, November 13, 1988

Last year, The Cosby Show's Huxtable clan descended on Spelman College to film an uplifting episode about the changing of presidents at "Hillman College," alma mater of Cliff, Claire and daughter Denise.

A week ago, Mr. Cosby returned to Spelman, where his daughter Erinn is a sometime student, and announced that he and his wife were contributing $20 million to build an academic center, establish professorships and beef up the college's already hefty $42 million endowment. Speaking at a gala celebrating the inauguration of Dr. Johnnetta B. Cole as the college's first black woman president, he said, "Mrs. Cosby and I wanted this woman to know how much we love this school."

Mr. Cosby, who holds a doctorate in education, is a longtime supporter of the country's traditionally black colleges. He sits on the board of Morehouse College and last year gave $1 million to Fisk University. But the $20 million gift is unprecedented. Last year the United Negro College Fund raised a total of only $44.1 million.

The gift is not only a boost for Spelman. It sends the message that black institutions of higher learning, far from being anachronistic survivors of the era of segregation, have an important part to play in the nation's educational future. The U.S. Census Bureau estimates that by the end of the century minorities will constitute one-third of all American workers. With a century's worth of experience educating the black and the disadvantaged, these schools represent an invaluable training ground for that work force.

Last February, at a banquet honoring the new president of Morehouse College, Mr. Cosby urged his audience to pony up as much as they could for black colleges. "It's time to seriously consider instead of donating $50, donate $200. Forget about $2.5 million, make it $10 million ... We want $10 million buildings." Although few have struck the "vein of gold in the side of the mountain" that he credited with making his huge gift possible, many can follow his word and example.

Newsday
New York City, New York, November 12, 1988

Bill Cosby and his wife, Camille, attribute their $20-million gift to Atlanta's Spelman College — one of more than 100 historically black colleges and universities — to a vein of gold they found in the side of a mountain.

Cosby is a highly popular and successful TV star. But we hope that others who share the Cosbys' African-American heritage will discover that they too have untapped resources from which to contribute to a group of American institutions they can truly call their own.

Spelman, like the other black colleges, was founded in the aftermath of the Civil War to educate former slaves; Spelman became the first college for black women in 1881.

The schools have largely depended on white philanthropy: Spelman was renamed in 1924 for John D. Rockefeller's mother-in-law, Laura C. Spelman, an early benefactor.

The generosity of the Cosbys' gift, however, is a welcome sign that blacks now possess the capability and will to claim and support these institutions as depositories and wellsprings of African-American life and culture.

THE KANSAS CITY STAR
Kansas City, Missouri, November 14, 1988

Bill Cosby has gathered friends and respect in assorted public roles. But now few can compete with Cosby as the philanthropist. The $20 million donation to Spelman College made by Cosby and his wife, Camille, deliberately nurtures higher education. That he honored it through a black, women's institution is additionally to Cosby's credit.

He's done something for higher education. He's done something for the waning practice of giving to higher education. The Cosby gift is the largest any individual has ever made to a black college.

The artist's gift is not a small one in anybody's reckoning. But it would be measured on a different scale by an Ivy League university secure with a multi-million-dollar endowment than by a private college for whom the tuition of a few students more or less figures significantly in balancing the budget.

There are such small colleges in the Kansas City area. A grand check would give them fresh life. The University of Missouri system as it campaigns for private support surely would welcome such a friend as Cosby.

Even for an elite facility such as Spelman College in Atlanta, $20 million must seem like untold wealth. Surely all supporters of a diversified higher education system hope the riches won't overwhelm a community accustomed to more modest budgeting.

Cosby said something important about what's valuable in an era when television personalities are more likely to pump their astronomical earnings into lavish mansions or costumes. He also took a position in a social and educational controversy. Experts disagree about the propriety of black colleges in the United States. Cosby affirmed there is a place for strong, black educational institutions. He gave Spelman College the security of an endowment. Now the 107-year-old college has the opportunity to thrive money can ensure.

St. Paul Pioneer Press & Dispatch

St. Paul, Minnesota, November 14, 1988

Bill and Camille Cosby's $20 million contribution to Spelman College, a black women's school in Atlanta, is noteworthy not only for the dollar amount of the gift, but for its strong endorsement of black colleges.

These institutions started when the doors of white universities were closed to blacks. And even though most American colleges and universities are now integrated, the 107 historically black schools continue to offer a needed alternative to thousands of students each year.

The United Negro College Fund schools, whose membership includes just under half of the black colleges, enrolls about 45,000 students. About 90 percent are on scholarships and many are the first in the family to attend college.

These schools produced the majority of this century's black professionals. Yet many are struggling financially and are in desperate need of support.

The Cosbys showed how deeply they believe in the United Negro College Fund motto, "A mind is a terrible thing to waste." Other Americans should follow their example and give generously.

The Dallas Morning News

Dallas, Texas, November 13, 1988

Money talks, they say. And comedian Bill Cosby's $20 million gift last week to Spelman College, a black women's college in Atlanta, says a great deal, not only about the uncommon generosity of the beloved entertainer but also about his firm belief in the special mission of the nation's historically black institutions of higher learning.

Mr. Cosby's gift comes at a time when many of these colleges are facing declining enrollments, evaporating scholarships and escalating costs. All of these problems are stretching to the limit the ability of the predominantly black institutions to provide a competitive education. Fewer than two of every 10 black students attend such schools.

True, the fact that more than 80 percent of today's black college students attend predominantly white institutions is one measure of the social progress achieved in this country in recent decades. But it would be a tragedy if the price of that progress were the demise of colleges that occupy a special, and important, niche in higher education.

The nation's 100 black colleges have a unique ability to provide their students with the kind of nurturing environment that produces results. That attention is especially important for youngsters from low-income families where neither parent has attended college. For many, a diploma from one of these schools means their ticket out of poverty.

As anyone who witnessed the recent closing of Bishop College in Dallas knows, the financial underpinnings of predominantly black institutions of higher learning are not as solid as they could be. Despite increases in government assistance in recent years, many schools still lack the resources necessary to prepare students for the next century.

That's why Mr. Cosby's gift has a significance beyond just its size. The donation is not only an expression of support for Spelman but also a challenge to other Americans — of all races — to support these institutions. That challenge must be met. Otherwise, more black colleges surely will close — and the nation will be the lesser for it.

The Boston Globe

Boston, Massachusetts, November 9, 1988

Bill Cosby's $20 million gift to Spelman College is a spectacular vote of confidence in the college and a catalyst that should spark support for other black colleges. It also is recognition that 34 years after the Supreme Court desegregation decision, these colleges are important in the nation's cultural life.

Starting with his 1960s role as a secret agent in the "I Spy" series, Cosby has amassed a fortune by portraying blacks who have assimilated themselves into white American society.

In his latest TV role, the wise Dr. Huxtable of "The Cosby Show," he has acknowledged some of the tensions that accompany assimilation. When his television daughter Denise was accepted at Princeton, he advised her to go to the fictional Hillman College in Atlanta. That suggestion mirrored his real-life daughter's decision to attend Spelman, a black women's college founded in Atlanta in 1884.

The creation of Spelman and other black colleges provided a means for blacks to work their way up from the serf-like conditions of the late-19th-century South. These colleges were repositories of black culture and the birthplaces of the black middle class.

Black colleges seemed to fade in the 1970s as white schools opened their doors and extended scholarships to black students. In the 1980s, black colleges experienced a resurgence as students felt a renewed need for the nurturing and intellectual growth that these schools are especially able to provide.

This emotional support is an important factor in academic success. Only about 20 percent of black college students attend black colleges, but about 40 percent of black college graduates each year are from these schools.

Johnetta B. Cole, Spelman's new president, said Cosby intended his gift as a challenge to other black Americans to help their colleges. It also should be a reminder to foundations and other philanthropies that black colleges are worthy of support.

Discrimination against blacks is not as blatant as it was when Spelman was founded, yet racial antagonism persists. Black colleges provide an invaluable buffer for students at a vulnerable time in their lives.

WORCESTER TELEGRAM

Worcester, Massachusetts, November 13, 1988

Bill Cosby is more than just the most popular performer on television. Evidently, he is also one of the most generous Americans, and his example should attract followers.

In donating a staggering $20 million to Spelman College, a black women's school in Atlanta, Cosby and his wife, Camille, managed to revive interest in black colleges that seemed to fade in the 1970s as white schools opened their doors to minorities.

The Cosby grant is a measure of the high esteem two successful Americans have for one particular college, but such a marvelous gift can also be seen as an invitation to others to follow suit. An investment in higher education, regardless of the size or color of the school, yields a return in the form of better life.

Donations of $20 million are not often, if ever, matched or exceeded anywhere in the eleemosynary realm. Gifts of that size can see the construction of whole new buildings, endow several professorships for years or result in major advances in scientific research. Most important, they can help young men and women get a better education.

Few people can display $20 million generosity. But many smaller gifts, say in the $25 or $100 range, can also make a difference for institutions of higher education. And those who give help make that difference.

Proposition 42
Stirs Controversy

The National Collegiate Athletic Association (NCAA) Jan. 11, 1989 approved a new rule that would end athletic scholarships to incoming freshmen who did not meet the NCAA's minimum academic standards. The new rule, Proposition 42, drew criticism for its possible effect of reducing funds available to economically disadvantaged students, both athletes and non-athletes.

Proposition 42, which would go into effect in August 1990, was passed at the NCAA's annual convention in San Francisco. The new rule would amend a bylaw known as Proposition 48. Under that rule, enacted in 1983, freshmen who did not earn a 2.0 grade-point average in high school and achieve a minimum result on one of two standardized entrance examinations could not participate in sports in their freshman year, but would be able to accept athletic scholarships for the year.

Such students were known as partial qualifiers. According to the NCAA, about 600 athletes per year – some 90% of them black – fell into that category. Under Proposition 42, partial qualifiers could not receive athletic scholarships in their freshman year. They could receive aid from other sources and could become eligible for scholarships after their first year.

The new rule was passed by representatives of member institutions and conferences, 163-154, after having been rejected the previous day, 159-151.

Critics of Proposition 42 said that schools would find ways to give aid to partial qualifiers – either through illegal means or from funds that would otherwise go to economically disadvantaged students who were not athletes. Opponents also argued that the standardized tests used to qualify students were racially biased.

One opponent, Georgetown basketball coach John Thompson, Jan. 14 protested the rule by walking off the court before a game against Boston College at the Capital Center in Landover, Md. Thompson did not attend Georgetown's next game.

Backers of the new rule argued that tightening athletic standards would force potential student-athletes to do better school work. According to a news analysis Jan. 13 in the *Washington Post*, the new rule could also save athletic departments some $6 million annually in reduced scholarships.

The Washington Post
Washington, D.C., January 16, 1989

THE COLLEGES, in their rules about which students can play the big sports, had a decent rule in place in Proposition 48. It let marginal academic performers enter college and receive athletic scholarships but made them sit out the first year until they showed they could do college-level work. The powerful Southeastern Conference, reacting to a scandal at one of its member schools, adopted a rule denying these first-year scholarships to academically marginal athletes, and last week this new rule—Proposition 42—was adopted, by a close vote, nationwide. Georgetown University coach John Thompson, whose school accepts no students who can't meet the Prop 48 standard, rose on a point of principle, declaring that the new rule penalizes the black students elsewhere who benefit most from the old one.

Mr. Thompson is right on the mark. No doubt there are schools, including those whose coaches and officials are now claiming the new rule is "racist," which prize only winning and make only the feeblest pretense of educating their young athletes. John Thompson's Georgetown, however, has a proven record of providing an education as well as an athletic program to youngsters who otherwise might get neither—not at Georgetown, anyway. When he says the new rule threatens the sports careers and life prospects of the young men who enter college under Proposition 48, he deserves to be heard.

This is not to concur in the shallow argument that there is something intrinsically "racist" about asking young athletes to meet certain academic standards. It is doubtless so that most of those who might suffer under the new dispensation are black. But some standard is necessary in order to ensure that the pressures of big-time college athletics, and the rewards to which they usher the few athletes who go on to the pros, do not banish study from the campus and leave only sport. It is a disservice to black athletes who work at their studies to suggest that the standard should be a phony one.

Still, there is a limit to how much of an academic arbiter the colleges' athletic association can be. In the end it depends, as it should, on the colleges themselves. Georgetown is a good model: it does well in sports and academics and does not need an intercollegiate association to instruct it in its responsibilities to its students.

The Hutchinson News
Hutchinson, Kansas, January 17, 1989

Georgetown University basketball coach John Thompson did something Saturday that ought to get a lot of people's attention.

The first thing he did was act like a gentleman.

That alone seems to be unusual for some coaches. Too many coaches and too many athletes find themselves the subjects of unfavorable news stories. Don't count coach Thompson among them.

Secondly, the coach made his statement in such a way as to spark debate on a significant social issue, something that should concern all citizens, including those who don't know a three-pointer from a hoop. And he didn't have to yell at anyone, insult anyone, or throw anything to get attention.

Coach Thompson walked off the basketball court Saturday before a game against Boston College. His action was meant to protest a recent ruling by the National Collegiate Athletic Association, the governing body of college athletics. The rule change prohibits scholarships to college freshmen with less than a minimum 2.0 grade point average and who failed to receive a minimum score on one of two standard entrance exams.

Coach Thompson thinks the rules are too strict and discriminate against students from a low socio-economic background.

We'll withhold judgment concerning the rules change, but one thing is clear. Coach Thompson did an important thing in a classy way. His actions told all undergraduates everywhere that you don't have to act like a buffoon to get attention or ignite a movement.

We need more coaches of Thompson's integrity and less of the other kind.

THE SACRAMENTO BEE
Sacramento, California, January 17, 1989

The protest walkout staged the other night by Georgetown University basketball coach John Thompson against the NCAA's new eligibility rule was out of character. Thompson has built a reputation as a coach who has high standards for his players, both on and off the basketball court. Why then should he object to the National Collegiate Athletic Association's having some minimal academic standards of its own?

Four years ago, to stop the athletic exploitation of academically unqualified freshmen, the NCAA passed Proposition 48, barring freshman athletic eligibility for students admitted with high school grade point averages below 2.0 and combined Scholastic Aptitude Test scores below 700. However, in a loophole, the NCAA permitted member colleges to give athletic scholarships to athletes who met one part of that standard. The result at several schools was scandal, as athletic departments engineered higher grades for ineligible freshman athletes. With its new Proposition 42, narrowly passed last week, the NCAA eliminated that loophole, forbidding member schools from giving athletic scholarships to students who don't meet the standards.

Thompson and other coaches charge that the rule is racist and is meant to drive black athletes out of major universities. He objects particularly to using college entrance test scores as a standard, charging that they are culturally biased.

That's an insult to black students. The majority of college-bound black students, and 80 percent of college-bound students as a whole, score above 700 on the SAT. While it's true that the new rule will deny athletic scholarships to about 600 students a year, most of them black, those scholarships won't disappear. They'll go instead to athletes, many of them also black, who may not have the same dazzling moves on the basketball court or football field, but who have paid more attention to the classroom and who will now be given an opportunity for scholarships that the superstars would have otherwise taken.

The NCAA's new rule sends a clear message to young athletes, their high schools and parents: You can't just dribble, pass or run your way into college. To win a scholarship, an athlete must put in some time with the books, too, learning enough to meet at least minimal academic levels. That rule may make life more difficult for coaches and some athletes, but it tells kids who need to be told that there are some standards in life that have nothing to do with jump shots and hip fakes.

THE BLADE
Toledo, Ohio, January 20, 1989

THE governing body which regulates collegiate athletics has finally decided that athletes must truly qualify as students first, which is the only proper position to take despite the arm-waving and cries of foul from a few big-school sports factories and some black coaches who fall back on a tired old theme: racism.

The NCAA's adoption of Proposition 42 will deny scholarships to incoming freshmen who fail to achieve 700 on the Scholastic Aptitude Test and don't have a 2.0 grade-point average. It is an extension of the milder but equally controversial Proposition 48, adopted three years ago, which denies an athlete already holding a scholarship a chance to play if his SAT scores and grades don't measure up.

Because nine out of 10 Proposition 48 students are black, blacks stand to be the most affected by the newer and tougher standards, which prompted the nation's best known black collegiate basketball coach, Georgetown's John Thompson, to boycott his team's recent games with Boston College and Providence College.

His objections to using the SAT as a measuring stick stem from his conviction that the test is culturally biased against blacks. If we assume there is some merit in that argument, the fact is that a SAT score of 700 is hardly an impossible dream — a perfect score is 1,600.

Those who feel that Proposition 42 is simply a black vs. white issue should be reminded that three largely black schools — Howard University, Florida A&M, and Maryland-Eastern Shore — voted for it. So did the predominantly black Mid-Eastern Athletic Conference.

Mr. Thompson and other critics of Proposition 42 seem to assume that blacks will fail, an ironic twist that would be branded as racist if it came from a prominent white coach.

Even if the NCAA's hidden agenda is to help smaller colleges grab some of the athletes that the powerhouse sports schools collect and hoard, its true success will come when it lifts the academic standards and achievements of the young people our colleges are supposed to be educating.

For every black athlete John Thompson sends on to professional basketball from Georgetown, thousands of others attend and then leave American colleges without even knowing how to read a newspaper or balance a checkbook.

Of course, the issue may be moot soon, anyway, because the pressure continues to grow for the NCAA to rescind Proposition 42.

Even so, if John Thompson really wants to boycott where it will do some good, let him grab a sign and march in front of the elementary schools and secondary schools which are failing to educate these kids in the first place.

The Oregonian
Portland, Oregon, January 24, 1989

There's furor in the sports world over a recent decision by the National Collegiate Athletic Association, but little about an important issue it raises.

The NCAA convention voted, narrowly, to deny athletic scholarships beginning in 1990 to college freshmen with weak academic records or low scores on standard aptitude tests.

John Thompson, the highly successful basketball coach at Georgetown University, is the most conspicuous among numerous coaches who have been protesting the new rule. Many of Thompson's players come from poor inner-city neighborhoods. Most of them, like Thompson himself, are black.

Refusing such a player an athletic scholarship even for one year amounts to denying him a college education for which his native intelligence may qualify him even if his test scores and prior educational record don't show it, Thompson has charged.

Thompson has a limited point. A college should be able to admit anyone it wishes, use athletic ability as one of its admission standards if it wants to and give a scholarship to anyone it thinks deserves it.

But the issue being missed is that a college is first of all an educational institution. It should be judged on what kind of educational job it does with the students it chooses to accept.

Most of Thompson's players graduate, but there have been cases of young men who spent four years at a college as athletes and left unable even to sign their own names. Their college exploited them for the fame and profit of a winning team. The NCAA's new rule recognizes that fact but puts most of the burden of failure on the student, not the college.

And what about that vast majority of minority young people who cannot play football or basketball well enough to gain the support and close supervision of a campus patron like John Thompson? Who is looking out for them?

Low income, and coming from families with no experience of attending college, make it difficult for many of them to see themselves as academicians. For those who do venture into the usually impersonal college world, the keys to success are their own motivation and the amount of help available to them when they need it.

The underrepresentation of minority students in higher education is a serious concern that colleges have an obligation to do something about. But simply admitting them is not enough. If the students are willing to work for it, the colleges also have an obligation to give them a fair chance to succeed once there, athletes or not.

The Miami Herald

Miami, Florida, January 24, 1989

MANY brilliant people — from chess masters to musical prodigies — suffer from a form of tunnel vision. They focus strongly on their special interests and ignore the surrounding contexts.

Maybe that's John Thompson's problem. He's the brilliant basketball coach at Georgetown University. Last year he coached the U.S. Olympic basketball team.

Right now, though, Coach Thompson unwisely is trying to overturn a new National Collegiate Athletic Association (NCAA) rule concerning athletes' eligibility. To dramatize his views, he has boycotted games.

The rule, Proposal 42, takes effect in the fall of 1990. It denies athletic scholarships to students who fail to achieve minimal levels on college-entrance exams *and* high-school grades. At present, marginal students may be admitted under rules that require a 2.0 grade-point average *or* minimal test scores (700 on the SAT), but not both.

Coach Thompson's obsession, to his credit, is not basketball but shaping young lives. At Georgetown he has encouraged his athletes to finish their degrees. Alas, there are too many other coaches whose obsession is winning. For them, the athletes are merely a means to that end.

To prevent the abuses that these coaches often tolerate or encourage, stricter rules are needed. Proposal 42 is only a start. Florida's university chancellor, Dr. Charles Reed, outlined some others recently to the presidents of NCAA colleges.

Chancellor Reed, himself a college athlete as an undergraduate, proposed four major changes: eliminate spring practice for football; end freshman participation; keep score, by schools and teams, on graduation rates and grades; and award scholarships only to those students whose test scores *and* grades predict collegiate success.

This is not as Draconian as it sounds. As tennis great Arthur Ashe pointed out in defending Proposal 42, "Seven hundred on the SAT exams — that's like a D average." Moreover, Mr. Ashe noted, raising the standards sends out the message that "if you want to play basketball or football or run track, you've got to hit the books."

Most college athletes never turn pro. For them to make a living after the cheering stops, they need a real education with real standards that begin with college admission. That's why Coach Thompson's protests, though well-meaning, are misguided.

THE PLAIN DEALER

Cleveland, Ohio, January 17, 1989

Though there are concerns about the effect a new NCAA rule will have on college athletics, there is a compelling argument for the higher standards of Proposition 42, which will require true student-athletes in the 1990-91 school year.

The new rule will deny scholarships to freshmen who don't score 700 out of a possible 1,600 points on the Scholastic Apptitude Test and don't have a 2.0 grade point average.

Under present rules, a freshman can receive an athletic scholarship by meeting one of the two criteria, though he is not eligible to compete in his first year. The change leaves him the option of either paying for tuition himself or applying for federal loans and grants.

Georgetown basketball coach John Thompson walked out of a game against Boston College this weekend to protest the change. He says it will adversely affect poor, minority students and deny them the only chance of attaining a degree. That might be true for a few; the NCAA estimates that 600 students a year meet one of the rule's requirements but not both.

Yet even Thompson admits that a 700 SAT score and a 2.0 GPA are not difficult to attain. Georgetown University won't accept any student-athletes who don't meet both requirements. Thompson's problem is that scholarships will be denied to freshmen. It's an important distinction, and stopgap alternatives are needed. Perhaps some students should be attending two-year institutions before entering a four-year college.

Proposition 42 *is* exclusionary; but more importantly, it presents a minimal standard for student-athletes to work toward. (Whether the SAT is culturally biased is a debate for another time.) The rule tells them that academic and athletic ability together warrant a scholarship, not athletic ability alone.

Too many student-athletes have been exploited for their athletic ability without any consideration of their college grades or their futures. The NCAA's attempt to emphasize academic performance has in mind the student's future beyond the court.

Federal Curbs Set on Race-Based Scholarships

Education Secretary Lamar Alexander Dec. 4, 1991 proposed new federal regulations concerning scholarships for minorities at colleges and universities that received federal funding. The proposals were issued following a seven-month review of current policy, in the wake of a controversial change announced in 1990 that had banned scholarships based solely on race.

Alexander proposed that scholarships based exclusively on an applicant's race be banned except in the following circumstances:

- When such scholarships were mandated by court to remedy past discrimination.
- When such scholarships were funded by Congress.
- When colleges used such scholarships to achieve campus diversity, so long as "race is not, in effect, a condition of eligibility for the scholarship."
- When such scholarships were funded by private donors and were awarded on the basis of need or to promote diversity, so long as the scholarships did not result in a denial of aid to other students.

Alexander said colleges would be given four years to implement the new rules and that none of the estimated 35,000 to 45,000 students who currently received such race-specific scholarships would have them revoked.

The proposed rules would be published in the Federal Register and would be subject to a three-month period of public comment before being finalized.

The Houston Post

Houston, Texas, December 13, 1991

THE BUSH ADMINISTRATION appears to have come up with a fairly good decision that bars the awarding of scholarships based solely on race. It still allows colleges receiving federal funds to use financial aid for racial, cultural and geographic balance.

The methods left open to choosing scholarship recipients can be fairly applied. According to Education Secretary Lamar Alexander, "some race-exclusive scholarships are legal" He was referring to awards from court desegregation orders, congressional mandates and private donors. In other cases, he said, "race may be a positive factor in awarding scholarships."

Conditions under which colleges and universities receiving federal funds may grant any financial aid include:

☐ Need. Awards to low-income students can be made without regard to race, even if it means such awards go disproportionately to minority students.

☐ To create diversity. Race can be considered as one factor among several when awarding scholarships to increase the variety of experiences, opinions, backgrounds and cultures.

☐ To remedy discrimination, fulfill congressional mandates or the wishes of private donors. Colleges may administer private-donor, minority-targeted scholarships where that aid does not limit the amount, type or terms of financial aid available.

This ruling was prompted by a controversy stirred up last year by the Education Department's assistant secretary for civil rights, Michael Williams. He held it would be a violation of civil rights laws for the Fiesta Bowl in Arizona to offer $100,000 in minority scholarships to the University of Louisville and the University of Alabama if their football teams played in the game.

The aid was offered by a private group to attract the football teams to play in the 1990 Fiesta Bowl after national criticism of the state of Arizona's refusal to honor Martin Luther King with a paid holiday.

About half of the 13 million U.S. college students receive financial aid. Of the 1.3 million minority students, only about 45,000 attend college with race-exclusive scholarships. But basically, the Constitution forbids all forms of racial discrimination, and scholarships that go to any student based on race are discriminatory.

That shouldn't happen because it tends to make the student discriminated against feel resentful, which in turn fuels racial intolerance. America doesn't need that.

Richmond Times-Dispatch

Richmond, Virginia, December 3, 1991

On the same November day President Bush was executing a full somersault on the quotas issue to the delight of race/ethnicity/gender/religion protectionists everywhere, Secretary of Education Lamar Alexander was standing fast, commendably, against the quotacrats in higher education's monopoly accrediting establishment.

In a letter to the chairman of his accreditation advisory committee, Mr. Alexander hammered those accrediting groups that try to "impose their own views of social policy on schools that clearly provide a quality education." Diversity of ideas, attitudes and cultural background is a healthy quality, but institutions should be free to define diversity according to their own aspirations without being intimidated by accreditors, the secretary declared.

The secretary's ire was raised originally by the attempt of the Philadelphia-based Middle States Association of Colleges and Schools to bully Bernard M. Baruch College of New York into implementing quotas for hiring of minority faculty and measures to raise the retention rates of minority students. Middle States also arrogantly sought to force a theological institution to violate an article of its faith by placing a woman on its governing board.

But Mr. Alexander did more than make an excellent statement. By proposing to end the policy that requires a college to be accredited before it may receive federal student financial aid, the secretary took what could be the first step toward cracking the accreditation monopoly. The ability to accept federally aided students is a life-or-death matter for many institutions. By freeing colleges from the accreditors' power to use student aid for blackmail purposes, the secretary may make it possible for colleges to bolt from politicized accreditors and, if they wish, to form new accrediting entities dedicated to academic quality.

The secretary proposes to end the accrediting/aid link by letting institutions qualify for a "pass" to qualify for student aid without formal accreditation. He wants his advisory committee to study further how that might be done, but one way would be to grant automatic eligibility to those institutions that have low default rates. When Mr. Alexander decides in January whether to continue to grant official federal recognition to Middle States, we hope he will use the occasion to strike another blow against monopoly control of accreditation.

Naturally, much of the accrediting and higher education establishment has been empurpled by Mr. Alexander's principled stand. To permit some colleges to avoid accreditation, huffed one president, in a more-or-less typical response, "would splinter the entire higher education community." Well, we can only hope so. Higher education could benefit from being less monolithic, less slavishly devoted to groupthink, more . . . diverse.

Yes, the diversity that educrats repeat as though it were a mantra is something they have too often transformed into the opposite — conformity and orthodoxy of thought. Let diversity flourish in accreditation so that institutions may choose between accreditors who will judge according to accepted academic standards and accreditors who will press their own political agendas.

The Christian Science Monitor

Boston, Massachusetts, January 23, 1989

JOHN THOMPSON, the winning basketball coach at Georgetown University, is not one of those coaches who take lightly the obligation of colleges and universities to educate student-athletes. Nor does Thompson, though he is black, believe that every black youth in America is "entitled" to a college education – especially if he can slam-dunk. Under his tough regimen, Georgetown basketball players – predominantly black – have one of the best graduation records in major college sports.

So when John Thompson protests a National Collegiate Athletic Association rule whose ostensible purpose is to stiffen admission requirements for college athletes, one takes notice. He has earned credibility on the issue.

Proposition 42, adopted by NCAA schools this month, limits athletic scholarships to students who maintain a 2.0 average in core high school courses and who also achieve certain minimum scores on standardized aptitude tests. The new rule modifies Proposition 48, under which athletes who had the grade-point average but fell below the test thresholds could receive scholarships, but were ineligible to play during their freshman year.

The majority of Proposition 48 students were black. The reason, according to some educators, is that standardized tests are culturally biased against blacks, particularly those from the ghetto. Experience shows, they add, that with tutoring and other remedial help during their year of ineligibility, many poor black athletes are able to perform college work.

Supporters of the new rule say they were trying to curb recruiting abuses. Opponents see suspect motives behind the vote, having to do with discrimination or with competitiveness among schools and conferences.

What's clear is that, as Thompson notes, some youths who previously would have had at least a shot at a college education will no longer have that opportunity (unless they can get other financing).

Like many in the US, we are concerned about the growing professionalization of college sports; so long as athletics purport to be part of an academic environment, the players should be young men and women with a capacity for higher education.

But we also believe in opening the doors of opportunity, especially for those to whom the doors have been barred unfairly.

The real scandal in college athletics has less to do with the way players enter the system than with the way they leave it. Most big colleges and universities have a dismal record when it comes to ensuring that scholarship athletes graduate. Too many coaches in the major, revenue-raising sports – abetted by see-no-evil administrators – only feign interest in players' education.

Some universities, through the leadership of coaches like John Thompson and equally strong-minded administrators, have proved that academic excellence is not incompatible with success in big-time athletics. The NCAA should be following the example of these institutions, rather than slamming the door on some minority athletes.

Richmond Times-Dispatch

Richmond, Virginia, January 23, 1989

Ideally, athletic prowess would be a minor consideration in university admissions. All people would go to college first to study and only secondarily to be a flanker back — or debater, student journalist, campus politician. Everyone knows, though, that in the portion of academe with big-time sports programs, that's not the "real world." And since it's not, the need has been for academic standards for athletic recruits high enough to ensure that they are students, or reasonable facsimiles, and not just hired hands performing to make stadium turnstiles click.

The NCAA's Proposition 48 made a good start a few years ago in seeing to it that collegiate sports recruits show some promise of being able to handle at least a light load of college academics. (Some, of course, handle much more than that.) It imposed an entrance requirement of a 700 minimum score (out of a possible 1600) on the Scholastic Aptitude Test and a 2.0 average in 11 "core" high school subjects. In a compromise, colleges were allowed to admit recruits who satisfied only one of those two criteria, give them their scholarship but hold them out of athletic competition during their freshman year. Now comes Proposition 42, narrowly adopted at the NCAA's recent San Francisco meeting, proposing to do away with that compromise. Georgetown University basketball coach John Thompson has led the charge against Proposition 42, going so far as to stage a one-man walkout before his Hoyas' games at the Capital Centre. We believe Mr. Thompson has a legitimate beef; already it seems likely that the NCAA will rescind Proposition 42 when it meets next January in Dallas. Mr. Thompson, who coached the U. S. Olympic team in Seoul, was the ideal person to raise the issue, because he has always recruited students who were capable of college work, and then has seen to it that they study. The Georgetown basketball program has consistently been among the nation's leaders in percentages of players who graduate. But though he was not personally affected, Mr. Thompson, who is black, was sensitive to the new rule's potential for depriving minority students of a chance of a lifetime to use a God-given skill to climb the ladder.

Indeed, it is easy to understand how Proposition 42 must have seemed an exercise in bad faith to those who feel that the SAT is being used unfairly against black athletes. That doesn't mean that "racism" is the culprit; the NCAA's Byzantine politics seems a more likely one. Nor does it mean that efforts to enforce minimum academic standards have come a cropper. The beauty of Proposition 48 is that it provides two warning signals of likely academic deficiencies suggesting a freshman should buckle down to studies before competing in sports: grade-point average and the SAT score. And it should be noted that the 700 minimum is more than 200 points below the average for all college-bound test-takers; thus, it is should not be a huge hurdle for future aspirants to college athletic scholarships who know well in advance that it's going to be there.

The best feature of an admittedly imperfect Proposition 48, in fact, is that it has signaled to high school athletes throughout the land that they are going to have to get serious about their studies. And yet a student-athlete who freezes when faced with a standardized test — as many creative people of all races do — is not absolutely denied a chance to use his talents as a ticket to a college education. The NCAA ought to let 48 continue to have its beneficial effect without injecting the divisive, potentially disruptive influence of 42.

The Des Moines Register

Des Moines, Iowa, January 21, 1989

The National Collegiate Athletic Association has coaches in an uproar over a rule that would deny athletic scholarships to students who can't meet minimum college-entrance standards.

The NCAA has good intentions. A student who cannot muster a "C" average in high school and a minimum score on college-entrance exams will probably fail in college. A college may be doing a youth no favor by granting him an athletic scholarship if he will ultimately fail to graduate.

The tragic story is all too familiar: The college dumps the kid after his athletic eligibility is used up, he's not quite good enough to make the pros, so a young man ends up back on the streets, having gone to college but not having acquired an education.

Still, some do beat the odds. Despite all the handicaps of a disadvantaged background and of the enormous time demands on a student-athlete, some academically "unqualified" students do end up with a degree and a future.

For some students, an athletic scholarship may be the only shot at a college education. If an athletic scholarship helps even a few break out of the ghetto, it's worthwhile, and the NCAA's rules ought to give athletes with sub-par academic qualifications at least one chance.

Perhaps the NCAA is going at the problem from the wrong end. Instead of barring academically deficient athletes from college, the approach might be to admit them, then make sure they are given a genuine chance to succeed. The NCAA should see to it that disadvantaged athletes are not merely kept eligible with snap courses but are given remedial instruction and then a real education.

Some rule changes might help. Scholarships should be good for five years, and freshmen should be barred from play. That would allow at least one year on campus without the pressure of competition and still leave four years for sports — and the chance at an education.

Minority Scholarship Policy Changed

The Education Department Dec. 18, 1990 announced a partial reversal of a controversial policy change that would have prohibited colleges and universities from awarding scholarships designated exclusively for minority students. The revision was announced at a news conference in Washington, D.C. by Michael Williams, the department's assistant secretary for civil rights, who had sparked the controversy with his earlier announcement of the policy change.

Williams said the department would now allow colleges that received federal funds to award scholarships to minority students if the money for those scholarships came from private donations or federal programs set up to aid minority students. A college's general operating funds could not be used for scholarships targeted exclusively at minorities, however. (Although no specific figures were available, most minority scholarships were reported to be funded by general college funds.

Colleges would be given a four-year transition period in which to phase in the new policy, Williams said.

Williams, who was black, insisted that he had been "legally correct" in his initial policy ruling but admitted that he had been "politically naive." The earlier policy change had generated a fire-storm of protest from educators and civil rights officials, and had led President George Bush to order the Education Department to reconsider its position.

President Bush Dec. 18 denied that the partial reversal represented a "flip-flop" on the part of his administration. "I've long been committed to affirmative action," he insisted at a news conference for editors of regional newspapers. He declared that he wanted "to continue these minority scholarships as best we can."

The partial reversal pleased neither critics of the previous policy change nor conservatives, who were generally opposed to affirmative action programs.

"It was not a clarification, it was not a retraction, it was a confusion," said Robert H. Atwell, president of the American Council on Education.

Several college administrators and civil rights groups pointed out that it would be difficult to distinguish between privately donated funds and a college's own operating funds, and that there was no legal precedent for doing so. "The distinction is not one that I've seen recognized in the law anywhere, said Janell Byrd of the NAACP Legal Defense and Educational Fund.

Conservative critics attacked the administration for caving in to political pressure. "We think the original policy statement was a correct statement of law," said John Scully, counsel to the Washington Legal Defense Foundation, which was considering a lawsuit over the reversal. "The current press release is a substitution of bad politics for good law," he added.

The Houston Post

Houston, Texas, December 18, 1990

THE BUSH ADMINISTRATION appears ready to pull back from last week's Education Department ruling that race-based minority scholarships are illegal. Beating a retreat may achieve a desirable result — helping to keep needy and worthy minority students on track educationally — but it also looks like a cop-out.

The 1964 Civil Rights Act clearly bars discrimination on the grounds of race, color or national origin in any program that gets federal financial assistance. That is what Assistant Education Secretary Michael Williams said.

It is all but certain that this section was written to curtail whites-only scholarship programs. Still, that isn't how it reads. So instead of various officials berating Williams, other solutions to the problem should be sought.

One is to change the law. That is the most direct (if politically thorny) response.

The other is to change how the scholarships are structured: Make them primarily based on financial need, and it will be mostly minorities who qualify. That is far from a perfect solution. But this world is imperfect, and even as minority-based scholarships stand now, many students fall tragically through the safety net. Who can say this change would worsen matters?

Only a bigoted few want minority students cut off from scholarships. Black college enrollment is dropping, and minorities' undergraduate enrollment greatly outstrips the numbers who actually achieve degrees. Such trends must be reversed, not exacerbated. The challenge now is to figure out to get the result we as a nation want without flouting current law.

Lincoln Journal

Lincoln, Nebraska, December 19, 1990

Sensibly beating a retreat, the U.S. Department of Education now says no, there won't be a total ban on financial aid aimed at minority students. Instead, colleges and universities will be able to award scholarships solely on the basis of race as long as only private funds are used.

The situation thus returns pretty much to what it was before an Education Department official last week proclaimed the startling prohibition, affecting both private and public funds. Most minority scholarship programs are supported by private funds.

Some questions linger regarding programs such as the Davis Scholarships at the University of Nebraska. Intended for minority students, they depend on a mix of public and private money. But presumably that program is in the clear. If not, NU could switch the funds to the private University of Nebraska Foundation.

U.S. society, unfortunately, is not colorblind. Minority scholarships provide a way to open higher education's doors to blacks, Hispanics and American Indians, helping them overcome the effects of racial discrimination. Foreclosing this kind of assistance, as the Education Department was seemingly intent on doing last week, understandably set off a storm of protest across the country.

It does not make sense that President Bush was in any way behind last week's bombshell. If nothing else, he did not want the political fallout from a scholarship ban following on that of his veto of a civil rights bill. After he called an Education Department official on the carpet, the revised policy followed quickly.

Thus the scholarship furor says less about the Bush administration's racial attitudes than about its ability to run a tight ship in Washington. An obscure assistant education secretary made the controversial announcement last week. Apparently Bush had no warning of it. Neither did the outgoing education secretary, Lauro Cavazos. The White House had to switch quickly to a damage-control mode.

Perhaps the incoming education secretary, Lamar Alexander, can bring more order and rationality to the department.

The Virginian-Pilot

Norfolk, Virginia, December 20, 1990

Last week Michael L. Williams, U.S. assistant secretary of education, ruled that "race-exclusive" scholarships are discriminatory, hence illegal under the Civil Rights Act of 1964. He said the government would cut off federal funds to all colleges that continued such aid. This week he said: Yes, but . . . there would be exceptions.

Defenders of race-based grants point to the need for affirmative action to overcome inequities rooted in years of segregation and prejudice.

As a concession to that view, the Bush administration partially retreated Tuesday. The revised provisions include a four-year delay in imposing the scholarship ban at private institutions "in order to permit universities to review their programs . . . and to assure that any students under scholarship, or being evaluated for a scholarship, do not suffer."

But amid all the confusion, one curious constant emerges in Mr. Williams' two announcements: Colleges that have desegregation agreements with Washington may continue to award race-based scholarships.

Presumably this would cover Virginia's public higher-education system. The Old Dominion, in reaching a compromise with the U.S. Office of Civil Rights in 1978, set goals for desegregating both predominantly white and predominantly black colleges. Under the agreement, the state offers incentives to attract students to institutions in which they are part of the minority race.

The state last revised its desegregation goals in 1983; Washington last reviewed them in 1986. Virginia, overall, has moved close to compliance in student-mixing. Records show that in 1989-90 white institutions attained 85 percent of their goal; black institutions, principally because of Norfolk State University's success in enrolling white students, 101 percent.

But under the agreement the federal government still monitors compliance with the state's commitment to enhance predominantly black Virginia State University.

The commonwealth maintains four race-based financial-aid programs, which total about $2.5 million a year: (1) graduate fellowships to black students, aimed at bolstering black faculty at state institutions; (2) payment of tuition and fees to both black and white graduates of Virginia community colleges who transfer to a senior state college at which they are in the minority; (3) scholarships to encourage white students to attend NSU and VSU; (4) supplements to fill out aid packages or replace student loans for blacks attending historically white institutions.

Obviously, then, the federal government thinks racially integrated campuses are so preferable to those where all or virtually all students are of the same race that it demands strenuous efforts by states to achieve racial integration.

Which raises troubling questions about Mr. Williams' finding that, for private institutions, race-based aid isn't legal.

If Washington considers racial diversity vital to the nation's interests — which the exception for certain public colleges implies — why should private schools be barred from striving for similar variety?

And how can race-based agreements with the federal government — such as Virginia's — supersede federal law?

The Washington Post

Washington, D.C., December 19, 1990

THE ADMINISTRATION tried yesterday to turn invisible on the divisive issue of reserving college scholarships for minority groups. To quell the controversy its own Education Department created, it reached for a neutral position. A new policy statement was silent on whether the federal government can restrict student aid to minorities, as it does in a few minor programs. It stood off as well from the question of whether state and local governments can impose such restrictions, saying only that the issue had been covered by the courts and was therefore beyond executive branch discretion.

As to universities, its revised view is that under the Civil Rights Act of 1964, they can't restrict aid to minority groups using their own funds but can administer restricted scholarship programs that are privately funded. The administration also has created a four-year "transition" or grace period during which there will be no active enforcement of the new rule. The idea, Assistant Secretary of Education Michael Williams said at a news conference, is not to put any student or university at immediate risk. This should be reassuring.

The main shift yesterday from what Mr. Williams had announced before had to do with university programs. He had earlier said they could not administer scholarships even privately financed for minority groups only, but most could have gotten around that ban, as even protesting higher education officials conceded. As Mr. Williams himself originally suggested, they could change the terms of the scholarships, give them to needy or otherwise disadvantaged applicants and achieve the same result, and they remained free in the name of diversity to make race or a comparable factor one consideration in the awarding of aid; it could just not be the overriding one. Mr. Williams, who issued the revised policy at the direction of the White House, continued to say yesterday that "I think we must be very careful about making any decisions, significant decisions, in this country that relate to individuals based upon race." He is right about that. He also said he had been "naive" in the earlier declaration of policy, and on that he's more than right.

Increased access to higher education is one of the great equalizers in this society. No administration should oppose it, and no administration can afford to appear to be an opponent. Any policy statement on scholarships needs to be set in the cement of commitment to this goal. There is still more for the administration to say on this subject.

The Phoenix Gazette

Phoenix, Arizona, December 20, 1990

Once again the Bush administration appears to be in disarray. The president was caught short by a U.S. Department of Education ruling that it is illegal for colleges and universities that receive federal funds to set aside scholarships on the basis of race.

The department acted against an offer by promoters of the Fiesta Bowl football game to set aside $100,000 for such scholarships.

Michael L. Williams, head of the Office of Civil Rights in the U.S. Department of Education, did not inform the White House before making the announcement.

Now, apparently at the behest of the president, the Education Department has backed away from a total ban on financial aid targeted for minorities. Colleges and universities will be allowed to award scholarships based solely on race as long as federal funds are not used. However, they are warned that the matter could end up in court, even if the department takes no action.

Williams' big mistake, in addition to not informing the White House, is that he attempted to force consistency upon federal policy.

Williams wanted to align department policy with the 1964 Civil Rights Law, which prohibits discrimination on grounds of race, color or national origin in any program or activity receiving federal financial assistance.

He might have reasoned that if race-specific federal policies are wrong, they are wrong even wher inspired by noble purpose.

He might also have made th error of attempting to read th president's lips. Bush recently ve toed civil rights legislation becaus he opposed the imposition race-based rules.

Former Assistant Secretary Education Chester Finn Jr. summ up Williams' dilemma: "We' known for years that you ca have all-white scholarships, a that's fine, but somehow it's b permissible to have all bl scholarships." The new pol Finn said, is "absolutely consis with President Bush's unhappi with the previous civil rights bil

Instead of telling the nation he was "disturbed" by the r and scurrying to placate cr Bush might have used the opp nity to clarify his administra position regarding prefer treatment and the goal colorblind society.

DESERET·NEWS
Salt Lake City, Utah, December 7, 1991

By opting this week for a new regulation banning college scholarships intended only for racial minorities, the Bush administration has put itself in an awkward position.

The position is the pratfall that inevitably results from trying to stand on two different stools placed too far apart to straddle.

Predictably, the result in this particular case is a new policy that pleases neither those wanting no race-based scholarships at all or those seeking more of them.

But these scholarships should be encouraged as a way of promoting diversity on campus. If the new regulation is not withdrawn, what's next? A ban on scholarships for students from Pittsburgh or some other specific geographical area? Or a ban on scholarships earmarked for young women of Latvian descent?

In announcing the ban, the administration outlined certain exceptions. The new regulation would allow race-exclusive scholarships if the money comes from private donors, if Congress creates such scholarships, if a college is under court order to desegregate, or if a state legislature or even a city government wants to remedy past discrimination at its public colleges based on "good evidence."

The regulation sounds like more exception than rule. But even a couple of the exceptions are bothersome. What specifically, for example, constitutes "good evidence" that would let a legislature or city council mandate scholarships only for racial minorities? And doesn't the exception for colleges under desegregation orders invite more lawsuits against more colleges?

Aside from such questions, the new regulation still puts Washington in the position of telling colleges what to do with their own money.

Instead of formulating the new rule, Washington should have let well enough alone. Better yet, the White House should have tried to repeal the misguided provision in the Civil Rights Act that evidently spawned the new regulation.

We're referring to the provision specifying that institutions accepting federal funds may not discriminate even in programs that don't use federal money.

In response to that provision, the administration a year ago proposed a total ban — without any of the new exceptions — on financial aid targeted for minorities, then quickly backed away from the ban following widespread criticism. Though the new regulation is better than the old one, it's worse than the status quo.

The best thing that can be said for the new regulation is that it won't take effect until March 9, leaving plenty of time for the public to register its objections and for the White House to change its mind.

Meanwhile, this episode should teach at least two pointed lessons:

One is that Washington needs to get out of the habit of threatening an entire institution just because the federal government has a quarrel with part of that institution.

The other is that if colleges and other organizations really want to eliminate such needlessly finicky federal meddling, the most effective way to do it is to reduce and even eliminate their dependence on money from Washington.

The Birmingham News
Birmingham, Alabama, December 5, 1991

Among the confusing, complicated and contradictory facets of a new policy on race-based scholarships issued by the U.S. Department of Education Wednesday, one axiom is clear:

Uncle Sam knows best (even when Uncle Sam doesn't know why).

There will be sound and fury over the new guidelines.

Conservatives will applaud the Bush administration's tough stand against reverse discrimination. And maybe that is what's wanted here; a political counterbalance to the president's signing of the Civil Rights Act of 1991.

Liberals will condemn it as another example of how civil rights policies are being grossly undermined.

But the guidelines signify little.

Of all the students in American colleges, only about 1 percent have scholarships set up on strict racial criteria. Only about 3 percent of minority students have them.

Still, there is a principle to be upheld. Which brings up the obvious question: what is the principle to be upheld? To which the federal government answers, "Huh?"

Is the principle that no student should be given a scholarship just because of his or her race? Not really. No student ever was. Even that infinitely small number of students awarded race-exclusive aid had to demonstrate they were also scholars.

This new policy doesn't prohibit race-based scholarships either. They may still be awarded if backed by private financing. They are also OK if established by Congress or mandated by courts or legislatures.

But colleges may lose federal funding if they initiate such scholarships to attract minority students themselves.

Congress, courts and legislatures know more about scholarships than do college administrators? Now there's an uncomfortable thought.

This all has to be clarified in such detail because the same Congress that creates race-exclusive scholarships itself passed a law a few years ago which seems to outlaw them.

Perhaps there is an overriding principle here after all: He who has the gold makes the rules. If you want Uncle Sam's gold, here's another rule for you, whatever it's worth.

The Washington Post
Washington, D.C., December 12, 1991

DIVERSITY in academe, college accreditation and student financial aid have been mixed up in a stew for some time now, just long enough for the issue to come to a good, rolling boil. Secretary of Education Lamar Alexander turned up the heat last spring when he questioned the "diversity standards" used by one of the regional accrediting groups. The Middle States Association of Colleges and Universities had threatened to delay or withdraw accreditation of several schools when it found "unbalanced" faculties or governing boards—that is to say, the racial or gender mix was not to its liking.

A college's diversity—its racial and gender balance—can contribute directly to its educational value. But the makeup of the student body, faculty and trustees (unlike the size of the library or a school's finances) should not be among the concerns of an accrediting group. As Secretary Alexander has pointed out, the authorized "diversity policemen" are the Justice Department and the Education Department's Office for Civil Rights, which enforce compliance with the carefully crafted anti-discrimination laws and other fairness rules.

The Education Department is now considering withdrawing its recognition of Middle States—a well-deserved smack if it didn't potentially hurt plenty of students who depend on financial aid (about half of all college students). Students are eligible for grants and federally guaranteed loans only if they attend accredited schools. What would happen to financially dependent students if the government were to turn its back on Middle States and its 500 affiliated schools?

Secretary Alexander has no intention of penalizing students. But he continues to question the relationship between federal financial aid and accreditation—as do some members of Congress reviewing the Higher Education Act. Why should a voluntary organization have the power to impose standards different from the government's—and to cut off federal aid to institutions that don't comply? And what about the school that can't abide by a particular accreditation standard but is by all accounts a worthy institution? Shouldn't it be eligible for federal aid anyway?

Secretary Alexander suggests granting institutions a "pass" for financial eligibility. What criteria would entitle schools to this "pass" and who would decide? The secretary doesn't have the answers, and the questions take him farther than he really wants to go. Competing certification would be fraught with pitfalls, and the federal government certainly shouldn't get into the business of defining standards for higher education. That's precisely what Congress sought to avoid when it asked associations such as Middle States to evaluate colleges.

Independent accreditation has served higher education and this country fairly well—and it has preserved a welcome diversity. There's no reason to redesign the entire system because of a quarrel over one standard that ironically would threaten the rich variety among institutions of higher learning. This politically charged standoff between Middle States and the government could be settled simply if the association would just back away from the troublesome clauses in its charter. (Amendments have already been offered, in fact, and a vote is pending this week.) But if it refuses, then Secretary Alexander needs the authority to grant aid to any aggrieved school that might come before his department.

FORT WORTH STAR-TELEGRAM
Fort Worth, Texas, December 11, 1991

In an effort to clarify whether race-exclusive scholarships are permissible under the 1964 Civil Rights Act, Education Secretary Lamar Alexander has proposed new regulations.

Unfortunately, the result of these regulations will be further confusion.

Early this year, Alexander delayed implementation of a decision by Education's assistant secretary for civil rights, Michael L. Williams, that had declared a Fiesta Bowl scholarship program illegal. The Fiesta Bowl scheme was born out of the flap about Arizona's refusal to declare a Martin Luther King Jr. holiday. To keep from being ostracized, the Phoenix-based Fiesta Bowl wanted to create $100,000 in scholarships for minority students. Williams said that would be discriminatory under the Civil Rights Act.

Now Alexander has spoken. He says the Fiesta Bowl scholarships are OK.

Actually, he is saying that the Bush administration opposes use of the Civil Rights Act and affirmative action to accomplish reverse discrimination. No quotas, to quote President Bush.

But Alexander is also saying that some categories of scholarships based on race are acceptable: when they remedy past discrimination, when Congress specifically created the scholarships or when a private donor paid for the scholarships and the scholarships do not result in other students being denied aid.

In other words, Alexander opposes race-exclusive scholarships but says most of them are all right. This makes a certain sense because many scholarships to U.S. colleges and universities have traditionally been directed at certain classes of students (children of ministers or missionaries, for instance, or those wishing to study a particular field or even those from a particular locale) without being considered discriminatory.

Educators who say Alexander is proposing the same thing Williams proposed are wrong. But educators who say the administration still is sending a confusing message to minority students and to those who administer scholarship aid are correct.

Since Alexander's proposed regulations are not really about education, and only add to the fog of Washington doublespeak, a legitimate question would be, "Why is this necessary?" The obvious answer is "presidential-year politics," which explains all kinds of nonsense these days.

The Des Moines Register
Des Moines, Iowa, December 11, 1991

A Bush administration proposal to ban college scholarships based exclusively on race panders to right-wingers whose support the president fears losing to the likes of David Duke and Patrick J. Buchanan.

Aimed at satisfying white Americans who feel cheated by affirmative action, the proposal downgrades race as a factor that can be considered in awarding scholarships. The move helps cloak racism in respectable garb since it also appeals to critics who legitimately question the wisdom of preferential policies for minorities.

Practically speaking, the new rules may have little effect on the nearly 45,000 scholarships awarded on the basis of race. Education Secretary Lamar Alexander said last week that race-exclusive scholarships would be allowed when used to provide redress for proven discrimination, when Congress created the scholarships, or when a private source donated the money and it did not cause aid to be denied to other students. He also said race could be used as a factor in awarding scholarships aimed at increasing racial diversity on campus. In short, it does not appear that the number of scholarships awarded minority students necessarily will be significantly diminished.

Even so, there's plenty of cause to worry. First, confusion over the new rules may discourage some qualified minorities from applying for scholarships. And the new paperwork those rules will entail may discourage colleges — especially those already lukewarm about racial diversity on campus — from helping minority students obtain scholarships.

The proposal will not be adopted until after a 90-day period for public comment. Though unnecessary and yet another example of negative race politics on the part of the White House, the new policy need not be allowed to squelch diversity on campus. Minority students, their parents and administrators should not be cowed by the Bush administration's tactics.

The New York Times
New York City, New York, December 6, 1991

Education Secretary Lamar Alexander has found a formula that may rescue the Bush Administration from an unnecessary, embarrassing flap over the legality of college scholarships based on race. He says race-based scholarships are legally questionable, thereby winning plaudits from conservatives who oppose affirmative action programs. But he also says that some race-exclusive scholarships are legal and that administrators may seek diversity on campus by using race as one factor in awarding aid.

That's a mixed signal, but a more positive one than the Education Department sent out a year ago when this controversy first surfaced.

The flap was precipitated by Michael Williams, the Education Department's Assistant Secretary for Civil Rights, who objected last December to an attempt by organizers of the Fiesta Bowl in Arizona to set up scholarship funds for minority students. Mr. Williams insisted that Federal law prohibited colleges from awarding scholarships on the basis of race unless under court order.

His pronouncement jeopardized a 20-year practice by colleges of setting aside special scholarship money to attract qualified minority students. Though these funds are a small fraction of total aid, they can help recruiters convince minority students that money is available for them.

Thus, college administrators and even the White House were stunned by Mr. Williams's interpretation. It was then up to Mr. Alexander, who took over as Secretary of Education in March, to defuse the controversy. After a seven-month review he now proposes a policy that would generally prohibit race-specific scholarships but would permit them if specially designated by Congress or a private donor or under a court order. This policy would have allowed the Fiesta Bowl scholarships that triggered this controversy because they were sponsored by a private donor.

At the same time, the new policy strongly endorses race as a factor that can be considered to create a diverse student body. It invites colleges to be creative in getting scholarships to minority students based on disadvantage, merit or other factors that are not race-exclusive.

That's a substantial improvement over Mr. Williams's pronouncement. But some colleges still wonder how far they can go in using their own funds to aid minority students. Their concerns need to be heard while the new proposal is subject to public comment from now until March.

The Boston Globe
Boston, Massachusetts, December 7, 1991

With the ink not quite dry on the Civil Rights Act, the Bush administration is up to its old tricks. Education Secretary Lamar Alexander's plan to pull the plug on publicly funded race-exclusive scholarships has all the markings of previous efforts to aggravate racial tensions.

Alexander acknowledges that among students of color receiving scholarships, 96 percent are not receiving those that fit the race-exclusive definition – scholarships that are awarded solely on the basis of race. By making an issue of the scholarships that do exist, he sends the message that students of color are receiving special privileges.

The scholarships, in fact, serve an important purpose. In some instances, they are used to attract students to institutions where certain racial groups have been historically underrepresented.

Even Alexander acknowledges this need. His new guidelines will allow for such scholarships at institutions under court-ordered desegregation. The guidelines also leave in place race-based scholarships mandated by courts or those funded by Congress or private sources.

During the debate over the Civil Rights Act, the Bush administration insisted that the bill would create a "lawyers' bonanza" by paving the way for alleged victims of discrimination to sue their employers. Yet Alexander's guidelines have the potential of creating a lawyers' bonanza of another kind, if they provide encouragement for white students to file reverse-discrimination suits.

Moreover, some schools may be less aggressive in their efforts to attract diverse student bodies if they think they may have to defend themselves in court. The guidelines also send the message that efforts to equalize opportunities and to correct past discrimination in higher education are no longer necessary.

The Seattle Times
Seattle, Washington, December 9, 1991

EDUCATION Secretary Lamar Alexander's proposed rule on minority-only college scholarships is so muddled it probably won't affect the actual distribution of scholarship money.

But student funding was never the real issue, anyway. The proposal is a symbolic blow against affirmative action, something President Bush desperately needs to appease conservatives for the coming political season.

Last April, the White House rescinded a declaration by Michael Williams, assistant secretary for civil rights in the Education Department, that all race-limited scholarships were illegal. The triggering event was a proposal by the organizers of the Fiesta Bowl in Arizona to establish a scholarship for minority students. After intense protest from universities and civil-rights groups, the White House backed away from Williams' questionable legal position.

In the wake of that fiasco, Alexander was asked to come up with a new policy. His solution allows race to be used as a factor in awarding scholarships to achieve ethnic diversity on college campuses — but only if white students are allowed to compete, too.

The privately funded Fiesta Bowl scholarship would be legal under the new rules if white students are not denied other types of funding. It's unclear what this limitation actually means.

Financial-aid offices, presumably, would go through the hoops of considering race as a "plus" factor in making grants. Scholarships that consistently are won by minorities may or may not be legal, since there's no rule on how much weight the race factor may be given.

Alexander's plan would cause needless confusion and resentment, particularly because the amount of money involved is so small. A survey by the American Council on Education found that less than 1 percent of all college students receive minority scholarships, and only 3 percent of minority students benefit from them.

Even so, these scholarships are tools that colleges need to attract minorities. As it is, the percentage of African American high-school graduates entering college has dropped from 33 percent in 1975 to 29 percent in 1990, even as percentage enrollment of white students has increased.

Educators need help in closing that gap, not more hurdles put up by the Bush administration.

CHICAGO Sun-Times
Chicago, Illinois, December 6, 1991

At first glance, it appears that the Bush administration might have dealt a major blow to minority scholarship programs by banning the award of college scholarships based on race. When a Bush administration official a year ago moved against "race-exclusive scholarships," an ensuing uproar forced the administration to back off, pending further study.

Now that the new policy is out, the reaction seems a bit more tempered, and a closer look might explain why:

Although it bans scholarships based solely on race, it still does not ban aid to remedy past discrimination or to fulfill congressional mandates. Race-based awards would also be allowed for promoting a variety of experiences, opinions and cultures on campus.

And the ban would still allow aid based on financial need, even if recipients are disproportionately members of minority groups.

Understanding the impact might be helped by examining affirmative action set-aside programs established by Chicago and other cities. To meet court tests, such programs (which in Chicago require city contractors to allot 21 percent of their business to minority business enterprises) must demonstrably address past discrimination.

Such a requirement hasn't crippled those programs; in fact, proving such past discrimination hasn't been all that difficult, and, we suspect, shouldn't be an insurmountable barrier for colleges. Even now, minorities remain underrepresented in higher education enrollment, retention and degrees.

And, as the Illinois State Board of Education has noted, the number of minority teachers has not kept up with the number of minority students.

A spokesman for Gov. Edgar said there is concern that the new rules could force a redesign of a new state program to entice more minorities into teaching. And reaction among Illinois college administrators ranges from a belief that the new rules would have little effect to fear that some important programs could be crippled. It may be a while before the actual impact is known.

For now, though, the important issue isn't whether the Bush administration gained or lost politically by this move.

What is important is making sure that despite the new policy, financial aid continues to flow to those who indeed have been hurt by past discrimination.

Newsday
New York City, New York, December 6, 1991

The hard facts are that the Bush administration's new rules banning colleges from awarding race-exclusive scholarships to attract minority students won't have much practical impact. Only about 35,000 of the 1.3 million minority students currently enrolled on the nation's four-year campuses receive such aid. The rest get scholarships that are available to everybody else, too.

So why the brouhaha?

Because as the Bush administration should know, the year-long struggle over this small but crucial type of program is symbolic. It has a chilling effect on minority students, who get yet another signal that American higher education is inhospitable to them and out of their reach. With minority enrollment already on the decline, this is unacceptable.

The controversy began when Assistant Education Secretary Michael Williams — acting without a policy review — advised organizers of the Fiesta Bowl football game they couldn't offer scholarships for minority students at two major universities. That would be discriminatory, Williams contended.

Turns out, however, a generation of law and tradition had made this type of scholarship routine — more than half of American campuses offer some form of race-targeted financial aid in an effort to move minorities into the ranks of those with college degrees. When educational leaders protested, the administration went back to the drawing board.

Now it's come up with a convoluted system of allowing colleges to provide such scholarships on the condition the money comes from private donors who designate the awards for minorities. The college could use its own funds for such scholarships only if it were meant to remedy past discrimination. And it could use its own money to award scholarships to promote campus "diversity" — including scholarships in which race is considered as *one factor* in awarding the prize.

Sound confusing? It is. Luckily, education officials say they will be able to comply and still keep money flowing to talented minority students. That's good. They've got to get the word that the funds are still available.

Meanwhile, the whole affair will go down as another attempt by the Bush administration to use racial politics to its advantage. And it has left scars — again.

DAILY ☒ NEWS
New York City, New York, December 9, 1991

On Thursday, Education Secretary Lamar Alexander proposed rules that would ban most race-exclusive scholarships. Instead of awarding support based solely on race, it would make race one of several factors to be considered in granting aid. Fine. But only a few such targeted scholarships exist. Why in the world is the Bush administration making them into such a big deal? Could this be another attempt at — perish the thought — playing racial politics?

Only 3% of minority-scholarship students are on race-exclusive scholarships. That's a tiny fraction of all college students. Yet such scholarships have been handled by the Bush administration as though, in the words of William Gray, former house Democratic whip, "some white child is being denied a right to higher education."

Race-exclusive scholarships deny no one an education. Nor do they help a huge proportion of college students. But they do provide one more opportunity for the administration to play the race card in the shoddiest way. That's the kind of opportunity that, sadly, this administration rarely chooses to pass up. And that is why characters such as David Duke can credibly claim to be speaking out the other side of Bush's mouth.

INDEX